SECURING THE WORLD ECONOMY

'In presenting this treasure trove of material Professor Clavin has performed a considerable service for all students of the League and its era'

Lorna Lloyd, *History*

Securing the World Economy

The Reinvention of the League of Nations, 1920–1946

PATRICIA CLAVIN

OXFORD
UNIVERSITY PRESS

OXFORD
UNIVERSITY PRESS

Great Clarendon Street, Oxford, OX2 6DP,
United Kingdom

Oxford University Press is a department of the University of Oxford.
It furthers the University's objective of excellence in research, scholarship,
and education by publishing worldwide. Oxford is a registered trade mark of
Oxford University Press in the UK and in certain other countries

First published 2013
First published in paperback 2015

Published in the United States of America by Oxford University Press
198 Madison Avenue, New York, NY 10016, United States of America

British Library Cataloguing in Publication Data
Data available

Library of Congress Cataloging in Publication Data
Data available

ISBN 978–0–19–957793–4 (Hbk.)
ISBN 978–0–19–876648–3 (Pbk.)

Acknowledgements

This is a history of associations—of people, ideas, policies, international organizations, and states—and writing it would not have been possible without the relationships that supported me. Work on it began in 2001 at Keele University, and from among my friends and colleagues there I would like to extend particular thanks to Anne Hughes, Andrew Rutherford, Mike Smith, and Alannah Tomkins, who also gave a warm welcome to Dr Jens-Wilhelm Wessels, a postdoctoral researcher who joined me there to work on the project. The multi-archival research on which the book is based was facilitated by a large research grant from the Arts and Humanities Council (AHRC), and by the project's adoption by the History Faculty of the University of Oxford and Jesus College Oxford when I moved here in 2003. I owe thanks to the Fellows and Principal of Jesus College, especially its lively community of historians, and my fellow tutors in History, Alexandra Gajda and Felicity Heal. Within the History Faculty special appreciation is due to Jane Caplan, Martin Conway, Gareth Davies, John Darwin, Christopher Haigh, Robert Gildea, John Robertson, Nick Stargardt, and Chris Wickham. Our treasured research officer, Aileen Mooney, deserves particular recognition. Her timely suggestion and assistance led me to apply for a British Academy Senior Research Fellowship, which helped turn a digital ocean of archival material into a book. I was honoured to be awarded the British Academy's 'Thank-Offering to Britain Research Fellowship', established by German–Jewish Refugees after the Second World War, some of whose donors have found their way into the pages of this text through their association with liberal internationalism. During this period of research leave, the Institute for Advanced Study in Princeton generously welcomed me as a visitor, and the Shelby White and Leon Levy Archives Center opened a new vista on the history of social science and rescue to me.

Margaret Macmillan once memorably claimed that only a 'handful of eccentrics' were interested in the history of the League of Nations.[1] We now number very many handfuls, who continue to enjoy the air of notoriety Margaret bestowed upon us. I am delighted to count myself among this group, and am grateful for their rich and diverse contributions to what sometimes felt like being in a remote corner of an isolated field when I began this research project. Among the friends to whom I am indebted are Anne Deighton, Madeleine Herren, Harold James, Sandrine Kott, Kiran Klaus Patel, Louis Pauly, Susan Pedersen, and Sunil Amrith, and I am particularly grateful to Pieter Briegel, Martin Ceadel, Glenda Sluga, Teresa Tomás Rangil, and Andrew Webster, who generously gave of their time to read parts of the text, however roughly hewn. Profound thanks are due to the archivists and libraries detailed in the bibliographic section of the book for their assistance,

---

[1] Margaret Macmillan, *Paris 1919: Six Months that Changed the World* (New York, 2001), 83.

and for permission to cite the materials they hold in their care. I am also grateful to Stephanie Ireland, Christopher Wheeler, and the very efficient production team at Oxford University Press.

I was sustained in my research by talking to different communities of students at schools, colleges, universities, and research institutes in Aarhus, Berlin, Cambridge, Copenhagen, Durham, Florence, Geneva, London, Manchester, Moscow, Oxford, Sydney, and Washington DC. Their enthusiasm was infectious, and some of the exchanges that resulted have lasted years, and continue to evolve. Here the International History Network put together by Hilde Henriksen Waage and Hanne Vik in Oslo deserves a particular mention. So, too, does the support of Tim Sanderson and the Calleva Foundation. In 2012 they provided the financial assistance that has enabled me to develop aspects of my work on the League into a new set of research questions and projects.

Conversations with people no longer here also shaped this work. My mother, Anneliese Clavin (Geburtsname Ricken), and Jens-Wilhelm Wessels both died suddenly within the same year. I am profoundly grateful to my family and friends who helped me through this, and the other unexpected challenges that confronted me during the writing of the book. They are now somewhat incredulous that it is, at last, 'finished'.

Here it is, and it is dedicated to them all.

Contents

Detailed Contents

Health at the heart of Europe 179
Economic appeasement 185
Rural dreams 193

6. Scrutiny and Strategy: Contesting Economic Depressions, 1937–1939 198
Business cycles and other journeys around the world 202
The hyperactive Depression Delegation 211
Prescriptions for the world economy 218
A world consuming and consumed 228

7. The League at War and in Pieces, 1939–1940 231
The case for reform 233
The 'Bruce Report' 240
War Begins 251
The fall of Avenol 258

8. Made in the USA, 1940–1943 267
Planning without plans 271
The challenge of the ILO 274
The League in Princeton 279
The Transition from War to Peace Economy 285
Food organized 294
Relief and reconstruction 297

9. The Architecture of a New World Order, 1944–1945 305
History meets monetary policy 308
The ghost of reparations past 319
Dumbarton Oaks 325
The quest for economic stability 329
The battle over employment 333
A watchtower for the world 335

Conclusion 341
Continuities 342
Discontinuities 351
Chronicle of a death foretold 357

Archival Sources and Bibliography 360
Index 385

Abbreviations

AMAE	Archives du Ministère des Affaires Etrangères, Paris
BA	Bundesarchiv, Abteilung Potsdam
BAK	Bundesarchiv, Abteilung Koblenz
BIS	Bank for International Settlements
Bodl.	Bodleian Library, University of Oxford
BoE	Archive of the Bank of England
CAEF	Centre des Archives Économiques et Financières, Paris
ECOSOC	Economic and Social Council
EEA	Exchange Equalization Account
EEC	European Economic Community
EFO	Economic and Financial Organization
EFTA	European Free Trade Association
EIS	Economic Intelligence Service
EU	European Union
FAO	Food and Agriculture Organization
FDR	Franklin Delano Roosevelt
FEA	Foreign Economic Administration
FRBNY	Archive of the Federal Reserve Bank of New York
GATT	General Agreement on Tariffs and Trade
GFM	Archive of the German Foreign Ministry
IAS	Institute for Advanced Study
IBRD	International Bank for Reconstruction and Development
IIA	International Institute for Agriculture
ILO	International Labour Organization
IMF	International Monetary Fund
ITO	International Trade Organization
LC	Manuscript Division, Library of Congress, Washington, DC
LNHO	League of Nations Heath Organization
LNU	League of Nations Union
LON	Archives of the League of Nations
LSE	London School of Economics
MFN	most favoured nation
Mudd	Seely Mudd Library, Princeton University, Princeton, NJ
NAA	National Archives of Australia
NARA	National Archives and Records Administration, College Park, Maryland
NGO	Non-governmental organization
ODNB	*Oxford Dictionary of National Biography,* online edn, October 2009
OFRRO	Office of Foreign Relief and Rehabilitation Operations
PPP	purchasing-power parity
RTAA	Reciprocal Tariff Agreement Act
SEC	Supreme Economic Council
TNA	The National Archives, Kew, Great Britain
ULC	University Library, University of Cambridge

UN	United Nations
UNO	United Nations Organization
UNOG	United Nations Office at Geneva
UNRRA	United Nations Relief and Rehabilitation Administration
WTO	World Trade Organization

Introduction

For thirty years after the First World War, humankind reeled from a series of financial catastrophes and economic depressions. This book tells the story of how during this period efforts to support global capitalism became a core objective of the League of Nations. In its lifetime, the world's first global intergovernmental organization confronted the powerful forces that influenced the world economy, to coordinate economic actors, and to articulate policies to take state and international agency in new directions. It is a history that resonates deeply with the global predicament of the early twenty-first century.

When it was founded in 1920, the League's only interest in international economics was the promotion of free trade. Central banks were charged with monetary policy, markets were to be set free, and the state was to be a nightwatchman. But the League was drawn into economics and finance by the exigencies of the post-war slump and hyperinflation in the early 1920s, and the onset of the Great Depression in 1929. Indeed, by the mid-1930s the League's undertakings in economics were so central to its self-identity that they formed the basis of attempts to reinvent the organization and its role in international relations. Its work continued through the economic emergency occasioned by the Second World War, where, from a new home in the USA, it resumed its now established role as a pathfinder, tracking the performance of the world economy, identifying routes back liberal capitalism, and mapping out policies and the lessons of the past for states and its successor international organizations to follow.

This history draws out the profound changes that took place in economic science, in government policy, and in ideas about the role of international organizations in sustaining economic security. By the Second World War, the League expounded the view that 'something was so radically wrong with the function of the economic system that, not the wisdom of this or that policy, but the fundamental assumptions of economic thought should be questioned'.[1] The performance of industry and agriculture was no longer the private concern of shareholders, trade unionists, and landowners; it had become 'a social function carried out in the interest of all'.[2]

It reflected the view that the experience of financial shocks and economic slump was as powerful a force of global change as war. Where the language of peace after

---

[1] League of Nations, *The Transition from War to Peace Economy: Report of the Delegation of Economic Depressions, Part I* (Geneva, 1943), 10.
[2] League of Nations, *The Transition from War to Peace Economy*, 16.

1918 divided the world into 'winners' and 'losers', the battle against economic depression should have united a world that faced the 'tragedy of forced unemployment'. That it led instead to a second world war cemented a conviction in the importance of economic stability for the prospects of peace. So did the shocking discovery of the 'coexistence of large unsalable stocks of foodstuffs and raw materials (part of which from time to time was deliberately destroyed), and want and deprivation suffered by the unemployed and partially employed' in a world where 'even in the richest countries a large proportion of the population was inadequately fed, inadequately housed, and inadequately clothed'.[3]

Whereas schemes for organizations to facilitate international peace had a centuries-old heritage, the notion of using a body such as the League of Nations to facilitate global economic and financial relations surfaced for the first time towards the end of the First World War. In Wilson's Fourteen Points it was articulated through an emphasis on free trade, framed in a liberal capitalist model of the world economy that the British and American peacemakers believed offered the best prospect for international prosperity and peace. This idea of a distinct intergovernmental organization dedicated to economic and financial relations faced powerful opposition from certain policy-makers and many of the world's central banks, and it took time for the self-conceived Economic and Financial Organization (EFO) to emerge. Until it was able to marshal personnel and support, the League's economic and financial arm was heavily reliant on a wider transnational network of financiers, economists, and political advisers. It was formed in efforts to stabilize financial crises in Austria, Hungary, Bulgaria, and Greece, but it was the impact of the Great Depression and its convention of two world economic conferences in 1927 and 1933 that allowed the EFO's resources and ambition to grow. As a result, this study's close focus on the unfolding history subverts the usual chronologies of the League's activities centred on the years before the Disarmament Conference or the Manchurian or Ethiopian crises. Here it is the years after, not before, 1930 that are of primary concern.

In many ways this is a lost history, and the EFO is itself something of an organization without a recorded past.[4] Yet many histories of the years between

---

[3] League of Nations, *The Transition from War to Peace Economy*, 16.

[4] This is the first study to be written based on a thorough investigation of its archives. Martin Hill, *The Economic and Financial Organization of the League of Nations: A Survey of Twenty-Five Years' Experience* (Washington, 1946), was drawn on his recollections and work for the Princeton Mission. Pioneering studies in the field is derived largely on its voluminous published record include works by Neil de Marchi, 'League of Nations Economists and the Ideal of Peaceful Change in the Decade of the "Thirties"', in Craufurd D. Goodwin (ed.), *Economics and National Security: A History of their Interaction. Annual Supplement to Volume 23, History of Political Economy* (London, 1991), 143–78; A. Alexander Menzies, 'Technical Assistance and the League of Nations', in United Nations Library, *The League of Nations in Retrospect: Proceedings of the Symposium* (Berlin and New York, 1983), 295–312. The most important studies to date have been by Louis Pauly, who foregrounds, in particular, the institution's legacies to the International Monetary Fund, where he was once employed, and uses oral testimony of key protagonists: Louis W. Pauly, 'The League of Nations and the Foreshadowing of the International Monetary Fund', *Princeton Essays in International Finance*, 201 (Dec. 1996), 1–52, and *Who Elected the Bankers? Surveillance and Control in the World Economy* (Ithaca, NY, 1997). Anthony M. Endres and Grant A. Fleming, *International Organizations and the*

1919 and 1946 have been written out of the published data and studies that the EFO produced. Its statistical compilations form the bedrock of comparative national and international economic histories; the conferences and meetings it organized became the stage on which historians have recounted the origins of the Second World War; many of the economists recruited to work for it made seminal contributions to the intellectual history of social science; its widely consulted accounts of the failure of the interwar economy formed the narrative backdrop to post-war planning after 1940; and its bureaucrats went on to found or lead new organizations after 1945. Partly because the publication record of the EFO was so voluminous, it was not readily apparent that the history of the institutional environment that powerfully shaped this work was missing, with its rich, wide-ranging archive long unexplored.

The history of the League's attempts to shape global economic and financial relations also remained in the shadows, because, while the organization sought to connect economics and finance to politics and society in pioneering and complex ways, economists and historians lost interest in studying these connections. Economists have been drawn to mathematical approaches (some of which have their origins in the League's scientific work); students of the intellectual history of economics have been inclined to study economic ideas, and social sciences generally, in relation to one another, in preference to studying their links to national or international policy; and historians have preferred to explore social and political relationships through the lens of cultural analysis. This is not to disavow the benefits or the insights gained from these approaches, but it helps to explain the neglect of the League's involvement in economic and financial relations compared with other aspects of its history.

Since the beginning of the twenty-first century there has been a great flowering of historical interest in the League of Nations. It was fuelled by the end of the cold war, and the dawn of a new age of multilateralism and insecurity in international relations on a scale last seen in the interwar period. A new wave of globalization, too, played its part in moving historians away from the same preoccupation with success and failure that framed contemporaries' view of the League solely as a means through which states navigated from one world war to the next.[5] Historians

---

Analysis of Economic Policy, 1919–1950 (Cambridge, 2002), is based largely on its published studies, and focuses on the EFO, and its contributions to the history of intellectual thought. But it neglects the historical context in which policy ideas were conceived and indiscriminately conflates League officials, League economists, members of the International Labour Organization (ILO), League committees, and delegations comprising national representatives. For the EFO's war origins, see Yann Decorzant, *La Société des Nations et la naissance d'une conception de la régulation économique internationale* (Brussels, 2011). For a study of its operations, see Patricia Clavin and Jens-Wilhelm Wessels, 'Understanding the Work of the Economic and Financial Organization of the League of Nations', *Contemporary European History Review*, 14/4 (2005), 475–6.

[5] Susan Pedersen, 'Back to the League of Nations', *American Historical Review*, 112/4 (2007), 1091–117. For details of scholars working on the League of Nations, see <http://www.leagueofnationshistory.org> (accessed 21 June 2012) and the History of International Organizations Network <http://www.apsun.ch/unoacademia/Home/page10149.html> (accessed 21 June 2012). For an online bibliographic and personnel database, see the League of Nations Search Engine <http://www.lonsea.de/> (accessed 21 June 2012).

have begun to build on the work of political scientists who were generally more interested in these organizations to move beyond a bifurcated division between those who regard global international organizations as autonomous actors in world politics and those who interpret them primarily as instruments of states' power, an epiphenomenon of the realist diplomatic game.[6] Insights from sociology have illuminated how institutions socialize their members, assigning international organizations the potential to generate shared causal and normative understandings that are the prerequisites and the resource base out of which collective action grows.[7] Historical research has enabled us to understand these processes on their own terms, and to do so it is necessary to work outwards from Geneva towards the nation states. This study attempts to give the League its due as an actor, or more properly as a company of actors, rather than treating it as merely a stage.

The EFO's approach to economics and finance was not always consistent. The book explores the contradictory conceptions of the 'international' economy, understood in relation to the powers and interests of nations and empires that marked its history. It explains why the League, in time, came to tolerate, and on occasions even facilitated, the promotion of protection for primary producers and regional networks of cooperation, while at the same time advocating a policy of free trade and a single, unified global economy. In monetary policy, in the early 1920s its actions endorsed the reconstitution of the globalizing gold standard monetary regime. But its views were transformed by experience and the information it gathered as to the mechanics and demands of the system, and the failure of states to coordinate policies in the 1930s. Similarly, in the 1940s, although the EFO was heavily engaged in the preparations for peace, it eschewed the language of 'planning' because of its associations with communism and fascism. It also stressed the importance of economic growth and the consumer economy for world peace, but one of the economists who began his professional career working at the League's Princeton Mission in 1940, Kenneth Boulding, was to become an influential critic, claiming that 'anyone who believes exponential growth can go on forever in a finite world is either a madman or an economist'.[8] It would become one of the most popular slogans of those who would seek to question the morality of the financial system after 2008. So it is that the League's contribution in the field of economic and financial relations is a rich demonstration of the paradox of outcomes.

This is also a history of ideas about capitalism, seen through the pragmatic eyes of the League secretariat in its search for 'practical' economics. Many of the economists whom the EFO recruited in a variety of capacities would become world renowned,

---

[6] Michael N. Barnett and Martha Finnemore, 'The Politics, Power, and Pathologies of International Organizations', *International Organization*, 53/4 (Autumn 1999), 699–732; Clive Archer, *International Organizations* (3rd edn; London, 2003), 68–73.

[7] See, e.g., J. G. March and J. P. Olsen, 'The Institutional Dynamics of International Political Orders', *International Organization*, 52 (1988), 943–69; Martha Finnemore, *National Interests in International Society* (Ithaca, NY, 1996); for an overview, see A. Wiener, 'Constructivism and Social Institutionalism', in M. Cini and A. Bourne (eds), *Palgrave Advances in European Union Studies* (Basingstoke, 2006), 35–55.

[8] Widely attributed to Kenneth Boulding. See, e.g., Jack Uldrich, *Jump the Curve: 50 Essential Strategies to help your company stay ahead of emerging technologies* (Avon, MA, 2008), 7.

including Gustav Cassel, Bertil Ohlin, Gottfried Haberler, Ragnar Nurkse, Jan Tinbergen, Tjalling Koopmans, Jacques Polak, and James Meade. Their work reaches deep into the history of economic thought, although it is possible to touch only briefly on this, and other relevant historigraphies, in a study written out of the archives. These men were survivors and students of some of the most turbulent episodes in the financial and economic history of the twentieth century. They became keenly interested in the relationship between economic ideas and state and international policy, and between cyclical downturn and financial crisis; they were experts in the history of inflation and deflation, and the search for stability and growth.

Throughout the time of the League, the world economy existed in a state of quasi emergency. It prompted the organization's secretariat to bring together discrete groups of social scientists, state officials, businessmen, financiers, farmers, and workers in a steady stream of conferences, meetings, and scientific investigations that enable us to recover afresh the varied and conflicting ways these groups understood the situation, and how their ideas related to policy. The organization's great range of interests and activities in the evolving architecture meant that, despite the outward appearance of a coherent structure, in practice the organization came to comprise different institutions and networks that pulled in different directions. This was both a weakness and a strength. The multiplicity of activities and perspectives frequently rendered the whole League ineffective in an international crisis, yet it simultaneously meant that, out of the diversity of its responses, information was exchanged, and national positions clarified in a process that, over time, opened up the possibility for different outcomes in the future. It also allowed for fruitful connections to be made across spheres, such as economics and health, or finance and security, which may have been impeded by the creation of discrete institutions. It speaks to an energetic striving for a 'new diplomacy' among communities that sought to replace state interest with a broader view of state's duties, and what historians have come to understand as a language of rights.[9]

The secretariat sustained many of these processes, and it looms large here, underlining that history is made as much by men in suits clutching notebooks as it is by those in bold uniforms carrying weapons. These individuals would never be described as colourful personalities, although they lived in colourful times, and were mostly male, although one of the EFO's section directors, Alexander Loveday, became anxious to advance the careers of women in his section, and they grew more visible in the crisis and war years of the League.

Therefore, an appreciation of the League's work needs to situate it in the *longue durée* of change in international relations in the twentieth century, and this history locates the locus of change in the people who worked for, or encountered, the League, and the ideas it helped to generate and disseminate about international relations. Over time, the EFO, or more precisely its secretariat and the experts it recruited to work with it, developed clear ideas on how to manage relations between

---

[9] Cornelia Navari, *Internationalism and the State in the Twentieth Century* (London, 2000), 252–68.

national and international economies, and the value of international and regional
organization in facilitating economic recovery and growth. For them, 'each period
of prosperity and depression is an historical individual', and each economic crisis
was 'embedded in a socio-economic structure of its own'.[10] Yet they also argued
that, for all the remarkable changes in the world economy between the mid-
nineteenth and mid-twentieth centuries, economic activity was characterized by
certain essential similarities, however different the economic and institutional
structures of individual countries might appear. The most obvious, shared characteristic was that economic progress had taken the form not of a steady hill
climb to new levels of output and well-being, but rather of 'spurts and rebounds',
'periods of prosperity and then depression', that should be understood in a global
context.[11]

As a result, they came to believe one of their core functions was not just to collate
global intelligence—a founding rationale—but to mitigate economic and financial
turmoil, and to safeguard liberal democratic values and peace. They privileged
technocratic cooperation—an early precursor to the principles underpinning the
Bretton Woods institutions and the European Economic Community, for which
many of its staff members went to work, and one that was predicated on a world
divided between capitalism and command economies. At the same time, the EFO's
secretariat and many of the social scientists who it hired became trenchant critics of
the actions and powers marshalled by member and non-member states that they
believed had worked against international coordination, cooperation, and peace. It
explains why during the course of the 1920s, and especially the subsequent decade
of ultra-nationalism of the 1930s, despite the League's shortcomings, many became
more, not less, convinced as to the utility of international organizations, especially
in the field of economic and financial relations. As the new world order was realized
in 1945, however, the League's Mission on economics and finance in Princeton was
neither an uncritical nor an impartial participant. Although it advocated the
primacy of social scientific expertise, the Princeton Mission argued that a world
organization of the future should not 'substitute for other forms of dictatorship a
new dictatorship of scholars. In the democratic world the final power must always
rest with the mass of people, with laymen.'[12]

The League of Nations was the emphatically descriptive name that the statesmen
at the Paris Peace Conference in 1919 intended would reinforce the authority of
member states rather than challenge it. The primacy of state sovereignty was

[10] League of Nations, *Economic Stability in the Post-War World: The Conditions of Prosperity after the Transition from War to Peace* (Geneva, 1945), 291. 'Technological knowledge, methods of production, degree of capital-intensity, number, quality and age distribution of the population, habits and preferences of the consumers, social institutions in the widest sense including the legal framework of society, practice in the matter of interventions of the State and other public bodies in the economic sphere, habits of payment, banking practice and so forth—all these practices change continuously, and are not exactly the same in any two cases' (Gottfried Haberler, *Prosperity and Depression* (rev. edn; Geneva, 1938), 177).
[11] League of Nations, *Economic Stability in the Post-War World*, 291–2.
[12] 'Report of the Director', 14 Oct. 1940, IAS, Records of the Office of the Director (Aydelotte), 1940; Alexander Loveday, *Reflections on International Administration* (Oxford, 1958), 36–7.

enshrined in the Covenant of the League and in the organizational structures and institutional practice that emerged. The League presented a vision of the world where the unit that counted was the nation state. Indeed, it was hidebound by this principle and by the need for unanimity among its members, or at least its most powerful members, as a precondition of action.[13] This carried the complication that among them were nation states that were also empire states, such as Britain, France, the Netherlands, and Belgium, or that aspired to empire, like Italy; while for others, such as Norway and Switzerland, internationalism was a defining feature of their national identity. This had important consequences both for the League's impact on international relations and for the impact of participation on members. It was characteristic of the ambiguities of the League that membership of the organization was attractive to former territories of the Austro-Hungarian Empire, or to dominions and colonies of Britain, because it provided access to a language of national rights and privileges, concepts and information, that for many of them was to shape their route to independent statehood. For Ireland, in 1919 in the throes of a war to be free of empire's reach, the League 'offered at once secure international recognition, not as a British Dominion'.[14] For small and middling powers and emerging states, Geneva gave a platform where they could be heard on terms of nominal equality with the great powers that had heretofore determined inter-national politics. More mundanely, it also provided access to other nation states and to intelligence without the expense of opening embassies and consulates around the world. Yet it was never a truly global organization. Its vista only ever comprised or reflected parts of the globe, never the whole. In particular, Africa surfaced largely as a subject of interest for the Council and the secretariat at the behest of Western powers—an object of the League, not an actor in its own right.

At the same time as the League sought to project a vision of international democracy onto the world, it had world visions projected onto it. Its diverse membership and the changing international context in which it operated meant there was no single and consistent view about what comprised the League, what it should do, and how it should function. 'The League' thus became a site where a plurality of views about global and regional coordination and cooperation were generated, and where they could be compared and could compete. In this sense, it was not a universe, offering one unique, essential view of the world and how it should be, but a multiverse: an international space–time that could and did spawn multiple universes. As the American director of the League's Information Section, Arthur Sweetser reflected, the rest of the world could challenge 'simplifie[d] European conceptions . . . of a single league at Geneva', and favour 'instead a bewilderment of nations'.[15]

---

[13] Zara Steiner, *The Lights that Failed: European International History, 1919–1933* (Oxford, 2007), 351–4; Christopher Thorne, *The Limits of Foreign Policy: The West, The League and the Far Eastern Crisis of 1931–1933* (London, 1972).

[14] Memo by Patrick Sarsfield O'Hegarty, 15 Sept. 1922, in Royal Irish Academy, *Documents on Irish Foreign Policy*, vol. 1, no. 320, NAI DT S3332.

[15] Memo by Sweetser, 'The League of Nations and the United States', 8 Feb. 1928, p. 4, LON R3567, 50/1683/1683.

The internationalisms embodied in the League had different roots: Jeremy Bentham's notion of 'international' as a term for laws that extended beyond the state; Immanuel Kant's vision of a permanent peace among nations, and the emergence in the late nineteenth century of non-governmental and international organizations dedicated to culture, communication, international standardization, and peace. It contained aspects of liberal (sometimes articulated as humanitarian) imperialism redolent with a language of rights, notably the rights of states in the West, and their 'responsibilities' towards the rest of the world, whose access to rights and resources were curtailed and increasingly controlled.

Aspects of this social agenda were activated when the Great Depression and the failure of intergovernmental cooperation caused the League to seek a more holistic approach to the economic crisis that embraced social health and welfare. The quality of the world's nutrition, housing, and access to employment, usually explored through the issue of public works at the International Labour Organization (ILO), were now all grist to its mill. After 1929, the worldwide economic crisis brought these issues, their relationship to economic policy, and the interconnections of the world economy more clearly into view than ever before. Throughout, the League also measured the performance of the non-Western economies that were of growing interest and importance following the recourse to closer imperial economic ties by the liberal democracies of Britain and France and the overtly racial empire-building projects of Japan, Germany, and Italy. In many parts of the world, including Europe, it was not just the 'Thirties' that were 'Hungry', but the decades either side of it. Charting the impact of the economic downturn on levels of employment and malnutrition were forces that its supporters used to reinvent the League.

The issue of who could metaphorically afford to butter their bread caused the League to reflect on the policy relationships between wealthier nations and poorer ones, predominately, but not exclusively, in Europe. An emerging sensitivity to the fat and the lean reflected and shaped a perspective on the world economy that was more conscious of the distribution of international wealth and the implications of its inequalities: by how the world was shaped by trading relations between industrial and primary producers; by patterns of international indebtedness and questions of reparation for the costs of war; and by the need for reconstruction aid and a host of issues that after 1945 would come under the umbrella of 'international development'.

In 1920 the prevailing view was that most societies were distinct and essentially non-comparable; the Western world was viewed as destined to remain different and separate from the societies of Africa and Asia. But during its lifetime the League— its voice amplified through the international network it sustained and given gravitas through the invocation of experience—came to place all societies of the world on a single, shared continuum from the least to the most developed, on the same trajectory towards a common project of 'modernization'. In a proto-theory of development, the EFO came to argue that the world's guiding objective should be 'the fullest possible use . . . of the resources of production, human and material, of the skill and enterprize of the individual . . . so as to attain and maintain in all countries a stable economy and rising standards of living'.[16] Equality and security, then, had an explicitly economic dimension, and, in this search for economic security, the League encountered one of the most challenging questions for economic policy in the modern world: how to respond to societies' diverse economic and social needs and resources on a plane of equality in international relations?

At the same time, the League's values could also be described as 'middle class' and 'protestant'. They were about respect for the ownership of property and assets, and the importance of self-improvement. The League was as much a 'state of mind' as an institution, or a range of treaties and conventions.[17] It respected the different needs of producers small and large, the wealthy, the less wealthy, and the poor, though it proved easier to measure and account for these differences than to develop and advocate policies that supported all parties. Working-class values and needs, of unionized, male urban workers at least, were both more evident and catered for in its sibling organization, the ILO. It was there that claims to 'proletarian internationalism' were primarily found, and intended to combat the claims of the USSR. Quite how international communism related to liberal internationalism in the interwar period is still unclear, but there is no doubt it played a central role as the defining 'other', especially in the field of economics, even after the USSR had joined the League.[18] It is also important to remember that industrial and state representatives, who formed the other two-thirds of the ILO's unique tripartite membership arrangement, primarily used it as a forum through which to promote improved labour productivity.

The League, and the ILO, became the focus of lobbying of all kinds, and not just from those who aspired to nationhood. Activists who lobbied at the League campaigned for the rights of women, children, slaves, and minority groups, producers' agreements on commodities such as wheat, sugar, and wine, and the monetization of silver. Movements dedicated to the causes of thrift, temperance, and international peace and disarmament also plied their cause. Expectations of independence were raised by its location in Geneva, away from the traditional spheres of power, even though petitioning the League was frequently mediated through states or national and international associations. As Britain's future Foreign Secretary, Lord Curzon, accurately predicted in April 1919, 'the League would experience many and great disappointments' as a result of the scale, and divergence, of hopes invested in it.[19] The ability of the League to meet the world's sometimes conflicting expectations depended, in large part, on the authority invested in it by member states, and this was strictly limited. By the end of 1920, forty-eight states had joined, yet key powerbrokers were absent. Germany became a member only in

---

[16] League of Nations, *The Transition from War to Peace Economy*, 113.

[17] Glenda Sluga, 'The Hancock Lecture, 2009: Was the Twentieth Century the Great Age of Internationalism?', *Australian Academy of Humanities Proceedings 2009* (Canberra, 2010), 162.

[18] Patricia Clavin, 'Interwar Internationalism: Conceptualising Transnational Thought and Action, 1919–1939', in Daniel Lacqua (ed.), *Internationalism Reconfigured: Transnational Ideas and Movements between the World Wars* (London, 2011), 5–6.

[19] Curzon to Hankey, *c.* Apr. 1919, in Stephen Roskill, *Hankey Man of Secrets*, ii. *1919–1931* (London, 1972), 66.

1926, and the USSR, a late participant, entered only in 1934, by which time other states were abandoning it, either out of ambition to form a world order that challenged the universalist values embodied in the League or motivated by the more prosaic need to economize. Before they joined, after they had left, or even if they never joined at all, the major powers shaped the agency of the League. This was especially true of the most famous non-member of all: the United States.

Throughout its lifetime the League continually needed to articulate the value of international cooperation to its members, and to demonstrate its achievements. The organization's battle for legitimacy was interminable. Such claims of 'success' were inevitably matched by accusations of failure, alternating tales of triumph and disaster, with little shade in between.[20] But it is impossible, perhaps even wrong-headed, to attempt to sidestep the binary of 'success' and 'failure', because the League's need for validation was conditioned by it. It subsequently also shaped policy-makers' and historians' search for the lessons of its history. Indeed, a clear-eyed recognition of why 'success' and 'failure' were fundamental to the contentions made by those who sought to act on the organization's behalf, and to the historical framing of the League, reveals much about the pressures it faced in asserting its value and role in interstate relations in a global climate where ideologies of nationalism and self-sufficiency were rife. It was imperative to make a strong and sustained case as to why and how the League brought something new to international relations so as to maintain member states' contributions to its work by sending officials, intelligence, and hard cash, and by tolerating League oversight and sometimes interference in their affairs.[21]

The League's successor organizations were not liberated from this history but enslaved by it: with the League as failure, they were the antithetical success stories. The United Nations Organization, in particular, remains trapped in the need to refute the charge that it 'was destined to the dustbin of history and the fate of the League of Nations'.[22] But, just as the origins of the League lay in nineteenth-century internationalism, so the League's interest in economics left a profound legacy for the global order that extended beyond 1946, transmitted through a dense institutional and personal network. The formal dates of the League's existence are parentheses within a much longer history. It served as an incubator for ideas and practices that continue to shape the twenty-first-century world.

---

[20] See, e.g., Beverly Nicols, *Cry Havoc!* (London, 1933), and Robert Edward Dell, *The Geneva Racket, 1920–1939* (London, 1941).

[21] League membership came to be calculated according to an assessment of the strength of the member's national economy. If the cost of the League, which totalled just over $5 million or £1,071,621 in 1929, were broken down into individual units (each worth just over $5,000), Britain contributed 105 units, France and Germany 79, Italy and Japan 60, India 56, China 46, Spain 40, Canada, 35, Poland 32, the Argentine and Czechoslovakia 29, Australia 27, and the Netherlands 23, surprisingly only one more than the much poorer Romania.

[22] Transcript of Press Conference by Secretary-General Kofi-Annan at United Nations Headquarters, 30 July 2003, United Nations Press Release Document SG/SM/8803 <http://www.un.org/News/Press/docs/2003/sgsm8803.doc.htm> (accessed 14 Oct. 2010).

1

The Multiverse of the League, 1920–1929

The founding fathers of the League of Nations had not intended the organization to contribute to economic reconstruction, or the operations of the world economy beyond a lofty pronouncement endorsing free trade. But a series of financial crises in Europe, notably in the successor states of central and eastern Europe, prompted it to gather economic and financial intelligence on national economies, and coordinate rescue efforts. The next step was to begin surveying the economic health of all regions, and then of the world as a whole. A combination of events were significant, notably in Austria, Hungary, Greece, and Bulgaria, and a series of conferences, in Brussels in 1920 and Geneva in 1927, fleshed out the bones of the League's economic operation. By the end of the decade an economic and financial organization had emerged, and it was only then that the League could claim an agency in economic and financial affairs in its own right. At first the handful of men charged with economic and financial issues relied upon a transnational arrangement of private agencies—banks, universities, scientific societies—and personal networks to make an impact. Their patterns of work created a cycle of international meetings about economic and financial policy, which was supported by the world's first international bureaucracy—the latter surprising national policy-makers by taking itself seriously. From inception, then, the League challenged expectations with the emergence of a strand of operation that the British and American architects of the new organization had sought to avoid: involvement in financial crises and economic reconstruction. But, at the same time as this 'technical' work moved in unexpected directions, the political challenges before the new organization made it clear the League was not going to be the millenarian 'bringer of light' anticipated by its most enthusiastic advocates.

BUILDING AN ORGANIZATION

As the internationalism of war gave way to the nationalism of peace, the expectation in 1920 that the League was largely to steer clear of financial and economic affairs was not an oversight, but a reflection of tensions between Allied and Associated powers. In particular, Britain and the United States feared the implications of League intervention on the already vexed issue of war debts owed by the Allies to the USA, and reparations owed by the Central Powers to the victors. Nor was there a precedent for intergovernmental cooperation in economics and finance in peacetime. The Covenant contained provision in Article 23 for the members of the

League 'to secure and maintain equitable treatment for the commerce of all Members of the League'. But, before trade could be considered, financial relations needed to be stabilized—particularly the widely fluctuating values of the world's leading currencies, which had left the gold standard to fight the war. Here the major powers' statesmen and central bankers feared the potential anarchy that might be unleashed by allowing the 'Geneva experiment' into such a sensitive area of policy-making, where international disagreement had the potential to trigger financial instability. As the world's premier financial powers, Britain and the USA set the tone, and their reticence was evidence of the widely held conviction that, when it came to economic policy, unlike diplomacy, there should be no break with the past. The state was expected to return to its pre-war role of 'nightwatchman' in a 'hands-off' policy regime that was believed to have brought unprecedented international economic growth before 1914. If coordination between national economies was necessary, it should be confined to the financial sphere and led by independent central banks.[1] However, the more economically vulnerable members of the wartime partnership, France and Italy, took a different view, and were keen for the cooperation to continue in peacetime. Within months Britain, having relinquished its role as the world's banker, came around to their perspective.[2]

The ideology of non-intervention was profoundly challenged by the context of peace. In 1920, rising levels of inflation, the end of the post-war boom, and the particularly difficult economic conditions faced by the new states of central and eastern Europe, the foster children of the League, all illustrated that the world economy was not likely to right itself. The successful Bolshevik revolution in Russia, moreover, offered the shocking realization of what could happen if capitalism's recovery failed. Influential, too, was lobbying by leading figures in economic science, a newly emerging discipline that was to become the dominant social science of the twentieth century. Especially eye-catching was the salvo fired by the economist John Maynard Keynes, who had represented the British government at the Paris Peace Conference. He castigated the statesmen for failing to see that the real challenge ahead was not rewriting the rules of the diplomatic game, but recognizing that the game had changed to one in which economic and financial stability and growth were central, both to the prospects of international peace, and to governments' claims for support and legitimacy from their electorate. Paris had delivered treaties but not a peace settlement. It was now imperative to consider *The Economic Consequences of the Peace*.[3]

---

[1] Derek Aldcroft, *From Versailles to Wall Street, 1919–1929* (London, 1977), 55–79, which draws heavily on the League's published evidence. Stephen A. Schuker, 'Origins of American Stabilization Policy in Europe: The Financial Dimension, 1918–1924', in Hans-Jürgen Schröder (ed.), *Confrontation and Cooperation: Germany and the United States in the Era of World War I* (Providence, RI, 1993), 377–407, and Michael J. Hogan, *Informal Entente: The Private Structure of Cooperation in Anglo-American Economic Diplomacy, 1918–1925* (Columbia, 1977), 33–56.

[2] Yann Decorzant, 'Internationalism and the Economic and Financial Organization of the League of Nations', in Daniel Lacqua (ed.), *Internationalism Reconfigured: Transnational Ideas and Movements between the World Wars* (London, 2011), 116–18.

[3] John Maynard Keynes, *The Economic Consequences of the Peace* (London, 1919). His views were endorsed by the mercurial publicist of internationalism, Norman Angell. See Norman Angell, *The*

Although often understood as a vituperative condemnation of the reparations imposed on Germany, the argument that Keynes was advancing was a much wider one about the need to put economic stability before territorial security. By the turn of the century a sophisticated notion of the complex network of mutual political obligations between rulers and the ruled had emerged. The trend was accelerated and cemented by the impact of the First World War, which changed forever the contract between citizens and subjects, and the governments that ruled over them. Total war required governments to organize their resources on an unprecedented scale, and forced the state to demand new sacrifices of all its citizens in the name of loyalty. Allegiance to the nation at war now entailed possible death, injury, bereavement, and upheaval. To sustain its war effort, the state was prompted to extend its obligations to its people and to make changes to the political system that such undertakings implied. The promise of benefits, of course, did not guarantee their delivery. Economic and fiscal policies and tools needed to be developed to match an emerging political and social agenda, and the battle for 'rights' that ensued over the coming decades also had important consequences for international relations. The need to provide greater social security for married women whose family income was imperilled by the death of their husbands in battle, for example, created widows' pension schemes that fuelled Allied claims for reparations from the Central Powers at the Paris negotiations. More broadly, the fortunes of political parties and the legitimacy of the state were now tied, far more than previously, to the prospects of economic stability and growth, and to the opportunities for employment. The international history of the interwar period was to be shaped profoundly by the search for economic solutions that could make good on these political claims. In the 1920s, governments largely pursued international routes out of this dilemma, which the League supported. By the 1930s, however, states everywhere resorted to economic nationalism to meet the frustrated expectations of their electorates, a trend the League sought to combat.[4]

But, in 1920, the League first needed to develop the authority and power to become involved in economic and financial diplomacy. Important precedents had been established in the First World War, with economic and financial cooperation between the Allies relating to food supplies, especially wheat, and in the arrangement of international credits from US banks, which created the war debts.[5] This cooperation spilled over in the peacetime drive to effect reconstruction in the devastated regions of western Europe through the Supreme Economic Council (SEC) founded by cabinet ministers from Britain, France, Belgium, Italy, and the United States in February 1919. The US government's withdrawal from active

Peace Treaty and the Economic Chaos of Europe (London, 1919), and Martin Ceadel, *Living the Great Illusion: Sir Norman Angell, 1872–1967* (Oxford, 2009), 240–1.

[4] Charles Maier, *In Search of Stability: Explorations in Historical Political Economy* (Cambridge, 1987), 1–16; Martin Conway and Pieter Romijn (eds.), *The War for Legitimacy in Politics and Culture, 1936–1946* (Oxford, 2008), 1–20.

[5] Kathleen Burk, *Britain, America and the Sinews of War, 1914–1918* (London, 1985); Martin Horn, *Britain, France and the Financing of the First World War* (Montreal, 2002); Decorzant, 'Internationalism', 115–34.

engagement with the SEC in July 1919, though never formally announced, acted as an important incentive to renew and widen collaboration among the Europeans beyond the immediate task of Belgian and French reconstruction. The need to re-engage the USA, given its emergence as the world's banker, was essential to the broader prospects of financial and economic reconstruction for the vanquished and the victors of the First World War.[6]

The founding drama of the League was primarily played out in the Council and the Assembly, which were the organization's two main governing bodies. The Assembly comprised members' delegates, while the Council was its smaller, higher authority. Its first permanent members were the British Empire, France, Italy, and Japan; these were later joined by Germany and the USSR. Members of the Assembly nominated and elected the remaining non-permanent members of the Council, who were allocated four seats in 1920, rising to six by 1933. It met for the first time on 16 January 1920 in Paris. The Assembly first convened in Geneva during November 1920, with meetings conducted in public, in keeping with the commitment to open diplomacy. The Council and Assembly were supported by a secretariat, and here too the legacy of wartime cooperation determined the personnel recruited to work for it. This was the world's first explicitly international civil service, and its activities lay at the centre of this history. It was established in London in 1920 under the direction of the Eton- and Oxford-educated civil servant Sir Eric Drummond, who became the organization's first Secretary-General. This task was very much business as usual for a British civil service well rehearsed in constructing overseas administrations, although the secretariat also borrowed notions and procedures from *de facto* worldwide organizations, such as the International Telegraph Union and the Universal Postal Union, and wartime inter-Allied committees.[7]

Drummond faced considerable challenges. Although the salary scale of League officials was often alleged to be overly generous by member states, money was in short supply and 'qualified' personnel were hard to come by. The work called for specialist skills, with lawyers and statisticians especially prized, as were those with a familiarity with (European) nations and languages. For ambitious young men, particularly those living in large, wealthier nation states, a career at home offered better prospects than one based abroad, which meant that the young men, and notably women, who went to work for the League were often driven by an enthusiasm for the 'Geneva spirit'. Jean Monnet was 30 years old when he became Assistant Secretary-General, for example, and it would be the destiny of many first hired by the League that they would still be working to facilitate international relations in the 1950s and 1960s.

[6] Burk, *Britain, America, and the Sinews of War*, 196–225; Horn, *Britain, France, and the Financing of the First World War*, 166–86.
[7] Marie-Cloud Smouts, *Les Organisations internationales* (Paris, 1995); Madeleine Herren, *Internationale Organisationen seit 1865: Eine Globalgeschichte der internationalen Ordnung* (Darmstadt, 2009).

The secretariat's core responsibilities were to carry out the preliminaries for meetings of the Council and Assembly, and the implementation of their instructions. But over time it assumed a broader role. Aside from essential administrative tasks—translating, publishing, and distributing documents and hosting teams of delegates and journalists—most of the preparatory drafting of documents and the technical groundwork for commissions and conferences were undertaken by the secretariat, where the League clung to the term 'technical' in preference to scientific. This was not because it feared its scientific work would fail to meet the standards of objectivity demanded by social scientists, but because it was aware that social science itself had a subjective quality. 'Technicians' working for the League were certainly influenced by American and West European efforts to model social science along the lines of natural science by stressing the production of an autonomous body of knowledge and the 'technological capacity for control'. But they did not seek to make such specific claims and associations for the work of the League. Rather, the stress on 'technical' activities emphasized a commitment to the collection, collation, and dissemination of knowledge in a practical application to the cause of world peace.

At its peak the secretariat as a whole compromised more than 600 personnel, whose work provided a continuity of expertise, with many members working for the League for a decade or more. The ethnic identities of individuals drawn to the League were more complex than the state-centred registration process could accommodate. Europeans predominated within the staff, with British and French officials holding the majority of senior posts. The status of bureaucracy, however, did not shield it from the dynamic impact of ideology, notably fascism and bolshevism, which cleaved state relations within the organization, as was evident almost immediately by Fascist Italy's attempts to control, and render Fascist, Italian nationals at the League. There was no doubt that the *esprit de corps* varied from section to section. In its lifetime the Economic and Financial Section was arguably less riven by ideology than departments engaged in the League's more overtly political work, where officials had a powerful role as advocates for international coordination and cooperation in their contacts with ministries of finance, trade, foreign affairs, and war, as well as businesses, banks, universities, and specialist organizations.

Member governments wanted League investigations to be limited to the 'ascertainment of fact'. Many of the studies published by the League, especially in the early years, were powerfully shaped by this condition, which, as the US State Department noted, impeded 'study of situations or matters when they fear that such a study may injure or result in criticism of them' and were 'carefully guarded' when it came to 'critical appraisal, theoretical judgements, distribution of praise or blame'.[8] It was ironic that the League's commitment to open diplomacy encouraged covert behaviour, but the secretariat, too, was prone to dissemblance.

---

[8] Memo by Feis, 'Report to the Advisory Committee on International Relations. Research Work Conducted in Geneva', June 1929, LON, Loveday, P140/11/in- and outgoing correspondence, 1928–9, pp. 3–4.

Because its purpose was couched in the claim that it was a non-political civil service, without responsibility for policy, and was therefore independent of power, it frequently attempted to conceal the political significance of issues it wanted to subject to international examination. Little wonder, then, that these tensions resulted in long, disjointed, and sometimes incoherent reports. But published studies did not reflect the intellectual engagement and vigorous exchange of ideas and information that took place in the meeting rooms or in correspondence when the reports were being drafted. As we shall see in the case of its economic and financial work, the secretariat grew bolder in identifying and asserting its views. It moved beyond its prescribed powers in ensuring League advocacy on these topics were heard.

AN ECONOMIC EXPERIMENT

In 1919, while the White House and Congress were loath to commit to renewed intergovernmental cooperation on economic and financial issues, other prominent American internationalists were keen to be involved. Notable among these were Herbert Hoover, the self-made millionaire who led humanitarian efforts to feed central Europe, and the New York-based bankers Paul M. Warburg and John Pierpoint Morgan, who had negotiated US war loans to Europe and were anxious to secure a return on their investments. Rallying behind a British proposal for a world financial conference, these American bankers and industrialists helped to mobilize a wide international network of finance and economic expertise out of that forged in war, with the determination to correct the failure to address finance and economics at Paris. Most striking was the coordination of a petition for financial cooperation, delivered to leading governments and newspapers, and signed by over 150 leading economists, including Keynes and his patron Arthur Pigou, and the Swedish economist Gustav Cassel; by the bankers Warburg, Morgan, Gerard Vissering, the President of the Bank of the Netherlands, and the British President of Lloyds Bank, Sir Richard Vassar Vassar-Smith; and by leading internationalists and humanitarians, such as Hoover, Lord Robert Cecil (whose experience administering Britain's wartime blockade and Chairmanship of the Supreme Economic Council meant he was eminently qualified to serve as a lobbyist for economic cooperation), and the Swiss President of the International Red Cross Committee Gustave Ador.[9]

It was thus misleading to disaggregate the contribution of an individual such as Keynes and attribute his agency alone, as some have, to the nascence of international financial cooperation. What was truly important was the cumulatively persuasive effect of this network of influential individuals on statesmen. It was

---

[9] For an attempt to pin the origins on a single progenitor, see Benny Carlson, 'Who was the Most Famous Economist in the World—Cassel or Keynes?' *The Economist as Yardstick, Journal of the History of Economic Thought*, 31/4 (Dec. 2009), 521–2. *The Economist* is not a neutral source, but rather a mouthpiece of the League in this period.

marked by the convocation of the League, indeed the world's first 'International Financial Conference', in Brussels between 24 September and 4 October 1920. It marked the second world conference after Paris in what would become known as the decade of 'diplomacy by conference'. For Maurice Hankey, the first Cabinet Secretary, who had been first choice as Secretary-General but who had declined the invitation, the League was the institutionalization of conference diplomacy that marked the great, peacemaking moments of history.[10]

The need to prepare for the conference prompted Drummond to create a new Economic and Financial Section under the direction of Sir Arthur Salter, Britain's former Minister for Shipping and secretary to the wartime Supreme Economic Council in Paris. He was aided by Monnet, with whom he was well acquainted from their joint work on the allied maritime transport council.[11] The challenge was attracting states to the conference table. The gathering was successively postponed, from May to July, and from July to September, becoming the first of many meetings to be impeded by the linked issues of the reparations, and outstanding war debts owed by the victor powers to each other, and primarily to the USA.

The calculation of how much should be charged had been entrusted by the Paris Conference to a Reparations Commission and not the League, to remove the issue from public debate, but the strategy failed. The protests of the new Weimar government against its treatment, assorted attempts at left-wing coups and right-wing putsches across Europe, and Keynes's salvo against the Paris treaties, which resounded around the world in a series of syndicated newspaper articles, stirred up a hornets' nest of international argument.[12] The richer countries of Europe, which at this stage still included Germany, may in fact have had sufficient monetary resources to clear their own path to currency stabilization, but the incumbent governments believed the domestic political costs were prohibitive.[13] It was easier to succumb to the expedient option of blaming other nations for their inflationary difficulties—in short to blame reparations, whereas the fundamental causes were war and the costs of reconstruction—and to plead for American financial assistance.

The French government was especially compromised as it needed US and British financial support for reconstruction but resisted the Anglo-American call to allow the Brussels financial conference to address reparations in relation to Europe's other financial problems. With Germany, Austria, Hungary, and Bulgaria slated to attend, France did not want to risk its policy agenda, in which reparations payments

---

[10] Maurice Hankey, *Diplomacy by Conference: Studies in Public Affairs, 1920–1946* (London, 1946), 21–39, 75; Roskill, *Hankey*, ii. 57–60, 64–7.

[11] Joseph S. Davis, 'World Currency and Banking: The First Brussels Financial Conference', *Review of Economics and Statistics*, 2/12 (Dec. 1920), 322–5. Salter was among those who had sought to link wartime proposals for a League to continued Allied economic cooperation.

[12] Bruce Kent, *The Spoils of War: The Politics, Economics, and Diplomacy of Reparations, 1981–1932* (Oxford, 1989), 17–55.

[13] Niall Ferguson, 'Constraints and Room for Manoeuvre in the German Inflation of the Early 1920s', *Economic History Review*, 49/4 (1996), 635–66.

formed a central plank, being sabotaged by a meeting at which other victors and the vanquished could reopen the issue. War debts, or 'political debts', as they were called by the European powers who wanted to retain their association with the sacrifices and promises made in the First World War, had to be distinguished from subsequent 'commercial loans' undertaken to rebuild currency stability. The European powers also wanted to keep reparations away from the meddling of the League of Nations.

Ultimately France could not resist the range of international pressures that demanded a meeting. Yet, for all that Germany's financial woes during the early 1920s have dominated historians' attention, equally, or even more, troubling to many commentators at the time were the deteriorating fortunes of other European nation states that had succeeded the former Empires, and the deficient responses of the world's diplomats and financiers. An economic failure at the heart of Europe threatened to leave millions destitute and create a dangerous power vacuum into which Bolshevik agitators, or (though less feared) military, revanchist leaders could surge. In exchanges among European leaders, the fate of the successor states of central and eastern Europe, products of the Paris Peace Conference and allies of France, demanded urgent attention. Even for the British, the possibilities of a League meeting seemed worth pursuing: the resort to the League reflected the wider move to integrate it into the heart of British diplomacy in 1920.[14]

In the eight months between the conference announcement and its convocation in Brussels in September, the inflationary spiral, and with it social and economic hardship, continued to worsen. For Austria, Germany, Hungary, and Poland, international financial aid was not optional but imperative to effect economic (re) construction and currency stabilization. The new Austrian republic succumbed to hyperinflation after October 1921, with a monthly inflation rate of 46 per cent and unemployment running at over 33 per cent; in Hungary inflation was to grow 33 per cent per month between March 1923 and February 1924, with rising un-employment and poverty levels to match.[15] The conference was called 'with a view to studying the financial crisis and looking for the means of remedying it and of mitigating the dangerous consequences arising from it', subject however to the very firm instruction that 'none of the questions which are the subject of the present negotiations between the Allies and Germany should be discussed at the Confer-ence'.[16] The proviso clearly underlined the limits of state willingness to open up key economic issues to League scrutiny. Rather, member states wanted to use the meeting to make the case to international financiers, notably in the USA, which

---

[14] An otherwise meticulous study of Britain's relationship with the League takes no account of the role of economics and finance in shaping Britain's relationship with the League once the organization was founded, although economic issues were there in the planning: Peter J. Yearwood, *Guarantee of Peace: The League of Nations in British Policy, 1914–1925* (Oxford, 2009), 66–7.

[15] Hyperinflation is defined in relation to episodes of chronic inflation, out of which it usually arises, by its fluctuating rate (it does not plateau) and its exponential acceleration. For an analysis of these episodes' impact on unemployment, and a revealing illustration of the degree to which economists continue to rely on EFO's data, see Elmus Wicker, 'Terminating Hyperinflation in the Dismembered Habsburg Monarch', *American Economic Review*, 76/3 (1986), 350–64.

[16] World Peace Foundation, *Report on the Brussels Financial Conference* (Boston, 1920), 2.

had assumed the role of the world's banker, for financial aid to central and eastern Europe. The conference was attended by eighty-six delegates from the banks and treasuries of thirty-nine nations, although significantly they were designated as 'experts' and not official government representatives.[17] Their declared intention was to exchange intelligence and ideas on how to combat an unprecedented financial crisis that was the result of an unprecedented war; they were there to analyse and recommend, not to set policy machinery into motion, and this framing put statisticians and economists centre stage.

To meet the Council's request to develop as complete a picture as possible as to the health of the global economy, the secretariat requested that states and their banks submit information on currency, public finance, international trade, retail prices, and coal production.[18] Alexander Loveday, a 30-year-old Scottish statistician hired by Salter in July 1919, took the lead in carefully sifting the data, developing interpretations, and offering commentaries on the different statistical methodologies applied by various countries to, for example, valuing international trade.[19] He was in charge of the fledgling Economic Intelligence Service that comprised part of Salter's section and established a preliminary conference on the standardization of national statistics for international use, which was seen as marking a 'great advance in the utilization of statistics' internationally.[20] But preparations did not end with intelligence gathering. The secretariat's request for members' policy suggestions on how to address the crisis went unanswered, so it commissioned proposals from prominent European economists and circulated them with its own. This resulted in individual papers by prominent economists Maffeo Pantaloni, Charles Gide, Gijsbert Bruins, Arthur Cecil Pigou, and Gustav Cassel, as well as their jointly drafted statement calling for governments to reduce their expenditure (singling out subsidies and military expenditure in particular), the resumption of international lending, and the restoration of the gold standard and normal patterns of trade. There were also, however, some marked differences of opinion between them, and here it was Cassel, in particular, who made the biggest impact.

His widely praised 'Memorandum on the World's Monetary Problems' set out the causes and dangers of inflation, and a subsequent text established the risks of deflation, in which he effectively dismissed the arguments of those who believed the rising levels of inflation could be explained simply by the post-war shortage of supplies.[21] Cassel offered a lucid and sophisticated multi-causal analysis of the financial crisis that was rooted in state behaviour during the war and immediate

---

[17] Of the major powers, only Russia, Turkey, Mexico, and Chile were absent. The USA was represented by Boston lawyer R. W. Boyden, who worked with the Reparation Commission.

[18] For the complete data set, see League of Nations, *Brussels Financial Conference, 1920: The Recommendations and their Application* (2 vols; Brussels, 1922), vol. i, C.10.M.7.1923.II.

[19] File 'Loveday, Alexander', LON, Personnel File, S820.

[20] Davis, 'World Currency and Banking', 350.

[21] Gustav Cassel, 'Memorandum on the World's Monetary Problems', was published as *The World's Monetary Problems* (London, 1921). See also League of Nations, *Supplement to Report No. XIII. (3.): Summary of Recommendations Included in the Memorandum on the World's Monetary Problems by Gustav Cassel* (London, 1921).

post-war period.[22] The cure, he proposed, was the internationally coordinated return to stable currencies, although it was predicated neither on the unadulterated reconstruction of the gold standard, nor on the need to force prices down before stabilization was effected. He argued that price stability was the key issue and he recognized deflation, particularly US deflationary policy (on which he offered an especially prescient and pointed commentary), potentially posed as great a danger as inflation to the future prospects of economic growth and social stability. In the direct, sometimes terse, language that was his hallmark, he also dismissed calls to re-establish exchange rates at the same rates as before the First World War—a step subsequently taken by the British government in April 1925 to demonstrate the virility of the British economy, with disastrous results.

Cassel also used the League as an opportunity to secure an international audience for studies he had been doing on developing the Ricardian doctrine of 'purchasing-power parity' (PPP). It was later adopted by countries, such as Belgium, as a means to calculate currency deflation in their toolkit to manage membership of the gold standard.[23] The concept lives on today as a means of comparing generalized standards of living between different nations. PPP linked fluctuating exchange rates to the prices paid for goods and services in any two countries, and helped to identify comparative inflation rates and transaction costs, although it struggled to include a cultural sensibility to the definition of a stable good.[24] What was really key in the 1919 debate triggered by Cassel's revival of a seventeenth-century idea was the emphasis it placed on *relative* prices, an essential motor in determining patterns of production and trade in a global economy. The relational quality of national economic performance and fortunes in reintegrating the world economy became a central motif of the Brussels Conference. It enabled government and independent experts to think in explicitly comparative terms about which states were coping well, which badly, and why.

Cassel and his colleagues helped the delegates develop a series of prescriptions for domestic action, but the Brussels Conference did not result in any substantive agreement. In central and eastern Europe, in particular, the inflationary crisis continued unabated. From the League's perspective, however, the meeting marked a significant departure in a number of new directions. First, the conference established its entitlement to engage in economic diplomacy. The secretariat had succeeded in gathering together a collection of advisers, financiers and statesmen—with only the latter engaging in some ungentlemanly sneering—who grappled with the central question of how to reinvigorate global capitalism.[25] This group

[22] Cassel, *The World's Monetary Problems*, summarized in *The Economist*, 21 Aug. 1920, p. 291; untitled review of Cassel's memos by N. R. Whitney, *American Economic Review*, 12/3 (Sept. 1922), 515–17.

[23] Isabelle Cassiers, *Croissance, crise et régulation en économie ouverte: La Belgique entre les deux guerres* (Brussels, 1989), 173–83.

[24] For a wider evaluation, see Paul A. Samuelson, 'Gustav Cassel's Scientific Innovations: Claims and Realities', *History of Political Economy*, 25/3 (1993), 515–27; Lars Magnasson, *Gustav Cassel, Popularizer and Enigmatic Walrasian* (London, 1991). A modern, simplified version of Cassel's PPP is the 'Big Mac Index'.

[25] Decorzant, 'Internationalism', 7–8.

endorsed Salter's assertion that governments and the League needed reliable and internationally comparative data against which to evaluate national performance, and to find coordinated, workable solutions to the financial crisis and economic reconstruction that would benefit the international economy as a whole. It was out of this recognition that the League of Nations was able to build an effective case for maintaining and developing its role in economic and financial relations.

Secondly, the conference determined the rudiments of what would become the League's methodological approach, markedly different from the central bank diplomacy that helped to reconstruct the international gold standard. The latter was characterized by elitism, an absence of accountability, and dogmatic commitment to the gold standard.[26] The League wanted to discuss economic and financial issues in the open, and to bring a heterodox community of experts from banks and the academe (albeit adhering in some measure or other to the tenets of liberal economics) together with politicians. It published a large and widely disseminated collection of well-received comparative intelligence on national financial and economic performance, and academic papers, such as that of Cassel, which gave it intellectual authority and an independent, critical perspective on the actions of nation states and financiers. Brussels also illustrated the League's ability to recruit nationally respected economists and to propel them onto the international stage. These were often people with a flair for self-promotion, the skill to communicate their ideas in more than one language, and the expertise to write reports informed by scientific insight that were intended to provoke a political response. The League's emerging working practices reflected the technocratic spirit of the age: as Frank Aydelotte, an Oxford-educated American educationalist and League enthusiast put it, 'the problems of the modern world' had proven themselves 'too complicated for rule-of-thumb solutions. They can be solved only by experts, by scholars.'[27]

Thirdly, the conference demonstrated a move to political independence by embracing Lloyd George's attempts to integrate Germany and the USSR into the European peace settlement, issuing invitations that had been so markedly absent in Paris.[28] The step was seen by *The Economist* 'as evidence of a dawning of sense among the leaders of the Allied peoples'.[29]

All this work reinforced the nascent section of the secretariat devoted to economic and financial issues, which was recognized in the only formal recommendation of the Brussels Conference: the establishment at the League of a provisional 'committee of bankers and businessmen to frame measures to give effect to certain decisions of the Conference'.[30] The resolution was a striking departure from the

---

[26] See, e.g., Liaquat Ahamed, *Lords of Finance, 1929: The Great Depression—and the Bankers who Broke the World* (London, 2010), 179–250.

[27] 'Report of the Director', 14 Oct. 1940, Library of the Institute for Advanced Study, Princeton.

[28] Cohrs is wrong to assert Genoa was the first post-war conference to which Germany and the USSR were invited. See Patrick O. Cohrs, *The Unfinished Peace after World War I: America, Britain and the Stabilisation of Europe, 1919–1932* (Cambridge, 2006), 73.

[29] Cassel, 'The World's Monetary Problems', *The Economist*, 21 Aug. 1920, p. 291.

[30] League of Nations, *The Committees of the League of Nations: Classified List and Essential Facts* (Geneva, 1945), 37. Walters misses these discrete origins. See Frank P. Walters, *A History of the League of Nations* (Oxford, 1952; 2nd edn, 1965), 77.

state-centred focus of the Covenant. The resulting Joint Provisional Economic and Financial Committee was not officially an intergovernmental forum, but rather a body made up of 'independent experts', in theory nominated by the Council but, as we shall see, frequently proposed by the secretariat. Committee members could originate from member and, crucially, non-member states, and need not represent their national governments in an official capacity. As a result, the provision opened up international space with the potential for frank negotiations on economic and financial questions. (The League's publications did not reflect this, because published reports of negotiations had to be agreed by all the participants, and so the gap between the archival and published record was often cavernous.) It was also kept deliberately unclear whether these 'experts' were to be bankers, businessmen, politicians, scientists, or civil servants, because it was recognized that these categories were porous—economists could become civil servants, civil servants went to work for central banks, and so on.[31] The main concern was to secure the best talent available—understood in terms of economic expertise, financial influences, and political links—to be supported by a designated section of the secretariat. Prior to Brussels, the League secretariat had one member of staff responsible for economic and financial intelligence; by 1922 it had thirty-six (the disarmament section could still boast only eleven members of staff, the mandates four, while those working on social questions, hygiene, and opium trafficking numbered two apiece).[32] Brussels had established a platform from which to imagine, categorize, and measure the world, and its regions and nations.[33] It was to generate the first global institution to attempt to measure and consistently to compare constituent parts of the world, giving statisticians a prominent and fast-growing role within the secretariat.

The novelty and importance of the new arrangement was recognized immediately, but the construction of this discrete economic and financial agency could not yet claim to be an organization in its own right. The word 'Provisional' was in the title precisely because there were those, including members of the British government, who feared that the creation of an economic and financial dimension to the League would impinge upon national sovereignty; invite consideration of sensitive central and commercial banking activities; and provide a new means through which other governments could challenge the British Empire, because it created the possibility to effect a multilateral diplomatic strategy on meagre resources.[34] The

---

[31] League of Nations, *The Committees of the League of Nations*, 37. This arrangement of a committee composed of 'independent experts' acting in lieu of national delegates when considering policy on an especially contentious subject is an approach that would also be adopted for the issue of disarmament. See Andrew Webster, 'Absolutely Irresponsible Amateurs: The Temporary Mixed Commission on Armaments, 1921–1924', *Australian Journal of Politics and History*, 54/3 (2008), 373–88.

[32] In 1920, the secretariat totalled 57 staff; by 1922 it stood at 218. The two major areas of growth were internal services (including office keepers, postal, and housekeeping staff, chauffeurs and lift boys) and the Economic and Financial Section. League of Nations, *Permanent Staff List of the Secretariat* (Geneva, 1920); *Staff List of the Secretariat* (Geneva, 1922), C.246 (a).M.137 (a).1922.X.

[33] An approach so far adopted primarily by historians of the nation state. See Michael Billig, *Banal Nationalism* (London, 1995).

[34] Victor-Yves Ghébali, 'The League of Nations and Functionalism', in A. J. R. Groom and Paul Taylor (eds), *Functionalism: Theory and Practice in International Relations* (London, 1975), 141–61.

French, the League's other major paymaster, shared this concern. Central bankers were also nervous of League intervention—one of the most outspoken critics was the President of the Federal Reserve Bank of New York, Benjamin Strong Jr, who effectively led the US banking system. International scrutiny, especially because the world public seemed so enthused by the League, risked unwelcome attention to their activities. By contrast, the approach of Montagu Norman, the Governor of the Bank of England, was to prove characteristically double-edged: he was keen to exclude the League from scrutinizing British and imperial financial affairs, but was willing to use Geneva to stabilize central and eastern Europe, and to secure access to American investment to effect the reconstruction of the international financial system disrupted by war and its aftermath.[35] Elsewhere central bankers in smaller European states had their backs to the wall, and hoped that the League would afford an opportunity to apply pressure upon, and to educate, the new world's banker as to what was expected of it in challenging times. It was clear the power to determine the agenda of financial diplomacy remained with the richest nation states and their central bankers, and notably with the League's most powerful refusnik, the USA.

Yet, once the momentous decision to create an intergovernmental and expert group, with its own civil service to coordinate international economic and financial relations, had been taken, the next major step in efforts to stabilize the world economy sidestepped the League. From 10 April to 19 May 1922, a successor conference, the 'International Economic and Financial Conference', was convened in Genoa under the auspices of the British and French governments, and not the League of Nations. This was so that the USA would attend. The Coolidge administration agreed to participate, albeit reluctantly, still arguing that the real challenges before Europe were political and that the continent needed to solve them without the intervention of the USA: reparations needed to be resolved, war debt payments to the USA resumed, and armaments expenditure curtailed. None of these issues, it argued, required the agency of the USA and hence none were permitted on the conference agenda.[36] The lack of unity among the former Allied and Associated powers was reinforced by French (and behind the scenes American) opposition to Britain's aspiration to invite Germany and the USSR to Genoa. Meanwhile, frustrated by their pariah status, the two outsiders took the bold step of signing the Rapallo Treaty on 16 April to restore diplomatic and trade relations between them. Their bilateral response, in part, reflected the wider breakdown of multilateral negotiations and demonstrated, paradoxically, the ability of isolated and

---

[35] Although we know much about their policies towards the Brussels and Genoa conferences, Norman's and Moreau's attitudes towards the League demand further investigation in the light of Peter Yearwood's stress on the centrality of the League to British foreign policy more generally in this period.
[36] Carole Fink, *The Genoa Conference: European Diplomacy, 1921–22* (Chapel Hill, NY, 1984), 69–105; Carole Fink, Axel Frohn, and Jürgen Heideking (eds), *Genoa, Rapallo and European Reconstruction in 1922* (Cambridge, 1991), esp. Peter Krüger, 'A Rainy Day, 6 April 1922: The Rapallo Treaty and the Cloudy Perspective for German Foreign Policy', 49–64; Kenneth Mouré, *The Gold Standard Illusion: France, the Bank of France, and the International Gold Standard, 1914–1939* (Oxford, 2002), 52–7.

ideologically opposed powers to make a deal on a bilateral basis in secret, in contrast to states with publicly declared and shared aims that sought multilateral agreement.[37]

On the face of it, negotiations at Genoa were no more productive than those held at Brussels. Although at Genoa delegations comprised government representatives as well as experts (the same ones who had attended Brussels), they again agreed that currency stabilization and the reconstruction of international trading patterns would best be served by a return to gold, but unanswered questions as to how and when to effect this hung in the air like stale cigar smoke.[38] Where the conference did make progress, after decisive intervention by delegates from the Bank of England, was in defining the mechanics of international monetary cooperation once countries had returned their currencies to gold. State delegates endorsed the principle of coordinated central bank cooperation to secure price levels as well as exchange stability, the approach as taken before 1914. In other words, the world's most powerful central banks agreed to work together to help any member currency threatened by depreciation. Given the world shortage of gold, it was also agreed that countries could top up their gold reserves with foreign exchange that was itself backed by gold (this invariably meant US dollars).

Although neither the Brussels nor the Genoa conference had brought the financial crisis to an end, both meetings produced advances, and discussions helped to clarify the key issues at hand. They identified the nations most at risk of economic and financial collapse, and established a consensus as to the best means to resolve the crisis: the reintroduction as promptly as possible of the international gold standard. From the European perspective, negotiations also determined that the preferred means by which this was to be effected was through the agency of central and commercial banks, supported when possible by the financial power of the United States. Although Lloyd George has been given the credit by some for the attempt to use economic cooperation as a means to facilitate a political rapprochement between the 'winners' and the 'losers' of Versailles, an international financial network stood behind this approach. And, while the conference strategy championed by Lloyd George may have sunk without trace after Genoa, the wider community of British policy advisers and financiers, notably Norman, remained in place. So, too, did the quest to re-create, as far as possible, the liberal economic order of the late nineteenth century that lived on in the minds of centrist politicians across Europe. Clear ideological lines around parties were harder to draw when it came to economics, as many social democrat (or in Britain Labour) politicians, as well as liberals, conservatives, moderate nationalists and centre political parties, cleaved to the 'world of 1913 [which] seemed to most of us a paradise from which we had been excluded by a flaming sword'.[39]

---

[37] Harmut Pogge von Strandmann, 'Rapallo—Strategy in Preventative Diplomacy: New Sources and Interpretations', in Volker R. Berghahn and Martin Kitchen (eds), *Germany in the Age of Total War* (London, 1981), 123–43.

[38] Charles Martin and Édouard Montpetit, *La Conférence de gênes en vue de la reconstruction économique de financière de l'Europe* (Ottawa, 1922).

[39] Arthur Salter, *Memoirs of a Public Servant* (London, 1961), 193.

Norman's stress on central bank cooperation at Genoa, though an approach that privileged a private, market-based solution rather than a public, intergovernmental one, moved away from ideas embodied in the League. Nevertheless it fore-grounded the need for multilateral cooperation among disparate groups within national political economies, and between states. The League was not yet trusted as a venue where these issues could be thrashed out, but it was becoming increasingly clear such a forum was needed. In the meantime, patterns of work were being established that made the organization an essential clearing house for the exchange of information, techniques, and contacts, and that brought the uneven, yet interwoven character of the global economy more clearly into view. The problem remained that the state with the financial power to give the League real clout, the USA, would not yet participate in its activities, proving that finance was not readily separated from politics. Indeed, for most states after the First World War, politics were all about finance. The battle for currency stability required governments to reduce budget deficits to match bankers' and economists' expectations; and businessmen, trade unions, and the general public had, in uneven measure, to fall into line if they wanted to avoid the political violence that already pock-marked central Europe. It took a further toxic dose of inflation in central and eastern Europe and the invasion of the Ruhr before the answers to the European crisis were found, and League intervention helped to establish an international agenda for future work.

STABILIZATION AND DEVELOPMENT: GOING EAST

The inflationary crisis of the new states on Germany's frontiers is usually con-sidered separately by historians, who present Weimar's restabilization as the prelude to the promising, but ultimately short-lived, European peace of the 1920s.[40] But, at the time, the connections and 'differences between' Germany and nations forged from the late Austro-Hungarian Empire were understood to be 'of degree rather than of kind'.[41] The League could not do much to help Germany's financial crisis, because it was not a member of the League; because the scale of the financial aid needed meant the USA (another non-member) had to participate to make any rescue package viable; and because divisions had opened up between Britain and France—the League's power-brokers—over Poincaré's decision to occupy the Ruhr in January 1923. The League did contribute, however, by offering assessments on

---

[40] International historians generally stress the 'primacy of economics' in their accounts of the 'failure' of Weimar Germany, while focusing on minority rights and the 'primacy of nationalism' in their narratives of democracy's collapse in other eastern and central European countries. See, e.g., Steiner, *The Lights that Failed*. For economic historians, the interconnection, articulated through capital flight and an infectious collapse in confidence, is much more obvious. See Barry Eichengreen, *Globalizing Capital: A History of the International Monetary System* (Princeton, 1996), 47–55.

[41] See 'Trade Doubts', *Manchester Guardian*, 23 Aug. 1921, p. 6; 'Difficulty of Doing Business', *New York Times*, 22 Jan. 1923, p. 22; 'From Private Correspondence', *The Scotsman*, 2 Nov. 1921, p. 7.

German capacity to pay to members of the Dawes Committee and more significantly, through the League coordinated rescue of Austria.[42]

As the custodian of the principle of self-determination through which the new
nations were articulated from the old Austro-Hungarian, Russian, German, and
Ottoman empires, the League had a special relationship with the successor states of
central and eastern Europe from the beginning. The Brussels Conference had
drawn attention to the desperate plight of the new Austrian republic, which had
inherited ballooning inflation, debts and reparations, an expensive and oversized
bureaucracy, and a starving population. In 1922, calculations by the League
secretariat indicated that, without outside help, the new state would be bankrupt
by the middle of June 1923. Lobby groups that had fought to found a League,
notably the British-based League of Nations Union, argued that the Economic and
Financial Section had demonstrated the case for action, and the organization
needed to step in to save not just Austria but all Europe from financial ruin.[43]

Formally, the League's intervention was triggered by the Allied Supreme Council's decision to decline the Austrian Chancellor Ignaz Seipel's pleas for help in
August 1922.[44] In fact, behind the scenes, efforts to put together a private Anglo-
American financial package to stabilize Austria had been developing for some time,
but it was when the Provisional Economic and Financial Committee of the League
became involved that a shared view of the problem and a viable solution emerged
between the distressed and the putative rescuers. This, in turn, generated sufficient
confidence for stability—financial, economic, and political—to take hold.[45] (It was
during this rescue that the League claimed for the first time to contain 'specialist
organizations', of which the provisional committee became an Economic and
Financial Organization, an EFO.)[46]

It was not the case that the League was immediately able to come to the rescue
where others had failed. Early League efforts to help Austria also came to naught. In
1921, it had helped to devise the Ter Meulen scheme, the brainchild of the Dutch
banker K. E. Ter Meulen, which marketed state-guaranteed bonds that proved
cumbersome and unattractive. The office opened by the League in London in 1921
to sell bonds in Austria closed without custom after a year. What changed in 1923
was that Salter returned to Geneva after his brief and unhappy sojourn as chairman
of the Reparations Commission, to take charge of the EFO. He used the newly

[42] Salter was the mediator. See Walters, *History of the League*, 262; Nathan Marcus, 'Credibility,
Confidence and Capital: Austrian Reconstruction and the Collapse of Global Finance, 1921–1931',
unpublished Ph.D. thesis, New York University, 2010, pp. 50–70.

[43] Drummond D. Fraser, *Credit or Chaos: The Ter Meulen Credit Scheme of the League of Nations*
(London, 1921); Marcus, 'Credibility, Confidence and Capital', 70–3.

[44] K. Klemperer, *Ignaz Seipel: Christian Statesman in a Time of Crisis* (Princeton, 1971); Walter
Layton and Charles Rist, *The Economic Situation of Austria* (Geneva, 1925); M. Healy, *Vienna and the
Fall of the Habsburg Empire: Total War and Everyday Life in World War I* (Cambridge, 2004); Herbert
Hoover, *Three Years World of the American Relief Administration in Austria* (Vienna, 1922).

[45] It received considerable, but not entirely flattering, publicity in Britain. See, e.g., A. M. Innes,
'The Ter Meulen Scheme', *Economic Journal*, 31/124 (Dec. 1921), 544–7; Frank Bayersdorf, ' "Credit
or Chaos"? The Austrian Stabilisation Programme of 1923 and the League of Nations', in Lacqua (ed.),
Internationalism Reconfigured, 136.

[46] League of Nations, *Staff List of the Secretariat* (Geneva, May 1922), C.246(a).M.137 (a).1922.X.

expanded office and wartime contacts to devise, with the cooperation of the Bank of England, a multilateral programme of private financial and intergovernmental support that brought stability, albeit at a hefty price, to Austria.[47]

Key, too, were relationships between Salter's young and enthusiastic staff, including Loveday and the Swedish economist Per Jacobsson, and British officials with whom the section developed long-standing associations, including Otto E. Niemeyer, chairman of the Financial Committee and a senior figure in the British Treasury, who went on to work for the Bank of England, and Henry Strakosch (a naturalized South African born in Vienna), who had close connections to Threadneedle Street. Together they persuaded the governments of Britain, France, Belgium, Italy, Czechoslovakia, the Netherlands, and Spain to guarantee bonds that would be marketed by major Austrian banks in New York and London.[48] These states were largely, but not exclusively, Council members, and, although the US administration did not sign up, J. P. Morgan & Co. was an important supporter and investor behind the scenes.[49] In return, the Austrian government offered up its state income from its monopoly on tobacco and customs revenues as collateral.

The financial security afforded foreign investors by this arrangement was reinforced by a series of extraordinary political guarantees that, for the first time, handed financial oversight of a nation state to an intergovernmental organization.[50] The Geneva Protocol negotiated through the League Council in October 1922 required Austria to establish an independent central bank and restabilize its currency on the international gold standard. (Remarkably, it was thus one of the first nations among those that had suspended their membership during the war to return to gold.) League intervention, and the measures it insisted the Austrian government take, made this restabilization credible. It agreed to a rigorous programme of fiscal retrenchment: food subsidies were cut and state expenditure was slashed. Some 50,000 civil servants were sacked, although pension costs of former officials who had once administered the empire remained a considerable drain on resources.[51] In Stefan Zweig's eulogy to the lost Austrian republic, this was the dark, hostile environment in which his *Post Office Girl* eked out her shamefully poor existence, set in painfully sharp relief by the thoughtless

[47] Arthur Salter, *Slave of the Lamp: A Public Servant's Notebook* (London, 1967), 95–8; Denis Rickett, 'Salter, (James) Arthur, Baron Salter (1881–1975)', *ODNB*.

[48] It was Strakosch who drew up the detailed plans for security and dissemination of the bonds. See Bayersdorf, '"Credit or Chaos"?', 10–11. Strakosch was also a vocal advocate in the British press, arguing for a 'gradual and cautious' British, but preferably multilateral, 'policy of [currency] stabilisation in Europe. See, e.g., 'Money and Stocks', *Manchester Guardian*, 6 Apr. 1922, p. 15.

[49] Bayersdorf, '"Credit or Chaos"?', 142–3. He argues that Morgan delayed participating in order to maximize the terms of J. P. Morgan's investment.

[50] A point powerfully stressed by Louis Pauly, who also poses the equally pertinent question of *Who Elected the Bankers? Surveillance and Control in the World Economy* (Ithaca, NY, 1997).

[51] For Marcus, it was League intervention alone that changed 'people's expectations about the political future and its economy and currency', and he offers a detailed account of its labours. See Marcus, 'Credibility, Confidence and Capital', 92–145. For the impact of pensions, see 'Minutes of 17th Session of the Financial Committee', LON, F.17th Session/P.V. 2(1) 1st Part.

beneficence of a wealthy American aunt who unexpectedly opens the door on a new world glittering with possibilities, only brutally to slam it shut.[52]

The international community's commitment and control over the formulation of Austria's path to recovery was reinforced by the appointment of a Commissioner General of Austrian Finances for the League, the former major of Rotterdam, Alfred Rudolph Zimmerman. A powerful personality and liberal of the classic nineteenth-century variety who had a deep antipathy to socialism and socialists, Zimmerman set up shop in 'Red Vienna', supported by experts from the League's Economic and Financial, and Information, Sections.[53] He collated and analysed intelligence as to Austria's budgetary and monetary performance, sending in monthly reports to the Council, which in turn authorized the release of tranches of financial aid to Austria. For the next two years Zimmerman enjoyed extraordinary powers, determining when and where Seipel's government spent or cut expenditure. His relations with Austrian politicians became deeply fractious, as he became the personification of unwelcome international interference in the new country's political and social programmes, which marked a subversion of the principle of national sovereignty that the League was supposed to hold so dear.

In immediate financial terms, however, Zimmerman delivered. By 1924, the Austrian budget was back in the black, and news of this League 'success' was widely publicized. Another member of the League team in Austria was the young Dutch journalist Adrianus Pelt, a member of the Information Section. In 1922 in Vienna, Pelt established a sophisticated strategy to disseminate 'good news' about Austria's recovery to reassure the markets and energize a virtuous circle of confidence that would facilitate its recovery. Salter and the Economic and Financial secretariat were central to this strategy, analysing and disseminating financial intelligence on Austrian performance supplied by Zimmerman, and drafting reports for Pelt to publish and for companies such as J. P. Morgan & Co. to pass on to investors.

J. P. Morgan's perspective was crucial, because its participation, secured in May 1923, brought in other European investors, notably from France and Italy, who were sufficiently reassured by the American interest to buy bonds themselves.[54] But progress was not straightforward. Persuading investors to buy bonds on longer terms, which were cheaper and more stable than short-term credits, took more time than Austria and the League would have liked. Nevertheless, within six months the Austrian economy had been stabilized. Montagu Norman was certainly keen for the bankers, and especially Morgan's, to take the credit, and grew rather resentful that the rest of the world preferred to praise instead the League's 'non-rationalistic

[52] Stefan Zweig, *The Post Office Girl* (London, 2009), 15.

[53] J. L. J. Bosmans, *De Nederlander Mr A. R. Zimmerman als Commissaris-Generaal van de Volkenbond in Oostenrijk 1922–1926* (Nijmegen, 1973); Alfred R. Zimmerman, *Principiële Staatkunde* (2nd edn; Rotterdam, 1932). Although Salter later claimed he was unaware of Zimmerman's anti-communism, it is clear Pelt left him in no doubt as to the major's anti-communist credentials, which had strong appeal in British financial circles. See Drummond and Monnet to Salter, 8 Dec. 1922, and Pelt to Salter, 31 Oct. 1922, LON Salter, S109 2/4/1.

[54] Mussolini's behaviour and that of his Italian Minister in Vienna, Orsini, however, were a frequent obstacle. See Zimmerman to Salter, 12 May 1923, LON, Salter, S109, 2/4/1.

& almost altruistic endeavours'.[55] While it was true that its economic and financial agency did not deserve all the acclaim showered upon it—it had not risked its own money in the crisis, because it had no stabilization funds of its own—its ability to marshal evidence and to disseminate it to the wider network of governmental and financial institutions was central to the rescue. The League was a constant voice in explaining why it was in the world's interest that the new republic be helped, and changed political debate and financial expectations within Austria. Its regular reports from the field added a dramatic counterpoint to liberal anxieties fuelled by the recent failed communist revolutions in eastern and central Europe and the recent Bolshevik victory in the Russian civil war.

The Austrian model was an important vindication of the League's broadening interest in economic and financial affairs, especially given the currency chaos unleashed in Germany following successive defaults on reparations and the Franco-Belgian invasion of the Ruhr launched on 11 January 1923. Austria validated the League's stress on coordination and cooperation. The 'ruhrnation' of Germany, as the press called it, which was taking place simultaneously, illustrated the likely consequences if these principles and the League were circumvented. France's unilateral decision to invade the Ruhr, with a reluctant Belgium in tow, stood in contrast to the internationalism of the rich 'uncles', the network of bankers coordinated by the League.[56] It was only later, as the EFO's staff numbers and reach grew, and the gold standard order began to fail, that this cooperation began to break down.

Historians disagree about whether the League's stabilization of Austria worked to the republic's advantage in the long run. There was certainly immediate pain—the higher the inflation rate the greater its acuity—and with stabilization came increased taxes, and cuts in state welfare and employment provision; real interest rates went up while opportunities to secure domestic credit declined. Not without justification, in the eyes of the popular press, the League Commissioner of Vienna took on the appearance of the Governor-General of an occupying colonial power. Austrian democracy was forever tainted in the eyes of nationalists for ceding fiscal sovereignty to an internationalist authority. However, without the League's intervention it is hard to see how Austria's crisis would have ended, and, when League oversight was removed in 1926, financial problems soon returned.[57] If, as Knut Borchardt famously put it, the Weimar Republic had 'no room to

---

[55] Cited in Bayersdorf, '"Credit or Chaos"?', 148.

[56] Niemeyer to Salter, 20 Aug. 1922, and Charron to Salter, 16 Aug. 1922, LON, Salter, S104, 2/8/2.

[57] For an overview of the options before Austria, see Jens-Wilhelm Wessels, *Economic Policy and Microeconomic Performance in Inter-War Europe: The Case of Austria, 1918–1938* (Stuttgart, 2007), 19–34. Marcus's demarcation of the debate challenges accounts that privilege the social and political pain occasioned by the League's intervention, especially to the left of Austrian politics, typified by Karl Ausch, *Als die Banken fielen: Zur Soziologie der politischen Korruption* (Vienna, 1968), 75–113. Rost van Tonningen's tenure as League Commissioner after 1926 underlines the League's preference for stability over democracy, and the potential for its agents to embrace the politics of the far right. See Peter Berger, *Im Schatten der Diktatur. Die Finanzdiplomatie des Verters des Völkerbundes in Österreich, Meinoud Marius Rost van Tonnigen, 1931–1936* (Vienna, 2000).

manœuvre' in response to the Wall Street crash because of the terms under which it stabilized in 1924, the same was true for Austria under League control after 1922.[58] Frustrated expectations of republican statehood were dashed by a financial weakness, which meant the country was able to develop policy only on terms that suited the world's dominant financial powers and that profoundly shook the confidence of many Austrian citizens in internationalism. (Their history was to find a powerful echo in the experience of decolonized powers after 1945.)

But all this lay in the future. In 1922 and 1923, the unfolding crisis in Europe meant statesmen's and citizens' time horizons were short, and what mattered was the present. In 1923, Hungary descended into hyperinflation too, and its crisis management was based on the Austrian model: a League-coordinated loan of £10 million secured by the state's customs revenues, tobacco and salt monopolies, and sugar taxes. These revenues were put directly into the hands of the League's Commissioner-General to Budapest, the 54-year-old Bostonian lawyer Jeremiah Smith Jr, who also had oversight of domestic expenditure. Because this state income was more than sufficient to cover the loan, there was no need, as there had been in the Austrian case, for the government to agree each step of its spending plans, which made life easier on Smith's and the League's reputation. This was not the only way in which the Hungarian experience differed from that in Austria.[59] While more than three-quarters of the Austrian population made their living from industry, finance, and trade, the bulk of Hungary's people earned their living from the land. This meant that, while Austria's descent into hyperinflation was faster, steeper, and more immediately painful, carrying as it did the threat of imminent starvation, stabilization appeared to deliver growth. In Hungary, by contrast, the onset of the disease was less immediate, and the economic recovery less convincing.

Salter concluded that, whatever hostility the League mission faced at the outset in Austria, it paled in comparison to the risks faced in Hungary, with its 'more intense national feeling, with a sterner and less pliant population', and with a history of political violence typified by Bela Kun's resort to 'a red terror to govern which caused the Romanian Army to march in, and when they left a White Terror replaced the Red'.[60] Between 1920 and 1923, Hungary made a more determined attempt than Austria to put its own house in order, and only when this had failed catastrophically did it take up League overtures, made through the Reparations Commission, the Council, and the EFO, for help. The financial arrangements and the League oversight in Hungary was predicated on the Austrian experience, although the sum loaned was half that granted to Austria, and there was less stress on austerity. Indeed, Salter argued that in Hungary the problem was that 'expenditure

[58] Carl-Ludwig Holtfrerich, 'Economic Policy Options and the End of the Weimar Republic', in Ian Kershaw (ed.), *Weimar: Why did German Democracy Fail?* (London, 1990), 58–91.
[59] 'Financial Reconstruction of Austria: Agreements Drawn up by the League of Nations and Signed at Geneva on 14th March 1924', LON R2935, C.185.M.53.1924.II. The role played by the League in initiating and coordinating negotiations is underplayed in Miklós Lojkó, *Meddling in Middle Europe: Britain and the 'Lands Between', 1919–1925* (Budapest, 2006), 81–7.
[60] 'The Reconstruction of Hungary', address delivered by Salter to Chatham House, 22 May 1924, pp. 2–5, attached to LON R2935, C.147.(1)/1924/II.

on certain services was obviously insufficient' and the challenge was to generate more income for the population and higher tax yields for the state.[61] The international politics also were more complex. Disputes raged over refugees, borders, and even the ownership of its former national archives. For the financial programme to work, the deal had to be signed off by Romania, Czechoslovakia, and Yugoslavia: Hungary's neighbours had good reason to fear its restoration. Salter's office and the League also negotiated directly with the Reparations Commission to fix the final sums owed by the Hungarian republic, which agreed to waive its claim to payment in favour of Hungary's new creditors to give the League-negotiated loan a fair wind. An open wound since 1920, the Hungarian reparations settlement agreed in 1924 was certainly a great deal more generous than that imposed on Germany: an annual average charge of ten million gold crowns for twenty years. The comparison, made widely at the time with Germany's reparation settlement, was striking: one British shilling was owed by every Hungarian per annum compared to forty-one schillings per annum outstanding for each German.

In Hungary, results appeared to come more efficaciously and with greater ease than in Austria. Within the year, the Hungarian pengö was stable and the budget was balanced. Salter took pride in the fact that, after the pressures exerted from above, there was proof that 'economic life was steadily growing from below'. But Smith's monthly reports indicated deep-seated anxieties regarding rural poverty and agricultural underperformance that Salter was less keen to advertise. The League's limited engagement with Poland's financial crisis also revealed a preference for 'strong', even autocratic, leadership, among some of its members. While Salter worried over Finance Minister Lóránt Hegedűs' 'tragic, impossible and misdirected' battle to stabilize the Hungarian crown that 'cost him his mind', Joseph Avenol, the French Deputy Secretary-General, strongly endorsed the 'drastic and far-reaching reforms' of Władysław Grabski that had brought financial stability to Poland at the price of democracy, negating the need for direct League intervention.[62] Although the League was not openly involved in the stabilization of the German economy, where foreign oversight was eschewed and where American bankers, unlike in Austria's case, took the commanding lead, confidence in the Dawes Plan (similar in structure to the League arrangements) was also shaped by these experiences.

It was not just Europe's new nations, or the free city of Danzig, that learned to lean on the League for financial support. After a series of failed attempts to secure credit on the open market in London, the Greek government approached the Council for help in February 1923. The immediate cause of the crisis was the influx of what was estimated by Fridjof Nansen, the League's High Commissioner for Refugees, to be more than 750,000 refugees, mostly women and children, into a

[61] 'The Reconstruction of Hungary', 8.
[62] 'The Reconstruction of Hungary', 2; Statement by Avenol, 'Minutes of the 13th Meeting of the Financial Committee, XVII Session', 12 Feb. 1925, LON, F/17 session/P.V. 13(1) 6th part, p. 9. A League-endorsed expert, Hilton Young, advised the Poles on how to create and operate a central bank.

country of four million, in the wake of the Greco-Turkish war in 1922–3.[63] The crisis put an intolerable strain on a Greek economy already weakened by the tripling of prices during the First World War, and the inflationary spiral continued unchecked. Although domestic financial difficulties were not part of the case presented by Greece to the League, the Financial Committee itself was motivated as much by the political ambition to quell 'revolutionary fever' as any humanitarian impulse.[64] The League, as in the case of Austria and Hungary, mediated between the debtors and the British financial authorities, and offered detailed advice on the type of security the market would require before extending what became a loan of £12.2 million (of which Greek banks and financial groups subscribed £2.5 million). This was largely some 1,250,000 square acres of land suitable for the cultivation of tobacco, cereal, and pastures (an echo of the Hungarian scheme, which hypothecated state revenue from these commodities), as well as houses and shops sold to the refugees on an instalment plan. Salter and his colleagues used their London-based network to develop the loan programme, but its financial management was handed to the International Financial Commission, which had been set up in 1898 following the Greek government's default of 1893, and coordinated through the League Refugee's Settlement Commission.[65] This meant the EFO was less involved than in the case of Austria or Hungary, but continued to play a direct role in advising the Bank of Greece on reforms necessary to secure membership of the gold standard in 1928, a process that necessitated a further League-backed loan of £7.5 million at 6 per cent interest.

The Greek scheme also formed the template for a loan of £4 million to support the settlement of 220,000 refugees in Bulgaria in 1926, with René Charron appointed League commissioner. Here, the link between League support for the loan and the creation of new, League-approved, statutes for the National Bank of Bulgaria was more immediate. A further loan of £5.4 million was granted to effect Bulgaria's currency stabilization, and arrangements for oversight were more akin to those of Hungary than of Greece.[66] In an episode worthy of much more sustained investigation by historians, the terms of this loan were the most hotly contested by other League members, notably Yugoslavia, which sought to control where the refugees be allowed to settle and to reduce the sums offered to Bulgaria.[67]

---

[63] Dimitri Pentzopoulos, *The Balkan Exchange of Minorities and its Impact on Greece* (Paris, 1962), 61–71; Louis P. Cassimatis, *American Influence in Greece, 1917–1929* (London, 1988).

[64] Statement by Henry Morgenthau Sen. to Council, in League of Nations, *The Settlement of Greek Refugees* (Geneva, 1924), C.524.M.187.1924.II.

[65] It was these bodies that sought to secure supplementary funding in 1925 and 1928 as the scheme's early success faltered, but it was the Financial Committee that oversaw the scheme's conclusion in 1930. See 'Thirty-Seventy Session of the Financial Commission [*sic*], 21 Jan. 1930', LON, P.V. F/37ème Session/P.V.4. The Financial Committee also provided similar support to Portugal.

[66] League of Nations, *The Settlement of Bulgarian Refugees* (Geneva, 1926), C.522.M.204.1926. II. US funds made up 40% of the stabilization loans to Greece and 33% to Bulgaria, while its contribution to refugee support was less (16% and 29% respectively). See also FRBNY memo by Klopenstock, 'The League of Nations' Financial Committee', 17 May 1943, FRBNY 4608.

[67] Ivanovitch to Drummond, 20 Aug. 1926, LON, C.471.1926.II.

What was already clear by 1924, however, was that the League's involvement in these stabilization crises legitimated its entitlement to intervene in economic and financial relations, and established important ideas and practices for the future. In the case of Austria, Hungary, Poland, Bulgaria, Yugoslavia, Romania, Czechoslovakia, and Estonia, where the League also supported a stabilization loan of £1.5 million in 1927, it also created a reciprocal relationship.[68] The Economic and Financial Section sustained an almost proprietorial interest in these countries' access to foreign credit and budgetary health. In time it was also to become committed to promoting these nations in rather patriarchal terms focused on their levels and terms of trade; industrialization; and the agricultural, physical, and social well-being of its citizens. The approach echoed ideas of humanitarian imperialism that shaped Europe's connections to the wider world in the nineteenth century and was later expanded by the League to embrace all agricultural Europe. In turn, many of the experts drawn into the orbit of the League in the 1920s and 1930s and who developed skills in the field went on to apply them beyond Europe's frontiers after 1945. Indeed, Nicholas Politis, the first Greek delegate to the assembly, publicly praised Sir John Campbell's 'practical knowledge thanks to his long colonial experience', which 'had been of the utmost value' in his work in Greece.[69] The traffic in personnel moved in both directions. Austria, in particular, became an important recruiting ground for staff that made glittering intellectual contributions to economic science and the work of the League.

In the West, by contrast, the world's wealthiest powers restabilized their currencies unilaterally, and with no reference to the League. Britain restabilized sterling in 1925 and France fixed the franc to gold unofficially in 1926 and formally in 1928, with other countries to which these states had close ties following. Throughout no attempt was made to coordinate the rate at which one country chose to stabilize with another. Cassel's warnings at Brussels were not heeded, and this national approach created problems that soon came home to roost. It left the pound sterling overvalued by around 10 per cent and the US dollar and French franc significantly undervalued. British economic performance, notably the health of its manufacturing sector, was listless on gold; French and American exporters, on the other hand, enjoyed considerable advantages. The experience was to shape attitudes towards the gold standard system, and the internationalism with which it was equated, when the world economy turned sour after 1929.

PATTERNS OF WORK

By 1924, the three main arms of the League's Economic and Financial Organization were in place, and the sobriquet 'provisional' in its title was quietly dropped.

---

[68] Estonia was the only party that consistently maintained full service of its League loan until July 1940.

[69] 'Minutes of 13th Session of Council', 14 Sept. 1924, LON, C.1282.1924.II. The colonial link was evident elsewhere: the vice-president of the Refugee Settlement Commission was John Hope Simpson, formerly of the Indian Colonial Service.

The first element of the operation was the Economic and Financial Section, its discrete secretariat. Formally, the secretariat was there to serve the interests of League members represented in the Council and the Assembly; in practice it developed its own policy agenda to effect coordination and cooperation in the world economy. The section exploited its responsibility to prepare both the agenda for meetings and the preparatory documentation to generate questions it believed that states should address. Salter was master of the ship, having been temporarily replaced during an absence chairing the Reparations Commission by Walter Layton, an economist and gifted statistician whom he had grown to know during wartime procurement negotiations with the USA and who in 1921 became the editor of weekly journal *The Economist*.[70] Layton retained close ties to the League, and *The Economist* became an important channel to economists, businessmen, politicians, and the international financial press, who regularly scanned its pages.[71] *The Economist* reflected his liberal internationalist vision, his commitment to the League, and his continued ties with former colleagues in Geneva, as well as his connections to the powerful circle of liberal British opinion-makers in which he moved, including Keynes, William Beveridge, and Gilbert Murray.

In interwar Britain, liberal ideas continued to be influential in public life, even if the parliamentary Liberal Party was divided and in decline.[72] Moreover, as the climate became more inclement for liberal ideas elsewhere in Europe, the League became an important international reinforcement, and eventually a sanctuary for liberals, like the Italian Pietro Stoppani, born in Milan in 1879, who joined the League in February 1923; significantly, he was also part of an American–Italian immigrant family. He went on to become Director of the Economic Section in 1930, when the secretariat was divided into two, with Loveday appointed Director of the Financial Section and the Economic Intelligence Service (EIS).[73] Stoppani should have replaced Salter, as he was the most senior official of the Economic and Financial Section. However, Britain and France opposed the move, arguing that there were already a considerable number of Italian directors of section—the fascist presence in the League was already uncomfortable—and that the onset of the Depression underlined the importance and interest in the work of the EFO. Stoppani, while an effective researcher and a good liberal, was regarded by the British as insufficiently combative. One option was to replace Salter with another Briton, but, in view of Stoppani's seniority among the section's officials, it was considered inappropriate to place an outsider above him. France, too, did not want

---

[70] For a keen appraisal of Layton's contribution to Liberal internationalism, see Richard S. Grayson, 'Layton, Walter Thomas, first Baron Layton (1884–1966)', *ODNB*.

[71] David Hubback, *No Ordinary Press Baron: A Life of Walter Layton* (London, 1985).

[72] Richard S. Grayson, *Liberals, International Relations and Appeasement: The Liberal Party, 1919–1939* (London, 2001).

[73] He was born in Milan on 6 Mar. 1879 and worked continuously for the League from 18 Feb. 1923 until 15 Oct. 1939, when his contract was terminated by Avenol. See Stoppani to Lester, 23 Nov. 1946, LON, Section Files, Personnel Files, S.888. The EIS provided intelligence used by the other sections of the League. Although it was described as a discrete section, its staff were effectively part of the Financial Section.

to see another Briton as section director, especially given what it saw as 'radical' developments in British financial policy in 1931. As a result, Drummond opted to split the section and to place Avenol formally in a coordinating position above the two directors; in practice, he played almost no role in their work, as Loveday and Stoppani were able to cooperate closely, although not without disagreement. The squabble over succession was not unusual at the League, as national rivalries surfaced with every senior appointment. The dispute also reflected the growing importance of the section and its directors.[74] By 1930, its staff had grown to fifty-six formal members, compared to nine permanent and four temporary staff employed by the Disarmament Section.[75]

In the 1920s, British leadership dominated economic and financial issues in the League, a perspective that was also facilitated by Drummond, and outside Geneva by Lloyd George and Norman. Officials from France, the League's second largest financial contributor, also rose to prominence. Monnet was there at the beginning, as was Pierre Quesnay, whose work for the Economic and Financial Section focused particularly on the task of Austrian reconstruction. In 1926, he became Director of Economic Studies at the Bank of France—a sign that working for the League could advance a career—where he had a significant influence on French monetary policy.[76] Once France had returned to the gold standard and became a staunch defender of orthodoxy, its political and banking delegates became increasingly visible in EFO, and their activities and perspective stood in sharp contrast to the pursuit of social justice through the ILO led by French socialist Albert Thomas.[77]

Members of the secretariat were usually recruited from League member states, and, although they were not necessarily nominated by their governments, inter-governmental connections were certainly important in endorsing their credentials. The men and women who worked for the secretariat did not slavishly follow the policy perspectives of the states of which they were citizens. In the Economic and Financial Section ties to government and academic circles were seen as much as a means through which to influence national policies as offices to which they were accountable. Stoppani, for example, found himself out of step with the rising fascist tide in Italy, and refused to give up his position in Geneva when instructed to do so by Rome. He declared himself 'an outsider to the Italian administration', and in any case a man 'would always prefer to serve an independent international organization than any government, my own included'.[78]

Unlike the ILO, which had offices in the field, the EFO, aside from a small office comprising three staff in London, did not. It relied on specialist advice from

---

[74] See note from the 'Délégation de la Republique Française' to the Foreign Minister, 29 Apr. 1930, AMAE, SDN/no. 164,/Secretariat, Directeurs de section,/1922–39.

[75] League of Nations, *Staff List of the Secretariat, Showing Nationalities and Salaries for 1930* (Geneva, Aug. 1930), C.186 (1).M.87 (1).1930.

[76] See, e.g., Mouré, *The Gold Standard Illusion*, 98–115.

[77] Francophone internationalism was a powerful force in the 1920s across Geneva, but dwindled in significance in the 1930s. And, while American voices were strong in the League, they were remarkably absent from the ILO for much of the 1920s. See memo by Sweetser, 'The League of Nations and the United States', 8 Feb. 1928, LON, R3567, 50/1683/1683.

[78] Stoppani to Lester, 23 Nov. 1946, LON, Section Files, Personnel Files, S.888.

scientific societies and intelligence from member and non-member states, to whom it sent lengthy and detailed questionnaires. The officials' work sounded mundane, but their labours were Herculean. States did not give up sensitive intelligence willingly, and even minor enquiries turned up major problems in attempts to reconcile economic data drawn from a variety of national, imperial, and mandate sources around the world.[79] When trying to compile the first snapshot of the modern chemical industry, for example, officials discovered what is understood by 'chemical industry varies considerably from country to country and as a result the reports we receive talk, in fact, about quite different industries'.[80]

Over time the EIS, and the Economic and Financial Sections, developed an extensive series of periodical and special publications and investigations. These included the annually published *Statistical Yearbook of the League of Nations*, the *Monthly Bulletin of Statistics*, *Money and Banking*, *International Trade Statistics*, *International Trade in Certain Raw Materials and Foodstuffs*, the *Review of World Trade*, *Balances of Payments*, *Survey of National Nutritional Policies*, and the *World Economic Survey*. The work required a continued effort to standardize methods in economic statistics between nations and agencies, a process that was managed by the League's Preparatory Committee on Statistics made up of members of the International Statistical Institute, the ILO, and the Economic Committee. Contemporaries recognized the League was 'more and more documenting contemporary life throughout the world'.[81] Most of these publication series were later continued by the United Nations. The compilations were supplemented by annual reports on the general economic situation published in the name of the Secretary-General—a practice initiated by Avenol in 1936—whose text was drafted entirely by the Economic and Financial Sections.

Its ability to recruit scientific advisers, and to set up specialist enquiries, formed the second main arm of the EFO. This scientific work of the League enabled the secretariat to increase the number of personnel at its disposal and to develop its role. Its comparative autonomy did not go unnoticed and made it the subject of envious jibes from other sections.[82] The secretariat brought some of the brightest talent in twentieth-century economics to Geneva. Here, the facilitative agency of American internationalists was instrumental. Sweetser attempted to persuade the Rockefeller Foundation to help fund an Institute of Research in Geneva on problems affecting world stability to help the League, but Abraham Flexner, the leading scientific adviser to the Rockefeller Foundation and future

---

[79] Although the EFO sought intelligence from every continent, from member and non-member alike, depending on the question under review there were notable gaps, generally the USSR and central and southern Africa, while parts of Central and South America and south-east Asia came more frequently, but never fully, into view.

[80] Loveday to Stoppani, 19 Aug. 1929, LON, Loveday, P140/11/outgoing correspondence, 1929. There is scope for more research on issues of definition and categorization within the League.

[81] Memo by Feis, 'Report to the Advisory Committee on International Relations: Research Work Conducted in Geneva', June 1929, LON, Loveday, P140/11/in- and outgoing correspondence, 1928–9.

[82] For an early appreciation of its autonomy, see Jean Siotis, 'The Institutions of the League of Nations', in United Nations Library, *The League of Nations in Retrospect*, 19–41.

founding Director of the Institute for Advanced Study, resisted Sweeter's formulation of their research relationship. Instead he awarded $2 million towards the creation of the League of Nations Library and opted for a more flexible funding arrangement, where financial aid would be given 'from time to time' to the League's scientific work, not to the League itself.[83] It served as early testament of Rockefeller's confidence in the League's technical work, and continued US determination to remain at arm's length from its political implications.[84]

Unlike the senior members of the secretariat who were recommended and recruited from the national civil service of member states, those seconded to work on 'scientific' projects, as we shall see in the case of the Rockefeller-funded research into business cycles, were nominated by a more diffuse and wide-ranging network of academic advisers and scientific societies. Cassel, for example, recommended Bertil Ohlin and Gunnar Myrdal, leading figures in the renowned Stockholm School of Economics and future Nobel prize-winners. They worked alongside a central figure in the Austrian School of Economics in Vienna, Gottfried Haberler, who was recommended to the League by his colleague Oskar Morgenstern. The League's research into business cycles is the most widely recognized dimension of its work, although the degree to which the institutional structure and political priorities of the League shaped the content of this intellectual project, and Geneva's contribution to individual economists' personal and professional development, have been little understood. What became almost familial entanglements among these young economists, facilitated by the agency of the League, have been obscured by the need to highlight the differences in their ideas. When their scientific work is returned to the context of Geneva, it is clear that the League provided essential grist to their development and to the substance of their disagreements as economists. There were also significant points of congruence between them, especially when compared to the ideas, role, and intent behind economic science in communist and fascist states that has been unhelpfully obscured by the attribution of national schools, such as the 'Swedish' to Ohlin or 'Austrian' to Haberler. Similarly problematic in a League context are the labels associated with the history of economic ideas of the period, notably 'proto-Keynes', 'Keynesian', and 'orthodox'. The application of economic ideas to the development of policy, particularly in an international setting, is far less studied or understood than the relationship between economic ideas, or indeed the relationship between one economist and another. In Geneva, the imperative for 'practical economics', a guiding theme of nineteenth-century liberal thought, promoted by the iconic Anti-Corn Law League, and articulated in values found in the cooperative movement also, was at the heart of its approach to stewarding capitalism.

[83] Katharina Rietzler, 'American Philanthropy and Cultural Diplomacy in the Interwar Years', *Historical Research*, 84/223 (Feb. 2011), 148–64.
[84] Report by Feis to the Advisory Committee on International Relations, 'Research Work Conducted in Geneva', June 1929, LON, Loveday, P140/11/in- and outgoing correspondence, 1928–9, p. 1.

Until 1930, however, the EFO's attempts to inform and reshape the world economy were dominated by its determination to coordinate rather than direct states' policies with the aspiration to return the world economy to the levels of growth and global exchange enjoyed before the First World War. It was a conception of the liberal world economy that reached to a time before the creation of the modern nation state and the First World War, and all the disruptive pressures it exerted on global economic and financial relations and the prospects of peace.

To this end, two intergovernmental committees that formed the third prong of the EFO's structure were critical: the Financial Committee and the Economic Committee. In 1923, the single provisional committee was divided into these two permanent committees, which were granted a mandate to examine economic and monetary questions, and to publish policy recommendations, informed by science, for the use of members and non-members alike. Participation in the Economic and Financial Committees was much less diverse, in intellectual, gender, and national terms, than in the EFO's secretariat or in the expert committees and commissions. In the secretariat, women appear in significant numbers in the middle ranks as statisticians as well as in junior clerical roles, and the Economic and Financial Section in the 1920s comprised staff from Czechoslovakia, Sweden, Italy, Britain, France, New Zealand, Poland, Austria, the Netherlands, Bulgaria, India, Romania, Switzerland, Ireland, Greece, and Denmark. These remained the predominate nationalities in the 1930s, although the categories do not necessarily reflect individuals' own sense of ethnicity evident in their personnel files. 'Ireland', for example, appeared as a discrete category in staff lists only after 1925. Although numerous staff described themselves as 'Irish', they were designated 'British', while Armenians were designated as such only in 1922.

By contrast, the Economic and Financial Committees' composition largely mirrored that of the states that had permanent seats on the Council, which was no great surprise, given that the latter controlled the process by which members were nominated, with the remainder given over to smaller member states. As a result, Britain, France, Italy, and Japan enjoyed permanent representation on the Economic and Financial Committees of the League. They were joined by Germany (until it left in 1933) and the USSR, which was granted a permanent seat on the Council in 1934.[85] A significant marker of the committees' growing importance came in 1927, when the United States agreed to participate, although American officials were still not employed in the Economic and Financial Sections, nor represented in the Second Committee of the Assembly, which was made up of Council members and served as the institutional link between the intergovernmental committees and the secretariat, and the Council and Assembly. Formally, the Second Committee directed the EFO's work, but in practice it frequently worked the other way around: the EFO's secretariat made suggestions to the intergovernmental committees and the Second Committee, which then, with the

---

[85] Italy was left unrepresented on the committees once it left the League in 1937, while Japanese delegates continued to serve on the committees for some time after Japan's withdrawal in 1933–4.

Council's blessing, nodded them through. Nevertheless, major initiatives by the secretariat required alliances with governments' representatives to carry them out.

It is important to appreciate the inner workings of the institution to understand how, in time, the reach, influence, and power of the secretariat came to extend far beyond the parameters of the constitutional configuration of the League. Not only was the EFO intellectually heterodox within the spectrum of capitalist economics; its national influences and ambitions ranged far beyond the formal membership of the League. Nowhere was this clearer than in the case of the United States. When its formal diplomatic relations with the League ended in 1919, Drummond was instructed by the American Raymond Fosdick, a short-lived Deputy Secretary-General of the League, that, if the organization had something really important to communicate to American internationalists, this was better facilitated by non-governmental US agencies (including the Rockefeller Foundation, where Fosdick returned as an employee) than through the State Department.[86] Transnational connections came to the rescue where intergovernmental relations in 1919 had failed.

THE POLITICS OF TRADE, AND THE TRADE OF POLITICS

After 1924, with its institutional apparatus in place, the currencies in Europe's heartlands stabilized, and its intellectual credentials in liberal economics established, the League turned its attention to the central issue of liberal internationalism, trade. The goal of free trade was articulated in Wilson's Fourteen Points, in the League's Covenant, and was concomitant to the reconstruction of the international gold standard order. The secretariat intended to help states deliver on this aim, and to liberate world markets to enable debtor nations to trade and so to earn essential hard currency to pay off commercial and political debts. By the mid-1920s, reducing protectionism was also part of efforts to safeguard the gold standard, allowing prices to fall in some parts of the world and rise in others to iron out what were suspected to be the overvaluation of some currencies (for example, the pound sterling) and the undervaluation of others (notably the French franc and the US dollar). By then, the League had emerged as the world's major site for monitoring and negotiating international protectionist practice. The universalist, global claims of the League of Nations were frequently presented as the antithesis to the idea of national protection and regional, notably European, solidarity. But the picture was contradictory. In 1925, for example, Aristide Briand, the French foreign minister, in Geneva proclaimed the Locarno treaties, which also helped to pave the way for Germany's accession into the League the following year, as 'the draft constitution of

---

[86] Raymond Fosdick, *Letters on the League of Nations* (Princeton, 1966), 65.

a European family within the orbit of the League of Nations . . . the beginning of a magnificent renewal of Europe'.[87]

The League of Nations helped to make the arguments and activities of national protectionists, colonial activists, and European unionists within nations visible to one another. Protectionist arguments were expressed in the context of calls for European union and colonial renewal (in the French and Dutch case the two aspirations were closely linked) and anti-Americanism.[88] At the same time, Americans' observation of trade discussions in Geneva and their participation in the technical work of the League exposed them to debtors' critiques of their debt and trade policy, which tied Europe to the need to sell in the US market to earn dollars to pay off its loans, while at the same time facing tariff arrangements, including the Fordney–McCumber Act of 1922, which raised the average American *ad valorem* tariff rate to 38.5 per cent. In the evocative words of an American banker, Benjamin Anderson, who had been involved in Austria's reconstruction: 'The debts of the outside world to us are ropes about the necks of our debtors, by means of which we pull them towards us. Our trade restrictions are pitchforks pressed against their bodies, by means of which we hold them off.'[89]

The secretariat was staffed almost entirely by proponents of classical liberalism, for whom free trade was an article of faith. Among member states, support for it ranged beyond the borders of party politics, and was articulated by leading internationalists calling, as Ramsay MacDonald put it, for the League to help forge an 'enormous federation of Free Trade nations'.[90] History ensured that for member states the association of free trade with British policy was automatic, but inside the League of Nations it was the Netherlands that was its most enthusiastic and consistent supporter.[91] Its commitment to trade liberalization lasted long after that of Britain failed, and Dutch leaders, notably Hendrikus Colijn, leader of the Revolutionary Party and Dutch premier, who served successive terms as chairman of the League's Economic and Financial Committees, oversaw a series of investigations into international protectionism. Among the Dutch elite, free trade was seen as the means to preserve its valuable export industries and imperial interests in South East Asia, and the ideology of the League (and the broader community of

[87] Quoted in Robert W. D. Boyce, *British Capitalism at the Crossroads, 1919–1932: A Study in Politics, Economics and International Relations* (Cambridge, 1987). 108; E. D. Keeton, *Briand's Locarno Policy: French Economics, Politics and Diplomacy, 1925–1929* (New York, 1987).

[88] See Anne-Isabelle Richard-Picchi, 'Colonialism and the European Movement in France and the Netherlands, 1925–1936', unpublished Ph.D. thesis, Cambridge University, 2010.

[89] Benjamin M. Anderson, in The Chase Bank (ed.), *The Chase Economic Bulletin*, 14 Mar. 1930, later cited by Gottfried Haberler, *The Theory of International Trade with its Applications to Commercial Policy* (London, 1936), 80; Edward S. Kaplan, *American Trade Policy, 1923–1995* (Westport, CT, 1996), 1–21.

[90] *Free Trader* (Dec. 1925), 265.

[91] R. T. Griffiths, 'Free Traders in a Protectionist World: The Foreign Policy of the Netherlands, 1930–1950', in S. Groenveld and M. Wintle (eds), *Britain and the Netherlands: State and Trade, Government and Economics in Britain and the Netherlands since the Middle Ages* (Zutphen, 1992), 152–68.

economists, financiers, and businessmen to whom it afforded access) reinforced their position at home when opposing Dutch farmers who were lobbying for greater protection. The Dutch delivered essential political support to the work of the secretariat on trade liberalization, which, in turn, helped the League to attract experts and politicians who were committed to free trade within nations whose trade policies were traditionally protectionist.

The first sustained attempt to establish its authority in trade relations came in September 1925, when Louis Loucheur proposed that the League convene an economic conference to tackle the rising tide of protectionist policies that, unchecked, had the potential to scupper the beneficial effects of Locarno.[92] With the argument put this way, the entire Assembly had little choice but enthusiastically to endorse the suggestion, and Salter and the Economic and Financial Section were charged with putting together the programme and materials. The intervention was timely. In January 1925, Germany had regained the power to impose tariffs denied to it by the Versailles Treaty, and French, Polish, Austrian, and Czech duties were also on the rise. But Loucheur, a close ally of Briand, was a surprising choice to lead what was presented as a coordinated League charge on trade protectionism.[93] A businessman who had made a fortune from establishing the largest network of electrical distribution companies in France before entering government during the war, Loucheur was famous for his enthusiasm for the French colonial mission in Africa, where he exhibited a great interest in coordinating electrical distribution— an exemplar of European efforts to master the world through science and technology. Inside the League, his renown lay in his formidable skills as a trade negotiator and in his interest in the League's electrification programmes for Europe. But Loucheur was no free-trader, and eyebrows were raised in London and The Hague, where statesmen feared his intervention in Geneva was the prelude to attempts to use the League as the launching pad for a protectionist United States of Europe.

Salter had to take a different view. There were risks in taking up Loucheur's rallying cry, but working at the behest of the League Council and Assembly, which had resolved on 24 September 1925 that the notion of a conference should be investigated, meant Salter's options were limited. On the plus side, the French proposal offered the chance to engage French energies in the League's economic work, and to bring the investigation and discussion of global trade protectionism firmly into the EFO's purview. *The Economist* swung firmly behind the initiative, at the same time as the secretariat was given the rationale and the power to elicit a huge amount of data from states regarding their protective quotas and tariffs. It marked a further expansion of the section's activities and staff roll—rising from

---

[92] It was part of an attempt to hold German revanchism in check. Robert W. D. Boyce, *The Great Interwar Crisis and the Collapse of Globalization* (London, 2009), 166–7.
[93] Coordinated because it coincided with calls for a League conference at the third Congress of the International Chamber of Commerce in Brussels in June 1925; League of Nations, '6th Assembly', *Official Journal* (Geneva 1925), 81. The League also provided a venue and network through which Loucheur could promote his interest in European electrification. See Vincent Lagendijk, *Electrifying Europe. The power of Europe in the construction of electricity networks* (Amsterdam, 2008), 51–67.

thirty-one to forty-five employees between 1925 and 1926, and forty-eight in 1927.[94]

The World Economic Conference met from 4 to 23 May 1927, and brought together 226 accredited experts from the worlds of social science, industry, finance, and agriculture, with 194 national delegates, together with experts in international trade with the secretariat. Following precedents established at the Brussels Conference, the USA and the USSR were invited to participate, as was Germany, in an important prelude to its full accession the following year. Expert participation in Brussels was a model too, and the conference placed particular emphasis on the value of expertise in the hope it would push politics to the margins to allow scientific evidence to speak to the benefits of freer trade. It was an international landmark in exploring the state of national and international recovery since the war, and in testing different strategies to effect economic relations between, and within, nation states.[95] The event opened with a series of individual statements from the conference President, Georges Theunis, the former Belgian Prime Minister, and the conference Vice-President, Loucheur, and Cassel, in recognition of distinct contributions to the Brussels Conference. Prominent on this occasion, too, was the voice of industrial and agricultural lobbyists, with Walter Runciman speaking for the International Chamber of Commerce, Max Muspratt for the Federation of British Industry, and Carl Friedrich von Siemens for the Reichsverbandes der Deutschen Industrie.

The main work of the conference was undertaken in special commissions, which explored, for example, the role of cartels and quotas in national recovery and international trade. The intellectual breadth and the variety of industry and expert perspectives the League mustered on trade meant discussion, not agreement, had always to be its declared intention. With individuals 'perfectly free to express their own opinions, delegates were perfectly free to arrive at any conclusion they wished, but not able to tie the hands of their respective governments'.[96] But there were some more concrete outcomes. First, the three-week gathering established the League's authority in the field and marked the first economic conference in history that claimed to be of and for the world, even if most of the discussion centred on European protectionism. Secondly, the narrative forged by the economic secretariat implicitly projected a progressive vision of a common global economy, which, facilitated by the agency of the League, would become more prosperous, entangled, and peaceful if tariff barriers, quotas, and other restrictive trade practices were reduced. The secretariat produced a large array of information to support deliberations, compiled the agenda, and segregated the discussion into distinct strands of

[94] Staff numbers of the other sections, by contrast, remained fairly static. The Mandates Section had six permanent and one or two temporary staff members, for example. See League of Nations, *Staff List of the Secretariat, Showing Nationalities and Salaries for 1925*, C.459.M.170.1925; for 1926, C.245.M.92.1926; for 1927, C.184.(1).M.62.(1).1927.

[95] League of Nations, *World Economic Conference, Geneva 1927: Final Report* (Geneva, 1927).

[96] H. J. Colijn, 'The World Economic Conference of 1927', *Annals of the American Academy of Political and Social Science*, Special Issue, 'Europe in 1927: An Economic Survey', 134 (Nov. 1927), 140.

tariff and quantitative restrictions, cartel arrangements, sanitary restrictions, and so on, producing a complete inventory of protectionist practices. Intriguingly, it had an open mind on cartels going into the conference, but its investigations led the secretariat to conclude that they were more likely to raise than lower protectionism.[97]

Thirdly, the diversity of groups represented in Geneva and the space afforded smaller nations and poorer producers the opportunity to explain why they opted for protectionism, and drew sustained international attention to the plight of agricultural producers. Fourth, while the case for protection was couched in positive terms—the need to safeguard employment levels, wages, or the environment, for example—French, German, Dutch, and Swiss delegates, in particular, narrated the global recourse to protectionism explicitly in relation to what they argued were failures in US policies, notably the aggressive efforts of the USA to undercut local producers overseas. Protection also enabled these powers to preserve their membership, hard fought, of the gold standard system, which was in the interest of the USA.[98] In short, despite the primacy of national and imperial politics in shaping individual state's policies, the blame for the global recourse to protection was laid squarely upon the USA.[99] The American penchant for protection, offset only by the occasional bilateral agreement to reduce tariffs that eschewed the principle of unconditional most-favoured-nation (MFN) status, flew in the face of its responsibilities as the world's banker. To the European liberals, US tariffs rubbed salt into their wounds, because US workers were, on average, more than twice as productive as their European counterparts, and did not appear to need protecting. They argued that American global power needed to take on the economic and financial attributes of the nineteenth century *Pax Britannica*, and, given its economic strength, it had little to fear, and much to gain, from opening its markets to the rest of the world.[100]

The lack of a firm resolution at the conference emphasized that, while League scientific work showed that levels of protectionism across Europe and the Americas were rising steadily, there was considerable scope for barriers to grow even higher. At the conference Layton warned delegates that, if the British public received the general impression from the meeting that 'the other European countries had no intention of doing anything', then they too were likely to demand protection. Although the thrust of British retaliation would not desist those intent on protection any more than it had dissuaded American or European protectionists, Britain's continued power as the world's leading import market, especially in

---

[97] Matthias Schulz, *Deutschland, der Völkerbund und die Frage der europäischen Wirtschaftsordnung, 1925–1933* (Hamburg, 1997), 110–51.

[98] Louis Loucheur, *Carnet secrets, 1980–1932*, ed. and annotated Jacques de Launay (Brussels, 1962), 159.

[99] Beth Simmons, *Who Adjusts? Domestic Sources of Foreign Economic Policy during the Interwar Years* (Princeton, 1994). Frank Trentmann has demonstrated that free trade had lost its appeal in domestic politics by 1920; see Frank Trentmann *Free Trade Nation: Commerce, Consumption, and Civil Society in Modern Britain* (Oxford, 2008). Nonetheless it remained a central plank of British policy for another thirteen years, thanks to international and imperial considerations.

[100] Colijn, 'The World Economic Conference of 1927'.

Europe, gave it considerable influence. To free-traders like Colijn, it was clear that the loss of the British import market would have severe consequences for France, Denmark, Germany, Norway, Sweden, Portugal, and many others.

The Anglo-Dutch axis helped liberal free-traders deliver the most important result of the conference, the endorsement of the unconditional MFN and multi-lateral trade negotiations as the goal and means to reduce global protectionism. The principle became a key element in the League's work, although Salter was prepared to 'admit certain exceptions to this clause . . . if they were to remain in touch with the realities of the situation'. One important 'reality' was that if, as happened in 1931, Britain moved to an imperial preference scheme that advantaged only colonial and dominion trade, it would be in violation of the clause. Tolerant at first, after Salter's departure from Geneva in the same year, the section was to become increasingly hostile to British, colonial, and dominion violation of the clause, and British protectionism more generally.[101]

The international adoption of unconditional MFN as the ideal standard of tariff conventions was an important step—the clause meant that the favourable terms of any trade agreement between two countries would be passed onto other nations with which they had MFN agreements. Until Daniel Serryys, director of the treaty department of the French Ministry of Commerce, declared his government in favour of it at the conference, it had not been a component of French or US tariff agreements with other nations. In the past this had put Britain, the Netherlands, and other free-trading nations at a marked disadvantage when bargaining for equitable treatment in foreign markets because they had no tariffs or quotas to surrender. The conference resolution did not mean that unconditional MFN was widely adopted overnight, but the League had now set a standard against which national and imperial trade policy could be seen to fail, and the resolution certainly registered with the free-trading and future US Secretary of State Cordell Hull and other internationalist groups in the USA.[102]

Yet, although the League had endorsed a new international standard, it had no power to enforce it. And binding the principle of unconditional MFN to the ambition for multilateral tariff reductions was a very tall order. Among European states, it had been common to engage in bilateral tariff deals that were then widened, when suitable, through the application of MFN. Stating its preference for multilateral negotiations over bilateral ones, a logical step given the League's desire to facilitate multilateral cooperation, meant it had now set the bar very high for international tariff negotiations. The history of the twentieth century was to demonstrate the importance of unconditional MFN to cutting tariffs, but it was also to show that bilateral negotiations proved more efficacious than multilateral ones—the more participants, the more elusive a successful outcome.

---

[101] Comment by Salter, 'Minutes of Directors' Meeting', 8 Oct. 1930, LON, R3565, 50/16937/767, p. 4.
[102] The conference and Hull's commitment to its resolutions surfaced in the Nobel Committee's award of the Peace Prize to Hull in Dec. 1945. See 'The Nobel Peace Prize 1945—Presentation Speech' <http:\nobelprize.org\nobel_prizes\peace\laureates\1945\press.html> (accessed 29 Sept. 2010).

After 1927, the reputation of the League of Nations was implicated in these failures as the EFO's Economic Committee was now handed the challenge by the conference delegates of turning the declared will of the assembled experts into binding international agreements. With more responsibility came greater risks.

After the World Conference, progress on the trade resolutions proved desultory, and this troubled the secretariat, especially when Briand's talk of renewing Europe shifted away from an economic to a political rationale, out of the EFO's purview, and back into the realm of intergovernmental political relations.[103] The Briand Plan for a 'United States of Europe' was proposed at a meeting of the League Assembly on 3 September 1929.[104] On the same day, the British and Belgian governments announced a counter-bid to European union at the League: a firm commitment to a two- or three-year-long 'tariff truce' that sought to fix states' current levels of protection to provide breathing space in which multilateral tariff agreements could be initiated.[105] While the truce was debated, outside the League the pace of change was quickening. Within days of the announcement of the Briand Plan and the tariff truce, the Dow Jones Industrial Average had peaked at a level it was not to reach again until 1954; a month later Briand was no longer Prime Minister in France, Stresemann was dead, and the Wall Street crash had wiped off more than $30 billion from the value of the New York Stock Exchange (a figure ten times greater than the annual budget of the US government).

Back in Geneva, the Assembly's support for a tariff truce provided the institutional case for the Economic and Financial Section to expand its studies concerning comparative agricultural prices and industrial products. It now had unparalleled practical and intellectual expertise in the field of protectionism, especially on comparative statistics.[106] But, although expert opinions expressed in Geneva between 1927 and 1929 set a broadly liberal tone, the sentiment needed political support. There was an attempt to generate it at a League conference on the customs truce in the spring of 1930. But after the Wall Street crash, the rapidly tightening credit and trading conditions and the deterioration of domestic demand made it all the more difficult to match words with policy. Drummond and Salter agreed that, at best, any truce would not 'be a legal engagement so much as a system which would create practical obstacles to an increase in tariffs'.[107] The deal that was subsequently struck, albeit with a hefty number of reservations, surpassed Salter's expectations (privately he gave it no more than three months), for it lasted until the end of a second world economic conference three and a half years later.

---

[103] 'Minutes of Directors' Meeting', 12 Nov. 1930, LON, R3565, 50/16937/767; Carl Hamilton Pegg, *Evolution of the European Idea, 1914–1932* (Chapel Hill, NC, 1983), 121–62.

[104] Cornelia Navari, 'Origins of the Briand Plan', *Diplomacy and Statecraft*, 3/1 (1992), 74–104.

[105] League of Nations, 'Records of the Tenth Assembly, Plenary Meetings', *Official Journal* (Geneva, 1929), 52.

[106] Staff numbers went up again too: rising from 56 in 1930 to 68. See, e.g., Loveday to Flux (Royal Statistical Society), 16 Sept. 1929, and Loveday to Lloyd, 28 June 1929, LON, Loveday, P140/11/ in- and outgoing correspondence, 1928–9.

[107] Comment by Salter, 'Minutes of Directors' Meeting', 6 Mar. 1930, LON, R3565, 50/16937/767, pp. 1–2.

Facing a new financial crisis and determined to reinvigorate the League, Salter and his colleagues in the EFO argued that the organization needed to present an outward semblance of optimism and to offer viable and focused policy solutions to international problems. Yet the plate-tectonic activity occasioned by the Great Depression disoriented liberal internationalists. After 1929, they were scrambling to weave together a new case to legitimize the League's place in the rapidly changing context of world affairs.

2

From Boom to Bust, 1929–1932

Although the League of Nations was not in the business of economic forecasting, the web of intelligence spun by the secretariat made it sensitive to vibrations of state and market behaviour. The challenge for the EFO was to decipher what the tremors signified and to decide what powers, if any, it could exercise in response. An additional complication for these watchmen of the world economy was that the signals were frequently contradictory. At the end of 1928, League reports showed the volume of world trade was higher than in any year since 1914. At the same time, from their 'point of view the tariff situation was bad; the furious wave of protection', especially in the USA, where the role of Congress, as both the 'proposer and maker of tariffs', was of particular concern.[1] Meanwhile, the gold standard enjoyed similarly mixed fortunes. The good news was that the fixed exchange system had a record number of members: forty-two currencies, representing and shaping the fate of their nations. But there were signs the system was exerting a troubling deflationary impact on some economies and the accumulation of substantial, and potentially destabilizing, gold reserves in others. Theoretically, the system should have facilitated the self-righting of the world economy. Practically, the behaviour of states, central banks, and societies stood in the way. Society intruded into the financial system, and either it or the financial system had to give.

BITTER-SWEET INTERNATIONALISM

In the spring of 1929 there were also big changes in the political world. In March, the inauguration of President Herbert Hoover offered opportunities and risk. It triggered a re-evaluation of what the League might expect from the world's major economy and what the USA could expect from the League. The American President, whose infamous failure to combat the Great Depression produced its own bitter language of hunger and fear in the slang of Hooverism, stood in sharp contrast to the expressions of hope and confidence of a new American presence in the world at the dawn of his presidency. In the wider world, the new President was famed for his humanitarian intervention. He had helped feed starving Belgians and Germans after the First World War, and was committed to the international welfare of the child, in part as a result of his experience as an engineer in Australia,

---

[1] 'Minutes of the Directors' Meeting', 13 Mar. 1929, LON, R3564, 50/2792/767.

New Zealand, Malaya, India, Burma, Ceylon, Egypt, South Africa, and China.[2] He was, for Sweetser, 'an important actor in the development of the present international situation at the Peace Conference', who, 'for eight years as Secretary of Commerce, has had unparalleled contact with America's whole economic system, especially abroad'. The President was 'a new type of man, with new methods of work and new lines of interest'. He was 'the engineer and man of science succeeding the life-long men of politics' such as Harding and Coolidge.[3]

Hoover's internationalist credentials did little to endear him to the American public, including his fellow Republicans, many of whom were suspicious of his intellectual gifts, and a grasp of languages that included Latin. His detractors complained he was 'a British gentleman and not an American in either thought or action'.[4] But these attributes held great appeal in Geneva, where the wave of enthusiasm in the secretariat at Hoover's election was such that Drummond issued a plea for public restraint. He did 'not wish [League officials] to prophesy in this difficult field'.[5] There was also great interest in Hoover's association with the Efficiency Movement of the Progressive Era, whose central tenet was that a technical solution existed for every economic and social problem. This struck a chord with the technocrats in Geneva, encouraged by Hoover's fulsome declaration in his acceptance speech to his party's nomination for the Presidency of his support for the League's 'endeavours to promote scientific, economic and social welfare and secure limitation of armaments'.[6]

But, if the League seemed no longer taboo in presidential politics, the EFO's members were not blind to Hoover's shortcomings, notably his inexperience at the sharp end of American politics, a limitation to which they were especially sensitive, because the same weakness had cost President Wilson and the League dearly. The secretariat was more impressed by his record as Secretary of State for Commerce, notably his creation of a network of commercial attachés around the world, and his interest in Central and South America, where his commitment to promoting the relationship between prosperity and peace resonated profoundly in the League. Under Hoover, liberal capitalism did not retreat into isolation, but the EFO was aware that beyond American shores it assumed a bitter-sweet flavour: US commercial loans totalled some $7.9 billion at the same time that international negotiations produced only a nominal reduction on interest payments levied on 'political debts'; the US proclaimed its liberal capitalism, while its level of trade protection rose throughout the period, and the Smoot–Hawley tariff in 1930, pushed it to a record-breaking 50 per cent.[7] Hoover did not escape

---

    [2] The chairman of the Belgian relief committee was Émile Franqui, who became the standing Belgian representative on the Finance Committee and at the BIS. See Lawrence G. Gelfand (ed.), *Herbert Hoover: The Great War and its Aftermath, 1914–1923* (Iowa, 1979).
    [3] Memo by Sweetser, 'Mr Hoover's Election', 12 Nov. 1928, LON R3567, 50/8371/1683.
    [4] e.g. 'Willis Excoriates Hoover', report by the Associated Press, *New York Times*, 4 Mar. 1928.
    [5] Minute by Drummond, 7 Nov. 1928, LON R3567, 50/8371/1683.
    [6] 'League Expects Aid in Work from Hoover', *New York Times*, 8 Nov. 1928.
    [7] William J. Barber, *From New Era to New Deal: Herbert Hoover, the Economists, and American Economic Policy, 1921–1933* (Cambridge, 1985), 65–103.

criticism that US economic internationalism seemed more about dampening down international retaliation against the USA than opening up American markets to products that had not been 'made in the USA'. The challenge this posed to the world was all the more pressing because between 1924 and 1929 American multinational firms expanded abroad faster than at any time before or since, selling products—cars and their components, radios, refrigerators, washing machines— cloaked in meanings of modernity that made them irresistible.[8]

Salter and his colleagues in the EFO's secretariat begrudgingly recognized the logic behind Hoover's commitment to protecting the wage levels of US workers who could not fall back on other forms of social protection. The idea that protecting the home market while safeguarding national wage levels had wide and increasing appeal on the left and right of global politics. Salter and League experts were also regular visitors to the USA, and understood the centrality of interest group politics and the role of Congress, distinct from the executive arm of the Presidency, in explaining the rapid escalation of American protectionism. Real change would 'only happen when the large exporting industries realized there was nothing to be got out of protection and when farmers saw that it was not the way in which agricultural relief was to be sought'.[9] (The relationship between protection- ism and farmers' well-being was always closer than in policies that sought to protect industrial labour.)

At the same time that the League was sizing up Hoover, the US executive commissioned a new appraisal of the League. In June 1929, Herbert Feis, the American economic adviser to the State Department, reported to the American foreign policy community on the work of the League of Nations. The EFO dominated his account. This was not just because when he visited Geneva he spent much of his time in the company of Loveday and Salter, but because the economic and financial dimension to the League's work had grown considerably in recent years, and embraced issues of considerable interest to the USA.[10] By 1929, its activities ranged from an established programme exploring international protec- tionism to new investigations into the conditions of depressed industries, notably coal and wheat production, the operation of cartels, the problem of double taxation and fiscal evasion, and a putative study in the depressed state of world agriculture (the EFO had put out feelers as to whether the League Council would support, and the International Institute for Agriculture in Rome would tolerate, a League- sponsored inquiry). These initiatives marked an assertive move into world agricul- ture that would bear fruit only later.

---

[8] Victoria de Grazia, *Irresistible Empire: America's Advance through 20th Century Europe* (Cambridge, MA, 2005); Stephen Kotkin, 'Modern Times: The Soviet Union and the Interwar Conjuncture', *Kritika: Explorations in Russian and Eurasian History*, 2/1 (Winter 2001), 111–64; A. Weinbaum, L. Thomas, P. Ramamurthy, U. Poiger, M. Dong, and T. Barlow (eds), *The Modern Girl around the World: Consumption, Modernity and Globalization* (Durham, NC, 2008).

[9] Comment by Salter, 'Minutes of the Directors' Meeting', 13 Mar. 1929, LON R3564, 50/2792/767.

[10] Feis to Loveday, 21 June 1929, LON, Loveday, P140/11/in- and outgoing correspondence, 1928–9.

Feis recognized also the League's interest in financial cooperation. Its early work on the 'financial restoration of Austria, Hungary, Greece etc. appeared completed'. Through it, the League had learned a great deal about the operation of central banks, and remained sensitive to renewed monetary threats to credit conditions and prices in Europe in particular. Behind the scenes in 1929, members of the EFO's financial section did what they could to support banking and intergovernmental negotiations for a new international scheme to replace the failing Dawes Plan, and signs of strain in the gold standard prompted the EFO to launch an investigation into the technical side of the problem, 'the purchasing power of gold'.[11] But, for all the EFO's recognized expertise, involvement in these financial questions remained a politically sensitive area. Central banks continued to guard their powers jealously, and states were nervous of drawing international attention to their own financial weaknesses for fear that would trigger further financial plagues upon their houses.

Feis's overview did more than tell the Americans that the League's economic and financial work was of increasing significance. The ever-growing list of issues with which the EFO was engaged, and the less than optimistic tone of its reports and statistical overviews of global economic performance, also reflected growing US concerns for the health of the world economy. With the gold standard reconstructed and the armistice more than a decade old, there were few signs that imbalances in the world economy were diminishing; every silver lining was obscured by ever-darkening clouds. The EFO, Feis acknowledged, was uniquely well placed to identify the problems in the world's economy, their respective interconnections, and their interplay with the particular situations of individual societies. These were the persistently depressed conditions for producers of key commodities (notably coal, wheat, and sugar); rising protectionist sentiment exemplified by the rise in quotas and tariffs; cartel arrangements that affected not just commodities and raw materials, but also semi-finished or fabricated goods, such as cement and steel girders, and high-value goods, including pharmaceuticals and electrical equipment; stalled tariff truce negotiations; and unevenness in the operations of the international gold standard. It was precisely these linkages that the EFO's secretariat had sought to underline in the standing inquiry established by the World Economic Conference of 1927 with its 'Investigation of Economic Trends tending to create or destroy conditions favourable to peace'. The problem for the League was that, as its civil servants recognized, analysing material under this heading 'would inevitably entail criticism of League members'.[12] After 1929, these criticisms, which extended far beyond the formal remit of the EFO's secretariat, ran the risk of imperilling not just the EFO, but the League too.

---

[11] Report by Feis to the Advisory Committee on International Relations, 'Research Work Conducted in Geneva', June 1929, LON, Loveday, P140/11/in- and outgoing correspondence, 1928–9, pp. 8–12. The EFO was also involved in the debate about a new international bank to support the Young Plan, which became the Bank for International Settlements (BIS).

[12] Charles P. Kindleberger, 'Commercial Policy between the Wars', in P. Matthias and S. Pollard (eds), *The Cambridge Economic History of Europe*, vol. VIII: *The Industrial Economies: The Development of Economic and Social Policies* (Cambridge, 1989), 161–96.

At the end of 1929, the paralysis in League efforts to free up the channels of trade were dealt a heavy blow by the collapse of the US stock market in October, and with it the cessation of US domestic and international lending, which had lubricated the global economy since 1924. The world was faltering, and it was defects in the operation of the international gold standard that helped to turn the 1929–30 recession into the greatest economic depression of the twentieth century and to transmit the effects of a crisis around the world.

INTERROGATING THE GOLD STANDARD

The League of Nations' efforts to understand and address the impact of the gold standard on the international economy marked a further stage in its evolving world role as it stepped, if not decisively then irrevocably, into the field of monetary policy. The special subcommittee on the 'Purchasing Power of Gold', which became known as the Gold Delegation, marked the first time an international organization questioned and raised concerns about the norms of monetary policy agreed by central bankers, who had overseen the arrangements, and national governments which signed up to them. By launching the inquiry into what were guarded and deeply sensitive issues, the EFO was pushing at the boundaries of what states would accept by way of international scrutiny and interference in monetary policy.[13]

Yet the pace of economic and political change wrong-footed the Gold Delegation from the moment the inquiry was mooted in the spring of 1928 to when it delivered its final report in the summer of 1932. The gap between its deliberations and the magnitude of the economic crisis made the delegation's work seem dated in relation to the immediate challenges facing governments and central banks, and irrelevant to the concerns of 'ordinary people' to whom the League also wanted to reach out. There was much more to its work than the final report on which historians have usually focused: there were six major meetings of the delegation, and a series of subsidiary meetings, which brought together more than twenty-five monetary experts from around the world, many of whom met repeatedly over the next fifteen years. The delegation published three substantial reports, a variety of supplementary commentaries, and a wealth of statistical information that remains a major resource for interwar monetary history.[14] These meetings and publications helped to identify existing positions and new trends in monetary policy.

The real contribution of the Gold Delegation lay in what went on behind closed doors: the private meetings that descended into heated rows, the double-dealing by

---

[13] Accounts of its history are generally based on the inquiry's final published report and condemn it as a failure, both on its own terms as a technical inquiry, and as a misconceived venture that sought to reimpose the gold standard order. See, e.g., Endres and Fleming, *International Organisations*, 73–7. Barry Eichengreen, *Golden Fetters: The Gold Standard and the Great Depression, 1919–1939* (Oxford, 1992), 198–203, says little about the committee but drew on the statistical materials it generated.

[14] Eichengreen, *Golden Fetters*, 198–203.

British bankers and officials, and a battle for political and public opinion that prompted delegates to leak information to the media and, for the first time in the EFO's history, to publish reports that dissented from a collective line. (Formally all participants had to agree on the contents of reports before they were published.) The spectacle of open dissent held grave dangers for the secretariat, which privately had grown increasingly critical of the system's operation. But consensus-building remained the name of the game, even if the economic science on which it was to be built was on the move. The secretariat continued to believe in the power of experts to generate unanimity among the states. This was the lesson of the 1927 World Economic Conference, and in 1930 it began to support calls for a new League-sponsored World Economic Conference that would bring experts and senior political figures together.

The EFO's origins were interwoven with the reconstruction of the gold standard, and its secretariat was well aware of its shortcomings. Salter knew that Norman, Strong, Émile Moreau, and Hjalmar Schacht had sought to address some of these through central bank diplomacy, although with limited success. But a key protagonist in the debate, Cassel, was closer to the EFO, and his 1928 book, which set out his views on the potential dangers of the current gold shortages, made a big impact on the secretariat, the British Treasury, and a number of independent economists, including John Maynard Keynes, an increasingly vociferous critic of the gold standard.[15] Drawing on Cassel's work, the EFO's secretariat identified two fundamental and interconnected problems with the way the gold standard system operated. First, some countries' national reserves were too low or 'tight' because gold was unevenly distributed around the world; and, secondly, that the supply of gold was insufficient to sustain the parity of currencies fixed on the gold standard. Inflation between 1914 and 1926 across much of Europe had resulted in higher price levels, and had caused a massive outflow of gold, primarily from there to the United States. The situation was compounded when, after 1926, it moved also in unpredicted quantities into France, thanks to the undervalued franc. At the same time, inflation had caused the value of gold (that is, its purchasing power) to fall, which meant that it was less profitable to mine gold.[16] In short, the world's supply of available gold was diminishing fast.

Meanwhile, demand for gold was rising. There were more national currencies than before 1914 that needed gold reserves to become a member of the gold standard club. More significantly, a number of currencies that had been gold standard members before the war decided to restabilize at pre-war gold parities, while actual price levels were considerably higher than before 1914. This meant a

---

[15] Gustav Cassel, *Post-War Monetary Stabilization* (New York, 1928). In early 1929, Keynes began to support and publicize Cassel's gold shortage theory and welcomed a League exploration of the gold question. See John Maynard Keynes, 'Is There Enough Gold? The League of Nations Inquiry', *The Nation and Athenaeum*, 19 Jan. 1929, repr. in *The Collected Writings of John Maynard Keynes*, xix. *Activities 1922–1929: The Return to Gold and Industrial Policy, Part II*, ed. Donald E. Moggridge (Cambridge, 1981), 775–80. See also John Maynard Keynes, *A Treatise on Money. Volume II. The Applied Theory of Money* (London, 1930).

[16] Lower profitability of gold mining resulted in lower annual gold-mining output.

greater volume of monetary gold was required as reserves in each country to support the increased need for international credit and the quantity of money in circulation.[17] If more gold could not be brought into the system, it would be impossible to expand the amount of credit available, and deflation would be the inevitable result in countries with low gold reserves. Having banished the scourge of inflation and facilitated stability and recovery, the gold standard now brought a very real threat of deflation in its place.

Clearly, the big question for central bankers, national governments, and the EFO was what to do in response. (The even bigger question as to whether the world required a fixed exchange mechanism remained unthinkable.) According to the economic orthodoxy, the answer was nothing. One of the great attractions of the system was the widely held view that it had the ability to correct itself. The expectation was that countries with limited, and in the long run insufficient, gold reserves would have to deflate their economies. This would be painful, but the gain was expected to be twofold. The rising price of gold would encourage more gold mining, thereby increasing the volume of monetary gold available and expanding the amount of credit available. As a result, prices would fall, making member economies becoming more competitive. Their balance of payments would then improve and eventually facilitate an inflow of gold to boost national reserves.

This theory was sorely tested by the practice. By 1928, some countries, notably Britain and Germany, had begun to experience serious deflationary pressures and the supposed self-righting properties of the gold system had not engaged. The supply of gold did not increase, and social and political tensions began to mount as governments struggled to manage the rising deficits in their balance of payments. Nor did central bank cooperation seem able to redress the growing imbalances. Disagreements began to appear between the central bankers. Strong, formerly one of Norman's closest allies, dismissed British fears of a worldwide liquidity crisis, and this American perspective was warmly endorsed by the Bank of France. Nor did the French and American banks support British schemes of establishing a general gold exchange standard based on sterling, which would have relieved the scramble for gold reserves.[18]

From the League's vantage point, the risks to international stability were becoming readily apparent, especially given the increasingly sharp divergence between French and American monetary fortunes on the one hand, and British and German ones on the other, with each of these major economies tied to a cluster of other nations and territories with whom they had economic and financial relationships. Thanks to their close connections to critics of the gold standard in

---

[17] This was especially the case when central banks set very high reserve ratios as well as high surplus reserves. The US Federal Reserve, the Bank of France, the Bank of England, and the Reichsbank held legal reserve ratios of between 35% and 50%. Ragnar Nurkse, *International Currency Experience: Lessons of the Inter-War Period* (Geneva, 1944), 96–7, and Eichengreen, *Golden Fetters*, 194–8.

[18] Barry Eichengreen, 'The Bank of France and the Sterilization of Gold, 1926–1932', in Barry Eichengreen, *Elusive Stability: Essays in the History of International Finance, 1919–1939* (Cambridge, 1990), 83–112. See also Strong to Norman, 27 Mar. 1928, BoE EID 4/102.

British financial circles within government, in the City, and in academia, Salter and Loveday were especially attuned to the mounting pressures on sterling.[19] Norman, with the support of the Treasury, decided to accept Salter's offer to use the League as an alternative forum to discuss the growing imbalances in the gold standard. It was not an easy step for him to take. Norman, like other central bankers, valued the independence of traditional central bank-dominated financial diplomacy, and, in the past, had been hostile to the EFO's effort to extend its remit. But he was reassured by Salter that the 'Gold Question' would be taken up in a way that would suit British objectives, thanks to the British dominance of the EFO's Economic and Financial Section, and the Financial Committee. In an effort to get his own way, while appearing to preserve the established conventions of central bank diplomacy, Norman told Strong and Moreau that he did not approve of the League looking into the operation of the gold standard while at the same time encouraging the secretariat to pursue the inquiry. It was a risky tactic for both the Bank of England and the League.[20]

In Geneva the call for an inquiry emerged via a bureaucratic side route: concerns regarding the purchasing power of gold were raised for the first time in May 1928 at the first session of the Economic Consultative Committee, a standing League committee that had been created in the wake of the 1927 World Economic Conference.[21] Because its composition reflected that of the conference, this committee was exceptionally large, comprising over fifty members, who represented national economic interest groups covering labour, business, agriculture, finance, industry, and commerce from various countries. By this means, the British agenda was well camouflaged. Six British representatives took part in the meeting, three of whom had a primary interest in bringing the gold question to the fore: Layton; Arthur Balfour, Chairman of the Committee on Trade and Industry; and Sydney Chapman, chief economic adviser to the British government and member of the Economic Committee of the League.[22] Behind the scenes, Layton was also in close contact with Henry Strakosch, the long-serving South African representative on the Financial Committee, and Otto Niemeyer, the British delegate to the Financial Committee. (They were very well known to Salter and Loveday.) Strakosch was an expert on gold production and its relationship to currency stabilization, thanks to his work as chairman of the Union Corporation, a South African gold-mining concern, and his membership of the Royal Commission on Indian Currency and Finance in 1925–6.[23]

[19] Peter Clarke, 'The Treasury's Analytical Model of the British Economy between the Wars', in Mary O. Furner and Barry Supple (eds), *The State and Economic Knowledge: The American and British Experiences* (Cambridge, 1990), 184.

[20] See Patricia Clavin and Jens-Wilhelm Wessels, 'Another Golden Idol? The League of Nations' Gold Delegation and the Great Depression, 1929–1932', *International History Review*, 26/4 (Dec. 2004), 709–944.

[21] Hill, *The Economic and Financial Organization*, 50.

[22] League of Nations, *Official Journal* (July 1928), 1126–9.

[23] Strakosch's ties to gold-mining interests meant that he had more than an academic interest in the problem. See Philip L. Cottrell, 'Norman, Strakosch and the Development of Central Banking: From

The range of support for the inquiry meant that, once Council approved it, the Financial Committee was able to get to work quickly, or as quickly as the administrative wheels in Geneva would permit. In its report to Council, the EFO linked the investigation to its long-standing engagement in the financial reconstruction in Austria and Hungary, the stability of which would be placed in jeopardy unless the question of exchange-rate fluctuations (currency movements in relation to gold) relative to price-level changes (fluctuations in the purchasing power of gold) was examined.[24] The project certainly seemed narrowly focused and technical, but, beyond these immediate parameters, the terms of the investigation were kept open. The specialist framing of the inquiry's terms by the secretariat was critical in concealing from League detractors the potentially explosive political implications of the inquiry's intention to assess 'the effect' of these fluctuations 'upon the economic life of nations'.[25] The search for these wider effects could raise contentious issues connected to US and French monetary policy and had the potential to question whether the gold standard system needed major reform.[26]

Salter recognized that the composition of the committee would be central to its effectiveness. It was essential, he argued, that the delegation bring together 'first-rank central bankers and economists', and not just members of the Financial Committee. But central bankers, including British ones, resisted the call to Geneva. Early nominees were Charles Rist, economist and deputy governor of the Bank of France, and Basil Blackett, closely affiliated to the British Treasury and the Bank of England—who were both prohibited from joining by the Governors of their respective central banks—and Alberto Pirelli, a former President of the International Chamber of Commerce and Managing Director of Pirelli and Co. in Milan.[27] Central bankers in France, Germany, and the United States attempted first to boycott, and then to limit the agenda and the composition of, the delegation.[28] But, once the Council had authorized the study, central bankers could obstruct, not stop, the undertaking, although doubts over the group's membership and the agenda meant that early momentum behind the initiative was soon lost.

Conception to Practice, 1919–1924', in Philip L. Cottrell (ed.), *Rebuilding the Financial System in Central and Eastern Europe, 1918–1994* (Aldershot, 1997), 30.

[24] 'Meeting of 31st Session', League of Nations, *Official Journal* (July 1928), 1032.

[25] Salter to Rist, 19 Dec. 1928, and Salter to Moreau, 19 Dec. 1928, LON R2963, 10E/5196/5196.

[26] Eichengreen is wrong to claim that the Gold Delegation 'diverted attention' away from more immediate threats to the system. Rather, this apparent preoccupation was a cover to address more fundamental problems—as proceedings were to demonstrate. See Eichengreen, *Golden Fetters*, 198–200. Sayers, also, failed to see the broader ambitions of the inquiry, characterizing the League's intention as to 'get the facts and report them accurately and fairly and let the banks of issue themselves deal with the question'. R. S. Sayers, *The Bank of England, 1891–1944* (3 vols; Cambridge, 1976), i. 349.

[27] Salter to Strakosch, 15 Jan. 1929, and Rist to Salter, 28 Dec. 1928, LON R2963, 10E/5196/5196; Sayers, *The Bank of England 1891–1944*, i. 349.

[28] Summary of a letter by Siepman, 20 Nov. 1928, BoE OV 48/2; Norman to Schacht, 13 Dec. 1928, BoE G 1/29; Schacht to Norman, 21 Dec. 1928, and Moreau to Norman, 28 Dec. 1928, BoE G 1/29. See also Moreau to Harrison, 24 Nov. 1928, and Harrison to Moreau, 19 Dec. 1928, FRBNY C798/1st File/League of Nations/Jan. 1927–Dec. 1929.

It took the League more than a year to form the Gold Delegation.[29] In February 1929, desperate to make progress and to take advantage of a new head at the Federal Reserve, Salter visited Strong's successor, George Harrison, in New York to see if the deadlock could be broken. Harrison made it clear to Salter that he would tolerate the inquiry only if certain conditions were met: only 'the most responsible people' should serve; proceedings should be slow; there should be no publicity; and there should be neither reports nor interim reports 'as to substance'. And even then Harrison refused to supply a delegate representing the board of the Federal Reserve. Choosing his words carefully, Salter did not agree but promised to 'make the study as unobjectionable as possible to the banks of issue'.[30]

The tortuous pace to establish the Gold Delegation and its eventual composition revealed the politically sensitive nature of the topic, and the ability of vested interests to stymie the EFO. It was significant that only smaller financial powers permitted members of their central bankers to join the delegation. These included Albert Janssen, Director of the national bank of Belgium and a former Minister of Finance, who was appointed chairman of the delegation; Leonardus J. A. Trip, Governor of the Dutch central bank and former Treasurer-General of the Netherlands; Feliks Mlynarski, Professor of Banking at the Academy of Commerce in Warsaw and Vice-Governor of the Bank of Poland; and Vilem Pospisil, Governor of the National Bank of Czechoslovakia. These men had an established association with the Financial Committee and continued to work closely with the EFO for most of the 1930s. The real intellectual weight behind the committee came from its 'expert' representation, most notably Cassel, but, while his views were held in high regard by the Economic and Financial Section and the British Treasury, American central bankers regarded him as a dangerous heretic who grossly overestimated the potential of monetary policy to shape economic, and indirectly political, outcomes.[31] And it was difficult for anyone who needed the support of American finance to gainsay these views.

Cassel's Swedish passport was a poor fig leaf to cover the fact that he essentially fell into the same camp as the British members of the Gold Delegation, which comprised Strakosch, the driving force behind the inquiry, and Reginald Mant, a member of the Council of India who had served alongside Strakosch on the Royal Commission on Indian Currency and Finance. American, French, Italian, and German representation on the delegation was by far the most politically and intellectually conservative, represented by Oliver M. W. Sprague, Professor of Banking and Finance at Harvard University, André de Chalendar, member of the Financial Committee and former Financial Attaché to the French Embassy in

[29] The Gold Delegation was finally appointed on 17 June 1929. It was particularly difficult to find Italian and French representatives. See League of Nations, *Official Journal* (July 1929), 1180.

[30] Memo by Harrison, 26 Feb. 1929, and conversation with Avenol, 26 Apr. 1929, FRBNY C798/ 1st File/League of Nations/Jan. 1927–Dec. 1929.

[31] Gustav Cassel, *Post-War Monetary Stabilization* (New York, 1928), and 'Note of Conversation between Arthur Salter and Benjamin Strong', 25 May 1928, BoE EID 4/102.

London, and Alberto Beneduce, President of the Credit Institute for Public Works in Rome. German representation came by way of Moritz Bonn.[32]

Behind closed doors it is clear the EFO's secretariat was far from impartial. It was firmly behind the position espoused by Cassel and Strakosch. As Walré de Bordes, a Dutch member of the secretariat and League secretary to the Gold Delegation, put it, 'it is not our role to convert all Committee members *before the meetings* to our opinion' (emphasis added). The issue was how best to proceed in persuading the 'orthodox' members of the delegation, and their respective nations, to come around to the Economic and Financial Section's view during the course of the Gold Delegation's work.[33] The delegation's first four-day-long meeting was in August 1929. Progress was slow.

MONEY DOCTORING

At the first meeting, Salter acknowledged the political sensitivity of the task that lay ahead. With fresh warnings from Harrison that the delegation had the potential to 'endanger future American co-operation with European central banks' still ringing in his ears, Salter urged delegation members to keep their respective central bank governors fully informed of the proceedings, and to exercise care when formulating anything that might be regarded as a proposal for a change in policy.[34] Strakosch and Cassel, with characteristic energy and impatience, on the other hand, urged the group to move quickly. In a warning that was to prove prescient, Strakosch counselled that an 'all-round contraction of credit, with all-round tendency for falling prices', was just a matter of time. In fact, it began within a matter of weeks. He also openly questioned the central banks' willingness to cooperate effectively to make the monetary system work. Cassel, too, foresaw 'grave economic danger' ahead.[35] They argued it was imperative the delegation warn the world of the problems with the Gold Standard by publishing a report to this effect as soon as possible.[36]

This was strong stuff. But theirs was a minority view, soon to be labelled as such by the rest of the committee, and at this stage a clear split in the delegation was avoided thanks only to the orthodox majority's numerical superiority. The

[32] League of Nations, *Official Journal* (Nov. 1929), 1708. League of Nations, *Interim Report of the Gold Delegation of the Financial Committee* (Geneva, 1930), 7.

[33] 'Note by the Secretariat on Purchasing Power of Gold—Summary', 28 Nov. 1928, LON R2958, 10E/8626/4346; de Bordes to Loveday, 29 Jan. 1930, LON R2963, 10E/12747/5196. In Nov. 1928, the secretariat circulated summaries of opinions on the gold question, drawing primarily on the work of Cassel, Irving Fisher, R. H. Hawtrey, and John Maynard Keynes. For the French perspective, see Arthur Turner, 'Anglo-French Financial Relations in the 1920s', *European History Quarterly*, 26 (1996), 31–55.

[34] Memo by Harrison, 26 Apr. 1929, FRBNY C798/1st File/League of Nations/Jan.1927–Dec. 1929.

[35] First Session, 'Minutes of the Third Meeting held at Geneva', 27 Aug. 1929, p. 26, LON R2964, 10E/14089/5196.

[36] First Session, 'Minutes of the Sixth Meeting held at Geneva', 29 Aug. 1929, p. 16, LON R2964, 10E/14089/5196.

procedural niceties of committee work in Geneva also provided cover. The orthodox members of the group corralled radical views into a lengthy and carefully
itemized plan of work intended to keep the delegation, and therefore Cassel and
Strakosch's argument with them, on the boil behind closed doors.[37] The Financial
Committee's subsequent report to the League Council noted only briefly that the
delegation had met, and sought to dampen down rumours of disunity within the
delegation. The minority group, however, was not to be quietened easily, and its
fervour was aided and abetted by the secretariat. Salter did his best to give
prominence to the work of the delegation and made sure the 'minority' views
were aired in the Second Committee, the Assembly committee dealing with
economic and financial questions, which met in September 1929—for which he
earned Strakosch's deep thanks.

By the time the Gold Delegation met again in June 1930, Cassel's and Strakosch's fears had been realized. Deflation and the scarcity of credit were biting
deeply, and would worsen after the firestorm of financial crises that hit the
following year. The collapse of the US stock market, the cessation of American
loans to Europe, and the ever-tightening deflationary pressures on countries whose
currencies were overvalued on gold meant the international climate became increasingly tense. In the second meeting, while matters of greater substance were
addressed when compared to the first meeting, negotiations were querulous and
slow because the stakes grew ever higher. The disagreements also became public
knowledge. Although Salter promised Harrison no reports would be published
until the end, in the summer of 1930 the delegation produced an *Interim Report* for
public distribution. Salter claimed he thought Harrison would not be too upset
because the primary focus of the report was 'technical', but in fact his only
concession was to sidestep any reference to the issue of the uneven distribution of
central bank gold reserves and exchange-rate policies.[38]

Although outnumbered in the delegation, Strakosch, Cassel, and Mant believed
their view might prevail in the longer term, and the secretariat was an important
source of advice and support to them. Behind the scenes, Loveday's role as principal
secretary to the delegation was pivotal. He shared their view that a shortage and
maldistribution of gold reserves had triggered damaging deflation, and that monetary policy needed to be examined anew in the face of the current climate.[39] But his

[37] Even this was not enough to forestall the Italian need to grandstand on behalf of gold orthodoxy
and to condemn the League for overstepping the boundaries of its authority. Beneduce resigned in
opposition to the delegation's agenda and was replaced by Guido Jung, President of the Instituto
Nazionale per l'Esportazione, who only ever attended one meeting of the Delegation. League of
Nations, *Official Journal* (Nov. 1929), 1708; Strakosch to Salter, 26 Sept. 1929, LON R2964, 10E/
14694/5196.
[38] Strakosch to Norman, 15 June 1930, BoE OV 48/3; League of Nations, *Interim Report* (1930).
[39] Loveday to Keynes, 25 July 1930, LON R2961, 10E/20721/4346. In Dec. 1928, Loveday
undertook a preliminary study for the Financial Committee regarding the supply and demand for gold
and agreed with Cassel that a 'fair degree of correspondence between variations in the stock of
monetary gold and variations in prices' existed. See Loveday, 'Factors Influencing the Supply and
Demand for Gold—An Approach to the Problem', 21 Dec. 1928, p. 19, LON R2957, 10E/8626/
4346.

powers to help Strakosch and his allies were limited. Loveday encouraged them to advance their opinions carefully, an approach endorsed by the British Treasury and banking circles. London helped the League put together an academically credible study, replete with extensive statistical appendices regarding the shortage of gold, which would demonstrate clearly that a serious liquidity crisis was imminent, if not already under way. This was intended to provide a springboard from which a wider community could criticize French and American gold sterilization policy, the imbalances in the international payments system, and the rapidly declining availability of credit thanks to successive interest-rate increases.[40] Indeed, by highlighting the links between these phenomena, the group around Strakosch had recognized the deflationary bias of the gold standard system and identified the means by which the Great Depression was to spread through the world economy.

Loveday and his staff in the Financial Section and the EIS collected an imposing amount of data on the price, supply, and movements of gold, analysed in the annex to the *Interim Report*.[41] In this, Loveday appeared to follow League 'non-politicized' diplomacy, but these materials were far from impartial; nor were their findings free from political implications. The reports on gold production compiled by experts in South Africa, Britain, the USA, Australia, India, and Japan were infused with the 'British' view of the problem. So, too, were supporting memoranda by Joseph Kitchin, Loveday, and Cassel, who, again in anticipation of present-day scholarship on the topic, argued that, while there had been short-term annual price level variations, the long-term price level had been stable in the nineteenth century because the annual increase of the stock of gold was sufficient to keep up with the increase in production and trade.[42] Cassel was particularly explicit in his condemnation of the existing monetary order, and questioned the benefits of the entire system.[43] It was a radical and prescient statement, which effectively predicted the unravelling of the gold standard that followed a year later.

The content of the *Interim Report* marked an important victory for Strakosch, Cassel, Mant, and League officials. Not only had they publicly expressed their views regarding the deflationary dangers inherent in the reconstructed gold standard; they had also, albeit circuitously, condemned the accumulation and sterilization of gold in the USA, France, and a number of other countries after 1928. They even

---

[40] The Delegation's preoccupation with the gold shortage theory has often been misunderstood. While the minority group certainly believed that a shortfall in the supply of gold had serious implications for the gold standard, it wanted more than a reduction of the central banks' note cover ratios, as suggested by Eichengreen and Balderston. See Eichengreen, *Golden Fetters*, 198–203; Theo Balderston, 'Introduction: The "Deflationary Bias" of the Interwar Gold Standard', in Theo Balderston (ed.), *The World Economy and National Economies in the Interwar Slump* (New York, 2003), 15 and n. 27.

[41] De Bordes to Trip, 17 May 1930, LON R2963, 10E/12747/5296. Loveday provided the theoretical framework for the statistical material. See, e.g., his 'Improvement of the Statistics of the Consumption of Gold', Sept. 1930, LON R2959, 10E/19973/4346.

[42] Micheal D. Bordo, 'The Classical Gold Standard: Some Lessons for Today', in Michael D. Bordo, *The Gold Standard and Related Regimes: Collected Essays* (Cambridge, 1999), 149–78.

[43] Gustav Cassel, 'II. Supply and Demand. Annex X. The Supply of Gold', in League of Nations, *Interim Report* (1930), 76.

managed to include the suggestion that central banks should drop the minimum legal reserves for gold cover, a proposal that, among other things, challenged the high reserve ratio for the Reichsmark set in the recently agreed Young Plan that proved a decisive consideration in Chancellor Brüning's catastrophic austerity budget of 1931.[44]

The secretariat now held its breath in anticipation of the international response. In London, it was broadly positive. At the Bank of England, Niemeyer hailed it as 'exceedingly useful' and expressed surprise that Strakosch had been able to convince the other delegation members 'to swallow so much of the true doctrine'.[45] The next step, it was agreed, was to ensure the League published the report quickly and circulated it widely, especially in the USA and France. In the meantime, however, key Americans, notably Jeremiah Smith at the Federal Reserve, began to argue that publication of the report should be delayed or even prevented. He warned that the *Interim Report* would intensify pressure on gold standard members who were already experiencing difficulties, and threatened that the USA was less likely to come to their aid because domestic opposition to American cooperation with Europe and the League would increase if the report caught the public eye.[46]

The timing of Smith's intervention came at an inopportune moment for the Bank of England and was crucial in determining Norman's response. Since August 1928, sterling had been struggling to cope with gold inflow into the USA, and, while sterling's reserve position had shown some improvement relative to the dollar by the spring of 1930, it continued to lose gold to France.[47] It was clear that future American cooperation was likely to be vital to sustain sterling on the gold standard.[48] Smith's views, coupled with news that Harrison's opposition to the delegation was more entrenched than ever, prompted Norman to support Harrison's calls to transfer some of the delegation's work to the less public forum of the newly established Bank for International Settlements (BIS). Although Norman was in close communication with Strakosch behind the scenes, the furore prompted the governor to tell his fellow central bankers that he had always been opposed to the delegation but had 'entirely failed to prevent or impede its activities'.[49]

There was nothing the central bankers could do to halt the *Interim Report*'s publication on 8 September 1930. It was a landmark: the first time an

[44] Knut Borchardt, 'Could and Should Germany Have Followed Great Britain in Leaving the Gold Standard?', in: *Journal of European Economic History*, 13/3 (Winter 1984), 490–3; Harold James, *The German Slump: Politics and Economics, 1924–1936* (Oxford, 2006; new edn, 2007), 285–319.
[45] Strakosch in a letter to the Bank of England, 15 June 1930, BoE OV 48/3; Niemeyer to Strakosch, 29 July 1930, BoE OV 9/264.
[46] Norman to Harrison, 29 Aug. 1930, BoE G 1/30. Strakosch to Niemeyer, 1 Sept. 1930, BoE OV 9/264. Harrison to Moreau, 19 Dec. 1928, FRBNY C798/1st File/League of Nations/Jan.1927–Dec. 1929. For the French reaction to the *Interim Report*, see Mouré, *The Gold Standard Illusion*, 191–3.
[47] Sayers, *The Bank of England 1891–1944*, i. 231–3.
[48] Harrison to Norman in cablegram, 4–5 Sept. 1930, BoE G 1/30.
[49] Norman to Harrison and Young, 6 Sept. 1930, BoE G 1/30. It was an open secret that Norman's influence on the Financial Committee, especially on its British members, was substantial. The French even claimed the committee was the Governor's personal agent. Lester V. Chandler, *Benjamin Strong, Central Banker* (Washington, 1958), 263.

intergovernmental organization had addressed pressing and fundamental questions of financial policy, and demanded an urgent response by the responsible monetary authorities. Copies of the report were issued to all member and non-member states.[50] But the League's devilish attempt to challenge the status quo of the gold standard was undone by the details. Most states and central banks claimed they were at a loss as to what do with the report, because it contained a huge and varied volume of statistical material, but no clear policy directions.[51] Nor could it—the League's hands were tied by its commitment to present an 'impartial', 'scientific', and collective view, and there was awareness of the risks to the League's prospects if it did not. Of greater use was the collection of memoranda, compiled and copy-edited by the secretariat but carrying the imprimatur of individual national experts, that accompanied the report.[52] The second of two such supporting memoranda by Strakosch, in particular, offered a trenchant critique of the 'excessive accumulation of gold' by the USA and France, and held the failure of central bank cooperation directly accountable for the deflation that had gripped Britain since 1929.[53]

Strakosch's view was challenged by Oliver M. W. Sprague, Professor of Banking and Finance at Harvard and the US delegate, in two memoranda in the *Interim Report* collection that restated the orthodox interpretation of the crisis: the balance of payments disequilibria were explained by external shocks to the system, notably war debts, reparations, and protectionism. But, in the context of the deflationary crisis that was beginning to grip the world, his staunch defence of American gold sterilization driven by the 'need to avoid inflation' struck many in Britain as bizarre.[54] Similar efforts to rebut what was widely called the 'British view' were also made in French memoranda submitted to the Gold Delegation. Taken together, however, the American and French perspectives were woolly and, at times, incoherent.[55] In intellectual terms, the 'British view' dominated both the report proper and the supporting memoranda and materials. Instead of engaging with the arguments, the Federal Reserve and the Bank of France complained about the League's decision to publish statements that included open criticisms of Franco-American monetary policy by internationally recognized experts, most notably Cassel.

[50] League of Nations, *Official Journal* (Nov. 1930), 1553. Smith resigned from the Financial Committee in protest.

[51] e.g. League of Nations, *Legislation on Gold* (Geneva, 1930).

[52] League of Nations, *Selected Documents Submitted to the Gold Delegation of the Financial Committee* (Geneva, 1930).

[53] Henry Strakosch, 'The Economic Consequences of Changes in the Value of Gold', in League of Nations, *Selected Documents Submitted to the Gold Delegation*, 28.

[54] Oliver M. W. Sprague, 'The Working of the Gold Standard under Present Conditions', in League of Nations, *Selected Documents Submitted to the Gold Delegation*, 53–6. This paper had first been published under the title 'Price Stabilization', *American Economic Review*, 19/1 (Mar. 1929), 61–8.

[55] For the French view, see Jacques Rueff, in League of Nations, *Selected Documents Submitted to the Gold Delegation*, 42–52.

But there were also those in Britain who railed against the way the delegation had given birth to a view that was being categorized as 'British'. By covertly supporting the League's gold inquiry, Norman had hoped to internationalize problems with the system's operation in order to improve it. But, from Norman's perspective, it was now unhelpful to have an international discussion that identified the cause of wholesale reform (if not dissolution) of the gold standard system with a 'British view', because it alienated the United States, the financial powerhouse on whom Britain would depend for aid when sterling was faced with speculative pressure the Bank of England alone could not contain. Moreau's and Harrison's vehement rejection of the *Interim Report* brought an end to Norman's double-dealing—there were no more supportive discussions with Strakosch and Niemeyer on how to advance the inquiry in Geneva, while declaring his opposition to the Gold Delega-tion's work to his fellow central bankers. Britain's weak financial condition by the late summer of 1930 meant Norman had no choice but to distance himself from Strakosch.[56] Indeed, it was clear the delegation was so divided that the search for consensus was futile, and the public exposure of their disagreement held greater risks for sterling than any other currency, because the formulation of a 'British view' brought into question its very commitment to the system in the eyes of the world.

The next meeting of the delegation in November 1930 confirmed Norman's assessment. The French government and the Banque de France set their face against the delegation altogether, arguing that the League should suppress the publication of the final report, the draft of which was now in circulation, as it would become highly destabilizing if the world became aware of the extent of divisions among members of the gold standard. But the best the orthodox group could secure was a lengthy postponement. Assured of a platform at the League, Strakosch did not give up easily. Now that their support from the Bank of England had fallen away, he and Cassel renewed their contacts to the British Treasury. Strakosch and the EFO knew the Treasury was interested in exploring the issue of gold outflows from Britain with France, and was keen to explore anew reparations that it believed were destabilizing the German economy and international credit. So, while the Treasury did not want to postpone the work of the delegation any further, and favoured the publication of a compromise final report (its ideas about what it should comprise were vague), it needed to keep France on side. Unlike the USA, France was also a full and important member of the League and was therefore especially sensitive to being condemned by the agency which it supported.[57] Even before the Gold Delegation reconvened in January 1931, public speculation was mounting with regard to the League's role in fuelling tensions in Anglo-French relations.[58] On 9 January 1931, *The New York Times* reported: 'Paris Gold Session at New Deadlock—British and French Disagree on Publication of Report by League

[56] Norman now supported Harrison's call that the BIS take over the inquiry. See Norman to Gates W. McGarrah, 16 Sept. 1930, BoE G 1/30.

[57] Leith-Ross to Strakosch, 11 Dec. 1930, TNA: PRO T188/15B; Kenneth Mouré, *Managing the Franc Poincaré: Economic Understanding and Political Constraint in French Monetary Policy, 1928–1936* (Cambridge, 1991), 51–65.

[58] *New York Times*, 9 Jan. 1931, p. 8.

Experts—Observers Much Worried'. Harrison was not worried, he was cross, commenting sourly that the delegation was 'a most unusual and haphazard set-up . . . considered largely in a political atmosphere'.[59]

The January sessions were very different in content and outcome from earlier meetings of the delegation. The depression had intensified and the question of gold reserve distribution and falling prices was more contentious than ever. There was now the obvious risk that the deflationary crisis, and therefore the economic crisis as a whole, might be blamed on the actions taken by the League and Great Britain, or on the Bank of France and the Federal Reserve System. All this produced a noticeable change in direction on the part of Loveday, whose preparatory documents for the meeting stressed the need for a unanimous final report.[60] With the British Treasury, too, endorsing this new move for conciliation, it was now Strakosch who found himself increasingly isolated, condemning the new drive for unanimity as pathetic 'pander[ing] to the French and their satellites, when the primary concern of the Gold Delegation's work should be the promotion of the right policy'.[61]

The *Second Interim Report*, published on 20 January 1931, far surpassed the standards set by the first *Interim Report* for obfuscation. It appeared to signal a determination within the delegation, and therefore the League, not to engage with the current financial and economic problems.[62] On closer reading, however, a much more orthodox statement regarding monetary policy emerged than that of the first report. Notably, the focus was on the role of non-monetary, economic, and political factors—budget deficits, protectionism, and wage rigidities.[63] Unlike the first *Interim Report*, the *Second Interim Report* accorded monetary policy, and therefore also the work of central banks, a minor role in its presentation of the workings of the international economy, with the message that the reconstructed gold standard was the right monetary tool, but one that could not function in current conditions.

Once again, the report was accompanied by a large array of supplementary materials. In contrast to the first *Interim Report*, this time only memoranda that set out the 'majority', orthodox view, or those that simply described gold reserve policies of central banks or states, were published.[64] A host of high-quality papers were sidelined, including contributions by the Austrian economist Gottfried Haberler, Strakosch, and Cassel, in favour of French and American memoranda

---

[59] Smith to Harrison, 10 Jan. 1931, and Harrison to Smith, 17 Jan. 1931, FRBNY C798/League of Nations/Jan. 1930–July 1943.

[60] De Bordes to Strakosch and Mlynarski, 18 Dec. 1930, LON R2966, 10E/23990/5196. Loveday's memos served as the basis for the *Second Interim Report*.

[61] Strakosch to Leith-Ross, 31 Dec. 1930, TNA: PRO T188/15B.

[62] League of Nations, *Second Interim Report of the Gold Delegation of the Financial Committee* (Geneva, 1931), 7.

[63] League of Nations, *Second Interim Report*, 8.

[64] Other materials were circulated and discussed. Loveday also wanted, but failed, to incorporate Keynes, who was finishing his two-volume *Treatise on Money*, which came out in autumn 1930. See Loveday to Keynes, 1 July 1930, Keynes to Loveday, 17 July 1930, and Loveday to Keynes, 25 July 1930, LON R2961, 10E/23523/4346.

that sought to defend their central banks' policies publicly.[65] It was telling indeed that the only British contribution to the collection was from the obscure Theodore Gregory, who argued that Britain's monetary difficulties could be explained by high domestic price levels—a view that was out of step with arguments made not only by British representatives within the delegation but by the British Treasury itself.[66] The secretariat had pulled back from the brink of identifying itself publicly with views articulated by its favoured expert advisers in the *Second Interim Report* in preference for a picture of international unity, however inchoate, intended to inspire confidence in the financial status quo and in the League project as a whole.[67] The furore over the first *Interim Report*, notably the French and American criticism of the League, and the divisions between its chief paymasters, Britain and France, meant the secretariat was unwilling to challenge key members and non-members to safeguard its institutional future and the reputation of its 'non-political' technical work. It was especially vulnerable to political pressures from both without and within the institution, because Salter's term in office had ended in 1930, and there was considerable disagreement between the Secretary-General's office, and between Britain and France, as to who should succeed him. With Stoppani made head of the Economic Section and Loveday put in charge of the Financial Section and the EIS, Salter's departure marked a turning point in the secretariat's strategy. Loveday and Stoppani thought it safer to retreat and regroup.

Through the delegation, the EFO had staked its claim for a role in facilitating and shaping international monetary policy but decided it was better to fight another day than to imperil its future prospects for intervention. (With the creation of the Bank for International Settlements in 1930, which subsequently claimed the crown as the world's oldest financial institution, it now also had a potential rival.) Developments beyond Geneva suggested, however, it was time for bold action, not institutional consolidation. The secretariat's attempt to regroup was dealt a series of serious blows by the banking crisis that first gripped Austria with the collapse of the Creditanstalt in May 1931, then moved across to Hungary, Bulgaria, Yugoslavia, Czechoslovakia, and Germany in the same month. By the latter half of 1931, all these countries had resorted to exchange controls designed to limit the outflow of gold and foreign currency. The international operation of the gold standard was profoundly compromised, and so increasingly was the liberal capitalist ideology in which it was embedded. Currency controls significantly extended state power to intervene in the domestic economy, and the financial crisis helped to bring to power political parties that sought to exploit these new monetary borders to reinforce their national and racial frontiers.

More immediately, the gold-induced credit crunch again prompted the postponement of the delegation's work. In February 1931, it had been agreed that the

---

[65] See minutes of Third Session, Nov. 1930, LON R2966/7, 10E/24231/5196.

[66] Gregory taught at the LSE and was a member of the Macmillan Committee on Industry and Finance (1929–31). See Theodore Gregory, 'The Causes of Gold Movements into and out of Great Britain, 1925 to 1929', in League of Nations, *Selected Documents on the Distribution of Gold*, 21–37.

[67] Ian A. Drummond, *The Floating Pound and the Sterling Area, 1931–1939* (Cambridge, 1981), 133.

delegation should meet in June and August to complete a final report for submission to the September session of the League Assembly.[68] These plans were subsumed, rather than energized, by the banking crisis. Meetings of the delegation were postponed until January 1932, because governments gave priority to the domestic financial emergencies, and, by the time it met again, the international context had changed dramatically. Britain, followed by more than twenty other countries, left the gold standard in September 1931, as the liquidity crisis that Strakosch and Cassel had predicted came to pass. Paradoxically, the development weakened the EFO's position. The British Treasury completely withdrew its support for the minority group on the Gold Delegation, since it was no longer interested in internationally coordinated monetary policies after the devaluation of sterling. The development had a dramatic impact of the Anglo-EFO axis that had been central to the organization since its foundation in 1920. At the same time, the sterling crisis prompted France and the USA to reaffirm their commitment to orthodoxy.[69]

ORTHODOXY ABANDONED

When Salter next returned to Geneva in an official capacity in September 1931, it was as Chairman of the British delegation to the Assembly, where his first duty was to announce Britain's departure from the gold standard. His colours as a gold standard sceptic were now firmly nailed to the mast, and a furious row followed between the British and French delegates, each launching into a spirited defence of his nation's monetary and economic policies. Arguments that had previously taken place behind the closed committee doors of the delegation now erupted on the floor of the Assembly hall before the world's press. While Salter connected war debts and reparations to the deflation and blamed the uneven distribution of gold reserves for the depression, Pierre-Étienne Flandin, French Finance Minister and Chairman of the French delegation, repudiated these accusations. He pointed the finger firmly at Britain, announcing that the gold standard had been undermined by its imprudent and unorthodox economic policies. While Salter endorsed inflationary measures as a remedy to counter the depression, Flandin believed in the automatism of the free market to settle price levels. And, while Salter called for an Assembly resolution to press for new political and financial 'leads' to support the EFO's efforts to find a way out of the economic crisis and urged the Gold Delegation to 'hasten its final report with the practical conclusions at which it arrived', France demurred.[70] The resolution that resulted from Salter's intervention was, as the American Consul in Geneva, Prentiss Gilbert, pointed out, just another 'vacuous

[68] De Bordes to Cassel, 3 Feb. 1931, and Roberts to de Bordes, 6 Feb. 1931, LON R2966, 10E/24130/5196.

[69] Mouré, *Managing the Franc Poincaré*, 80.

[70] Gilbert report to the Secretary of State, 'The Twelfth (1931) Assembly of the League of Nations—General Financial Discussion and Report', Geneva, 29 Dec. 1931, p. 14, NARA Records of the US State Department Record Group 59 (hereafter RG59), Box 2478, 500.C111/528.

call' for governments' promotion of international understanding and revival of international investments.[71]

The Gold Delegation almost collapsed completely in the wake of the financial 'catastrophe' of 1931. Strakosch, Mant, and Cassel called for further meetings and the publication of the final report as a matter of urgency, but the silence that greeted their calls was deafening. In frustration, the delegation's Acting Chairman, Trip, threatened to resign.[72] It was only the energy and diplomacy of Loveday and his associates in the Financial Section that kept the project afloat. There was no doubt that Loveday's anxiety was fuelled, in part, by the institutional implications of his predecessor having so firmly come out in favour of devaluation. The secretariat needed to rebuild its reputation for impartiality, and, with disaster now hanging over the League's mismanagement of the Japanese incursion into Manchuria, it seemed as if the standing of the organization as a whole was at stake. In the ensuing three months, Loveday worked continuously to ensure all members of the delegation were not only contacted but responded to League communications during the hiatus, and he prepared a draft final report for the rescheduled session of January 1932.[73]

The sixth and penultimate meeting of the Gold Delegation convened in Geneva in the second week of January 1932. But consensus was further away than ever. Instead, as Norman Davis, the American member of the Financial Committee, predicted, members of delegation 'were all lined up for a real fight', and a real fight is what they had. While four members of the original delegation opted to boycott proceedings, the remainder split openly into two opposing groups, in fundamental disagreement as to the causes of the crisis and the necessity of publishing a final report.[74] The final showdown came on 8 and 9 January, when the British-dominated group argued that 'recent events' demonstrated that the instability of the gold standard was 'even more far reaching and full of dangers than was generally understood' and demanded the immediate publication of a final report, which, as it happened, they had already prepared in draft form.[75] In what was to become known as the 'Minority Report', Strakosch outlined the minority group's main arguments: the breakdown of the gold standard had been caused by 'the combined result of the obligation to pay reparations and war debts, on the one side, and the unwillingness of the receiving countries to receive payment in the form of goods and services'. (This was an implicit criticism of American foreign economic

[71] Gilbert report to the Secretary of State, 'The Twelfth (1931) Assembly of the League of Nations'. 15–16.

[72] Trip to Loveday, 20 Nov. 1931, Chalendar to Loveday, 28 Nov. 1931, and Bonn to Loveday, 25 Nov. 1931, LON R2968, 10E/32836/5196.

[73] Loveday to Trip, 29 Oct. 1931, and Loveday to Cassel and Chalendar, 30 Nov. 1931, LON R2968, 10E/32836/5196. The Americans tried to convince Loveday that publication of the draft final report could 'intensify the unsettlement in monetary affairs'. See George E. Roberts to Loveday, 28 Dec. 1931, FRBNY C798/League of Nations/Jan. 1930–July 1943.

[74] See 'Minutes of the Sixth Session', 8 Jan. 1932, LON Comité Financier, Délégation de l'Or, F./Gold/5ème Ses./P.V./1–9/1931.

[75] Cassel to Loveday, 1 Dec. 1931, and Loveday to Cassel, 7 Dec. 1931, LON R2968, 10E/32836/5196. The group primarily comprised Cassel, Strakosch, and Mant.

policy.)[76] The dynamic had caused a massive accumulation of gold reserves in the USA and France, which, thanks to the sterilization of gold by the Federal Reserve and the Bank of France, caused the decline of general price levels, the key symptom of the crisis. Their recommendation was radical: currencies on gold should be devalued and governments should immediately undertake inflationary measures to raise prices. Economic historians would now judge that these money doctors were recommending the best policy choices to cure the crisis: devaluation and credit expansion.[77] (The implication of their argument was that the devaluation should be internationally coordinated by the EFO, although this was never spelled out.)

Other members of the Gold Delegation rejected the minority view entirely. They argued that the newly dubbed 'minority' group (formerly known as the 'British view') strayed far beyond its interpretation of the remit of the delegation's work, and were appalled by the suggestion of using 'inflationary measures' to counter the crisis. Publication was not imperative; rather it should now be avoided at all costs, for it was the least opportune moment to publish. At this, Strakosch lost his temper and threatened to resign, but this did not mean he would go quietly.[78] On the contrary: the minority, determined to generate a constituency in support of its call for policy change, declared its intention to pass a report outlining its views to the Financial Committee for publication. The move was strongly resisted by the 'majority group' and Trip, who was desperate to avoid official cognisance of the profound division of the delegation and to hide the open rift from the general public. More resignations were threatened, and Loveday's attempts to mediate between the two sides proved fruitless.

In a last-ditch attempt to prevent the minority group from publishing its work independently, it was decided that both sides would produce separate reports, which would be released at the same time.[79] Loveday and his section now abandoned the notion it had briefly harboured to facilitate a strategy of coordinated depreciation in response to the crisis. Its approach was resolutely one of safety first. It is also important not to lose sight of the fact that, although the majority group's money doctors had misdiagnosed what was ailing the world's economy, its work together formed an incipient gold bloc, and promoted a sense of west European solidarity in the face of the vagaries of Anglo-American monetary infidelity (of different kinds) to monetary orthodoxy, which was to become a familiar refrain in European relations in the twentieth century.

But, despite League efforts to moderate its message, and the spectacle of solidarity among the majority, Strakosch did 'not go gentle into that good night'. He urged the British Secretary of State for Foreign Affairs, John Simon, to condemn the majority's role in Council for the unpardonable delay in producing

[76] 'Minutes of the Sixth Session', 8 Jan. 1932, LON Comité Financier, Délégation de l'Or, F./Gold/5ème Ses./P.V./1–9/1931.
[77] See Barry Eichengreen and Peter Temin, '"Afterword": Counterfactual Histories of the Great Depression', in Balderston (ed.), *The World Economy and National Economies*, 212.
[78] 'Minutes of the Sixth Session', 8 Jan. 1932, LON Comité Financier, Délégation de l'Or, F./Gold/5ème Ses./P.V./1–9/1931.
[79] Trip to the President of the Gold Delegation, 10 Jan. 1932, LON R2963, 10E/12747/5196.

a final report.[80] But the attitude of the previously supportive British government towards the minority group had begun to change. Talk of international reforms to the operation of the gold standard now fell away, as the depreciation of the pound and cheap money became the cornerstones of British domestic and imperial economic strategy. Increasingly set on a national and, through the development of the sterling bloc, an imperial path to recovery, the British government was anxious to minimize the international repercussions of their break with gold. Like the Financial Section, Britain now placed the need for consensus ahead of the need to promote the 'right' policy in an international context. Guided by the Treasury, the Foreign Office began to support the majority view for fear that the minority report would be identified as an official British position.[81]

At this point, the Gold Delegation found a focus to bring unity to the disparate positions adopted by the minority and majority groups: reparations and war debts. In their final meeting, in May 1932, without an American present to object, all members of the delegation agreed that 'political debts' were an important cause in the depression and that a delegation report should act as a support for the forthcoming Lausanne Conference on reparations, due to open on 16 June. The conference itself was the culmination of British diplomacy and Anglo-French cooperation, in the wake of the 1931 banking crises.[82] Common sense being the better part of valour, Loveday and Stoppani sought to heal divisions, dispatch the Gold Delegation, and launch these new initiatives, which included a new inquiry into the 'Course and Phases' of the depression and the call for a World Economic Conference.

Loveday and John Bell Condliffe, a New Zealand economist and member of the Economic and Financial Section, attempted to write a joint, compromise draft of the final report, which, though it dropped the radical minority proposal for 'universal devaluation', still contained elements of the minority view.[83] But, much to Loveday's and Condliffe's frustration, these elements did not survive the endless redrafting by members of the majority group.[84] By this stage the minority and majority held separate meetings in Geneva, with members of the secretariat shuttling between the two. What resulted from this unseemly end was a messy compromise that satisfied no one. The majority's main objective now was to stop the minority group from proceeding unilaterally, so it was agreed that, while neither group should be permitted to submit a separate report, every member or group of members could send notes or memoranda of dissent to the Financial Section. These

[80] Strakosch to John Simon, 19 Jan. 1932, TNA: PRO FO 371/16452.

[81] The Foreign Office rescinded its earlier call that the minority group publish a separate report. See Leith-Ross to the Under-Secretary of State, 26 Jan. 1932, TNA: PRO FO 371/16452.

[82] De Bordes to Niemeyer, 13 May 1932, BoE OV 9/264; Mlynarski to de Bordes, 19 May 1932, LON R2962, 10E/34452/4346.

[83] A summary of the draft gold report was circulated by the secretariat. See 'Summary of Paragraphs of Draft Gold Report', 2 May 1932, LON R2962, 10E/34452/4346.

[84] Condliffe to Jung, 31 Mar. 1932, LON R2962, 10E/34452/4346.

would be added to a common compromise report to be drafted by the League officials and based primarily on the majority view.[85]

In the months that followed, it was the secretariat that kept the project afloat. It believed a report was still worth pursuing because of the imminent meeting in Lausanne and the accompanying expectation that it would bring an end to the painful saga of war debts and reparations. Among other benefits, it would salve Anglo-French economic and financial cooperation, which had been badly bruised by sterling's devaluation and arguments in the gold delegation. For a month after the delegation members had left Geneva, Loveday and his colleagues circulated and recirculated the paperwork, until they had a draft report that all the members were prepared to sign.[86] The minority made extensive use of the provision for the submission of notes of dissent, effectively lodging a revised version of its January report to the secretariat. But the secretariat's drive for unanimity in the main report proved too much for Cassel, who, with characteristic independent-mindedness, refused to sign the compromise report and submitted his own separate, unequivocal statement favouring depreciation, which promptly rekindled the whole dispute.[87] Otherwise, members of the minority group were content to let their views appear collectively, because, as the secretariat had made it clear, expressed in this way, they would be on an equal plane to those of the majority.

Strakosch, unlike Cassel, was less interested in ensuring his scientific integrity than that his message reached a wider public. Once it was agreed that the minority view would be published under League auspices, albeit as one of two parts of the final *Report of the Gold Delegation*, he flagrantly disregarded protocol and passed a copy of the final report to the British press on 7 June 1932 in an attempt to determine its press coverage.[88] Both *The Times* and *The Economist*, unsurprisingly given Strakosch's connections to the editors, gave the report extensive coverage and highlighted the deep cleavage of opinion between the main body of the report and the minority view, before coming down firmly on the side of the latter.[89] When it came to publicity, the minority group trounced the majority group, and the same month saw the publication of Cassel's Rhodes Memorial Lectures, which went even further than the minority report in explicitly condemning American and French monetary policies.[90]

[85] De Bordes to Mant, Strakosch, and Janssen, 14 May 1932, LON R2962, 10E/34452/4346.
[86] De Bordes to members of the Financial Committee, 13 May 1932, LON R2962, 10E/34452/4346.
[87] No minutes were kept of the final meeting of the delegation. See Cassel to de Bordes, and de Bordes to Cassel, 25 May 1932, LON R2962, 10E/34452/4346.
[88] When advertising the report, the League described it as 'unanimous, except for a few dissenting notes on particular problems touched in the report'. See League of Nations, *Review of World Production, 1925–1931* (Geneva, 1932), 2.
[89] *The Economist*, 11 June 1932, p. 1277; 'World Money Policy—Return to Gold urged—League Report', *The Times*, 10 June 1932, p. 14.
[90] Gustav Cassel, *The Crisis in the World's Monetary System: Being the Rhodes Memorial Lectures Delivered in the Trinity Term 1932* (Oxford, 1932), 63–98. Loveday was also asked to advise on the Chatham House 1930–1 investigation into 'The International Functions of Gold', which was shaped by the League inquiry and Cassel's work. See Stephen King-Hale to Loveday, 13 Nov. 1929, LON, Loveday, P140/11/in- and outgoing correspondence, 1928–9.

There is no doubt that intellectually both the Financial and the Economic Sections sided with Strakosch, and believed in the scientific and political value in the longer term of the frank exchange of ideas, but it continued to aspire to a semblance of public unanimity before powerful national critics who had baulked at the League's intervention in monetary policy. The final report demonstrated the limits of its ability to promote policy innovation. It was a mass of conflicting opinions and overwhelming detail. The majority view in the final report set out an orthodox interpretation of the depression and the breakdown of the gold standard, which concluded that political intervention prevented the gold standard mechanism from functioning properly in the 'imperfectly restored world econ-omy'.[91] In short, it presented the answer to problems with the gold standard as less political intervention, not more, and avoided the question posed by Cassel, by Strakosch, and indirectly by the secretariat as to whether the gold standard had caused the depression. Its recommendation was curt, and phrased with one eye on the forthcoming Lausanne Conference: a final settlement of reparations and war debts as a main precondition for the restoration of the gold standard system.

Remarkably, in financial circles, the report was regarded as a success. Gates W. McGarrah, the American President of the BIS, was so enthused by its lucid and positive declaration in support of the gold standard that he planned to issue an official statement from the BIS to endorse it and asked Harrison to sanction such a move.[92] The latter flatly rejected the idea.[93] The British Treasury, by contrast, highlighted the report's 'patchwork composition'—the majority report as a reflec-tion of the views of the gold standard countries, led by France, and the minority report a different and important point of view, even if it was one it did not feel able to endorse publicly.[94]

The minority's notes of dissent in the report, too, covered ground well travelled in previous statements. Cassel, Mant, and Strakosch blamed the large accumulation of French and American gold reserves, gold sterilization, and the protectionist trade policies of these countries for the deflation.[95] Their argument was that only by abandoning the gold standard could countries end the deflation and enjoy a new monetary freedom that would help to secure economic recovery. In effect, they commended the depreciation of sterling as the model the world should follow—something the British government itself had eschewed.[96] But the minority group's break with orthodoxy was kept within limits. It still argued that, in the long run,

[91] League of Nations, *Report of the Gold Delegation*, 21.

[92] Fraser to Harrison, 27 June 1932, FRBNY C798/League of Nations/Jan. 1930–July 1943.

[93] E. M. Despres to Allan Sproul, 31 Oct. 1932, FRBNY C798/League of Nations/Jan. 1930–July 1943.

[94] Memo by Hopkins, undated, TNA: PRO T175/70; Mouré, *The Gold Standard Illusion*, 176.

[95] The original minority report was submitted in Jan. 1932. See 'Report on the Causes and Effects of the Recent Increase in the Purchasing Power of Gold', LON R2962, 10E/34031/4346.

[96] Patricia Clavin, *The Failure of Economic Diplomacy, Britain, France, Germany and the United States, 1931–1936* (London, 1996), 19–23, 45–9, 61–5.

it would be necessary to reform the gold standard and secure a rapprochement between the sterling bloc and countries still on gold.[97]

The views expressed by the minority group were an important step towards a gradual move away from an orthodox and passive approach to monetary policy towards a heightened awareness of the increasing necessity for policies promoting economic growth, but there was still some way to go.[98] Although the minority had formulated relatively radical propositions in its challenge to gold standard orthodoxy, an international system of cooperation and control, as propounded in the Bretton Woods agreements, was beyond its imagination. So, too, was a monetary system based on flexible exchange rates.[99] In the short term, there was certainly no clear line of development from the innovative aspects of the Gold Delegation's work to innovation in monetary policy, as in the United States in March 1933, for example. What it is possible to demonstrate out of the history of the delegation is that the reports were widely circulated and its data heavily consulted. The information on gold supply and prices mapped the system's global operation for the first time and was drawn on by the architects of the Bretton Woods system, and its work was the subject of bitter and repeated debate in Europe and the United States. Out of these arguments, later policies grew.

The delegation made the League the first international body to discuss the necessity for a pro-active monetary policy to raise and stabilize prices. Public criticism of the delegation's irrelevance stung the secretariat because, from its perspective, the League had been unable to make headway because of the deeply divided position of nation states. Keen to address the desperate economic problems faced by ordinary citizens, on the one hand, and states, on the other, in 1931 the EFO put its energy into two new initiatives. Neither was launched expressly by its own hand, but both sought to combat the Great Depression. The first was a 'Study of the Course and Phases of the Present Depression', more familiarly described by historians as research into business cycles. The second was to endorse, support, and provide the intellectual framework for a British-led proposal for a World Economic Conference that was to become the defining event in international economic and financial relations of the decade.

SCIENCE VERSUS POLICY

These initiatives took the League's diplomacy in two distinct directions: the first, the business cycle inquiry, was a road that brought to international prominence

---

[97] League of Nations, *Report of the Gold Delegation*, 69–73. BIS experts also came to recommend a coordinated devaluation and a return to fixed exchange rates. See Stephen A. Schuker, 'The Gold Exchange Standard: A Reinterpretation', in Marc Flandreau, Carl-Ludwig Holtfrerich, and Harold James (eds), *International Financial History in the Twentieth Century: System and Anarchy* (Washington, 2003), 92.

[98] See, e.g., Rufus S. Tucker, 'Gold and the General Price Level', *Review of Economic Statistics*, 16/1 (Jan.1934), 8–16.

[99] Nurkse, *International Currency Experience*, 14, and Ragnar Nurkse, 'International Monetary Policy and the Search for Economic Stability', *American Economic Review*, 37/2 (May 1947), 576.

new ideas and fresh, and sometimes contradictory, approaches to economic and financial relations. The second, the world economic conference, aimed to facilitate cooperation between governments and, where possible, to encourage coordination of initiatives taken on a national and regional level. The first project, and others that followed, typically became identified with an individual social scientist, although in practice the work was sustained by a wide network of scholars and the secretariat. The latter demanded intergovernmental cooperation, and was a vast undertaking absorbing the bulk of the secretariat's resources in the service of members and non-member states. Both roads carried risks and opportunities for the EFO. Its Economic and Financial Sections were much more at ease handling the special 'scientific' investigations, where they had more say, often proposing both the subject and the most appropriate expert to members of the Economic or Financial Committee—as was the case in the business cycle inquiry, as we shall see in Chapter 6. But the secretariat also intended these specialist enquiries to cross-pollinate with its state-centred work, given its intention, articulated in the 1930 Assembly resolution, not just to compare but also to coordinate governments' responses to the economic crisis. A specialist inquiry certainly ran fewer risks that the EFO would come under attack from central banks (although this group became less of a threat as the gold standard fractured) or from finance ministers from governments of the world's more powerful economies. But it could be controversial nonetheless.

That the League's economic and financial activities appeared more clearly bifurcated than before prompted the secretariat to assess once again the needs of the world's poorer powers. The League wanted to help them through the unfolding crises—the EIS expended a great deal of energy tracking their economies in 1930–2 and the secretariat made several attempts to promote agricultural credit schemes to help farmers in central and eastern Europe obtain loans at reasonable terms of interest.[100] But, with the history of League intervention in Austria and Hungary still raw in local memories, its internationalism was perceived as much as a threat as a support to national sovereignty. It prompted first Salter in 1930, and later Loveday and Stoppani in 1931, to wonder whether the role of oversight was a poisoned chalice. Perhaps it would be better for the EFO 'to give advice to members of the League without taking any responsibility in regard to the accept-ance of such advice...to remove the fear felt by some states that a request for advice might involve League interference in financial policy'.[101] In time, the question would grow only more urgent. How was the secretariat to remain intellectually independent, while sustaining the support and consent of the League's diverse membership of nation states on which its activities depended?

---

[100] See, in particular, its role in the International Agricultural Mortgage Credit Company, 'International Agricultural Mortgage Credit Company Convention', LON R2901/2910.

[101] Comment by Loveday, 'Minutes of Directors' Meeting', 12 Feb. 1930, pp. 3–4, LON R3565, 50/25831/767, Directors Meetings 1931; Comment by Salter, 'Minutes of Directors' Meeting', 8 Oct. 1930, LON R3565, 50/16937/767, Directors Meetings 1930, p. 4.

Indeed, as the economic climate deteriorated, so did the context of diplomatic relations and with it the resources on which the League could draw to sustain its work. Life in Geneva continued to be replete with dichotomies. In February 1930, at precisely the moment when work on the foundations for the new Palais des Nations designed by five separate architects (because the jury could not decide on who had won an international competition) was beginning in the grounds of a former zoo, the directors of sections were in a meeting to discuss the likely financial implications of the mounting economic crisis. Drummond and his colleagues knew states would cut back on their remittances at a time when financial pressures on the League were increasing, because of the disarmament conference and growing expectations of greater League engagement with economic and financial issues. In 1929, Drummond had been able to secure a sizeable increase in member contributions, primarily to support the disarmament conference, but he was under no illusions: 'a number of countries had accepted it most reluctantly and had made it plain that if there was an increase next year they would have to reconsider their position in the League.' Member states remained the League's lifeblood and the basis on which its legitimacy was built, and, just as nation states began to reduce spending in 1930, so it became important 'in the larger interests of the League to exercise the strictest economy'.[102]

If the need to spend more at precisely the moment resources became scarce was one tension that strained the fabric of the League, rising expectations that the League should 'do something' to tackle the economic crisis became another. By 1931 it was clear the organization could not stand idly by. The growing ranks of the world's poor were little more than ghostly figures in Geneva, but the EFO's officials could feel the icy chill of their suffering nonetheless, detailed in the statistics they collated on the ever-deteriorating performance of the world economy. The organization's efforts to coordinate a reduction in international protectionism and to tackle imbalances in the gold standard were interventions of a kind, the intention behind them being to create conditions in which the world economy could correct itself of its own accord. While Salter and his colleagues believed that, since the Wall Street crash, discussion in the Economic and Financial Committees had become 'more real', the sharp differences between states that this trend reflected were also making life more difficult. The secretariat and the experts with whom it was in close contact recognized the problem: the acute depression was 'not suitable for the advance of that liberal economic policy with which the League had hitherto been associated'. The crisis inevitably forced states onto a 'defensive attitude and a search for arrangements calculated to yield immediate benefits'.[103] This defence included radical new ideas about the value of state planning and national self-sufficiency.

There could be no doubt that the constellation of economic and political forces inside states prompted greater recourse to national and imperial self-defence

---

[102] Comment by Drummond, 'Minutes of Directors' Meeting', 12 Nov. 1930, p. 5, 1930, LON R3565, 50/16937/767.
[103] Comment by Salter, 'Minutes of Directors' Meeting', 8 Oct. 1930, p. 4, LON R3565, 50/16937/767.

during the course of 1930. The world was fragmenting in old and new ways, although it was also clear that the economic crisis created a commonality of experience across borders, visible in the human tragedy of rising numbers of individuals who were unemployed or underemployed and rendered destitute by the crisis. In September 1930, this groundswell of experience of 'the losses suffered by society' prompted the Assembly to widen the expectations of the EFO 'to undertake the study of the course and phases of the present depression and the circumstances which led up to it'.[104] The secretariat was the logical site for such an international inquiry, given its links to current research into business cycles being undertaken by 'Conjecture' or business cycle institutes across Europe. American private philanthropy was also a determining element. The Rockefeller Foundation sponsored, among others, the Austrian Institute for Trade Cycle Research in Vienna and the Dutch Economic Institute, and subsequently became paymaster of the business cycle inquiry at the League. Although very much the silent, junior partner, Rockerfeller gave the EFO more than $10 million between 1930 and 1940, with both organizations wanting to understand the operation of the international economy and, in particular, the origins of the Great Depression.[105]

But what the secretariat regarded primarily as a scientific exchange (its views on this were to change) was propelled into the political spotlight and widened to include a specific focus on unemployment by debate within the Assembly. Loveday put it down to 'Labour governments' who had pushed for action with a 'rather forlorn hope' that it would help them meet voters' expectations to safeguard employment and welfare provision while their hands were tied by the rigours of gold standard membership.[106] The focus on unemployment resonated with Loveday, because this aspect of the inquiry had deep roots in the ILO's research programme begun in 1924 'for preventing periodic crises in unemployment'.[107] It became a much broader study, covering workers' wages, living standards, and

[104] Memo by Loveday, 28 Oct. 1929, p. 10, LON R2982, 10D/2256/2256.
[105] The Rockefeller Foundation sponsored forty-six different institutions, including the Statistical Institute of Economic Research in Sofia, the Economic Institute of the Polish Academy of Sciences, the Romanian Institute of Social Science in Bucharest, the Institute of Economics and History in Copenhagen, the London and Cambridge Economic Service, the Oxford Institute of Statistics, l'Institut Scientifique de Recherches Économiques et Sociales run by Charles Rist, and a number of research programmes at the LSE. It, of course, was also a vital connection between social science research in the USA, notably at Harvard and Chicago and Europe. Between 1929 and 1939, the Dutch, Austrian, and Danish institutes received an average of £4,692 per year; the central and east European grants ranged between $1,000 and $7,000 per annum, but with a much lower average of £2,515 per annum. See Katharina Rietzler, 'American Foundations and the "Scientific Study" of International Relations in Europe, 1910–1940', unpublished Ph.D. thesis, University College, London, 2009, 276. For an assessment of its role in social scientific work in the League of Nations, see Ludovic Tournes, 'La Philanthrope americaine et l'Europe: Contribution à une histoire transnationale de L'Americanisation', Université Paris-I Panthéon-Sorbonne, unpublished habilitation, 2008, ii. 292–360.
[106] Loveday to Jacobsson, 1 Oct. 1930, LON, Loveday, P142a,/outgoing correspondence, 1930.
[107] Endres and Fleming, *International Organisations*, 17–30; Olivier Feiertag, 'Albert Thomas, les débuts du BIT et la crise économique mondiale de 1920–1923', in A. Aglan, O. Feiertag, and D. Kevonian (eds), 'Albert Thomas, société mondiale et internationalisme, réseaux et institutions des années 1890 aux années 1930, actes des journées d'études des 19 et 20 janvier 2007', *Cahiers d'IRICE*, 2 (2008), 127–55.

working practices, which, of course, underlined the degree to which the ILO's concerns related to the more general field of economic and financial relations that now also comprised the EFO's remit. In the 1920s, the interactions between the ILO and the EFO were strained. Although the EFO relied upon the ILO's statistical work in the field of employment, much of which was published in the *Official Bulletin*, the EFO's secretariat was anxious its technical work would not be compromised by the accusations of partiality directed at the scientific work of the ILO. The contrasting institutional roles and approaches were embodied in the very different temperaments and political dispositions of their leaders, the cerebral liberal Salter at the EFO, and the passionate socialist Albert Thomas at the ILO. But the emerging economic crisis generated both new expectations and new pressures on the resources of both organizations that took time to negotiate. The business cycle marked the pithead of what became a rich seam of intellectual engagement by the League as to the causes of and possible remedies for economic depression over the next fourteen years.

Thomas, until his sudden death in 1932, shared the view of Salter's opposite number in the health organization, Ludwik Rajchman, that the economic crisis meant the secretariat needed to become more proactive in attempting to shape political debates in the Assembly. They had to ensure particular subjects would be discussed to bring governments around to the League's expert opinion on how to tackle a problem. This way, discussions would be 'better prepared and more concentrated' (although the word orchestrated would have been more appropriate).[108] Nor, they argued, was it right 'that the debates of the Second Committee [the inter-governmental committee that was notionally in charge of the EFO] should be of a technical character'.[109] In Thomas's and Rajchman's minds, questions of political interest and ideology needed to be addressed directly. This approach was anathema to Salter, Loveday, and Stoppani, who claimed, until the mid-1930s at least, that the EFO's perspective was apolitical. They were not so naive as to believe this contention without qualification, but maintained that the objective of scientific impartiality strengthened the EFO's right to assert a fresh, international perspective that would shape the highly politicized policy agendas of member states.

In this, the workings of the Gold Delegation marked a significant if perverse breakthrough for the League. Not only did its tortured path redouble secretariat efforts to provoke a more creative response on the part of governments to the economic crisis; in time it also forged a more productive relationship between the EFO and the ILO. The appointment of Briton Harold Butler as Thomas's successor undoubtedly helped, but so did the fact that the Gold Delegation report was the last major piece of League advice that gave pre-eminence to the monetary aspects of the business cycle. The fast-paced banking crisis in the summer of 1931 opened up

---

[108] Comment by Rajchman, 'Minutes of Directors' Meeting', 8 Oct. 1930, p. 4, LON R3565, 50/16937/767.

[109] Rajchman, 'Minutes of Directors' Meeting', 8 Oct. 1930, p. 4, LON R3565, 50/16937/767.

new questions and approaches to managing the world's ever-changing economic fortunes.

In 1931, Bertil Ohlin, the rising star of Swedish economic and political life, a colleague of Cassel, and a student of League stalwarts in the USA, including economists Frank W. Taussig and John Williams, arrived in Geneva.[110] Ohlin was charged with coordinating and writing the report to meet the Assembly's demand that the League understand 'The Course and Phases of the World Economic Depression'.[111] Historians of the renowned Stockholm School of macroeconomics have scoured its pages in vain for evidence of the school's intellectual imprint. But, if Ohlin's acute sensitivity to 'international independencies', especially in the framework of an open world economy, was the hallmark of Swedish research on business cycles in this period, it was also a product of the broader intellectual and practical experience of the League of Nations. It was precisely because Ohlin was likely to reflect the League perspective that he had been selected to write the report, and secretariat practices and direction played a major role in shaping the study.

In consultation with Loveday, Ohlin established three primary fields of investigation: the causes of the economic depression; problems that affected agricultural producers in particular; and unemployment. The secretariat then sent out letters to fifty-six states around the world requesting information relevant to these spheres and arranged meetings with leading groups of economists in Britain, France, and the United States, with 'Conjecture' institutes, and with specialist national economic advisory bodies in the search for data and ideas.[112] Loveday invited key figures to Geneva from these organizations in Europe, North America, and Japan, taking care that 'governments should not choose whom they liked to represent their Economic Councils'. He was interested not in the presidents of these associations, but in their most forward-looking thinkers, including men like Keynes, who could not attend (his place was taken by Arthur Henderson), and Frederich Hayek, who did.[113]

The global search for information was reflected in a report that underscored the 'length, depth and universality' of the depression. Ohlin highlighted the variety of interdependencies between countries in the global economy and showed how the interconnectedness of economic relationships meant national economies and their peoples would inevitably be shaped by international forces, even if states adopted policies intended to isolate them. The ebb and flow of demand, trade, and investment might mutate under state direction, but could never be fully controlled

[110] Taussig, the internationally renowned student and proponent of liberal trade, was as important as an international facilitator. For a student's-eye view of the Harvard department, see Valdemar Carlson, 'The Education of an Economist before the Great Depression: Harvard's Economics Department in the 1920s', *American Journal of Economics and Sociology*, 27/1 (Jan. 1968), 101–11.

[111] Bertil Ohlin, *The Course and Phases of the World Economic Depression* (Geneva, 1931).

[112] For Loveday's assessment as to the strengths and weaknesses of possible participants, see his memo 'Study of the Course and Phases of the Present Economic Depression', 28 Oct. 1929, LON 10D R2889.

[113] For a full list, see 'Liste des Représentants des Conseils Économiques Nationaux et des Instituts de Recherches Économiques à La Réunion du 2 mars 1931', 2 Mar. 1931, LON 10D R2890.

or insulated. He identified four principal elements that had transmitted the crisis from one country to another after 1929. The first was the reduction in the demand and international trade of commodities (notably raw materials), particularly in the cases of Bolivia, Malaya, Chile, Egypt, Ecuador, Finland, India, Mexico, the Dutch East Indies, New Zealand, Paraguay, Peru, Uruguay, and Venezuela. Secondly, it was clear agricultural producers found it difficult to adapt to the precipitous falls in demand and in prices, so that the trade balances and purchasing power of primary producers deteriorated markedly. This left farmers poorer than other groups within society, an issue that was all the more pressing given the problems affecting world agriculture since the end of the First World War. No part of the world was free from problems affecting agricultural production, but they were acute where food production dominated the economic landscape, as in Argentina, Australia, the Balkan countries, Brazil, Canada, Colombia, Cuba, and Hungary.

The third key interdependency was the impact of international capital movements (the collapses of international investment that fed banking crises and speculation against the national currency), which, Ohlin emphasized, in the 1920s hit poorer countries that had become reliant on the inflow of foreign capital in order to join the gold standard club promoted by the richer powers. Here, Austria, Hungary, Czechoslovakia, Greece, Japan, and Poland secured a mention as being especially disadvantaged.[114] Britain, too, was identified as a country very dependent on foreign conditions, but in its case because so much of its wealth came from exporting manufactured goods and from earnings made by overseas investment, while the United States and Germany were sensitive to falls in the demand for their manufactured exports. The final aspect of global economic interdependency Ohlin highlighted was the increasing resort to restrictive trade policies and competitive currency depreciation as the cycle of the world economy continued downward. (His fire was directed not at the decision to leave the gold standard but the failure thereafter to coordinate monetary policies.)

Throughout, Ohlin was careful to acknowledge that the economies of some countries appeared less sensitive to the overall health of the world economy—among them the Baltic countries, Belgium, Denmark, France, Italy, the Irish Free State, the Netherlands, Norway, Russia, Spain, Sweden, and Switzerland—but, in so doing, he also demonstrated other connections and vulnerabilities. The Danish economy, for example, was more dependent on Britain than on the world as a whole; in short, it stood at one remove from the crisis, but not invulnerable. The Dutch, Belgians, and French had been partially insulated by the favourable terms under which they returned to gold, but that might not remain the case, especially given the interdependencies of the continental Europe as a whole. There was also the open question of how imperial ties, notably to south-east Asia and Africa, would shape future prospects. In common with his colleagues, however, Ohlin preferred to present European

---

[114] Ohlin was privy to the commissioners' monthly reports on Austria and Hungary. See, e.g., Royall Tyler to Chairman of the Financial Committee, May 1930, LON 10E, R2935, C.147/1930/11.

powers as nation states with particular economic and financial ties to the wider world than to use the more challenging and emotive framework of empire.

The prognosis for the Irish Free State and Spain, too, was bitter-sweet; their apparent detachment from the worst of the crisis was read as a sign of the low level of their economic development since 1920, which, unless addressed, would impede their ability to flourish once the world economy entered a new phase of growth. Ohlin's emphasis on the interdependency of the world economy is commonplace in any history of the Great Depression, but in 1931 the variety and significance of economic and financial ties that comprised the international economy were only beginning to be understood. In this, the report also enabled the EFO to bridge the technical with the diplomatic side of its work. Ohlin's report was widely disseminated as part of preparations for the World Economic Conference and went on to structure the discursive strands of the conference.

THE ORIGINS OF THE WORLD
ECONOMIC CONFERENCE

The genesis of the London conference lay with Herbert Hoover's diplomatic efforts to tackle the Great Depression in the spring of 1931, when the banking crisis swept Europe like a bushfire. By then, League officials, like the American public, were much less enamoured of a President who had hitherto proven impervious to calls for action at home and abroad as the crisis deepened. And, when action came, his wider purposes were far from clear. In June 1931, he facilitated multilateral negotiations that secured a debt moratorium to postpone for one year all payments, of both principal and interest, of intergovernmental debts owed by Britain, France, and their allies to the USA and of reparations owed by the defeated central powers to the Allies. It was in the midst of these negotiations that the idea for a world conference to explore the wider questions posed by the collapse of the world economy was first proposed.

But in 1931 the call for a second world economic conference was not taken up. Instead, the moratorium became the only state-sponsored attempt to effect international cooperation to combat the depression. Hoover hoped the measure would give governments and the international credit system valuable breathing space, but it was no match for the pace of economic and political fortunes. Instead, the new National Government in Britain and the cabinet of Heinrich Brüning in Germany sought to capitalize on the moratorium by using it as a springboard for a new initiative to rid Europe and the world of war debts and reparations for good. Chancellor Neville Chamberlain led the way by vigorously and mistakenly arguing that the moratorium had demonstrated that the White House had finally recognized that war debts and reparations were linked. Woodrow Wilson had not recognized the connection in 1919, and neither Hoover nor his successor, Franklin D. Roosevelt, was later to alter this position. Yet Hoover's meetings with French Prime Minister Pierre Laval in October 1931 muddied the waters sufficiently for the French government to be open to Chamberlain's proposal to reduce German reparation payments further without a prior agreement from the USA on French war debts. After this meeting, Hoover's notion that 'the initiative on this matter should be taken early by the European powers' was interpreted by Britain and France, not just as a demand to act with some urgency to help Germany, but that the reduction, or indeed even the end of reparations, would be reciprocated by favourable action on war debts in Washington.[115]

Given that the EFO's collective view, as its national members sought to form a '*general* standpoint' (emphasis in original) that the 'intensive struggle and acute depression clearly distinguishable' from the difficult conditions of 1930 was explained 'almost entirely by the grave financial disorders' since July 1931, it seemed obtuse to focus on reparations and war debts. Why did the League secretariat, and the major European powers and the USA, appear to accept Chancellor Brüning's rhetoric that removing the burden of reparations would benefit, not just Germany, but the European and the global economy? For the EFO, the situation of all central and eastern European powers was critical. Reparations were the best means to draw attention to the increasingly heavy weight of debt on the world's poorer nations since 1929—'an Eastern and Central European farmer requires 150 kg wheat to pay off interest which he could pay off with 50 kg before the crisis began'—and the fact that countries' financial interests were often 'utterly at variance with their economic interest'. Financial pressures explained why protectionist measures were now strangling the global economy.[116]

For national politicians and financiers, other elements also came into the calculation to put debts centre stage. Reparations were no longer the intolerable burden on the German economy they had been in the first years of the Weimar Republic thanks to the US-sponsored Dawes Plan. After 1924, the German economy appeared to recover, thanks to a steady stream of US capital that lured it into accumulating a commercial debt of more than 25 per cent of its national income. Beneath the veneer of recovery, as Stresemann famously claimed in 1928, Germany was dancing on a volcano. Taken together, reparations and Dawes loans created a sizeable debt overhang—in 1930 its commercial debts stood at 30 milliard (thousand million) RM, which investors began to doubt Germany could ever pay off.[117]

The same could be said of the war debts owed to the United States. In the first years after the war, the principal and interest owed to the United States was a significant item on British and French national budgets. In 1926, the French managed to secure more favourable terms with the US authorities in the Mellon–Bérenger Accords. This left Britain and its allies disadvantaged, although the drain on their national budgets was offset by the depreciation of sterling after September

[115] Hoover–Laval communiqué, in *Papers Relating to the Foreign Relations of the United States, 1931* (Washington, 1947–), ii. 252.

[116] League of Nations, 'Work of the Economic Committee during its Thirty-Seventh Session', *Official Journal* (Mar. 1932), 588–9.

[117] See Albrecht Ritschl, *Deutschlands Krise und Konjunktur 1924–1934: Binnenkonjunktur, Auslandsverschuldung und Reparationsproblem zwischen Dawes-Plan und Transfersperre* (Berlin, 2002), 18–20, 107–42.

1931.[118] By then, the challenge of war debts owed to the United States was as much political as economic, or, as Chamberlain put it, 'how to persuade our own people to pay the taxation involved'.[119] Hidden from the public gaze was a more potent financial dimension to the international crisis surrounding German indebtedness: the interdependence of the banking system. In August and September 1931, Germany's overseas creditors, notably the American banks that had extended commercial loans through the Dawes and Young plans, and British banks that had given emergency loans to their German counterparts during the financial crisis, voluntarily agreed to freeze their credits inside Germany under 'Standstill Agreements'. Accepted on all sides as a short-term necessity, the Standstill Agreements became a long-term, gnawing hardship for Germany's creditors.[120] The City of London was increasingly worried that many in Germany had begun to blur the distinction between commercial and intergovernmental political debts, and supported the notion that political debts should be abolished to save the contractual agreements of the private market.

For Germany, too, the Standstill Agreements had important consequences for the future direction of policy, enabling both the last Weimar and the future National Socialist governments to sustain the country's foreign trade and, in theory, borrow more on existing credit lines. They effectively liberated the German state from the 'rules of the gold standard', giving it increased independence to formulate economic and monetary policy along unorthodox lines, which the Nazis exploited to considerable effect in the push for rearmament.[121]

The financial crisis of 1931 acted as a powerful accelerant on the already energetic flames of nationalism burning around the world. The irony was that it also worked to bind ever tighter the interests of the world's major powers and specifically the welfare of powerful communities of international financiers. This dynamic resonated within the League during the lifetime of the Gold Delegation Inquiry. It was immediately recognized in Britain, too, because of the exposure of British banks to a potential German default was an additional strain on Britain's already stretched financial system and culminated in a sterling crisis that would force the pound from the gold standard. In the minds of British policy-makers, the debt crisis and the convertibility crisis were linked, and their conviction was shared by their counterparts in central Europe and Latin America. Here, Treasury thinking was powerfully shaped by the logic of Cassel and Strakosch: with political debts out of the way, market forces would be better able to redistribute the world monetary resources and facilitate recovery.[122] And it was the Treasury that primarily shaped British foreign economic policy.[123]

---

[118] Benjamin D. Rhodes, 'Reassessing "Uncle Shylock": The United States and the French War Debt, 1917–1929', *Journal of American History*, 55/4 (Mar. 1969), 787–803.

[119] Quoted in Schuker, 'Origins of American Stabilization Policy in Europe', 398.

[120] Neil Forbes, *Doing Business with the Nazis: Britain's Economic and Financial Relations with Germany, 1931–1939* (London, 2000), 39–132.

[121] Clavin, *Failure of Economic Diplomacy*, 100–9, 181–5.

[122] Memo by Leith-Ross, 16 Jan. 1932, TNA: PRO T160, F12929/1; memo by Strakosch, 15 Dec. 1932, TNA: PRO T172.

[123] The Foreign Office and the Federation of British Industries, by contrast, feared the implications of a Germany freed from the shackles of reparations.

The case for an international agreement to liberate Germany (central Europe featured much less prominently) from the burden of reparations was also easily made to a British public schooled by Keynes's treatise on *The Economic Consequences of the Peace*, which had captured its imagination.[124] The 'harshness' of Versailles had become entwined with frustration in the progress of international disarmament, making Germany, as the US Secretary of State Henry Stimson put it, 'the key log' in the 'European jam'.[125] In October 1931, Ramsay MacDonald, head of a new National Government, believed that taking a 'big bold lead in the world' on debts would give the impression of dynamism. In practice, British policy was led on the issue by Chamberlain. He was not cut from the same internationalist cloth as MacDonald, but he, too, had a global vision. In his case, it centred on a reinvigorated British Empire, of which the sterling area now formed a critical part, and so meeting and shaping international expectations of British leadership in the search for economic peace offered an opportunity to quell international hostility to the floating pound and Britain's incipient move to general and imperial protection. So, too, would a resolution to tackle economic and political instability (in Chamberlain's mind the two were inextricably interwoven) at the heart of Europe, freeing Britain to focus its security policy on what really mattered: the British Empire.[126] An improvement in Anglo-French relations was a key element of this strategy, and the Treasury was prepared to exploit French interest in British monetary policy and mislead if it helped deliver an end to political debts, calculating 'it could not hurt' if 'France thought stabilization to be closer to reality if they adopted British reparation and debt policy'.[127] This strategy, effective in the short term, would come back to haunt Anglo-French relations and the League.

Although the terms of the Lausanne Conference explicitly excluded political debts, the League had a strong vested interest in the health of Anglo-French relations. In June 1932, it watched events of the meeting nearby, convened to effect a final settlement of reparations, with the studied disinterest of the passionately interested. Central to British efforts was the expectation that, once the issue of reparations had been resolved among the Europeans, the United States would offer a corresponding settlement on war debts. But the chances of American concessions dissipated as its own national crisis deepened and Hoover retreated into the isolated sanctuary of the Oval Office. The spectre of a 'united European front of debtors' began to haunt his administration and a beleaguered Congress, which, disgusted by news that Germany and France were spending increasing amounts on defence and

---

[124] Matthias Peter, *John Maynard Keynes und die britische Deutschlandpolitik. Machtanspruch und ökonomische Realität im Zeitalter der Weltkriege, 1919–1946* (Munich, 1997), 29–57.

[125] Stimson to MacDonald, 29 Dec. 1931, TNA: PRO PRO 30/69/679.

[126] After Sept. 1931 the Australian, New Zealand, and South African pound was pegged to sterling not gold. Egypt and Iraq, a British mandate until 1932, for whom Britain was a major export market, followed suit. Canada preferred to shadow US monetary policy. John Darwin, *The Empire Project: The Rise and Fall of the British World-System, 1830–1970* (Cambridge, 2009), 430–9. For his view of global politics and how it shaped his global strategies as premier, see Keith Neilsen, *Britain, Soviet Russia and the Collapse of the Versailles Order, 1919–1939* (Cambridge, 2006), 212–312.

[127] Memo by Leith-Ross, 11 Aug. 1931, TNA: PRO T188/21; Claudel to Herriot, 1 June 1932, AMAE Y/Internat/73.

Britain was retreating into its Empire, professed itself 'bored of selfish European interests'.[128]

It was in this context that the idea of couching the debt negotiations in a broader economic and financial conference resurfaced in the spring of 1932. But the event that turned this, and the notion of a reparation settlement, into the basis for a Europe-wide rapprochement that would have global implications was the formation of a new left-leaning French cabinet under the leadership of Édouard Herriot in early May. The replacement of Brüning, who had put reparations at the heart of his foreign policy, with the ultra-conservative Franz von Papen on 30 May 1932 brought no pause in the Anglo-French initiative. It should have. Although Brüning had long resorted to ruling German democracy by presidential decree, he was less implicated in the rise of political violence and the lurch to a right-wing style of authoritarian leadership exemplified by Papen and the National Socialists who hovered in the wings behind him.

The Lausanne Conference, which met from 26 June to 9 July, marked a remarkable reversal from earlier League and Franco-German expectations that Hoover would take a leading role. Instead, it was Chamberlain and Herriot who thrashed out the terms of the final settlement. With a final German payment of 3 billion RM, which was never paid, and a fudge on the war guilt clause, the reparations slate was wiped clean. French agreement to the deal, reversing a decade-long policy on reparations in which much was invested, was that Britain and France would cooperate closely together. The public version of the agreement stressed its contribution to the 'development of confidence between nations in a mutual sprit of reconciliation, collaboration and justice'. But this lofty rhetoric was promptly undermined by newspapers' publication of the details of their secret 'gentleman's agreement', which made clear the eventual ratification of the deal was conditional on a satisfactory arrangement being reached between Belgium, Italy, France, and Great Britain, on the one hand, and the United States, on the other. Should the plan fail, as it would, then, in theory, the established reparations arrangements under the Dawes and Young plans would be reinstated. The Americans reacted with fury and dismay. The secret pact smacked of the discredited diplomacy of the world before 1918, to which it was publicly opposed. The White House did not take kindly to the arm-twisting tactic that the *fait accompli* presented.[129]

Here the League and the open diplomacy that was its trademark came to the rescue of the Europeans. Enshrined in the fifth article of the Lausanne agreement—signed but 30 miles from Geneva in the plush surroundings of the Beau-Rivage Hotel—was the call for the League of Nations to convene a world economic conference to address war debts and other economic and financial issues that were contributing to the slump. The secretariat knew it was a poisoned Anglo-French

---

[128] Memo by Stimson, 11 Jan. 1932, in *Papers Relating to the Foreign Relations of the United States*, i (1932).

[129] Twenty-one years later the incident still smarted: Hoover chose to reprint the furious exchange of transatlantic correspondence relating to the secret agreement in his diary: Herbert Hoover, *The Memoirs of Herbert Hoover, 1929–1941* (New York, 1953), 171–3.

chalice but had to accept it. Although experience had taught it that more focused initiatives had a greater chance of success, the conference was the ultimate in networking opportunities. It would assemble all the constituents of the world's economy—governments, central bankers, businesses, workers' representatives, and economists—in the League's name to grapple with the worst economic crisis the world had faced. News that the USA was to be a leading participant was also an allure. The World Economic Conference offered the possibility of a resolution to insecurities afflicting the world economies and the uncertainties facing all. Agreement, debate, disagreement, and haggling beckoned. The League may not have been liked or feared, but it was trusted sufficiently to host the event. The challenge of meeting these global expectations was now laid at the EFO's door.

3

Conferences and their (Dis)contents, 1933–1934

The World Financial and Economic Conference, as it was renamed by the League, lies at the heart of the Great Depression.[1] Preparations for it were extensive and included the convocation of two Preparatory Commissions in Geneva and a flurry of diplomatic missions in the spring of 1933 to the USA, where Franklin Delano Roosevelt was waiting in the wings to assume the Presidency. His was not the only election to presage the conference, with the appointment of Adolf Hitler as German Chancellor having the most far-reaching consequences. When it convened in London between 12 June and 27 July, the World Economic Conference marked the first and only attempt to move international cooperation away from an obsession with debts onto wider terrain. It was the key opportunity by which the world might have been spared crushing economic conditions that continued with little respite for twenty years. It was a truly global event, assembling delegates from sixty-five nation states, including representatives from ten non-member territories as well as intergovernmental and non-governmental organizations, to deliberate schemes to raise world prices, stimulate demand, and roll back barriers to world trade. The history of the world conference was told and retold by subsequent generations of economists and historians, many of whom witnessed the collapse of the conference first hand, or who were exposed to a narrative of failure that placed responsibility for the debacle firmly on the shoulders of the United States.[2]

The story has been told invariably through the lens of state agency, with the British cast as charming but ineffective hosts, the United States as the disruptive party guest, while the delegates attending from Nazi Germany feasted handsomely on the spectacle of international disunity. From the outset, Britain decisively shaped the design of the conference, aided by the appointment of the Foreign Secretary John Simon as chairman of the Organizing Committee, with Hankey responsible for liaising with Geneva regarding the logistical arrangements.

Because of this national focus, it is often overlooked that the World Economic Conference was formally convened under the auspices of the League of Nations;

---

[1] The directors of section agreed the new title to mimic the structure of the Economic and Financial Organization. See General Discussion, 'Minutes of Directors' Meeting', 15 Sept. 1932, pp. 2–3, LON R3565, 50/34358/767.

[2] Barry Eichengreen, 'The Origins and Nature of the Great Slump', *Economic History Review*, 47/2 (1992), 13–39; Patricia Clavin, 'The World Economic Conference, 1933: The Failure of British Internationalism', *Journal of Modern European Economic History*, 20/3 (1991), 489–527.

that its agenda and supplementary materials were prepared and shaped by the Economic and Financial Sections; that its structure mimicked that of the League; and that the conference was funded largely out of its coffers. In the minds of contemporaries, however, the event was associated with the organization, which, as so often, bore the risk and could take none of the credit. It was also the League of Nations that helped to turn the lessons of London into a process that ultimately realigned the machinery of political and economic relations, and to produce a conference namesake—the United Nations Financial and Economic Conference—to make good on the experience of 1933.

THE HOST WITH THE MOST

The World Economic Conference was held in London because it coincided almost exactly with the proposed start of the League of Nations Disarmament Conference in Geneva, which had been in preparation since 1925. In 1932 and 1933, the Disarmament Conference and a busy programme of Assembly, ILO, and Mandate Commission meetings were set to swallow most of the League's annual budget and almost all of its personnel and physical resources. Leave entitlements for League staff were cancelled, and pressure on space meant that an alternative conference venue had to be found. The London event marked a considerable advance on its 1927 predecessor of the same name, because the agenda included monetary issues and comprised both senior government ministers and nominated expert advisers, the former appearing on 'the scene for action after the play has been completely written'.[3] Ministerial representation was essential to turn fine ideas into political reality, but behind the scenes it was the EFO's secretariat, and its close advisers, who wanted to direct events.

First, the League strove to build the set in the EFO's image. Aside from the Organizing Committee, there was a Preparatory Committee of Experts, which comprised an economic and a financial subcommittee. Nation states were responsible for determining who might be nominated, although the secretariat made unsolicited suggestions. In an extension of past practice, the League also sought to involve other interested parties, notably the ILO, which proposed nominees from government, employers' and workers' groups, and a committee of International Chamber of Commerce, put together especially for the event (on whose advisory council served the American Leo Pasvolsky).[4] Some institutional participants were not welcomed so enthusiastically, among them the Rome-based International Institute for Agriculture (IIA), whose perceived inefficiencies and fascist leanings unsurprisingly gave rise to a troubled relationship with the EFO.[5] From

---

[3] Memo by Feis, 3 June 1932, NARA RG59 550.S1/43.

[4] Memo from the Chambre de Commerce Internationale, 12 Dec. 1932, LON R2669, 10A/38039/38039, Box R 2669; 'Delegation of the International Labour Office to the Preparatory Commission', 23 Nov. 1932, LON R2669, 10A/38039/38039.

[5] De Michelis to Simon, 3 Nov. 1932, LON R2669, 10A/38094/38039.

the latter's perspective, however, the most delicate negotiations surrounded the participation of the BIS. It, like the EFO's section directors, had been identified in the final act of the Lausanne Conference as particularly well qualified to offer expert advice to the World Economic Conference. But, whereas in 1930 the two institutions had shared common cause in safeguarding gold standard orthodoxy, since 1931 their perspectives had diverged.[6]

Widening the conference remit to consider monetary policy made the BIS an obvious participant, especially as the conference aimed to include central bankers. But the notion that the EFO and the BIS might prepare an agenda that would expose central banks to public scrutiny was something the BIS preferred to avoid: it had shunned the EFO's calls for joint initiatives to help countries in crisis in central and eastern Europe in 1930 and 1931, and wanted to keep 'its skirts clear' of initiatives that were overtly political, notably the call for European Union in 1931.[7]

And cooperation at arm's length had emerged between the EFO and the BIS. The Financial Section and Committee regularly exchanged intelligence and opinions on conditions relating to the operation of the gold standard and financial stability, and the preparations for the conference were to bring them into closer contact. As a result, a healthy element of competition between them began to develop when it came to proffering financial advice, and fed into what was to become a lively rivalry between Loveday and one of the rising young stars of the BIS, his former colleague Per Jacobsson. Although the BIS disapproved of the Economic and Financial Sections' interventions into policy and politics, it also admired aspects of their work, notably the early work of the Gold Delegation. Indeed, suspicious of the degree to which the Financial Section had been seduced by the British taste for depreciation, in 1931 the BIS wanted to pick up the work of the Gold Delegation where the EFO had left off as its contribution to preparations for the conference. After all, the bank of central banks was 'in its very nature, par excellence, the place to discuss' the operation of the gold standard. But it was stymied by an institutional structure that privileged the position of the world's most powerful central banks, and it could no more persuade its national members to open up 'sensitive' topics to international discussion than could the League secretariat. In this case, it was Governor Moret, Governor of the Banque de France, who was the stumbling block. He certainly did 'not care what the League says about the gold situation, because they are a group of politicians or theoreticians'; and while he was prepared to discuss French gold policy with 'governors of central banks', he was not ready 'to pursue it through the medium of the BIS'.[8]

By contrast, delegates representing smaller economies on gold wanted closer ties with the BIS as 'a banking institution with funds occasionally available for

---

[6] Avenol to Fraser, 6 Oct. 1931, LON R2669, 10A/38729/85039.
[7] Fraser to Harrison, 18 Sept. 1931, BIS, McGarrah Papers, 7.18(2), File 47.
[8] McGarrah to Beneduce, 30 Dec. 1930, BIS, McGarrah Papers, 7.18(9), File 27.

investment' and with unrivalled access to the international network of central bankers.[9] But the underlying challenge to closer collaboration between the EFO and the BIS lay in the degree to which the financial landscape had changed since 1930. The London conference was the first occasion where the BIS would make a public presentation of its activities, describing itself as a 'club of central bankers, where they can meet, interchange information, make themselves acquainted with the problems in respective markets and develop those personal contacts which can often prove so useful'.[10] This, of course, privileged the position of the central banks, whereas the EFO, so the BIS argued, was governed by representatives of government finance ministries. While there was some overlap in representation and function, the League's commitment to open diplomacy stood in contrast to the BIS's determination to 'avoid silly rumours' and 'indiscriminate publicity' by abstaining from any kind of public engagement, which approach set it apart from 'all other international organizations'.[11] This commitment to the values of confidentiality and status—or, in the language of its critics, a culture of secrecy and privilege—was to bring challenges of its own for the BIS and its relations with the axis powers in the future.[12] But more immediately dramatic consequences came from the creation of the sterling area following the pound's depreciation, and the floatation of the US dollar in April 1933. In countries with depreciated currencies, central bankers no longer ruled the financial roost, while those still tied to gold became increasingly defensive. These changes were reflected immediately in the Financial Committee, which included government representatives of newly floated currencies, but not in the BIS.[13] During the preparations for the World Conference and in its immediate aftermath, the question of how to restructure the architecture of international financial relations was a major talking point between financiers and economists associated with both organizations, but there were few ready answers. After the economic conference their relations remained confined to informal lunches and telephone calls until the war in 1940 forced a clean break.

---

[9] Davis to Fraser, 3 Sept. 1931, BIS, McGarrah Papers, 7.18(9), File 92; McGarrah to Schacht, 6 Nov. 1933, BIS, McGarrah Papers, 6.14, Box 1; McGarrah to Mylanarski, 31 Oct. 1933, BIS, McGarrah Papers, 6.14, Box 1. The BIS archives contain a full complement of League financial publications as well as drafts circulated for comment of key publications between 1931 and 1933. See, e.g., BIS, League of Nations, 7.8 RD06, File 7a.

[10] Memo by Jacobsson, 'Tasks of the BIS', 16 May 1933, BIS, Per Jacobsson Papers, 7/18 (11), Box Jac 1, File H.S. 25.

[11] Fraser to Davis, 4 Sept. 1931, BIS, McGarrah Papers, Box 7.18(9), File 92.

[12] Gianni Toniolo, *Central Bank Cooperation at the Bank for International Settlements, 1930–1973* (Cambridge, 2005), 201–59.

[13] The Treasury and EFO sought to improve the coordination of financial activities and cooperative arrangements between the EFO and the BIS, but the French, the Italians, and the Germans opposed it. The position of the Americans was ambiguous. The Federal Reserve Board was nervous of the consequences for central bank and BIS autonomy, while Roosevelt's administration was concerned about how public opinion might receive news of its closer association with the League and 'old-style' financial diplomacy, on the other. See McGarrah to Mlynarski, 31 Oct. 1933, and McGarrah to Schacht, 6 Nov. 1933, BIS, McGarrah Papers, 6.14, Box 1.

THE DEVIL IN THE PREPARATION

By October 1932, there had been several meetings of the conference Organizing Committee, and Loveday and Stoppani told Hankey what would be required. They estimated there would be more than 700 delegates representing 67 invited governments. They also posed questions to which they had ready solutions in Geneva yet no answer for London: where would these men and women meet, sleep, eat, and negotiate, who would interpret for them, type and transmit communications on their behalf, transport them and clean up after them when they left? Hankey helped find a venue large enough to host the event and support for the stretched officials of the League. But the great spirit of cooperation that the League effected with MacDonald's cabinet office, the Foreign Office, and the Stationery Department should not be equated with easy relations with the Treasury, and, when the Treasury tried to impose itself on the practical arrangements, Stoppani and Loveday refused to provide additional information outside the usual channels.[14]

For the most part, officials on both sides congratulated themselves for the efficiency with which preparations proceeded in an atmosphere of mutual appreciation that reflected how far the EFO's administrative culture replicated that of the British civil service. Hankey's and Stoppani's joint scouting expeditions delivered the Geological Museum as the surrogate Assembly Hall, with access to the lobbies of the Natural History Museum next door for social events and publication displays. Carpenters and builders were commissioned to embellish facilities, including an extra ladies' rest room (to accommodate the large number of female clerical workers) and a special platform in the main hall, from which King George V would deliver the opening speech. (Stoppani and Loveday were a little surprised when the palace and the Foreign Office invited the newly appointed Secretary-General of the League, Joseph Avenol, to stand on the podium alongside the King and the conference president MacDonald for the opening ceremony.[15]) The opening events were to be broadcast around the world through a coordinated effort of wireless communication of 400 different stations arranged jointly by the League, the British Broadcasting Corporation, the BBC Empire, and the Columbia Broadcasting System in America. Great pains were also taken to ensure the broadcast was received in Europe, in North and South America, and in the furthest corners of the European Empires—something that was pioneering for its day. The League, however, resisted calls, to which later transatlantic broadcasters were to succumb, to move back the opening speeches to a later hour to suit audiences in North America.[16] Given that the League was convening abroad, planning the logistics ran surprisingly smoothly. Within the institution, the conference provided a launch pad both for Avenol's career as Secretary-General, a post

---

[14] Herlsey to Steneck, 31 May 1933, and Stencek to Hersley, 2 June 1933, LON R4634, 10D/1400/517.

[15] For correspondence relating to the arrangements, see LON R4633, 10D/597/597.

[16] Cummings to Avenol, 15 May 1933, LON R4635, 10D/4187/597.

he assumed while in London, and for Stoppani and Loveday, who did most of the groundwork, once again expanding the reach of their agency within the League.

While the practicalities were resolved, the need to finalize an agenda that would give the conference purpose became increasingly pressing. This task, by contrast, fell solely to the Economic and Financial Sections. As before, the challenge for the EFO as a discrete agency intended to facilitate economic growth was that its structure privileged consensus between all parties as the means to effect cooperation. This stood in the way of its ability to recommend what the secretariat believed were the 'right' policies to states to combat the depression. What the world needed was not consensus, but detachment and flexibility. This would enable policy-makers to break free from the fettered mentality of the gold standard system. So, the secretariat had to make the best use of the experts invited to participate in the Preparatory Commission charged with drafting an agenda and policy recommendations to push governments in directions they did not necessarily want to go. Economic science had to shine, which meant that states had to nominate delegates to the Preparatory Committee who had important ideas and perspectives to share, and who, at the same time, were able to work within League conventions.

Early nominations to the first meeting of the preparatory conference in Geneva on 31 October 1931 were not encouraging. On the one hand, the fact that Hoover's administration had agreed to the Financial Section's suggestion that US Governor James Cox should chair the all-important Monetary Commission was good news, because it underlined US commitment to the conference. Cox had been the Democrat Presidential candidate in 1920 and was a Wilsonian who had favoured US entry into the League of Nations. He would oversee the work of two major preparatory financial committees, the first of which was intended to be innovative and address 'immediate measures for financial reconstruction': credit policy, price levels, how to limit monetary fluctuations, exchange control, indebtedness, and questions relating to the resumption of international lending. However, a less favourable omen was the insistence of the USA, France, and other gold standard states that Cox preside over a second committee to focus on 'permanent measures for the reestablishment of the international gold standard', including central bank cooperation, the distribution of gold, and, as a sop to India, China, and the powerful silver-producing lobby in the USA, the price of silver.[17]

The perspective from the chair of the Economic Commission was also one of orthodoxy. Its chairman was Colijn, who had a well-known preference for low tariffs. But, as in the Monetary Commission, the range of issues identified for discussion pointed to the contradictory directions in national policies. Three smaller committees were given a more open-ended brief to study commercial policy; the production and marketing of primary products; and subsidies and sanitary restrictions. These committees gave voice to a variety of protectionist impulses from primary producers and imperial consumers that pulled in a very different direction from free trade. A further indication of how the League could

---

[17] Clavin, *Failure of Economic Diplomacy*, 39–40.

spawn and facilitate the international interaction of contradictory economic policies came with the creation of a fourth subcommittee under Colijn on international public works. Here, the ILO became an invaluable partner in defining the landscape of the task ahead.[18]

The framework of the conference reflected the practical and intellectual model the EFO had developed since 1920, which proved remarkably durable. During the Second World War it provided the first point of reference for economists, civil servants, and politicians in the United States, Great Britain, and elsewhere engaged in planning the post-war economic order. But it was the conference's expert delegates who gave it life, although, thanks to the guiding hand of nation states, not a life of their own. For the British government, Chamberlain and the Treasury quickly gained the upper hand in choosing the experts. The suggestion from Geneva that Keynes, Strakosch, or Ralph Hawtrey, the 53-year-old economist and Director of Financial Enquiries at the Treasury, represent Britain was promptly dismissed, as Chamberlain regarded them as 'too extreme' and 'unreliable'.[19] The Treasury preferred the 'safe hands' of Leith-Ross as its nominee to the Economic Commission, who, in his role as liaison between the Treasury and the Board of Trade, would offer a controlled presentation of British depreciation and trade policy to an international audience.

These were sensitive topics, as the appointment of Layton, the outspoken advocate of British depreciation, as Britain's representative to the Monetary Commission illustrated.[20] Layton had many admirers overseas, for his credentials as a free trader, but it was these that caused him to resign noisily from the Monetary Commission weeks later in protest against what he saw as the 'rigidity' of British tariff policy after Britain had signed up to imperial preference at Ottawa. Layton's act signalled his public despair that the British government no longer equated national economic well-being with the interests of the international economy. The episode reinforced Chamberlain's determination to retain control over Britain's performance on the League stage, and his loyal adviser at the Treasury, Frederick Phillips, replaced Layton. The Treasury's nominations caused disquiet in Geneva and in London too, where the Foreign Office reflected how British protectionism and the economic conference had the potential to shift British foreign policy in directions over which the Foreign Office had no say. As Victor Wellesley, Under-Secretary of State at the Foreign Office, warned his colleagues, 'if it is not clear at the start that we consider that these financial and economic questions cannot be

---

[18] The ILO delegation comprised Weigert (Germany) representing the government group, Oersted (Denmark) for the employers' group, and Jouhaux (France) for the workers. Despite intensive lobbying, the Parisian International Chamber of Commerce, the International Institute for Commerce based in Brussels, and the International Cooperative Alliance in London were not allowed to attend delegations, but contributed lengthy memos. See Simon to Trip, 6 Oct. 1932, LON R2671, 10A/38756/38756.

[19] Clavin, *Failure of Economic Diplomacy*, 40.

[20] See Lammers to Neurath, 10 Sept. 1932, TNA: PRO GFM 33/1230, 3177/D683889, and Bernsdorff to Neurath, 29 Oct. 1932, TNA: PRO GFM 9245/E65901; Coleman to Stimson, 25 Oct. 1932, NARA RG59 550.S1/330.

divorced from foreign policy', there was a serious risk that everything would be approached from 'its economic and financial side to the exclusion of wider political considerations'.[21] Later critics of Chamberlain's appeasement of Hitler's government could not have put it very much better.

As their economic and financial policies had undergone less change, the French and German governments had rather more success at disguising their rising economic nationalism, at least at the preparatory stage of the conference. The French government nominated old Geneva hands, the well-respected Deputy Governor of the Bank of France Charles Rist, and two civil servants, Paul Elbel of the Ministry for Trade and Industry, and Jean Parmentier, Director-General of the Ministry for Trade and Industry. Germany, too, never lost sight of the potentially explosive political implications of the conference and sent only 'reliable' civil servants: Hans Ernst Posse, head of the Economics Ministry, was nominated to the economic commission and Wilhelm Vocke, a member of the Reichsbank Direckorium, to its monetary counterpart. Behind the scenes in Germany, the experienced diplomat Karl Ritter, who had directed the Foreign Ministry's reparation and trade strategy, skilfully guided German policy preparations for the conference, intending to 'wait to heap the odium for failure onto others, while ensuring that Germany reaped the benefits'.[22]

If European representation on the Preparatory Committee was cut from the resolute cloth of grey civil-servant flannel, the American government opted for trusty academic tweed. Edmund Day, Director of Social Science at the Rockefeller Foundation, was nominated to the Economics Commission, and John H. Williams, Professor of Economics at Harvard University, was to serve on the monetary side. While Day was connected to some of the more progressive schools of economic and social thought in the USA, Williams was identified largely with economic orthodoxy. Aged 45, he was comparatively young and relatively junior within a Harvard economics department that had been set alive by the recent arrival of Joseph Schumpeter, and, through another colleague in the department, Taussig, Williams had developed strong connections to other economists associated with the League.[23] The study of economics in the 1920s, still developing its identity as a discrete science, was distinguished by its integration as a scholarly network and its dedication to public service.

Within this wider network, Williams was seen as orthodox but not dogmatic, and useful because of his political connections. He was highly regarded as an authority on monetary reform and international finance, and combined his strong theoretical understanding with—in the words of Harvard lawyer Felix Frankfurter, an Austrian-born an American enthusiast of the League and a confidant to both Stimson and

[21] Memo by Wellesley, 25 July 1932, TNA: PRO FO 371/16418, W8647/8034/50.
[22] Neurath to Krogmann, 9 Aug. 1933, TNA: PRO GFM 33/1231, 3177/D684405; Lorenz to Lammers, 17 June 1933, BA R43II/365a.
[23] When Schumpeter was asked to list possible honorary members for the American Economic Association in 1944, all his nominees were closely associated with the League. His selection was subsequetly endorsed by Viner. See Schumpeter to Willets, 1 May 1944, and Viner to Schumpeter, 21 May 1944, Mudd, Viner, Box 2, Folder 23.

Roosevelt—a feeling 'for the importance of having a hand in practical affairs'.[24] Williams also worked as a ghost writer for Ogden Mills, Under-Secretary of State at the US Treasury, and as an adviser to the Federal Reserve Bank of New York. (He later became its Vice-President and Research Director.) Williams was held in considerable esteem by the US Department of Commerce, where he was commissioned to prepare reliable statistics on the US balance of payments—a task that brought him into frequent contact with Loveday.[25]

The implications of the American nominations were complex. Day and Williams lacked direct political power or accountability, which caused the government appointees of Britain, France, and Germany to the Preparatory Committee, for example, to try to bypass them and speak instead to Frederic M. Sackett, US Ambassador to Germany, and Feis, who was sent to Geneva to support the American expert representatives.[26] The European delegates' attempted subversion of the American team did not go unnoticed in Washington, but Hoover was not overly concerned. He had taken the League's request for 'expert' nominations at face value, because he did not want Williams and Day to 'act as spokesmen of definite official policy' and because he knew his presidency was in its death throes.[27] However, Hoover remained committed enough to the value of international cooperation to attempt to shape FDR's policy towards the conference in January 1933. If it was a lame-duck delegation, as many alleged, it is worth noting that the American experts were among the most senior figures to be appointed to a publicly accountable, intergovernmental committee on economic and monetary policy since 1919. Moreover, these nominations, in contrast to those of most member states, went some way to meeting the League's call that committee representatives have sufficient intellectual firepower and 'creative energy to escape traditional policy limitations'.[28] Innovative policy suggestions, however, would still need political support and commitment, and this Day and Williams did not have (some might also question their creative capacity). In the event, European disquiet as to the political firepower of the US delegation did not really matter for the first preparatory meeting, because much of it was given over to recriminations over sterling's depreciation.

On 31 October 1932, the first meeting of the Preparatory Commission convened in Geneva on a day bathed in brilliant autumnal sunshine. But the bright light flooding into the committee rooms did little to lift the gloomy mood of many of the participants or to illuminate the discussions, which revolved almost entirely around Britain's departure from the gold standard and the creation of the sterling

---

[24] Frankfurter to Feis, 13 Oct. 1932, LC, Feis: 34. For alternative nominations, see Feis to Stimson, 2 Oct. 1932, NARA RG59 550.S1/120½.

[25] Barber, *From New Era to New Deal*, 206. For a major attempt to reassert Williams's contribution to international economics, see Pier Francesco Asso and Luca Fiorito, 'A Scholar in Action in Interwar America: John H. Williams' Contributions to Trade Theory and International Monetary Reform', *Quaderni*, 430 (2004), 1–38 <http://www.econ-pol.unisi.it/quaderni/430.pdf> (accessed 6 Jan. 2009).

[26] For Sackett's central role, see Bernard V. Burke, *Ambassador Frederic Sackett and the Collapse of the Weimar Republic, 1930–1933: The United States and Hitler's Rise to Power* (Cambridge, 1995).

[27] Castle to Williams and Day, 17 Oct. 1932, NARA RG59 550.S1/283.

[28] Memo by Trip, 8 Nov. 1932, TNA: PRO FO371/16420.

area. The Geneva meeting provided the first opportunity for governments to interrogate this dramatic development, much to the discomfort of the British delegates, who complained to their government back home of having to act like 'lumps of cement' in the face of vehement and united international criticism.[29] In both the Monetary and Economic Commissions, French, German, Italian, Dutch, Japanese, Belgian, and American representatives were quick to turn the discussion of almost every issue back to the depreciation of sterling, with no representatives of the thirty-five national members of the sterling area to help the British fight their corner. 'Stabilisation was like the Polish question,' the British complained, in a reference to the Paris Peace Conference.[30]

Abandoning gold had overturned a cardinal tenet of more than a century of British monetary policy and was followed by only vague promises that there would be a return to the gold standard when prices were right. Phillips swaddled his case for sterling's depreciation in quotations from the *Final Report of the Gold Delegation* on the problems of the gold standard and from the 'Financial Resolutions of the Ottawa Conference', which offered a vigorous statement of the need to raise prices on behalf of the primary producers: 'the world could not support further deflation . . . it would lead to the bankruptcy of raw material producing countries.'[31] But, despite the merits of the case, which was not nearly as selfless as Phillips presented, the British government should not have been surprised by the strength of international anger, although it was never likely to deliver what the majority of the delegates wanted: namely that the British government face up to its responsibilities to take the lead by a return to gold. In Geneva, one move Britain could have made was to make a forceful case for coordinated devaluation by all the remaining members of the gold standard, because it would have broken the vicious deflationary cycle of the Great Depression. But, although the break by sterling and its associated currencies with gold had indicated the future path to recovery, Britain was in no mood to proselytize, and other governments were unlikely to listen. While Britain had confidence in its own abilities to manage sterling's flotation, notably through the exchange equalization account, it had less faith that other countries had the financial acumen or will to do so, and 'currency chaos' could be the outcome. It also feared losing the comparative trading advantage, especially important for an economy that, according to League calculations, still exported around 80 per cent of its GDP.

Political considerations dominated British policy in a way they had not in the minority report of the Gold Delegation. To this end, the British government argued that the fluctuation in sterling's value was caused primarily 'by the unresolved war debts question'. No one accepted this position, but there was an obvious advantage to the world's debtors, dominant among the League members and chief of which was Germany, in exploiting it. Britain's line provided an opportunity for

[29] Memo by Niemeyer, 30 Nov. 1932, BoE OV4/PN72.
[30] Rodd to Hopkins, 3 Nov. 1932, BoE OV4/PN72.
[31] 'Analytical Summary of the Second Meeting of the Monetary Sub-Committee', 1 Nov. 1932, LON R2671, 10A/39643/39643.

the Reich to renew its attack against the volume of state indebtedness more generally, particularly its own, although it opted to ignore the fact that the falling value of the pound and the later depreciation of the US dollar significantly reduced the amount Germany had to pay. The League secretariat was alive to the complexities of international debts, but, although host of the preparatory meetings, it had no authority to intervene on a question that brought only risk to its endeavours.

Despite the challenges, by October 1932, the Financial and Economic Sections had drafted the twelve-page preparatory agenda for the meetings, furnished more than thirty-four preparatory documents that established the narrative of the causes and course of the Great Depression, and given shape and some coherence to what were very large divergences in national policy. National differences received a thorough airing at twelve lengthy meetings of the first Preparatory Commission. At the first session, economic policy and public works were very much the poor relations to monetary policy. On the agenda for discussion was a comparison of the behaviour and fortunes of nations on and off gold, and those states that had adopted exchange control; questions pertaining to the operation of the gold standard; the role and price of silver; and an evaluation of other proposals regarding international currency systems. The second major item identified by the League was the 'level of prices', and the concept's application to gold and non-gold currencies, along with how to attain a 'desirable level'. Then came questions relating to exchange control, capital movements, the world's international financial machinery, and, finally, the relationship between financial structures and practice.[32] The challenge, as Williams put it, was for the preparatory meetings 'to discuss the problems in the spirit of experts rather than as representatives of national interests'.[33]

It was also apparent that, while all the delegates agreed that monetary policy was defined in relation to the gold standard, and that there were shortcomings in the system's operation, there was no consensus as to how these problems could be addressed. To circumvent imminent deadlock, the Financial Section proposed the early meetings of the Financial Commission be confined to a 'preliminary exchange of views', although it sought to give it direction by interjecting that the world's most powerful nations 'would have a determinant influence on general monetary development... and on the institutional arrangements for monetary co-operation'.[34] Framing the discussion in this way was as close as the section could come towards arguing that it was imperative that Britain, France, and the USA should encourage the conference to bolster the EFO's position in the architecture of international relations.

[32] 'Draft List of Financial Questions Prepared by the Financial Section', 31 Oct. 1932, LON R2671, 10A/38753/39643.
[33] Despite Williams's reputation as a staunch defender of the gold standard, he was far from uncritical, announcing that 'since the war neither of the fundamental assumptions of the gold standard had been fulfilled, i.e. there had been no flexibility in the economic system, and there had been too rapid change'. See 'Analytical Summary of the First Meeting of the Monetary Sub-Committee', 31 Oct. 1932, LON R2671, 10A/1518/39643.
[34] Draft note, 'Work of the Financial Sub-Committee of the Preparatory Committee', 4 Nov. 1933, LON R2671, 10A/38753/39643.

Questions relating to the independence of central banks, the quality of their collaboration with the BIS, and the character of cooperation between the BIS and the EFO were also on the agenda. The Financial Section called for the creation of a separate committee at the conference to consider using the limited resources of the BIS to help currencies to stay or return to gold, and to ask what greater central bank coordination and cooperation might deliver. Leon Fraser stressed that central bank cooperation was essential because of its ability to provide credit to stabilize the system, and 'above all relief credits'. He adopted a more open approach than might have been expected in his willingness to explore the limits on central banks' ability to prioritize international financial stabilization, because, as they were currently constituted, central banks were required to hold reserves against internal as well as external liabilities, which made it difficult to distinguish between reserves required for both purposes. Fraser's stress on the national and international obligations of central banks made it clear that no central bank had sufficient reserves to call 'surplus', and this fundamentally affected their ability to extend help to others in crisis. There was also widespread agreement in the expert monetary committee that it would be necessary to accept a 'new parity' to enable some currencies that had resorted to exchange control and clearing agreements to return to gold.[35]

The preparatory Monetary Commission offered up a banquet of issues so large that participants invariably had indigestion. They succumbed to offering only 'vague recommendations'. John Williams proposed an alternative approach: to arrive 'at real solutions by studying certain positions of particular importance because they implicated others, for example, the case of Germany and the Danubian countries or that of the United Kingdom and the Scandinavian countries'.[36] The idea was risky. The interwoven and at the same time increasingly detached character of the central and east European economy was a cause close to the EFO's heart, but it was also one that the British, French, and US governments, for various political reasons, did not want to engage. A detailed study of the sterling bloc had similarly awkward implications: an opportunity to put pressure on the British government to mend its 'irresponsible' ways or the chance to explore the potentialities of currency depreciation and regional coordination. Williams's suggestion, at the end of a day-long meeting, was met with stony silence by national representatives. When the commission reconvened the following day, the Europeans, led by Rist, Trip, and Phillips, responded with a coordinated statement, that the main priority must be to solve 'political and economic problems relating to inter-state debts'. Only when these debts had been 'solved' would it be possible to take 'concrete steps towards economic and financial reconstruction'.[37]

[35] 'Analytical Summary of the Fifth Meeting of the Monetary Sub-Committee', 2 Nov. 1932, LON R2671, 10A/39643/39643.

[36] For the Economic and Financial Section's role in raising the Stresa Fund and issues relating to the role of international institutions, see 'Analytical Summary of the Eighth Meeting of the Monetary Sub-Committee', 4 Nov. 1932, LON R2671, 10A/39643/39643.

[37] 'Analytical Summary of the Fifth Meeting of the Monetary Sub-Committee', 2 Nov. 1932, LON R2671, 10A/39643/39643.

An obvious question was why neither Loveday nor Stoppani supported Williams? Why was the EFO instead prepared to go along with the British war debt agenda when it was potentially toxic to European and American relations, to League–American relations, and to the prospects of the economic conference? The answer lay largely in the League's long-standing special relationship with eastern and central Europe. The recommendations of the Stresa Conference convened in September 1932 to consider the region's economic and financial conditions were put before the Preparatory Commission, along with a directing gloss by the Economic Section. In it Stoppani pointed out that the anti-depression strategy of countries with the world's stronger financial systems, notably Britain, France, and the United States, after 1930, had been to lower their interest rates (this was obviously easier for the floating pound) and to convert debts taken out on higher rates of interest to new, lower rates. He could not criticize these developments *per se*: they were voluntary and made good financial sense for the parties concerned. But it meant debtors in the wealthy West were paying much less to borrow money, 'in striking contrast to the very high rates of interest which are, or should be, paid in the international market by the poorest debtors for their old debts'. The real challenge was that 'in countries where distress is greatest—for instance, the countries of Central and Eastern Europe—in order to keep their currency on gold interest rates had to remain high and their balance of payments brought into equilibrium'. This was an impossibly tall order, given that in order to do so the prices of their exports had to rise, and, because these countries could neither obtain cheap money nor abandon gold without international support, it 'would not be possible to do very much' to help. He abruptly corrected the British Empire delegates at the meetings who declared what was needed to save the world was ' "higher prices for primary products *and* cheap money". What they meant was probably "higher prices for primary products *by* cheap money." ' (Emphases in original.)[38] It was this desire to do something about the indebtedness of states in which it had an established interest that seduced the EFO's section leaders into accepting the British line that international indebtedness needed to be reduced across the board. Without international support, this option was not open to these countries, and there was no escaping Anglo-French determination on war debts, however much the League secretariat and the Americans might wish it away.[39]

The risk of stalemate in preparations for the conference increased when the British government, in the light of the first wave of preparatory meetings in Geneva, decided to reinforce its position on debts 'to insist on the settlement of war debts first of all'.[40] It was a tactic intended to free Britain from isolation over the floating pound, and shifted some of the risk of the conference's potential failure onto the League. Nor was the danger minimized by US insistence that war debts

[38] 'First Reflections on the Preparatory Commission's Task in Regard to International Trade', 26 Oct. 1932, LON R2671, 10A/39755/38756.
[39] 'Analytical Summary of the Sixth and Seventh Meetings of the Monetary Sub-Committee', 3 Nov. 1932, LON R2671, 10A/39643/39643.
[40] Memo by Leith-Ross, 'The Prospects of the Conference', 21 Dec. 1932, TNA: PRO T177/72.

remained off the conference agenda, as it exposed the League afresh when other participating powers attempted to bring political debts back into the frame. Having secured enthusiastic American support for the conference from Hoover, and, crucially, the incoming Roosevelt, Britain now faced the danger that, if it pushed the cause of war debt reduction too hard, the USA would abandon the conference. To the secretariat, Britain's obsession with war debts, coupled with its new reluctance to discuss the performance of the gold standard regime, was further evidence of a new British irresponsibility in economic affairs.

In the winter of 1932, there was no indication of an early resolution to the issue of political debts. The next war debts payment from Britain and France fell due to the United States on 12 December, immediately after the conclusion of the first sitting of the Preparatory Commission and shortly before the second session was to convene in Geneva. Britain was due to pay $95,000,000 and the French government the considerably smaller interest-only payment of $19,216,437. Both governments anticipated that their cooperation, the world conference, and Hoover's resounding loss to his Democrat opponent had all worked to increase their leverage on Hoover's lame-duck administration. It proved to be a grave miscalculation. First, while the Anglo-French Gentleman's Agreement had delivered the Lausanne Agreement with Germany, it had weakened their individual negotiating positions with the United States. Hoover and Stimson continued to recognize, as they had at the time of the Hoover Moratorium, that Britain faced bigger economic challenges than France and had less favourable debt terms (though the situation had eased since sterling's depreciation). The French, on the other hand, had no balance of sympathy in the USA against which they might draw. Americans' frustration towards the French position on international disarmament, fresh in their minds, thanks to preparations for the League Disarmament Conference, was sharpened by a monetary policy in France that saw it accumulate increasing reserves of gold by sterilizing gold flows that came into the country. The inflow of gold bullion swelling Marianne's coffers via the operation of the gold standard meant France was not in a position to argue, as had Britain, that exporting gold to the USA to pay for its war debts would put the stability of its currency at risk. American resentment was also fed by US Treasury calculations that, while French war debts had been reduced by 50 per cent since 1926, and those of Italy (which was now clinging to Anglo-French coat-tails in the negotiations) by 68 per cent, British debts had been eased by only 18 per cent.[41] The Anglo-French Gentleman's Agreement muddied what the USA saw as the very different situations of Britain and France. The British and French, in the meantime, were equally frustrated with the USA: had it not called for European solidarity in the face of the economic crisis?

Public opinion was an additional, potent dimension to this already heady mix. The general public in the United States were understandably unwilling to release foreign debtors from their obligations when no one would set the Americans free from the burden of personal debt. In Britain, too, opinion was hardening against

---

[41] 'Interview with Hoover', 20 Apr. 1932, Mudd, Krock, Box 1, Book 1; memo by Treasury, Oct. 1932, TNA: PRO T175/76.

what was perceived to be the prioritizing of the interests of wealthy American banks ahead of British public services. In popular cartoons this perception was stained with anti-Semitism: the USA was represented by a fat Uncle Shylock or a super-sized presidential jockey (Hoover's corpulence was a gift to the European comic imagination) flogging an emaciated European horse. It was all very painful for Prime Minister Ramsay MacDonald, who for two years had sought to place 'friendship and closer co-operation' with the USA as the 'cornerstone' of his foreign policy.[42]

While British and American public opinion grumbled *sotto voce* at the other's demands, however, French public opinion was in open revolt, with disastrous consequences for Franco-American diplomatic relations. In the December negotiations, both Britain and France threatened debt default in the face of American unwillingness to offer new concessions. The French economic case was weak, but a sense of political outrage was shared across political parties, and by all sections of French society. It was directed towards the Americans who had failed to recognize the financial and material sacrifices France had made during and after the First World War, and who, with the British, had 'tricked' France into making reparation concessions to Germany through the Hoover–Laval declaration and the Gentleman's Agreement. Herriot's impassioned plea on 13 December 1932 to the Chamber of Deputies not to default and that 'developments on the other side of the Rhine might soon leave France in desperate need of powerful friends' was not enough.[43] Ten days later, France reneged on its war debts to the United States. It now became impossible for either Hoover or the incoming President Roosevelt to be seen to consort publicly with the French government. Britain stopped short of defaulting for fear of damaging the government and the City of London's international reputation as a debtor and creditor by making a token payment on its war debts to the United States pending further negotiation in 1933. After the passage of the Johnson Act in 1934, neither the French nor the British government (the act did not recognize unauthorized partial payments) was able to borrow money from the United States again. This was to have profound consequences for their diplomatic relations.

French wrangling over the war debt payment also ruptured Herriot's coalition government, and the world had to adjust again to a new Prime Minister and French cabinet, headed temporarily by the former Foreign Secretary, Joseph Paul-Boncour. Within weeks it was replaced by another radical-dominated government led by Édouard Daladier. This was the first of a new round of leadership changes at the top of governments in the winter of 1932–3. On 30 January 1933, the short-lived cabinet of Kurt von Schleicher, who had replaced the beneficiary of the Lausanne agreement Franz von Papen in November 1932, was in turn supplanted as Chancellor by Adolf Hitler. This whirling carousel of national leaders

---

[42] Granville to Simon, 6 Dec. 1932, Bodl., Western Manuscripts, Private Papers of John Simon, Simon 73; Lindsay to Simon, 10 Nov. 1932, TNA: PRO T160/417, F6677/06. For cartoons, see, e.g., Sidney 'George' Stube, *Daily Express*, cartoon campaign, 3 Mar. 1932, 21 Nov. 1932, 26 Nov. 1932, 30 Nov. 1932, 23 Jan. 1933, and 2 Nov. 1933.

[43] Clavin, *Failure of Economic Diplomacy*, 53–9.

and the acrimonious breakdown of war debt negotiations spelt new trouble for the preparations for the economic conference, and for the League. Although it was to be another three months before Roosevelt formally took charge, the very public spat over debts was unhelpful to US–League relations at a formative stage in their evolution.

For the British Treasury, however, international disagreement over war debts was a source of solace. It cracked open the united line of attack against the floating pound mustered by France, Italy, Germany, the Benelux countries, and the USA—many of whom would become members of a new 'gold bloc' at the London Conference. War debts created lines of disagreement that ran across, rather than parallel to, divisions over monetary policy and were criss-crossed again by varying perspectives on trade, commodity agreements, and public works. The behaviour of the Treasury also shattered any remaining secretariat illusions of the almost un-questioned sense of common purpose between them enjoyed in the 1920s. In a break with established League practice, it had been agreed that the Preparatory Commission could meet *in camera* to facilitate the kind of free and direct discussion that many, notably British, members of the EFO had complained was impossible to achieve in its public deliberations for fear of upsetting the markets. Chamberlain, Phillips, and Leith-Ross had supported the decision, but, in Geneva, the British members of the Preparatory Commission leaked news of each complaint over French protective quotas, central European blocked accounts, and American tariffs. Loveday and Stoppani protested bitterly to their contacts in the Foreign Office in London about the British delegation's behaviour at the meeting, but glossed over their irritation to the wider world with the well-honed skill for dissemblance of the international civil servant. The general public, they announced, was not worried by the details of disagreement, but rather heartened by the spirit of cooperation that the Geneva meeting itself demonstrated. But, in reality, the public took a different view, its imagination embittered by what was now perceived as the disintegration of economic internationalism. Privately, Loveday and Stoppani shared public appre-hension about the depth of disagreement. After a decade of battling to facilitate international economic and financial negotiations, they knew the devil was in the detail, and the number of demons they faced was multiplying.[44]

RESPONSIBILITY WITHOUT POWER

The first Preparatory Commission for the World Economic Conference had certainly helped to clarify national positions, but it was also manifest that states' priorities differed so markedly there was no obvious policy territory on which agreement could be built in time for the main event. To resolve this, the conference Organizing Committee agreed that the second session of the Preparatory Commis-sion should focus on publishing an annotated agenda on which to base the

---

[44] Memo by Stoppani, 'Instructions relatives à la prochaine session de la commission préparatoire d'experts', 19 Nov. 1932, LON R2671, 10A/38756/38756.

conference discussions, rather than a series of 'pious resolutions which no one intends to carry out'.[45] The move pushed the responsibility for the next stage squarely onto EFO's secretariat, which was charged with providing the annotations for the *ordre du jour annoté* by the final week of January 1933. The change produced an immediate role reversal between national delegates on the Preparatory Committee and the secretariat: the former supplying details on national monetary and economic policy as required by the League, with the secretariat teasing out areas of possible agreement and drafting the agenda. The secretariat knew its hand in defining the agenda of the conference was strengthened by this decision, but also that it had no new authority to affect agreement other than the power of rational suasion.[46]

National experts were almost unanimous in their relief at their demotion, and offered few new materials or concrete proposals at the second meeting. There were two notable exceptions: the first was Leith-Ross, whose long-standing personal connections to Loveday and unique role bridging the Treasury, the Board of Trade, and the Foreign Office meant he was seen to be to some degree independent of Chamberlain. He offered extensive and influential criticism of Loveday's draft of the monetary side of the agenda that privileged the deflationary case.[47] The American expert delegation was the second. It wanted the secretariat to make a clear statement in favour of the new administration's professed interest in trade liberalization.[48] The secretariat were sympathetic, delaying the next schedule meeting in Geneva for as long as possible to allow the Americans time to prepare, at the request of John Foster Dulles, future Secretary of State to the State Department, a businessman with extensive European connections and a member of the American delegation in Geneva.[49] The second meeting of the Preparatory Commission was pushed back as far as was practicable, to 9 January, and the secretariat was heartened to learn that, owing to unprecedented exchanges between Stimson and Roosevelt, 'some measure of understanding' was effected that would enable the USA 'to share effectively in the work' of the Second Commission.[50] Although these encounters between the Republican and Democrat administrations have generally been seen as domestic in origin, much of their original impetus lay in the urging of the EFO's secretariat and the American internationalists who supported it.[51]

When the Preparatory Commission reconvened in Geneva, the secretariat had barely ten days to secure the delegates' approval of the annotated agenda so that it

[45] Leith-Ross to Stoppani, 20 Oct. 1932, LON R2671, 10A/39421/38756.
[46] Minute by Loveday, 2 Dec. 1932, LON R2671, 10A/39421/38756.
[47] This did not go unnoticed by the BIS. 'Aide-Memoire for Discussion in Governors' Meeting on 11th December 1932', BIS, 7.18(4), HUL 6.
[48] Davis to Stimson, 8 Dec. 1932, NARA RG59 550.S1/386.
[49] Note by Stencek, 'Record of Telephonic Conversation with Mr Dulles', 9 Dec. 1932, LON R2671, 10A/39421/38756.
[50] Day to Stoppani, 27 Dec. 1932, LON R2671, 10A/39421/38756.
[51] See, e.g., Herbert Feis, *Nineteen Thirty Three: Characters in Crisis* (New York, 1966), 79–86; Robert Dallek, *Franklin D. Roosevelt and American Foreign Policy, 1932–1945* (New York, 1979), 35–44; David M. Kennedy, *Freedom from Fear: The American People in Depression and War, 1929–1945* (Oxford, 1999), 105–59.

could be presented to the conference organizers in time for their meeting of 25 January 1933. Stoppani gave the project direction in two critical respects. First, he impressed upon his young colleagues in the Economic and Financial Sections who were drafting the annotated agenda, and the national representatives of the commission who had to approve it, that they were living in extraordinary times. The central issue, therefore, was to identify certain provisional and 'modest, necessary' targets for international policy coordination and cooperation to which most nations could agree. 'The best way to promote long-term developments', he argued at the second session of the Preparatory Commission, 'was to concentrate on immediate necessities.' Here the 'whole economic history of the United Kingdom' was the model to emulate, for it proved 'the advantages of concentrating on the needs of the moment'. Although Stoppani decided not to comment on whether the depreciation of sterling fitted into his evaluation of the reflexive British economic model, the second meeting of the Preparatory Commission was certainly much less preoccupied with the consequences of the floating pound than the first. This time, the discussion of the sterling bloc was more nuanced. Norway, thanks to the spirited interventions of Gunnar Jahn, a statistician, economist, and future finance minister and governor of its central bank led the way. He was a vocal supporter of the floating pound who emphasized that the 'experience of Norway, as a member of the sterling group almost from the first, was distinctly more encouraging than that of many countries still on gold'. Its mercantile marine, the fourth largest in the world after Britain, the USA, and Japan, was thriving, and, while there was a 'certain percentage of unemployment in Norway, it was nothing in comparison with the percentages of some of the countries that had stayed on gold'. But Norway still favoured an eventual return to gold, the date of which would depend on British policy. Jahn's intervention helped facilitate a general momentum around the EFO's view that it was essential for the agenda to concentrate on a few key points and not a far-reaching programme, for 'that way danger lay'.[52]

Stoppani set the tone. The secretariat was determined to use the annotated agenda not simply as a document around which to organize a world conference, but as a wider framework to shape the League's efforts to improve the rapport between nations and the prospects of economic and monetary coordination. The objective was to stabilize the current situation, so that over time the alpine barriers now ranged across the global economy could be rolled back. Stoppani argued that it was pointless to argue about whether quotas, prohibitive levels of duty, licences, or surtaxes were more damaging; all affected international trade in different ways. He wanted large nations to engage with League efforts to unclog international trade in the search for what he called a 'new middle way' beyond a 'completely rigid most-

---

[52] 'Monetary and Economic Conference. Preparatory Commission of Experts. Second Session. Provisional Minutes of the Fourth Meeting', 10 Jan. 1933, LON R4637, 10D/608/3821. For an introduction into Jahn's wide-ranging involvement in the League's work, see his entry, *NSD PolSys— Data om det politiske system*, 'Biografier 1905–1945 Gunnar Jahn' http://www.nsd.uib.no/polsys/ index.cfm? urlname=polsys&lan=&MenuItem=N1_1&ChildItem=&State=collapse&UttakNr=33& person=18066 (accessed 10 Oct. 2009). The sterling bloc grew more attractive, because it was demonstrably well managed through the operations of the Exchange Equalization Account.

favoured-nations system', although he remained dangerously ignorant of how price-fixing agreements on a global scale could work against the interests of small producers.[53]

The purpose of the conference should not be the 'unrealistic' quest for a tariff-free world, but rather to help move towards that which had existed before the financial crises of 1931, a world premised on a system of 'simple custom duties'. Nor should it demand that producer agreements be abandoned outright—notably commodity agreements relating to wheat, coal, dyestuffs, and meat. His central message was that, before the summer of 1931, international trade in peacetime, for all the talk directed against producer agreements and tariffs, had functioned as satisfactorily as might have been expected, but the situation had been changed fundamentally by the banking crises of 1931. From that moment onwards, 'the machinery of finance and currency was more or less out of gear', and it was essential that the League ensure states did not allow the search for a perfect outcome to get in the way of a good one. For Stoppani, 'the return to liberty of trading constitutes the *adequate* operation which must of necessity accompany the repair of the monetary machinery' (emphasis in original).[54] This tolerance for protection, while simultaneously arguing for its reduction, set up an inherent tension in League economic policy at the world conference and beyond, which saw it arguing for tariff reductions, on the one hand, and facilitating the agreement of producer agreements, on the other.

From this assessment came Stoppani's second essential contribution to the history of the conference: the Preparatory Commission should propose a stabilization of trade relations by some means—the idea was later widened to encompass currency fluctuations—that would freeze the world in a distinct moment to ensure the present situation could not deteriorate any further. From this stable foundation, there would then be a chance to build.[55] The idea was hardly novel. It had been introduced at the World Economic Conference of 1927 but had withered on the vine by 1931. In 1927, Britain had been one of its chief supporters, but, through the introduction of its General Tariff and then imperial preference in 1932, Britain became not only one of the last countries to abandon the truce, but also one of the first to lodge its opposition to a new one. Imperial preference also opened up the thorny question of exceptions to the tariff truce, or 'Prohibitions Convention' as it was known formally, which in 1927 related to coal, dyestuffs, and scrap iron agreed largely between European producers.[56] Imperial preference agreements between Britain and imperial producers agreed at the Ottawa Conference added a

[53] Note by Stoppani, 'First Reflections on the Preparatory Commission's Task in Regard to International Trade', 26 Oct. 1932, p. 18, LON R2671, 10A/39755/38756.

[54] Note by Stoppani, 'First Reflections on the Preparatory Commission's Task in Regard to International Trade', 26 Oct. 1932, pp. 6–8, LON R2671, 10A/39755/38756.

[55] Note by Stoppani, 'First Reflections on the Preparatory Commission's Task in Regard to International Trade', 26 Oct. 1932, pp. 6–8, LON R2671, 10A/39755/38756. Memo by Stoppani, 'Instructions relatives à la prochaine session de la commission préparatoire d'experts', 19 Nov. 1932, LON R2671, 10A/38756/38756.

[56] The production and trade in these commodities and the agreements surrounding them were the subject of extensive study by the League.

significant level of complexity, because these countries now reserved the right to safeguard their newly agreed quotas on primary products, primarily meat and grain.[57] Stoppani and his colleagues believed this was a problematic, but not an insurmountable, obstacle. Britain's commitment to free trade, now consigned to history, had shaped both the League and Britain's relationship to it. At the same time, in the mind of League officials, Britain was 'spatially and intellectually semi-detached' in its trade relations, for it looked 'partly to Europe and partly to the various parts of its Empire which are scattered all over the world'.[58] The diversity of its interests and the degree to which its economy remained dependent on international trade made it special. Although Britain was no longer committed to free trade, it certainly recognized the advantages of freer trade, and it might be easier to facilitate international negotiations now that the British government, too, had protectionist weapons in its arsenal. The EFO did not fall into the trap that has ensnared some historians of conflating British economic nationalism with its entire commercial and financial policy. After 1931, trade policy and sterling operations were certainly less high-minded than in the heyday of *Pax Britannica*, but the volume and variety of British trading and currency operations still gave it unrivalled global influence.[59]

The Economic Section's sanguine approach to what effectively marked the end of British leadership in the League on questions of economic liberalism was also shaped by the attitude of the United States. The new administration's enthusiasm for freer trade gave the League a new national hook on which to hang its commitment for liberal trade to general and multilateral tariff reductions for the World Economic Conference in particular. It was also facilitated by a significant personal link between Geneva and Washington during the transition from one administration to the next in the shape of Norman Davis, the long-serving US delegate to the Geneva Disarmament Conference. A southern Democrat, Davis, like Secretary of State-elect Hull, had an established interest in free trade.

By January 1933, diplomatic chatter in Europe and Central and South America about the incoming administration's trade policy merged with Stoppani's revival of the tariff truce, to generate an expectation that the USA would sponsor a tariff truce for the world conference before moving to initiate multilateral tariff negotiations. Viewing this development from Geneva rather than Washington brings out the League's central role in shaping and facilitating the initiative. It was Stoppani who helped the American representatives in Geneva and Washington frame their generally articulated interest in trade liberalization into a proposal to inaugurate a tariff truce. The secretariat also worked on Argentina, the Netherlands, and

---

[57] The Economic Section mistakenly thought British reservations would apply to meat exports only rather than the full range of goods covered by imperial preference.

[58] Note by Stoppani, 'First Reflections on the Preparatory Commission's Task in Regard to International Trade', 26 Oct. 1932, LON R2671, 10A/39755/38756. This emerged as a key theme in the work of Tim Rooth, *British Protectionism and the International Economy: Overseas Commercial Policy in the 1930s* (Cambridge, 1993), and David Edgerton, *Britain's War Machine. Weapons, Resources and Experts in the Second World War* (London, 2011).

[59] Rooth, *British Protectionism*, 99–144.

Norway to stoke up international interest and remind the USA and Britain that 'big powers would make or mar the conference'.[60]

In the draft annotated agenda, the Economic Section set out the various means by which protectionist schemes could be dismantled: universal percentage reductions, regional agreements, bilateral negations, and even autonomous action by a single government. But the needs of significant groups of producers were also recognized.[61] By granting exceptions to key commodities such as coal, wheat, and meat, it would be possible, Stoppani argued, 'for large groups of countries, which are determined to lower barriers to trade among themselves, to frame agreements to that end' without one 'single non-participatory country' that enjoyed most-favoured rights with one of the group impeding negotiations. Stoppani's proposal, with the predictable dissention of Germany and Italy, found wide favour in the Preparatory Commission.

In 1933, governments around the world were unaware of Geneva's subtle moves in shaping the presentation of US trade policy on the international stage, and this was exactly how Stoppani wanted it.[62] He frequently exchanged his ideas with Davis, Day, and Williams. The signs for an American lead on trade looked positive in January 1933, when President-Elect Roosevelt established a new committee to coordinate the development of US policy at the League's World Economic Conference and to represent the USA at the conference under Hull's leadership. The committee, in a fashion that was to typify the contradictory character of the New Deal, comprised departments and interest groups with very different visions for the development of US economic, financial, and foreign policy. It was chaired by James P. Warburg, a New York banker with well-established links to Europe, who was joined by Davis, Sackett, Feis, and members of Roosevelt's Brains Trust, including Raymond Moley and the new Assistant Secretary of State for Agriculture, Rexford Tugwell.[63] During the lifetime of the committee, old-style central banker diplomacy confronted state department enthusiasm for freer trade, and the New Dealers' emphasis on the primacy of price inflation and domestic recovery.

But, at first, the eclectic character of Roosevelt's conference committee was lost on observers overseas in Geneva, London, Paris, Rome, and Berlin. What stood out for them was the continuity of US representation in Geneva—notably that Davis remained in post. It was seen as an apparent indicator both of his importance, and that the USA had taken up the call for a tariff truce sponsored by the League of Nations. It meant the European governments had to take American claims of a new internationalism seriously, especially as they were accompanied by Davis's repeated assertions that the truce was merely a prelude to a bold US initiative on

---

[60] 'Monetary and Economic Conference: Preparatory Commission of Experts. Second Session. Provisional Minutes of the Fourth Meeting', LON R4637, 10D/608/3821.

[61] 'Monetary and Economic Conference. Preparatory Commission of Experts. Economic Sub-Committee. Draft Report', 17 Jan. 1933, LON R4637, 10D/1070/735.

[62] Stoppani, 'First Reflections on the Preparatory Commission's Task in Regard to International Trade', 26 Oct. 1932, pp. 8–12, 25–31, LON R2671, 10A/39755/38756.

[63] Day and Williams were unhappy at this turn of events. See Warburg, Diary Entry, Butler Warburg, vol. 1, 22 Jan. 1933, p. 86.

tariffs. The German Foreign Ministry was particularly perturbed by the danger that the economic conference had awoken the USA from 'its dormant pose of economic isolation' and might prompt greater involvement in European affairs, a development that would be deeply unwelcome.[64] More troubling still for the wider ambitions of the revisionist powers was the spectre of US internationalism reinvigorated through the agency of the League, especially if the tariff truce revived British liberalism, triggering a joint Anglo-American initiative to break down tariff walls as a prelude to more effective Anglo-American cooperation in preparations for the Geneva Disarmament Conference.

Two developments heightened German fears of a new cooperative tenor in British, French, and American relations facilitated by the secretariat. The first was that Loveday found a formulation on monetary stability for the annotated agenda that everyone could accept. The annotated agenda called for the conference participants, 'especially larger countries', on gold to declare their intention of 'pursuing a policy of low money rates and liberal credit such as to permit a rise in wholesale prices to take place', while authorities in countries on paper standards would 'endeavour to maintain their exchange within certain defined limits, at least as regards any downward movements'. Loveday's framing of the problem remained overtly orthodox: the absence of inflation since 1924 by returning to gold was an achievement of which the 'responsible authorities might feel justifiably proud'. But it was also critical: the return to gold 'in the last ten years had hardly been a great success'; and advantages the sterling area had enjoyed since abandoning gold were not denied.[65]

This formulation united the divergent monetary policies of those committed to gold, and central banks and governments that had abandoned it in search of higher prices, cheaper money, and greater budgetary flexibility. It became the basis for a temporary stabilization agreement to be negotiated between the major central banks for the duration of the conference, and was the monetary equivalent to Stoppani's tariff truce, intended to stabilize currency fluctuations while negotiations proceeded to matters of substance.[66] But, instead of anchoring negotiations, it became the rock against which the conference famously foundered.

THE WASHINGTON PRELUDE

The second outcome of Davis's intimacy with Stoppani and Loveday, and the cooperative tenor of discussions at the second Preparatory Commission in Geneva, was Roosevelt's decision of 20 January 1933 to invite the British delegation to

---

[64] US protectionism legitimated the Reichsbank's charge that Germany could not gain sufficient access to the US market to earn dollars to pay off loan obligations that in reality the Nazis had no intention of honouring. See Posse to Ritter, 14 Jan. 1933, TNA: PRO GFM 33/1231, 3177/D84055.

[65] 'Monetary and Economic Conference. Preparatory Commission of Experts. Monetary Sub-Commission, Draft Report (Revised)', 16 Jan. 1933, LON R4637, 10D/871/675.

[66] Patricia Clavin, '"The Fetishes of So-Called International Bankers": Central Bank Cooperation for the World Economic Conference, 1932–3', *Contemporary European History*, 1/3 (1992), 281–311.

Washington to discuss trade, stabilization, and war debts. Davis suggested a number of times to Roosevelt that he should come to Europe, to support the work of the Preparatory Commission and to attend the world conference. Although tempted, FDR believed that he was needed at home and that any concession he might offer in a European setting, as his old friend Frankfurter (yet another of Roosevelt's circle who was widely known in Geneva) advised him, would be perceived as one that 'those clever devils in Europe had hornswoggled from you'.[67] FDR's response, much to British chagrin, was to widen the invitation to all European, Asian, and Latin American countries participating in the conference to come to see him in Washington.

The British perspective on the invitation was telling. MacDonald was enthusiastic about the prospect, especially as FDR had moved the goalposts from expert to ministerial talks. Either unknowing or uncomprehending of foreign-policy differences between the two administrations, MacDonald was excited by the prospect of helping to present the new President 'before Congress as a man making a concerted attack on the difficulties of the economic situation with the British government beside him'.[68] Neither Chamberlain, the Treasury, nor the Board of Trade aspired to such lofty dreams. FDR's enthusiasm for the conference made them nervous.[69] It scuppered any last prospect that the conference would meet during Hoover's presidency, and the chance that he would make concessions on war debts, a move far less likely of the new incumbent. There was also the danger the intergovernmental dimension would highlight transatlantic divisions over currency and trade.

FDR's decision to invite the French government next was by no means without political risks for him, given the French default of its war debts that December. Daladier helped by nominating his predecessor Herriot as his representative, and the dangers to FDR were borne out when Georges Bonnet and Chamberlain publically reaffirmed their loyalty to the Lausanne Agreement and scepticism as to the USA's proclaimed commitment to lower tariffs shortly before arriving in Washington.[70]

League officials, on the other hand, were encouraged by FDR's adoption of the League agenda as a programme for diplomatic action in Washington, but could only look on powerlessly that spring, as one foreign visit after another to the White House failed to bear diplomatic fruit. The British delegation (MacDonald and Leith-Ross) were the first of eleven foreign missions received by FDR, most of whom, like FDR's British visitors, were regulars at the League meetings. Canada, China, Japan, Chile, Mexico, Brazil, Argentina, and France all sent special

[67] Frankfurter to Roosevelt, 12 Nov. 1932, LC, Frankfurter Reel 60.

[68] Committee Meeting, 6 Feb. 1933, TNA: PRO Cab 27/548; Lothian to Simon, 16 Feb. 1933, Bodl., Western Manuscripts, Private Papers of John Simon, Simon 2.

[69] MacDonald to Baldwin, 23 Mar. 1933, ULC, Baldwin 121.

[70] The French visit to London and the publicity surrounding it were orchestrated by Chamberlain. See Clavin, *Failure of Economic Diplomacy*, 82–3. Personal relations between FDR and Chamberlain were forever poisoned by these early exchanges. D. C. Watt, *Personalities and Policies: Studies in the Formulation of British Foreign Policy in the Twentieth Century* (Notre Dame, IN, 1965), 40–52.

delegations, and there were thirty additional special ambassadorial meetings with representatives from Austria, Romania, Poland, and Norway to discuss the anno- tated agenda.[71] The agenda for cooperation may have originated with the League secretariat, but it was not there to help direct the meetings, and as it stood the agenda offered too broad a menu to serve as the basis for the bilateral encounters between the US executive and its foreign visitors. There was also scope to discuss issues beyond the remit of the League, notably war debts.

Intergovernmental relations now moved in directions that were harmful gen- erally to the prospects for the conference and therefore for the League, especially as the atmosphere began to deteriorate between Britain, France, and the United States—the great 'liberal' powers upon whom League fortunes depended. On 19 April, the financial world was rocked by the news that FDR had decided to take the US dollar off the gold standard. Speculation that the new President would take this step had flourished since his election, fuelled in particular by the dramatic fall in US primary prices (farm commodities alone were valued at 40.6 per cent of their levels in 1926), and the long-standing difficulties faced by US domestic banks, which were failing in their thousands.[72] FDR's bold decision to float the dollar inspired confidence in the market and captured the imagination of the general public. Britain and its associated sterling bloc countries declared they had been 'forced' from gold because of the speculative pressures on their reserves, but gold stocks in the Federal Reserve System remained around $4,000 million.[73]

Over the next months, the dollar's value dropped by some 40 per cent, inflating domestic prices and providing the USA with an overseas trading advantage similar to that which Britain had begun to enjoy some eighteen months earlier. Interest rates fell, making the prospect of renewed borrowing at home, if not overseas, a more realistic possibility. FDR's assertive measures to stabilize the US banking system at the same time increased the likelihood that banks would also be in a position to lend, and the President was now freed from the budgetary strictures of the gold standard regime. (The size of the American deficit remained modest, never rising above $3.5 billion until the United States began the drive to rearm in 1938.[74]) The reality of FDR's cautious approach to government spending, and the very vocal complaints of financiers and investors who feared a weaker dollar, demonstrated that, while the orthodoxy of the gold standard no longer reigned supreme, the rationale that underpinned it still had an intellectual and political value for powerful groups in the national economy. Paradoxically, the rousing economic effects of the US dollar and the sterling bloc reinforced their perspective as to the power of the market—in this case money markets—to shape economic outcomes. In stepping in to liberate

---

[71] That FDR and the State Department were using a League agenda as the basis for these discussions has been hitherto obscured.

[72] In 1931 alone, 2,291 banks had collapsed. See Elmus Wicker, *The Banking Panics of the Great Depression* (New York, 1996).

[73] *The Economist*, 22 Apr. 1933.

[74] For a useful tabulation, see Peter Fearon, 'Hoover, Roosevelt and American Economic Policy during the 1930s', in W. R. Garside (ed.), *Capitalism in Crisis: International Responses to the Great Depression* (London, 1993), 141.

the nation state from the effects of gold standard orthodoxy, FDR also strengthened the power of markets (not central bankers) to challenge the will of the state. Chamberlain was to learn this lesson anew when speculative pressure weakened sterling and threatened to sabotage Britain's efforts to rearm after 1937.

The international reaction to FDR's move was similarly mixed. Stoppani and Loveday recognized the unprecedented intellectual and practical impact of the administration of the world's largest economy adopting currency depreciation as a policy to fight depression. Business communities in the sterling area, for example, argued that a carefully managed dollar devaluation would boost the global economy as American demand, particularly for primary imports, would revive. Trade unionists, too, recognized that national economies might suffer some disadvantages in the short term, but the power of the rising American tide had the potential to lift most economies from the slough of depression, and improve the conditions of the working man. Inside the gold bloc, on the other hand, these perspectives were less clear cut. Export-oriented industries in France could profit if American demand revived, but were more likely to lose out to American producers, as the exchange rate of the French franc remained tied to gold. For most constituents of the French political economy in 1933, the psychology of the gold standard order, and the social, political, and economic order it conveyed, remained potent. It was a pattern mirrored in other gold states.

Not that the various interests that comprised the political economies within (and across) countries had much time to formulate their view or find the necessary diplomatic language to give it expression. When the depreciation of the dollar was announced, assorted heads of state, or their representatives, were on board ship, bobbing across the Atlantic on their way to meet the President. Two days later, on 21 April, the first to arrive were MacDonald and Herriot. Planned ceremonies of welcome were hastily cancelled.[75] MacDonald's line, supplied by the British Treasury and advisers at the Bank of England, was cautious. The British government was not interested, as some trade unionists and economists such as Keynes suggested, in coordinating its monetary policy with the USA.

For those still committed to gold, of course, the turn of events had more threatening implications. The Italian government was quick to imagine an 'Anglo-Saxon' conspiracy designed to sabotage the stability of the gold bloc. Hitler's government declined to offer an official response but was privately fearful that FDR had re-energized Anglo-French solidarity, exemplified by the Gentleman's Agreement on war debts. The response of the French press was as frenzied as the Italian, even if the French government managed a more balanced diplomacy, which sought to elicit details of when the USA might return to gold rather than to condemn the move and its author outright. The prospect of imminent debt talks in Washington instilled discipline in Daladier's cabinet and the Bank of France, who were anxious to ensure that the already poor tenor of Franco-American relations was not soured further by intemperate claims. It was easier said than done,

---

[75] Leith-Ross, Frederick, *Money Talks: Fifty Years of International Finance: The Autobiography of Sir Frederick Leith-Ross* (London, 1968), 160–1.

however. Speculative pressure on the gold franc had already begun to mount, and within the week the French government sought to arrange a £30 million loan from the Bank of England. The step provided a new means to reinforce the ties between the fate of the French franc and British banks (as they had between British finance and German loans to potent effect after 1931). Indeed, what French statesmen called 'the vulgarization of sterling' remained a greater focus of French ire than the floating dollar, given that eighteen months on, despite the improvement in their fortunes, members of the sterling bloc showed no signs of returning to gold.

Over time the diplomatic encounters mediated or facilitated by the League were important to changing attitudes towards the gold standard. Policy lessons were acquired, not from learned texts or discrete tutorials in economics in a domestic setting, so much as from the hustle and bustle of intergovernmental and transnational encounters. Thanks to the agency of the League, the years from 1930 to 1933 were thick with them, and, although these exchanges mostly laid bare disagreements, out of them views were made plain, experience distilled, and policy choices emerged. The process was exemplified by the move of the French arch defender of the gold franc at the Preparatory Commission in 1932, Paul Reynaud, to favour devaluation by early 1934.[76] Actors were watching and learning from one another, imagining potential economic and political futures in the longer term.

But the ties of the past were not easily undone, especially the emotional and moral obligations of the First World War and the bonds they had produced. The dissolution of war debts was the prize the Europeans hoped to take from Washington, with the prospective economic conference acting as the lever. But the week-long negotiations on debts left the affair unresolved, frustrating both Leith-Ross and Herriot. Instead, the White House and the array of American office-holders and special advisers fielded by the President referred time and again to the League's draft annotated agenda for the conference as the basis for their discussions. Uncoupled from Loveday and Stoppani's direction, the agenda unleashed a medley of ideas and desires between those who wanted the League to support a move to economic liberalism (the State Department), and those who wanted the focus to be better conditions for primary producers (New Dealers and members of the Brains Trust). The apparent absence of coherence among the American negotiators was not lost on British or French representatives, nor on observers in Geneva who sought to make sense of the new administration and its foreign policy; nor was what Chamberlain labelled continued American 'intransigence' on war debts, which, from the British perspective, undermined the value of the conference. The League officials in Geneva had to put on a brave face and clung to a vision of a reinvigorated US internationalism. After all, the White House had consulted the secretariat as to whom it should invite to Washington that spring and had adopted the two main policy plans devised by Stoppani and Loveday: to stabilize international trade

---

[76] Mouré, *The Gold Standard Illusion*, 209–11.

relations through a tariff truce, on the one hand, and floating currencies via a temporary stabilization agreement, on the other.

FDR and the State Department used League memoranda as a means to resolve the war debt imbroglio by proposing a 'general initiative' that traded war debts against a reduction in British tariffs or French quotas. When this failed, Warburg developed a complex new scheme, nicknamed 'the Bunny', which exchanged debt amelioration against currency stabilization, at least on a *de facto* or temporary basis.[77] This scheme, and there were others, involved trading armaments for debt reductions and was the logical outcome of an attempt to reduce the range of issues opened up by the League's economic and disarmament conferences into some sort of 'manageable' concentration. This notion made sense only on a very superficial level, given the complexities of linking debts, protectionism, unmanaged currency depreciation, blocked exchange systems, and a mounting arms race. The President was desperate to show Congress that any concessions made to European powers on debts offered some advantages to the USA. In his April meetings, FDR implored the British and French delegations to recognize the domestic pressures that his extensive legislative programme placed on his relations with Congress and the centrality of public opinion to US foreign policy.

But the British and French governments faced urgent claims imposed by their own constellation of domestic interest groups and imperial and international obligations, which could not be jettisoned easily. FDR's generalizing approach did not match the Europeans' painstaking preparations on debts (and their absence of preparation on trade). To them, his stance betrayed an impatience to settle world affairs so he could turn his attention back to American concerns. For the European statesmen, the possibility of agreement lay in the detail, and FDR had no time for details. By the same token, this preoccupation with specificity meant MacDonald and Herriot missed the novelty of FDR's renewed engagement with international affairs, given that his election had focused solely on the USA's domestic problems.

In February and March 1933, Loveday's call for a temporary stabilization agreement in the annotated agenda also prompted a new series of meetings between central bankers and finance ministers. Although the context of these meetings had been dramatically transformed by the USA's new monetary policy, Loveday's formulation allowed the USA to move comfortably from the gold-backed camp to that of floating currencies in a pact in which governments and central banks of floating currencies would agree to maintain currency movements within agreed limits, while countries with gold-backed currencies declared their intention to lower interest rates and liberalize credit and gold movements. But the plans of central bankers' themselves had been thrown into disarray by the dollar's flotation. The BIS was forced to abandon its proposed convention on central banking, Governors Harrison and Moret ditched schemes for a joint declaration on gold policy, and Warburg gave up detailed proposals for coordinating currency

---

[77] Memo by Warburg, June 1933, FDR PSF, Diplomatic Grt Britain.

movements between the world's three major currencies. Talk of an international stabilization fund also floundered.

It proved impossible to come up with a deal in Washington. Loveday's formulation remained the basis of negotiations, but these were out of his hands and in those of treasury officials and bankers. Both he and Stoppani were disappointed at the discord in Anglo-American monetary relations, when it should now have been easier to effect cooperation. Dollar depreciation at last offered the chance to break out of the familiar League pattern: the 'smaller powers' spoke out in favour of concerted action through the League, and the 'big powers' stood in their way. There was more promise when it came to trade relations. Far from abandoning the tariff truce, as the British officials had hoped, all the White House's bilateral meetings underlined American commitment to the scheme. The administration hoped the truce would give a 'psychological boost to world trade' and externally and internally strengthen Hull's hand in sustaining FDR's support for his planned Reciprocal Tariff Agreement Act (RTAA).[78] From this a wider regional engagement, notably with Central and South America, and global engagement could follow. The challenge for Hull was that the depreciation of the dollar had introduced a new element of uncertainty. To his frustration it was the British who repeatedly pointed out to him and FDR, though not to gold bloc countries who were its victims, that currency depreciation was an indirect form of protectionism. It was doubly irritating, for Hull had hoped to secure his first reciprocal agreement to cut tariffs with Britain.[79] The implications of British reluctance to sign the truce were not confined to Anglo-American relations. The authorship of the tariff freeze, unlike the stabilization agreement, lay with the League, and it was there under the auspices of the final meeting of the Organizing Committee, convened in April 1933, that League agency succeeded where FDR and Hull had failed.

FINAL PREPARATIONS

On the same day that Herriot and MacDonald bade farewell to Roosevelt in Washington, the Organizing Committee met at the Foreign Office in London. Ignoring Avenol's advice to proceed slowly, the section directors' relief at reassuming some level of control over the event was palpable.[80] With little over six weeks remaining, and with London, and not Geneva, the venue, there was much to do. Although the British government was giving some assistance, notably its document production service, which undertook to print the voluminous papers required by the League and national delegates in English and French, the majority of administrative support came from the League. Within short order, Loveday and in particular Stoppani ensured that 144 League employees were transported and

---

[78] Hull to Davis, 5 May 1933, NARA RG59 500.S1/729.
[79] Davis to Hull, 13 May 1933, NARA RG59 500.S1/769.
[80] Carr to League of Nations, 19 Apr. 1933, and Stencek to Loveday, 1 Apr. 1933, LON R4637, 10D/997/997.

accommodated in London. Photographs of the conference halls and the world's newsmen went on to record an all-male event, but almost 70 per cent of the League delegation was made up of women.

Staff with skills in foreign language, economics, and statistics were scarce and in especially high demand. Stoppani had turned down an offer from the International Filene and Finlay Translator System company for free installation and use of its technology to facilitate simultaneous translation into delegates' native languages. Instead, special emphasis was placed on French as the second language of the conference. The French-language competence of the British Foreign Office was not regarded as adequate, and the League supplemented its own staff with additional translators and readers from the Imprimerie Nationale Paris.

The League's specialist equipment, including French keyboard typewriters, travelled by van, and its support staff by train, and senior staff—the Secretary-General Stoppani, Loveday, and Sweetser—made their way by car. Accommodation was similarly stratified. Avenol and the senior officials stayed at the South Kensington Hotel, and their staff in boarding houses across central and west London to cut overheads. Parsimony and propriety were uppermost in the official mind. Loveday's and Stoppani's entertainment allowance was the princely sum of £5.00 a day; Sweetser, responsible for liaising with the world's press, had £12.00 a day to spend. Times were tough, and it was neither seemly nor possible for the League to be lavish. Every telephone call and every bus ticket was carefully itemized, and there was much wrangling with the British government, whose cost-tracking was much less extensive or efficient than the League's, over who was responsible for picking up the bill for the conference. The agreed formula was that the League would calculate what it would have cost to host the event in Geneva and pay this to the Cabinet Office. The British government would then pay the remainder, including the cost of transporting almost a third of the secretariat to London.[81]

The cost and the stakes for the League were rising. Junior officials frantically worked on the practical arrangements; last-minute instructions about the need to wear morning dress to honour the King at the inaugural ceremony were issued; Stoppani drafted the opening speech for the British King—an exceptional task for a League official. But a much greater challenge in the time left was finding a basis on which the secretariat could advance the conference agenda among the participating powers. In its desperation to stabilize international economic relations, ameliorate the conditions of the world economy for producers and consumers, and sustain, if not enhance, the legitimacy of their own agency, Stoppani and Loveday continued to attempt to drive policy in two directions, now that monetary relations were not

---

[81] The final account of the conference, compiled in May 1934, itemized and totalled British expenditure at £26,184 and that of the League (excluding preparatory meetings) at 184,850 Swiss F. See 'Statement of Cost of the Monetary and Economic Conference', 7 Aug. 1934, LON R4633, 10D/1261/597. When it came to paying what was owed to the British government, the issue of the pound's appreciation between 1933 and 1934 was a sensitive one. The League insisted in paying up its account at the 1933 exchange rate of 17.808 Swiss F. to the pound, which meant that Britain paid more than twice as much as the League.

up for discussion in London: a tariff freeze and producers' agreements on dairy products, wine, timber, coal, and copper.[82]

The tariff truce had become the big ticket item. On 29 April at the organizing meeting in London, Davis reasserted both FDR's commitment to the truce despite the lukewarm international response to date, and the determination of the American delegation to present the truce as its own to the conference; it would, in effect, become the London meeting's first positive and concrete act of agreement. (It should be remembered there were no other proposals on the table.) Far from abandoning the truce in the face of international opposition, the USA reasserted its determination. Davis, with Stoppani's support, attempted to push members of the Organizing Committee one step further by proposing that they should put their energy behind it by passing a resolution emphasizing their conviction as to the 'urgency' and 'essential' quality of the truce by committing their governments to its terms with immediate effect.[83] Uproar followed. The Belgian and Norwegian delegates liked the idea, but de Fleuriau, Leopold von Hoesch, Dino Grandi, and Tsunco Matsudaira, representing the French, German, Italian, and Japanese governments respectively, denounced Davis's flagrant attempt to turn the committee into a lobby for a particular initiative. Hoesch, Grandi, and Matsudaira did not care if they fell out with the Americans. The situation was more painful for de Fleuriau, because it compromised French relations with the Economic and Financial Sections. Davis's reassurance that 'the proposal was not put forward by the United States government with any selfish idea, but wholly with the idea of making the conference a success', fell on deaf ears.[84] No government, as the Americans had hoped, abandoned protectionist measures that were already in train and most signed up with a long list of reservations to cover trade restrictions that were in the process of being ratified.

Many took their lead from the British government. Much to MacDonald's embarrassment, while he assured the American people that their cousins across the Atlantic were anxious to cooperate with them, the London government was 'moving rapidly in the opposite direction'. The Treasury and Board of Trade's 'petty objections', as the State Department called them, included changes to the Ottawa quotas on eggs and bacon, freshly modified by negotiations with Denmark, and on tariffs relating to fabric gloves, pottery, and baskets. These were passed into law before Britain would sign up to the truce.[85] If these steps took Britain further from the USA, it was not moving towards the Dominions. The latter's frustrations with the preferential deal signed with the British government had begun to smart,

---

[82] These were largely abandoned by 1934. See Colijn's report to MacDonald, 29 Nov. 1933, LON R4636, 10/6518/597.

[83] 'Council Committee for the Organisation of the Monetary and Economic Conference. Summary of the Meeeting Held in the Foreign Office', 29 Apr. 1933, LON R4637, 10D/3881/997; Stoppani to Stencek, 29 Apr. 1933, LON R4634, 10D/1400/317.

[84] 'Council Committee for the Organisation of the Monetary and Economic Conference. Summary of the Meeeting Held in the Foreign Office', 29 Apr. 1933, p. 6, LON R4637, 10D/3881/997.

[85] Atherton to Hull, 1 May 1933, *Foreign Relations of the United States 1933*, i. 584–8; Hamilton to Leith-Ross, 26 Apr. 1933, TNA: PRO BT 11/198; Davis to Hull, 5 May 1933, NARA RG59 550.S1/718.

and the Board of Trade decided not to consult them about the truce, for fear of 'making them nervous'. What it failed to recognize was that the hybrid identity, part nation and part colony, of Australia, New Zealand, Canada, and South Africa meant that, in accepting their invitations to join the conference, they had effectively joined the truce in any case as sovereign members of the League of Nations.

If negotiations to preserve cheap access to the staples of British cuisine rubbed salt into Hull's already smarting wounds because Britain prioritized trade relations with Denmark over those with the USA, his mood was not improved when Japan, Italy, and others followed British policy. The behaviour of Germany was especially telling. The very public spat over the tariff truce, coming on top of stalemate in Anglo-American war debt negotiations (which resulted in a second 'token' payment in June 1933), encouraged Germany to sign the truce under 'declared reservations so general as to render their acceptance nugatory'.[86] The Third Reich was typical of other states in its willingness to blame nations for its protectionist impulse when the real impetus for these measures lay at home.

These were difficult days for the League. Where the tariff truce was to be proof to the world that FDR aspired to 'establish a degree of co-operation with other nations that would surprise the American people', the President in turn was astonished at the range of international and European hostility directed towards him.[87] The list of published reservations made it clear no state was in a mood to take a vacation from raising tariffs. The truce was signed, but the prospects for intergovernmental cooperation on trade in London were now bleak.

The only potential benefit was that, after eight months, international discussion about Hull's enthusiasm for RTAA, whether FDR would support the bill, and the potential merits of the tariff truce had helped to refine positions inside and outside the USA. If states wanted to improve their political relations with one another, it was clear where concessions had to be found, and compromises, however unhappy, made. But, until war was imminent and the limits of their domestic strategies clear, this was difficult for Britain, France, and the United States, given the variance in the priorities of their national recovery strategies and vision of the world economy. In 1933, the search for agreement moved elsewhere on the agenda. It put renewed attention back to the question of stabilization, the League's proposals for special assistance for central and eastern Europe, and challenges faced by the world's primary producers.

The idea to coordinate international action to raise primary prices had come not from the secretariat of the League of Nations, but from producer groups who lobbied the League to participate in the London conference, and states where agricultural producers formed part of a larger story of depression and poverty.

[86] Hoesch to Neurath, 9 May 1933, TNA: PRO GFM 9245/E652096; Auswärtiges Amt, *Akten zur deutschen auswärtigen Politik 1918–1945* (Baden-Baden, 1950–), Series C, vol. I, 1, Reichskabinett meeting, no. 210, 5 May 1933, p. 380.
[87] Davis to Stimson, 22 Nov. 1932, NARA RG59 500.S1/354; Fosdick to Sweetser, 22 Mar. 1933, LC, Sweetser: 31; Prittwitz to Ritter, 29 Oct. 1932, R2/9960; Claudel to Paul-Boncour, 27 Feb. 1933, no. 349, Ministère des Affaires Étrangères, *Documents diplomatiques français* (Paris, 1929–86), Series 1932–5, vol. 2; Lindsay to Simon, 20 Dec. 1932, TNA: PRO T188/68.

League support in efforts to raise the price of wheat became an important illustrative case and it took the EFO in a very different direction from its explicit support for liberal free trade, towards endorsing efforts to restrict the production of commodities and artificially raising prices. Inconsistent it may have been in the realm of economic thought, but in terms of practical politics and economics it complemented the League's determination to reflect the concerns of its members, to be able to signal a 'success' at the conference, and to reinforce the claims for the agency of the League in economic and financial affairs. It also matched the League's differentiated view of a world where poor farmers of member and non-member sovereign states needed to be accommodated and balanced against one another. This was exemplified by its special experience in central and eastern Europe, a community that required paternal care from its wealthier neighbours.

Wheat received the most attention. Between 1927 and 1933 the League facilitated over twenty different conferences on the subject of wheat production and prices. But, in May 1933, the issue, like the tariff truce and currency reform, was rejuvenated by developments in the USA. On 12 May the Agricultural Adjustment Act cleared congress, and with it came provision to control the amount of acreage put into production. For the Americans, an international agreement was an essential corollary to the scheme.[88] It was they who insisted to Stoppani and Loveday that US interest was far more than a 'gesture', and asked them to convene a meeting of the world's leading wheat producers, the USA, Canada, Argentina, and Australia.[89] To protect the League, Loveday sought to keep discussions out of the public eye, and he proposed the delegates meeting in Geneva should attend a session of the Economic Committee and convene separately in another room to reach an agreement among themselves without the intervention of the League. The camouflage was uncomfortable; as was the spectacle of the world's wealthier agricultural producers attempting to control the market and he demanded other wheat producers, notably in Hungary, Yugoslavia, and Romania, be brought into the negotiations as a matter of urgency.

This exposed the League's real interest in the distribution of production within Europe. Stoppani and Loveday were keen to foster the new US administration's willingness to use the League as a site of international negotiation, even if the economic measures it was interested in advocating also had a nationalist dimension. The Economic and Financial Sections were flattered that the USA had asked the League to host negotiations between the world's major wheat producers within three weeks of FDR's inauguration, and wheat talks in Geneva opened just as the Agricultural Administration Act passed into law. But Loveday and Stoppani were well aware that

[88] Fritz Georg von Gravenitz, 'Internationalismus in der Zwischenkriegszeit Deutschland und Frankreich in der globalen Agrarkrise', unpublished Ph.D. thesis, European University Institute, 2011, p. 256; Joseph Stancliffe Davis, *Wheat and the AAA* (Stanford, CA, 1935), 301–5.
[89] 'Record of a Conversation between Prentiss Gilbert, Loveday and Stencek', 21 Apr. 1933, LON R4634, 10D/2506/597. Gilbert was the only American to serve on the Council of the League of Nations, but shortcomings in his performance undermined the secretariat and the US State Department's confidence in him, and encouraged them to fall back onto Norman Davis and less formal diplomatic channels.

the basis on which the USA wanted to facilitate cooperation through the League posed significant problems for the institution itself. Talks on limiting national wheat production would do nothing to tackle protectionism; had obvious drawbacks as a strategy unless restrictions were widely adopted, since raising prices while forcing production down in one part of the globe tended to encourage other producers elsewhere to grow more; and favoured large producers over smaller ones. Progress would come only if the Americans were prepared to appoint someone who was 'really prepared to push the matter'.[90] They did: Ambassador Hans Morgenthau Sen., FDR's new Director of the Farm Board, Democrat Party stalwart, father of FDR's Treasury Secretary, and former Chairman of League Greek Resettlement. Stoppani and Loveday were content to leave him to it; their cautious mood was heightened by the determination of the IIA and the Italian government to intrude on the talks.

THE WORLD ECONOMIC CONFERENCE CONVENES

On 29 May, Stoppani delivered drafts of the opening speeches for the King and the conference president MacDonald. It was the Economic and Financial Sections' final act of preparation and executive agency.[91] Their role as stage manager and playwright was at an end. The fate of the conference now lay in the hands of government representatives. Economic experts and central bankers were in attendance and offered a network of resources on which the League sought to draw to keep the conference on track, but the stars of the show, and potentially the villains of the piece, were always the governments.

The cartoon chroniclers of the League, the Hungarian Jews Alois Derso and Emery Kelen, depicted the opening ceremony of the conference as a gladiatorial contest set in the Coliseum in Rome in place of imperial London.[92] A toga-clad George V, flanked by the similarly attired President of the Conference MacDonald, Avenol, and Chamberlain, reviewed the legions of national delegates, their shields emblazoned with the symbols of their national currencies, parading before them. The image was both apposite and prescient. When the conference opened formally on 12 June, newsreels and the world's press captured the arresting site of more than 1,000 delegates in full ceremonial dress squeezed into the comparatively small and unventilated museum. It was more than the unseasonably warm London weather that echoed Rome. The King, channelling Stoppani, spoke of 'one of the most important international gatherings so far held in history' and its common mission to seek a 'renewal of the steady improvement in the material conditions of life, which the past has led the world to expect'.[93]

---

[90] 'Record of a Conversation between Prentiss Gilbert, Loveday and Stencek', 21 Apr. 1933, LON R4634, 10D/2506/597.

[91] Stoppani to Hankey and enclosures, 29 May, LON R4633, 10D/597/597.

[92] Derso and Kelen, 'The Gladiators', 12 July 1933, Mudd, Derso and Kelen Collection, MC205, Box 20.

[93] Memo by Stoppani, 'Draft Inaugural Speech by the King', 30 May 1933, LON R4633, 10D/597/597.

But, within half an hour, the conference had been dragged down to hand-to-hand combat by Chamberlain. In charge of the British national delegation, he gave the first speech delivered by a delegation head, and swiftly introduced a break with the agreed protocol by making direct reference to the damage caused by war debts to the world economy. The American delegation, led by Hull, was infuriated, especially as FDR's administration had accepted two 'token' payments. (Indeed, the British and the BIS considered this an important outcome of the conference.[94]) Instead, the US public were treated to an ill-judged and unhappy reminder of the USA's last major venture—the First World War—and the spectacle of Britain, the apex of the world's largest empire, threatening to default on its debts to an impoverished American people. It was swiftly followed by a public reminder from Daladier that the French Empire was already in default and rumours that Germany was making debt payments to British banks while reneging on payments owed to American creditors.

The spectre that emerged of European bankers doing backroom deals to the disadvantage of the American taxpayer was, predictably, deeply unwelcome in the White House. The public fear and Congressional suspicion of internationalism that would threaten FDR's recovery programme was made much worse by private negotiations that opened at the Bank of England on 10 June. These talks between central bankers from Britain, the USA, France, the BIS, and League officials were intended to deliver the temporary stabilization agreement, which was to provide a stable monetary basis on which discussions to remove barriers to trade could be advanced. Instead, it became the immediate reason for the breakdown of the conference. Events down the road at the Bank of England were a strange throwback to secret diplomacy. While Loveday's intention had been for the stabilization agreement to assert the primacy of talks on protectionism and the EFO's role in facilitating monetary negotiations, the initiative also threw a lifeline to central bankers who wanted to reassert the old monetary order.

In October 1932, the board of the Federal Reserve System had declined to send anyone to the preparatory meetings for the conference, because it wanted 'to avoid any embarrassment to central banks or any invasion into their field of activity'.[95] By the time the conference convened, FDR's decision to abandon gold meant the monetary landscape and hence Governor Harrison's place within it, had changed dramatically. Life was only a little easier for Governor Norman. Although he enjoyed closer relations than his counterpart in the USA with the British Treasury when it came to the evolution of national monetary policy, Norman too had begun to feel a rising sense of isolation, as Chamberlain and the Treasury's authority and powers grew. Norman accepted the Treasury's emphasis on lowering interest rates and raising prices, but he was less comfortable with the primacy given to imperial financial relations over those with Europe and the United States, which the Treasury's strategy implied, and often warned against any plan that would 'react

---

[94] Per Jacobsson Diary, Diary Entry, 5 July 1933, BIS, Per Jacobsson Papers, 1/18 (11), Diary Vol. A.19, 1933.
[95] Memo by Crane, 12 Sept. 1932, FRBNY C.747.41; telephone conversations between Mills and Harrison, 27 Sept. 1932, 28 Sept. 1932, and 11 Nov. 1932, FRBNY 2012.2.

disadvantageously on . . . our foreign central banking friends'.[96] The floating pound and what came to be regarded by both the Bank of England and the Treasury in 1933 as FDR's generally erratic monetary policy threatened to 'increase American export competition and produce a new crop of exchange controls' that would work to Britain's disadvantage. For central bankers, then, the preparations for the world conference had underlined the degree to which central banks, until 1931 the centre of the monetary universe, were increasingly exiled to the periphery.[97]

Only for France was the situation different. The French government remained committed to the gold order and the Banque de France's central role in sustaining it. On the opening day of the stabilization talks, Moret, Daladier, and Georges Bonnet, Minister for Finance, attempted to direct proceedings by expressing grave new fears for the continued stability of the French franc and other gold-backed currencies, which triggered renewed speculative pressure, in particular on the Dutch guilder, the very thing stabilization negotiations was supposed to prevent. Rumours now swirled around hotels and bars among the watching delegates and the press that what France was attempting to negotiate was not a temporary stabilization agreement, but a permanent one. It was also clear to delegates that certain members of the US delegation in London, notably Harrison, were not unsympathetic to the French and Dutch plight, especially when the French couched their policy in a wish to follow an American lead, for if they had to 'wait for the British we would have to wait for a very long time'.[98]

Apart from the brief prelude of the opening ceremony at the Geological Museum, therefore, all eyes and ears were trained on the stabilization meetings at the Bank of England and the offices of the British Treasury. Divisions within the American delegation quickly opened up. Harrison confessed to other members of his team, Cox and Professor Oliver Spargue, that he wanted to commit the USA to a more permanent stabilization arrangement. Back in New York, Emanuel Goldenweiser, who, like Sprague, was widely known and admired in Europe, lobbied FDR on Harrison's behalf, suggesting that a US commitment to a substantial stabilization deal might induce France to resume war debts payments (although there was no evidence for this).[99] Cox and Sprague, on the other hand, urged caution. Anything other than a temporary deal could backfire against Harrison and the Federal Reserve Board at home, and ultimately limit US action abroad too. It was wise counsel. So was their analysis that it was better to put the onus back on the French and the British, because the former was 'somewhat confused' about how to effect the technical arrangements for a permanent deal, and the latter clearly did not want anything more than a temporary agreement in any case.[100]

---

[96] Norman to Harrison, 14 Apr. 1933, BoE OV 732/8.

[97] Record of conversation between Norman and Harrison, 26 May 1933, FRBNY 3125.4.

[98] Paul-Boncour to de Laboulaye, 14 May 1933, No. 274, Ministère des Affaires Étrangères, (*Documents diplomatiques français*), Series 1932–5, vol. 2; Tyrell to Simon, 10 June 1933, TNA: PRO FO 371/173–6, W 6858/5/50.

[99] Memo by Goldenweiser, 16 June 1933, LC, Goldenweiser Papers; Per Jacobsson Diary, Diary Entry, July 1933, BIS, Per Jacobsson Papers, pp. 4, 5–9.

[100] For a fuller account, see Clavin ' "The Fetishes of So-Called International Bankers" '.

After five days of wrangling, the bankers began to draw up a plan, and two days later, on 17 June, it was ready for circulation to the national governments of the three countries concerned. The deal was largely Norman's work. In it, the Bank of England agreed to hold the exchange rate of sterling between 121 and 124 schillings per ounce of gold and set aside 3 million ounces for the purpose. For its part, the Federal Reserve declared its intention to maintain the dollar between $4.79 and $4.73 to 100 French francs or around $4.00 against the floating pound, and reserved 700 million ounces of gold to do so. (Again, there was talk of a common stabilization fund, which ran into the sand because the French refused to contribute to a stabilization fund for others, as their currency was already stable.[101]) The technical arrangements were perfectly respectable, and Loveday and his colleagues breathed a deep sigh of relief.

But what happened next fatally wounded the prospects for the conference. The injury did not stem primarily from the technical arrangements, though it did not help that, as soon as they learned of the deal, markets began to trade heavily against the dollar. Instead, the culprit was the short written declaration by the three central banks that a return to gold 'was the ultimate aim of their policy'.[102] The document, and the diplomatic and press circus around it, was redolent of central bank diplomacy of an age discredited by the collapse of the world economy. It was not what the League-sponsored intergovernmental conference, nor its commitment to open diplomacy, was supposed to be about.

The declaration lit a slow-burning fuse. International speculation centred on the possibility that Roosevelt might reject the declaration because the agreed dollar rate was too high. But the bigger issue for Roosevelt was that the destiny of the conference appeared to have fallen into the hands of the bankers. He urged Hull to return international attention to the issues under deliberation in the main conference hall, notably relating to freeing the world from economic nationalism. Too much attention was being given to 'exchange stability of banker-influenced cabinets'.[103] On the same day, Warburg received the dark warning from Washington: 'it's dead' and the time had come to 'bind the wounds'.[104] But, with the bit firmly between their teeth, the French were not prepared to let the matter drop and were urged on by discussions with representatives of other gold-backed currencies, which underlined rising market speculation against the Dutch guilder, the Swiss franc, the Italian lira, and all the other gold currencies. The French now directed their fire onto the British, threatening to leave the conference unless Britain agreed to commit to some

---

[101] Suggestions for a common fund were not new. They evolved out of the 1932 Stresa Conference on Danubian reconstruction that inspired several plans formulated along similar lines, including the Franqui, Kisch, Kindersley, and Henderson plans, and the League-sponsored International Agricultural Mortgage Credit Company, which the EFO promoted between Sept. 1930 and Aug. 1931.

[102] 'Stabilisation Declaration', 17 June 1933, BoE CT 118.01; Drummond, *The Floating Pound*, 164–5.

[103] Roosevelt to Hull, 20 June 1933, NARA RG59 550.S1/Monetary stabil./25.

[104] Warburg, Diary Entry, Butler Warburg, vol. 1, 21 Jan. 1933, p. 83.

form of restabilized pound in the near future. To add to the pressure, the Dominions began to lobby the British government to drop the discussion of stabilization, and ally itself with the inflationary position adopted by the United States.[105]

Almost three weeks in, and the business of the conference had been entirely highjacked by the very issue the League had sought to avoid from the start: currency stabilization. By the end of June, the central bankers were trying to draft a new temporary agreement with an altogether much more general statement about the future direction of their monetary policy—much along the lines of Loveday's original proposal—and some big names were attached to promoting the effort: Raymond Moley, one of FDR's financial gurus on the New Deal, had flown in from the USA; Keynes and Walter Lippmann now pitched in to help explain the new agreement to the press. It contained no advertised stabilization rates, but simply reaffirmed the commitment of those nations on gold to remain there, the importance of the gold standard as a medium of exchange, and the intention of those off gold to return to it when 'proper conditions' allowed.[106]

By 1 July a moment of calm at last had been effected. But not for the first time the central bankers had misjudged the true ramifications of what was unfolding. Their reveries were rudely interrupted by what within hours became known as the 'bombshell message' that blasted from Roosevelt's yacht, moored at Buzzards Bay off the coast of Cape Cod where he was holidaying. It took everyone on the other side of the Atlantic by surprise, though it should not have done so. True, the language was unusually frank and direct for a diplomatic exchange, but it came from a President noted for his ability to reach out to the man and woman in the street, and his message rang out as clear as the bell on his yacht. It is worth citing at length because it demonstrated how far FDR had taken on board the League secretariat's formulation of the conference agenda, now lost amid bickering between governments and banks. It announced his belief that 'it was a catastrophe amounting to a world tragedy, if the great Conference of Nations . . . should . . . allow itself to be diverted by the proposal of a purely artificial and temporary experiment affecting the monetary exchange of a few nations only' (those committed to gold). It was time for the world to put the 'old fetishes of so-called international bankers' of the gold standard behind it.[107] Remote from the proceedings, the President had the necessary distance to see the conference had gone down the monetary cul-de-sac the secretariat had sought to avert since October 1932. But the strength of Roosevelt's language left no way back.

The impact was dramatic. The value of the dollar continued to fall, much to the delight of New Dealers intent on raising American prices, and pressure mounted on countries still attached to gold who, in response to the 'bombshell', issued their first formal declaration of gold bloc solidarity. France, Italy, Poland, Holland, Belgium, and Switzerland were the co-signatories. Schacht declined to sign on Germany's

[105] Meeting between the British and French Delegates, 22 June 1933, TNA: PRO Cab 29/142; meeting between the British and Empire Delegation, 30 June 1933, TNA: PRO Cab 29/142.
[106] Meeting of the gold bloc, British and American representatives, 28 June 1933, TNA: PRO Cab 29/142.
[107] *Foreign Relations of the United States 1933*, i. 673–4.

behalf, because he wanted a free hand and was committed to securing a deal on German commercial debts with the Americans. He was, therefore, reluctant to embrace the gold bloc in its public condemnation of the USA. The world's press and most of the conference participants declared the world economic conference over before it had begun.[108]

THE END OF THE PARTY

The 'bombshell message' was a sobering moment. The US delegation in London was now cruelly exposed, but charges levied by Britain, France, Italy, and others that the conference was in crisis because of FDR and policy divisions within the American delegation were greatly exaggerated.[109] FDR had only ever agreed to sign up to a temporary stabilization agreement, and everyone was aware the President was far more interested in other aspects of the conference agenda, notably raising prices and reducing tariffs. Indeed, the Democrat administration had shown greater interest in the agenda promoted by the League for the conference than any other government. But the President's intemperate language and the shattered stabilization agreement provided the conference participants, some of whom the USA had hoped would sign trade deals under the auspices of a future RTAA, with the opportunity to express their scepticism regarding US internationalism more generally, especially after FDR withdrew the act from the legislative programme for 1933 while Hull was en route to London. (It was reintroduced the following year.) Save for Latin American countries, who used the London venue to continue conversations with the US administration that were to culminate in the Montevideo Conference that December, the USA was left to feel the full force of self-righteous European disdain. European attempts to forgo debt payments to the USA and disinterest in trade negotiations were lost amid the welter of condemnation that blamed the USA for 'smashing' the conference.[110]

If it had been divided before the 'bombshell message', the US delegation was certainly united after it, sharing the President's conviction that the responsibility for the stalled conference was not theirs but was rather put down to Britain and France. The latter had sought to discredit US policy for 'certain clear objectives' of their

[108] 'Meeting between the British Delegation and the Gold Bloc', 3 July 1933, TNA: PRO Cab 29/142; Schacht to Dreyse, 6 July 1933, TNA: PRO GFM 33/1231, 3177/D684361.

[109] Moley's arrival certainly gave the impression that Hull was not in command, but it was Feis's pointed account in *Nineteen Thirty Three* that largely set historians on this trail. However, Feis was also motivated by his animus towards Hull, who had increasingly sidelined him as Economic Adviser. At the time, the Economic Adviser had a different view, recognizing American statesmen 'were not angels', but it was the British who were behaving with a 'diminished sense of international responsibility that was very likely to stand in the way of any about turn in the whole course of international relations'. See Feis to Frankfurter, 8 Nov. 1933, Library of Congress, Washington, Private Papers of Herbert Feis, Box 123.

[110] Neville Chamberlain to Ida Chamberlain, 15 July 1933, Birmingham 18/1/836. Mouré, *Managing the Franc Poincaré*, 118–19; Eichengreen, *Golden Fetters*, 346–7.

own.[111] Nor were those objectives realized. In 1934, Congress moved to punish national debtors who had reneged on their obligations in the Johnson Act, and the desultory state of trilateral relations between Britain, France, and the USA meant FDR had no interest in mustering the political will to oppose it or other neutrality legislation that followed in its wake during his first term in office.

But, while government delegates could walk away from the Geological Museum like teenagers whose party was out of control, it was the League of Nations that was left to clean up the mess. The first step was to deal with the practical side. The conference had to be wound up. In the planning, the secretariat had anticipated the event would last at least two months; it had sat for barely four weeks. The fate of the daily conference *Journal* that detailed proceedings was sadly telling. Within twelve hours of the close of business each day, 400 copies of the *Journal* summarizing discussions in the committee rooms and plenary sessions were distributed to members of the world's press, and a further 700 copies were circulated among national representatives as well as being sent out to their governments back home in both French and English editions. The translation was meticulous, and the standard of production impressively high. The problem was that, within two weeks of the conference opening, the editors were desperately short of copy, because the business of the conference had ground to a halt.[112] Negotiations that were still running, such as the commodity agreements for sugar and wine, were moved seamlessly to Geneva. Other topics, such as ILO–League proposals for international public works schemes and discussions that it had hoped to facilitate on raw materials and cartelization were also absorbed into the EFO's regular programme of work.

The disappointing outcome of intergovernmental negotiations in London was greeted with stoic, silent resignation by the secretariat. The twists and turns of the stabilization saga had certainly taxed the staff—Loveday was taken seriously ill before the conference began and was run ragged during the stabilization negotiations.[113] But the outcome was not a surprise, given the conflicting pattern of expectations and priorities established at Lausanne and revealed at the preparatory meetings in Geneva and Washington. Although the negotiations had failed to create common ground between the states, they established a clear view of state priorities and where the EFO might, or would not, make a difference. Trade liberalization, facilitating depreciation, and exploring the particular conditions faced by the world's primary producers emerged as future possible routes along which the EFO might guide the world to economic recovery.

At the same time, the conference had exposed the very real limitations of the EFO's tactical ability to coordinate the actions of states and effect cooperation between them. The grand scale of intergovernmental, multilateral cooperation on a range of issues to which the conference aspired had delivered few positive outcomes. Instead, the Economic and Financial Sections concluded that a new strategy

[111] Roosevelt to Hull, 24 June 1933, NARA RG59 550.S1/Monetary stab./47.
[112] For publication and translation arrangements, see LON R4634, 10D/1164/597.
[113] Per Jacobsson Diary, Diary Entries, 24 June 1933, 28 June 1933, 30 June 1933, 13 July 1933, BIS, Per Jacobsson Papers, 7/18 (11).

was needed. It would focus on the causes and potential responses to the depression, defined on a very broad basis, and work to maximize League financial and intellectual resources, and its ability to control and shape outcomes. This led to the strengthening of intra-sectional relationships within the League, notably between the EFO, the Health and Social Sections, and the ILO. Stoppani and Loveday were clear that intra-institutional pressures and the changing context of international relations in the world at large meant that in the future the EFO would need to exercise greater caution with its dealings with states. The financial climate was now inclement. In 1932, the British civil servant Sir Malcolm Ramsay was seconded to Geneva to begin the first of what would become a series of rounds of 'efficiency drives' that reflected the diminishing financial and political resources on which the League and heads of section could draw, although EFO staff levels remained steady.[114] The failure of the Disarmament Conference at the end of that year, and the continued financial pressures on member states, led a rising number of member states to question the value of affiliation.

Responses to the Great Depression meant that, even in the case of those member states for whom disassociation was not an option, the character of relations between the state and the agents of the League was undergoing significant change. The British case was stark. The evolution of British economic and financial policy since September 1931 led the secretariat to conclude that, while it was intellectually in sympathy with sterling's devaluation and coordination within the sterling area, it was less comfortable with the ideology of imperial regeneration and economic nationalism that underpinned it. Under Chamberlain's indomitable leadership, British economic policy was now frequently out of step with the ethos of the League. The Economic and Financial Sections retained important intellectual ties to the liberal and international study schools, and to leading economists in Cambridge, Oxford, and London. But the policies and power of the British imperial state were no longer congruent with the interests of the organization. The space left by Britain created room for France to assert its views in the EFO, although its protectionism had proven problematic in the past and remained so in the 1930s. The Netherlands, Belgium, and Sweden emerged to take a greater role in directing the intergovernmental dimension of the League's work in the economic and financial committees. But the League needed a state champion with the economic muscle and vision to unlock what the secretariat saw as the frustrated potential of the liberal capitalist economy for growth and peace. For the Economic and Financial Sections, and the advisers clustered around them, that power was the USA.

---

[114] General Discussion, 'Minutes of Directors' Meeting', 8 June 1932, LON R3565, 50/34358/767. Ramsay's particular focus was the salaries paid to League civil servants, which were generally believed to be too high. In 1921, the Nobelmaire Commission concluded that remuneration of League personnel should be higher than that of the best-paid civil servants of merit from Britain (at that time the best paid in the world). It was deemed inappropriate to pay lesser salaries for equal work to citizens of different countries. In the wake of the depression it was agreed section directors would need to take more responsibility for the expenditure in their sections, which had previously been delegated to a junior member of each unit.

4

All Things Trade and Currency, All Nations Great and Small, 1933–1936

The years between the London conference of 1933 and the Tripartite Stabilization Agreement signed in 1936 were the dull days of diplomacy. There were neither crises, agreements, nor dust-ups, and the period is little studied as a result. Yet the view from Geneva reveals this as an important period of transition. It was then it became clear that currency controls and restrictions on overseas trade that reshaped relationships between national and imperial territories, and that had been announced to the League as 'emergency' policy responses, had arrived to stay. Walls had gone up around economies. In 1929, the proportion of world trade affected by tariffs was less than 10 per cent, by 1934 it was over 50 per cent. Yet the League remained an important medium through which nations attempted to make sense of their changing international relations.[1] The secretariat continued to inform and to attempt to direct these processes in ways it believed were conducive to the League's own, also now changing, priorities. After 1933, grand conferences and talk of coordinated recovery programmes linking monetary coordination, freer trade, and debt reduction lay in the past as new means were sought to achieve international peace and capitalism.

Two examples of state-driven economic nationalism came to preoccupy the minds of economists and financiers working for, or connected to, the League of Nations. The first was that of Germany and the changes wrought to its economy, society, and foreign policy under the impact of National Socialism. In 1926, Germany's accession to membership was a landmark in the League's aspirations to act as redeemer and stabilizer of international relations, offering the opportunity to resolve rancorous issues left undone by the peace settlement and to enable the world to move on from the First World War. But now Germany began to undermine the world order, demanding living space in the East at the World Economic Conference and abandoning the League Disarmament Conference and the organization itself in October 1933. With its society and economy put to the service of increasingly aggressive foreign-policy ambitions, Hitler now menaced as the League's destroyer, and the situation raised questions as to how to handle Germany, and the other aggressor states. It also led to a growing estrangement between Stoppani and Loveday, on the one hand, and Avenol, on the other.

---

[1] Michael Tracy, *Government and Agriculture in Western Europe* (3rd edn; London, 1989), 146.

Nor was Germany alone in renouncing its membership. Japan, too, had first threatened and then announced its resignation from the League in March 1933, while Central and South American membership numbers, already fluctuating in the 1920s with Costa Rica's departure announced in January 1925 and Brazil's in June 1926, saw the further losses of Guatemala and Nicaragua in 1936 and El Salvador the following year. The membership of the League and the EFO was shifting in terms of the composition of the individual national political economies it comprised, and the pattern of overall membership. If some nations fell away from the League, the USSR was moving closer, facilitated by the limits Stalin imposed on communist internationalism, and by the USA's recognition of the Bolshevik state in November 1933.

The secretariat knew it had to understand the changing character of its membership and adapt if the League was to survive. For the EFO, the urgency of the challenge was underlined by the continued depreciation of sterling and the US dollar. If the secretariat applauded some of the economic benefits it brought, the absence of international consensus, as the gold bloc cleaved to orthodoxy, created a formidable obstacle to international coordination and cooperation. More immediately, the divergent monetary paths of the sterling bloc, on the one hand, and the gold bloc, on the other, posed demonstrable risks to the Anglo-French axis on which life in the secretariat turned.

The second member state whose policies gave the EFO's secretariat pause for thought was Great Britain. The relationship between state and society in Britain had not been fundamentally reshaped by the impact of the Great Depression in the way it had in Germany, and the political resolution of the British financial crisis in a National Government was far less radical than the political polarization of Germany that produced the NS-Staat. Nonetheless, in 1931 and 1932 British economic foreign policy had been transformed. The shift away from economic internationalism predicated on gold standard orthodoxy and free trade profoundly compromised Britain's claim to leadership in the EFO, and with it the secretariat's ability and willingness to rely on British support for its activities.[2] Although the Financial and Economic Sections had become low-key advocates of currency depreciation, they were increasingly at odds with British policy in other areas, notably on trade, on the value of public works in providing targeted help, and on the need to develop central and eastern Europe.

But at the same time as the EFO's secretariat found itself increasingly alienated from British policy, tensions between member states, evident in the Economic and Financial Committees over the breakdown of the gold standard, began to dissipate. With Germany never having been a significant player in the EFO, this change was notable in relations between Britain and France. By July 1934, the French Finance Ministry conceded the monetary question was no longer the burning issue it had

---

[2] For a striking example of how the League used the history of British internationalism to illustrate the model working of the world economy and the challenges it faced by its retreat into economic nationalism, see, e.g., League of Nations, *Remarks on the Present Phase of International Economic Relations* (Geneva, 1935), C.344.M.174, 40–1.

been among members of the League's Financial Committee.[3] The regular, iterative rounds of intergovernmental meetings had enabled most, if not all, states to grow accustomed to the reality and implications of floating currencies, and to accept that one era in monetary history was drawing to a close. Quite what form that end would take, and what would come next, however, remained open and troubling questions.

If the value of Britain to the League's economic agenda was in decline, the EFO was now also less useful to Britain. (Its utility to the British government would undergo something of a revival with the outbreak of the war.) For other states, the new semi-detached attitude of the British to the EFO proved to be liberating, allowing space for new ideas and approaches to supersede British preoccupations. French interest in the League's financial and economic agenda was notably on the rise, a shift that presented obstacles and opportunities. The biggest barrier to greater French engagement was that the government of National Union, inaugurated in the wake of the most serious urban riots to grip the Third Republic, remained as committed to gold as previous regimes. In their past encounters with the EFO, successive French governments had denounced both depreciation and devaluation (at the time, the former meant floating the currency, the latter revaluing it at a new, fixed exchange rate) as a remedy for its economic woes, and for those of the gold bloc. This was very different from the views of the sterling bloc, and the EFO's secretariat, but in 1934 the latter was encouraged to find in its informal exchanges in the corridors and dining rooms of Geneva that the hardened, external face of French monetary orthodoxy had begun to soften. With life increasingly tough on gold, France, and other members of the gold bloc, began to reach out to the League for financial support and intellectual reinforcement.

At the same time as France sought out the EFO, no nation's economic and political concerns were becoming as important to its staff as those of the USA. The secretariat had monitored the consolidation of US monetary policy—Roosevelt had abandoned what the secretariat regarded as his outlandish gold-buying programme in January 1934—and recovery with interest. Most significantly from its perspective, the passage of the RTAA into law marked a new stage in US trade policy and, potentially, foreign policy on which the League could build.[4]

These new trends were evident at the 41st meeting of the Economic and Financial Committees in July 1934. Outwardly little seemed to have changed. Loveday and Stoppani, the ever-resourceful outriders of internationalism, continued compiling an agenda with enough scheduled items to keep delegates talking for two months, not the scheduled two days of the meeting. High on the list, as usual, were the issues of currency stability, price levels, and the burden of debt bearing down on the world's poorer economies, but in 1934 the content of the

[3] Letter and attached note from Baumont to the French Foreign Minister, 21 July 1934, AMAE, SDN, IJ/Organisation Économique et Financière de la Société des Nations/Comité Économique/ Juillet 1934–Septembre 1937, no. 1184.

[4] Scott Sumner, 'Roosevelt, Warren, and the Gold-Buying Program of 1933', *Research in Economic History*, 20 (2001), 135–72; Loveday, 'Report to the Secretary-General on Mission to Canada and the United States, October–November 1934', p. 19, LON R4605, 10C/13175/9854.

discussion changed significantly. Evidence in the *World Economic Survey* and EIS statistical reports, summarized in the secretariat's accompanying commentary, meant there could now be no denying either the upturn under way in currencies that abandoned gold or the crippling levels of protection that stood in the way of recovery in the longer term. It encouraged Leith-Ross to become increasingly bold in his characterization of the British policy model. Gone was the language of 'temporary', 'forced', and 'unavoidable' depreciation that had characterized its discussions with gold bloc ministers between 1931 and 1933. Britain's currency depreciation was now gleefully represented as the best, if not the sole, route to recovery. 'Other countries, instead of harping on the necessity of stabilization, ought to consider what their policy was to be, on the assumption that [British] stabilisation was not likely to be practicable for some considerable time.'[5] Many delegates from the gold bloc agreed with him, but this did not mean, as Leith-Ross acknowledged to his superiors in the Treasury, that Austria, Italy, or Switzerland was coming around to Britain's way of thinking. What it did signify was that the time had come to abandon sterile discussions of currency stabilization, and to progress, if necessary, without the British government.

That summer, the secretariat opened up two new topics for exploration and discussion. The first was the Economic and Financial Sections' proposal to launch a systematic inquiry into 'the Chief Aspects of Government Intervention in Economic Life'.[6] The League intended to move decisively to study the impact of public works programmes, a field that, until the London economic conference, the ILO regarded as its own, signalling the secretariat's determination to understand the character and impact of state expenditure on economy and society more generally. The American delegate was especially enthused by the proposal, reporting that it produced 'unquestionably the frankest discussion that had ever been held in the Economic Committee . . . it had brought out into the open the issues which have developed among countries in the way of conflicting policy.'[7] It marked the EFO's move away from efforts to facilitate intergovernmental coordination in the short term towards informing and reshaping the ideas that underpinned their policies in the longer term. It was becoming more a think tank and less a talking shop. More immediately, it led to a new publication series, 'Remarks on the Present Phase of International Economic Relations', produced annually in the 1930s, which charted the changing composition of the political economies of member and non-member states, and the contemporary history of the depression.[8]

The second new item shifted the focus away from the study of national coordination more firmly in the direction that the EFO's secretariat wanted to see policy develop, with the inauguration of a large-scale investigation into 'the trend of commercial policy in the United States'. By singling out this national case study

[5] Leith-Ross to Ashton Gwatkin, 23 July 1934, TNA: PRO FO371/18497, W 7043/1195/50.

[6] Memo by Rogers, 30 June 1934, NARA RG59, 500.C1199/129.

[7] Willard L. Thorp to James Harvey Rogers, 'Concerning the 41st Session of the Economic Committee Held at the League of Nations', 30 July 1934, NARA RG59, 500.C1199/129.

[8] For the first issue, see League of Nations, *Remarks on the Present Phase of International Economic Relations*, (Geneva, 1935), 52.

for attention—it was unprecedented for the secretariat to identify a policy with a particular nation state, whether member or non-member—Loveday and Stoppani underlined their view that the RTAA had shifted the course of US trade policy in a liberal direction in several ways. Notably, Congress delegated its tariff-negotiating powers to the executive and surrendered its authority to legislate duties on specific goods. Its powers were now framed simply in terms of whether or not the RTAA should be continued, and the threshold of political support needed for members of Congress to approve tariff cuts was also reduced. The RTAA strengthened the hand of the President, and reinforced the move to economic policies that benefited the USA as a whole, boosting the influence of exporters, and reducing the influence of powerful, often regional, protectionist lobby groups.[9] By endorsing the RTAA, EFO's secretariat identified a new champion for economic liberalism, and aimed to bring their appreciation of US trade policy to the wider world.

THE CHALLENGE OF CLEARING

Although much of the secretariat's time was given over to work that would later culminate in the positive security agenda and in the Depression Delegation, it did not mean an end to state agency in the EFO. In 1934, French interest in the organization, in abeyance since the days of the Briand Plan, resurfaced in a French-sponsored initiative to address international clearing. France was on the verge of implosion, but taking the time to launch an international initiative to address clearing arrangements was not as irrelevant as it first appeared.[10] The primary purpose of clearing agreements was to sustain trade and other commercial transactions with countries that had imposed exchange controls (by 1934 this applied to all France's partners in eastern and central Europe, with the exception of Czechoslovakia). They were overlain with compensation agreements intended to recompense debtors who were disadvantaged by the controls. Compensation agreements widened the protective field of clearing from monetary exchanges to commercial arrangements. Their general intention was to maintain a certain balance between imports and exports between two countries, but invariably they resulted in state attempts to use the need for imports as a basis to 'encourage' the other to take its exports. The declared purpose of clearing and compensation arrangements was the preservation of exchange parity of currencies on the gold standard. Yet, taken together, they represented a new vision for international transactions through a complex and sophisticated set of bilateral arrangements that gave nations with large debts and important import markets, notably Germany, considerable leverage over their creditors and trading partners. The controls implemented in 1931 to manage German financial weakness had,

---

[9] Douglas A. Irwin, Petros C. Mavroidis, and Alan O. Sykes, *The Genesis of GATT* (Cambridge, 2008), 8–9. Loveday's and Stoppani's reading of the legislation was far more penetrating and sympathetic than that of the British, French, or German governments.

[10] For domestic conditions, see Julian Jackson, *The Popular Front in France: Defending Democracy, 1934–38* (Cambridge, 1988), 30–51.

perversely, brought the National Socialist tools it used to its economic advantage. (Germany also used bilateral negotiations with its creditors to divide and rule, as dramatically illustrated in 1933 and 1934 when Schacht secured a deal that favoured British creditors and Anglo-German trade relations to the perceived detriment of its creditors in the USA.[11])

As Britain distanced itself from the EFO after 1933, the Economic Committee became increasingly open as a venue from which France might inculcate a sense of solidarity among the remaining countries on gold, many of whom had imposed clearing and were developing compensation agreements. And for all governments, including those in the sterling bloc and the USA, which had not imposed currency controls, international clearing and compensation negotiations afforded the opportunity to pacify powerful economic and financial interest groups at home.[12] Moreover, very little was known about either clearing or compensation arrangements, because the deals were made at times of crisis and were negotiated on a bilateral basis. Details were scarce beyond the immediate circle of those involved in their negotiation or operation, and it was difficult to develop an accurate reading of their scale and impact on the international economy. The French government used this widely recognized intelligence deficit as the hook on which to hang its request for the League's help.[13] As René Massigli of the Foreign Ministry told the EFO, it was important for the international community to pool its intelligence and expertise on the character and comparative utility of complicated clearing agreements and administrative structures. The French government presented its interest in the subject as value 'neutral' when compared to Britain and the United States, because, unlike the 'Anglo-Saxons', it did not condemn clearing mechanisms outright and, it argued, nor should the EFO. (The secretariat was known to be hostile.) What was needed was a 'technical' investigation that would establish: the methods used to effect clearing; whether the agreements reduced or increased trade; and the broader economic and political consequences if such agreements continued to be adopted across the global economy.[14] The League could then work to simplify and move clearing onto a multilateral basis—by negotiating deals between groups of interested parties—that would minimize their stifling effect on international trade.

Loveday and Stoppani were deeply troubled about the French initiative, but proved incapable of resisting it. They complained about the lack of consultation. Lucien Lamoureux, the Minister for Commerce, Foreign Minister Louis Barthou, and Louis Germain-Martin, the Finance Minister, bypassed them, going straight

---

[11] Forbes, *Doing Business with the Nazis*, 66–132; Scott Newton, *Profits of Peace: The Political Economy of Anglo-German Appeasement* (Oxford, 1996), 33–52.

[12] Arnold A. Offner, 'Appeasement Revisited: The United States, Great Britain and Germany 1933–1940', *Journal of American History*, 64/2 (1977), 373–93. The USA exported more to Germany than to any other state in 1933, 1934, and 1938, and our knowledge of German–US trade between 1939 and 1941 remains sketchy.

[13] Memo by Baumont, 'Note pour Monsieur Fouque-DuParc', 11 Aug. 1934, AMAE, SDN, IJ/Questions Économiques et Financières/Accord de Compensation et de Clearing/Mai 1934–Janvier 1935, no. 1323.

[14] Baumont to Barthou, 21 July 1934, AMAE, SDN, IJ/Organisation Économique et Financière de la Société des Nations/ Comité Économique/ Juillet 1934–Septembre 1937, no. 1184.

to the Second Committee of the Assembly and Avenol. As a result, Loveday and Stoppani had good grounds to fear the EFO could end up negotiating multilateral clearing deals between members of the gold bloc.[15] French thinking was certainly advanced. Although publicly declaring it was confident its clearing offices would be able to repatriate monies owed on its trade surpluses overseas in time, privately it was deeply troubled by the amount held in blocked accounts, and the cumbersome bilateral mechanism by which it was repaid. It would be far more efficient, the Quai d'Orsay told Stoppani, to create an international body through which the accounts would be cleared; in other words, some form of international payments union. It would not solve the problems with clearing overnight—it remained likely countries would continue to import goods from countries where they already had blocked accounts—but a multilateral clearing union would both standardize the process and render it more transparent. More immediately for France, it would help to build trade connections between members of the gold bloc and to demystify negotiations under way between the British and German governments, on the one hand, and the USA and Germany, on the other.[16]

Stoppani and Loveday were not persuaded by these arguments, but under pressure from Avenol they had little choice but to go along with the investigation.[17] They insisted, however, it be framed in the widest possible terms, for clearing and compensation agreements were, as Loveday put it, 'not much more than a mouse-hole in the Chinese Wall' of protection, and what was needed was a 'report on the wall itself'.[18] France's determination to stamp its mark and its perspective on the inquiry—evident too in its energetic lobbying among select members of the Financial Committee in Geneva, notably Austria, Britain, Belgium, Hungary, Italy, the Netherlands, and Czechoslovakia—was viewed with disquiet by the secretariat. An 'anxious' Stoppani wrote to his contacts in Britain, Australia, Canada, India, and Ireland 'without wasting time' to urge them to send 'competent' delegates with a sufficient grasp of the issues at stake to the Second Committee meeting to ensure the League's inquiry was 'framed in the round—commercial, monetary, and financial'.[19] He also wrote to Prentiss Gilbert, the US Consul in Geneva, to ensure his US 'collaborators' would be present when the French initiative was discussed at the Second Committee.

Stoppani's anxiety would have tipped into outright alarm had he known that at first the US response to the news of an inquiry was unreservedly positive because it

---

[15] Note of conversation between Loveday and Stoppani, 28 Aug. 1934, LON R4400, 10A/12852/2874.

[16] Unsigned memo, 'Note pour Monsieur Massigli', 4 Sept. 1934, AMAE, SDN, IJ/Questions Économiques et Financières/Accord de Compensation et de Clearing/Mai 1934–Janvier 1935, no. 1323.

[17] Memo of conversation between Loveday and Stoppani, 28 Aug. 1934, LON R4400, 10A/12852/2874.

[18] Loveday to Hill, 12 Sept. 1934, LON, Loveday, P143/14–15/outgoing correspondence, 1934–5.

[19] In the first instance, these were Economic Committee delegates Leith-Ross, McDougall, Riddell, Lindsay, and Cremins respectively. See letter from Stoppani, 4 Sept. 1934, LON R4400, 10A/12852/2874.

believed the inquiry would dovetail and inform a State Department-sponsored study of clearing agreements that was already under way.[20] US officials failed to register Stoppani's inference that, unless the forces of opposition to clearing and compensation marshalled their diplomatic resources, the inquiry could head off in unwelcome directions, notably the possibility of using the compensation side of the arrangements to negotiate multilateral import and export deals with members of the gold bloc.[21]

This danger became abundantly clear when the French government hastily convened a first meeting of the Clearing Committee only days after the Assembly Second Committee had approved the proposal. It met for the first time in Paris—not Geneva—on 18 October 1934, coinciding with the opening of the Gold Conference in Brussels, which brought together foreign, finance, and ministers of commerce from France, Belgium, the Netherlands, Switzerland, Luxembourg, Poland, and Italy. The meeting reaffirmed these countries' commitment to a range of monetary policies that the sterling bloc, the USA, and EFO's secretariat believed were damaging their economic health and that of the international economy. The gold bloc countries agreed to set up what they called a 'General Commission' and a range of subcommittees to study ways of increasing world trade through bilateral negotiations. (The latter was an echo of what Loveday and Stoppani feared the French had in mind for the League inquiry). The reinvigoration of gold bloc solidarity was signalled to the world on 20 October by the 'Brussels Protocol', which announced the members' intention to raise trade between them by 10 per cent within a year. It was followed by further meetings in Geneva that, although not under the auspices of the EFO, were attended by members of the secretariat, and at which EIS materials on clearing and bilateral agreements formed the mainstay of discussions.[22]

Behind these technical discussions and their imperative to unblock the world economy lay politics. The Geneva Clearing Committee formed part of a wider French initiative to bolster the gold bloc and its ties to countries that did, or that France hoped would, support the wider aims of French security policy in Europe. The haste with which France acted was intended to avoid giving the 'Anglo-Saxons' a determining voice in the inquiry's framework, but, forewarned by Loveday, Britain insisted that representatives from the Treasury and the Bank of England (Leith-Ross and Niemeyer respectively) serve on the committee. The French response was to match the British demand. It, too, insisted on another delegate,

---

[20] Feis to Stoppani, 21 Aug. 1934, and Stoppani to Feis, 28 Aug. 1934, LON R4402, 10A/13154/3100.

[21] The USA also missed the point that France wanted to confine its investigation to Europe because Latin American arrangements were different. Feis to Stoppani, 4 Oct. 1934, LON R4402, 10A/13154/3100.

[22] The French and Belgians considered Stoppani's involvement especially important. Note from French Ambassador in Brussels to Laval (Foreign Minister), 15 Oct. 1934, CAEF, B.57/7–74/ Relations Commerciales 1918–40, Questions Financiers/Bloc Or, 1934–5. For details of the Brussels Protocol, see 'Brussels Protocol', *Foreign Relations of the United States, 1934*, i. 609–10.

giving them two representatives each on the committee—everyone else had one—except for the USA, which had none.

It was this wrangling over committee membership that roused the Americans from their torpor. The Parisian picture of gold bloc solidarity may have been little more than a brassy front, but it now risked impugning the economic international-ism of the League, and so FDR demanded that the United States be granted 'full participation rights to express and record its views as any other member govern-ment' in the Clearing Committee's work.[23] It triggered a flurry of activity in Geneva, for, despite the fact that the USA had participated in a wide range of League committees since 1927, this was the first time it had demanded 'full rights of participation'. It did not just throw up awkward procedural questions about who had the power to issue such an invitation. It also exposed that gold bloc members of the Clearing Committee did not want the Americans to contribute; it was the secretariat and the British who wanted to see the Americans involved.[24] And, although FDR's demand for 'full rights' was a rhetorical flourish, it did not stop US internationalists wondering in vain whether it carried a deeper signifi-cance. Why explicitly demand full participation rights 'when it [the USA] had always had the chance to participate as fully as it desired in any previous League undertaking'.[25]

For the secretariat, however, it was essential that the USA should not just participate in, but dominate, the inquiry. By early November, much to their relief, Stoppani and Loveday had managed to regain some control of this runaway train.[26] With the Americans on board, the work of the Clearing Committee was reformu-lated to bring it closer to the position of the USA and the secretariat. Elements of the French programme remained, notably the determination to secure detailed information from governments as to the nature and extent of their clearing arrangements: the League asked to see complete texts of the agreements and facilitated standardized reporting of their functioning and effects. But any sugges-tion that clearing systems should be extended and moved onto a multilateral basis was gone. In its place came the more critically articulated purpose: to determine 'the repercussions of the clearing agreements on the trade of the contracting parties with third countries . . . and on the internal economic situation of contracting parties'.[27]

[23] William Phillips to Roosevelt, 31 Oct. 1934, NARA RG59, 840.515/Gold Bloc/25A.

[24] Baumont to de Panafieu, 2 Nov. 1934, AMAE, SDN, IJ/Questions Économiques et Financières/Accord de Compensation et de Clearing/Mai 1934–Janvier 1935, no. 1323; Stoppani to Pospisil, 5 Nov. 1934, LON R4422/13878/13878.

[25] Sweetser to Stoppani, 12 Nov. 1934, LON R4422, 10A/13878/13878.

[26] The issue of American participation also raised the question of whether the League should extend invitations to other non-members, notably Germany, but the secretariat rejected the idea.

[27] Note by Stoppani in 'Annex—Special Points to be Considered in the Study of Clearing Agreements', 1 November 1934 attached to Gilbert's report to Hull, 7 November 1934, NARA, RG 59, 840.515/Gold Bloc/25. Stoppani to French Foreign Ministry concerning, AMAE, SDN, IJ/Questions Économiques et Financières/Accord de Compensation et de Clearing/Mai 1934–Janvier 1935, no. 1323.

Stoppani and Loveday were able to assure the State Department and the White House that the investigation now had 'a very different feeling from that which was left after the first meeting of the Joint Committee', and that the evidence before them demonstrated that 'almost everywhere in Europe clearing is far from considered desirable and different states drag those agreements along like a heavy burden'. This optimistic interpretation of the data reflected the longer-term ambition of the secretariat's diplomacy to work as closely as possible with the United States. As important as reassuring Americans that European economic diplomacy could be reoriented towards a liberal capitalist agenda was the determination of the EFO officials to impress FDR that the League of Nations 'will certainly not fail to take the necessary measures for actual and complete collaboration'. Indeed, this intention was 'emphatically expressed' in a special mission by Loveday to the USA in 1934.[28]

MISSION AMERICA

It was in the 1930s that 'mission diplomacy', which frequently became mission impossible, came of age. The advent of the aeroplane combined with celebrity media coverage helped to make the stuffy world of high finance glamorous and accessible. The melodramatic 'mercy dash', exemplified by Raymond Moley's aeroplane diplomacy to save the 1933 London Conference, remained rare.[29] More common was the practice of fact-finding missions, of which there were a large number in the 1930s, directed at 'pioneering' economic projects in Nazi Germany, the Soviet Union, and the USA. But the League did not have the same freedom as states to determine where and when it might send envoys. As curious as EFO officials were about developments in Germany, the Nazis' stormy rejection of the League in 1933 put it out of bounds. Roosevelt's New Deal proved a similar draw for economists and statesmen. Keynes and William Beveridge both visited the USA in 1934, and here the League was allowed to venture. In October 1934, Loveday began a two-month tour of governments and learned bodies in the USA and Canada.[30]

The Canadian portion of Loveday's tour was focused on updating Canadian contacts on the performance of the world economy and developments within the EFO and the League. When it came to Loveday's sojourn in the USA, however, the focus was to gather rather than impart intelligence. Loveday publicly claimed the purpose of his visit was to 'study the economic and social revolution taking place', but privately he admitted he was not 'tracing the recovery programme in any detail' because the New Deal was 'confessedly experimental . . . and at present it's

---

[28] Smets to Feis, 20 Nov. 1934, LC Feis, Box 17, File 'H Miscellaneous 1933–1937'.

[29] It was the first recorded example of a practice that became commonplace in the 1960s. See Feis, *Nineteen Thirty Three*, 198–206.

[30] Beveridge advised Loveday on appointments for the secretariat, particularly difficult-to-fill posts in non-European economics. See Loveday to Beveridge, 15 May 1935, LON, Loveday, P143/14–15/ outgoing correspondence, 1934–5.

difficult to judge its effectiveness'. The bulk of Loveday's time in the USA was given over to studying Hull's new commercial policy and the US perspective of the League clearing and compensation inquiry. His aim was to confirm the internationalist credentials of the Roosevelt administration, and to bring the USA closer to the EFO. Loveday's meetings in the State Department and the White House left him in little doubt that US officials were 'anxious to effect a radical change in its commercial policy' and wanted his help to 'establish contact with persons concerned with commercial policy in Europe'.[31] Nor did Loveday read much into the running spat between Hull and George Peek, which misled observers in the British Treasury who were hostile to the RTAA into concluding that FDR was not enthusiastic about Hull's programme. Loveday's judgement was more perceptive. He recognized that the widely reported squabble between Hull and Peek was 'characteristic' of the 'political–administrative arrangements of the administration' but of 'little significant importance in determining the trend of policy'. Loveday rightly identified that the RTAA was likely to become a key plank of American economic foreign policy, which the departments of State, Commerce, Agriculture and Treasury and the US Tariff Commission came to support unanimously.[32]

His visit to the USA also increased Loveday's sensitivity to the 'violent sectional opposition' within and beyond Congress to the administration's efforts to liberalize international trade, recognizing a great deal would depend upon 'how far the President is prepared to go in the face of the opposition'.[33] Domestic debates about the RTAA prompted different interest groups in the US economy to bare their teeth, which provided useful intelligence to Loveday, who was encouraged by the variety and strength of sectional interests that declared themselves in favour of liberalizing the US trade regime: farmers who were anxious to sell more of their produce overseas, and industrialists who wanted to exploit the dollar's depreciation, who saw no end to the rising costs of the New Deal if international trade and the world economy did not revive, and who believed 'the adoption of such a policy would be a vital blow to the National Recovery Administration'.[34] True, the liberal direction of Hull's trade policy sat uneasily with the more protectionist and nationalist elements of the New Deal, but this did not mean the commitment to reduce the barriers to trade around the American economy was not radical in its own right, especially as the administration's intention was to negotiate on a multilateral as well as a bilateral basis. The fact that the RTAA enshrined the US commitment to unconditional MFN as the basis for agreement was very significant—British liberalism was the unashamed model—giving the USA 'a better

[31] Loveday (in Washington) to Stoppani, 19 Nov. 1934, LON R4422, 10A/13878/13878; Loveday to Avenol, 'Mission to Canada and the US', 29 Dec. 1934, LON R4605, 10C/13175/9854.
[32] Loveday to Avenol, 'Mission to Canada and the US', 29 Dec. 1934, LON R4605, 10C/13175/9854
[33] Loveday to Avenol, 'Mission to Canada and the US', 29 Dec. 1934, LON R4605, 10C/13175/9854
[34] Loveday to Avenol, 'Mission to Canada and the US', 29 Dec. 1934, LON R4605, 10C/13175/9854

tactical position to insist upon being given the lowest tariff rates without any compensating concessions'.[35]

The qualitative difference in American economic foreign policy by 1934, communicated to the world, in part, through the Economic and Financial Sections, was recognized by the French, who commended the 'pragmatic' approach of the new American trade policy—notably that the agreements were to be ratified by Presidential proclamation without submission to the Senate for ratification, and that the RTAA was informed and 'conducted by professors who were led by historical experience'. However, French officials believed international politics stood in the way. Hull's overtures to the Europeans had fallen on fallow ground at the world economic conference and he had come to 'feel he was among enemies'.[36] The subsequent Montevideo conference, by comparison, put him among friends, a contrast underlined by the fact that Hull was able to lay the groundwork for eight separate agreements with countries in Latin America.

In contrast to Paris, Geneva did not view the world in such starkly divided terms. Hull's success in Latin American countries, which, of course, made up an important proportion of League membership in the 1930s, proved the value of the RTAA to Stoppani and Loveday. Over the coming years, the American initiative on trade was to become a key feature in the EFO's efforts to revitalize its economic and financial diplomacy, to reaffirm the value of the League more generally, and to make up for the decline, in particular, in British interest and commitment to the organization. But at the same time as the secretariat was to place a refreshed version of American economic liberalism at the heart of its work, in 1934, in Loveday's words, the world remained to be convinced that the USA was 'serious and meant business'. It was down to the League to help, which, in return, would help the League. Loveday returned to Geneva at the start of 1935 persuaded of a growing desire in American official, banking, and commercial circles 'for closer international cooperation'. Binding America to the economic heart of the League had become his central, long-term ambition.

BACK TO CLEARING

Loveday's mission to the USA helped transform the tone and direction of the second meeting of the Clearing Committee in March 1935, as did the inclusion of a US delegate, Oscar Ryder, a Harvard-trained economist and member of the US Tariff Commission known affectionately as 'Ha Ha'. The discussion and materials provided by the League—notably a detailed analysis of the effects of clearing on international trade and a summary of governments' responses to the EFO questionnaire on clearing circulated in October 1938—hung on the central thread that

[35] Loveday to Avenol, 'Mission to Canada and the US', 29 Dec. 1934, LON R4605, 10C/13175/9854

[36] Beaumont to Barthou, 21 July 1934, AMAE SDN, IJ/Organisation Économique et Financière/Comité Economomique 41ᵉ à 46ᵉ Session/Juillet 1934–Septembre 1937, no. 1184.

clearing regimes and compensation arrangements were demonstrably bad for international trade.[37] Stoppani took the lead in arguing that the League should unequivocally condemn clearing, articulating what he described as the majority view, which saw exchange control as the cause and the perpetuator of clearing agreements. He exonerated countries that had floated their currencies of responsibility because 'the origins of the clearing system lay not in monetary instability but in the non-negotiability of the currency', putting the blame firmly with countries that had sought to defend their parity on the gold standard by methods that violated 'the rules of the game'.[38] It was a remarkably explicit statement of the secretariat's view that currency depreciation or devaluation was preferable to exchange control. So, far from leading the Clearing Committee, France found itself marginalized in the face of open opposition led by the Economic Section. Gold bloc solidarity crumbled, as did French hopes of using the League as a site to negotiate clearing agreements on a multilateral basis.

Shepherded by Stoppani and Loveday, the Clearing Committee agreed it was important to connect its treatment of clearing to the wider need to free the international economy from the shackles of protection.[39] The coherence of their shared view was revealed in a memorandum circulated by Stoppani shortly before the second session of the Clearing Committee, which strongly criticized the gold bloc countries' violation of the rules of the gold standard, notably quotas and gold sterilization, and the continued deflation of their national economies.[40] He was equally scathing of the contribution to international relations of the Brussels Protocol, noting that intra-group trade between its members had increased little since its inception and that, in general, the gold bloc's determination to protect its national interest by whatever controls necessary had merely exacerbated the general tendency to protectionism. (The report contained an especially damning section on the deterioration of trade relations between the gold bloc and the sterling area.) Stoppani then turned his fire on British policy to argue that what the world needed was a concerted effort to reduce the levels of international protectionism and the coordinated restabilization of currently floating currencies at new, agreed exchange rates. Only by increasing trade, he argued, would the currencies of the gold bloc and sterling areas be relieved of the speculative

[37] Economic Section report for the Economic Committee, 'Les Problèmes des Accords de Clearing et du Controle des Devises', 1 Sept. 1936, LON R4401, 10A/25435/2874. Guarneri, Rueff, Ohlin, Clay, and Basch all submitted memos on the origin, impact, and implications of the clearing agreements.
[38] Record of meeting, 'Joint Committee for the Study of Compensation and Clearing Agreements—Second Session—Held at Geneva from 25th to 30th March 1935', 26 Apr. 1935, LON R4422, File 10A/14496/13878. See also Gilbert to Hull, 14 June 1935, NARA RG59 840.515/ Gold Bloc/84.
[39] Loveday and Stoppani sought to manage intergovernmental exchange at every turn. See memo entitled 'Loveday Conversation with M. Stoppani re. Procedure at Assembly', 28 Aug. 1934, LON R4400, 10A/12852/2874.
[40] Memorandum by Stoppani, 'Economic Committee—Studies concerning the Problem of Closer European Economic Relations—Third Series—Essential Figures of the Trade of the Gold Bloc Countries among themselves and with Germany, the United Kingdom and the United States', 8 Mar. 1935, LON R4400, 10A/12852/2874.

pressures they faced, and, at the same time, reduce the trade barriers between them, allowing price levels between the two groups to adjust.[41] The answer, he concluded, was that trade talks between the sterling area (especially Britain) and the gold bloc countries should begin immediately.

Although this was a technical report, the opinions expressed in it were anything but impartial and apolitical. They were certainly too much for Avenol, who considered Stoppani's memorandum to be so inflammatory that he immediately banned the secretariat from publishing it.[42] The Secretary-General was motivated by his well-known desire to avoid offending member states, and notably one with whom his sympathies as an economically orthodox French patriot lay.[43] But Avenol's ban did not stop it from being circulated by Stoppani and Loveday through their high-level contacts in foreign ministries and treasuries, including those of Britain, France, and the United States.[44] Tough times for the economic liberalism emboldened Stoppani and Loveday. It was not the first or the only occasion EFO officials refused to allow League protocol or Avenol to prevent them disseminating their views.

In the meetings of the Clearing Committee itself, the secretariat view dominated. Indeed, the French representatives found themselves alone in arguing that the clearing 'system' was a 'compromise [measure] that could be improved upon' to which it had resorted to sustain their exports because 'their natural markets were closed to them owing to the monetary conditions of larger countries' (a barbed remark directed at the sterling and dollar areas). It was striking, too, that French delegates were bereft of support from gold bloc members, who eyed French gold reserves with envy and who saw France as a large market that had become closed to them. Without fresh injections of capital and financial support, they would rather keep the clearing system as it was.

Among the government delegates, none was more vociferous about the degree to which clearing 'dislocated and canalized world trade' than Ryder, who was congratulated by Hull and Feis for his role in 'leading' the committee to the 'right' conclusion.[45] In reality, however, Ryder articulated the secretariat's view as much as US policy, and reflected a wider set of connections established over the years between the State Department, the White House, and the Federal Reserve Bank through, among others, Williams, Day, Ryder, Goldenweiser, and W. R. Burgess, Deputy Governor at the Federal Reserve Bank. After 1933 these were supplemented by new people and new departments, including Henry Chalmers, Chief of Division of Foreign Trade at the Department of Commerce, Assistant Secretary

[41] A coordinated devaluation of the gold bloc currencies was also, by implication, a possibility.
[42] Dennis to Rappard, 25 Mar. 1935, LON R4420, 10A/11620/13878.
[43] Dennis to Rappard, 25 Mar. 1935, LON R4420, 10A/11620/13878.
[44] See Gilbert, 'Transmitting English/French Translations of Extract from Secretariat Memorandum Concerning Commerce of the Gold Bloc', 7 May 1935, NARA RG59, 840.515/ Gold Bloc/7.
[45] Hull to Ryder and Hull to Ryder, 9 Apr. 1935, NARA RG59, 840.515/Gold Bloc/73A. For Davis's comparatively limited role, see correspondence of Norman H. Davis in file 'League of Nations—Financial Committee 1931–1937', LC, Davis, Box 34.

of State Leo Pasvolsky, Harry Dexter White, whom Loveday and Stoppani first encountered as part of preparations for Tripartite Stabilization negotiations in 1936, and, a critical figure, the Chicago-based economist Jacob Viner.[46] Like many key American internationalists and social scientists associated with the EFO, Viner was born outside the USA, in his case in Romania, from where he settled in the USA via Canada. Viner was the consummate networker. Respected for his intellectual powers, he was also greatly valued by economists, statisticians, and politicians for his inter-personal skills and his grasp of current thinking in the fields of economics and statistics. He acted as official and unofficial consultant to hundreds of academic and professional appointments, working as a vital conduit in the transfer of people and ideas between Europe and the USA, frequently through the mediating hub of Geneva in the 1930s and after the 1940s through the Institute of Advanced Studies and the attendant US university and philanthropic network.

The Clearing Committee's report was formally presented to Council on 25 September 1936. It came out firmly against clearing and compensation agreements, concluding, just as historians would later, that clearing systems were the consequence of two main elements: first, a fear of inflation and exchange depreciation and, secondly, an anxiety that exchange control would trigger exclusion from international markets or an inability to service international debts, or both. Especially significant from the Americans' perspective was the report's emphasis on the negative effects of clearing on the 'commercial and financial interests of third countries' (that is, countries like the United States, which were largely excluded from the arrangements) and on the fact that most signatories of such agreements were in clear violation of MFN.[47]

But there was not a complete convergence of US and secretariat views. Indeed, the final report betrayed more about the direction in which secretariat wanted to take international economic relations than the views of government representatives on the committee. It strongly echoed Stoppani's memoranda on clearing, and contained elements that irked the State Department, especially the view that creditor countries had to take a more understanding line with debtors who were struggling to earn sufficient foreign currency to repay their overseas debts.[48] Loveday and Stoppani, were certainly satisfied by their handiwork, believing the report to be the most important the EFO had published in five years, and they set about commissioning two economic journalists to frame its conclusions in more 'populist language'.[49]

[46] For a list of Loveday's key contacts in 1935, see Loveday to Norberg, 9 Mar. 1935, LON, Loveday, P143/14–15/outgoing correspondence, 1934–5, which also reveals the advice he and Stoppani gave, in this case to the Svenska Handelsbanken, on how to cultivate links to the United States.

[47] League of Nations, *Enquiry into International Clearing* (Geneva, 1935), II.B.6. (Here the League adopted the form 'Enquiry' in preference to 'Inquiry', which it also used in an official context.)

[48] Deimel cable to Feis, 1 Apr. 1935, NARA RG59, 840.515/Gold Bloc/69; League of Nations, 'Work of the Economic Committee during its Forty-Fourth Session, Held at Geneva from 7th to 12th September 1936: The Problem of Clearing Agreements and Exchange Control', *Official Journal* (Nov. 1936), annex 1619, 1330–2.

[49] Loveday to Pelt, 17 Apr. 1935, and Loveday to Cummings, 3 May 1935, LON R4422, 10A/17619/13878.

Their view stood in sharp contrast to the view of the French delegates on the committee, frustrated by the end result that unquestionably favoured the Anglo-Saxon perspective.[50] French disappointment reflected broader trends afoot as the failure of gold bloc coordination in Geneva demonstrated the now rapidly failing gold bloc, which received a further blow in May 1935, when Belgium, a key ally, abandoned gold. But, when the report was returned to the hands of government delegates at the League Assembly in September 1935, France was able to stymie resolutions proposed by the sterling bloc members calling for the League to promote currency devaluation as a means to combat depression, and the removal of exchange controls by some of the worst offenders, Germany, Hungary, and Bulgaria. Instead, the remaining members of the gold bloc passed resolutions that pulled in the opposite direction, with Poland and the Netherlands arguing that the Clearing Committee should remain in session and identify means by which the clearing system and compensation arrangements could be improved and perpetu-ated. Behind the scenes, Britain too was anxious to curtail the League's interest in clearing because of its 'special importance' to the Anglo-German relations—well known to the secretariat—which meant the Treasury was opposed to any multilat-eral approach on the topic.[51] The outcome was a characteristic reminder of the obstacles facing the EFO's carefully crafted 'technical' solutions when they were transposed into the broader framework of interstate relations.

The politics of international financial relations remained dynamic and prone to rapid change. While in Geneva in March, Leith-Ross had a number of private conversations with Rueff, who intimated that his position and that of his govern-ment was beginning to move. Since the depreciation of sterling, there had been debate among the gold bloc members as to whether Great Britain should be invited to participate in trade negotiations, either with the gold bloc collective or on a bilateral basis, but throughout France had been adamant that Britain had to stabilize the pound before trade negotiations could be countenanced. Rueff and Flandin now offered Britain the opportunity to enter trade negotiations with the gold bloc without preconditions, an opportunity Leith-Ross believed Britain should seize, if only to manage the imminent devaluations of the gold bloc members. But many in the Treasury disagreed. Phillips, Hopkins, Chamberlain, and Norman concluded British 'intervention might do more harm than good'; that Rueff and Flandin represented a minority view, and that talking to them would only antagonize other countries (notably Germany, and, to a lesser extent, Switzerland and the Netherlands) while bringing France a little closer to depreci-ation.[52] For them, France was clearly not a priority, although Leith-Ross was instructed to use further meetings of the EFO to discern how far depreciation

---

[50] French delegates also felt abandoned by Stucki and Di Nola, who failed to turn up at the, all important, final meeting.
[51] Waley to Makins, 9 Oct. 1935, TNA: PRO FO371/19681, W425/422/50; memo by Lloyd, 'Report on London Interviews', 19–30 Oct. 1936, LON R4422, 10A/24322/14617.
[52] Leith-Ross to Phillips, 26 Mar. 1935 and Phillips to Chamberlain and Hopkins, 30 Mar. 1935, TNA: PRO T160/840, 13427/2.

was a realistic possibility for members of the gold bloc. In Geneva, the secretariat had anticipated the request.

ENDINGS

The chronology of the Great Depression has been set in history by the loss-leaders not its laggards. Britain and the sterling bloc countries were among the first to suffer the pain of credit contraction and price deflation in the 1920s, and were the first to surface from its deepest troughs. Next came the USA and those economies most entangled with it in the Americas. In 1935, these landmarks, and others, began to be charted on an overtly global and comparative scale by a new League initiative to assess 'The General Position of Economic Relations at the Present Time'. It was an unexciting title, but it did exactly what it claimed. Indeed, the very generality of its remit gave the secretariat and the EIS the opportunity to address a wide range of issues and, critically, to present them in an interrelated and more overtly political fashion than it had before. Aside from detailed materials exploring the evolution of American economic foreign policy, Stoppani and Loveday prepared an extensive annotated agenda, and each subject was supported by a vast array of detailed notes. The 'General Report of Economic Situation, and in Particular on International Economic Relations' was backed up by League memoranda on the 'Evolution of Commercial Policy since the Crisis' and on 'Various Restrictive Measures', papers on agricultural protectionism, a note on 'International Economic Collaborations: Regional Agreements', detailed trade statistics, and a 'Chronological Table of Commercial Treaties and Agreements that had been Concluded, Ratified, and Brought into Effect'.[53]

The study of 'Economic Relations at the Present Time' sought to be universal in its ambit, but the secretariat's intention was to use its work to facilitate a new examination of international protectionism and what it believed to be the virtuous example of American policy exemplified by developments in US–Latin American trade agreements and in negotiations, begun in February 1935, between the US and Belgian governments.[54] Among the lengthiest documents compiled by the Economic Section was a report on US commercial policy, going into exhaustive detail on US deals with Brazil and Cuba, and the recent US–Belgian trade agreement to demonstrate the very favourable impact of unconditional MFN status on the co-signatories. Negotiations with Belgium were seen as especially significant in the 'official mind' of the League, because they offered demonstrable evidence of the USA taking positive steps to engage with the heart of Europe.

By lauding measures that expressed the American intent to liberalize the world economy, the secretariat demonstrated an increasing willingness to criticize policies of member and non-members at variance with those of the United States. The

[53] See Gilbert to Hull, NARA RG59, 500.C1199/139.
[54] The US–Belgian negotiations have been little studied by historians. A rare account appears in Simmons, *Who Adjusts?*, 241–55.

materials it garnered on the state of world trade supported the US position that Germany, France, and the USSR discriminated 'unduly' against others. The secretariat now unequivocally opposed the French position that the restabilization of floating currencies was a fundamental precondition to trade negotiations, and British policy that currencies had to achieve greater equilibrium than they held at present before trade negotiations would be fruitful.[55] Currency stabilization was desirable and would facilitate trade negotiations, but the gold standard required reform before that was practicable.

Taken together, the work of the Clearing Committee and the RTAA study marked a clean break with the secretariat's past efforts to build consensus around a liberal internationalism exemplified by British policy in the 1920s. The investigation into clearing was presented to the Economic Committee as a manifesto for action, calling for multilateral RTAA-style tariff reductions and some sort of currency agreement that would represent a landmark in relations between the major economic blocs (gold bloc, sterling group, and the USA) and, equally importantly, raise the prestige of the League. The State Department was undoubtedly excited by the possibility of such a deal, but Stoppani and Loveday understood that, without the commitment of key states, there was little likelihood of the Economic Committee delivering it. Like the Americans, they, too, appreciated the new candour in its meetings, but knew it was facilitated, in part, because so many issues divided delegates. They no longer sought to preserve even the outward impression of consensus in the League as they had in the past because it now had little value, given the trouble brewing in Ethiopia and the Rhineland. Everything, and at the same time nothing, was at stake.

Yet for Loveday, Stoppani, and their colleagues in the sections it became all the more important to articulate what they understood to be the EFO's values and ambitions as part of wider efforts to save the League. For the organization, the crisis over Ethiopia began at the end of 1934, when Italian and Ethiopian troops clashed at Walwal, and Emperor Hailie Salassie requested arbitration from the League. Its response was shockingly ineffective. The League's ambiguous relationship to imperialism seduced some into believing Mussolini's claim that he had invaded the sovereign state and fellow League member to rid it of slavery—the organization had agreed a Convention in 1926 to Suppress the Slave Trade and Slavery.[56] League paralysis was also a consequence of Anglo-French attempts to retain Mussolini's favour for their own ends, and because Italy was a long-standing council member whose nationals were widely employed in a number of League committees. As a result, it took the League over a year to condemn the Italian action, and by then its deplorable treatment of Ethiopians was played out at the Assembly, where its leader, Haile Selassie, forlornly implored it for help.

[55] Memo by EFO, 'Development of the Commercial Policy of the United States since June 1934—Summary of Official or Semi-Official Statements and Other Information', 8 Mar. 1935, copy attached to Gilbert's report to Hull, 10 Apr. 1935, NARA RG59, 500.C1199/137.

[56] Jean Allain, 'Slavery and the League of Nations: Ethiopia as a Civilised Nation', *Journal of the History of International Law*,.8 (2006), 213–44; Amalia Ribi, 'Humanitarian Imperialism. The Politics of Anti-Slavery Activism in the Inter-War Years', Unpublished D.Phil. University of Oxford, 2006.

With an increasing sense of urgency, the League's efforts at economic diplomacy were related directly to these iconic political events. The Ethiopian catastrophe was protracted, and throughout Avenol, and Loveday and Stoppani, albeit with different end goals in mind, became eager for the League to redouble its efforts in the economic sphere. Avenol proposed regular meetings at the League between leading economic and finance ministers (a form of prototype G8 arrangement through which Avenol wanted to include the aggressor powers), while Loveday, by contrast, began to pursue greater power and independence for EFO from the League in the hope of bringing the USA on board and reinforcing the League's commitment to economic liberalism. He was also frustrated by the limitations of intergovernmental consensus imposed on the economic and financial committees, and began to advocate the creation of an 'independent' economic and financial organization comprising government ministers and a beefed-up secretariat, because, as things stood, there were grave limits on what the EFO could do when it came to criticizing state policies. This programme for reform, and the disagreement it provoked between Loveday and Avenol, was to resurface with renewed vigour in 1938.[57]

But, while the Ethiopian crisis smouldered, the more immediate issue for the EFO was the impact of the Belgian devaluation in March 1935 and the US–Belgian tariff agreement, which once again renewed French interest in multilateral financial diplomacy. In June 1935, these developments prompted the Belgian Prime Minster Paul Van Zeeland, supported by the French, to call for the reopening of the mothballed World Economic Conference.[58] The French move against gold was confirmed at a meeting of the Financial Committee in Paris in late August and at the 43rd meeting of the Economic Committee in Geneva that opened on 2 September, where France announced it had come around to the view that, as currencies rates had largely been stable for over a year, it was 'now time to do something in the field of trade restrictions. *De jure* stabilisation could not be expected.'[59] Keeping the faith with gold was left to the Swiss delegate, who demanded, as France once had, that only the gold standard offered a real guarantee of currency stability that would allow protective barriers to fall. The response of James Harvey Rogers, monetary adviser to FDR and a prominent critic of Smoot-Hawley, was swift and sharp.[60] Stucki was being 'completely unrealistic'. No

[57] Report by Dayras, 15 July 1935, AMAE, SDN, IJ/Organisation Économique et Financière, Comité Economique/Composition Comité Economique/Réunions Interministérielles, 1926–40, 1927–9, no. 1172.

[58] Laroche to Barthou, Telg. 47, 17 July, AMAE, Y/Internationale, 1918–1940/Dossier General: Situation Financière 1935.

[59] Report by Rogers and Gilbert, 'Proceedings of the Economic Committee of the League of Nations—Forty-Third Session—Geneva, September 1935', NARA RG59, 500.C1199/165, 31–2; Stoppani to Boissard, Rueff, and Coulondre, 23 Aug. 1935, AMAE, SDN/IJ/Questions Économique, no. 1154; Rowe-Dutton to Leith-Ross, 1 Oct. 1935, TNA: PRO T188/120.

[60] James Harvey Rodgers and Carlton J. H. Hayes, *The Process of Inflation in France, 1914–1927* (New York, 1929), and the especially well-regarded James Harvey Rodgers *America Weighs her Gold* (New Haven, 1931). James Harvey Rogers also studied the monetary systems of Japan, India, and China, taught at the Geneva School of International Studies for ten years, and served on the Economic Committee of the League for the USA between 1933 and 1937.

country, he rejoined, could give Switzerland the kind of guarantee it sought. There followed an energetic and authoritative rebuttal of gold standard orthodoxy and a call that the committee explicitly recommend currency depreciation and cheap money, which would greatly increase the supply of available money around the world and bring global recovery with it. The 'time was ripe for trade liberalization through the League', he provocatively suggested, because 'large portions of the world were currently operating under stable dollar and sterling standards'.[61]

At this point, discussions in the meeting became so heated that Loveday had to call for an emergency tea-break, which did little to cool off tempers inflamed by Rogers, and the French *volte-face* on the primacy of gold stabilization. Swiss and Polish resentment was especially pronounced. It was clear the French move away from gold was inexorable—there was no mistaking the conviction of its delegation, led by Paul Elbel, President of the Radical-Socialist parliamentary group, a former Director of Economic Relations in the French Ministry of Commerce and President of the Economic Committee of the League. (Within a year, Elbel began to lobby for an international currency issued under the guarantee of the League of Nations.) And this, combined with Rogers's forthright attack, meant that the remaining gold bloc members wanted to remove previously agreed sections of the proposed financial committee report that praised the improved performance of the British economy since depreciation, alongside the agreed call that quotas be reduced. Rowe-Dutton and Stoppani fought back, and the wrangling was all too much for Rogers. European protectionism was 'insane', he declared, 'to pay 7,000 Swiss francs [£2,300] for a Ford which costs $550 in America is too absurd. Europe was depriving itself of a higher standard of living', and for what?[62]

The question helped to focus minds, not onto the bigger issue of the primary purpose of economic policy—there was rarely space for these kinds of considerations—but on the more mundane question of what should go in the report. The US delegates and Loveday and Stoppani began to fret over the implications of an open display of disagreement. Would it neuter or nourish the EFO's work? How would the US position be interpreted? And what would it mean for the League? Rather than present a false consensus, Loveday and Stoppani suggested that the Economic Committee put two options before the world. Should states take measures to revive international trade before attempting to stabilize their national currencies? Or should currencies be stabilized and then trade liberalized? Britain and the United States rejected the notion that there was a choice, and pushed for trade liberalization; the Swiss and Poles, in turn, demanded the report be suppressed. As the meeting descended into farce, the delegates were brought to their

[61] Report by Rogers and Gilbert, 'Proceedings of the Economic Committee of the League of Nations—Forty-Third Session—Geneva, September 1935', pp. 31–2, 37–8, NARA RG59, 500.C1199/165.

[62] Report by Rogers and Gilbert, 'Proceedings of the Economic Committee of the League of Nations—Forty-Third Session—Geneva, September 1935', p. 53, NARA RG59, 500.C1199/165. Elbel leaned heavily on the reports of the 1935 and 1936 Economic And Financial Committees in his treatment of 'The Problem of Peace: Political Entanglements, Psychological Difficulties, Economic Realities', *Annals of Public and Cooperative Economics*, 14/3 (1937), 436–59.

senses when Miyoji Ito, the Japanese delegate (who still participated in economic and financial committee meetings although Japan was no longer a full member of the League), wanted to revise the sentence reading 'economic anarchy leads to propaganda for war' to read '"social" war'.[63] Heated discussion disintegrated into laughter as everyone, except the unfortunate Ito, in the midst of a lonely campaign to preserve Japan's formal membership of the League, saw the funny side. While humour may have reminded them of their common humanity, it could not overcome divisions on policy, the absence of a common vision, or the threat these divisions posed to the League.

'BEFORE THE EYES OF THE WORLD'

Although the delegates were deeply divided, there was no escaping the relentless grind of the League machinery, which meant that by the end of September an agreed report of some description had to go forward from the Economic and Financial Committees to the Second Committee and Assembly. As usual, the need for a public show of unanimity meant that the final report cobbled together by the secretariat did not reflect the obvious rift between the dollar/sterling group and the gold bloc/debtor states, nor that France was moving from one side to the other. Nevertheless, by default, it sought to create a 'world view'. *Remarks on the Present Phase of International Economic Relations* offered generalities on the global capitalist economy and the secretariat's unconvincingly positive spin on what had been bitter discussions and a frustrating outcome by emphasizing international agreement on the damage caused by all types of protectionist restrictions, including currency manipulation. The approach neatly sidestepped policy recommendations, be they to tariff cuts, exchange controls, or currency devaluation. More significantly, the report abandoned the League's usual emphasis on state policy to stress instead the commonality of experience between producers and consumers, around the world, in an attempt to show the folly and danger of condemning 'foreign' economies:

foreigners are purchasers of *our* products; they are those who have to pay *us* the interest on the capital we have lent them; they are those who, by transporting their goods to our country and our goods to their country, would provide work for *our* railways and *our* shipping, who, visiting us as tourists, would spend their money in *our* hotels and *our* shops. In short, these '*foreigners*' are an indispensable link in the chain of our activities, or, to express it more aptly, they are members of our body economic: to impoverish them is to impoverish ourselves.[64]

---

[63] Report by Rogers and Gilbert, 'Proceedings of the Economic Committee of the League of Nations—Forty-Third Session—Geneva, September 1935', p. 57, NARA RG59, 500.C1199/165. On Japan's relations to the League more generally, see Thomas W. Burkman, *Japan and the League of Nations: Empire and World Order, 1914–1938* (Honolulu, 2008), 194–209.

[64] League of Nations, *Remarks on the Present Phase of International Economic Relations* (Geneva, 1935), 10. Emphasis in the original.

These were Stoppani's and Loveday's words. They were in the preparatory materials that had gone to delegates and were heard once again at the opening meetings of the Second Committee of the League. It was their attempt to counter the bickering over trade and currency to promote a new agenda on 'positive security' that promoted human development, of which more in Chapter 5, and sought to bypass these issues and the state agencies that controlled them.

But the power of the state was not easily circumvented. The high-powered French delegation to the Second Committee and Assembly was augmented by Bonnet, now Minister of Commerce, and Rueff, Joint Director of Mouvement Général des Fonds at the Finance Ministry; formally its representatives were the senior diplomat Charles Rochat, and Senator Joseph Paul-Boncour. Sensing something was up, Germany sent an observer to the League for the first time since its abrupt departure in 1933: Dr A.H. Haak, an attaché of the German Legation in Berne, although his observer status did not grant him entry to where the real action was taking place.[65] The night before the Second Committee convened, Loveday and Stoppani hosted a private dinner party for French, British, and US officials, at which Bonnet was the guest of honour. Before the first course was served, Bonnet, with a dramatic flourish, took to the floor to announce that France planned to revalue its currency and wished to do so—in contrast to Britain in 1931 and the USA in 1933—through multilateral negotiation at the League. The organization's members, he asserted, needed to break free from what he described as their 'natural reluctance' to address the question of monetary stability directly because of its importance to the wider context of diplomatic affairs, although this did not mean directly confronting central bankers and finance ministries overseas whose support France needed.

The British were somewhat taken aback by the energy of the Franco-League initiative, and took a non-committal line by asking for further details of the French proposal.[66] These were not long in coming. The following day, first in bilateral meetings with the British delegation, and then at a full meeting of the Second Committee, the French offered their terms for what they called a 'wide-ranging commercial agreement' that would see France move away from its internationally vilified quota system to an internationally agreed general tariff. In return, the sterling area currencies were expected to maintain their exchange parities within 10 per cent of their present exchange value for the duration of negotiations. Although reminiscent of the London temporary stabilization agreement, French policy had moved on. Paris no longer sought the restabilization of sterling as its ultimate aim, and declared itself ready to move from quotas to a more transparent system of protection from which, in theory at least, it should be easier to negotiate reductions. The Americans regarded the proposal as a 'turning point in French

[65] Note from Le Ministre de l'Interieur, le Directeur Général de la Sûreté Nationale to the President du Conseil, 7 Sept. 1935, AMAE, Serié SDN/ASSEMBLEE, Seizième Session, Mai 1935–Juillet 1936, no. 101.
[66] Burgin to Phillips, 18 Sept. 1935, TNA: PRO FO371/19601, W8250/31/50.

commercial policy', and delegates from the British Commonwealth, too, welcomed the fact that France was at last moving towards a more liberal economic policy.[67]

The 'sticking-point', or so it seemed to US observers, was 'British intransigence', with French and secretariat officials also disappointed that Britain was 'decidedly unresponsive' to the proposal. The problem, they rightly concluded, was as much political as economic: with a British election pending, its statesmen were not happy 'to commit themselves in any way even to temporary stabilization', and it was natural enough for the British to be hostile to a French initiative launched with little advanced warning before 'the eyes of the world in Geneva'. Charron believed that Britain needed time to reflect upon the details of the proposal, and was encouraged by the favourable response of the Danes, the Dutch, the Swedes, the Norwegians, the Argentinians, the Mexicans, the Australians, and the Belgians— nations with both stable and floating currencies.[68] Such unanimity was rare and reflected a new confidence in the ability to negotiate tariff reductions between states with different monetary regimes.

The EFO's secretariat believed it would be a real step forward if wrangling over currency stability could be put to one side. It would at last be free of the precondition of currency stabilization most states put on any EFO-sponsored proposals for multilateral tariff reductions, clearing, and agreements to effect a better deal for the world's primary producers. The French proposal also offered a number of specific benefits: it marked a further international endorsement of the RTAA and American participation in the EFO. (Leo Pasvolsky provided much of the supporting documentation for the secretariat's work and the French proposal, and briefed the press on both sides of the Atlantic.) It could also shore up the position of Rueff, and other 'sound-minded' officials in France who wanted to return the country to the norms of liberal capitalism, and who were vulnerable to right-wing reactionary pressures. If Bonnet did not receive international support, 'there was a danger that France would again retire behind her fortress of quotas and a great opportunity would be lost'.[69] The secretariat and collaborators in France and the USA believed the time to strike a deal was now. The problem was that this was not how the British saw it.

Chamberlain took the lead on British policy. Disregarding the League, he used his Mansion House speech of 2 October 1935 to issue a very public rebuttal of the French proposal, in which he argued that the French were using the League to exploit American enthusiasm for tariff reductions in order to favour the gold franc. He rejected the notion that France was attempting to cultivate international support for its devaluation.[70] Other British voices, notably those of Leith-Ross

[67] Gilbert's report to Hull, 'Speech by French Minister of Commerce before the Second Committee of the Assembly of the League of Nations', 20 Sept. 1935, NARA RG59, 500.C111/891.
[68] Gilbert's report to Hull, 'xvith (1935) session of the assembly of the league of nations—Report on the Work of the Second Committee Respecting Economic and Financial Questions', 3 Oct. 1935, NARA RG59, 500.C111/902.
[69] Gilbert's report to Hull, 'Session of the assembly of the league of nations—Report on the Work of the Second Committee Respecting Economic and Financial Questions', 3 Oct. 1935, NARA RG59, 500.C111/902. Gazel to the Quai D'Orsay, 21 Sept. 1935, AMAE, Y/Internationale, 1918–1949/ Dossier general: situation financière 1935, no. 221.
[70] Text of Mansion House speech, 2 Oct. 1935, TNA: PRO, FO371/19601, W8628/31/50.

and Eden, were more conciliatory, but they were powerless against Chamberlain's determination to retain a free hand in his European policy. As a result, the resolutions passed at the League in response to Bonnet's proposal were an awkward fudge of Anglo-French views. They acknowledged tariff reductions were important but did not specify how countries were to negotiate them on a multilateral basis, nor how far the principle of unconditional MFN should be applied. (Britain, for example, did not pass on privileges from imperial preference to its other MFN trading partners.) In response, the secretariat immediately launched an inquiry into the MFN clause. Bonnet's initiative may not have reshaped the diplomatic landscape in ways Loveday and Stoppani had hoped, but a bilateral Franco-American trade and currency deal could still deliver wider benefits, and they were determined not to let the momentum behind the initiative lapse.

There were reasons to be cheerful: the Americans were clearly very enthusiastic about the League's efforts to promote multilateral tariff reductions. Hull had bombarded participants of the Second Committee's discussions with congratulatory telegrams regarding the 'large measure of agreement between so many countries', which he hoped would lead to 'effective agreements without too much delay'; this state enthusiasm was mirrored in equally positive responses to much of the press coverage in France and the Americas, and behind the scenes the US administration was doing what it could to stoke this enthusiasm.[71] But there was also cause for concern. The debate had prompted the Second Committee to endorse the Chilean call for the League to study whether a scheme of 'integral compensation', the so-called Milhaud Plan, would facilitate trade, and directed the secretariat to work alongside the BIS on clearing 'in order to devise a means of bringing Germany back into the picture'.[72] Loveday and Stoppani were far from enthused by the instruction. It ran directly counter to their attempts to condemn German trade and monetary policy for violating the norms of liberal internationalism, and their efforts to keep the BIS at arm's length. But, while they were unhappy with the Second Committee's directive, it came with a silver lining: the authority to study 'any other projects or measures designed to extend international trade and to give it greater freedom'. In short, *carte blanche* to explore anything that could reasonably come under the heading of the 'problems of international trade' without prior state approval.[73]

At the end of 1935, the secretariat worried that the League presented an incoherent vision of the world economy before, in Stoppani's words, the 'eyes of the world': it favoured floating currencies, but continued to support those states, notably France, that were clinging to gold by their fingertips; it preferred free trade,

---

[71] Marriner to Hull, 30 Sept. 1935, NARA RG59, 500.C111/895; Hull to the diplomatic officers of the American Republics, 1 Oct. 1935, *Foreign Relations of the United States 1935*, i. 525–6; Rowe-Dutton to Leith-Ross, 1 Oct. 1935, TNA: PRO T188/120.

[72] Gilbert to Hull, report, 'Recent Developments Respecting Resolution of the XVIth Assembly on Economic and Financial Questions', 2 Dec. 1935, NARA RG59, 500.C1199/177.

[73] Records of the Sixteenth Ordinary Session of the Assembly—Meetings of the Committees—Minutes of the Second Committee (Technical Questions), in League of Nations, *Official Journal*, Special Supplement, No. 140 (Oct. 1935), p. 77.

but it was not averse to exploring the 'benefits' of clearing and compensation agreements; it denounced German autarky, yet it was looking for ways to bring Germany back into the EFO; its secretariat was increasingly hostile to British economic foreign policy, but Britain remained its chief paymaster and British economists were key supporters; and it was increasingly enthused by US commercial policy, yet the USA had signed few deals of economic significance and in real terms was no closer to League membership than it had been in 1927. It had become undeniable that the policies that had shaped the EFO's founding and its development were firmly in the past. While the vision of a liberal capitalist economy and the benefits it would bring to the world remained unchanged, the EFO's civil servants and expert advisers were uncertain where the paths they sought to carve out of the forest of protectionism and depreciation would take them. At the same time it was clear that states acting on their own, whatever their political inclinations, had not found the policy recipe for economic growth.

The League was lost in other ways. Just as the 1935 meeting of the Assembly closed, Mussolini launched a full-scale military assault on Ethiopia, and the crisis invoked significant divisions within the League: between member nations who wanted to take decisive action to support the Ethiopian Emperor Hailie Selassie and those who did not; between Council members who endorsed the notion of sanctions and those who did not; and between Italian members of the secretariat who openly showed their support for Mussolini's action and those who were appalled by the Italian invasion. The most conspicuously treacherous act of Mussolini's supporters in the employ of the League was their decision to give up their salaries to present Mussolini with a bar of gold to bolster Italian gold reserves, which had been put under additional pressure following the implementation of League sanctions.[74]

Stoppani was the most senior Italian in the secretariat to oppose *Il Duce's* action. He ignored governmental pressure to return to Rome and resisted Mussolini in the best way he knew how: by developing the progress he believed had been made towards a cooperative, multilateral agreement on trade and currency devaluation so as, in his words, to 'attain its highest objective, namely international peace'.[75] Over the next twelve months, in the face of considerable apathy, if not hostility, on the part of the League's principal progenitors—the United States, France, and Britain—and obstruction on the part of Avenol, Stoppani sought to make the Economic Committee the agent of an international and financial agreement among the world's great powers to combat the damage done by the sanctions fiasco and the continued deterioration of international relations. The previous year's work had given him grounds to believe trade negotiations could take place in the context of floating exchange rates and provide an international platform to help gold bloc members face an increasingly uncertain future, with greater engagement from the United States.[76]

[74] Arthur W. Rovine, *The First Fifty Years: The Secretary-General in World Politics 1920–1970* (Leiden, 1970), 129–31

[75] Stoppani to Halifax, 3 Aug. 1936, TNA: PRO T188/148.

[76] Rovine, *The First Fifty Years*,.131; Gilbert to Hull, 'Question of Meeting of Economic Committee—Most-Favored-Nation Clause', 24 Mar. 1936, NARA RG59, 500.C1199/189.

In the first half of 1936, the final act of the ugly drama over Ethiopia was played out in Geneva. The crisis prompted the League to take the unprecedented step of calling an extraordinary meeting of the Assembly in June, at which, amid acrimonious scenes, sanctions against Italy were abandoned. Shortly afterwards, the international order established at the Paris Peace Conference received a further weighty blow when German troops marched west and remilitarized the Rhineland, contrary to the provisions of both the Versailles and Locarno treaties. Loveday's and Stoppani's worst fears were now realized. They, like many Liberal internationalists, recognized that time was fast running out for the League. Stoppani was so desperate that he launched an emergency action of his own. Abandoning what was an explicit, but increasingly resented and violated, code of practice that every League initiative had to be as inclusive and open as possible, Stoppani proposed an international economic agreement between the United States, Britain, and France, on the one hand, and Germany and Italy, on the other. (Another variation on the scheme included the USSR.) There were four key steps to his proposal. First, persuade Britain and the United States to fix the parity of sterling and the US dollar in relation to one another for at least two years. Secondly, use this Anglo-American currency axis to persuade countries practising exchange control to abandon it by offering a number of incentives, including guarantees to buy their exports. The third step would be a revision of debt schedules. Finally, in return, these and a much wider circle of countries would be encouraged to abandon quotas and tariffs by a wider commitment to currency stabilization. (The inclusion of the 'have-not' powers was by far the least developed part of the programme, and Stoppani privately believed it would not get that far.) The key objective was to effect multilateral cooperation between the leading liberal capitalist states. A crucial element of this final step would be the negotiated revaluation of currencies through a revised mechanism of international exchange. The plan was bold. To give it political clout, in July 1936 Stoppani called on Paul Van Zeeland, the Belgian economist and former central banker who was currently President of the League Assembly, to take up the mission on the League's behalf.

The scheme set out the path away from nationalism to a newly reintegrated international economy, but it did so in a political vacuum. Van Zeeland, as requested, supported the call for the world to 'make a comprehensive and strenuous effort to set in motion an international economic revival'.[77] Stoppani also organized a series of personal meetings with national representatives, including those from Britain, France, the USA, Belgium, the Netherlands, Denmark, and the Commonwealth.[78] Among the latter group, the Australians gave him particular cause for hope. Stanley Bruce and McDougall, from the Australian Commission in London, promised Stoppani their support, arguing that Britain should be more receptive to

[77] Van Zeeland's closing speech attached to Gilbert's report to Hull, 'Possible Developments of Discussions on Economic Questions in Forthcoming Session of Economic Committee and the Assembly of the League', 14 July 1936, NARA RG59, 500.C1199/202.
[78] Walters to Strang, 4 July 1936, TNA: PRO FO371/20474, W6109/79/98; Baumont to Coulondre, 9 July, CAEF, B.98/I1, Relations Commerciales, 1918–1940, Société des Nations,; Everett to Hull, 10 July 1936, NARA RG59 500.C1199/201.

French overtures for a monetary and trading agreement. This would then be the means to recast the system of imperial preference into a 'low tariff group which could then be joined by France and other countries'—a far better option, as far as McDougall was concerned, than bilateral deals.[79] The end of imperial preference would do much 'to counter German claims for colonies', and, when the White House and the State Department heard of the proposal, they warmly agreed. McDougall, Loveday, and Stoppani were united in their view that the real problem in international relations was 'the do-nothing policy of the United Kingdom' that would change only if the 'United States put pressure on London'; without this, the British 'might block any economic move by the League'.[80] Stoppani recognized this was not a request to which the USA could readily accede; after all Roosevelt faced a testing presidential election in 1936. So, not for the first time, he suggested American officials hide their economic internationalism beneath the League's petticoats and 'exploit the opportunity for anonymity' in the committee rooms of Geneva to negotiate a deal, because it circumvented the risks of antagonizing domestic public opinion.[81]

The British response to Stoppani's plan was not uniformly hostile. The Treasury and the Board of Trade did not take Australian disenchantment or the need to raise food prices seriously. Foreign Secretary Anthony Eden, on the other hand, was more enthusiastic, because the proposal offered the chance to re-energize 'British leadership' at the League, and the possibility of a 'useful agreement with the Americans and the French'.[82] But neither he nor Stoppani, who arrived in London that July 'convinced of the gravity of impending dangers', was able to bring the Treasury around.[83] The key to understanding its opposition lay less in the content of the deal—after all, Britain offered its own range of economic and financial concessions to Germany and Japan in an effort to neutralize their territorial ambitions—than in the fact that it meant relinquishing control of the process to the Foreign Office and the EFO. The Treasury now recognized French devaluation was increasingly likely but believed it was best not discussed in the open forum of the League, where it would be difficult to protect the pound, and argued that it was in Britain's interests to approach Germany and Italy solely on a bilateral basis. Treasury officials agreed to reject the secretariat's call for a strong British lead on an initiative that was 'wholly academic in the circumstances of today & the foreseeable future'.[84] While it could 'not prevent the questions being ventilated, we ought to ensure that the conclusions are limited to pious platitudes'.[85]

---

[79] 'Memorandum by Mr F. L. McDougall', 16 July 1936, LON R4422, 10A/24322/14627.

[80] Thompson to Feis, 21 July 1936, NARA RG59, 500.C1199/205; Jebb, record of conversation with Bruce, 10 June 1936, TNA: PRO T160/63.

[81] Thompson to Feis, 21 July 1936, NARA RG59, 500.C1199/205.

[82] Eden to Runciman, 17 July 1936, and Eden to Chamberlain, 12 Aug. 1936, TNA: PRO T160/633.

[83] Stoppani to Halifax, 11 Aug. 1936; TNA: PRO T188.148; Eden to Chamberlain, 12 Aug. 1936, and Chamberlain to Eden, 25 Aug. 1936, TNA: PRO T160/633.

[84] Fisher to Hopkins and Hall, 25 July 1936, TNA: PRO T160/633.

[85] Chamberlain to Fisher and Fergusson, 31 July 1936, TNA: PRO T160/633.

When Stoppani arrived at his next stop in Paris on 1 August, however, he conveyed little of the British opposition to his plan to the French or, subsequently, to Italian and Belgian officials. Instead, he glossed over the details of his proposal and focused on the central message that multilateral negotiations would be a force for peace, a means to construct a new Europe, and the basis from which progressive social programmes could be launched. This was rather different from the way he had pitched his ideas to the British. To the French, he underlined the crucial point on which the secretariat and Britain were agreed: the 'fundamental and decisive role' to be played by France if such an initiative were to get off the ground.[86]

He also placed much greater emphasis on the monetary component. In discussions with officials in the foreign and finance ministries, Robert Coulondre, Charles Spinasse, and Massigli, Stoppani argued that the key step was a 'normalization' of French currency relations between states with free currencies. From this, all good things would follow, notably an end to clearing, freer trade, and a resumption of international lending.[87] The fact that British support was the linchpin of Stoppani's initiative, and his tendency to skirt over Treasury opposition in favour of Foreign Office support, were reflected in his contacts with the Americans. They were similarly told by Stoppani that the British had been 'surprisingly receptive' to his overtures. The dissemblance was sufficient to maintain the momentum for inter-governmental action, at least for the time being. Stoppani arranged to bring the principal British, French, and American actors together for a set of private meetings under cover of the 44th Economic Committee meeting in Geneva, scheduled for September 1936.

American sources in Paris endorsed Stoppani's claim to the US administration that there was a favourable combination of circumstances permitting a considerable and long-desired change in the monetary and commercial policy of France. The report prompted a flurry of activity in the departments of State, Trade, and Commerce over whom they might send to Switzerland. Henry Grady was the most obvious choice, but he was committed to the Democrat election campaign, so the talented young economist Leo Pasvolsky, who had already been in extended contact with the EFO's sections, was chosen to accompany Rogers. Pasvolsky, a Russian émigré and graduate of the University of Geneva, was nervous. It was his first mission as special assistant to the secretary of state, and he had been attached to the Trade Agreements Division of the State Department for only a year. What if the other officials at Geneva wanted to discuss monetary policy? Not only did he lack the authority to comment; he was critical of some aspects of FDR's monetary policies. But these concerns, and his general lack of experience in diplomatic negotiations, were swept away by an enthused Hull, who knew he had chosen well. Pasvolsky had covered and argued for US admission into the League in 1919

[86] Memo by Stoppani, 'Enquête auprès des Gouvernements principaux au sujet d'une action urgente de normalisation économique comme moyen de reprise et d'apaisement politique', 4 Aug. 1936, AMAE, SDN, IJ/Questions Économiques et Financières, Politique Commerciale, Mai–Juin 1939, no. 1399.

[87] Stoppani to Massigli, 7 Aug. 1936, AMAE, SDN, IJ/Questions Économiques et Financières/ Politique Commerciale, Mai–Juin 1939, no. 1399.

as a journalist, and had closely monitored its economic work since.[88] Hull packed
him off to Geneva after a thorough briefing, armed with several thick files on State
Department trade policy. It was the beginning of a remarkable career in international relations.

GOVERNMENTS' LAST HURRAH

The Economic Committee that opened in Geneva on 7 September 1936 was to be
the last meeting of its history at which the secretariat harboured any real hopes for
intergovernmental cooperation. The meeting marked the crystallization of its
efforts since 1933 to promote trade liberalization in the context of fluctuating
currencies, to signal renewed American economic internationalism, and to forge an
'information-based' response to the political and economic dangers posed by
German and Italian nationalism. The report that emerged from this, the committee's 44th meeting, was more concise than many that came before it, which was all
the more notable because the number of delegates was exceptionally large.[89] The
agenda was a mixture of the familiar and unfamiliar. Familiar was its comprehensive
quality; novel was the secretariat's determination, in unspoken alliance with the
Americans, to steer the discussion firmly to what it regarded as the most important
item on the agenda: 'an inquiry into the present state of economic relations', that
would enable the USA to lead a determined charge for multilateral tariff negotiations with the world's major capitalist powers.

The information placed before the committee on the state of the world economy, and the economic health of individual members, was extensive. It comprised
the report of the clearing inquiry; an overview of exchange control mechanisms;
and details the EIS had been able to gather on the volume and value of global trade,
and the terms of recently negotiated trade agreements, sometimes wrested from the
hands of reluctant government representatives or gleaned from published printed
sources. No measure of economic defence, however small, was spared scrutiny,
including sanitary conventions applied on the grounds of maintaining 'national
health'. Indeed, the secretariat had called for an international Nutrition Commission to test such claims, but the proposal received short shrift from national
delegates who believed the question, rather like trying to define and measure
poverty—another secretariat proposal—was too political a topic to address in the
difficult prevailing international climate. (Stoppani's response was to suggest that

---

[88] Pasvolsky's intellectual interests and publications strongly reflected League preoccupations and
League materials. See, e.g., Leo Pasvolsky, *Economic Nationalism and the Danubian States* (New York,
1928), *Bulgaria's Economic Position with Special Reference to the Reparation Problem and the Work of the
League of Nations* (Washington, 1930), *War Debts and Economic Prosperity* (Washington, 1932), and
Gold: A World Problem (Philadelphia, 1933).

[89] The delegates were: Rogers and Pasvolsky (USA); Andrews (Canada), Comolli (Argentina). The
Europeans were: Jebb (Britain), Dolezal (Poland), Elbel and Rueff (France), Jahn (Norway), De Nickl
(Hungary), Rosenblum (USSR), Schueller (Austria), Stucki (Switzerland), Ibl (CSR), Simoni (Italy),
and Van Langenhove (Belgium).

each country should create its own nutrition commission and then coordinate its work with the League.) This was in contrast to a Soviet-sponsored call for an internationally agreed convention on customs statistics, which fell by the wayside in the absence of support from either the secretariat or member states.

The secretariat remained determined to make headway in promoting bilateral—preferably multilateral—tariff reductions linked to monetary agreement that would facilitate a revaluation of the French franc, but steering the committee in this direction proved difficult, especially with Leith-Ross as chairman of the committee. The discussion of what the secretariat, in the preparatory paper for the meeting called 'the partial eclipse of the Most-Favoured-Nation-Clause' was especially discomforting for Leith-Ross, and his rebuttals that the League 'put too much emphasis on the necessity of a continuous expansion of world trade' were absurd.[90] The unsolicited support by Poland and Switzerland did not help him feel any happier in denouncing what had once been a standard feature of British trade policy. But, despite his opposition, the secretariat did not retreat from its view that protectionism was the greatest obstacle to the world's fragile recovery. There were signs economies were returning to health—visible in higher prices for primary and manufactured goods and reduced levels of unemployment—but the revival was confined almost entirely to domestic markets. World trade was still some 8 per cent below levels of 1929, a deeply worrying trend that was all the more significant because until 1914 world trade had increased practically without interruption throughout the history of mankind.

Leith-Ross was driven to uncharacteristically intemperate outbursts because he was forced repeatedly to defend Britain's inconsistent application of MFN compromised through imperial preference. Britain's harshest critic was Leo Pasvolsky, who was terrier-like in his determination to challenge the British bulldog. Pasvolsky dominated the discussion. He intervened repeatedly, fought aggressively, and won debates, sparing Stoppani the awkward business of trying to intervene to shape the discussion when his role as head of the Economic Section gave him the power to facilitate but not to direct. Although new in post and with a background in journalism, Pasvolsky was clearly no junior 'economic expert', but an adviser who had mastery of his brief and Hull's ear, and whose star was on the rise in the administration.

Pasvolsky's commanding performance was not the only surprise for hardened veterans of the Economic Committee. So, too, was his stress on the variety of means through which tariff agreements might be reached, the US willingness to work through the EFO, and its acceptance of the 'necessity for compromises in the transition period'.[91] Pasvolsky argued that the meeting's final report should outline

[90] League of Nations Economic Committee Report to Council, *Remarks on the Present Phase of International Economic Relations* (Geneva, September 1936), 4; 'Remarks on the Present Phase of International Economic Relations (September 1937): Carrying out the Programme of the Tripartite Declaration of September 1936', League of Nations, *Official Journal*, annex 1681 (1937), 1212.

[91] Gilbert's report to Hull entitled 'Meeting of Economic Committee of the League of Nations', 18 September 1936, annex attached 'Third Session—Tuesday, 8 September 1936, at 10:15 a.m.', p. 31, NARA RG59, 500.C1199/238199/238.

the very many routes to concluding tariff agreements, including the coordination of quotas with flat rate tariffs. The main thing, Pasvolsky argued, was that countries agree the primary aim of abolishing restrictive measures, and develop a common conception as to the precise meaning and practice of MFN status to reinforce the value of the clause to international relations in the longer term. The League's work had revealed not just existing obstacles to its operation, but divergences in how the clause was interpreted, as well as states and constituent groups in the international political economy that were fundamentally opposed to it. The US experts led the way in demanding that the secretariat investigate these disparities to facilitate more effective cooperation in the future.[92] Their engagement and commitment throughout underlined the Economic Section's claims regarding the 'novel and significant' shift in American policy at the start of the meeting: 'the United States have never up to the present been prepared to reduce or to consolidate Customs duties in favour of other countries. They have always treated tariff policy as a purely international question, to be settled without regard to others. They are now prepared to admit this view is mistaken and opposed to their own interests.'[93]

Rogers provided the political context so that delegates could understand the shifts afoot in American policy. It was true, he said, that the USA believed it had fought off the Great Depression by drawing on its own economic resources, and by increasing its sense of 'independence from other countries and a rising cynicism regarding European matters and the League of Nations'. But it was important for the world to be able to distinguish between the views of the American elite and the general public. FDR's administration, he argued, was 'the most internationally-minded since that of President Wilson...[Its] government officials recognize clearly that a great many of its economic difficulties arise from the present international situation.' Its internationalism was evident in two key strands of its diplomacy: its willingness to respond when countries sought tariff agreements via the RTAA, and its desire to help countries who wanted or needed to depreciate their currencies, including, most recently, Belgium. Langenhove interjected: Belgium's deflation had not been 'deliberate but was imposed upon the country by the force of circumstances beyond the government's control' (it was ever thus), but the key to Belgium's recovery in the longer term was indeed American assistance, and the prospects of a general international recovery, orchestrated by the world's major economic powers.

The exchange between Rogers and Langenhove encapsulated two areas of unanimity between the participants at the meeting. The first was not new, but had been orchestrated by the secretariat into a clear refrain: that the way to move international relations forward was for the world's 'big powers' ('great' had become an unfashionable and inappropriate 'epithet') to act together soon to agree an economic route through the world's pressing economic and political difficulties.

---

[92] League of Nations, *Economic Committee, Equality of Treatment in the Present State of International Commercial Relations: The Most-Favoured-Nation Clause* (Geneva, 1936), C.367.M.250.1936.II.B.

[93] Memo by the EFO, 'Trend of Commercial Policy since March 1935—Note by the Secretariat', 4 Sept. 1936, NARA RG59, 500.C1199/219.

The second area of agreement, in a historic reversal of views expressed five years earlier, was the near unanimous view that currency depreciation or revaluation was an effective route to recovery and was inevitable for currencies presently still committed to gold if the world wanted to avoid yet more currency controls. The British Treasury was not alone in recognizing that, for the first time, the League revealed a consensus of opinion 'in favour of the devaluation of over-valued currencies'.[94] Italy struck back. It celebrated the gold standard and autarky too: national economic independence was required for political dependence, and there was much bristling when it boasted 'the creation of a new colonial empire has acted as a great stimulus to production'.[95] (Although Ethiopia abandoned the League in May 1936, Italy did not announce its decision to leave until December 1937, and during the intervening period it made increasingly inflammatory remarks.) The two lines of agreement were set out in Stoppani's draft final report, but Leith-Ross refused to allow it to go forward to the Assembly. With the support of the Soviet delegate, he exploited his position as chairman to dilute proposals of multilateral cooperation.[96]

The Financial Committee also came to Leith-Ross's aid. It opened two days after its economic counterpart and was even more non-committal: it pulled back from issuing a blanket endorsement of currency depreciation as the route to recovery. It also disliked the notion of bringing the world's major powers to explore co-ordinated currency depreciation and tariff cuts. The view partly reflected the natural conservatism of finance ministers and central bankers who made up this committee when compared to what they regarded as their more 'politicized' counterparts on the Economic Committee, but it also reflected the continued sway of the Treasury in this committee. Its chairman, Niemeyer, scotched French hopes that the Americans would host a conference of the world's principal powers, and sought to temper Stoppani's enthusiasm to use the imminent devaluation of the French franc as a means of salvaging the League. To underline that the real power in international relations lay elsewhere, while the committee was in session, secret talks opened between French, British, and American central bankers to facilitate the managed depreciation of the French franc.[97]

In some respects, the resultant Tripartite Agreement and the published report of the Economic Committee, endorsed by both the Second Committee and the League Assembly, constituted a vindication of the British and US monetary policy since they had abandoned gold. Past and present gold bloc members viewed it as a victory for what had become known as 'Anglo-Saxon' monetary policy. But,

[94] Treasury note on report of the Economic Committee, 24 Sept. 1936, TNA: PRO T160/633.

[95] Gilbert's report to Hull entitled 'Meeting of Economic Committee of the League of Nations', 18 Sept. 1936, annex attached, 'Seventh Session—Thursday, 10 September 1936, at 10:15 a.m.', and 'Tenth Session—Friday, 11 September 1936, at 3:30 p.m.', NARA RG59, 500.C1199/238199/238; Leith-Ross to Phillips, 12 Sept. 1936, TNA: PRO T188/120.

[96] Pasvolsky and Stoppani strongly opposed this step. See Gilbert's report to Hull entitled 'Meeting of Economic Committee of the League of Nations', 18 Sept. 1936, annex attached, 'Tenth Session—Friday, 11 September 1936, at 3:30 p.m.', p. 11, NARA RG59 500.C1199/238199/238.

[97] S. V. O. Clarke, *Exchange-Rate Stabilization in the Mid-1930s: Negotiating the Tripartite Agreement* (Princeton, 1977).

while Chamberlain, Niemeyer, and Phillips took a certain satisfaction in the development, they were not prepared to accede to the entreaties of Hull and other internationalist-minded Americans, on the one hand, and Rueff and Charles Corbin, the French Ambassador in London, on the other, to couple the announcement of the Tripartite Stabilization Agreement with a League-sponsored initiative in economic diplomacy.[98] Hull and Rueff wanted to build on the agreement before the hard-fought momentum for agreement between the three countries was lost, but Chamberlain stood firm in his view that attempting to widen arrangements to incorporate economic and political issues of any kind would lead only to 'disaster'.[99]

When it became clear there was no progress on tariff reduction to be had in Geneva, Hull did not hide his disappointment. The final resolution of the Assembly was horribly 'watered down', he complained.[100] During Economic Committee meetings, Stoppani and Pasvolsky told Hull that, if French delegates attempted to stress the value of intergovernmental cooperation through Geneva, the 'British might be suspicious and might not want to play ball'—indeed, French delegates had maintained a studied silence in both the Economic and Financial committees— whereas a strong American endorsement as to the value of multilateral cooperation through the Tripartite Stabilization Agreement was much more likely to deliver British support and could 'strengthen France in discussions with Germany'.[101] But, as it transpired, neither Pasvolsky's push in Geneva, nor the Tripartite Stabilization Agreement delivered the necessary momentum. Hull and Stoppani both reached the same conclusion: it was not the League that had failed to deliver but its leading member state, Britain. When challenged, the British government hid the primacy of its imperial economic and security agenda that determined policy priorities behind a caricature of national character that eschewed 'some large-scale and dramatic gesture which would by itself herald in a new era of prosperity for the world . . . apt to prefer, as is our British way, a pragmatic approach to economic problems'. Pragmatism, it was claimed, meant keeping the League and internationalists in the USA and in France firmly at arm's length.[102]

---

[98] Memo by Stoppani, 13 Oct. 1936, AMAE, SDN, IJ/Questions Économiques, Organisation Économique et Financière/Œuvre économique et financière de la SDN, 1930–6, no. 1154; Corbin to Laval, 6 Oct. 1936, AMAE, SDN, IJ/Questions Économiques et Financières, Politique Commerciale, Mai 1933–Juin 1939, no. 1399. Henri Spaak also expressed deep frustration with Britain's position.

[99] Chamberlain to Ida Chamberlain, 7 Mar. 1937, Birmingham 18/1/997. For Corbin's importance and the degree to which successive French governments sought to influence their relations with Italy and Germany by exerting diplomatic pressure on London rather than Rome or Berlin, see Martin Thomas, *Britain, France and Appeasement: Anglo-French Relations in the Popular Front Era* (Oxford and New York, 1996).

[100] Hoden to Massigli, 23 Nov. 1936, AMAE, SDN, IJ/Organisation Économique et Financière de la Société des Nations, Comité Économique, 41e à 46e Session, Juillet 1934–Septembre 1937, no. 1184; Chamberlain to Morrison, 6 Oct. 1936, TNA: PRO T160/633.

[101] Gilbert to Hull, 17 Sept. 1936, NARA RG59, 500.C1199/227; Stoppani to Massigli, 14 Sept. 1936, AMAE, SDN, IJ/Questions Économiques et Financières, Politique Commerciale, Mai 1933– Juin 1939, no. 1399.

[102] League of Nations, 'Records of the Seventeenth Ordinary Session of the Assembly—Meetings of the Committees—Minutes of the Second Committee', *Official Journal*, Special Supplement No. 157 (Geneva 1936), 37–47.

So it was with a heavy heart that, by the end of 1936, the EFO's secretariat concluded that paths through which it had sought to reopen international economic and financial cooperation since 1934 had reached a dead-end. The EFO's contribution to international monetary policy had come a long way since the start of the Great Depression. It now openly championed the cheap money policy of the British Treasury and the USA, and had helped to sustain many of the intellectual and personal connections that facilitated members of the gold bloc, notably France, to move in that direction. It also promoted RTAA-style multilateral tariff reductions, although to less effect. Yet, if the journeys along these paths had produced different outcomes, they demonstrated clearly that the political support extended by member states to the League and embodied in its secretariat remained fleeting and conditional. Indeed, if the EFO's remit had expanded considerably from its narrow focus on intelligence gathering in the 1920s, the powerbase of League members on which it could depend to carry out that work had shrunk markedly. By the end of 1936, Hull glowered that British conduct, echoed in the behaviour of aggressive economic nationalists such as Italy and Germany, meant he had little choice but to abandon the League and to 'keep negotiations on the doorstep of every nation'.[103]

The entrenchment of Italian and German economic nationalist and imperialist ambitions had proven beyond the EFO's means to combat them, and, whatever hopes Stoppani and Loveday might have harboured to promote France's place in the EFO, the waves of economic, political, and social crises rippling through the Third Republic meant France returned to traditional financial channels when it became clear, as in preparatory negotiations for the Tripartite Stabilization Agreement, that the EFO could deliver neither unequivocal nor immediate results. More troubling for the EFO than the USA's retraction or renewed French indifference, however, was the demise of its most important champion, the British government. Stoppani and Loveday confirmed their assessment of the uninterested and sometimes even disdainful performance of British delegates, during a mission to London in the autumn of 1936 to assess whether the ministerial changes inaugurated by the Baldwin government would lead to a revival of British internationalism. The reports made gloomy reading. 'Protectionist-thinking' had gained ground 'in every British ministry' and was supported by powerful lobbies, the British Chamber of Commerce and the Federation of British Industry recently and unequivocally stating their support for protectionism.[104]

The Tripartite Stabilization Agreement signed between the US, British, and French governments in September 1936 outside the auspices of the League reinforced the secretariat's diagnosis that its energy was better spent elsewhere

---

[103] Hull quoted by Feis to Stoppani, 5 Nov. 1936, and passed on by Marcel Hoden to Massigli, 23 Nov. 1936, AMAE, SDN, IJ/Organisation Économique et Financière de la Société des Nations/ Comité Économique, 41ᵉ à 46ᵉ Session, Juillet 1934–Septembre 1937, no. 1184.

[104] John Colville replaced William Morrison at the Treasury; Morrison became Minister of Agriculture. Favourable contacts in the Treasury were now thin on the ground. See Lloyd memo, 'London Interviews in October 1936', 5 Nov. 1936, LON R4422, 10A/24322/14627. Loveday to Norberg, 9 Mar.1945, LON, Loveday, P143/14–15/outgoing correspondence, 1934–5.

than in the battle to preserve intergovernmental relations. The primacy of old-school diplomacy was not surprising, given the need for states to appear in control of their monetary destiny to reassure both their electorates and the markets, and French economists and policy-makers, for example, invariably downplayed Geneva's contribution to reshaping their view of the gold standard. By the end of October members of the now defunct gold bloc, notably Belgium, the Netherlands, and Switzerland, also signed the Tripartite Agreement.[105]

The deal expressed the signatories' commitment that any subsequent devaluation of the franc would similarly be the product of international cooperation. But in May 1938 the French government was forced to devalue the French franc unilaterally as government cooperation failed once again. By then the Economic and Financial Sections had long given up hope of coordinating monetary or indeed economic relations between nation states whose values and interests had given birth to the League. The secretariat's experience and analysis of these powers' economic and monetary policies between 1934 and 1936 had extinguished what remained of the aspiration to promote British or French internationalism as a means to foster the universal values claimed by the League. Nor, it calculated, would the USA be riding to the rescue any time soon.

But, disenchanted as the secretariat may have been by the policies of member states, it neither could, nor desired, to be free of the demand to do something to oppose the threat posed by Fascist internationalism. In the opening lines of the Tripartite Stabilization Agreement, the USA, Britain, and France affirmed their common desire to restore order to international economic relations and 'to pursue a policy which will tend to promote prosperity in the world and to improve the standard of living of peoples' in language that was redolent of the League.[106] The declaration reflected and confirmed a trend already under way in its work: to divert its energy and focus away from governments and towards individuals. The search for an agenda to restore liberal capitalism and to promote the prospects of peace now turned towards the everyday concerns of the world's citizens.

---

[105] Ian A. Drummond, *London, Washington and the Management of Franc 1936–1939* (Princeton, 1979), 3–10.

[106] 'Declaration by the United States, the United Kingdom and France effected by simultaneous announcements in Washington, London and Paris', 25 Sept. 1936, Department of Treasury Press Release, 25 Sept. 1936, at Avalon Project, Yale University <http://avalon.law.yale.edu/20th_century/usmu001.asp#1> (accessed 2 May 2009); 'Exposé des Motifs of the Devaluation Law', issued by the Popular Front, Paris, 28 Sept. 1938, p. 2, TNA: PRO T160/685.

5

Society and Economy in Global Partnership, 1935–1938

By 1935, key elements of the international economic settlement of the 1920s had gone for good, and competition gripped international relations. As notions of planning increasingly framed economic debate within states, the aspiration to return to nineteenth-century-style economic liberalism seemed an eccentric goal. The slump promoted a climate of national introspection where the 'international' seemed at best irrelevant, at worst a threat. The collapse of the World Economic Conference of 1933, and the failure of the EFO's subsequent initiatives on trade and clearing, demonstrated that a League governed by the primacy of national sovereignty was left deeply vulnerable when nation states opted to ignore its procedures and ideals. For the EFO's secretariat, the answer to the crisis was to redouble League efforts to inculcate a broader view of states' duties, as well as rights, to the societies they represented and to the international economy as a whole.

Within the League the creative foment around planning and welfare, the emerging debate about the structure of the League, and the crisis in global security with first Asia, now Africa, and soon Europe at war, re-energized and recast some of the diverse ways of thinking about what comprised security evident both in late nineteenth-century internationalism and at the founding of the League. The new approach of the League of Nations to 'global security' emphasized the relationship between the world's richest producers and its poorer ones, and its genesis lay in the earth. Agriculture and primary production became the focus of new work, as the League's assessment of the Great Depression in 1934 emphasized two major yet divergent trends in the world economy: the steady and substantial recovery in aggregate industrial production, and the near complete collapse of international trade.

As we have seen, this second problem was the focus of considerable League interest as its secretariat sought to hitch the organization's long-standing commitment to trade liberalization onto the emerging American preoccupation with freer trade after 1932. But Loveday and his colleagues in Geneva, in particular, were aware that, while their statistical analyses threw the 'stagnation of trade into very clear relief . . . they conceal the lack of balance in the world, the unevenness of the progress and the variety of national experience'.[1] With work under way to unravel

---

[1] Loveday, 'Note on Economic Conditions, 1934/35', p. 3, LON Loveday, P143/14–15/outgoing correspondence, 1934–5.

'the causes which have led to the striking contrast in conditions or the extent to which industry has been stimulated into activity by government orders for armaments', the EFO's secretariat believed that in the future the 'unevenness in the degrees of recovery constitutes a danger and impediment to global stability'.[2] For the Secretariat the key to understanding the challenge before the world lay in two parts: the unequal recovery and development of the economy on a national, regional, and global scale; secondly, recognizing the challenges before the world's poorest producers because they were hit especially hard. By League calculations at the end of 1934, the value of trade had fallen to little more than a third of what it had been in 1928, and, while there were signs of economic recovery by 1934, the prices on world markets remained very low. This divergence in the world economy identified by the EFO was interpreted as a danger to global economic recovery and international security. It produced a policy response and language of 'development' in the secretariat that is more usually identified with the years after 1945.

There was also a monetary dimension to the problems of the poorer, primary-producing nation states drawn out by its study of clearing and compensation agreements, and raw material production. National and regional fortunes varied considerably between those territories that had disconnected their currencies from gold and had escaped from the downward pressure of falling prices, and those that maintained their currencies and the mechanism of the gold standard. There 'the effects of falling prices have been concentrated with constantly increasing intensity', and as a result primary producers were being 'punished' disproportionately for continuing to adhere to norms of monetary internationalism once advocated by the League.[3] Since the financial crisis of 1931, their only recourse had been to adopt various national measures to support their own producers, which, in turn, depressed demand overseas yet further—a point reinforced by the recent history of Romania, Germany, Greece, Italy, and Hungary among others.

Although framed in global terms, the political and cultural core of this insight derived from Europe. Consideration was given to the challenges facing primary producers on other continents, including Japan, Chile, India, Argentina, China, Colombia, Costa Rica, Ecuador, the USA, Guatemala, New Zealand, Egypt, Iran, Iraq, Palestine, Burma, Mexico, Ceylon, Cuba, 'Manchukuo', the Philippines, Siam, Sudan, Syria, the Straits Settlements, the Union of South Africa, as well as other British, French, and Italian colonies and protectorates. But the comparatively comprehensive treatment of European primary production reflected the balance of power in the organization, its better data on the region, and the view that addressing the needs of this continent's poorest producers held the key to fostering an economic growth and stability that would improve European, and ultimately global, security.[4]

---

[2] Loveday, 'Note on Economic Conditions, 1934/35', p. 5, LON Loveday, P 143/14–15/outgoing correspondence, 1934–5.

[3] Loveday, 'Note on Economic Conditions, 1934/35', p. 6, LON Loveday, P 143/14–15/outgoing correspondence, 1934–5.

[4] See, e.g., memo by the EFO, 'Economic Committee, Regulation of International Trade', 1 Sept. 1936, LON R4407, 10A/29627/3826.

At the same time, as a consequence of its engagement with the wider consequences of the depression, the League began to move from a preoccupation with
agricultural production to a broader concept centred on the quality of 'rural life'. It
was directed towards individuals, not governments that claimed to represent them,
to the environment in which they lived, and the specific commodities they
produced. Some seventy-five years later a similar logic was paraded, purportedly
for the first time, in the more genuinely global frame of the Human Security agenda
of the United Nations.[5] Self-evidently, neither the challenges nor the opportunities
were new. The report could have been drafted by Loveday and Stoppani.

Stalemate in attempts to facilitate intergovernmental cooperation, and interest in
developing new approaches to the challenge of security, also led to a reorientation
within the practice of the League of Nations. The secretariat became more effective
in overcoming intra-sectional divisions—'Social', 'Economics and Finance', and
'Communication'—and breaking through the practical and sometimes ideological
barriers that divided them from the semi-detached LNHO and ILO. This was best
illustrated in the work of the 'Mixed Committee on the Problem of Nutrition'
appointed in 1935, which comprised an intra-sectional committee of officials from
the LNHO, the ILO, the IIA, and the Economic and Financial Sections, which
dominated (although the committee also included three Americans).[6] For Loveday,
there was a painful irony that, at a time when much of the world had come to
believe the League was almost entirely irrelevant to international relations, these
new schemes placed so great a burden on its administrative machinery that the
organization was at risk of breaking down, 'not for lack of will or intelligence, but
because there is a limit to the physical endurance of the staff'.[7]

There followed other 'mixed' ventures that bound the 'social' more closely to
international economics than before. By 1938 a new Advisory Committee on Social
Questions had been established, authorized by the Council to develop programmes
with the ILO and the LNHO. This work altered the League's previously narrow
focus on child well-being to one of family welfare, and set up new programmes for
the training of social workers as well as for the rehabilitation of prostitutes, penal
reform, and assistance to indigent foreigners.[8] And it was in this context, with
increasing urgency, that League officials also decided to revisit the question of the
organization's structure: how and in what ways the organization might reshape

[5] United Nations Commission on Human Security 2003, *Human Security Now* (New York, 2003),
2–4.
[6] The EFO had four represenatives while other agencies fielded between one and two staff
members. Loveday drew up the guidelines for the Mixed Committee's composition. See Loveday,
'Note: Steps to be Taken in Pursuance of the Assembly Resolution on Nutrition', *c.* July 1935, LON,
Loveday, P143/14–15/outgoing correspondence, 1934–5. See also the Burnet–Aykroyd Report,
Quarterly Bulletin of the Health Organisation, IV/2, June 1935. The EFO also nominated specialist
economists.
[7] Loveday to Aghnides, 1 Nov. 1935, LON, Loveday, P143/14–15/outgoing correspondence,
1934–5.
[8] Dominque Marshall, 'The Formation of Childhood as an Object of International Relations: The
Child Welfare Committee and the Declaration of Children's Rights of the League of Nations',
International Journal of Children's Rights, 7/2 (1999), 103–47; Iris Borowy, *Coming to Terms with
World Health. The League of Nations Organization 1921–1946* (Frankfurt Am Main, 2009), 167–236.

itself to remain connected to the rapidly changing world while safeguarding its essential values. Although the will to internationalism had become alien to the world's major powers, for every watchful, smaller state, however, national and international interests were inherently more difficult to uncouple. In western Europe these powers remained more engaged with the League, while the fate of central, eastern, and southern Europe was the focus of much preoccupation.

'POSITIVE SECURITY'

In the summer of 1935 there was a renewed debate in Geneva about how to re-energize the 1919 suggestion of the South African Prime Minister, Jan Smuts, that the real value of the League would be its 'practical' work. The League should take a hands-on approach to the 'government of man' and 'occupy the position which has been rendered vacant by the destruction of so many of the old European Empires'. Smuts's vision was an imperial one in which the League became the 'natural master of the [European] house' that nursed the peoples of central and eastern Europe to 'economic and political independence'.[9] By the 1930s, although notions of practical cooperation, as we shall see, retained a strong paternal dimension, they were framed in less overtly imperial terms by other participants in the debate, which drew in students and practitioners of international relations, and institutions associated with the League, including the Institut Universitaire des Hautes Études Internationales. Another protagonist was the latter's co-founder, William Emmanuel Rappard, the Swiss diplomat and historian who had been instrumental in bringing the League to Geneva, who now asserted that 'the main purpose of the League, the prevention of war, could perhaps be more readily and more effectively served by the consolidation of peace than by the repression of violence'.[10] The growth of a collective system of international relations strong and effective enough to prevent war obviously remained an essential goal. But, with the number of failures in this regard rapidly outweighing the triumphs, it was time to switch emphasis to the 'technical international collaboration through the League . . . which in some instances has blazed a significant new trail towards rational government of the world, which presupposes, if not a super-state, at least a supra-national loyalty—i.e. a loyalty to mankind as a whole'.[11]

---

[9] Jan C. Smuts, *The League of Nations: A Practical Suggestion* (London, 1919), pp. v–vi. For the longevity of Smuts's voice in international affairs, see Mark Mazower, *No Enchanted Palace: The End of Empire and the Ideological Origins of the United Nations* (Princeton, 2009), 28–65. The absence of economics and finance in Smuts's text is striking.

[10] William E. Rappard, *The Common Menace of Economic and Military Armaments: The Eighth Richard Cobden Lecture* (London, 1936), 37. Memo by Pitman Potter, 'Positive Security: The Development of World Cooperative Services', forwarded as first confidential draft for Loveday's comment, see Potter to Loveday, 3 June 1935, LON, Loveday, P143/14–15/outgoing correspondence, 1934–5.

[11] Pitman Potter, 'Positive Security: The Development of World Cooperative Services', 27 Mar. 1935, p. 2, LON, Loveday, P143/14–15/outgoing correspondence, 1934–5.

There were others who shared Rappard's functionalist view that technical collaboration was an antidote to the brutal world of realism. As his colleague at the Institute in Geneva, the American Pitman Potter, claimed, 'whatever may be said in criticism of the League of Nations—and admittedly much may be said—it offered useful cooperative services to its members'. Potter was the author of the best-selling textbooks that exemplified the liberal view of international relations that were widely used in British and US universities in the period. His 1935 study of 'the Development of World Cooperative services' highlighted the work of the League's Social, Health, Economic and Financial, and Information services, and made the case for change. There were a 'number of other services crying out to be organized'. What stood in the way was not international imagination but the membership: 'the fear of Governments lest their "sovereignty" be infringed'. This was manifest

first in an attempt to limit the League's activity through the withholding of funds; the total annual expenditure today amounts to less than half the outlay of a single battleship. Secondly, by seeing to it that no organised attempt shall be made by the League itself [the secretariat] to educate public opinion about the revolutionary principles enshrined in the Covenant and the equally revolutionary technique of administration and service developed by the League during the first decade of its existence.[12]

His implication was clear. The League was being sabotaged by member governments from within and it was imperative that the 'true' League, the secretariat and associations and unions that supported it around the world, should formulate an effective response. Potter suggested the initiative be called 'Positive Security'.[13]

Potter was a founding figure in the study of international relations in the United States, which was dominated by Wilsonian legalism and was identified with an approach to international relations that came to be branded 'idealist' by more forceful critics of the League of Nations, such as E. H. Carr. Like these other pioneers of international relations theory, Carr had encountered the organization personally as a lowly third secretary in the British foreign office who had served with distinction at the Paris Peace Conference. Carr condemned the passionate desire of men such as Potter to avoid war as 'utopian', placing it in contrast to the 'realist' school of international relations that stressed the primacy of the state in world politics. In his seminal *Twenty-Years Crisis*, he explained how the League of Nations was a product of the Enlightenment faith in reason, individual liberty, social openness, and human progress. Yet, even as staunch a League critic as Carr was moved to recognize that it was the experts who commanded the greatest respect in the corridors of the League, while 'diplomats were long regarded with suspicion'.[14]

---

[12] Pitman Potter, 'Positive Security: The Development of World Cooperative Services', 27 Mar.1935, p. 2, LON, Loveday, P143/14–15/outgoing correspondence, 1934–5.

[13] Pitman Potter, 'Positive Security: The Development of World Cooperative Services', 27 Mar. 1935, p. 2, LON, Loveday, P143/14–15/outgoing correspondence, 1934–5.

[14] Carr's claim was unqualified. See E. H. Carr, *Twenty-Years Crisis* (London, 1939), 102. It is a view found, too, in the work of J. A. Hobson, who in other respects was also a forceful critic of the League. See David Long, *Towards a New Liberal Internationalism: The International Theory of J. A. Hobson* (Cambridge, 1996), 159–83.

This stress on expertise was taken up by 'functionalist' theory, another discrete strand of international relations thought that emerged in relation to the League, although one that is more usually identified with the period after 1950.[15] It challenged realist assumptions about the primacy of the state, stressed the practical and intellectual interdependencies of world politics, and is closely associated with the Romanian-born naturalized British scholar David Mitrany, who played an important role in efforts to prioritize the economic and financial activities of the League of Nations.[16] Like Carr, Mitrany was never formally employed by the organization, yet his career similarly traversed the organization in a number of ways. He was an adviser to the League of Nations and the British government on the League mission in Austria in 1922; he worked with the Carnegie Foundation on a number of projects relating to the economic and social impact of the war; and the EFO frequently consulted him for his expertise on European peasantry. His appointment in 1933 as Professor of the School of Economics and Politics at the Institute of Advanced Study in Princeton, too, would prove of special value.[17]

In 1932 and 1933, Mitrany gave a series of influential lectures in the USA, published as *The Progress of International Government*, that called for international organizations to work with and for people; to cooperate on issues and matters that united not divided; to consider the common interests of individuals and peoples; and to look for solutions by function and form.[18] Criticisms as forthright as those of Potter of the League's membership could not, of course, be made by the secretariat itself, given its subservient role to the nation states, but, if these shots against the sovereign members of the League were being fired by supporters outside the organization, the secretariat helped to fashion the bullets.

For members of the Economic and Financial Sections and their associates, it was important that the League meet the challenge of positive security on a practical as well as on an intellectual basis, bringing together ideas from the fields of social and economic science. Here, the Mixed Committee on Nutrition played a series of essential roles. Not only was it as the first major committee to establish wide-ranging administrative and political connections between internal agencies of the League and external organizations; it also created a discursive arena in which the relationship between the fields of health, society, and the economy could be explored. The interconnection between these issues in intellectual and practical terms was widely recognized in the second half of the nineteenth century when the fight against hunger was an international cause célèbre. But, while the impact of the Great Depression led to the rediscovery of hunger as a major international issue from the obscurity in which it had languished since 1919, in the meantime, scientific understanding and national and international structures had separated

---

[15] Torbjörn L. Knutsen, *A History of International Relations Theory: An Introduction* (Manchester, 1992), 196–207, 226–8.

[16] David Mitrany, *The Functional Theory of Politics* (London, 1975), 8, 16–17, 38.

[17] LSE, Mitrany, Boxes 19 and 20, correspondence about the League officials such as Salter, Loveday, and Polak. Mitrany, like Salter, Butler, and Loveday, also had strong ties to Oxford.

[18] David Mitrany, *The Progress of International Government* (London, 1933).

the science of nutrition from an appreciation of the economic and social circumstances that left people undernourished.

BREAD AND BUTTER INTERNATIONALISM

Scientific and political developments during and after the First World War enabled scientists to define and measure hunger in objective and universal ways—a process of standardization that was common to so much of the League's work. In this, the LNHO played a central role, emphasizing the importance of data collection and testing in the setting of the sanitized, neutral laboratory, which, like the EIS, was intended to insulate scientists from competing ideological forces and political pressures. It also facilitated the internationalization of a biomedical view of hunger. Developments, including the discovery of vitamins and of the role played by minerals, widened and changed the meaning of 'hunger' from a phenomenon denoting a quantitative lack of food to a closer association with the new term 'malnutrition'. This had led to a fundamental redefinition of hunger in terms of the quality of diet and health, a biological condition amenable to a range of bio-medical and social scientific forms of measurement and treatment. In the international context, British expertise took a leading role; scientific pioneers associated with these developments were the indefatigable Glasgow University-trained nutritionist John Boyd Orr, and Wallace R. Aykroyd, the LNHO's first nutritionist, who studied malnutrition in Romania in 1933 and 1934 became director of the Coonoor Nutrition Research Laboratory in south India in 1935. Shaped in large part by imperial concerns, British engagement and interest in questions of food also offered a way around foot-dragging on questions of international trade and monetary cooperation. But, in an international setting, an understanding of nutrition also offered a new way to tackle the crisis in primary production and under-consumption.[19]

If the credit for the League's nutrition programme generally goes to Boyd Orr, the acclaim for the development of a welfare ethic within the League is generally bestowed upon Stanley M. Bruce, a former Australian Prime Minister and subsequent Resident Minister and then High Commissioner in London. But behind both Orr and Bruce stood Frank Lidgett McDougall, a man whose life's work was to link together the themes of international security, trade, the quality of rural life, and health. Formally, he was Economic Adviser to the High Commissioner for Australia, holding concurrent appointments on the Commonwealth Council for Scientific Research, the Commonwealth Development and Migration

---

[19] James Vernon, *Hunger: A Modern History* (Cambridge, MA, 2007), 98–145, underlines Britain's importance, although the League's work challenges the tension he sees emerging in British policy and in the LNHO 'between nutrition as a biological science and nutrition as a social science' (pp. 113–14); Paul Weindling, 'The Role of International Organizations in Setting Nutritional Standards in the 1920s and 1930s', in Harmke Kamminga and Andrew Cunningham (eds), *The Science and the Culture of Nutrition, 1840–1940* (Amsterdam, 1995), 319–32.

Commission, the Empire marketing board, and after 1927 as Australia's standing delegate to the Economic Committee of the EFO.

McDougall's career behind the scenes in Geneva, London, and Rome in the service of the United Nations FAO after 1945 made him the League's foremost *éminence grise*. His importance to the development of a League agenda on 'positive security' shines through its archival record, and he was the only official named in the guidelines drawn up for the Mixed Committee on Nutrition. McDougall brought Boyd Orr to Geneva, and nutrition from the purview of the LNHO onto a wider platform. McDougall's relationship to Bruce was equally important. It facilitated McDougall's entry into international society and brought him into contact with some of the world's most powerful men and women.[20] When McDougall died aged 73 in 1958, Bruce claimed: 'I'll never really know whether Bruce made McDougall or McDougall made Bruce, but whichever way it was, it was a damn fine combination.'[21] Bruce had the public pedigree in politics, national and international, leading the Australian delegation to the Imperial Conference in Ottawa in 1932 and the World Economic Conference in 1933 that helped to launch McDougall's career, but it was McDougall, judged a 'fascinating and brilliant' man by the British Foreign Office, who had the long-standing interest in primary production and agricultural science that came to be associated with Bruce.[22] McDougall was never in any doubt about where the ideological power in their relationship lay: 'I influenced Bruce to be a progressive.'[23]

McDougall claimed first and foremost to be an Australian 'working farmer', but, from the start of his working relationship with Bruce in 1922, he framed questions of agriculture with global politics in mind.[24] Although not the progenitor of preferential trade within the British Empire and Commonwealth, he was one of its most effective advocates, working hard to refine and to popularize the notion politicians and officials, and the general public.[25] But McDougall's biggest triumph—he was credited with securing the all-important agreement of Chancellor Neville Chamberlain to preferential trade agreements at the Imperial Conference at Ottawa in 1932—became his greatest disappointment. It was then he realized that sheltered markets in Britain for the empire's agricultural produce and for British industrial goods in the empire did not provide the answer to questions about the

[20] For his role in Australian politics context, see Sean Turnell, 'F. L. McDougall: Éminence grise of Australian Economic Diplomacy', *Australian Economic History Review*, 40/1 (2000), 51–70; for his early life and imperial economics, consult John B. O'Brien, 'F. L. McDougall and the Origins of the FAO', *Australian Journal of Politics and History*, 46/2 (2000), 164–74.

[21] Bruce cited by Ina Mary Cumpston, *Lord Bruce of Melbourne* (London, 1989), 40.

[22] Tallents to Ohlin, 17 June 1931, LON, R2889, 10D/24139/23630. Both Dubin and Ghébali fail to see beyond Bruce. See Martin D. Dubin, 'Towards the Bruce Report: The Economic and Social Programs of the League of Nations in the Avenol Era', in United Nations Library, *The League of Nations in Retrospect* (Geneva, 1983) 48; Victor-Yves Ghébali, *La Réforme Bruce, 1939–1940: 50 ans de la Société des Nations* (Geneva, 1970), 9–15.

[23] H. M. G. Jebb, *The Memoirs of Lord Gladwyn* (London, 1972), 63.

[24] O'Brien, 'F. L. McDougall and the Origins of the FAO', 164.

[25] He often described himself as an 'artist in propaganda'. See, e.g., F. L. McDougall to Norman McDougall (brother), 13 July 1924, ANA, McDougall, A2910 442/13/67, part 1.

Commonwealth's future agricultural and industrial development.[26] What should have been a major milestone of his career instead became a significant turning point. Imperial preference did not go far enough to secure livelihoods and at the same time stymied the Dominions' ability to negotiate better terms in other, non-imperial markets and to promote their own industrial development. His disillusion-ment with imperial preference was more rapid than most, but it became typical.

Throughout the 1920s, imperial preference was closely associated with the needs of white producers in the British Empire whose campaign for imperial preference had racist and survivalist overtones. The real eye-opener for McDougall was his work in the Economic Committee, as part of preparations for the World Economic Conference, which led him to see the paradox of 'restriction policies to control plenty in a poverty stricken world'.[27] He began to argue that, where possible, tariff barriers should be reduced in favour of the movement of goods (and ultimately people) so that the quality and quantity of food, and the standard of living for all, could be improved. In this way, the League's inconsistent approach to world trade and primary production that saw it supporting free trade and seeking to widen the US reciprocal tariff programme, on the one hand, and facilitating the negotiation of commodity agreements, on wheat in 1933 and on sugar in 1937, on the other, now began to sprout new fruit. The League had brought the world to McDougall and provided him with an instrument through which to see and transpose trends evident in the relationship between trade and economic development within the British Empire and Commonwealth into a global framework, one that explicitly embraced the needs of European farmers as much as colonial ones. For him, nutrition and consumption came to hold the key to economic growth and global security.

In the 1930s, McDougall became the author of successive papers on global agriculture, including reports written for both the League's Nutrition Inquiry and the Depression Delegation, an investigation launched in 1938 into the causes and remedies of economic crisis. Organization came first for McDougall and content second. He, like many in the wider community of agriculturalists interested in the science of food production, was frustrated by the limitations of the IIA, and argued the world needed a much more effective source of comparative international infor-mation on primary production. The IIA was increasingly seen as a creature of unsavoury fascist 'representatives of European farming interests that considered it undesirable for the institute to identify itself with consumer interests lest this might result in pressure for the lowering of prices paid to farmers and for decreasing protective duties'.[28] His was not a solitary view. Members of the Economic and Financial Sections, and the United States administration, when political sensitivities

---

[26] J. H. Thomas and Malcolm MacDonald credited McDougall with a decisive role. See O'Brien, 'F. L. McDougall and the Origins of the FAO', 166.

[27] See O'Brien, 'F. L. McDougall and the Origins of the FAO', 167.

[28] Memo by McDougall, 'The Committee on the Structure and Functions of the Economic and Financial Organizations', 2 Mar. 1938, TNA: PRO FO371/22517, W3240/41/98, p. 6.

allowed, supported moves by McDougall and the Economic Committee to break links to the institute and create an agricultural section at the League.[29]

The League's relationship with the IIA was never clearly defined and operated on an ad hoc basis, in part because the EFO, whether under Salter, or under Stoppani's and Loveday's joint direction, did not want to place 'limits on the development of the League's economic action' through a formal arrangement.[30] The EFO respected the IIA's established track record in gathering material on agricultural and economic intelligence since its foundation in 1905, and relied on its data on agricultural output, but grew increasingly frustrated by the 'deficiency and unpunctuality' of its statistical compilations. In 1934, Loveday became so exasperated, he dispatched two staff members, the Swede Johan Rosenborg and the Pole Gregorz Frumkin, Editor of the *Statistical Yearbook*, to Rome to go through the long series of questions thoroughly with the various branches of the Institute in the hope it will create 'a proper working system . . . for the future'.[31] But the limits of his office meant Loveday was powerless to do more, and, in the meantime, the problem rumbled on.

The notion of 'positive security' provided the EFO with a means to assert its primacy over the IAA. But it did more than that. Questions relating to health and nutrition became significant because of the potential impact on primary production, habits of consumption, economic recovery, and the prospects of world peace. It was the same logic that had made nutrition central to the discussion of colonial development, which, in turn, remoulded the political economy of the British Empire around a discourse that tied development more clearly to rural welfare.[32] The commonwealth and imperial dimension was reflected through the League, too, with Africa as the early site of investigation for the relationship between agricultural production and nutrition. The League's creation of transnational networks that contributed to the reshaping of British colonial policy is eye-catching, where Aykroyd's conclusion that widespread malnutrition in the colonies was arresting their potential for economic development had an important impact.[33] But similarly important and less well-studied processes were at work in French and Dutch imperial relations, and in Central and South America,

---

[29] Report by Feis to the Advisory Committee on International Relations, 'Research Work Conducted in Geneva', June 1929, LON, Loveday, P140/11/in and outgoing correspondence, 1928–9. Sweetser complained that the IIA's shortcomings meant the USA was establishing its own global network of agricultural commissoners, thereby nationalizing what he believed 'should be international'. See memo by Sweetser, 'Condition in the United States', 16 July 1930, LON, R3567, 50/21727/1683, p. 14.

[30] Comment by Salter, 'Minutes of Directors' Meeting', 12 Nov. 1930, LON, R3565, 50/16937/767, Directors Meetings, 1930.

[31] Cumpston, *Lord Bruce of Melbourne*, 144; Loveday to Treasurer and General Secretary, 4 Sept. 1934, LON, Loveday, P143/14–15/outgoing correspondence, 1934–5.

[32] Stephen Constantine, *The Making of British Colonial Development Policy, 1914–1949* (London, 1984), 232–46.

[33] Sunil Amrith, *Decolonizing International Health: India and Southeast Asia, 1930–1945* (London, 2006), 28–34.

where the League sponsored an Intergovernmental Conference on Rural Hygiene for Latin American countries in Mexico in 1938.[34]

The primary laboratory for the League, however, and the region of concern that underpinned the Mixed Committee on Nutrition, were not Africa or Asia but central and eastern Europe, where the League had had a sustained interest since 1919. Here, coupling economic development with health was promoted by McDougall and Loveday as a means of advancing the region's economic and social improvement, reinternationalizing the economy, and addressing the emerging security crisis. Loveday's interest in agriculture, though less immediately apparent than McDougall's, given his financial brief, was no less passionate. As was evident in his early published work on India and in his frequent trips to central and Danubian Europe (his wife was Romanian), Loveday was a keen visitor of local farms. He understood the importance of agriculture to both the economic and the political fortunes of Europe, continually garnering information from the world's more successful agricultural producers in the aspiration it would help its poorer ones. In preparation for a visit to the Americas in 1934, for example, he wrote to the Canadian Prime Minister, Richard Bradford Bennett, that his work had 'brought me very much in contact with agricultural states in Central and Eastern Europe, and I am anxious to see something of the prairie provinces in addition to Ottawa, Montreal and Toronto'; on his mission to North America, he travelled 'as far West as Winnipeg' before visiting some of the plain lands of the USA.[35] The League's sensitivity to the diversity of local experience and the value of that diversity—so much less evident in the modernizing, development projects of the period after 1945—emanated from its commitment to scientific fieldwork and the ingrained habit of comparison, local, regional, national, and global, that evolved within the institution during its twenty-six-year life span. While it is true that the League's policies stressed that indigenous food cultures needed to be standardized and modernized, they also recognized that food had a culturally specific social value.

In 1935, McDougall and Loveday planned how a new initiative on agriculture and health could 'best be handled at the forthcoming Assembly'.[36] They agreed that, although their scheme owed much to the LNHO's work, notably the 1931 LNHO European Conference on Rural Hygiene—a term whose meaning in the 1930s included the promotion of health as well as sanitary conditions—and the Pan-African Health Conference of 1935, it was important that any new step should foreground the relationship between health, primary production, and trade. Economic development and trade were their primary concern, and they anticipated that, by adding nutrition and health into the mix, they would be able to depoliticize issues relating to agriculture and reinforce an air of scientific impartiality that would

---

[34] Warwick Anderson, *The Cultivation of Whiteness: Science, Health and Racial Destiny in Australia* (Melbourne, 2002), 212–35; Paul Weindling, 'The League of Nations Health Organization and the Rise of Latin American Participation', *História, Ciências, Saúde—Manguinhos*, 13/3 (2006), 1–14.

[35] Loveday to Bennett, 19 Sept. 1934, LON, Loveday, P143/14–15/outgoing correspondence, 1934–5. See also Alexander Loveday, *The History and Economics of Indian Famines* (Oxford, 1914).

[36] McDougall to Loveday, 14 Aug. 1935, LON, Loveday, P143/14–15/outgoing correspondence, 1934–5.

capture some of the international momentum and goodwill built up by the LNHO (in contrast to the fractious response that League investigations into trade and raw materials frequently engendered). At the September meeting of the Assembly in 1935, McDougall and Loveday crafted a speech for Bruce in which he stressed that the world needed to lower tariff barriers, increase market access to industrial countries for agricultural producers, and reduce the scandalous level of poverty in agrarian countries. It argued there should also be a greater awareness that promoting good nutrition would increase demand for primary products, and that, as agricultural producers became wealthier, so they would be better able to buy more exports. Tariff barriers and quotas would gradually fall and the world would be set fair on the virtuous circle towards democracy and free trade. Of course, the benefits of trade liberalization was a long-held ideal of the League, and so too was Bruce's attack on the fashion for self-sufficiency in Europe, which carried the malodorous smell of imperial rivalry that had characterized European relations before the First World War.

Bruce offered an especially pointed critique of European provincialism and its attempt to make European nations or regions self-sufficient in food: it was a parochial policy that ignored the well-being of peoples beyond Europe's frontiers, perpetuated inefficiency within Europe, kept European living standards low, and made its citizens unhealthy. He called upon members of the League to recognize the simultaneous existence of millions of hungry people in a world where there were also huge agricultural surpluses. Not only should the LNHO collect data on national efforts to improve nutrition, but the mixed committee of agricultural, economic, and health experts should broaden the ambit of inquiry to report on the 'agricultural and economic effects of improved nutrition'.[37] Bruce's appeal to the assembly was supported by intensive lobbying behind the scenes by McDougall and Loveday, who tirelessly reminded members of the Economic and Financial Committees that, while there were around seventy sovereign states in the world and eighty-five countries of economic significance with which the League needed to engage, only ten of these could be described primarily as industrial countries. Of these three were totalitarian and the other seven absorbed more than 44 per cent of the world's primary exports. This, alone, they argued demonstrated that it was essential to keep the position of different agricultural producers firmly in view.[38] Bruce was later to boast that what became the first systematic international investigation into human nutrition was primarily conceived and promoted by Australia. But in reality the initiative was sustained because of the large degree of support it commanded across the secretariat and within the offices of the LNHO and the ILO. There was more truth in his claim that the idea for a Mixed Committee

[37] League of Nations, 'Minutes of the Eighty-Ninth Session of Council', 28 Sept. 1935, *Official Journal*, 16/11: 1208.
[38] League of Nations, 'Minutes of the Economic Committee, 49th Session', 30 Mar. 1939, pp. 5–6, Comité Économique, P.V., vol. 16, 1935–9, 'Procès-Verbaux, 42–49 Sessions'.

inquiry into nutrition 'was completely economic and had no humanitarian back-ground'.[39] It bore witness to the importance of economic development and security to the committee's inception. The inclusion of food science and rhetoric of 'malnutrition' that enabled east and central Europeans, and others, to become the objects of humanitarian sympathy and agency came later.

The most important publication that resulted from this work was the mixed report on 'The Relation of Nutrition to Health, Agriculture and Economic Policy' published in 1937. It quickly became an important part of the EFO's extended policy agenda, and helped to generate a remodelled policy language that focused on the relationships between food, agriculture, trade, economic stability, social well-being, and housing. In it, McDougall, Loveday, Stoppani, and other League associates argued that the needs of primary producers had to be integrated more effectively into international relations, and, in particular, industrialized countries should concentrate agricultural production on milk and fruit to meet their domes-tic markets' need for perishables, but, for the good of their own economic development and the balance of the world economy as a whole, they should produce less wheat, sugar, and cereals—the world's major traded commodities.[40] The report and supplementary materials were sensitive to the national, regional, and global dimension in its analysis.

Thereafter, the ILO and the LNHO continued to make separate enquiries into nutrition, the former being interested in its impact on labour productivity and well-being (with hunger presented as an impediment to modernization), and the latter concerned with its relationship to health more generally. Although League members rejected McDougall's proposal to set up a League international nutrition committee in 1938, nineteen members established national nutrition committees, which were rapidly absorbed into war preparations instead.[41] But, in a pattern reflected in the EFO's work in other fields, success in establishing a set of univer-sally applicable statistical standards, in this case a set of dietary minimum require-ments published as *The Physiological Bases of Nutrition*, came more readily. The clarity of these recommendations, and the alacrity with which they were taken up by doctors, public health officials, social workers, and teachers, demonstrated once again both the potential and the perils of the technical agenda of the League. Statistics were hard to come by and standards were contested, but the EFO's secretariat believed these challenges were easier to resolve than what the League believed was the biggest question before it: how to reach a wider public without running into interference from states.

The legacy of inter-institutional engagement in the Mixed Committee on Nutrition, and the personal networks that grew out of its work, were also import-ant. They marked a significant step forward in cooperation between the different sections of the League of Nations. The Social Section was now more aware of what

---

[39] Cumpston, *Lord Bruce of Melbourne*, 146.
[40] League of Nations, *Final Report of the Mixed Committee of the League of Nations on the Relation of Nutrition to Health, Agriculture and Economic Policy* (Geneva, 1937), 151–73.
[41] Cumpston, *Lord Bruce of Melbourne*, 148.

the EFO could provide by way of intellectual support, economic intelligence, and political contacts; and the authority and centrality of the EFO as the prime coordinating agency within the League were redoubled. Inter-institutional cooperation, notably between the ILO and the Economic and the Financial Sections, also became more consistent and sustained. In the 1930s, the rhetoric of improving 'living standards' fulfilled an important coordinating function, at once eye-catching, morally just, and yet sufficiently flexible to accommodate the different meanings that League bodies and outside agents might ascribe to it. As the 'Final Report of the Mixed Committee' put it, economic and social policies needed to be developed in relation to one another with a common emphasis on 'living standards'. This, far more than the abstract topics relating to monetary relations and trade, would revive the interest and enthusiasm of the 'common people' in the work of the League and in international cooperation more generally.[42]

WHAT'S IN A LIVING STANDARD?

The Tripartite Stabilization Agreement of September 1936 expressed the common aim of the United States, Britain, and France to raise the 'living standards of peoples'.[43] The prominence of this global commitment to raise the minimum required for humans to live in dignity was a potent echo of the nutrition debate. The public pledge not only reflected the debate about positive security under way in the League, but was another tool used by officials in Geneva to renew their role and authority in international relations. They had a long-standing interest in living standards, which was more a term of art than a stable concept. In the late 1920s, the ILO was the first international agency to try to grapple with the problem by trying to compare living standards between Europe and the USA—an initiative that generated painful headaches for its director and its staff. But, if living standards created as much dispute as agreement between states, and engendered a variety of disparate remedies, the ILO and the League at least played an important part in generating the claim for international agency and a global perspective on the topic, and their work helped to stabilize the term's meaning in international relations.[44]

The approach of co-signatories of the Stabilization Agreement, invariably, was more narrowly prescribed. For France, the focus on living standards, although couched in an international perspective, was directed primarily at a domestic audience. The Popular Front's commitment to raising living standards ran through

[42] League of Nations, *Final Report of the Mixed Committee of the League of Nations on the Relation of Nutrition to Health, Agriculture and Economic Policy*, 34.

[43] Department of US Treasury Press Release, 'Declaration by the United States, the United Kingdom and France Effected by Simultaneous Announcements in Washington, London and Paris', 25 Sept. 1936, Avalon Project, Yale University <http://avalon.law.yale.edu/20th_century/usmu001.asp#1> (accessed 2 May 2009); 'Exposé des Motifs of the Devaluation Law', issued by the Popular Front, Paris, 28 Sept. 1938, TNA: PRO T160/685.

[44] Victoria de Grazia underlines the importance of living standards to the articulation and competition between varieties of capitalism in the USA and Europe. See de Grazia, *Irresistible Empire*, 76–126.

it as through a stick of seaside rock. The promises of a forty-hour week, paid holidays, increased agricultural prices, and public works schemes were intended to raise the purchasing power of urban and rural communities, and most importantly to secure economic revival. It was also embedded in the Popular Front's commitment on entering office to maintain French membership of the gold standard so as to safeguard middle-class savings and fixed incomes. The painful reality, however, was that, as both MacDonald's 'enforced' departure and Roosevelt's rejection of the gold standard demonstrated, increased government spending and gold standard membership were incompatible. The depreciation of the French franc facilitated by the Tripartite Stabilization Agreement fuelled an already enhanced sense of middle-class imperilment thanks to the broad socialist coalition of support on which the Popular Front was based. The international promise to raise living standards was meant to counter it, and included a promised 'move definitely in the direction of freer trade in order to keep down the cost of living'.[45]

If the primacy of living standards in French political rhetoric derived from the Popular Front's determination, as far as possible, not to 'split the classes' in the political economy, it also reflected broader trends in Britain, the United States, and elsewhere, which had recast earlier debates about living standards in the wake of the Great Depression. The ILO inquiry, which opened in April 1929, reflected the widespread assumption that higher living standards would be brought about by increasing wages. The ILO venture had its origins in its unlikely coupling with the Ford Corporation and the Twentieth Century Fund, bank-rolled by the Bostonian department store magnate Edward Filene, an ardent internationalist and a great fan of Henry Ford, who contributed $25,000 towards the cost of the ILO–Ford project. Although the ILO Director Albert Thomas complained about the terms and timetable set by his sponsors that jeopardized the ILO's claim to scientific impartiality and his mission to promote workers' rights, he believed it a price worth paying, because living standards held the key to employment and international peace.[46]

The Ford Motor Company wanted the ILO to furnish it with information regarding the living costs of European workers in order to determine the pay scales in the seventeen cities in twelve countries where it had or intended establishing production plants. The ILO had compiled statistics on the wages and hours worked by industrial workers since 1923, and Thomas hoped that an investigation would reveal 'how much a Parisian, German etc. worker would need to expend if his general standard of living was to be approximately equivalent to that of his Detroit counterpart'.[47] European trade unions and businessmen, meanwhile, suspected the

---

[45] 'Statement of the French Government Relating to the Monetary Agreement Reached between France, United States and Great Britain', 25 Sept. 1936, Annex VII, TNA: PRO T160/877.

[46] De Grazia, *Irresistible Empire*, 78–83.

[47] Memo of interview between Lyndall Urwick and Sir Percival Perry, London, 26 Sept. 1929, ILO, Box 1, T 101/0/1, Ford–Filene Enquiry File. For the findings, see Social Science Research Council and the International Labour Office, *International Wage Comparisons: A Report of Two International Conferences and a Critical Review of Available Statistical Data* (New York and Manchester,

real impetus behind the inquiry was Ford's determination to garner intelligence that would enable him to undermine European car production, while luring the best skilled workers away from domestic producers with higher wages.

Yet it was precisely Ford's commitment to higher wages that seduced Thomas into running the inquiry. The chance to foster greater US involvement in the activities of the ILO was an additional impetus, especially as the USA had decided to participate fully in the League's intergovernmental and expert committees in 1927. (Indeed, the USA became a full member of the ILO in 1934.) But, as so often in the ILO's and EFO's experience of specialist inquiries, it was only once the work was under way that the real conceptual and practical difficulties of the project became clear. It quickly became apparent that no one had any real idea of the living standard of the average Ford-worker in Detroit as against which European stand-ards were to be measured. ILO employees in Detroit spent over eight months pouring over pay slips, wives' household account books, and the ephemera of daily life that recorded how families spent their hard-earned cash. European investigators in cities as far west as Cork, and as far east as Warsaw and Istanbul, too, found their lives given over to collecting materials that would have been at home in a Kurt Schwitters collage. Although the ILO enjoyed the benefit of experienced field agents and local offices, unlike the EFO's secretariat, which largely collected data by correspondence, intelligence remained hard to acquire because their inquiries touched political, commercial, and cultural sensitivities.

The cultural challenge was fundamental. It was comparatively easy to compare wage rates on an international basis, even if workers' payments included non-monetary benefits, at a time when the issue of currency fluctuations was theoretic-ally neutralized by the gold standard. It was much harder to determine which items were deemed essential to everyday life in all parts of the world, and constituted the basket of goods, services, and amenities on which standards of living might be determined and compared. Here, taste and traditions collided both between and among different regions and nations of Europe, and with the Americans against whom the Europeans were to be evaluated. As the British professor of industrial relations John Hilton put it in a review of the ILO study, 'the fantasy of a universal identical basic budget' was sorely tested by the 'French worker [who] inclines to wine, coffee and veal, where the English worker fancies beer, tea and bacon', while the renowned French sociologist and economist François Simiand condemned the initiative, which was 'by its very nature impossible either of formulation or of attainment'.[48]

So, when the EFO resurrected 'living standards' as a means to effect the revival of economic internationalism almost a decade later, it was aware of the challenges.

1932). For an overview of the ILO's work in the field of wage rates, see J. W. Nixon, 'Work of [the] International Labour Office', *Statistical and Social Inquiry Society of Ireland*, 91 (1937–8), 69–86.

[48] John Hilton, 'International Wage Comparisons', *Economic Journal*, 43/171 (Sept. 1933), 480; Marjorie Beale, *The Modernist Enterprise: French Elites and the Threat of Modernity, 1900–1940* (Stanford, CA, 1999), 145–64. See also the later work of the Hungarian-born American economist Tibor Scitovsky.

This time the starting point was to recognize the difference between an American conception of the good life, which consisted of a decent income for lots of people spent individually by purchasing all the goods that enabled them to live comfortably, and European notions, which emphasized the 'manner', not the standard, of living—a rhetoric that stressed quality, taste, and preference as much as quantity and price in the market.[49] Although the League Assembly preferred the term 'human well-being', the EFO's 'Sub-Committee on the Standard of Living', set up in 1938, with the ubiquitous McDougall as chairman and the British economist Noel Hall as special adviser, preferred the terminology and possibilities afforded by standardization. At the same time, the EFO subcommittee sought to traverse the divide between a 'style' and a 'standard' of living by widening the latter notion to include physical as well as material well-being, and to incorporate agricultural workers and the unemployed, as well as urban workers, into their analysis.[50] Its nine-man membership marked another mixed venture and included the German Otto Olsen, representing the League's hygiene section, and ILO statisticians Hans Staehle and J. W. Nixon, the new Chief of the ILO's statistical office.[51] Other members of the committee were Rappard, Loveday, and Stoppani, as well as the Polish François Dolézal and the French Socialist-Radical Paul Elbel, both longstanding governmental delegates to the Economic Committee. Elbel's participation was especially significant. In 1929, the French government had been so hostile to Thomas's adoption of the American definition of living standards that it withdrew from the ILO inquiry. Although Elbel continued to argue that a 'phrase such as *l'accroissement du bien-être humain* would have a much greater appeal in France', and would remind governments, and the League itself, of this 'essential duty', his participation challenges the contemporary view that French economists and sociologists were aloof from living standards research in the 1930s.[52] The ILO, too, was keen to put the earlier inquiry behind it, describing its 1929 work 'in the nature of a pre-requisite', tacitly acknowledging its conceptual, practical (shortfalls in data), and geographic limitations.[53] The group agreed to make use of interesting work on production and consumption in Asia, China, and Africa, and integrate notions of cultural preference and a physical well-being with the development of a basic standard of living that was transferable around the world, which would be facilitated and ultimately guaranteed by the reopening of the international economy.

---

[49] De Grazia, *Irresistible Empire*, 94–5.

[50] Hall had just completed work on the Political and Economic Planning Organization's report on living standards in the UK and had a long-standing interest in Australian trade policy and social health. See Noel F. Hall, '"Trade Diversion"—An Australian Interlude', *Economica*, 5/17 (1938), 1–11.

[51] Comment by Noel Hall, Minutes of Third Meeting, 'Sub-Committee on the Standard of Living', 2 Dec. 1938, p. 2, LON R4468, 10A/36292/35663.

[52] Minutes of Third Meeting, 'Sub-Committee on the Standard of Living', 2 Dec. 1938, p. 5, LON R4468, 10A/36292/35663. The French pioneer in the field of living standards Maurice Halbwachs complained that the French ignored overseas reasearch, a view repeated by Beale, *The Modernist Enterprise*, 145–64.

[53] Comments by Staehle and Hall, Minutes of Third Meeting, 'Sub-Committee on the Standard of Living', 2 Dec. 1938, pp. 2–4, LON R4468, 10A/36292/35663.

And this was the crux of the issue for the Economic and Financial Sections. Although there were risks, the ILO–Ford inquiry had demonstrated the potential of living standards to capture the international imagination. There was a need to 'go on [because] knowledgeable ignorance' was better than 'ignorant knowledge', and after 1933 the world was full of those with 'loud confidence as to the exact truth, whatever they would like to be the truth'.[54] The rhetoric of raising living standards had been used and abused to considerable effect by fascists and communists, and it was time for liberal internationalists to fight back. Although the League Committee on Standards of Living explored how it might best contribute to the new scientific work in France, Britain, and the United States on the meanings, value, and nature of living standards, the group was primarily gripped, in Elbel's words, by 'a more dynamic [global] purpose. How were they to liberate and set in motion the enormous potentialities which existed of increased production and consumption? There were millions of people in the world who lack sufficient food, clothing, accommodation and education facilities, while at the same time the possibilities of increasing production were almost unlimited.'[55]

For historians, the emergence of the 'standard of living' defines the moment when the phenomena of consumption emerged in its own right.[56] Framed within the agenda of the League of Nations, the notion of a 'standard of living' became a lens through which to see the world as an object to be improved by liberal capitalism, western science, and international organization. But living standards were also conceived as a means to reinforce connections between those interested in promoting the values and practices of liberal capitalism, interwoven as some of these were with imperialism, against the forces of fascism and communism. It was no accident that in the same breath that Elbel made this grand pronouncement on behalf of global development in the League, he announced that the US Ambassador in Paris, William Bullitt, entirely agreed that, in furthering this aim, the 'League would have the sympathy of all countries', most importantly, McDougall and Loveday added *sotto voce*, the United States.[57] Living standards were one of the great battlegrounds of the Great Depression. National Socialists, Fascist, nationalist, and authoritarian political parties and governments claimed they would fight to improve them for the men, women, and children they claimed as their own, but saw the resources from which such improvement would come as finite. In the 1930s, theirs was a struggle, potentially a war, for the 'right sort' of material, human and physical, that would raise living standards for the chosen, and see them deteriorate markedly for selected ethnic and political categories.

Centrists, liberals, and socialists dedicated to reforming capitalism, and not to destroying it, on the other hand, retained their faith in a capitalist model that

---

[54] Hilton, 'International Wage Comparisons', 481.

[55] Comment by Elbel, Minutes of Third Meeting, 'Sub-Committee on the Standard of Living', 2 Dec. 1938, pp. 2–4, LON R4468, 10A/36292/35663.

[56] Judith G. Coffin, 'A "Standard" of Living? European Perspectives on Class and Consumption in the Early Twentieth Century', *International Labor and Working-Class History*, 55 (1999), 6.

[57] Minutes of Third Meeting, 'Sub-Committee on the Standard of Living', 2 Dec. 1938, p. 5, LON R4468, 10A/36292/35663.

posited cooperation between nations and held out the potential of open financial and trading markets to deliver increased growth and rising living standards for everyone. Yet by 1936 the gyrations of the international economy, and wave after wave of nationalist, uncoordinated, 'emergency' measures, had assumed an air of permanence, and produced a siege mentality in democratic politics. The emergence of 'Keynesian' ideas of demand management, with its express focus on the need to manage consumption during an economic downturn as a means both to effect recovery and to sustain living standards, impressed the Economic and Financial Sections and their advisers, such as McDougall, because of its stress on the importance of consumption. Ideas about demand management were focused primarily on national conditions, but the group wanted to understand the implications for the international. The question of living standards and its intimate relationship with consumption therefore also enabled the League to open a new perspective on questions that had preoccupied the EFO since 1930: how was the international economy to be reopened? How might the myriad benefits offered to the world by internationalism and international organizations be reasserted and secured?

The Great Depression encouraged states to present themselves as the protectors of the welfare of their citizens. An international (and comparative) perspective was essential if such assertions were to be challenged and tested. For Rappard, no power was beyond reproach. Despite what they maintained, states were not necessarily 'concerned to increase the general welfare. There were plenty of phenomena which went to belie such contention—armaments, for instance, and certain aspects of customs policy.' The fact that the 'strength of totalitarian systems lay largely in this claim to represent the interests of the whole population' underlined the political power of living standards, and the need for such assertions to be measured and contested. For democracies, on the other hand, international agency could make a different contribution, given that 'in democracies different groups jostled to get their interests represented', which resulted 'in many countries' in the 'desire to protect certain classes . . . in opposition to the general welfare'.[58]

McDougall's primary motivation as chairman of the committee—and the participants were unanimous in crediting the Australian for taking the lead on the issue—was to highlight the potential of living standards both to facilitate international unity and to iron out global inequality. (The nutrition agenda coincidentally also furthered the interests of Australian primary producers.) It was a logic echoed in the appeal of former Foreign Secretary Anthony Eden in the British House of Commons in November 1938 that it was impossible to separate the question of national unity from that of the standard of living of the poorer sections of the population: if the government was to get the nation to fight in times of war, it needed to 'devote as much attention to the provision of housing, nourishment and

---

[58] Minutes of Third Meeting, 'Sub-Committee on the Standard of Living', 2 Dec. 1938, p. 8, LON R4468, 10A/36292/35663

sunlight as we do to the provision of arms'.[59] Eden's call to arms borrowed heavily
on the positive security agenda of the organization at which he had been a
committed and regular visitor, entering cabinet in June 1935 as a minister for
League of Nations affairs (without a portfolio). For him the two overwhelming
tasks before the nation were 'security and the well-being of our people . . . we have
to rearm and rebuild'.[60] For McDougall, too, a close focus on improving the
'manner of life' in democracies would enable the League to alter the timbre of
international relations. To this end, it was essential to combine and coordinate the
specific studies being undertaken by the League, the ILO, and other international
communities, including the scientific world and the cooperative movement, and to
spell out their findings in relation to how they shaped the living standards of every
man, woman, and child. The League agencies had to 'evolve new technical methods
of getting knowledge across . . . to evolve a process for the translation of these
studies into general terms comprehensible by the public'.[61]

The issue of how the League should communicate to a wider public was a
challenge to which the EFO's secretariat returned repeatedly, and McDougall's
concerted effort to energize debate about living standards and human well-being
within the EFO and the ILO marked a new stage in the interrelationship of those
agencies. If notions of positive security had helped to increase the EFO's sensitivity
to social issues, it also helped the ILO to widen its focus from the urban worker to
rural communities and the unemployed.[62] As concepts of human well-being and
consumption were recast in these international organizations, the work and its
range were facilitated by long-established personal friendships between many of the
key protagonists, including Loveday and the Oxford-educated Englishman Harold
Butler, who succeeded Thomas at the helm of the ILO in 1932. The latter sought
to ensure that, as the ILO began to range more widely into economic policy, 'there
was no question of it [the ILO] preparing memoranda or other documents which
would in anyway overlap with the work of the League or other international
bodies'.[63] Although the new tone of Anglo-Saxon bonhomie facilitated cooperation
between the EFO and the ILO on one level, it also alienated others. As cosy as their
personal and professional relations may have been, they were underpinned by a
shared criticism of British economic nationalism and disappointed by the efficacy
of Roosevelt's New Deal as a means of effecting economic recovery in the United
States; but Loveday and Butler agreed the effects of his social reform programme
were more 'generally tacitly accepted by the business world than the business world
itself realizes or would ever admit', and was being mimicked in countries such as

[59] *Hansard*, HC Deb, 10 Nov. 1938, vol. 341, col. 378.
[60] *Hansard*, HC Deb, 10 Nov. 1938, vol. 341, col. 378.
[61] Minutes of Third Meeting, 'Sub-Committee on the Standard of Living', 2 Dec. 1938, LON
R4468, 10A/36292/35663, p. 4.
[62] Amalia Ribi Forclaz, 'A New Target for International Social Reform: The International Labour
Organization and Working and Living Conditions in Agriculture in the Interwar Years', *Contemporary
European History*, 20/3 (2011), 307–29.
[63] Butler to Loveday, 7 Jan. 1935, LON, Loveday P143/15–15/outgoing correspondence, 1934–5.
Maurette's Economic Group at the ILO held periodic meetings with the Economic and Financial
Sections to ensure there was no overlap and to explore where collaboration was possible.

Canada.[64] Their economics harked back to an older brand of economic liberalism, one that admired the Gladstonian emphasis on free trade as a means to drive down prices and push up living standards for the poor. It was global in orientation, albeit a world that was the object of their benevolence rather than the subject of their engagement. And, if the Great Depression had helped to link economic science to social and biological science more firmly than before, it was a development given impetus and a tighter geographic focus by the growing storm clouds of war building over Europe.

HEALTH AT THE HEART OF EUROPE

The new emphasis on physical well-being in relation to living standards and primary production within the framework of 'positive security' was not seen as distinct from the League's efforts to arbitrate disputes in international relations. Unlike the rigorously compartmentalized areas of science and policy design, in the messy world of international politics, 'positive security' and 'hard security', the latter represented by the sanctity of national borders and the resources used to protect them, blended into a lumpy mix. The plight of central European and Danubian states became a talisman for the interconnectedness of agricultural production, nutrition, and health. The fate of Romania, Yugoslavia, Bulgaria, Hungary, Austria, and Czechoslovakia was of particular concern, the latter less because of the problems of its own agricultural sector than because it was imperilled by the vulnerability of the states around it. In one of a series of his widely circulated papers on 'Standards of Living in Eastern Europe', McDougall outlined the desperate plight of 'about a quarter of the 60 million peasants of eastern Europe that do not produce enough to enable them to get enough bread to eat throughout the year'.[65] Details of the estimate comprised three million hungry Poles in the south of the country, two million in the east, and a further one and a half million in its central territories. One million people in Hungary were malnourished (25 per cent of its population), 150,000 in Slovenia, half a million in Ruthenia (a staggering 80 per cent of the total population), two million in Transylvania, half a million in 'the Old Kingdom of Romania, one and a half million in Bulgaria, and three and a half million in Yugoslavia': some fifteen and a half million souls in all.

The analysis was not tied to the Great Depression in particular. Rather, the situation was presented as a vicious, persistent cycle of rural undercapitalization, underproductivity, underemployment, malnourishment, pervasive misery, and over-population. Indeed, in MacDougall's mind, rural overpopulation was a much more prevalent problem than urban overpopulation, because conditions on the land were

[64] Butler to Loveday, 7 Jan. 1935, LON, Loveday, P143/14–15/outgoing correspondence, 1934–5; Loveday to Avenol, 29 Dec. 1934, LON R4605, 10C/13175/9854.
[65] Memo by McDougall, 'Standards of Living in Eastern Europe', Oct. 1938, LON R4453, 10A/3303/326649.

so poor. To members of the League secretariat, the deterioration of rural life in the territories liberated into statehood by the Paris Peace agreements had come to demonstrate the need for greater international intervention, both by international organizations and by the coordinated action of nation states, to facilitate the diversification of production and the promotion of 'better equipment and organization', with more attention being given to the health and well-being of rural communities.[66]

Romania, Hungary, and Yugoslavia were singled out for special attention by the Economic and Financial Sections—Romania because it was there that the 'worst type of diet' was found, consisting 'almost entirely of maize pudding, with the consequence that the health of the Romanian peasantry is very bad'. Infant mortality was measured at 18 per cent, the highest in Europe, with diseases associated with malnutrition, including debility (general weakness), rachitis (fragile bones), gastro-enteritis, pellagra (a niacin deficiency), and goitre affecting up to 30 per cent of peasants in villages investigated by League missions. In both Romania and Hungary the problem was attributed to the type of farming: land was cultivated too intensively and ineffectively. The interests of landless agricultural labourers, on the other hand, were illustrated through the case of Yugoslavia, where the average family income 'of farm labourers with little or no land of their own was about 6*d*. per day, enough to buy two-and-half kilos of bread for the whole family until the winter-time', when work dried up and they had to 'eat oats, wild grasses and weeds to exist until the next harvest', when they could work again.[67] McDougall and his colleagues acknowledged that, although these examples were chosen from 'the poorest and worst-fed peasants, the conditions are typical of many millions' around the world. In this way, the undernourished east European became the imagined universal peasant, and this debate about economic and social security allowed Asian colonial states—and Asian nationalist intellectuals without state power—to envisage their place in a world of nations. At the same time, these discussions played into the existing (even rising) concern of politicians in the United States, Australia, and other settler colonies, with agrarian poverty and population growth in Asia viewed as a threat that stood to send thousands of unwanted migrants to their shores.[68]

But it was in central and Danubian Europe that the Economic and Financial Sections most closely monitored the deteriorating conditions. It measured the dramatic decline in agricultural prices, especially in relation to industrial goods: in Romania they fell by nearly 56 per cent between 1929 and 1934, whereas the prices of industrial goods used in agriculture fell by 19 per cent; in Hungary there

---

[66] Memo by McDougall, 'Standards of Living in Eastern Europe', Oct. 1938, LON R4453, 10A/3303/326649.

[67] Significantly, the family unit and the unit of production were merged in this analysis to become the family farm—the talisman of post-war European agriculture. Memo by McDougall, 'Standards of Living in Eastern Europe', Oct. 1938, LON R4453, 10A/3303/326649; Sunil Amrith and Patricia Clavin, 'Feeding the World: Connecting Europe and Asia, 1933–1945', for a special supplement of *Past and Present* on Transnational Movements and Organizations edited by Rana Mitter and Matthew Hilton, forthcoming.

[68] Sunil Amrith, 'Food and Welfare in India, *c*.1900–1950', *Comparative Studies in Society and History*, 50/4 (2008), 1010–35.

was a 70 per cent gap between agricultural and industrial prices. Over the same period, peasant incomes declined by 58 per cent in Romania, 59 per cent in Poland, and 36 per cent in Hungary.[69] The price and income declines were catastrophic for these overwhelmingly agricultural countries, and the League was especially struck by the degree to which the declining fortunes of agriculture reversed some of the considerable gains in development made in the region. During the 1920s, it argued, the use of fertilizers had trebled in Yugoslavia and quadrupled in Hungary, but in the 1930s their use stopped almost entirely. Whereas west European farmers used 100–300 kilograms of fertilizer per 10,000 square metres in the 1930s, in Yugoslavia levels had fallen to a negligible 7 kilograms and 2.6 kilograms per 10,000 square metres in Poland. With unemployment now rife, more people than ever were living off the land, yet the increase in manpower caused yields to fall not rise, because the land was being exploited more intensively to feed the many more mouths dependent on it when unemployed urban workers returned to the already stretched family landholdings. Considerations of short-term survival ruled the day. Sugar-beet yields fell by 5–10 per cent in Poland, Romania, Hungary, Bulgaria, and Yugoslavia; wheat yields fell by a dramatic 20 per cent on 1920s figures, and were actually some 4 per cent below levels attained between 1919 and 1931 in Romania and Poland.

Nor was there much comfort to be had from falling prices, for in agricultural Europe they had not resulted in the significant reductions in the cost of living that had been recorded elsewhere. The comparison between west, and central and eastern, Europe was stark. The Financial Section calculated that, between 1931 and 1936, the 'cost of living' in Britain had fallen by 45 per cent from 1929 (relative to the gold-based prices of 1929), whereas it had dropped by only 26 per cent in Austria and 39 per cent in Poland. Central and eastern European farmers had precious little, if any, surplus produce to sell, and the terms of trade were firmly against them. Equipment essential to raise living standards for the farm or for the home was prohibitively expensive, and the problem was worsened by the impact of tariffs and cartels that pushed industrial prices even higher.[70] The view of the EFO's secretariat was that the policies of nationally elected governments, regardless of their peasant-friendly rhetoric, were failing them with demands for tax payments and debt servicing pushing peasants ever deeper into poverty.[71]

Central and eastern Europe seemed to be travelling backwards in time. Precious advancements in agricultural production achieved in the first two decades of the

[69] In the same way that H. Hessell Tiltman, *Peasant Europe* (London, 1936), influenced the EFO's work, so League statistics continued to underpin the English-language scholarship on the region. See, e.g., Ivan T. Berend, *Decades of Crisis: Central and Eastern Europe before World War II* (Berkeley and Los Angeles, 1998; 2003 edn.), 256–7.

[70] The League was also a pioneer in collating and categorizing information about industrial cartels whose protective capacity for industry also impressed the secretariat as to the potential value of collective price deals for agricultural goods.

[71] Memo by Financial Section, 'Gold Price Levels, October 1926', Geneva, 5 Dec. 1936, LON Economic and Financial Committee Bound Documents, Documents du Comité Financier, vol. XLIX, F.1505–70. Striking was the absence of any sustained investigation of the pattern of landholding. See, by contrast, S. D. Zagoroff, J. Vegh, and A. D. Bilimovich, *The Agricultural Economy of the Danubian Countries, 1935–45* (Stanford, CA, 1955), 29–46.

twentieth century had not just stopped but were being reversed. Such changes of fortune had more than economic and social consequences as they strengthened the hold of authoritarian governments in power across the region, with the 'noble' exception of Czechoslovakia. The region's politics helped to distance it from democratic Europe and the USA, which increasingly regarded central and eastern Europe with suspicion and distaste. But, if indifference had begun to characterize the attitude of the Great Powers, most strikingly those of France, whose Little Entente alliances were increasingly viewed as a liability rather than an indemnity, the financial network sustained by the League recognized that the region needed renewed access to foreign credit but it lacked the will to revive earlier credit schemes. Instead of finding a means to support the region financially, the Western powers turned the problem on its head, and used central and eastern Europe as a tool to contain, if not to neutralize, the National Socialist threat by allowing German economic penetration through the 'strategy' of economic appeasement. In 1936, the EFO's research laid bare the decline of French trade with central Europe and the scale of German penetration of the region, and it questioned the intentions and implications behind Germany's creation of a *Grossraumwirtschaft* (large-area economy) that would provide a self-sufficient economic area in its backyard. Between 1929 and 1937, the EFO calculated south-eastern Europe supplied 37 per cent of German wheat imports, 35 per cent of its meat, 31 per cent of its lard, 61 per cent of all the tobacco smoked in Germany, and more than 62 per cent of the bauxite needed for German industry.

These trade deals that gave 'preferential access' to German markets for central and eastern European primary producers (in much the same vein as the Ottawa agreements, which had also proved disadvantageous to the primary producer), became increasingly oppressive and coercive. As the League's study of clearing and compensation agreements had made clear, these were essentially barter agreements. In the first known arrangement of this kind signed between Germany and Hungary in February 1934, for example, 90 per cent of Hungarian exports to Germany were paid for by deliveries determined by German industry, and only 10 per cent could be used by Hungary to buy raw materials and other goods of strategic importance, with only two million Reichsmarks available to Hungary as part of the deal. It was grossly disadvantageous, and, as primary prices began to recover after 1933, Hungary was anxious to sell elsewhere, especially to countries prepared to pay in hard currency. But, when it sought to break free or negotiate more favourable terms, bullying and default were Germany's answer. It was a pattern repeated elsewhere, and by the end of 1936 Germany had accumulated nearly five hundred million Reichsmarks in credits in the Reichsbank nominally owed to its south-eastern European trade partners alone.[72] And, where Germany enjoyed economic domination, it also harboured political ambitions.

---

[72] David Kaiser, *Economic Diplomacy and the Origins of the Second World War, 1930–1939* (Princeton, 1980), 155–9; Berend, *Decades of Crisis*, 274–6.

The problem was laid out with stark clarity in the work of the Economic Committee's subcommittee on Raw Materials set up in October 1936.[73] It was instigated by the Economic and Financial Sections, and the debtor nations of central and eastern Europe in the Economic and Financial Committees, and was a continuation of the League's work on clearing and compensation agreements, this time seen from the perspective of supply. Supply was very much the issue of the moment, with world rearmament proceeding apace everywhere after 1936. As a result, demand and prices so long depressed began to recover significantly. The committee was divided into two groups: the first studied the supply of raw materials, including in its remit the impact of exchange controls on that supply; and the second explored how raw materials were purchased and paid for, with a special focus on access to foreign exchange and the impact of import controls. It was intended to reveal the extent to which the search for raw materials was shaping German, Italian, and Japanese foreign policy, on the one hand, and the fate of primary producing nations, on the other.

The hostility of the axis powers to inquiry was to be expected, but the British government also feared the political implications of renewed League intervention on the topic. First, it complained, the geographic remit of the inquiry was left open, and the committee chairman, Leith-Ross, under firm instructions from London, made it clear colonies had to be excluded from the inquiry. Their inclusion risked reinforcing demands for colonial territories from the 'have-not' powers and high-lighted tensions in intra-imperial economics between colonial and dominion 'producers' and British 'consumers' that the British government did not want aired at the League.[74] (As the committee's work coincided with a meeting of the Imperial Conference in London, these issues were especially delicate.) Secondly, the British were concerned that the Balkan countries, the focus of secretariat interest were 'much too heavily represented', while the 'have-not' powers with whom Britain wanted to reach accommodation were embodied in a sole 'taciturn Japan-ese'. So, having complained it feared Axis demands, the British also contrarily complained that without Italy or Germany there would be no opportunity for appeasement. Nor, from the secretariat's perspective, should there be. The aspir-ation was to highlight how credit shortages and the fall in agricultural prices sustained exchange control and the rest of central and eastern Europe's dependency on Germany. As Leith-Ross grumbled, the committee offered the opportunity, vigorously exploited by, in his words, 'verbose Poles', to call for a long-term settlement of their foreign debt obligations and a central bank credit or normaliza-tion fund on which they might draw to ease their exchange pressures and access to essential supplies. Britain, the only major creditor of the region on the committee (the French delegate failed to turn up), feared that publicizing and giving credence

---

[73] The Assembly meeting of Oct. 1936 established its terms of reference, and it met in camera. League of Nations, *Official Journal*, 20 Mar. 1937, 18/2: 106–7.

[74] Shackle to Leith-Ross, 8 May 1937, and Leith-Ross to Stoppani, 19 May 1937, TNA: PRO FO371/21247, W9168/393/98. For the surrounding discussion with the Foreign and Colonial Offices, see TNA: PRO FO371/21247, W8864/393/98.

to these needs would serve as the 'jumping off ground for further demands',[75] or, as Ashton-Gwatkin put it, that 'credit facilities' (presumably largely supplied by London) 'should be made available for France's friends in central Europe'.[76]

Leith-Ross insisted that the report be redrafted to excise these demands. He shifted the focus from economic relations between states onto questions relating to the performance and behaviour of national economies by asking why states could not buy what they needed, given that raw materials could be purchased freely on the world market. The strategy redirected attention from prices and credit shortages evident on the international market, back to exchange controls and the use to which nations were putting scarce hard currency resources, including the purchase of armaments.[77] Beneath the logic of economics lay the expediency of politics. The British recognized the secretariat intended to draw Britain and France into a renewed effort to helping the states on Germany's eastern frontier just as Britain was trying to extract itself from that part of the world and was encouraging France to do the same.[78] The EFO's sections emphasized how the difficulties experienced by Germany, Italy, and Japan were 'largely of their own making, as distinct from the cases of Poland and the Balkan countries, whose difficulties were largely the reaction of the great powers'.[79] Indeed, Stoppani's suggestion that the committee report apportion 'blame fairly and squarely' on Germany, Italy, and Japan triggered a vigorous response from the Treasury, the Board of Trade, and even Vansittart in the Foreign Office, demanding Stoppani's draft report be suppressed before news of it 'leaked' because the condemnation of German, Italian, and Japanese economic foreign policies together in a single League document had 'explosive' implications.[80] Stoppani certainly shared some of the British fears that such an approach might prompt the 'three naughty powers to react against the League'.[81] But he and Loveday were also deeply frustrated by their failure to condemn those whose policies worked directly against the liberal internationalist values of the organization, and by their inability to find support for those values, and the initiatives they sought to launch to uphold them, among member governments.

[75] Note by Leith-Ross, 9 July 1937, p. 3, TNA: PRO FO 371/30699, C5139/71/62.
[76] Minute by Ashton-Gwatkin, 13 May 1937, TNA: PRO FO371/21247, W9940/393/98.
[77] Leith-Ross to Stoppani, 19 May 1937, TNA: PRO FO371/21247, W9168/393/98; memo by Clauson, 20 July 1937, TNA: PRO FO371/21247, W8864/393/98; League of Nations, 'Work of the Economic Committee at its Forty-Seventh Session 6th–7th December 1937', *Official Journal*, 18, annex 1695: 175–8.
[78] Minute by Ashton-Gwatkin of conversation with Avenol, 13 May 1937, TNA: PRO FO371/21247, W9940/393/98. Britain was also concerned that the Raw Materials inquiry would aim to 'open colonial markets'.
[79] Leith-Ross to Phillips, Hopkins, and Fisher, 22 July 1937, TNA: PRO FO371/21247, W14587/393/98.
[80] See minute by Gwatkin, 6 Aug. 1937, TNA: PRO FO371/21247, W15417/393/98.
[81] Stoppani to Leith-Ross, 28 July 1937, and Vansittart to Leith-Ross, 16 Aug. 1937, TNA: PRO FO371/21247, W15417/393/98. Although Stoppani and Loveday were united in their frustation with British internationalism, they did not always agree on strategy. Early in the Raw Materials inquiry Loveday complained vehemently that Stoppani had written the sections on the impact of indebtedness on raw material producers without his prior consultation. See Loveday to Stoppani, 10 June 1937, Nuffield, Loveday, File 177.

ECONOMIC APPEASEMENT

The ignominious tale of how Germany was allowed free rein in central and eastern European trade has been told largely from the perspective of nation states. It is a history of misguided British, duplicitous French, and irresponsible American interventions. But, aside from intergovernmental relations at the League, the secretariat and the scientific community around the organization, too, were part of the failed attempt to answer the questions posed to liberal internationalism by the aggressor powers through the application of economic appeasement. Many of the ideas and personal connections that informed and sustained the diplomatic missions of Van Zeeland, Colijn, and the Belgian financier Maurice Frère leaned on intelligence and concepts developed by the economic and financial agency of the League. Yet, at the same time, as the raw materials committee revealed, members of the EFO's secretariat had become consistent critics of the notion that economic concessions to Germany, allowing it unassailable economic domination of Europe's heartlands, would be sufficient to quell its hunger for territorial annexation and provide the British with their desired 'general settlement' to the European question.[82]

In January 1937, Van Zeeland dusted down Stoppani's July 1936 proposal for an economic agreement between the USA and the European powers to liberalize trade at a meeting of the currently moribund World Economic Conference.[83] Rather than focusing on Democratic solidarity, however, Van Zeeland suggested that Germany should be approached first, and without the agency of the League. At first the French government and the British Foreign Office objected to this suggestion; however, officials in the Treasury and the Board of Trade took a different view. They encouraged Van Zeeland and were instrumental in securing French assent. In April 1937, after none too gentle prodding from the British, the French government formally invited the Belgian to make an inquiry of leading governments as to the possibility of dismantling the weapons of economic nationalism. The initiative was divided into two parts: the first would see his compatriot Frère tour the capitals of Europe; on the second leg, Van Zeeland would travel to Washington to sound out the Roosevelt administration.[84] There was an air of desperation around Frère's and Van Zeeland's diplomacy, made more pungent by the recourse to military law against the Rexist agitation inside Belgium, and the country's abandonment of its military alliance with France, and reversion to

---

[82] Klaus Jaitner, 'Aspekte britischer Deutschlandspolitik', in Josef Becker and Klaus Hildebrand (eds), *Internationale Beziehungen in der Weltwirtschaftskrise, 1929–1933* (Munich, 1980), 21–38; Andrew Crozier, *Appeasement and Germany's Last Bid for the Colonies* (London, 1988), 245–7; Newton, *Profits for Peace*.

[83] See, e.g., Callum A. Macdonald, *The United States, Britain and Appeasement* (London, 1981), 1–15, and J. Simon Rolfe, *Franklin Roosevelt's Foreign Policy and the Welles Mission* (London, 2007), 60–1.

[84] Sussdorf to Hull, 27 May 1937, NARA SD 600.0051, World Programme/133.

'neutrality' under Van Zeeland's premiership.[85] In contrast to Stoppani, Van Zeeland wanted to revive the World Economic Conference as a first step, and that meant involving the USA. But Van Zeeland's confidence that he could 'handle the Americans' was misplaced, especially in the wake of the Munich Conference in September 1938 that saw President Roosevelt and the State Department resolutely turn against making further concessions to Hitler.[86]

Although it was Stoppani who had drawn Van Zeeland into his plans in 1936, the secretariat sought to keep its distance from the Van Zeeland mission; and the Belgians, though drawing on League documentation and rhetoric about the importance of economic security for peace, did not involve them. Stoppani's and Loveday's view was that Frère was being treated to hackneyed reproductions of great power diplomacy on his grand tour of Berlin, The Hague, Paris, Berne, and Rome but learned nothing new. They were right: France emphasized the need for 'monetary security' facilitated through a general stabilization of currencies; so did Italy. The Netherlands and Switzerland offered more general approbations of economic cooperation, while the best that Britain could offer was the 'hope' that it would not need to increase tariffs further. In meetings in Brussels and Berlin, Hjalmar Schacht aired his tired and unconvincing claim that, if Germany's colonies were returned, either through territorial transfer or a ninety-nine-year lease, it would restore some sort of equilibrium in international relations.[87]

Schacht had been trying to sell colonial settlement as the prelude to general settlement of German demands in Europe—a strategy that was born, in part, of his desire to outwit his rival Hermann Göring—and retain his position as Minister for Economics and Plenipotentiary for the War Economy since 1933. It was a competition Schacht lost, and few took his prognostications seriously. Vansittart signalled his distaste for 'this ancient and dirty game', whose passing had been marked by the creation of the League of Nations, some of whose members 'at least had League principles', while British imperial enthusiasts feared that a renewed German imperial presence on the African continent would mark a return to the disastrous Anglo-German colonial rivalries of the past.[88] The Treasury, whether playing for time or anxious to leave no stone unturned in the search for peace, persuaded the Cabinet to keep the colonial question open, and encouraged the reluctant French to do so too. However, it and the Board of Trade had also reached the view that, if economic concessions were to be made, they should be offered not to Germany but to the US government, which had long wanted to open

---

[85] The primacy of economic and financial concerns also shaped his chairmanship of the International Refugee Committee, a role he assumed in 1939. See Carter Goodrich, 'Possibilities and Limits of International Control of Migration', *Millbank Memorial Fund Quarterly*, 25/2 (1947), 155–6.

[86] Jonathan E. Helmreich, *United States Relations with Belgium and the Congo, 1940–1960* (Newark, NJ, 1998), 11; Barbara Farnham, *Roosevelt and the Munich Crisis: A Study in Political Decision-Making* (Princeton, 1997), 137–62.

[87] Crozier, *Appeasement*, 248–9.

[88] Crozier, *Appeasement*, 97. On the Schacht–Göring rivalry, see R. J. Overy, *Hermann Göring: The Iron Man* (London, 1984), 40–7.

negotiations on a reciprocal tariff trade agreement with Britain. In 1937, the Treasury and the Board of Trade indicated their desire for a trade deal with the USA, although, as Stoppani and Loveday rightly observed, the Treasury was the main reason the temperature of Anglo-American economic relations had remained so cold for the previous five years. The Anglo-American bilateral trade negotiations reached a successful political, if not protection-shattering, conclusion in November 1938, and prompted Van Zeeland to try to take some credit because 'his ideas' had made such an impact on the White House and the State Department and at the Council for Foreign Relations in New York.[89]

Van Zeeland's report, published in January 1938, demonstrated he had imbibed much from the League. Its opening pages emphasized the relationship between economic depression, nationalism, and falling standards of living, and proffered a cure of trade liberalization.[90] The description of key problems of international relations was the stuff of countless League reports, Economic and Financial Committee meetings, and special inquiries and missions since 1932. The challenge before the world, as Van Zeeland put it, was that, while politicians could agree on the disease, they did not agree on a remedy. In broad terms, his proposed way forward also contained powerful echoes of the EFO: multilateral and bilateral trade agreements based on MFN, the reduction of quotas, and, more importantly, the dissolution of exchange control and clearing systems. The report called for some form of coordinated monetary system—a heavily modified gold standard perhaps—and a transition fund to be set up at the BIS to ease the conversion of heavily managed currencies back to the international fold (another measure advocated earlier through the League and taken up by planners in the Second World War).[91] Yet, for all that the secretariat might have agreed with the content, it believed the focus of this agenda of cooperation should be the world's remaining democracies, not the axis powers. Moreover, Van Zeeland recommended that treatment for the 'have-not' powers' deficiency of raw materials was in direct opposition to anything the secretariat would recommend. He proposed transforming the mandates into genuine international control 'from an economic and a political point of view'; an open-door system of trade practised on the (hardly to be recommended) basis of Belgian arrangements in the Congo for extant colonies; or the creation of 'privileged companies' set up on strict grounds of economic impartiality to supply raw materials, preferably for industrial goods, to facilitate the 'development' of these territories. It was no accident that Van Zeeland anticipated that the arrangements would fall primarily under the remit of the League mandates' commission. It also, however, viewed the proposals with hostility.[92]

---

[89] 'Record of Conversation between Welles and Van Zeeland', 25 June 1937, NARA RG59 600.0031/World Programme/142½; Crozier, *Appeasement*, 250–1.

[90] Wilson to Hull, 'Memorandum & Enclosure of Van Zeeland Report', 1 Feb. 1938, NARA RG59 600.0031/World Programme/303.

[91] The Americans were particularly sceptical of the proposal for a Common Fund. See Lindsay to Foreign Office, 13 Jan. 1938, TNA: PRO FO371/21623 C276/63/62.

[92] Osumaka Likaka, *Naming Colonialism: History and Collective Memory in the Congo, 1870–1960* (Madison, WI, 2005), 102–18.

   The American and French reception of the Van Zeeland report was distinctly frosty. They were not about to take advice from the Belgians on how to manage colonial economies. The former complained that Van Zeeland failed to privilege trade liberalization sufficiently; the latter said the same of currency stabilization.[93] In London, however, those who remained deeply committed to appeasement in its different forms, Chamberlain, Ashton-Gwatkin, and Neville Henderson, were less dismissive and continued to harbour hopes that the Van Zeeland report offered sufficient recognition of German and Italian economic difficulties to reinvigorate talks.[94]

   But what of the League of Nations officials whose work had helped to shape the emphasis on trade liberalization, gold standard reform, and living standards articulated by Van Zeeland and Frère? Unlike the attitude of member states, the distaste of the Economic and Financial Sections for the Van Zeeland mission was palpable from the outset. It was deeply hostile to the fact that Van Zeeland's approach was premised on the methodology of great power diplomacy in which the lesser powers acted as interlocutor, and where the League had no place. Five years of surveying axis power economic performance and diplomacy had made it clear to Loveday and Stoppani that the practitioners of autarky did not want to return to an international system premised on the values embodied in the League. They were privy also to confidential views from contacts—in the Bulgarian National Bank, for example— that were less than complimentary about the 'cynically demagogic and rude utterances of Herr Schacht as well as the patronizing attitude he deemed fit to adopt towards his hosts'.[95] It all confirmed Loveday's and Stoppani's view that Germany should no longer be allowed to hold centre-stage. Although Italy and Japan remained for them minor players compared to the power and potential of the German economy, it did not blind them to the rising anti-Semitism in Italy. (That same year, Loveday approached the Bank of England, the Federal Reserve Board, the BIS, and elsewhere to find work for the former member and chairman of the Economic Committee, the Jewish Italian Professor Angelo Di Nola.[96]) Instead, Loveday and Stoppani argued, the primary questions for the democracies were: how to shore up what remained of the structures and practices of liberal capitalism; how could the successor states, which it regarded as its foster children, be supported; and could cooperation be improved between the democratic powers that continued to claim they subscribed to the values of the League?

---

   [93] Note from the Sous-Directeur de la SDN, 'Visite de M. Charron', 3 Mar. 1938, AMAE, Questions Économiques/Organisation Économique et Financière/Œuvre économique et financière de la SDN, 1937–1938, no. 1155.
   [94] Britain was prepared to finance a new round of visits by Van Zeeland to Rome, Berlin, and Washington despite indications that the USA (Welles aside) was less than enthusiastic. See Cabinet discussions 'Cab. Conclusions 3 (38)' and Foreign Office reflections thereon in TNA: PRO FO371/21624, C756/63/62.
   [95] Loveday to D. Crena de Iongh, 28 Dec. 1937, LON, Loveday, P144/15–16/outgoing correspondence, 1935–7.
   [96] Loveday to Jacobsson, 21 Dec. 1938, LON, Loveday, P144/15–16/outgoing correspondence, 1935–7.

Their views were strongly held, yet the section directors had to hold their tongues because they had no right to make their disquiet public; nor did they wish to imperil the League further by expressing views on a subject that divided its member states. Loveday's and Stoppani's stony silence on the topic of Van Zeeland's adventures meant they were frozen out by the Belgian government. Loveday had to approach national embassies for news as to the mission's progress, and his office received a copy of the mission's report only on the day of its official publication, 26 January 1938.[97] States had received draft and final copies considerably earlier, and the British government had enjoyed extensive consultation with Van Zeeland and Frère over what should go into it.[98]

Although Loveday did not complain about Van Zeeland's mission directly to the British government, news of his disapproval nevertheless seeped through to London and caused officials in the Treasury to fizz: 'it had been evident for some time past that Mr Loveday is occasionally actuated by personal animus against the representatives of the Treasury and the Bank of England.'[99] The French Foreign Ministry, on the other hand, had considerable sympathy with what it understood as Loveday's 'lack of faith' in Van Zeeland.[100] The head of the Financial Section may not have been able to denounce a diplomacy that he regarded as reckless without putting his post and the League's credibility on the line, but he was able to launch an initiative intended to 'counteract the proposals attributed to Van Zeeland'.[101] In the spring of 1938, he decided once more to promote the cause of League reform, which was listed as a substantive item on the forthcoming agenda of the Council. The news was greeted by another sour note of complaint from the British Treasury, which regarded Van Zeeland's 'effort to secure economic collaboration with Germany and Italy' as having 'far better prospects of success than any tinkering with the present League machinery'.[102] But it was evident when the Belgian Foreign Minister Paul-Henri Spaak asked, via the French Foreign Ministry, that Frère be allowed to join the committee on League reform that Loveday and his team had regained some of the authority they had lost in the tussle with Van Zeeland.[103]

The question of League reform automatically ensured the involvement of Secretary-General Avenol, who had a long-established interest in the subject. But, as we shall see later, while Avenol and Loveday agreed on the need for reform, the two men had different motives and objectives. For Avenol, reform was about efficiency, supporting the smaller countries of Europe, and safeguarding what he believed to

---

[97] Loveday to Leith-Ross, 16 Apr. 1938, LON R4384, 10A/32252/1778.

[98] Van Zeeland to Avenol, 26 Jan. 1938, LON R4440, 10A/32556/32556. For consultation with the British, see Leith-Ross to Chamberlain, 20 Jan. 1938, TNA: PRO FO371/21623, C368/63/62.

[99] Minute by Makins, 20 Jan. 1938, TNA: PRO FO371/22516, W891/41/98.

[100] Note from the Sous-Directeur de la SDN, 'Visite de M. Charron', 3 Mar. 1938, AMAE, SDN, Questions Économiques/Organisation/Économique et Financière/Œuvre économique et financière de la SDN, 1937–8, no.1155.

[101] Loveday to Westman, 21 Dec. 1937, LON R484, 10A/32252/1778.

[102] Leith-Ross to Ashton-Gwatkin, 3 Jan. 1938, TNA: PRO FO371/22516, W147/41/98.

[103] French Foreign Ministry to Massigli, 1 Jan. 1938, AMAE, SDN, Questions Économiques/ Organisation Économique et Financière/Œuvre économique et financière de la SDN, 1937–8, no.1155.

be the League's reputation for neutrality; for Loveday, restructuring the League was intended to put the EFO at the centre of the League's agenda and profile.[104] His aspiration was to make the League a beacon of liberal capitalist values irresistible to the United States, and in the long term to help to bolster the weaker nations that were so evidently subject to the whims of the strong.[105] If Avenol was the public face of the reform agenda, the British Treasury was in no doubt that it was 'a put-up job between Mr Loveday and Mr McDougall, the former hoping to score off the Treasury, and the latter hoping for the position of an economic "éminence grise"'.[106] Loveday's intention may not have been quite as base as the Treasury's paranoia suggested, but there is no doubt he wanted to challenge British preoccupations with appeasing Germany. McDougall, on the other hand, was motivated less by the desire to make Bruce an 'economic superman'—a charge levied by the Treasury—and more by the desire to propel agricultural issues onto the world stage.[107]

McDougall's demand that the group working on League reform address the glaring gap in the architecture of international relations regarding the needs of agriculture was widely circulated. He also called for 'the social aspect' to be properly considered 'if the economic and financial side of the League is to function with high efficiency and if this aspect of the League's work is to achieve the importance it demands'.[108] Bruce became chairman of the committee, which then took his name, but, for McDougall and Loveday, the committee was never about appeasement. They wanted to address what McDougall called 'the dawning realization among the masses in many countries that poverty is not inevitable, but due to the faults in the productive and distributive systems that now renders action to secure improved living standards a matter of urgency to Governments'. True, in 1935 and 1936 McDougall's documents on the subject sometimes carried the title 'economic appeasement', but by 1938 the term had been dropped. The label was useful in catching the eye of a British government deeply committed to a strategy of appeasement, but a military settlement was much less important than McDougall's drive to recast British foreign policy from a preoccupation with hard security into 'a direct attack upon low standards of living both on the national and international plane ... [which] are required to demonstrate that democratic countries can achieve for their peoples greater comfort and well-being than can the Fascist or Communists states'.[109]

[104] Conversation between Leith-Ross and Avenol, reported to Harvey, 25 Apr. 1938, TNA: PRO FO371/22517, W5329/42/98.

[105] In 1938, Loveday wanted to approach the Americans to join discussions about restructuring directly but claimed 'Avenol was against it'. See Makins to Ashton-Gwatkin, 29 Jan. 1938, TNA: PRO FO371/22517, W1467/41/98. The Treasury was completely opposed to US involvement, wanting Anglo-American relations to be in state hands. See Leith-Ross to Harvey, 25 Apr. 1938, TNA: PRO FO371/22517, W5329/42/98.

[106] Minute by Makins, 21 Jan. 1938, TNA: PRO FO371/22516, W891/41/98.

[107] McDougall to Stevenson, 9 Mar. 1938, TNA: PRO FO 371/22517, W2340/41/98.

[108] Memo by McDougall, 'The Committee on the Structure and Functions of the Economic and Financial Organizations', 2 Mar. 1938, TNA: PRO FO371/22517, W3240/41/98.

[109] Memo drafted by McDougall and submitted by Bruce, 'Economic Appeasement', 21 Dec. 1936, pp 1–3, TNA: PRO PRO30/69/1569.

McDougall's ideological vision was intended to counter that of the Third Reich. What he called 'Western Civilization' always came first when he presented his ideas, and, 'although only a small percentage of the population' in these countries 'suffer from a lack of wheat or sugar it is clear that at least 50 per cent of the population goes short of the desirable quantities of protective foods (milk, dairy products, fruit, vegetables and egg)'. In central and eastern Europe, the general standard of nutrition was 'deplorably low', while in the Far East 'most people are in a state of malnutrition all of the time' and in the Tropics 'the relation between nutrition and resistance to tropical diseases makes it clear that this of major importance, especially in Africa'.[110] There were striking omissions in McDougall's vision, none more so than one of the most active regional groupings in the League, South America. Shortcomings were evident, too, in the crass simplification of 'the Tropics' and in the general insensitivity to indigenous tastes and habits when it came to food. In contrast to Aykroyd's view of food, McDougall's vision lacked finesse and any space for these territories to act as agents in their own right. Instead, his was a world view through which the League and the world's major powers imposed their ideas onto the peoples they wanted 'to help'. At the same time, McDougall was intent on confronting, not ceding, to the world's authoritarian and repressive powers. 'We prefer butter, and we propose to collaborate with all nations who will join with us in securing more butter', he declared in these culturally specific terms. The intention was not to offer concessions to Germany, but rather for the USA, Britain and its Dominion allies, and the European powers to make 'large scale moves for the restoration of world trade and for the improvement of living standards' that would affect a large number of European countries beneficially and would give Germany 'a peaceful way out of her difficulties', because it was widely known that living standards in the Reich were low and were likely to fall further, with recourse to war the likely outcome.[111]

McDougall also stressed the importance of international agency, and readily accept his ideas had been born and shaped by the League, the LNHO, and the ILO. But he believed reform would not bring Germany, Italy, or Japan back to the League. Nor would it bring greater American involvement than had been secured already. The Roosevelt administration took a close interest in the appointment of American members to the Economic and Financial Committee; indeed, 'it would not be possible to appoint more effective representation than has already been achieved'. But the key issue, as McDougall put it, was that, 'owing to the present lack of prestige of the League in the political field', it had become essential that its work on the 'social, economic and financial side be recognized as being of great

---

[110] Memo by McDougall, 1 Mar. 1938, TNA FO371/22517, W3279/4/98.

[111] Memo drafted by McDougall and submitted by Bruce, 'Economic Appeasement', 21 Dec. 1936, pp.13–14, TNA: PRO PRO 30/69/1569. Shortages in food, oil, and coal were behind Nazi ambitions to possess the Ukraine and invade the USSR. See Adam Tooze, *The Wages of Destruction: The Making and Breaking of the Nazi Economy* (London, 2006), 418–25, and B. E. Kroener, R. D. Müller, and H. Umbreit, *Germany and the Second World War: Organization and Mobilization of the German Sphere of Power: Wartime Administration, Economy and Manpower Resources, 1942–44/5* (Oxford, 2003), 673–5.

importance to the interest of State members and indeed of all nations'. If they were able to build on the League's record here, then, in due course, 'a solid foundation would be laid upon which the League's political prestige might gradually be re-established'.[112] This continued emphasis on the vulnerabilities of central and eastern European nations and their disadvantaged relations to richer states was a thorn in the side of Chamberlain, now Prime Minister, and Foreign Secretary Lord Halifax, who condemned France's 'unreal' attempt to sustain its ties to Romania, Yugoslavia, and Czechoslovakia.[113]

The call for reform in 1938 sought to downplay the League's political activities and questions about membership. It was a reaction against great power failure to support the League's disarmament and collective-security agenda, and marked the crystallization of a determination to prioritize and to separate economic, financial, and social activities from the League's political agenda, and to reinforce the organization's relationship to the world's remaining liberal democracies. The reform movement also reflected the technocratic notion of internationalism favoured by Loveday, McDougall, and those who described themselves as 'pure experts and pukka members of the secretariat', weary and disillusioned with the behaviour of the representatives of member states, whether they be self-styled totalitarian powers or the world's leading democracies.[114] The determination to stress the primacy of the League's economic and financial agenda came from a broad coalition of individuals forged around the agency of the EFO's secretariat and a collective agreement that, 'if real progress is to be made in international economic collaboration and the revival of world trade, the policies advocated must be put forward on grounds which will arouse the interests of the great mass of people'.[115] This would necessitate a significant reinforcement of the organization's economic and social aims, in liaison with the ILO, notably with regard to nutrition and standards of living.

In 1938, the French, British, and American governments were hostile to the idea of reform; they were to change their minds in 1939.[116] There was no need for it, they claimed, because the League had an 'immense programme'; and the demo-cratic governments were 'co-operating with all these various committees' without hesitation (a claim the secretariat would dispute). But they were also sceptical, even fearful, of the implications for nation states of Loveday's call for 'the development

[112] Memo by McDougall, 'The Committee on the Structure and Functions of the Economic and Financial Organizations', 2 Mar. 1938, pp. 2–3, TNA: PRO FO371/22517, W3240/41/98.

[113] Halifax quoted in Neilson, *Britain, Soviet Russia and the Collapse of the Versailles Order*, 259. For an overview as to how and why French policy changed, see Peter Jackson, *France and the Nazi Menace: Intelligence and Policy-Making, 1933–1939* (Oxford, 2000), 314–78, and Thomas, *Britain, France and Appeasement*, 177–97.

[114] Loveday to Hall, 14 Sept. 1936, LON, Loveday P144/15–17/outgoing correspondence, 1935–7.

[115] Loveday to Leith-Ross, 25 Oct. 1938, LON, Loveday P145/in- and outgoing correspondence, 2nd half 1938.

[116] Bonnet was reported to be unenthusiastic as to the prospects of reform; so, too, was Feis, although his influence in the US Administration was now limited. Rowe-Dutton to Leith-Ross, 19 Apr. 1938, TNA: PRO FO371/22517, W 5238/41/98.

of international policies through the instrumentality of the League'. Not only 'must practical action in such matters as nutrition, housing etc. rest with various Governments', but,

so long as the enquiries appeal only to the democratic nations, there is some danger in stressing overmuch the need for better conditions and housing and higher standards of life as the effect is to accentuate the disparity between their standards and those of the totalitarian Powers and to make it more difficult for democratic Powers to organise their peoples for the sacrifices that they may be called upon to make.[117]

In short, British, French, and US reservations were not about the implications of a reform that increased the League's powers in economic and social policy. Rather, what was at stake was the power of governments to ensure its citizens were prepared to make the necessary sacrifices if and when war came. There was the added fear that the record of democracies would not compare well with the welfare provisions trailed by the dictators. The League, the democracies argued, should be confined to having 'a long range effect on Government policies by educating public opinion in the different countries'; decisions on economic and social policy needed to remain in the hands of government.[118] Member states wanted the League confined to performing a valuable service by educating public opinion as to the values of liberal internationalism, yet recognized that, if unchecked, the League could encourage citizens to demand policies that were different from those being pursued by the polity of which they were a member.

Loveday, Stoppani, and like-minded colleagues, such as McDougall, grasped this challenge almost intuitively. It was why they promoted practical steps both to support and to confront states' policies and interests through inquiries, commissions, and conferences. The process generated a network of individuals that endorsed their work, and, in time, an international consensus for some of their ideas. Even the initiatives that 'failed'—and most of them did—helped to form lessons for the future. In the longer term, the EFO laid a path to new forms of internationalism during and after the Second World War, and, more immediately, its work in the field of agriculture and living standards coalesced in a conference on European rural life. Its history overshadowed by the outbreak of the war, the preparations for this conference revealed the interest of indigenous groups, farmers' unions, and departments of state responsible for agriculture and trade in regional and global organization.

RURAL DREAMS

The conference on European Rural Life scheduled for September 1939, organized by the EFO's secretariat, was the final act in the League's food diplomacy.[119] As for

[117] Harvey to Cleverly, 9 Mar. 1938, pp. 6–7, TNA: PRO FO371/22517, W3279/41/98.
[118] Harvey to Cleverly, 9 Mar. 1938, p. 7, TNA: PRO FO371/22517, W3279/41/98.
[119] Amrith, *Decolonizing International Health*, 36–42.

the conference on Rural Hygiene, which met in the Dutch East Indies in 1937, the intention was to highlight the needs of the world's poorest producers and consumers, categorized by state and by region, with no regard to ideological or imperial affiliation. Both events offered a different way of seeing the constituents of the world economy and how they might be arranged. During the 1930s, the number of regionally oriented reports and initiatives in the League was striking. At the same time, Europe remained at the centre of its concerns. The crisis in peasant production was identified strongly with Europe, and the boundaries of the conference mapped out the ideological cleavages of Europe's present and were a foreboding of its future. As in any process of border drawing, there were geographical limits on participation. Germany was invited, but no one expected it to attend. The USSR, however, did not receive an invitation, and the EFO had to explain this, because, unlike initiatives on currency stabilization or trade liberalization, the terms of the inquiry did not establish an a priori basis for its exclusion. The case was made on 'technical grounds': while only 19 per cent of the world's population resided in Europe (excluding the USSR) on a landmass that comprised no more than 4 per cent of its total land area, 'in normal years, the value of Europe's total trade (imports plus exports) was about equal to the trade of the whole of the rest of the world'. Including the USSR would distort this perspective, because it was 'largely a self-contained economic unit, and her trade is very small in comparison with her area or population'.[120] In short, including the USSR would distort the very special feature of European agriculture—large numbers of people, toiling on small, privately owned farms in a densely populated area. The argument did not stand up to close scrutiny, but the same logic also enabled the EFO to include Britain, and to ignore the distorting impact of empire. Britain was the leading importer of every traded commodity except rye, and for several products, notably beef, bacon, canned meat, butter, cheese, and eggs, the UK's imports were greater than the rest of Europe combined. Britain's significance as a global importer of cereal was unparalleled, taking in nearly half of Europe's exported wheat and one-third of the world total, and stood in dramatic contrast to French practice, which was shaped by regulations that required millers to produce flour comprising at least 87 per cent wheat grown in France or its North African colonies or Germany, whose National Socialist government trumpeted the protection and promotion of German agriculture as part of its racial vision.[121]

When it came to even the most basic tasks, the USSR confounded the League. The EFO's capitalist orientation meant it had little to do with it, but it was charged with calculating its membership contributions when the USSR joined in September 1934. Loveday warned the League Supervisory Commission that his department had taken the Soviet state at its word and valued 'the rouble at par', when in reality

---

[120] League of Nations, *Europe's Trade: A Study of the Trade of European Countries with Each Other and with the Rest of the World* (Geneva, 1941), 5–7.

[121] Britain's experience was hardly typical of Europe. In 1938, Britain imported around two-thirds of its food stuffs and agriculture represented only 3.2% of national income. Alan F. Wilt, *Food for War: Agriculture and Rearmament in Britain before the Second World War* (Oxford, 2001), 2.

its market value was 'certainly well below par, and Russia has, so far as one can judge, been indulging in inflation for a number of years now. However, even about that inflation we are ignorant as price indices are not available.' Nor did the USSR's advertised budget figures help, for they were 'not really comparable at all with budgets for other countries'. It defied the ways and means used by the League to understand and shape the world economy. What, of course, was undeniable was the striking increase in Russian output during the Depression, a time when production elsewhere around the world had fallen equally dramatically. It meant Russia emerged alongside Great Britain and France as one of the top three nations on the allocation list for contributions to the League finances. Yet, Loveday argued, the League somehow needed to take into account that its population was 'of course living very close to the subsistence level—or dying'. This meant that the amount the USSR should contribute to the coffers of the League had 'to be determined on political grounds rather than on economic or financial'.[122]

The work of the Preparatory Committee for the Conference on Rural Life met in Geneva in 1938, carefully categorizing and quantifying Europe to show how its agriculture was disadvantaged in comparison to North America. Fears about rising numbers of population in a world where migration was tightly controlled, as in its condemnation of tariffs, also played a role. It presented 'the pressure of population in Europe at its greatest, not in the densely populated highly industrialised regions, but in the least developed agricultural countries'.[123] Moreover, the pattern of disadvantage that typified the relations between European 'agricultural' and 'indus-trial countries' also operated within individual polities. In almost every aspect of European life in the 1930s, the preparatory committee argued, agricultural produc-ers were disadvantaged in relation to their fellow citizens. The economic and financial vulnerability of agriculture was clear, and explained these population groups' recourse to the extreme Left (in parts of Spain), and, more visibly, the Right (almost everywhere else in Europe) of the political spectrum. The anomaly of agriculture's situation came from the fact that its impact on the lives of individuals and its importance in domestic and international affairs far out-weighed its significance in the performance of the European economy as a whole. Their feeble economies militated against them as international actors, and, without the support of international agency, left them at the mercy of larger, predatory powers.[124]

The solution, the EFO argued, lay in European hands, for, while industrial Europe (defined by the League as Austria, Czechoslovakia, Belgium, France, Germany, Italy, the Netherlands, Sweden, Switzerland, and Britain) had important trading relations with the wider world, the eighteen leading agricultural states in

---

[122] Loveday to Réveillaud, 15 Sept. 1934, LON, Loveday, P143/14–15/outgoing correspondence, 1934–5.
[123] League of Nations, *Europe's Trade*, 69–70.
[124] Stoppani to Loveday, 26 May 1937, and 'Annotated Agenda of the 45th Session of the Economic Committee, 9 June 1937', LON R4383, 10A/1778/1778. René Charron and the French government were very active participants.

Europe were very largely dependent on these ten European industrial states.[125] The latter 'obtained approximately two-thirds of their imports from them and consigned three-quarters of their exports to them'. In other words, poor European countries were especially dependent on intra-European trade for their survival, whereas richer, predominately industrialized European countries relied on their trading relationships beyond Europe's frontiers.[126] Therefore, the problems of small peasant farmers could be solved by greater European collaboration.

The case developed and advanced by McDougall and the Economic Committee was tightly woven. The first strand was to maintain the pressure to find a resolution to the problems posed by clearing and rampant protectionism. The second element was to hope that its work on the question of raw materials would bear fruit. Thirdly, it argued, the work of the Depression Delegation, set up by the League Council in January 1938 to report on 'measures which might be employed with a view to the prevention and mitigation of economic depressions', would give close attention to 'policies which might ensure a greater degree of stability in the economic systems of non-industrialised states'.[127] The rural conference was postponed because of the outbreak of war, yet the materials prepared for this long-forgotten event in the spring and summer of 1939 demonstrated how far the League of Nations had come to espouse values, ideas, and technical know-how that were to become central not just to the reconstruction of Europe after 1945, but to development economics that sought to shape the world.

Key was the League's argument that Europe's rural communities had to be understood in the round. The exploration of 'rural life' was intended to be all-embracing, with separate and careful attention paid to farmers' 'economic situation' and their 'standard of life'.[128] The European Conference on Rural Life, moreover, was distinguished by some interesting departures in the practices of the League. For the first time, it explicitly sought to guard against the homogenization of nations' particularities, by asking delegates to consider local and national traditions—a recognition perhaps of the deep cultural and political resonance of these communities that faced imminent destruction from a variety of sources: military, economic, political, and cultural. Countries were encouraged to prepare individual monographs on national conditions under a framework determined by the League to form 'the living matter of conference discussions'.[129]

These documents were as much about imagination as quantifiable facts. The front cover of the monograph on British rural life, depicting a small antiquated farm, could have been composed by Constable; the pamphlet on Poland was

---

[125] 'Though it was recognised the dividing line between these industrialised countries and the others is necessarily somewhat arbitrary' (League of Nations, *Europe's Trade*, 14).

[126] League of Nations, *Europe's Trade*, 8.

[127] League of Nations, 'Delegation on Economic Depressions', LON R4454, 10A/33303/32649.

[128] McDougall, 'Economic Depression and the Standard of Life', June 1938, LON R4454, 10A/33303/32649.

[129] Stoppani to Gunn, 17 May 1939, LON R4459, 10A/36631/33684; League of Nations, *European Conference on Rural Life: Report of the Preparatory Committee on the Work of its First Session* (Geneva, 1938), C.161.M.101.

illustrated by a Polish farmer in heroic pose with heavy woven wicker-basket, sowing his field by hand; the front cover of the Norwegian booklet was illustrated by an elderly Norwegian fisherman and his wife in full national costume staring glassily out to sea. Although the conference was never to meet, the documents on European agricultural production, like so much League intelligence, served as important seed corn to those who later fought for a more integrated European economy, and who articulated the special place of European agriculture within it. The iconic status these League materials accorded to the family farm in its presentation of European agriculture formed an early exposition of what was to become a central theme in the work of the EEC (although 'peasant Europe' was no more). The League was a forerunner of the 'Europeanizing process' that was borrowed from, and found echoes in, the (western) Europeanization of agriculture in the period after 1945. Indeed, the separation of Europe into East and West that underpinned and facilitated the projects of European union was evident too as it noted the 'profound differences between the manner of life of the rural populations of Eastern and Western Europe'.[130] The conference showed how European agriculture might be compared to that of the rest of the world, and was part of a League call for parallel conferences on African, Asian, and Central and South American agricultural issues. It became fundamental to the League's assessment of the causes and cures for economic downturns in 1938 as the Depression Delegation formally began.

[130] Memo by Stoppani, 'Rapport de M. Stoppani sur son voyage avec M. Baumont en Bulgarie et en Yugoslavie (6–24 Novembre 1938)', LON R4457, 10A/34147/33563.

6

Scrutiny and Strategy: Contesting Economic Depressions, 1937–1939

'Why was it', Bertil Ohlin asked colleagues at a League meeting in 1938, 'that public opinion was prepared to tolerate budget deficits when preparing for war, but was so resistant to them when it comes to fighting economic depression and extreme social hardship?'[1] With an insight and exactitude that characterized his distinguished career as an economist, but often hampered his political prospects as a Swedish Liberal politician, Ohlin identified the central paradox of international economic relations in the late 1930s. With the remilitarization of the Rhineland in 1936, the eruption of Civil War in Spain, and the opening of what was to become the first front of the Second World War with Japan's renewed assault on China in 1937, state expenditure on rearmament reached new and unparalleled heights. As the Economic Committee reported in June 1937, 'vast armament programmes' were absorbing 'a high proportion of public revenue and of industrial activity, tending not only to impoverish the state but also to distort the economic situation'. At the same time, 'unemployment and the under-consumption of many commodities' remained widespread.[2] Over the next two years, the acceleration of state expenditure, whether for the purpose of attack or defence, was spectacular when set against what now appeared the small scale of state deficits that had triggered the collapse of confidence in some of the world's largest economies in 1931. Deficits accrued in combating the depression were small too. Even in the United States, welfare expenditure triggered by the New Deal peaked at only 3 per cent of GDP, whereas military expenditure rose to 16 per cent of GDP just after Pearl Harbor and 35.6 per cent of GDP per annum between 1943 and 1945. (Throughout the 1950s twice as much was spent on the military as on welfare.[3])

Ohlin's preoccupation with the acceptable norm of state indebtedness struck at the heart of the fundamental shift in economic science and its application to policy in the 1930s—a trend the EFO monitored, and with which it engaged. The historical shorthand for this development is the rise of 'Keynesian economics'. Yet, while there was no doubt that *The General Theory of Employment, Interest and*

---

[1] Minutes of meeting, 'Delegation on Economic Depressions: First Session, Third Meeting', 30 June 1938, p.1, LON R4454, 10A/36595/32649.

[2] League of Nations, 'World of the Economic Committee at its Forty-Fifth Session', 9–15 June 1937, C.280.M.181.1937.II.B, p. 1206.

[3] John Joseph Wallis, 'Lessons from the Political Economy of the New Deal', *Oxford Review of Economic Policy*, 26/4 (2010), 442–62.

Money published in 1936 marked a fundamental advance in economic science, the notion of a 'Keynesian revolution' that emerged subsequently does not do justice to the variety and range of Keynes's contributions to economic theory and policy—including reversals of his earlier positions—that helped shape economic debate in the EFO's lifetime. Keynes's incisive interventions contributed to the organization's foundation; its disillusionment with the gold standard; and its support for deficit-spending and measures to stimulate consumption. Keynes's skill as a communicator of economic ideas to a wider public was envied by his peers, but the evidence of whether his, or any other theoretical insights, were reshaping government policy is far from conclusive. Most politicians discovered the economic and political benefits of deficit finance through the accident of policy choices, often when their priority was to extend or defend their national frontiers as much as a response to developments in economic science.

Keynes's particular insight in the economics of depression was to place less emphasis on measures aimed at stimulating consumption, such as the reduction of base rates, increasing the cash reserves available to commercial banks, currency depreciation, and social insurance schemes (some of which entailed allowing the national deficit to rise), and to concentrate instead on measures designed to stimulate investment in national economies.[4] In the inter-war period, these ideas were generally associated with schemes for national and international public works, and their renown owed much to the work of Swedish and German economists and to the ILO and EFO. During the 1920s, the ILO launched a series of investigations into the utility of public works to combat depression, and, at the 1933 World Economic Conference, the ILO and the Economic and Financial Sections promoted public work schemes to help central and eastern Europe, albeit with little tangible success.[5] During the course of the 1930s, however, measures to secure societies' 'welfare' that necessitated social insurance and budget deficits had come to be appreciated by all economists, even those, according to Haberler, 'who usually held very different views' on policies used to counter economic downturns.[6] At the same time, internationally minded liberal economists were painfully aware that deficit-financing was a means widely deployed by the Third Reich in the drive to rearm. Moreover, deficit-spending did little to overcome 'beggar-thy-neighbour' policies that stifled global economic recovery and, alongside the pressures unleashed by rearmament, was once more tipping the world economy deeper into depression in 1937.

That year also brought renewed and very public questions about the League's continued role in international relations when Italy formally withdrew from the League on 11 December. At first the declaration did not trigger the repercussions against the League the secretariat feared—neither member governments nor public

[4] Roger E. Backhouse and Bradley W. Bateman, *Capitalist Revolutionary: John Maynard Keynes* (Cambridge, MA, 2011).
[5] Feiertag, 'Albert Thomas', 106–26, 157–79.
[6] Haberler's intervention, 'Minutes of the First Session, Third Meeting (Private)', 30 June, pp. 1–2, LON R4454, 10A/36595/32649.

opinion in the member states and the USA appeared to consider it an important or surprising development. But when it was followed by a German declaration that the *Reich* would never return to the organization, the sense of crisis in Geneva escalated significantly. Hitherto, the German government had spoken of returning under various conditions, and, to make matters worse, its denunciation of the League formed part of the announcement of the new Rome–Berlin–Tokyo Axis. The alliance hoped its first result would be the organization's destruction.

This *Sturm und Drang* against the League was met with stony silence from the remaining member states, and it took the secretariat, notably Under-Secretary-General Frank Walters, to galvanize them into a response. The countries concerned, he argued, had been waging a campaign against the League for the past three years, and what made the rising trend of hostility so dangerous was that it was one sided: London and Paris needed to take the lead in defending the institution. In response, the French Foreign Ministry consulted the Foreign Office, where at first opinion was divided. Roger Makins, the League's point man in Whitehall, argued forcefully for a coordinated international response, but objected to Walters's suggestion that any 'conversations with Germany and Italy were conditional on a preliminary undertaking to return to the League'.[7] Others in the Foreign Office, on the other hand, wanted Britain to issue a unilateral response, and it was left to Alexander Cadogan, who had realized his dream of promotion to the role of Permanent Under-Secretary to the Foreign Office only weeks before and who knew the League intimately from his time in charge of the FO's League of Nations section, to craft the British response. He ruled out the possibility of a joint Anglo-French declaration, and more emphatically, the offer of a tripartite announcement with the USSR, made by the Soviet Ambassador to Paris, Jakov Souritz.[8] Cadogan proposed instead coordinated statements of support for the League by principal delegations at the forthcoming meeting of the Council. But, again, the idea of joint action was killed off, this time by Chamberlain, which left Walters and Avenol to do the coordinating, using Britain's and France's declared intention to make unilateral declarations of support at the Council as the means to enlist other powers.[9] The statements were formally presented at the hundredth meeting of the Council on 25 January 1938.

It was at this meeting that the EFO announced its intention to take its work on the 'problem of depressions' to a new level. It would survey and assess state policies to combat depression, and differentiate between measures 'adopted as expedients intended to meet some exceptionally critical situation' and those 'constituting an

[7] Minutes by Makins, Stevenson, and Cadogan, 14–15 Jan. 1938, TNA: PRO FO371/22507, W473/3/98.
[8] 'Note on Conversation with Cadogan', 13 Jan. 1938, TNA: PRO FO371/22507, W473/3/98; Phipps to Cadogan, 12 Jan. 1938, TNA: PRO FO371/22507, W486/3/98. In fact, France did pass a preliminary draft of the proposed declaration to the Foreign Office; see Minute by Vigier, undated, *c.*5 Jan. 1938, TNA: PRO FO371/22507, W542/3/98.
[9] Unsigned memo, 'Sir A. Cadogan's Draft as Amended by the Prime Minister', 14 Jan. 1938, TNA: PRO FO371/22407, W542/3/98.

inherent part of a systemic endeavour to revive activity'.[10] So far, so familiar. The inquiry's terms seemed a new gloss on work undertaken in the past; however, what underpinned it was the determination of the EFO's secretariat, and the persons of 'special competence' it brought to Geneva, to exploit the work of this subsequently constituted 'Depression Delegation' to avoid the stricture that League officials were not authorized to make policy recommendations. In the past, the secretariat circumvented this in a variety of ways, but it still had a significant impact on its work. By 1938, Loveday and Stoppani were agreed the time for circumspection was gone. In the battle to save the League, and the values it ascribed to it, the Economic and Financial Sections became increasingly bold in their recommendations and manœuvres—a trend that would put pressure on relationships between the League and its remaining sponsors.

The Depression Delegation was born of the EFO's unique ringside view on development of national and imperial trade and finance through the intergovern-mental committees, and by the more distant, commentary-box perspective afforded by the sections' and the EIS's scientific work. It was the latter that led the secretariat to conclude that governments absorbed economic ideas into policy in an unsatis-factorily haphazard way that stymied League efforts to coordinate policy develop-ments and facilitate cooperation. Providing governments with the best advice available as to which was the 'right policy' would address this problem head on, and reshape attitudes towards the League and economic internationalism in the longer term.

Time was running out for the League. The secretariat knew it, and yet it sought to play the long game with an initiative that drew the EFO further into the realm of ideas, and away from immediate efforts to effect international coordination. At the time, most economists were preoccupied with understanding what they saw as causal chains between different elements in national and international economies, the fluctuations in economic aggregates, and the marked undulations of business cycles. Understanding these fluctuations, and their relationships to one another, would help elucidate the workings of economic life, and enable economists to recommend policies to avoid or at least to mitigate the impact of more dramatic movements on key constituents on economies and societies. The delegation there-fore reflected, and reinforced, this wider trend in economic science.

And what better vantage point from which to watch and learn to navigate than the bridge of the world's premier intergovernmental organization? It afforded a unique resource from which to draw and justify generalizations for policies to combat financial and economic crises of the future. When compared to today's standards, these forecasts, and theories on which they were based, were very accessible for non-theorists, notably businessmen, investors, and policy-makers.[11] The secretariat also wanted to encourage economists to develop an integrated and

---

[10] League of Nations, 'Assembly Resolutions', *Official Journal* (Feb. 1938), 157.

[11] For the business community's interest in forecasting, with so-called business cycle dinners, see Tobias F. Rötheli, 'Business Forecasting and the Development of Business Cycle Theory', *History of Political Economy* 39/3 (2007), 481–510.

global perspective on the threat depressions posed, even if the League's claim to universality was undermined by the reality of its membership. Economists who worked for the League and the government representatives who participated in its meetings, commissions, delegations, and conferences, and who read its publications, learned much more about other parts of the world and the connections of their national economy to the international system than they otherwise would have done. Although their work did not yet accommodate business forecasting, they helped expose a demand for it. Indeed, for economists employed by the League, the learning experience was not confined to the world of the mind. When the British economist James Meade, whose personal and professional life was shaped by a variety of connections to the League, was charged with preparing the *World Economic Survey*, he was urged by Loveday to travel widely, especially in central and eastern Europe and the USA, so that he saw 'a little of the world about which he is writing'.[12] Loveday nurtured his young staff, identifying Folke Hilgerdt also as someone whose work would benefit greatly if he were able 'to get away for a time and work out in peace a certain number of problems which are maturing in his mind, and have at the same time the occasion of meeting and discussing with economists in this country or that'.[13]

The Depression Delegation aspired not just to remake the world outside, but to remake the League. Following the pattern established by the failure of the World Economic Conference in 1933, which had prompted the Economic and Financial Sections fundamentally to reappraise their relations with other sections within the League of Nations to the Council and Assembly, and to widen its definition of 'economic' and 'financial' to embrace social, physical, and even environmental welfare, the Depression Delegation was another 'mixed committee'. The work of the Depression Delegation therefore had important implications for the way its participants and target audience imagined a new architecture for international relations to combat economic depression. As the international situation deteriorated, the Depression Delegation, far more than any other strand of the League's work, became a project oriented towards the future, imagined in a space and time when capitalism might be rebuilt.

BUSINESS CYCLES AND OTHER JOURNEYS AROUND THE WORLD

The Depression Delegation's intellectual genesis lay in the business cycle studies funded by the Rockefeller Foundation in 1931, and begun by Ohlin. His was the

---

[12] In 1938, Meade visited Hungary, Czechoslovakia, Poland, and Romania. See Loveday to Avenol, 24 Aug. 1938, LON R4605, 10C/35083/9854. Meade was an enthusiastic member of the Oxford branch of the League of Nations Union, where he met his wife, who was the branch secretary. Susan Howson, 'Meade, James Edward (1907–1995)', *ODNB*.

[13] Loveday to van Sickle, 6 July 1934, LON, Loveday, P143/14–15/outgoing correspondence 1934.

first in a series of single-author studies of the business cycle on which the organization's early scientific reputation was built, and in 1938 he returned to Geneva to become one of the prime movers in the Depression Delegation. Ohlin's work prefigured two further studies undertaken under the auspices of the Rockefeller programme that became renowned pieces of work in their own right. The first was Gottfried Haberler's *Prosperity and Depression: A Theoretical Analysis of Cyclical Movements*, formally published in 1937. The second comprised two reports by Jan Tinbergen: *Statistical Testing of Business Cycle Theories* and *Business Cycles in the United States of America 1919–1932*, which appeared in two parts in 1939.[14]

Loveday was able to recruit Haberler in 1932 because the attractions of Geneva afforded the opportunity for career development and a refuge from Viennese politics. *Prosperity and Depression* was the culmination of five years' work, and by the time it was published Haberler was safely ensconced at Harvard, although he made regular trips back to Geneva to participate in the Depression Delegation and to keep abreast of events in Europe. *Prosperity and Depression* marked a further step in the EFO's public move away from the gold standard orthodoxy started by the work of the Gold Delegation. As we have seen, in private the secretariat sided with the minority view and against the majority perspective articulated in the *Report of the Gold Delegation*, which favoured a monetary explanation for the downturn of 1929, and a policy response centred on allowing prices to adjust (that is, to continue to fall) in the expectation that this would eventually facilitate a recovery in demand. Haberler took the minority view a stage further in his determination to orient economists and policy-makers away from a preoccupation with price stability, because ensuring stable prices was not a sufficient defence against crises and depressions. Price levels, he argued, were frequently a misleading guide. Instead, attention should be focused on the role of credit policy, which had a deeper and more fundamental influence on the whole economy.[15]

Haberler's scientific contribution to understanding the causes of the depression was to stress that overinvestment, rather than the malfunctioning of the gold standard, was the central cause of the Great Depression, and a source of potential instability in the future. The core element of overinvestment theory, which economists associate with the 'Austrian' or 'Hayekian' school, was an unstable supply of bank credit, which caused long-run rates of interest and temporary money market interest rates to diverge and to distort the time profile of capital investment.[16] It was an authoritative survey of pre-Keynesian research into business cycles.[17] In simple terms, Haberler emphasized the need for banks to make credit available to investors at low rates of interest during periods of crisis (certainly lower

[14] Jan Tinbergen, *Statistical Testing of Business-Cycle Theories* (Geneva, 1939). This text also circulated in report form in 1938. Jan Tinbergen, *Business Cycles in the United States of America 1919–1932* (Geneva, 1939).

[15] Haberler, *Prosperity and Depression*, 116–17.

[16] See Endres and Fleming, *International Organizations*, 36–7.

[17] To unravel its place in the history of economic thought further, see Mauro Boianovsky and Hans-Michael Trautwein, 'Haberler, the League of Nations, and the Quest for Consensus in Business Cycle Theory in the 1930s', *History of Political Economy*, 38/1 (2006), 45–89.

than would be necessary to attract savers). Without it, business would be slow to innovate and financiers would raise interest rates to make up for the shortfalls in their investments. Lost investments and business collapse were the inevitable consequences.

He was not explicit about the geo-political framework of his argument; however, Haberler's focus was on the individual: how personal instincts, judgements, and decisions shaped economic and political outcomes. At the same time, the processes he outlined, his scientific conclusions, and his ideological predisposition were implicitly global. The scientific achievement of *Prosperity and Depression* was to offer an incisive critique of economic thinking on booms and slumps at a critical moment in the history of economic science. It coincided with the formulation of complete mathematical models of business cycles by Ragnar Frisch, Paul Samuelson, and, of course, Keynes's celebrated reformulation of macroeconomic theory.[18] Equally important from the perspective of international economic foreign policy, Haberler's work reinforced the League's view on the critical role played by investment, and on the impact the behaviour of large economies had on all members of the world economy. It formed an essential strand of the League's critique of the 'irresponsibility' of American short-term lending to Europe, which, when it petered out after 1928, caused these countries' economic fortunes to nose-dive and their politics to lurch away from the values of liberal internationalism.[19]

Prosperity and Depression became one of the most successful publications of the League. Haberler produced an amended edition in 1939, and the text was reprinted again, this time under the auspices of Princeton University Press, occasioning a bitter spat with Columbia University Press, which had published other League works during the war and resented relinquishing the rights, even temporarily, because the book sold so well. It continued its success into the 1960s, long after the League itself had been dissolved, reaching a fifth published edition in 1964. When he moved to Harvard in 1936, Haberler not only worked alongside the more distinguished Joseph Schumpeter, but moved into his house. (Haberler generously invited his former colleagues in Geneva to stay with them on visits to the USA, but most trembled at the thought.) His relocation did not end his association with the

[18] Olav Bjerkholt, 'Ragnar Frisch's Business Cycle Approach: The Genesis of the Propagation and Impulse Model', *European Journal of the History of Economic Thought*, 14/3 (2007), 449–86; Paul Samuelson, 'Interactions between the Multiplier Analysis and the Principle of Acceleration', *Review of Economists and Statistics*, 21/2 (1939), 75–8. Interestingly, Siven later credited Bertil Ohlin and Erik Lundberg with far greater influence on Samuelson's ideas than Alvin Hansen; Hansen was primarily the conduit through which the ideas of the Swedish delegation members were transmitted to the USA. Roy Harrod was an equally important influence. He also studied under Jacob Viner and Frank Knight. See Claes-Henric Siven, 'Heertje Heemeijer and Samuelson on the Origins of Samuelson's Multiplier-Accelerator Model', *History of Political Economy*, 35/2 (2003), 323–7. Hansen was primarily familiar with Ohlin and Lundberg's work thanks to the League of Nations.

[19] Loveday to Butler, 27 Feb. 1935, LON, Loveday, P143/14–15/outgoing correspondence, 1934–5. Haberler also cooperated closely with Dr Staehle of the ILO on questions of statistical technique and data, finding his help 'on these questions extremely useful'. Endres and Fleming were the first to stress the value of this cooperation but miss its wider significance in the dynamic of competitive-cooperation in ILO–League relations. See Endres and Fleming, *International Organizations*, 35–7.

League, but it did prompt a further widening of the business cycle research network with the appointment of another bright young scholar who was also to make a seminal contribution to the history of economic thought: the Dutchman Jan Tinbergen.

It may be a shorthand of history to attribute intellectual innovations to individuals, but the process of consultation, learning, and borrowing makes for a considerably messier reality. To hone the text, Loveday developed what Robbins subsequently called the 'Haberler-like method': 'a strong statement about the usefulness of the [League] fellowship system and various ideas cropped up about putting good men in the right milieu to work on a big subject and at a certain stage call in a select committee to discuss preliminary results and future plans'.[20] In July 1935, the EFO's offices were 'lousy with economists' meeting to discuss Haberler's draft, including 'J. M. Clark, D. H. Robertson, Lionel Robbins, Wilhelm Röpke, Oskar Anderson, Oskar Morgenstern, Edward Lipinski, H. F. Hall, Ohlin and Hansen'.[21] This was underlined in the next stage of the business cycle project in 1936. The position had been reached 'in which various theories contained in the Systematic Analysis of Business Cycle Theories have been submitted for comment and suggestions to about a hundred economists in various countries', and what was now required was an economist with skills at 'statistical presentation and verification with a view to establishing experimentally their content and claims to validity'. The post offered a generous salary of 400 Swiss francs a month. The specification for Haberler's successor was: 'English or French-speaking with some knowledge of other languages; a knowledge of German would be useful. University training in economics was not necessary. Essential desiderata are quickness and accuracy in calculation, and orderliness.'

The 33-year-old Tinbergen more than met these requirements.[22] Born in The Hague, he had a Ph.D. in Physics, while his early published work, commissioned by the Dutch government's Central Bureau for Statistics, attempted to construct a dynamic model of the Dutch economy comprising thirty-eight simultaneous dynamic equations. It was ample demonstration of his qualifications in the field of business cycle theory, and that politics were irrelevant when it came to the EFO's scientific appointments. While Haberler's politics had lain on the right of the political spectrum, Tinbergen's were on the left, although both men shared an interest and commitment to internationalism. In the 1920s, Tinbergen was very active in student socialist politics, founding a student social club and a student newspaper publishing articles that decried the suffering of the poor in the post-war economic crises. By the early 1930s, he had graduated to the board of the scientific bureau of the *Sociaal Democratische Arbeiders Partij* (the Dutch Social Democratic Workers' Party) and was a key contributor to the party's 'Plan of Labour', which included schema to increase employment opportunities, nationalize strategic

---

[20] Condliffe to Viner, 24 July 1936, Mudd, Viner, MC135, Box 7, File 5.
[21] Condliffe to Viner, 1 July 1935, Mudd, Viner, MC135, Box 7, File 5.
[22] Loveday to Deputy Secretary-General in charge of Internal Administration, 2 Mar. 1935, LON, Loveday, P143/14–15/outgoing correspondence, 1934–5. For Tinbergen's reflections on his time in Geneva and the development of his model, see Jan R. Magnus and Mary S. Morgan, 'The ET Interview: Professor J. Tinbergen', *Econometric Theory*, 3/1 (1987), 117–42.

industries, improve social benefits for the unemployed, and break the continued stranglehold of the gold standard on the Dutch economy. Although his party was kept from government in the 1935 elections, its campaign increased the pressure on the Guilder and helped to 'persuade' the liberal-confessional centre of Dutch politics to abandon monetary orthodoxy in 1936.

Tinbergen, then, was well versed in the monetary and political issues that shaped the EFO. His principal publications for the League also proved him to be, in Loveday's words, a 'modest but tenacious' investigator of the deep statistical underpinnings of business cycles.[23] These were pioneering studies, less for their immediate conclusions than for the importance of the methodology that Tinbergen developed and expounded. The first study constructed a series of aggregate economic models, and the second offered some tentative estimates of coefficients in his multi-equation models for the United States. In later years, Tinbergen consolidated and built on these foundations in ways that were to earn him, alongside Frisch, the first Nobel Prize in Economics. In both works his primary purpose, and one that Loveday strongly endorsed, was to underline the value of adopting quantitative methodology to measure—the studies were distinguished by the large number of tests to which Tinbergen subjected the data—and understand the character of the relationship between different economic variables.

Although the contribution of econometrics to war and post-war economics was considerable, the implications of Tinbergen's work for national and especially international economic policy at the time were rather limited, other than highlighting, as had his predecessors in the business cycle research programme, the interconnectedness of global monetary and economic processes.[24] All three business cyclists, Ohlin, Haberler, and Tinbergen, were criticized at the time by other economists for their failure to 'set out policy priorities or explicit policy prescriptions for each country', in contrast to ILO economists, who were much more forthright in advocating specific policies to combat employment.[25] But the ILO, unfettered by the primacy of intergovernmental cooperation, enjoyed freedoms the EFO did not. In 1931, while it is true scientific caution partly explained Ohlin's hesitation to offer precise recommendations, he, like Haberler and Tinbergen, were also expressively discouraged by the League from drawing conclusions in the form of policy recommendations.

Keynes, uninterested, rather than ignorant of institutional restrictions imposed on Tinbergen's position, wrote a famous and highly critical review of the first of Tinbergen's League-based publications.[26] His critique of Tinbergen revealed as much about Keynes's unawareness of developments in econometrics as

[23] Loveday to Radice, 2 Nov. 1939, LON, Loveday, P146/19/in- and outgoing correspondence, 2nd half 1939, part 1.
[24] For an incisive review of the League of Nation's reports and their importance to the field of Econometrics, see Mary S. Morgan, *The History of Econometric Ideas* (Cambridge, 1991), 108–21.
[25] Endres and Fleming, *International Organizations*, 35.
[26] J. M. Keynes, 'The League of Nations: Professor Tinbergen's Method', *Economic Journal*, 49/195 (1939), 558–69.

shortcomings in Tinbergen's model. For Keynes, the study's decisive flaw was that it had failed to explain 'fully and carefully the conditions which the economic material must satisfy if the application of the method is to be fruitful'[27]—in other words, that economic techniques were useful only when there was a correct and complete list of causes and when all the causal factors were independent of one another, could be measured, and existed in a linear relationship to one another, and, finally, that issues such as time lags and trends were dealt with adequately. The review caused a sensation, in part because of Keynes's rhetorical flourish. In response, Loveday was characteristically supportive of the young Tinbergen, shoring him up with a gentle reminder that one of the key objects of his first volume 'was to give rise to discussion on the methods adopted'. Indeed, 'it was very useful that Keynes had jumped in at once in this way and the fact he has reviewed the book so promptly himself is a proof that he attaches importance to it, however critical he may be'.[28] It was the quality and profile of the debate that was important, and the opportunity Keynes had afforded needed to be followed up by a coordinated response in the pages of the *Economic Journal*. Tinbergen consulted his colleagues, and, although the plans for a synchronized riposte was superseded by the outbreak of the Second World War, he published an effective defence of his work in an immediate reply as well as an article the following year, arguing that his focus on the most significant explanatory variables was sufficient for his method to provide good measurements of relationships.[29]

There is no doubt that aspects of Keynes's review were hurtful, perhaps none more so than the view of Tinbergen that 'the worst of him is that he is much more interested in getting on with the job than in spending time in deciding whether the job is worth getting on with'.[30] In fact, Tinbergen had made great efforts to consult widely before embarking on his study, but Keynes's critique of his methodology did not come as a complete surprise; nor were aspects of his criticisms new to economists pioneering econometric methods. It may be that Keynes expressed himself so vehemently because he had made similar points in more temperate language in response to the EFO's widely circulated earlier draft of Tinbergen's work. Other members of the League had attempted to warn the Dutchman of methodological and empirical shortcomings, which caused them to reflect more generally on the challenges before economists and statisticians. In 1938, the League Committee of Statistical Experts reported to the Depression Delegation's regret that 'there was no common agreement . . . as to the meaning of such basic terms as "savings", "capital" or investments'.[31] Nor did the quality of national statistics escape the EFO's scrutiny. British statistics, for example, harboured 'the radical fault' of being but 'a by-product of administration' so that, 'however excellent

---

[27] Keynes, 'Professor Tinbergen's Method', 559.

[28] Loveday to Tinbergen, 16 Nov. 1939, LON, Loveday, P146/19/in- and outgoing correspondence, 2nd half 1939, part 1.

[29] Tinbergen, 'On a Method of Statistical Business-Cycle Research: A Reply'.

[30] Keynes, 'Professor Tinbergen's Method', 568.

[31] League of Nations, 'Committee of Statistical Experts Report' (1938), 7.

certain branches of statistics may be, taken as a whole they are defective, illogical and inadequate'.[32]

Keynes's public rebuke that the League continued to closet away its best economists to drown their 'sorrows in arithmetic' and to work on 'computors' was a source of succour as well as irritation.[33] By the time Keynes's review was published, the work of the delegation had begun, and its intention was to offer the policy direction on depression that Keynes had demanded, and Keynes knew of its work. His relations with the EFO were complex. He had supported the World Economic Conference, offered detailed critiques of the Depression Delegation's work in correspondence, and was held in high regard by many members of the secretariat. He had little time for the niceties of diplomacy or political convention, however, so his impatience with the EFO's inability to give unequivocal direction for policy was long-standing; ironically it was shared by many inside the institution. But Keynes's suspicion of the potential implications of the econometric drive to measure, formulate, and test pointed to a new and potentially dangerous dawn for economic science, as for him the econometric method 'withdraws from the operation of the method all those economic problems where political, social and psychological factors, including such things as government policy, the progress of invention and the state of expectations may be significant'.[34]

When Tinbergen returned to the Netherlands in 1939, his place was taken by two other Dutchmen, Jacques Polak and Tjalling Koopmans, both hired by Loveday on the strength of Tinbergen's recommendations. In Geneva, Polak's work returned to a central preoccupation of the League: what caused depressions to spread from one part of the economy to the next, and from one country to another? His interest was the processes of international trade and payments, and he produced an explicit model of how fluctuations in one economy were propagated in others by focusing on what caused the value of national currencies to fluctuate in terms of foreign currencies. He showed how changes in the exchange rate of national currencies were affected by the fundamentals of economy, which included prices indices, interest rates, and employment levels; and how quickly fluctuations in trade and payments were transmitted around the world, regardless of currency exchange rates. He also demonstrated how the global movement of capital shaped and was itself shaped by the business cycle, and how it could disseminate depression around the world. Polak highlighted, in particular, the destructive impact of short-term capital movements, a perspective that was taken up some thirty years later with renewed force in the writings of Charles Kindleberger, who blamed the global

[32] Loveday to Noel Hall (National Institute of Economic and Social Research), 17 July 1939, LON, Loveday, P146/19/in- and outgoing correspondence, 2nd half 1939, part 1.

[33] Keynes, 'Professor Tinbergen's Method', 561.

[34] Keynes, 'Professor Tinbergen's Method', 562–3; de Marchi, 'League of Nations Economists and the Ideal of Peaceful Change in the Decade of the Thirties', 164–5. Dennis Robertson was an important contributor to the delegation's work, but asked for his name to be omitted from any published reports for fear Keynes would hold its conclusions against him. It was a difficult period in their relations for other reasons. See Donald Moggridge, 'Keynes and his Correspondence', in Roger E. Backhouse and Bradley W. Bateman (eds), *The Cambridge Companion to Keynes* (Cambridge, 2006), 136–59.

economic downturn on irresponsible short-term American lending overseas, which collapsed when the American economy turned inward and downward in 1929. Having assumed the mantle of the banker to the world from Britain during the First World War, the United States failed to recognize its responsibility by refusing to act as a lender of last resort when this was needed.[35] Kindleberger's elegant account dominated historians' understanding of the Great Depression from the 1970s until the early 1990s, when it was superseded by an explanation that attributes it to the operations of the gold standard and the failure of multilateral cooperation (not hegemonic failure).

Yet it is possible to see the origins of Kindleberger's account in his early writing on *Short Term Capital Movements*, published in 1937, and through this connection to the transnational network sustained by the EFO.[36] Although primarily known as an economic historian at MIT in Boston, between 1936 and 1939 Kindleberger spent part of his early career at the Federal Reserve Bank of New York, from 1939 to 1940 he was at the BIS, and on the Board of Governors of the Federal Reserve System before joining the State Department and the Office of Economic Security Policy, a move facilitated by Alvin Hansen. Thereafter, he was a counsellor to the Marshall Plan.[37] This personal history undoubtedly helped to shape his history-writing as the foremost exponent of the historical narrative of American irresponsibility in the 1930s. Although the League was preoccupied with sustaining a multilateral framework of international relations, the secretariat consistently sought to distinguish between the equal rights of states, and the differentiated power base and policy options available to national economies that conferred special responsibilities on the USA.[38]

The League enabled business cycle theorists to achieve the credibility they craved; they also gave credibility to the League.[39] It developed the organization's connections to what Loveday regarded as important scientific developments in statistics and economics taking place in the Americas in the late 1930s, and served as unequivocal proof of the Economic and Financial Section's almost unerring eye for talent.[40] Koopmans, too, went on to secure the Nobel Prize in Economics, establishing an intellectual and personal kinship with Meade, who arrived in

[35] Charles P. Kindleberger, *The World in Depression, 1929–1939* (Berkeley and Los Angeles, 1973; 2nd edn, 1986).

[36] Charles P. Kindleberger, *International Short-Term Capital Movements* (New York, 1937). This work lent on studies by Ohlin, Angell, and Iversen.

[37] Oral History Interview with Charles P. Kindleberger, 16 July 1973, by Richard D. McKinzie, Harry S. Truman Library and Museum <http://www.trumanlibrary.org/oralhist/kindbrgr.htm# transcript,> para. [7] (accessed 10 June 2009).

[38] Harold James, 'International Order after the Financial Crisis', *International Affairs*, 87/3 (2011), 525–37.

[39] Tinbergen to Loveday, 13 Nov. 1939, LON, Loveday, P146/19/in- and outgoing correspondence, 2nd half 1939, part 1.

[40] The genesis of the League inquiry lies partly also in the work of the International Institute of Statistics, which put together a committee of exceptional strength under its auspices in Mexico, to study business cycles. For further details of this link, see Loveday to Avenol, 25 Apr. 1934, LON, Loveday, P143/14–15/outgoing correspondence, 1934.

Geneva at the same time and who later shared the Nobel Prize with Ohlin.[41] These
economists contributed to the League, and the organization gave them an unrivalled platform for their intellectual and professional development, whether
scientific conferences devoted to discussing the methods, or the type of analysis
the League should apply to its statistical testing of business cycle theories. One such
event, co-hosted by the EFO, the University of Geneva, and the International
Institute for Intellectual Cooperation, explored 'Applications of Probability Calcu-
lus', which was very beneficial to the group. It was the League that also facilitated
Koopmans's regular meetings with R. A. Fisher, whose new paradigm for statistics
became a feature of econometric analysis thanks to the Dutchman's work, and that
dispatched him to Britain to meet Jacob Marschak, with whom he developed a long
and significant professional relationship.[42] They were reunited in 1943 in Chicago
when Marschak became research director—Koopmans was to be his successor—of
the Cowles Commission with its pioneering drive to develop an explicit 'probabil-
istic framework' and the concept of a simultaneous equations model began in
earnest.[43] Loveday, in particular, laid great stress on the importance of wide-
ranging personal networks as well as intellectual cross-fertilization and such attributes undoubtedly facilitated the business cycle studies' great conceptual clarity.
The degree of co-ordination and orchestrated networking was remarkable and was
reflected similarly in Meade's League–Rockefeller sponsored visit to the USA from
October to December 1939.[44]

The diplomatic and intellectual journeys doggedly undertaken by these business
cyclists charted the world economy and the League's place within it in new ways.
Coming from Sweden, Austria, and the Netherlands, these citizens of the world's
so-called lesser powers became global players on the strength of their technical

[41] Between 1969 and 1977 four Nobel prizes in economics went to men who had worked for
the EFO.
[42] Koopmans's report on Mission to London, Oxford, and Cambridge, 5 June 1939, LON R4605,
10C/39705/9854. He had meetings at the Board of Trade, Ministry of Labour, National Institute for
Economic and Social Research, Bank of England, Midland Bank, Lazard Brothers, *The Economist*, FBI,
Federation of Iron and Steel Manufacturers, Society of Motor Manufacturers and Traders,
Shipbuilding Conference, Lloyds Register, University Institute of Statistics, Institute of Agricultural
Economics, and economists at the LSE, Cambridge (notably Kahn and Harrod), and Oxford. For
Geneva meetings facilitated by Loveday, see Koopmans to Loveday, 20 July 1939, LON R4605, 10C/
39705/9854. The League's instrumental role in bringing Koopmans to Britain in 1939, Princeton in
1940, Washington when he was hired by the British Shipping Mission led by Arthur Salter in 1942,
and later Chicago was entirely lost in Herbert E. Scarf, *Tjalling Charles Koopmans, 1910–1985*
(Washington, 1995), and Edmond Malinvaud, 'The Scientific Papers of Tjalling C. Koopmans:
A Review Article', *Journal of Economic Literature*, 10/3 (1972), 798–802.
[43] Carl F. Christ, 'The Cowels Commission's Contributions to Econometrics at Chicago, 1939–
1955', *Journal of Economic Literature*, 32/1 (1994), 30–59. The EFO experts at Chicago included
Viner, Boulding, H. Simons, and Frank Knight, yet were atypical of the monetarism that would
become identified with the Chicago School in recognizing imperfections in markets. Carter Goodrich
of the ILO was also a graduate. See Malcolm Rutherford, 'Chicago Economics and Institutionalism', in
Ross B. Emmett (ed.), *The Elgar Companion to the Chicago School of Economics* (Cheltenham, 2010),
25–39.
[44] Loveday to Avenol, 25 May 1939, and Meade to Kittredge, 25 May 1939, LON R4605,
10C/38333/9854.

expertise. Their efforts were more broadly reflected in the distinguished contribution made by Europe's smaller nations to the League, among which representatives from Scandinavia, central and eastern Europe, the Netherlands, Belgium, and Ireland were especially pronounced. But, if this was a 'diplomacy of expertise', traditional elements of diplomacy and privilege helped to determine who gained access to the network.[45] Educated at the best universities in the West, with connections to the academy of modern economics, undoubtedly the fastest-growing social science, these men all hailed from countries and economies with a strong international orientation. Imperial trade had made their countries powerful, and the different histories of their empires had increased their intellectual sensitivity to global interconnectedness. Moreover, international markets remained central to their nations' fortunes, as did traditional intergovernmental rivalries, particularly between the USSR, the Axis powers, and the Allies. There were to be some notable gaps. The treatment of China and the USSR was sketchy; Africa was barely considered except through the prism of empire. These economists may have sought scientific objectivity, but there is no doubt they had an emotional relationship with their subject. Sweden, Austria, and the Netherlands may have been perceived as smaller nations by Britain or the USA, but they were medium-sized economic powers, interconnected and vital to the European and world economies. After 1945, the careers of Haberler, Tinbergen, Koopmans, Hilgerdt, Polak, and many others were distinguished by continued and high-level service in international organizations, and by a persistent and newly formulated preoccupation with what were now called developing economies.

THE HYPERACTIVE DEPRESSION DELEGATION

The work of the special delegation on economic depressions sought to build on the political and intellectual capital of Ohlin, Haberler, and Tinbergen.[46] With war looming and membership of the League falling away, the preoccupation with economic depression gave the impression that the League and its economists were busy fighting the last war rather than preparing for the next one. But for the Economic and Financial Sections and their associated committees, the battle against the causes of economic depression had never ended. Ohlin's 1931 report 'The Course and Phases of the World Economic Depression' was incorporated, with only minor amendment, as the preamble to the work, because its emphasis on the dense complexity of global economic relationships underlined a predominant theme of the secretariat's work—namely, that only the international coordination

---

[45] Thomas Cayet, Paul-André Rosental, and Marie Thébaud-Sorger, 'How International Organizations Compete: Occupational Safety and Health at the ILO, a Diplomacy of Expertise', *Journal of Modern European History*, 7/2 (2009), 174–96.
[46] League of Nations, 'Work of the Economic Committee at its 47th Session' *Official Journal*, (Feb. 1938), 178.

of national recovery strategies and the creation of a sustained and agreed global perspective on international economic relations would truly rid the world of the depressive scourge. As it stood, even if preparations for war were to push the depression aside, the relief would be temporary. Unless the world economy was reformed, depression would be back with a vengeance as soon as the fighting stopped.

Following the pattern established by the League's Mixed Committee on the Problem of Nutrition, the Council accepted Loveday's proposal that the delegation's membership should extend to sibling organizations and to those 'outside' the Geneva family. In reality, however, the delegation was dominated by the EFO. The first tier of membership came from the intergovernmental Financial Committee. The principal figure was Frederick Phillips, a deputy permanent Secretary to the British Treasury and chairman of the Financial Committee, who also served as the delegation's chairman. He was joined by McDougall; Winfield Riefler, an American economist, member of the Institute for Advanced Study and adviser to the US Treasury; and Risto Ryti, a former head of the Finnish Finance Ministry and Governor of the Bank of Finland, who was called away urgently from the delegation in August 1939 when Finland faced the imminent threat of war with the USSR and Germany.

To their number were added a group of economists who were officially designated 'outside experts', as they were not in the pay of the League, but who really were insiders, because they had all served on either the EIS or the EFO expert committees in one capacity or another: the Austrian economist Oskar Morgenstern, substituted in the early meetings by Haberler, who was so enthusiastic a participant he declined to retire when Morgenstern returned; Ohlin; and the Deputy Governor of the Banque de France and Treasury official Jacques Rueff. What they all had in common was a commitment to the League. What they did not share was an agreed view on what caused economic crises or how they should be tackled. The participants in the Depression Delegation were associated with various schools of economic thought, ranging from the classically orthodox, notably Ryti and Rueff, representatives of what was to become new orthodoxy led by Haberler, to the varieties of Keynesianism exemplified by Ohlin. These four men alone demonstrated the degree to which labels like 'orthodox' and 'Keynesian' were problematic in the fluid context of international economic relations and the evolution of economic science in the period.

EFO's secretariat added to this rich mix. They included the head of section, Loveday; the Canadian Louis Rasminsky; the Estonian Ragnar Nurkse; the Swede Arthur Rosenborg; the Pole Grzegorz Frumkin; Meade; Koopmans; the Frenchman René Charron, and the American Royall Tyler, who joined the delegation from a posting as League Commissioner in Hungary. The broadening of the delegation's membership came with the addition of Carter Goodrich, an American ILO economist who, like Harold Butler, attended delegation meetings (although this was not widely publicized at the time), and was well known to members of the Economic and Financial Sections, although the EFO was identified as the senior partner in the collaboration.[47] It marked the continuation of the wider meaning ascribed to the term 'economic' since the onset of the Great Depression, which had caused the issues and policies ascribed in 1919 under the distinct headings of 'social', 'economic', and 'financial' to shift. Important, often creative, tensions between the EFO and the ILO remained unresolved throughout the lifetime of the League, but the delegation was a site at which ideas on how to reinternationalize the world economy were explored alongside key elements of the agenda for positive security—economic, social, cultural, and physical well-being—and the utility of welfare provision.

The secretariat of the EFO served as the engine room of the inquiry. The first stage involved sending out requests to League members and non-members to provide information on their recovery policies. Letters and questionnaires dispatched from Avenol's office asked governments to offer a brief summary of measures adopted 'with a view to reviving economic activity' and an overview of more permanent steps taken 'to prevent or mitigate depressions in the future'. The committee was less interested in 'expedients intended to meet some exceptionally critical situation' than in those that were part of a 'systematic endeavour to revive activity'. The League sought to set the tone of the national inquiry and response: the exercise would have real value only if governments were willing to adopt a scientific rather than a political approach and to add their own candid views as to the 'relative effectiveness of the various measures adopted'.[48]

The delegation's call for the collective economic good to be placed above domestic political self-interest was always ambitious, never more so than at a time when the climate of permanent diplomatic crisis was likely to darken further with the outbreak of global war. Indeed, the most immediate obstacle facing the call to share economic intelligence was not political pride but national self-defence. Many governments did not reply to the League's survey (notably France); and of those that did, Afghanistan, Belgium, Britain, Burma, Cuba, Finland, Hungary, India, Latvia, Siam, and Uruguay were judged by the secretariat to have missed the distinction between temporary and permanent measures, and to have said little that was of scientific or political interest. The Argentinian, Bulgarian, Iraqi, Swedish, and US governments took rather more care, distinguishing carefully between the emergency response and permanent protection. Most remarkable was the American answer, both for the speed of reply—it was the first to arrive in the EFO's postbox—and for the care taken over the exposition. Sweetser believed it to be 'the most concise overall statement the government has yet made' on its recovery policies.[49] This did not mean it was short. At seventy pages, the American overview

---

[47] Minutes of the first meeting, 'Délégation pour l'étude des dépressions économiques', undated June 1938, LON R4454, 10A/36595/32649; memo by Avenol, 18 Feb. 1938, LON R4450, 10A/ 32446/32446.

[48] Memo by Avenol, 18 Feb. 1938, LON R4450, 10A/32446/32446.

[49] Sweetser to Loveday, 16 June 1938, and 'The Recovery Program in the United States', National Resources Committee on behalf of Cordell Hull, 5 May 1938, LON R4450, 10A/34038/32446. The report was compiled by the National Resources Committee and approved by Harold Ickes and Hull.

was ten times longer than most other replies, which was in part an expression of US determination to sell the New Deal programme to the wider world.

However, the League was interested as much in the collective mentality the process exposed as in individual responses. The national reports were collated to form an overview of measures states had taken, paying particular attention to steps known to have been adopted but about which previously no account had been offered to the international community, and policies on which states refused to be drawn. Silence spoke volumes when it came to monetary policy; as Rasminsky noted, 'the most remarkable feature common to practically all Government replies is the absence of definite statements regarding the adoption of exchange depreci-ation as a deliberate measure of government policy.' Britain clung to its predictable refrain that the decision to devalue had been 'forced upon the Government', and that the EEA 'was not used, was never intended to be used, to impose any given rate of exchange on the market', an assertion that was met with the scepticism it deserved in Geneva. Sweden, the United States, and the Netherlands instead sought to gloss over their strategic decision to abandon gold rather than explain it, while Belgium failed to mention it altogether. Only the Chilean government was bold enough to announce its break with gold standard orthodoxy on the principle that central bank policy 'should be directed primarily towards maintaining the relative internal stability of the currency than towards maintaining [external] exchange stability'.[50]

The notion of international responsibility still determined a sufficiently healthy respect among this group of nations to prompt them to respond to the delegation's inquiry, but all the replies devoted a great deal more attention to internal credit policy. Almost all countries were prepared to acknowledge they had taken steps to promote easy money and reduce interest rates. Once again, Britain's response was singled out by the secretariat for its evasive brevity, in sharp contrast to the US and Chilean responses, which were extensive and placed great stress on the beneficial impact of cheap money.[51]

Countries were more forthcoming generally on banking policy, although most governments implied they had introduced new legislation governing central and commercial banks rather than offer precise details (notably Argentina, Belgium, Bulgaria, Hungary, Romania, and the United States)—of measures conceived to ease the current depression and to prevent similar crises in the future. Initiatives that were classified as 'banking reorganization', on the other hand, largely came under the 'emergency' banner, although some of them had longer-term anti-cyclical properties: debt moratoria, conversion of short-term debts, reduction of rates of interest on certain categories of debts, the granting of special credits to banks, agriculture, industry, shipping, and building, and the creation of special

[50] Note by the Secretariat, 'Summary of Government Replies to the Economic Depressions Enquiry', 11 Nov.1938, LON R4450, 10A/34383/32446.

[51] Report from the Central Bank of Chile, 'On the Subject Dealt with in the Questionnaire from the League of Nations Secretariat concerning Economic Depressions', 5 Sept. 1938, LON R4450, 10A/34383/32446; 'The Recovery Program in the United States', National Resources Committee on behalf of Cordell Hull, 5 May 1938, LON R4450, 10A/34038/32446.

credit institutions to provide credits to banks and particular classes of producers or consumers. Here Argentina, Belgium, Bulgaria, Cuba, Hungary, Iraq, Latvia, the Netherlands, Panama, Romania, Siam, and the United States were distinguished.

The EFO's secretariat noted that states still remained very reluctant to discuss the condition of their national budgets or their policies towards them; even the otherwise forthcoming USA avoided the issue. The implication was that budget orthodoxy continued to reign supreme. Only the Swedes distinguished themselves in a submission, jointly crafted by its Finance Minister, Ernst Wigforss, and the Minister for Social Affairs Gustav Möller, who stressed that Sweden did not seek to balance its national budget yearly, but over a business cycle; their primary intention was to soothe troubled economic waters, not to demonstrate fiscal probity; not to subvert the state but to reinforce it and to make it stronger and wealthier in the long run. When the delegation began its formal work, the Swedish approach to national budgets was taken up with great enthusiasm by Loveday and Rasminsky and championed in the draft report and during the Second World War in all League documents on post-war planning. The evidence on taxation policy, on the other hand, generated conflicting evidence and was of less interest to the delegation. The Belgian, Iraqi, and Dutch governments had opted to refund taxes to stimulate demand; Hungary had exonerated certain groups from taxation; meanwhile the United States had introduced new taxes and Sweden had increased them. Iraq had also engaged in extensive fiscal reform.

More consistent and striking was the importance attached by states to agricultural policy, even in countries where industry dominated, such as Belgium, the Netherlands, and the United States. (The Dutch report spent twice as long detailing the measures to help agriculture than those to help industry.) The result was to reinforce the secretariat's conviction of food's cultural, social, and political importance to governments and its value to the League (or any successor organization) as an issue through which to promote internationalization and global improvement. The secretariat categorized agricultural measures under six headings: the regulation of markets (especially the creation of monopolies); price regulation that centred on steps either to increase prices or to guarantee prices; subsidization of farmers (Belgium, Britain, the USA, and Uruguay); the restriction of cultivation and breeding (Argentina, Bulgaria, the Netherlands, and Romania); participation in international restriction schemes (India); the reorientation of agricultural production (Afghanistan, Burma, Iraq, Latvia, the Netherlands, and Siam); reforestation (Afghanistan and Siam). In addition, it identified individual instances of measures that could be worthy of further investigation, such as the destruction of agricultural products in Panama.[52]

The account of industrial policy drawn up by the secretariat from the national submissions stressed how predominately agricultural countries, in particular,

---

[52] Note by the Secretariat, 'Summary of Government Replies to the Economic Depressions Enquiry', 11 Nov. 1938, LON R4450, 10A/34383/32446. Fishing also received a brief mention, where it was noted that Britain had introduced special legislation to regulate the quantity and quality of supplies of fish.

adopted 'numerous measures to develop home industrial production'. Schemes in Bulgaria, Hungary, Romania, Latvia, and Burma were singled out for particular attention, and regarded as more remarkable than state creation of new industries in Belgium and the Netherlands. Britain and the USA, by contrast, had opted to reorganize industry by introducing statutory schemes administered by the coal, iron and steel, and cotton industries, while the US National Recovery Administration provided a code that sought to make competition 'fair'. That parts of this legislation had been declared unconstitutional did not prevent FDR's administration from lauding its innovative qualities overseas, and its 'powerful stimulus to the restoration of national morale'.[53] Sweden, the United States, and Latvia also placed great stress on the restorative qualities of increased building activity.

Governments' response on public works was less clear-cut. Most replies were vague as to the benefits accrued and silent as to whether the schemes were financed by taxation or increased government borrowing, with only the Swedish and Belgian governments offering details—the former funding public works by increased state borrowing, the latter by a revaluation of the National Bank's gold reserves, which generated a fund to finance expenditure normally covered by borrowing. Britain, again, proved characteristically unforthcoming, making no mention of public works in its submission, and alluding only briefly to commercial policy.[54] The Treasury had declined to reply to the League's request in detail because, as Ashton-Gwatkin noted, while the British submission to the League offered 'the most useful explanation and defence of British commercial and agricultural policy since the depression of 1931 . . . The financial side is weak [yet] "cheap money" and the great conversion of 1932 played the most important part in our measures against depression'. He recognized the secretariat 'would want details of public works expenditure, road building, encouragement of housing, etc.'.[55] But neither he nor many of his colleagues in the Foreign Office or the Treasury wanted to supply them. Indeed, so frustrated were the Geneva officials with the paucity of detail that Rasminsky, who was to draft the report of the delegation's conclusions, made Phillips promise he would supply more details on the volume of public works, building construction, and commodity stocks.[56]

Many replies also ducked the issue of trade policy, and those that did reply— Argentina, Britain, Bulgaria, India, Latvia, the Netherlands, Romania, and Uruguay—focused on quotas and import controls, and not on tariffs more generally. This was not surprising given that the latter were much more difficult to justify in an international context. Most countries preferred to make international political capital out of measures adopted to promote exports by stressing the role of national

[53] 'The Recovery Program in the United States', National Resources Committee on behalf of Cordell Hull, 5 May 1938, p. 2, LON R4450, 10A/34038/32446.

[54] 'Statement on Economic Depressions', prepared by the Treasury and the Board of Trade, 30 Aug. 1938, LON R4451, 10A/35134/32446.

[55] Minute by Ashton-Gwatkin, 7 July 1938, TNA FO371/22517, W8090/41/98.

[56] Rasminsky wanted to test Kuznets's work on 'commodity flow and capital formation' in the USA in the British case but needed data, in the worst case pertaining to just one or two years, to do so. See Rasminsky to Kuznets, 7 Aug. 1939, LON R4451, 10A/35134/32446.

defence. Only the United States made great play of trade liberalization as a preferred path to national and international economic revival.

Human capital barely featured. Education and training were treated cursorily, and only Belgium, Cuba, Sweden, and the USA reported their efforts to freeze or raise wages, reduce working hours, and introduce annual holidays with pay. The secretariat saw this as a real weakness in national responses, compounded by governments' failures to attempt 'to co-ordinate particular measures into a systematic programme of a deliberate anti-depression policy' and to 'formulate a declaration of principles underlying business cycle policy or to take into account the theoretical background or implications of the various measures adopted with a view to preventing or mitigating depressions'.[57] Governments remained reactive rather than proactive in the field of anti-depression policy.

To overcome the gaps, the secretariat supplemented its overview of the governmental reports with an extraordinary series of studies based both on its own research and the work of other leading economists in Europe and the United States. The opening page of the secretariat's study compiled on 'The Measurement of the Volume of Saving', for example, offered a critical review of the comparative statistical materials available to the international community on national saving levels from publications in the *Vierteljahrshefte zur Konjunkturforschung*, published in Berlin; the *Swedish Unemployment* Report *Unitas*, published by the Nordiska Foeringsbanken; L. W. R Soutendijk's 'Methoden tot het vaststellen van den Omvang der Besparen', published in Haarlem; and T. Lescure, 'L'Epargne en France, 1914–1934', published in Paris in 1936, which offered a broad estimate of private wealth in France.[58]

Before the delegation convened for its first formal meeting, a whirlwind of papers circulated among its members. There were fifty-two preparatory reports, each approximately fifty pages in length, divided by the secretariat into four parts. The first related to 'Economic Depressions and Economic Structure'; the second, 'Policies Directed towards Greater Stability of Total Demand'; the third 'Policies Specifically Directed towards Greater Stability in Capital Formation'; and the final part focused on 'Policies Specially Relevant to States Producing Primary Products'. These formed the basis of subsequent discussions, which comprised seven private meetings in June 1938, followed by six meetings in November, with a final round of meetings in July 1939.

The materials compiled by the secretariat built on research and communication with other economists throughout the 1930s, sustained through the League and the academies of economics and statistics in Britain, the United States, France, Sweden,

---

[57] Note by the Secretariat, 'Summary of Government Replies to the Economic Depressions Enquiry', 11 Nov. 1938, pp. 9–10, LON R4450, 10A/34383/32446.

[58] It included another pointed analysis on how national accounting methods and/or information policy fell short of what was needed for effective international measurement and comparison. See Note by Secretariat, 'Measurement of the Volume of Saving', 23 Nov. 1938, LON R4453, 10A/33303/32649.

Germany, Australia, and Canada.[59] These materials offered a detailed snapshot of the web of economic science available to the League and, in its critique of this work, a picture of how the League would reconfigure the world economy to face up to what it saw as the ever present and grave danger of economic depression. Evaluating the Depression Delegation's contribution to the history of economic thought, therefore, must take into account not just the quality of particular economic ideas or the contribution of specific economists. It must also explore its contribution to the collation, articulation, and dissemination of economic concepts and intelligence to some but not others, and its role in framing the world economy and giving it geographic shape and content.

PRESCRIPTIONS FOR THE WORLD ECONOMY

Loveday's team was rarely complacent about the quality of its work. Koopman's note on food stocks, for example, was judged by Loveday to be 'very thin . . . not at all adequate' and he urged Koopmans to supplement it with Beveridge's research on the effect of harvest on employment and prices presented before the British Association in Cambridge in 1938.[60] The amount of work and effort the secretariat put into the delegation, at a time when the League faced considerable political and financial pressures, reflected the importance of the delegation to Loveday and his colleagues. Their preparatory reports and statistical compilations were among the first materials to be packed up and shipped to the USA when Loveday and his colleagues fled to Princeton. The secretariat was at pains to maintain its, and the delegation's, scientific impartiality and practical ambition in offering states an overview of what policies have been proposed and used in recent years to combat or prevent depression, with 'no attempt made to analyse their theoretical background' nor to focus on the 'details of the mechanisms suggested for implementing them'.[61]

It implied that the League's assessment of national economic policy, and the architecture of international relations and world economy in which it was situated, was value-free; this was not just an unattainable goal, but—from the League's perspective—ultimately an undesirable one. The secretariat, and its advisers were steeped in the values and ideas of economic liberalism. Their challenge was not to

[59] The secretariat also reproduced and circulated new studies that appeared during the delegation's lifetime, including John Maynard Keynes, 'The Policy of Government Storage of Foodstuffs and Raw Materials', *Economic Journal*, 48 (Sept. 1938), 449–60.

[60] Loveday to Rasminsky, 9 Nov. 1938, LON R4453, 10A/33303/32649. Jose Harris, *William Beveridge: A Biography* (Oxford, 1977), 351–2. Harris implies it was Harold Wilson who shaped Beveridge's view in *Full Employment in a Free Society* that depressions were triggered by a fall in employment of exporting industries, which in turn was caused by a decline in demand among primary-producing countries. See William Beveridge, *Full Employment in a Free Society* (London, 1944), 294–306. But this view had been expounded at great length in a series of publications and conferences sponsored by the League and known to Beveridge.

[61] Note by the Secretariat, 'Summary of Some Measures Recently Proposed with a View to Preventing and Mitigating Depressions', 4 May 1938, p. 1, LON R4453, 10A/33303/32649.

replace but to adapt this ideology in the changing landscape of national and international economics and politics. For members of the secretariat and the delegation, the underlying assumption of the desirability to produce 'a more positive programme for laissez-faire' was so obvious that there was no need for an explicit discussion about ideology, beyond a cursory debate about the degree of state intervention, which was regarded as necessary but in need of constraint.[62] Equally, there was no extended discussion of the radical alternatives of communism and fascism. Although Schachtian economics formed a counterpoint to their deliberations, the future-oriented policy agenda of the delegation liberated it from the EFO's past preoccupation with the behaviour and performance of the Third Reich that dominated the diplomatic horizon. The absence of Soviet-style command economics was less surprising given its already marginal place in the League, though the secretariat was interested in exploring 'socialist economics' (the term preferred by delegation members who were hostile to the idea) that related to schemes for national and international public works.

Ohlin frequently complained of the 'deplorable' poverty of a public imagination that equated deficit financing with public works when 'in reality economic policy was many-sided'.[63] Public works served as a springboard for a wider assault on the classical assumption that, in the words of Dennis Robertson, 'economic stability can be achieved only at the cost of material progress'.[64] To this end, Loveday, Rasminsky, and Koopmans prepared a summary of all the preparatory materials, and divided the agenda into two key questions: how to increase the stability of the world economy, and how to deal with depressions. The distinction was significant. Although it appeared to suggest that depressions were crises worthy of distinct, short-term measures, it also implied that the economic system's fluctuations explored in the theoretical and empirical work of Haberler, Tinbergen, and Koopmans needed to be moderated on a permanent basis for the sake of peace. The secretariat sought to steer the delegation collective away from the classical proposition of 'allowing the crisis to take its course', giving only cursory attention to the Austrian school's proposition that the challenge before a world economy in depression was to 'aim to adjust to the reduced level of monetary circulation', before throwing its weight firmly in the other direction.[65]

The discussion of monetary policy did not detain the delegates for long, in sharp contrast to the League's attempts to combat depression in the early 1930s. When, on 1 July, Loveday proposed 'that the delegation would be wiser to keep out of monetary controversy if it wished to influence depression policy', the rest of the

---

[62] Note by the Secretariat, 'Summary of Some Measures Recently Proposed with a View to Preventing and Mitigating Depressions', 4 May 1938, pp. 5–6, LON R4453, 10A/33303/32649.

[63] Ohlin's intervention, 'Provisional Minutes, Fourth Meeting (Private)', 30 June, pp. 32–5, LON R4454, 10A/36595/32649.

[64] D. H. Robertson, *Banking Policy and the Price Level: An Essay in the Theory of the Trade Cycle* (London, 1926), 22, cited in Note by the Secretariat, 'Summary of Some Measures Recently Proposed with a View to Preventing and Mitigating Depressions', 4 May 1938, pp. 5–6, LON R4453, 10A/33303/32649.

[65] Note by the Secretariat, 'Summary of Some Measures Recently Proposed with a View to Preventing and Mitigating Depressions', 4 May 1938, LON R4453, 10A/33303/32649.

delegation readily agreed.[66] Loveday had particular reason to be cautious. Weeks earlier, he had advocated that the United States take urgent steps to increase its money supply and resume long-term lending; and that the British and French governments keep interest rates low and liquidity high, and accept increasing levels of state expenditure in a paper to be published in the annual series 'Some Aspects of the Present Economic Situation'. He was motivated by a desire to ensure these countries did the 'right thing' both to combat the renewed threat of depression, and to manage the economic and political pressures unleashed by rearmament. But it was rare for the EFO's secretariat to offer such direct comment for public consumption, and the State Department quickly intervened to warn Loveday that 'in the present circumstances such a report might receive an unusual degree of publicity in the United States and that he might wish to consider carefully what the effects of such publicity might be'. If the Americans feared domestic embarrassment, the British were more critical of Loveday. Treasury officials muttered darkly of Loveday's 'radical' turn, articulating 'proposals relating to this country which might have emanated from Keynes or any other Opposition speaker'.[67] However, it did not stop the Treasury delighting in Loveday's critique of the rather limp fiscal stimulus afforded by Roosevelt's New Deal, 'which would furnish the anti-Roosevelt press with material enough to last until the November elections'.[68] Only Phillips echoed US concerns, warning Loveday of the dangers such criticism posed to nascent American internationalism and its deepening relationship with the League. Loveday quickly saw the point and watered down his article.

It was not that the delegation was bereft of ideas on monetary policy, but it accepted Loveday's view that it lacked the international leverage to effect the take-up of any proposals, and any controversy would obscure the rest of its work. In fact, monetary policy was discussed at some length, but comparatively little of these discussions made it into the draft report. Ohlin was the most forthright in consigning the gold standard order to the dustbin of history; no one in the secretariat or among the economists sought to defend it, although there was agreement that monetary policies needed to be coordinated. There was warm praise for the monthly meetings of leading central bankers at the BIS, although most delegates agreed the world needed more comprehensive dialogue and coordination between nation states.[69] The BIS and the Tripartite Agreement were a start, but they recognized these arrangements excluded much of the world: as Phillips asked rhetorically, 'was there anything to be said for monetary agreements . . . of the three

[66] Loveday's comments, 'Provisional Minutes, Fifth Meeting (Private)', 1 July 1938, p. 19, LON R4454, 10A/36595/32649.

[67] Bucknell to Hull, 'Sixty-sixth Session of the Financial Committee of the League of Nations', 15 July 1938, NARA RG59, 5000.C1198/140. For details of Loveday's note, see 'Some Aspects of the Present Economic Situation', 9 June 1938, pp. 51–87, LON, Financial Committee Bound Documents, 1936–8. A copy of this document also accompanied Bucknell's report to Hull.

[68] Phillips, minute to Hopkins, 29 July 1938, TNA: PRO FO371/22518, W10199/41/98.

[69] De Bodres would telephone to find out how the meetings went. Recounted in Toniolo, *Central Bank Cooperation*, 199–200.

major monetary powers and the small number of very wealthy powers which had adhered to the Tripartite Agreement when others were left out of the account?'[70]

Only Rueff and Ryti, who had considerable political and intellectual capital invested in the gold standard order, advocated some sort of return to 'golden fetters'. All members were agreed, however, on the power of domestic pressures to shape monetary policy and, in turn, on the impact of monetary forces on the nation state and its peoples. This domestic perspective had been strikingly absent in Britain's decision to return to gold at its pre-war parity of $4.86 in 1925, and on the terms of gold standard membership imposed on the Weimar Republic when its return to gold was facilitated via the Dawes Plan in 1924. The secretariat and most delegates recognized the economic advantages that individual nations had enjoyed by leaving gold, but argued that, when pursued on an individual, widespread, and uncoordinated basis, depreciation held tremendous risks for the world economy as a whole. Coordination here, as in all things, was its mantra.[71] In the opening session, it was Ohlin, again, who posed the big question before them: 'what kind of agreement would reduce the risk of shock in the monetary system and increase the power of resistance to inevitable shocks.' And how far, added Rueff, 'was one country willing to pay for the policy of another country' in the interests of the world economy as a whole?'[72]

The delegation also agreed there was virtual accord among analysts of business cycles that the credit system was singularly important in producing or permitting fluctuations in real income that marked the difference between depression and boom. But, for all their professed 'unanimity regarding the necessity of controlling the monetary circulation in the interest of stability', there was no consensus regarding the criteria to be applied to that end, and no agreed view on how success should be measured. Should policy-makers try to stabilize wholesale prices, retail prices, the cost of living, or some other sort of general price index? And the next question followed: how should one intervene? 'What' asked the League, were 'the techniques of control'?[73]

It acknowledged the mounting scepticism among economists, and their colleagues working in the world's most powerful finance ministries, as to the limited effectiveness of central bank operations to restrict variations in money supply, investment, and the running of the national and international economy. But,

[70] Comment by Phillips, 'Provisional Minutes, Fifth Meeting (Private)', 1 July 1938, p. 19, LON R4454, 10A/36595/32649.
[71] General discussion in 'Provisional Minutes, Fifth Meeting (Private)', 1 July 1938, p. 21, LON R4454, 10A/36595/32649.
[72] Comments by Ohlin and Rueff, 'Provisional Minutes, Fifth Meeting (Private)', 1 July 1938, pp. 1, 18, LON R4454, 10A/36595/32649.
[73] Note by the Secretariat, 'Summary of Some Measures Recently Proposed with a View to Preventing and Mitigating Depressions', 4 May 1938, LON R4453, 10A/33303/32649. Aside from League materials, this one study alone drew on the writings of J. M. Keynes, D. H. Robertson, J. M. Clark, Sumner H. Slichter, Ralph Hawtrey, Lionel Robbins, Roy Harrod, H. C. Simons, Irving Fisher, Paul H. Douglas, Alvin Hansen, Johan Akerman, James Meade, Nicholas Kaldor, and Frank Graham.

again, while it was easy to agree that the behaviour of money was significant, there was no consensus as to the nature of the threat its movements could pose or how to manage them. Despite ten years of deflationary pressure, discussion in the meetings, as so often before in the League, turned first to the potential danger of cheap money. Nurkse, drawing on recent work by Lionel Robbins and Ryti for the delegation, argued that it was imperative to remain ever vigilant for the spectre of inflation. Loveday and Ohlin, on the other hand, focused on the benefits of cheap money as an aid to stability and the danger of dear money, and to support their case wielded Keynes at his most biblical as he cautioned the world to avoid dear money 'as we would hell-fire'.[74]

This brought the delegation onto the challenge of managing stock market volatility. Although the relationship between stock market gyrations and the stability of the real economy was far from clear, most delegates sided with Keynes's and Roy Harrod's published views that it was unhelpful to manage credit policy as a check on stock exchange speculation. More contentious within the group was the question of how far states should extend their powers to control commercial bank reserves beyond the use of discount and open-market operations. The secretariat furnished the delegation with an account of recent central banks' open-market operations in equities, and with a report from the Federal Reserve Board of the USA that suggested that its reserve requirements should be based not solely on the absolute volume of deposits but also on the rapidity of their turnover.[75] It drew attention to recent proposals for the reform of the commercial banking arm that started from the proposition that it was fundamentally wrong for monetary circulation to be determined by the lending policy of commercial banks because it 'introduces undesirable elasticity into the monetary circulation'. Centre stage here was Irving Fisher's call for '100 per cent Money', advertised in H. C. Simons's call for 'A Positive Program for Laissez-Faire', which proposed that commercial banks in the USA (and potentially elsewhere) be reconstituted as safety-deposit institutions, maintaining 100 per cent reserves against their deposits, and therefore being unable to create or destroy effective money. Instead, banks would derive their income from service charges, and the function of lending would be taken over by investment trusts, which would obtain funds by the sale of their own stock. As a result, 'the supply of money could then only be altered by the central bank operating in conjunction with state fiscal policy'. The system would then be rounded off with some definite rule of policy, 'such as the stabilization of the quantity of money, or total monetary turnover, etc.'. More important at this stage than determining the exact nature of the monetary rules was that they should be 'definite and unambiguous'. Here the political sensibilities were all significant: 'the rule should be chosen with regard to the political possibilities of securing adherence

[74] Note by the Secretariat, 'Summary of Some Measures Recently Proposed with a View to Preventing and Mitigating Depressions', 4 May 1938, LON R4453, 10A/33303/32649.

[75] Note by the Secretariat, 'Summary of Some Measures Recently Proposed with a View to Preventing and Mitigating Depressions', 4 May 1938, LON R4453, 10A/33303/32649.

to it over long periods' and needed to be robust enough 'that strong sentiments against tinkering with the currency can be regimented around it'.[76]

Reflecting what Loveday and Rasminsky reported to the delegation as the collective and the growing doubts of economists as to the ability of the established, 'ordinary' instruments of banking policy to control monetary circulation, the preparatory materials and discussion in the meetings devoted more attention to fiscal policy, both as an agent of stability and as a depression-busting tool. The secretariat's unequivocal view was that governments needed to recognize budgetary policy as a potent force for stability: when private spending was reduced, government needed to increase the volume of money in circulation by spending more than it collected in revenues. When private spending was high, it should attempt to reduce monetary circulation by spending less than it collected. The key challenge for the delegation and the international economic community as a whole was to educate elite and general public opinion as to the wisdom of this approach. The easy equation between state and household budgets in the public's mind had to be eradicated. Ohlin, as before, was most vehement on the importance of this point, but Loveday and Rasminsky were equally determined 'of the vital importance that the public understood the real economic issue'.[77] If fiscal measures

are to be adopted as permanent measures of policy, it is obvious that there is an urgent necessity to prepare public opinion for them . . . In particular, it is essential to prepare businessmen that it is not necessarily sound policy to balance the budget once every twelve months; for if confidence is disturbed by the measures enumerated, they will not of course have the effects they desire.

In the privacy of the Geneva meeting room, Loveday heaped praise upon Sweden, 'which had an excellent administration and a public highly educated on economic matters', and opprobrium on France, 'where the public seemed singularly ignorant. That being so, perhaps the delegation should concentrate on educating public opinion to understand that a deficit in bad times was not necessarily a bad thing.' The United States had shown the way, witnessing a 'big change in public opinion . . . where it was beginning to be realized since 1928 that a deficit was not necessarily ruinous'. Moreover, if 'a deficit during a depression was viewed as an asset rather than an economic liability', business confidence would improve rather than deteriorate as it had during 1929 and 1930.[78] Robertson added his voice by warning of the dangers

[76] Note by the Secretariat, 'Summary of Some Measures Recently Proposed with a View to Preventing and Mitigating Depressions', 4 May 1938, pp. 5–6, LON R4453, 10A/33303/32649.

[77] Ohlin made this point in his opening comments at the first meeting at the first session. See Minutes of the first meeting, 'Delegation pour l'étude des depressions économiques', 29 June 1938, pp. 3–4, LON R4454, 10A/36595/32649; Loveday's comments, 'Delegation on Economic Depressions: First Session, Third Meeting', 30 June 1938, p. 15, LON R4454, 10A/36595/32649. Ohlin's frustration with public opinion was such that he 'was not in favour of letting the public know too much about the existence of special funds'. This had worked to Sweden's advantage in 1927 to 1931, when 'substantial surpluses were accumulated unknown to the public' that provided the initial cushion against depression.

[78] Loveday's comments, 'Provisional minutes, Delegation on Economic Depressions: First Session, Third Meeting', 30 June 1938, pp. 13–14, LON R4454, 10A/36595/32649.

posed if national governments sought to make 'prestige-capital out of one-another's budgetary difficulties'. He called for the delegation to encourage 'international organs of journalism and of journalism in general to cooperate to induce an atmosphere' in which the world could avoid 'the shame-faced shuffling of one country after another into budgetary disequilibrium, to the accompaniment of the pious rebukes of its neighbours' in ways that acted as 'a potent reinforcement of exchange dislocation and international depression'.[79]

Quite how this recognition as to the value of public education and the role of journalists was to be translated into a new strategy for public education in contemporary economics was unclear. Riefler cautioned of the dangers to EFO of trying to engage with public opinion directly. Repeatedly in 1931 and 1932, leading financiers in the USA had urged 'the American public to keep their money in the banks, and this turned out to be bad advice'. Unlike Ohlin and Loveday, he professed a deep aversion to 'urging action the validity of which depended on a great variety of circumstances'. In the end, 'attempts to affect economic activity' by propaganda backfired more often than they succeeded.[80] Riefler's view reflected the traditional EFO perspective, which consistently privileged the technical side of its operations and assumed that political engagement ran the risk of driving an already damaged League yet deeper into unpopularity. Indeed, rather than raise its profile, as world war loomed many agencies within the League had begun to fold inwards in the face of declining support from member states and widespread public disillusionment. The League's publicity budget, always small, was declining fast, and its strategies for disseminating information to the public remained underdeveloped, especially with regard to economics and finance. In short, public education was an area that neither Loveday nor his colleagues in the secretariat were well qualified or positioned to tackle directly.

The depth of the challenge regarding 'deficit education' was clear, even within the delegation. Rueff and Ryti, in particular, put up fierce and continued resistance to the notion of budget deficits. The latter flatly declared he was not in favour of deficits of any kind 'because they destroyed confidence'. Neither scientific unity in the supplementary materials presented to delegates, nor impassioned argument, swayed them. When the discussion moved from the efficacy of public works schemes as a tool to combat depression, new divisions opened up. Here, Phillips and Haberler professed themselves sceptics. By contrast, Ohlin declared the work of the Swedish Unemployment Commission the best advertisement in the world for public works. As he put it, public works did not exist 'simply to make a deficit. It was more important to provide employment where it was most needed and to create new employment to prevent' the national economy from sliding out of kilter.[81] Unity was restored to some degree when Ryti introduced the distinction

[79] Memo by D. H. Robertson, 'Note on Measures to Promote Recovery from Depression', 26 May 1939, pp. 3–4, LON R4453, 10A/33303/32649.

[80] Provisional minutes, 'Delegation on Economic Depressions: First Session, Third Meeting', 30 June 1938, pp. 22–3, LON R4454, 10A/36595/32649.

[81] Provisional minutes, 'Delegation on Economic Depressions: First Session, Third Meeting', 30 June 1938, pp. 22–3, LON R4454, 10A/36595/32649.

between 'developed' and 'undeveloped' economies, arguing 'that in highly developed countries it was difficult to devise a public works policy which would be of permanent benefit. In undeveloped economies, on the other hand it was easier to select a public works policy which would remedy some defect in the country's equipment.' Even for this arch economic conservative, intervention was tolerable, even beneficial, when directed at the less 'advanced'.[82]

Loveday asked how states could slow down and preferably stop capital expenditure altogether on public works when the economy was in good health, and yet ensure public works schemes were planned and 'ready to go' when depression struck 'to avoid overlapping delay and waste'. Decisive, too, was the question of when and where the provision for capital expenditure should be made in the national budget. Ideally, Loveday, Ohlin, and Carter counselled, 'money required to pay for public works should be voted well in advance so as to be available at the first sign of decline'—a clear-cut policy but one that was politically unlikely. Nation states may be prepared to dedicate economic resources to preparing for war in times of peace, but were much more resistant to preparing for economic hardship in times of prosperity. The advocates of deficit spending admitted that the 'repayment of public debt during a boom would appear to require some special consideration' and Harrod offered a way out of the political conundrum posed by deficit spending.[83] He proposed creating an expert non-political body concerned with the study of trade cycle conditions—the so-called Commissioners of the Currency Equalization Account—whose task would be to determine the degree of 'unbalance' required in the national budget to create stability or recovery in times of crisis. The Finance Minister in any country that adopted the scheme would be responsible for balancing the budget in the ordinary way, but the commissioners could, acting on their own initiative, 'hand over to him at any time funds which he could treat as ordinary revenue'. This would take the politics out of stability and deficit financing, or at least put it at one remove from the Treasury (and, of course, political accountability). Commissioners would also have the duty of collecting surpluses when they could without precipitating a depression. They should be given absolute power to demand a surplus when it was clear the home economy was booming—for example, when wage rises outstripped any probable increases in the cost of living or when national demand for labour exceeded current supply. The secretariat and Ohlin thought it an idea worthy of exploration (Haberler was much more sceptical), but Ryti, Rueff, and Phillips, tellingly the delegates in government service, were not persuaded.[84]

Nothing made the delegates more irritable than the discussions as to how far deficits served as a tool to promote stability or aid economic management. While those happy to tolerate red ink on the balance sheets in the fight against

[82] Comment by Ryti, 'Provisional Minutes, Fourth Meeting (Private)', 30 June, p. 4, LON R4454, 10A/36595/32649.

[83] 'Provisional Minutes, Fourth Meeting (Private)', 30 June, pp. 9–10, LON R4454, 10A/36595/32649. The issue of funding was taken up at subsequent meetings, but no agreement was reached.

[84] See, for example, the general discussion in sixth and seventh meetings of the first session, 'Provisional Minutes', 1 and 2 July 1938, LON R4454, 10A/36595/32649.

depression now had the upper hand—a sign of how far the League and economics had both come since 1929—they had yet to win the argument. Agreement came more easily on the question of whether it was worth spending money, and in times of depression incurring debt, on social security. The financial pressure exerted by welfare provision, especially unemployment insurance, was no longer contentious, even for the Americans (although this was to change during and after the Second World War). Even the fiercest opponents of other forms of deficit finance recognized that the benefits of social security far outweighed the cost, especially because of its ability to sustain demand and thereby act as an agent of economic stability. As Haberler pointed out, unemployment benefits 'in recent years had been recommended by many economists, even those who usually held very different views . . . they had the advantage they could be applied more quickly than public works programmes, and did not involve either such a large measure of interference in the economic system or the permanent extension of government intervention in general'. Budget deficits incurred this way had become politically acceptable even among those groups in the political economy who generally 'opposed the extension of government activities'.[85] The discussion also provided the opportunity to explore more radical proposals, including James Meade's suggestion that, when the index of unemployment reached a certain level, the state should extend 'consumer credits' to old age pensioners and all insured workers. Meade's targeted form of fiscal stimulus and his stress on the inequality of the distribution of national and, by implication international, wealth was a concern shared by the secretariat, but his ideas received a cooler reception from Phillips, Rueff, Ryti, and Haberler.[86]

The discussion's focus on sustaining and stimulating consumption during times of crisis led to a greater nuance and equivocation on the question of wages. While it was still recognized that wages would and should fall during a depression, there was growing acceptance of the potential risks to sustaining consumption and confidence among workers, on economic, social, and political grounds. Ohlin's view that it was 'imperative to show the public there was no reason why people who had comfortable and secure incomes should cut down their expenditure during a depression' was enthusiastically taken up by the EFO's secretariat and developed at length for the benefit of delegation members who remained resistant to the view that had been expressed for the first time by Ohlin in 1931.[87] Similarly, while it argued it was important for states to pay attention to rigidities in the political economy—unit costs of labour, capital, and certain key prices—this was much less a focus of interest than it had been in the 1920s. Here

[85] Haberler's comments, 'Provisional Minutes, Delegation on Economic Depressions: First Session, Third Meeting', 30 June 1938, pp. 3–4, LON R4454, 10A/36595/32649.

[86] Note by the Secretariat, 'Summary of Some Measures Recently Proposed with a View to Preventing and Mitigating Depressions', 4 May 1938, pp. 20–1, LON R4453, 10A/33303/32649. 'Provisional Minutes, Fourth Meeting (Private)', 30 June, pp. 16–17, LON R4454, 10A/36595/32649; James Meade, *An Introduction to Economic Analysis and Policy* (Oxford, 1936), 49–60.

[87] Comment by Ohlin, 'Provisional Minutes, Delegation on Economic Depressions: First Session, Third Meeting', 30 June 1938, p. 22, LON R4454, 10A/36595/32649. Ohlin was credited with foreshadowing a lively debate on the role of wages initiated by the Stockholm School and some of Keynes's followers.

the stress was technocratic. States were urged to develop effective tools to measure if, for example, wages were imposing too great a burden on companies in the battle for recovery by reference to 'some sort of price index, preferably an index of wholesale prices'. The cake could also be sliced differently to ask whether wages were too low having regards to the interests of living standards, physical health, and the levels of consumption needed to sustain economic growth. The question of how far trade unions made wage rates more or less flexible was similarly ambiguous. The evidence, the EFO announced, 'falls on both sides', and it moved away from a past emphasis on wage reductions to a 'broad conclusion that wage policy should aim at stability in the general level of wages'.[88] Only monopolies were seen to have an entirely malign influence on the prospects both for growth in times of prosperity and for recovery in times of depression. Here Robinson and Rueff were the EFO's chosen authorities, but this view was more than the reaction to market monopolies.[89] These economists—in a trend evident also among US economists in this period—were reacting against the drive towards monopoly by organized labour and political parties too. They saw the increasing arbitrary use of state power and controls in civil society in relation to mounting empirical evidence—where the League had made a weighty contribution—which contradicted the model of perfect competition; both were trends that profoundly endangered the future prospects of a free and democratic society.[90]

That the markets were imperfect was evident in the similar consensus that there was a periodic yet regular tendency towards excessive or unproductive investment by the private sector. Again, the delegates agreed on the challenge for a national political economy was how to address it. The international dimension of the challenge was not beyond their imagination, but it was intertwined with the fraught history of war debts owed to the United States, and the failed Dawes and Young Plans that had left international investors significantly out of pocket. The secretariat placed a number of options before the delegates. Keynes's proposal for 'direct control of investment activity' by the state was presented as the 'most far-reaching' by the secretariat in such a way as to guarantee it would find little support among any of the delegates. His call in the *General Theory* for the 'comprehensive socialisation of investment' was cited verbatim in the preparatory materials as an instance of the most 'extreme' proposition. The term 'socialization' alone pushed him to the edge of the secretariat's known world and too close to the soviet command economy for members of the delegation. It was rejected without much discussion.[91]

[88] Note by the Secretariat, 'Delegation on Economic Depressions. Basis of Discussion for Report. Part B. Economic Depressions and Economic Structure', 27 June 1939, pp. 1–11, LON R4453, 10A/33303/32669.

[89] Note by the Secretariat, 'Delegation on Economic Depressions. Synthesis of Discussion at First Session on Recovery Policy', 30 Nov. 1938, p. 6, LON R4453, 10A/33303/32649.

[90] Maria Teresa Tomas Rangil, 'The Role of Self-Interest and Rationality in the Explanation of International and Civil Wars, 1942–2005', unpub. Ph.D. Thesis, Université de Paris Ouest Nanterre-La Défense (2010), 29–35.

[91] Recognizing the inflammatory implications, the secretariat also recorded that Keynes was at pains to point out it was 'not the ownership of the instruments of production which it is important for the

Rasminsky and Loveday thought rather more of Alvin Hansen's proposal for the creation of a national (and potentially international) Capital Issues Board, which would approve securities before they were offered to the public. 'The board would limit the volume of investment, guide its flow, and prevent the influx of capital into overdeveloped industries.' The secretariat recognized the scheme would not be able to deliver all that Hansen promised. It would, for example, be unable to control the volume of investment, because it had no power over the volume of credit, but the board would offer oversight as to the character of investments and their implications for the world economy as a whole. Hansen's suggestion that the board would help to redirect the chronic tendency in the world's rich industrial communities to invest in 'capital goods in alarming prominence', which trapped the world in the past rather than invested in its future, was an important insight.[92] To break the trend set before the First World War, Hansen suggested—and the point was emphasized by Robertson—investment should be directed towards enlarging the proportion of total output destined for immediate consumption and so reduce the relative importance of the capital goods industries to national economies.

A WORLD CONSUMING AND CONSUMED

Promoting consumption around the world held deep attractions for the League secretariat. As McDougall, drawing on the positive security agenda put it before the Depression Delegation, 'not only is there widespread poverty today among the greater part of the world's population, implying a level of consumption far below any reasonable minimum standard of living, but during a depression, the standard of life of many of those who were formerly reasonably well off is frequently forced below the minimum'.[93] In the preparatory materials, the delegation's meetings, and the draft report prepared for dissemination in the spring of 1939, consumption took centre-stage. For the world as a whole the delegation advocated 'any measures designed to increase the demand for conventional necessities', provided they did 'not reduce national savings and national income' and were 'desirable to combat depression even when they do affect national savings'. This was not just an agenda for deficit spending, but 'unemployment insurance for maintaining income in bad times': for richer countries there was a need for 'any measures that tend to imbed a greater proportion of total demand in social customs'. This came with the caveat that too much consumer credit risked accentuating economic fluctuations, as, 'since the amount of credit outstanding is generally at its maximum at the top of the boom', there was a danger of helping people to buy more only when times were

---

State to assume'. Note by the Secretariat, 'Delegation on Economic Depressions. Synthesis of Discussion at First Session on Recovery Policy', 30 Nov. 1938, p. 6, LON R4453, 10A/33303/32649.

[92] Note by the Secretariat, 'Delegation on Economic Depressions. Synthesis of Discussion at First Session on Recovery Policy', 30 Nov. 1938, p. 6, LON R4453, 10A/33303/32649.

[93] Note by the Secretariat, 'Summary of Memorandum by Mr McDougall: The Standard of Living and Trade Depressions', LON R4453, 10A/33303/32649.

good, and 'postponing demand for longer when the boom is past'.[94] So, for all that the promotion of consumption has been associated with Americanization of the world, here it was being advocated predominately by Europeans and members of the British Commonwealth. The empirical underpinnings of the delegation's case were global, although Europe, the British Commonwealth, India, and the Americas dominated its mental map, with other territories intruding primarily when they were connected to a European Empire or a League Mandate, as in the case of Java or Iraq.

By the time the delegation completed its report in the summer of 1939, few doubted war was coming. Lines of communication were seizing up and delegates struggled to get to Geneva for the July meetings to finalize the report so that it could be published.[95] Inevitably, the League became increasingly introverted and individuals worried about what the future held both for them, their families (the position of staff members whose homelands were absorbed into the territories covered by the Nazi–Soviet pact was to become particularly acute), and the organization, which was threatened with oblivion. As the world retreated into separate camps, the Depression Delegation's efforts to elaborate a new architecture with specialized institutions to facilitate economic and financial relations that would administer its prescriptions for fighting economic depression were put aside in the battle to save the League.[96] There was also more scientific work to be done: every discussion ended with the delegates compiling a list of issues that needed further investigation.[97] The delegation's approach led it to emphasize that it was shortcomings in science, not the complex character of the political economy, that resulted in 'contradictory and inconclusive proposals . . . The observation and measurement of economic phenomena has not yet been pushed to the point when certain crucial elements in the alternation between prosperity and depression are fully elucidated and understood.'[98]

In Geneva, the crisis over the League's future revived the question of the institution's reform, which was used by Loveday and his colleagues to lobby for an

[94] Note by Loveday, 'How Far Could it be Anticipated that an Increase in Consumers' Demand for Food and Equipment of Simpler Types Would Have a Stabilising Effect On the Trade Cycle?', LON R445, 10A/33303/32649.

[95] On the struggle for publication and the continued disagreements between the orthodox members from Finland and France and the altogether less orthodox secretariat, see Rasminsky to Rueff, 14 Jan. 1939, LON R4453, 10A/32669/32649.

[96] Note by the Secretariat, 'Delegation on Economic Depressions. Synthesis of Discussion at First Session on Recovery Policy', 30 Nov. 1938, pp. 33–5, LON R4453, 10A/33303/32649.

[97] See, e.g., general discussion, 'Provisional Minutes, Sixth Meeting (Private)', 1 July 1938, pp. 19–20, LON R4454, 10A/36595/32649.

[98] They went on: 'Need more data to verify business cycles. Some of the basic elements, such as savings, investment, consumers' purchases, incomes, unused productive capacity and stocks have not yet been satisfactorily measured. Other relationships, such as the relationship between income distribution and savings, between consumption and profits, between interest rates and savings, and between interest rates and the quantity and velocity of the circulation of money also need further analysis' ('Provisional Minutes, Sixth Meeting (Private)', 1 July 1938, pp. 19–20, LON R4454, 10A/36595/32649).

institutional home for the Depression Delegation, 'a permanent machinery . . . for the exchange of information and the co-ordination of policies' of the world's political economy.[99] As we shall see in the next chapter, the proposal resulted in a tug of war within the secretariat, and between the Axis and Allied powers.[100] The Economic and Financial Sections began to talk about how the League's machinery and its values could help inform and set the agenda for reconstruction once the war had been won, implicitly connecting it to the Allies' side. Here the work of the Depression Delegation was key, and its empirical focus on the history of the interwar economy chimed with FDR's concern to learn the lessons of the past, while its orientation towards the future and the transnational network that sustained it would connect the delegation directly to the centre of US planning after 1941.

What was lost from view when the work of the Depression Delegation was absorbed into planning for post-war reconstruction were the wider insights it afforded on economic depressions and how to combat them. Not only was the group well-qualified and intellectually diverse; most of the participants had practical experience of policy as members of, or as advisers to, national governments, and had witnessed a considerable variety of economic crises, ranging from the pressures of financing total war (1914–18), war and post-war inflation, demobilization and economic reorientation (1918–24), and the Great Depression. The group was never likely to fall prey to a hubristic claim that it could put an end to boom and bust. Indeed the reverse was true. The delegation consistently stressed that the policy emphasis should be on the mitigation rather than the prevention of depression. Although it attached the greatest importance to economic stability, in the absence of what it called 'complete knowledge of the fundamental causes of depressions', it was easier to agree depressions were evil and treat their symptoms than to propose pervasive and permanent measures that might also curb the prospects of future prosperity. In this the delegation knowingly set itself in direct opposition to the trends represented in the alternative worlds offered by soviet-style communism and German National Socialism.[101] By its reasoning, economic crises, by definition, could not be anticipated precisely because of the economy's capacity for invention and growth. If the world wanted development, prosperity, and liberty, then the key challenge was to remain alert to the threat of depression, and to be ready with a variety of appropriate policies, within a coherent architecture of international coordination and cooperation, to handle the crisis when it came. Because come it would.

---

[99] Note by the Secretariat, 'Delegation on Economic Depressions. Synthesis of Discussion at First Session on Recovery Policy', 30 Nov. 1938, p. 21, LON R4453, 10A/33303/32649.

[100] Comment by McDougall, 'Provisional Minutes, Fourth Meeting (Private)', 30 June, pp. 16–17, LON R4454, 10A/36595/32649.

[101] By this stage there was universal recognition among economists that the cumulative contraction of monetary demand is the most important element in depression. Once it has started to feed on itself, in the absence of effective intervention to offset it, it continues far beyond the point required to correct any maladjustment to which it may originally have been due.

7

The League at War and in Pieces, 1939–1940

In August 1939, the League of Nations published a special report, entitled *The Development of International Co-operation in Economic and Social Affairs*, which proposed a radical overhaul of the organization. It came at a critical moment for the League. War in Europe would bring unparalleled political, financial, and logistical challenges. Colonial war in Ethiopia, civil war in Spain, and the start of war in China left the League buckling, and events in 1939 demonstrated conclusively its failure to achieve the primary goal of world peace defined for it by Woodrow Wilson. The report argued that many of the 'really vital problems' of international cooperation did 'not lend themselves to settlement by formal conferences and treaties', and suggested 'the primary object of international co-operation should be rather mutual help than reciprocal contract—above all, the exchange of knowledge and the fruits of experience'.[1] It was the yield of two key reforming tendencies within the League: the first that initiated by Loveday after 1933, consolidated in the 1938 Coordination Committee, chaired by the former Australian Prime Minister, Stanley Bruce; the second that of a small committee, led by Avenol but also chaired by Bruce, on 'The Development of International Co-Operation in Economic and Social Affairs'. (The overlap has caused confusion for historians, who tend to regard the two committees as one.) It is this latter committee that became known as the Bruce Committee.

The two committees were born of shared impulses. The first was to underline the League's pioneering contribution to the creation and dissemination of technical expertise on a huge range of economic and social questions. It sought to shift criticism of its work away from what it regarded as a '1920s' mentality that 'assumed international co-operation necessarily implied international contractual obligations, and that success could be measured by the [number of] new obligations entered into'.[2] The argument also connected to a widespread perception in the League, with world war seemingly inevitable, that the depoliticization of its activities was a matter of survival. In reality, few League members genuinely believed that the League could become an apolitical agent for international cooperation on economic and social affairs. Rather, the EFO's secretariat hoped that the humanitarian dimension of its intellectual programme, and the emergence of a universal

---

[1] League of Nations, *The Development of International Co-operation in Economic and Social Affairs: Report of the Special Committee* (Geneva, 1939), 11.
[2] League of Nations, *The Development of International Co-operation in Economic and Social Affairs*, 11–12.

language of economic and social entitlement, would provide a fresh basis on which diverse individuals and groups within the organization could support it, if for very different reasons.

The second impulse for reform was more evident among the social scientists whose work underpinned the initiative where the drive to improve living standards through international organization reflected a quest for academic freedom. As states, democratic or authoritarian, extended their reach into academic life, this vision offered intellectual freedom and scientific possibilities that were increasingly rare. And the third impulse that gave rise to the Bruce Committee was more long-standing: to give the League renewed relevance. Again, notions of what effectiveness meant to different groups within the organization and to the wider world varied considerably. But all could agree on the importance of economic recovery.

In the autumn of 1939, as the League's very existence hung in the balance, the reform debate also became of particular use to Avenol. His reputation as an administrative reformer was part of the appeal of his appointment as Secretary-General in 1933, but relations between his office and the EFO were troubled, and their cooperation between 1938 and 1939 proved to be superficial and short-lived. By spring 1940, Avenol's and Loveday's apparently shared views on structural reform within the League were unmasked as diametrically opposed, not so much for the organizational changes they suggested as for the political positions that underpinned them. Avenol was revealed as a supporter of Vichy and banished from Geneva, and the technical agencies of the League left Switzerland in a dramatic bid to escape the isolation into which a Nazi-occupied Europe threatened to place them. The struggle between Avenol and the EFO revealed their opposed visions for the future of Europe and the world: the first, embodied in Loveday, was the aspiration to return to the values of economic liberalism of 1920s Europe that were now represented largely in the political ideals embodied in the governance of the United States and Britain; the second, a radical new vision, championed by Avenol, of an authoritarian internationalist 'block centred on Germany, Italy, France and Spain'.[3]

The divided climate within the League and the hostile international environment outside it posed fundamental questions: if, and when, war came, should the League remain in Geneva? Did the organization primarily comprise its buildings and employees, or were the ideas and networks it helped to generate more important to its institutional integrity? How would it cope with fewer members and even less money? And, at the heart of the dilemmas before it: what was the purpose of an organization dedicated to international peace at a time of almost universal war? The answers the League fashioned to these challenges were drawn exclusively from its work in the economic and social fields, offering a radically restructured League and a reinvigorated zeal to reform the world.

---

[3] Livingston to Halifax, 21 June 1940, and minute by Makins, 25 June 1940, TNA: PRO FO371/ 24440, C7391/6953/98.

THE CASE FOR REFORM

The outbreak of war in Europe made Avenol's claim that he intended to set the League on a 'new basis' by reforming it seem perverse.[4] How could the Secretary-General argue it stood on the brink of forging a new framework for diplomacy when much of the world had succumbed to war? Even between the countries that had succeeded in avoiding war, key among them the Americas, the political will for any kind of broad-based international cooperation was missing. But the report of the Special Committee on the Development of International Co-operation in Economic and Social Affairs offered a mature appreciation of the limitations of states when it came to tackling vital and pressing economic, social, and health issues in the language of globalization more typically associated with the early twenty-first century:

The world, for all its political severance, is growing daily closer knit; its means of communication daily more rapid; its instruments for the spread of knowledge daily more efficient. At the same time, the constituent parts of the world, for all their diversity of political outlook, are growing in many respects more similar; agricultural states are becoming rapidly industrialised, industrial states are stimulating their agriculture. Nothing is more striking in this connection, or more characteristic, than the swift development of the great Asiatic countries.[5]

The reform movement within the League had a long and complex history. It was the result of years of frustration within the institution and the different constituencies that supported it. Central among them were the EFO's sections, which had seen initiatives repeatedly thwarted, not just by the governments from which they had come to expect opposition—Germany, Italy, and Japan—but from the League's chief political sponsors. The EFO's efforts to advance to talks on the levels of international protectionism, for example, were met by the fierce and sustained opposition of the British Treasury from 1933 and 1937, while the League was not able to get very much closer to the USA because the intergovernmental (political) structure of the League inhibited greater American involvement.

Although Avenol's credentials as a reformer in the early stages of his career at the League are undisputed, his focus was on efficiency more than efficacy. Once he had been appointed Secretary-General, peace-keeping concerns devoured his time, and his personality and work habits meant discussion of reform was deferred. Although he frequently declared himself partial to League reorganization, he did not develop formal plans for it.[6] Instead, between 1933 and 1938 it was the EFO's secretariat that initiated and maintained the momentum for reform. Its perspective on the

---

[4] Avenol to individual member states of the League of Nations, 25 July 1940, TNA: PRO FO371/24441, C7982/6953/98.

[5] League of Nations, *The Development of International Co-operation in Economic and Social Affairs*, 7.

[6] A view also supported by James Barros, *Betrayal from Within: Joseph Avenol, Secretary-General of the League of Nations, 1933–1940* (New Haven, 1969), 30.

question was very different from Avenol's. The sections' long-standing commitment to bringing economic and financial issues to the fore was strengthened by
their exasperation at the League's political inertia. Their analysis and political
experience had persuaded them of the power and potential of economic coordination, coupled with questions of social welfare, were central to international
peace. The structure and priorities of the League of Nations had to be redesigned
to reflect this recognition. They had facilitated the largely ignored report on League
reform by Viscount Cranborne, Eden's assistant, and it was only as the League
staggered through another international crisis occasioned this time by the event of
full-blown war between Japan and China in 1937 that Avenol stepped in to assist
the EFO's efforts. In January 1938, he asked the Council to create a committee to
study the question of reform, and on 5 May it duly inaugurated the Committee on
the Structure and Functions of the Economic and Financial Organization.

Bruce was made chairman, and the other committee members included Leith-
Ross; Frère; Georges Brunet of France; Caracciolo Parra-Pérez, historian and
Venezuelan minister to Switzerland; Tytus Komarnicki of Poland; Karl Westman
of Sweden; and Humphrey Hume Wrong of Canada, a future Ambassador to
Washington. Also present, though unrecorded in the minutes, was an unnamed
American observer, possibly Pasvolsky, who was invited along by Loveday. As
usual, behind the scenes Loveday and Stoppani sought to steer the committee,
drafting key proposals and preparing the materials that went before it, recruiting
Butler, now retired from the ILO, to help.[7] The absence of political muscle was
unsurprising in the circumstances. The main aim was to generate a viable structure
that would 'save' the organization and at the same time attract American support.
Loveday, in particular, was conscious that the League would need to tread warily if
it wanted to draw the United States further into its activities.

Indeed, in some ways Loveday and Stoppani saw the reform movement as a
jointly orchestrated public offensive between bureaucrats in Geneva and Washington to highlight the League's contribution to international economic and
social relations. They worked closely with members of the State Department,
especially Pasvolsky, and were instrumental in facilitating the visit by Bruce and
McDougall to Washington in December 1938. It was no accident that it was
this trusted duo who were sent to explore American views on the League's
economic, financial and social agenda, just after the Munich Conference and
before Avenol's scheduled appointment at the League exhibition pavilion in the
1939 New York World's Fair. The intention was for Bruce and McDougall to
present the innovative face of the League to Roosevelt's administration. True,
the usual topics of commercial policy and its relationship to the world diplomatic

[7] Memo by Butler, 'Committee on the Development of International Cooperation in Technical, Social and Humanitarian Fields', 4 Aug. 1939, LON R5805, 50/38620/38332. Winant was quietly supportive of moves to give economic and social questions a bigger role in the League, but also anxious to make clear that any changes within the League would not affect 'the autonomy or competence of the ILO'. See Winant to Avenol, 11 Dec. 1939, LON R5805, 50/39259/382332.

crisis were raised: it was the assured route to an audience at the State Department. But the approach of the Australians was very different from that employed by the British Board of Trade in the Anglo-American Trade Agreement negotiations of the same year. In a series of meetings with senior officials of the State Department, including Henry Wallace, the Treasury, the Tariff Commission, the Department of Agriculture, Secretary of State for Labor, Francis Perkins, and leading figures of the Brookings Institute, the Australians spoke of their nation's innovations in nutrition and habits of consumption in the years after 1935, and how these concerns were central to the League. Their message was an effort to heal the divisions between protectionists and free traders, farmers and industrialists, and nationalists and internationalists that had divided Roosevelt's foreign policy since his election in November 1932.

Centre-stage in Bruce's and McDougall's presentation was their emphasis that economic and social policies should be developed together with a common stress on 'living standards'. This approach of 'Positive Security', far more than the 'abstract' topics of monetary and trade diplomacy, could revive the interest and enthusiasm of what they called 'common people' in the work of the League and international cooperation more generally. Using a rhetoric that also tapped into FDR's New Deal, Bruce and McDougall proposed to the Americans that the League should now pursue a 'bottom-up' rather than a 'top-down' approach to diplomacy in an attempt to reinvigorate the popular appeal that accompanied the organization's foundation.[8] Its new mission would be to show 'average people' how their living conditions were affected by their governments' policies; they could then shape their own lives, national politics, and ultimately the wider world from this new, more informed perspective. The League's initiative on nutrition, Bruce and McDougall argued, was a perfect case in point. It was a topic to which 'all men and their families' could relate, and was connected to key issues in international trade. (That the failures in agricultural politics had had explosive consequences for democratic politics was readily apparent to speaker and audience.) The Australians then outlined how the EFO had developed a 'new approach' to economic diplomacy in recent years. In McDougall's words, 'the new technique was to assist nations in the solution of national problems by means of an international inquiry followed by a report to Governments containing suggestions and recommendations'. The EFO's role was 'to act as a clearing house of information and as a focal point for discussion', a necessary step to generate the transnational and international support for any agreement. This was sophistry. The language of planning and development suggested coherence in the evolution of the EFO's strategy in the 1930s, whereas the change in emphasis from conference diplomacy and multilateral agreements, to one founded on popular appeal coupled with 'scientific inquiry', had to do with frustration as much as utility. The approach had also been designed to lure the United States further into cooperation with the League, given the increasingly

---

[8] A. J. Badger, *The New Deal: The Depression Years, 1933–1940* (London, 1990), 146–97; Michael Parrish, *Anxious Decades. America in Prosperity and Depression, 1920–1941* (New York, 1992), 405–20.

apparent shortcomings of British internationalism since 1931. All the same, the recognition that economic diplomacy was a conversation rather than a fixed agreement was a potent one.[9]

Notably, Bruce and McDougall emphasized how the nutrition inquiry had generated a remodelled policy language for agricultural production and trade policy, which considered both national and international perspectives. It had stressed that industrialized countries should concentrate their agricultural production on milk and fruit to meet their domestic markets for perishables, but, for the good of their own economies and the wider world, they should produce less wheat, sugar, and cereals. Had the League's recommendation been taken up, the positive implications for the world and US economy were obvious: increased levels of trade for primary producers; and increased levels of exports for industrial economies, for, as the poor became wealthier, so they would be more able to buy exports. Tariff barriers and quotas would gradually fall away, and the world would be set fair on the virtuous circle towards freer trade. The way out of persistent protectionist logjams that snarled up international trade relations would be internationally negotiated schemes to regulate the production and trade of particular commodities, notably wheat and sugar.

It was a canny presentation, carefully tailored to the needs of the US administration. The liberal rhetoric and pro-trade stance were designed to appeal to the State Department, while the commodity agreements and the sensitivity to price levels sugared the pill for the Agricultural and Treasury departments. Bruce's own views on the need for greater international sensitivity to the needs of primary producers had evolved since his speech at the World Conference of 1933, which had been a thinly veiled attack on British trade policy and the failed promise of the Ottawa agreements.[10] Now he and the EFO presented freer trade as a development best secured by tying it closely to social policies that would safeguard the well-being of the poor members of society. An altered pattern of production, coupled with social policies intended to ameliorate the worst effects of free trade, would enable countries to drop protective barriers and reintegrate their economies into the international economy as a whole.

Bruce's political make-up, as Australian nationalist, Anglophile, and League enthusiast, made him an ideal recruit to the cause of reform. He, like FDR, could be a 'chameleon on plaid'—Herbert Hoover's famous description of his successor. In Australian politics Bruce was famed for being the most 'British' of Australian Prime Ministers, but in the League he was distinguished by his commitment to internationalism. He was certainly well connected in Britain, but he was regarded with suspicion in some quarters, notable the Treasury, because of his role in Commonwealth and European politics where he was close to the free-trading Dutch. Bruce also had a complicated relationship with Avenol, as did anyone who

---

[9] Memo by Bruce, 'Visit to Washington: 19 December to 23 December 1938', undated, NARA RG59, SD 500.C1191nutrition, 144½.

[10] Dubin, 'Towards the Bruce Report', 48.

sought to reaffirm and strengthen the liberal internationalist mission of the League at the expense of its proclaimed universalism.

A pledge to reform the League had been part of Avenol's election platform as Secretary-General, and had formed the basis of stalled initiatives in 1935 and 1936. Yet ultimately it was Loveday, rather than Avenol or Bruce, who drove the cause of reform forward.[11] He, and his colleagues in the Economic and Financial Sections were determined that international economic policy should connect to 'social reality', a view that was influenced by extensive consultation with senior figures within the US administration—a process coordinated by Loveday and Sweetser— including Francis Perkins, Henry Morgenthau Junior, Sumner Welles, Pasvolsky, Hull, and FDR, stretching back many years.[12] Bruce's diplomatic experience, coupled with his long-standing commitment to a form of socially responsible economic liberalism and Loveday's and Stoppani's confidence in him, made the urbane Australian the ideal public face for the renewed reform agenda. He also had the support of key national groups within the League. It was also not true, as Dubin claimed, that 'the Britishers' were uniformly hostile to notions of a League reformed around a combined economic and social agenda. Some members in the British camp were in favour of the initiative. The Foreign Office was broadly supportive, and Leith-Ross, too, frequently risked Chamberlain's ire by stressing that League policy on trade and commerce should now always seek to address the issue 'from the standard of living angle'.[13]

The reform initiative appeared to have support in the highest quarters in the USA. In May 1938, Roosevelt had told Sweetser that the League should 'abandon its political activities', disband the Council, and concentrate on non-political questions. As usual, Sweetser's enthusiasm for the League and his aspiration for a more internationalist White House prompted him to exaggerate the significance of this remark. It was highly probable, he concluded in a report to Avenol and Loveday, that the USA might join an 'independent Economic and Financial Organisation'.[14] Given FDR's highly sensitive antennae to domestic opinion, this was never likely, but it did no harm to the reform movement if other League members believed it, and it remains unclear what FDR understood by the word 'politics' in this context. Loveday and his colleagues certainly never believed politics

[11] Dubin's account is confused and his argument disregards an important clue buried within his own discussion where he notes that the Committee on the Structure and Functions of the Economic and Financial Organization accepted 'a report Loveday had drafted even before the committee had met'. Dubin, 'Towards the Bruce Report', 53.
[12] For an account of the negotiations surrounding the visit, see Sweetser to Avenol, 22 Mar. 1939, AMAE, Papiers Argents: Avenol, vol. 30, États-Unis (1933–40). The volume includes Pasvolsky's proposal for reform, where he argued it would be 'very effective if several branches of the League work, while still remaining grouped around a common centre and Secretariat could, now that each of them has developed a considerable law, tradition and personnel of its own, be given a somewhat autonomous status whereby States non-Members of the League might be able to co-operate on a basis of full equality, as the United States now does in the Labor Office and might do in the Court'. He even imagined a fixed date for annual meetings in Geneva on technical questions, arguing it would provide non-member states with a great possibility for cooperation.
[13] Harpham to Charron, 9 Jan. 1939, LON R4422, 10A/32974/32974.
[14] Sweetser quoted in Dubin, 'Towards the Bruce Report', 54.

could be taken out of issues like trade protection, measures to tackle unemployment, agricultural production, public works schemes, or monetary cooperation. Loveday's intention was to limit the power of 'rogue' states that sabotaged the work of the League, and reinforce the role of the USA. It is likely that FDR had the same understanding. The language and thinking of the time were reflected in the nomenclature and structure of the League, where 'political' activities encompassed disarmament and the peace-keeping activities of the Council and the Assembly. The 'technical activities' on the League, on the other hand, covered the activities of the EFO, the LNHO, and divisions, for example, concerned with intellectual cooperation. Yet these could hardly be described as apolitical.[15]

The pro-reform circles in the League, alongside foreign office officials in Britain, France, and the Netherlands sympathetic to the cause, professed they were greatly encouraged by the enthusiasm with which Bruce's and McDougall's proposals had been received in Washington. Hull had spoken before of his support for the work of the Economic Committee in 'very warm terms', but he now announced America was all in favour of 'more economic co-operation' with the League.[16] His praise was not merely expressed privately, but was declared to the American public and to the key allies in Central and South America at the Pan-American Conference in February 1939. 'The League of Nations has been responsible', the Secretary of State declared, 'for the development of mutual exchange and discussion of ideas and methods to a greater extent and in more fields of humanitarian and scientific endeavour than any other organisation in history'.[17] The language was fulsome and commendation carefully crafted and 'approved all the way up' to the President.[18]

The 'tone of unreserved cordiality, not at all characteristic of the State Department', surprised the British Foreign Office, which was vigilant for any sign of US internationalism that would favour Britain. But any warmth League reform might have engendered across the Atlantic was promptly undone by a characteristic icy blast from Chamberlain, who, in the same week, challenged Hull to translate his enthusiasm into greater financial support.[19] More substantial were the concerns of the British Foreign Office. It worried about the likely implications this new, publicly expressed pro-League, and particularly pro-EFO, position would have on Congressional opinion and American public opinion more generally. Would it help the League or Britain or France? Or would it further impede Roosevelt's ability to help those at risk from Axis aggression? And had the Prime Minister's response increased the risk?[20]

---

[15] See Andrew Webster, 'The Transnational Dream: Politicians, Diplomats and Soldiers in the League of Nations' Pursuit of International Disarmament', *Contemporary European History*, 14/4 (2005), 493–518.
[16] Harpham to Charron, 9 Jan. 1939, LON R4422, 10A/32974/32974.
[17] League of Nations, *The Development of International Co-operation in Economic and Social Affairs*, 17.
[18] Sweetser to Avenol, 22 Feb. 1939, AMAE, Papiers Argents: Avenol, vol. 30, États-Unis (1933–40).
[19] Walters to Randall, 23 Feb. 1939, TNA: PRO FO371/24038, W3660.
[20] The Foreign Office's gloomy mood deepened by Chamberlain's declared unwillingness to discuss trade and monetary issues and their relationship to peace with the US government. See Walters to

But American and League horizons were set beyond those of an emerging 'special relationship', and were motivated, in part, by the need for some good publicity: Avenol because his leadership was under increasing pressure, and Hull because supporting the League's economic work on protectionism was part of a wider ambition to show American solidarity with the values of democracy threatened in Europe and the Far East. American internationalism was still nascent, and attempts to encourage it could easily backfire. Smuts anticipated the problem, writing to Cecil that 'action from the British side' on behalf of the League 'may not prove helpful'; America's attitude to the League was more likely to be modified 'by world events now transpiring in the East' than by the actions of the League itself.[21]

In the event, however, while the Munich Agreement and its aftermath prompted Roosevelt's break with appeasement and cemented the USA's move to a foreign policy that sought national security through a global strategy, America's attitude towards the League was not so much transformed as transmuted into plans for a new international organization. The opaque quality of FDR's diplomacy frustrated many, including Loveday. In March 1939, he tried to draw the Americans into the open, penning a strongly worded memorandum for the Depression Delegation on the German system of trade and exchange controls, which posited that Germany would have to go to war in the near future to keep the whole system from collapse.[22] It triggered a stark response from Henry Grady, who argued that German economics flew in the face of current US trade policy, which was 'the only one consistent with democracy and free enterprise in international relations'.[23] The exchange caused a sensation at the forty-ninth (and as it turned out penultimate) meeting of the Economic Committee, which opened in Geneva on 27 March 1939. Not only had Grady's words been sanctioned by Hull and FDR: the former took the opportunity to call for a new tough commercial policy towards the totalitarian states. It was time to go on the counter-offensive, establishing a preferential trading group of countries that understood the meaning of fair play; conditions of entry to this club included abandoning exchange controls and reducing levels of protectionism.

But discussions did not get very far.[24] Only the Finns and Australians declared themselves broadly in favour of Grady's plan. The general view, however, was that now was not the time for a radical solution to the problem of blocked accounts. Representatives from Hungary, Romania, Poland, Yugoslavia, and Belgium warmly agreed, but offered a different spin: when it came to trade, they countered, Germany was the country offering the guarantees, while their trade with France,

Randall, 23 Feb. 1939, and minute by Randall, 28 Feb.1939, TNA: PRO FO371/24038, W3600, and *Hansard*, House of Commons, 27 Feb.1939, vol. 344, cols 890–1.

[21] Smuts to Cecil, 6 Dec. 1938, TNA: PRO FO371/24038, W3383.

[22] It was a conclusion recently reconfirmed by Adam Tooze, *The Wages of Destruction: The Making and Breaking of the Nazi Economy* (London, 2006). 285–367.

[23] Grady to Secretariat and members of Economic Committee, 25 Mar. 1939, LON, Princeton Office, C1737/ No.1 (2), 35–9.

[24] Report on the Work of the Economic Committee submitted to the Council on 23 May 1939, League of Nations, *Official Journal* (May–June 1939), 229–301.

Britain, the USA, and the Netherlands continued to decline. This was certainly not the moment, the Hungarian Alfred de Nickl declared, for the EFO to publish a report that put political considerations above economic ones. De Nickl was wrong on two counts: in 1939, economics was politics, and this was precisely the time to put politics before economics. There were not to be many such moments left to the League, as the rump of Czechoslovakia remaining after the butchery of the Munich agreement was absorbed into the German Empire. For several weeks afterwards, there was continued deliberation of Grady's proposal in Britain and France. Their responses were characteristically uncoordinated, but were remarkably similar. Both declared themselves willing to cooperate with the Americans and to see a reduction in trade and exchange control. The langauge was emollient: had France itself not proposed a bloc of '*états bon payeurs*' in 1933? But Grady's proposal would only damage relations between countries who were politically willing but economically unable to join. In France, Grady's proposal triggered an extended consideration on a theoretical and practical level as to the nature of commercial relations between free market and exchange control economies. These were questions the country was to face again in more urgent form after the fall of France in 1940, and, like the rest of the world, with the onset of the cold war: could two opposing economic systems coexist, or would one inevitably yield to the other, for either political or economic reasons, as Grady had implied? Did bilateral arrangements between competing systems ultimately weaken free market economies? Was compromise of any kind by free market economies with a totalitarian economy evidence of weakness on their part? Perhaps economic pressure on totalitarian states, rather than concession, was the basis on which international trade would reach a more profitable basis for all concerned? Were not the key weapons of war economic, and was now the time to make a stand in EFO and the League more generally?[25]

While members deliberated, time was running out, and the EFO was in deep trouble. And always, when trouble runs deeps, it comes in a variety of forms: the first was the EFO's rapidly deteriorating relations with Avenol and the Secretary-General's increasingly erratic and unpredictable behaviour; the second was war in Europe, and the now unavoidable question of whether there was any future for the League and multilateral cooperation at a time when the world was almost completely divided into warring parts.

THE 'BRUCE REPORT'

After March 1939, the reform process was overshadowed by actions of Avenol, who has been viewed variously by historians as attempting to dissolve the League to save Swiss neutrality or as trying to bring it into the fold of the totalitarian powers in

---

[25] Memo by Elbel and comments by the Sous-Direction de la SDN at the Quai d'Orsay, 31 Mar. 1939, AMAE, Relations Commerciales/Société des Nations/ B.83 sd VI, Comité Économique, 1 Feb. 1938–1 July 1939.

1940. As we have seen, the protracted reform process was motivated and shaped, in particular, by the frustration of the EFO secretariat with the failure of multilateral diplomacy to combat the Great Depression, and by the world's inability to address the ever-expanding gap between rich and poor economies after 1933.[26] Avenol's role in the reform movement of 1938 and 1940, on the other hand, is more difficult to assess, because his interventions were characterized by a strange mixture of laziness and audacity that typified his career.[27]

In the spring of 1939, the Secretary-General became an inconsistent force in an unreliable world. The escalation of tension between the Axis powers and Europe's remaining democracies triggered by the invasion of Prague on 14–15 March, Mussolini's threat of war with France on 26 March, and Britain's guarantee of Polish security, rounded off by Mussolini's invasion of Albania, which prompted British guarantees to Greece and Romania, demarcated the lines of military engagement. War was now widely predicted, but there were still surprises, none bigger than the announcement of the Nazi–Soviet Pact in August 1939. New turns in the increasingly twisted world of international relations were replicated in Avenol's erratic behaviour in the small world of Geneva. On 11 April, the Secretary-General suddenly abandoned his plans for meetings with the American administration in New York timed to coincide with the opening of the League of Nations' pavilion. He declared he could not leave Geneva at a time when there was a chance that Axis forces might use the League as a pretext to violate Swiss neutrality, invade the country, and seize the League. There was as much intelligence to support this fantasy as there was truth in Avenol's grandiloquent claim that, if an emergency arose, 'the presence of the chief often had an encouraging effect'.[28] During the next eighteen months the opposite happened. Avenol's presence served only to demoralize and to endanger the League.

The formalities of the planned visit were still observed: Avenol's speech to the world's fair was read by the head of the Secretariat's Information Section, Adrianus Pelt, and the various League, foreign, and American officials assembled in New York and Washington praised the League's contribution to 'human welfare' rather than world peace. But Avenol's determination to remain in Geneva, and the public reasons he gave for it, infuriated some of his colleagues in the secretariat, who argued there was not much the Secretary-General could do from Switzerland, and the likelihood of war made it all the more important to build cooperative bridges with the United States. In April and May 1939, there were other aspects to Avenol's diplomacy that smacked more of burning bridges than building them. Inside the

[26] Dubin and Barros explored the reform process through the committee instituted by Avenol in May 1939 and understandably missed the wider context, and the EFO's leading role, in shaping the proposed change. Those working primarily from the papers of Bruce and Avenol have naturally emphasized their role as actors. Bruce's biographer Cumpston, similarly, was wrong to see the Australian as a prime mover. Bruce was an effective public spokesman, but the intellectual force behind the special committee on the Development of International Co-operation in Economic and Social Affairs was drawn from within the EFO.

[27] Barros, *Betrayal from Within*, 20–1.

[28] Bucknall on conversation with Avenol, 11 Apr. 1939, reported to Hull, and Hull to Avenol, 19 Apr. 1939, NARA RG 59, 500.C113/174–5.

League, Avenol dismissed the suggestion of Deputy Secretary-General, Sean Lester, that the League should be used 'as a rallying point' for anti-Axis forces and Loveday's notion that the League could facilitate reconstruction. If war broke out, Avenol argued, League staff numbers would need to be further reduced and he predicted that, in the event of a German invasion of Poland, 'the majority of states would remain neutral'. In Avenol's view, it was essential that the League stay neutral too: 'it should not be used as an instrument of the belligerents.'[29] Despite the Axis powers' consistent violation of international treaties and conventions, and the values embodied both in the League and in international law, for Avenol neutrality meant that the League should never take sides. It carried the implication that, once at war, states might not just opt to rescind their membership of the League; they might relinquish their right to it. The position of the EFO's secretariat was very different. It had been openly critical of the economic and financial policies of the Axis for some time and, in effect, demanded that the League stand for certain principles and beliefs. This meant taking sides with the Allies.

In the fevered climate of the Palais des Nations, declaring the League should support one side over the other was a risky business. The dismissal of Avenol's long-time chef de cabinet, the Frenchman Marcel Hoden, for his allegedly having 'opinions for mobilization, for war' in October 1938 caused a sensation.[30] Since January 1939, Avenol had overseen the work of the Axe Committee, which sacked more than 300 men and women during the course of the year, although the overall picture remains unclear as to who left out of choice and who was fired. When Avenol told the State Department of his renewed intention to dismiss fifty to sixty members of the League's secretariat, he made the startling claim that these cuts were a result of the British and French governments 'bringing pressure on the Secretary-General to "purge" the Secretariat of officials who [had] leftist tendencies or who for other reasons [had] been outspoken in their reply to the dictatorships'.[31] There is no evidence to support this claim, and the criteria for the redundancies were determined by Avenol. What was not in any doubt was that the League was in serious financial difficulties because of member withdrawals and because members wanted to reduce their, already small, contributions. In December 1938, Avenol told Halifax that only 87 per cent of the League's contributions for the year had been received.[32]

The combination of financial and political pressures explains Avenol's decision in May 1939 to seize control of the reform agenda that was formally the responsibility of the Committee on the Structure and Functions of the Economic and Financial Organization. At a private meeting of the Council on 23 May, he proposed the Council set up 'a very small committee of persons qualified by their experience' to report in September 1939. He declared his intention was to build on

[29] Bucknall on conversation with Avenol, 11 Apr. 1939, reported to Hull, and Hull to Avenol, 19 Apr. 1939, NARA RG 59, 500.C113/174–5.

[30] Barros, *Betrayal from Within*, 174–84.

[31] Bucknell to Hull, 28 Oct. 1938, NARA, RG 59, 500.C113/160.

[32] Barros, *Betrayal from Within*, 186.

the dialogue 'so happily inaugurated with the United States' and requested Council to authorize him, in conjunction with Bruce, who would chair the committee, to select the other members.[33] Not only did these actions violate the procedures by which committee membership was normally determined; the committee also lacked a fixed directive. Avenol offered only generalities: the committee should devise appropriate organizational changes to make economic and social collaboration more effective and to promote active participation in the League's work by all nations (that is, whether they were members of the League or not). Though he agreed to be chairman, Bruce was uneasy about the way Avenol had imposed himself on the reform agenda, especially as the Secretary-General had informed neither Bruce nor Loveday of his proposal before putting it to Council, and Bruce was anxious that the manner of its launch, as well as the direction of the Secretary-General's scheme, 'might kill the political side of the League without giving birth to anything new'.[34]

Reluctantly therefore, and only after seeking the advice of the British Foreign Office, did Bruce accept the nomination. He was joined on the committee by Daniel Serruys; Francisco Tudela; Maurice Bourquin, a Belgian diplomat and professor at the University of Geneva; Helio Lobo, from Brazil, representing a non-member state; and Wrong, the only survivor of the Structure and Functions Committee. France and Norway, recognizing the importance of the agenda and dangers before the committee, rejected Avenol's suggested nominations, and insisted on more senior representation. France chose Charles Rist, the pre-eminent French economist and president of the Scientific Institute for Economic and Social Research in Paris, and the Scandinavian countries agreed on Carl J. Hambro, president of the Norwegian Sorting and chairman of the League's Supervisory Commission. He was joined by Kyriakos Varvaressos, former finance minister, and deputy governor of the Bank of Greece. Two key nations were missing—the USA and Great Britain, although under the terms of the committee they were free to contribute members.

These national delegates, like Bruce and Loveday, were primarily interested in preserving and promoting the League's economic work, not in reform *per se*. The State Department, too, made it clear to Pelt that any reorganization of the League's work should not be too explicit about facilitating the participation of non-member states. The risks to both parties were financial, political, and practical. Between 1936 and 1937, the United States had contributed some $15,000 to cover American participation in League meetings. The money had come from a general Congressional fund with no awkward questions asked. If Avenol issued an open invitation to Washington to discuss its reorganization, and this were refused by Congress, then the State Department would no longer be in a position to make financial contributions as before. Indeed, any kind of cooperation would become impossible, and the Americans were clearly interested in continued involvement.

---

[33] Dubin overlooks this key (dis)junction in the Bruce Report's history. Dubin,'Towards the Bruce Report', 56.

[34] Loveday to Tyler, 5 July 1939, LON R4422, 10A/32974/32974.

Their commitment to the League's technical agenda was long established, and their support for the reform agenda was made apparent again in a series of high-level meetings with Pelt.

If the US administration wanted to participate actively in the debate on the reform of the League, but desisted for fear of the potential political fallout, especially in an election year, the British did not want to take part at all. There was suspicion on both sides of the Atlantic. Treasury opposition to much of the League's economic agenda was long established, so the attempt to reinforce its economic activities, and to couple them with the organization's social agenda, was likely to engender fresh hostility. Leith-Ross, back from his failed diplomatic mission in China, was of little help this time, and the Foreign Office, often a source of support to Loveday and to the League more generally, was now under the leadership of a hostile Halifax rather than the League-friendly Eden. Lord Cranborne's historic involvement with the reform agenda made him a natural participant, but he was ill, and Avenol, for reasons of his own, did not try too hard to find a British replacement. It was left to Harold Butler, now warden of Nuffield College, Oxford, to nominate himself in late July 1939. Throughout the negotiations, the Treasury and the Foreign Office made their suspicion of Avenol's motives clear. Unlike the French, they had recognized that Avenol's new committee effectively usurped the power of the Co-ordination Committee, also chaired by Bruce, but led by the EFO.[35] (The Co-ordination Committee closed up shop on 24 June.)[36] The Foreign Office was worried also that Avenol's preoccupation with membership was not really directed so much at recruiting the United States: reinvolving Germany, Italy, and Spain might be the prize he was truly pursuing.[37] British fears were not allayed by the decision to hold the new committee's meetings in Paris.[38] Nor was Vladimir Pastuhov's explanation reassuring: it was 'a means of insulating the committee from the unwanted influences in the secretariat and permanent government missions stationed in Geneva'.[39]

Rumour and suspicion dogged the committee meeting held from 7 to 12 August 1939. Avenol insisted no minutes at all be taken, but covert discussion between Loveday and Lester reveal the rising tensions within the League, and the demarcations that were to appear dramatically between its personnel during the crisis of 1940.[40] Before the first meeting, Avenol declared his central aim was to 'extend and make more efficient in the widest possible sense international co-operation in the technical and social fields . . . as an

---

[35] Note by Sous-Directeur de la SDN of the Quai D'Orsay, 9 June 1939, AMAE, SDN/ IJ-Questions Économiques/Organisation Économique et Financière/Comité économique/Composition Comité économique/Réunions intermistérielles, 1926–40, 1937–9, no. 1172.

[36] Report of the Co-ordination Committee, 24 June 1939, LON R4468, 10A/38576/38576.

[37] Walters to Randall, 29 June 1939, TNA: PRO FO371/24039, W10161.

[38] Hill to Wilson, 9 June 1939, LON R5805, 50/38247/38247.

[39] Dubin, 'Towards the Bruce Report', 58.

[40] Loveday was sent early drafts of Avenol's preparatory papers by Lester. See memo by Hill, 'Rough Notes of Meetings of Bruce Cttee, 1939', LON, Hill P84/1–15, 1937–46.

important component of peace and to strengthen the position of the League'. It is worth quoting at length for it draws out the problems—and at the same time the appeal—of his approach:

All States who desire to collaborate in this work, whether Members of the League or not, should feel that they can do so without having to take into consideration any possible repercussions of a political character. They should feel that they have at their disposal a machinery which it is a part of their normal administrative action to use at every point where the national administration finds the need of consultation of the international aspect of any question which it may be considering.[41]

There was common ground here with ideas floated in 1937 and 1938 by the EFO, but Avenol's view that reform should 'clear away all hesitations based on the idea that co-operation in this [economic and social] work involves political commitments' was not one Loveday or his section shared. They were all too aware of the many political dimensions to economic and social policy, and that ultimately political commitment was required to make any economic or financial agreement binding and effective.[42]

It is clear from Avenol's correspondence in 1939 with the directors of all the League Sections that his main preoccupation was membership not reform. He asked them for an analysis of their organizations' work based on a comparison of the impact of member with non-member states, and asked them to differentiate between the role of countries that had never joined the League and those that had recently surrendered their membership. The tone of Loveday's response to the question of 'defection' (his word) was uncompromising when it came to Germany, Italy, and Japan: they did not cooperate with the EFO; nor had they done so to any measurable degree for almost a decade. This contrasted with the behaviour of South American countries which had recently rescinded their membership of the League to save money and in the wake of improved relations with the USA (the main target of their foreign policies). They continued to work with the EFO, sending in statistical and other intelligence. Of the non-member states, the USA, Brazil, Chile, Venezuela, Peru, and Hungary all enjoyed membership of various EFO committees. But there were also drawbacks to this type of participation: they had no representation in the Assembly and Council, which meant they could not initiate new projects in the EFO; and, aside from ad hoc contributions, they did not share in the EFO's running costs, which was a topic very much at the forefront of everyone's mind.

---

[41] See memo by Secretary-General Avenol, 'Committee on the Development of International Co-operation in Technical, Social and Humanitarian Fields', 6 July 1939, TNA: PRO FO371/24039, W11041. The word 'humanitarian' was suggested for the title by Hill. For an earlier draft, see memo by Hill, 'Rough Notes of Meetings of Bruce Cttee, 1939', LON, Hill P84/1–15, 1937–46.
[42] Dubin is insensitive to these differences and credits Avenol with views on this issue that were largely Loveday's. Compare Dubin, 'Towards the Bruce Report', 64, with Avenol to Loveday, Renborg, Rasmus Skylstad, Eugène Vigier, Branko Lukac, and Raymond Gautier, 5 July 1939, LON R5805, 50/38743/38332; and memo by Avenol, 6 July 1939, 'Committee on the Development of International Co-operation in Technical, Social and Humanitarian Fields', TNA: PRO FO371/24039, W11041.

These first two obstacles were well known and, as we have seen, the EFO's secretariat had evolved effective ways to circumvent them by consulting widely with non-members with whom it was interested in cooperating, and taking the initiative in launching new projects via the Second Committee. The EFO had also proven an effective fund-raiser from private sources. A more serious obstacle, to Loveday's mind, was the fact that non-members could not be represented in the secretariat, which, of course, he regarded as the real driving force behind the League. He believed that the current constitution of the League was a problem because the 'political body' of the League was something 'of which many states now were shy' when it came to collaboration in economic and financial questions. 'It is this fact and not the absence of Italy, Germany and Japan that is serious to us, for Italy, Germany and Japan are not really prepared to co-operate at all in international affairs.'[43] Loveday repeated this point a number of times in his response to Avenol, probably because he expected it to be ignored. It was further evidence of the suspicion with which he viewed the Secretary's new enthusiasm for constitutional reform.

When it came to restructuring, Loveday reiterated his view that the 'obvious solution was to separate the EFO from the political League body' (this sentence surfaced *verbatim* in the final report). But he went further than Avenol's proposal to offer 'associated non-Member status', which would give non-members the right to direct the League's economic, financial, health, and social work independently of Council and Assembly oversight. Instead, he proposed creating a new Central Committee as the coordinating body (no one picked up on the irony of the soviet-style nomenclature), coupled with an obligation to pay contributions to support these 'technical bodies'. Loveday argued that the concept of 'membership' had to be interpreted more broadly. It needed to become more inclusive, moving away from politicians at the head of a government and 'fonctionnaires at the bottom'—the former were 'ignorant' and the latter 'too expert to be constructive'. He demanded that, if economic and social cooperation were to be moved to the heart of the League's work, then a reorganized EFO must also comprise representatives from 'those occupations or interests whose personal income is directly affected by the correct solution of economic and financial problems'. The ambition and deliberately inclusive language was evocative both of the League's early claims to promote international democracy, and of the constitution of the ILO.[44] But, at the same time, it did not mean that Loveday believed there was more than one path to economic prosperity and social stability. The Great Depression had cemented in his mind the 'correct solution': a liberal trading regime and floating currencies pegged eventually in a flexible arrangement in relation to gold were essential, supported by social policies to ameliorate some of the

---

[43] Loveday to Lester, 11 July 1939, LON R5805, 50/38743/38332.
[44] At the news that Arnal was urging Rist to encourage the League Organizing Committee to allow employer organizations and labour unions to join the Central Committee, the ILO for the first time expressed its concern that the EFO was now straying into its territory. See Arnal to the Quai d'Orsay, 13 Dec. 1939, AMAE, Série SDN, Questions Économiques/Organisation Économique et Financier/ Œuvre économique et financière de la SDN, 1939–40, no. 1156.

potentially challenging effects of market liberalism on social cohesion and political stability. He believed in the power of scientific expertise and democratic debate to persuade doubters.

For all this to happen, Loveday argued that the League needed to establish an entirely fresh legal foundation, one free from the shadow of the Treaty of Versailles. The Assembly committees, too, he suggested, required reform so that their work could become a rolling process rather than a series of meetings that culminated in an annual conference. Loveday proposed that, at the first meeting of any future Assembly committee, government representatives should nominate particular states that would, in turn, identify non-governmental representatives from industry, commerce, finance, labour, agricultural, and consumer interest groups at a second meeting. From this arrangement it followed that any meetings and all activities would involve more non-governmental than governmental representation. National governments, however, would still have an important voice, because they would be in charge of the budget committee for the conferences. (It is hard to imagine that the responsibility for raising and managing the budget would make up for the loss of political control that Loveday's scheme envisaged.) The policies developed at the conference would then be pursued by its selected government and non-governmental representatives in the Central Committee. This final recommendation was regarded as fundamental by Loveday. The Central Committee would provide an important element of continuity and, equally significantly, facilitate change, liberating the League from the 'vicious circle of the same old gentlemen' that had come to dominate its diplomacy. His proposal offered 'an automatic procedure by which the younger coming men in different countries may be drawn into international affairs'.[45]

Loveday was consulted by the other heads of section, who used his memorandum as the basis of their reply to Avenol.[46] Only Bertil Renborg, head of the Opium Section, struck a different note, reporting that, although Germany, Italy, and Japan had ceased to be active members of the Opium Section, Germany still fulfilled some of the obligations of the convention and sent in annual reports. Spain, Hungary, many South American countries, and the United States, all non-members of the League, were still involved. Indeed, the USA was its most active participant, which was facilitated by the fact that the Central Opium Board was not formally part of the League; in short, the board made great play of its independence. This and the fact that, as Renborg noted, 'opium activities are largely based on international conventions already ratified and accepted by practically all States [meant that] the international structure of the Drug organization is already a fait accompli'.[47]

The exchanges between the Secretary-General and his heads of section in August exposed the difference in emphasis between Avenol, who was preoccupied with the

---

[45] There were strong echoes here of Loveday's memos on EFO reform presented in early 1938. See Loveday to Lester, 11 July 1939, LON R5805, 50/38743/38332.
[46] See Hill's summary of the replies, undated, LON R5805, 50/38743/38332.
[47] Renborg to Lester, 18 July 1939, LON 5805, 50/38743/388332.

issue of nation states' membership and all that followed from it, and Loveday, who, leading the heads of section on questions of reform, was much more interested in foregrounding the economic and social work of the League, and opening it to a wider constituency. This message was advanced even more vehemently by Butler, who argued that the new structure proposed by Loveday would enable the League to reconnect with a public who were largely unaware it 'dealt with the great economic problems of the day apart from its publications, which are highly valued in technical circles but are above the heads of the ordinary public'. Butler's language was forthright:

In normal times, a gradual transformation might be carried out over a number of years. In present circumstances, patching and tinkering will not meet the situation. The impression produced by an apparently half-hearted effort will not be such as to restrain the departure of doubtful members or to encourage the approach of non-member states. Nor will it strike the imagination of what a large section of the public in many countries which still cling to its faith in the League and is looking for some outward sign of revival.[48]

These were bold words, but Avenol's decision to hold committee meetings in Paris were widely read as a sign of weakness, not strength. Rumour and counter-rumour as to what was truly afoot dogged proceedings, and Butler complained there was a 'nauseating' preoccupation with position of the totalitarian powers.[49] The air was so thick with desperation and mistrust during the discussions the delegates could almost taste it. Members of the committee saw only risks before them, succinctly summarized by Hill: any suggested reforms should not change the legal basis of the League because these would require external ratification, which in turn would lead to new and dangerous debates 'on the principle of League membership'; any new autonomous organization, even if it were to 'offer temporary stimulus to inter-national co-operation on economic, social and humanitarian questions', might not be in the interests of the League in the long run.

But there was to be no long run.[50] The committee's report was issued on 22 August, published simultaneously in English, French, Spanish, Portuguese, and Norwegian, and disseminated widely and promptly. But it was wasted effort. As the US State Department put it, the important questions the report posed and sought to answer about the future arrangement of international relations were secondary to the immediate question before the world: 'war or no war'.[51] The day after the USA thanked the League for the report, Hitler invaded Poland, and further meetings to consider the document were immediately cancelled.

[48] Memo by Butler, 'Committee on the Development of International Co-operation in Technical, Social and Humanitarian Fields', 4 Aug. 1939, LON R5805, 50/38620/38332.

[49] Minute by Butler, 27 July 1939, TNA: PRO FO371/24039, W11041. Speculation abroad focused less on the issue of 'American membership', words forbidden by the US administration, than on the prospect that Avenol was seeking some sort of accommodation with the totalitarian powers.

[50] Memo by Hill, 'Objectives and Pitfalls: Rough notes of the Bruce Cttee.', c.10 Aug. 1939, LON, Hill P84/1–15, 1937–46.

[51] McDougall reflecting the wider reaction to the Bruce Report in the State Department. McDougall to Moffa, 30 Aug. 1939, NARA RG59, 500.C/995.

The report, drawing on materials prepared by Loveday, was, in his words, intended to 'tell our story and [be] a picture of our achievements', and the successes it identified reflected the EFO's determination to place economic cooperation centre-stage and highlighted its work on commercial policy, nutrition, economic depression, demography, the standard of living, finance, and accomplishments in the 'social field—health, drug trafficking and the welfare of women and children'. Financial cooperation on taxation and exchange control, for example, was also folded into the economic sphere, while important League work on more contentious topics, such as the treatment of refugees and trusteeship, were missing from the list. It was only after the history of the League's contribution to social and economic relations was told that the report moved on to the proposed reforms, although it was these that grabbed the headlines at the time and have held the historical imagination since.[52]

Predominant in the Bruce Report's case for institutional change was the intention to give powers that were not members of the League the opportunity to 'co-operate to the fullest extent' in its work. For the American historian Dubin, the report's novelty lay in its emphasis on American participation. But the EFO's entire history was characterized by efforts to involve the Americans as far as possible, and Barros's account of Avenol's attempts to accommodate Nazi Germany and Vichy France in 1940 makes it difficult to interpret the Secretary-General's position so generously. Nor was Avenol's bias towards the dictatorships something that only became apparent with the benefit of hindsight. In 1939, the British Foreign Office, in particular, was acutely aware that incorporating non-members into future League work opened up the possibility of providing the Axis powers with a legitimate route back into the committee rooms of the League.

These lurid fears in Whitehall said more about the Foreign Office, which did not take the trouble to read the report properly, than the proposed reform, which, in fact, continued to impose real limits on non-member participation. The primary intention of the reform was to restrict the power of the Second Committee (the committee that sat between the EFO and the Assembly and Council that notionally directed the EFO's work) and replace it by a Central Committee. The report did not propose, as was asserted in some quarters, to abolish the Council and Assembly altogether. Loveday and Bruce had consistently rejected any notion of an autonomous economic and financial organization. In their mind, it was important to preserve an intergovernmental dimension to the process of economic and financial cooperation, otherwise there was a danger that the EFO could become the tool of a particular financial interest group, or simply irrelevant. Only Avenol, in 1937 and 1938, had proposed making the EFO autonomous, which betrayed his uninterest in the issues underpinning the EFO's drive for reform, and the limits of his control over Bruce and Loveday.[53] The Bruce Committee had rejected Avenol's proposals then too.

[52] Memo by Hill, 'Rough Notes of Bruce meeting', LON Hill P84/1–15, 1937–1946.
[53] Phipps to Halifax, 5 Mar. 1938, TNA: PRO FO371/22517 W3015/41/98; and Bucknell to Hull, 11 Mar. 1938, NARA, RG59, 500.C 1/115.

In this respect, Loveday won the day. Rather than be autonomous of the Council and the Assembly, the Central Committee would replace the Second Committee but—and this was the key point for the EFO—could include non-League members. Non-member states would play a leading role and the principle of co-option, so effective on the special committees set up by the EFO to look at issues such as gold supply, raw material production, and trade, could be implemented at the highest directive level. Crucially, and again in a sharp break with past League practice, all Central Committee business was to be decided 'by a majority of members present'. Gone was the principle of unanimity, which had made negotiation and publication in the League such a miserable business. In short, the Central Committee would have an extraordinary degree of independence when compared to the established structure of League organizations. It could draw up its own procedures, approve its own agenda, elect its own president and bureau, appoint members to the main League standing committees (the intergovernmental committees), and establish its own subcommittees to examine questions of particular interest. Its budget was to be determined in negotiation with the Secretary-General; and it was to report to him and the League membership as a whole but once a year. (This structural skeleton would resurface in organizations established after 1943.) But, because it remained contained within the League, the totalitarian powers would not be able to join, because they had rejected the institution and its values.

To the uninitiated, the proposal appeared to give the EFO and the social division of the League the same independent status enjoyed by the ILO and the LNHO. But, in reality, the restructuring proposed was far more profound and wide-ranging than simply reducing states' control. It was intended to make economic and social work the primary mission of the League, and, in another significant development unnoticed by historians, coupled the League's economic with its social agenda. Where economics, finance, health, and society had been discrete aspects of the League's work, the new structure proposed binding economic with social concerns in an arrangement that would have profound implications for the EFO, the Social Section, the LNHO, and the ILO. The proposed structural change reflected a trend that was evident in the EFO's work from the mid-1930s onwards and was to underpin its contribution to post-war reconstruction and a new world order after 1945: that, while liberal economics offered the best hope for sustained economic growth and world peace, national and international government had to recognize that not everyone benefited equally from free market economics. Social and health policies were essential to ameliorate their sometimes challenging effects and to underline the responsibilities of the world's richer members to its poorer ones. Development should be at the core of their contribution to global relations.

Striking, too, were some of the intellectual tensions evident within the Bruce Report. On the one hand, it sought to underline to national governments the value of the League: that the challenges governments faced could not be solved by national action alone, and that economic convergence and interdependence underscored the value of both coordinating policies and sharing expertize and experience across frontiers. On the other hand, the obvious conclusion of its historical account of events since 1920 was that governments were largely unsuccessful at managing man's affairs. It presented a picture in which states were often powerless in the face of disease, economic crisis, and technological change, and unable to provide an effective answer to the 'continual growth in the material and intellectual demands which men make of life'.[54] If this was unpalatable to governments, the appeal to the public in 1939 was equally unconvincing. Despite its stress of potential mass support for an integrated economic and social international programme, and its determination that the humanitarian work of the League be 'more generally known', in practical terms the EFO's response was to advocate a retreat into an institutional structure that put technical expertise before democratic representation. It was, perhaps, an understandable response given the divided, fractious and violent world of the late 1930s, a climate from which the secretariat itself was not immune.

WAR BEGINS

The outbreak of war in Europe on the 3 September 1939 is generally seen to mark the end of the League of Nations. Formally this was not the case: during the next six years, until the ceremony held to mark its official dissolution in April 1946, the organization soldiered on in a variety of guises and locations.[55] But in September 1939 neither its founding charters nor the eyrie of Swiss neutrality could protect it from the divisions that the war exposed between its remaining members, and between its own employees. The League, at the heart of the world order proclaimed in 1919, twenty years later was now a sideshow to the main event: the USSR was expelled from the League of Nations on 14 December 1939 in the wake of its invasion of Finland. The event was generally characterized by historians as the final act of a League's career riddled with hypocrisy and ineptitude: inept because, of course, the USSR was to become the primary means by which the National Socialist tide was staunched in Europe; hypocritical because neither Germany, Japan, nor Italy had been banished from the League for international transgressions that later were judged as more severe than those of the USSR.[56] (This verdict underestimates the degree to which the USSR's presence was at best tolerated within the League.) It was in sharp contrast to the USA, which was certainly the

---

[54] Instead, the report evoked the clamour for international democracy that accompanied the founding of the League, with modern communications 'making men and women all over the world more keenly aware of the wide gap between the actual and potential conditions of their lives ... impatient to hear that some real and concerted effort is being made to raise the standard of their lives nearer to what it might become' (League of Nations, *The Development of International Co-operation in Economic and Social Affairs*, 9).

[55] The League of Nations Assembly concluded its twentieth session and held its twenty-first session in Geneva to suspend the organization. During the preceding months, a variety of its subsidiary institutions, such as the Permanent Court of International Justice, were disbanded before being reconstituted as new agencies of the United Nations, in this case the International Court of Justice created in January 1946.

[56] Zara Steiner, *Triumph of the Dark European International History, 1933–1940* (Oxford, 2011), 1059–60; Bernard Wasserstein, *Barbarism and Civilization: A History of Europe in our Time* (Oxford, 2007), 292.

most influential outsider inside the League, and in 1940 was to become the EFO's saviour.

Expelling the USSR was the Council's final act. The Council and the League Assembly did not reconvene until April 1946, although the secretariat and associated agencies of the League continued to work throughout. Ironically, war had brought about aspects of the reform envisaged by the Bruce Report, because the Council and Assembly now fell away as directing agencies of the League. As a result, Avenol had more autonomy (with his actions and loyalty coming under increased question), while Loveday stepped back, and sought to reinvigorate the EFO's programme of work launching a series of diplomatic missions to North, Central and South America and to the British Empire. The EFO was now engaged in the EFO's own battle for survival that made clear the importance of vigorous and determined leadership, ambitious and able team members, a creative and relevant policy agenda, and the value of powerful friends in a war to keep the ideas of economic internationalism alive.

From January 1939 onwards, Loveday devoted as much time as possible to a detailed consideration of what he envisaged would be the key policy issues when war came, and for reconstruction once it was over. A proactive approach to these issues would not just give the EFO and the League a future; it would also generate a shared vision of the future for liberal democratic states and capitalism around the globe. To help with this work he recruited Koopmans and the Oxford-trained economist Edward Albert Radice, a former financier and Secretary-General of the New Fabian Research Bureau and Oxford economist. He also consulted close colleagues in the secretariat and the Rockefeller Foundation.[57]

The EFO's remit, of course, meant that it was comparatively easy to redirect its focus from the present to the future. While national governments worried about how best to wage the war, Loveday's concern was rather how to secure the peace once it had been won. Their starting point, however, was the same: to use the First World War as a basis from which to explore and learn from past mistakes. The EFO believed the end of the war threatened renewed and immediate economic depression, but it argued that as grave a threat was a post-war consumption boom and subsequent downturn, which had helped tip the world economy into inflation, and, in some quarters, hyperinflation, in the early 1920s. The result of these preoccupations was a large and ambitious programme of study, which, in the chaos and uncertainty triggered by the outbreak of war, took careful management by Loveday. Circumstances within the League and beyond the Palais des Nations were now changing constantly, while member states remained anxious that the EFO meet its commitments to deliver international economic intelligence and analysis to support their war plans.

On 19 September, Loveday announced that the majority of the EFO would devote its attention, in the short term at least, to gathering economic intelligence on the rapidly evolving economic situation, while the EIS would begin developing

---

[57] At the time of his re-secondment to the League, Radice was teaching economics at the Wesleyan University in Connecticut, and he joined the British Ministry of Economic Warfare in 1940.

detailed analyses of three main areas: likely post-war problems, economic distortions, and 'the development of new tendencies' in the world economy. The composition of these distinct elements was subject to considerable evolution over the coming months, but structure of the analysis remained the same, centring, first, on an assessment of past experience and current changes triggered by the war; secondly, on determining likely future structural transformations; and, thirdly, on possible policy developments in the future.

The general assumptions underpinning Loveday's analysis, supported in memoranda by Radice and Koopmans, were proven broadly correct. He rightly identified and planned for all the short-term dislocations brought about by the end of the war: demobilization, physical destruction, industrial overcapacity and dislocation, trade restriction, inflation, and high prices for essential commodities. He rightly calculated that there was a good chance governments might prepare for these contingencies, but believed it was much less likely that states would have either the resources or the foresight to dedicate sufficient attention to the long-term international issues on which a return to peace and prosperity ultimately depended. It was therefore essential that the EFO attempt to measure and assess likely changes to: the distribution of international investments and gold reserves, the growth of indebtedness, the expansion of American creditor power, and the accelerated industrialization of territories outside Europe—in other words, the wider international situation. Loveday's real powers of foresight and ambition, however, were left for the final section of his plan for the EFO's war work, which dealt with the 'probable changes in policy and outlook'. This agenda embraced contentious issues, given that it required the EFO's officials to speculate on the basis of very limited evidence, and to think about politics as much as economics. Indeed, Loveday wanted his officials to be able to offer arguments and policies to counter what he believed would be the widespread 'reluctance to abandon controls', and to anticipate the 'acceptance by governments of the obligation to furnish employment . . . the public demand for public works . . . the acceptance of the claim for a more equitable distribution of wealth . . . the adaptation of the fiscal system to make this possible, and the growth of national insurance schemes'.[58]

Koopmans, for one, was uncomfortable with the degree to which this final element required him to move beyond the scientific, evidence-based practice of the EFO's work.[59] But the remainder of his colleagues within the EFO's secretariat recognized the need to demonstrate ambition and unity in the face of the destructive forces at work inside and outside the League. As Loveday put it in his presentation to Avenol when his plans were complete, the EFO's and the EIS's working assumption was that 'there was no longer one economic world, but a medley of warring fragments and peaceful areas', and that future research must be more sensitive to the character of change 'whether temporary or permanent,

[58] This work is summarized in a memo by Loveday, 'Division of Work', 5 Oct. 1939, and Loveday to Radice, 19 Sept. 1939, Radice to Loveday, 11 Sept. 1939, and Koopmans to Loveday, 11 Sept. 1939, all in LON R4468, 10A/39148/39148.
[59] Koopmans to Loveday, 25 Sept. 1939, LON R4468, 10A/39148/39148.

deliberate or incidental'.[60] The intellectual firepower that Loveday was able to bring to these new challenges was considerable. He drew extensively on the work undertaken for the Depression Delegation, and by early October Folke Hilgerdt was analysing current national balance of payments profiles, Eugène Derobert was assessing the impact of war on international trade and commercial policy, Nurkse was working on the impact of government policy and other factors on currency, banking, and credit, and Tyler was considering changes in public finance. At the head of the pack were Koopmans and Meade, who were responsible for wide-ranging briefs that brought all these different strands together. Meade's task was to assess the character of structural change in the international economy and its relationship to government policy, while Koopmans analysed the period from 1914 to 1923 with the ambition to understand the lessons of history necessary for a successful 'transition from war to peace economy', later to become the title of the influential report.[61]

Less easily secured were the political and financial resources to sustain this programme of work in the longer term, although quite what the longer term might comprise was anyone's guess in the winter of 1939. Avenol's consent to Loveday's programme of work was not given easily, but his grudging endorsement was indicative that the Secretary-General had not abandoned the etiquette of League internationalism just yet and acknowledged British and US support for Loveday's plans.[62] Loveday was anxious to secure a broad base of support among the British government for the EFO's programme. Building on Koopmans's visit to Britain in the summer of 1939, Loveday visited London in January 1940 and was given unequivocal support for the details of his mission and the preservation of the League—a commitment that was to be dramatically tested within a matter of weeks. He also took the opportunity to meet and assess a variety of study groups and opinion-makers, notably the Royal Institute of International Affairs (Chatham House), the Political and Economic Planning group (PEP), the LSE, and the Oxford Institute of Statistics. Among the economists and journalists he consulted were Thomas Balogh and A. M. Carr-Saunders, the chairman of the 'Consultative Conference on Co-ordination of Research in the Economic and Social Sciences in Wartime', a standing conference sponsored by Chatham House intended to coordinate the burgeoning number of committees working on post-war economic and social problems. But, perhaps inevitably, Loveday did not think much of the current research undertaken by British non-governmental organizations. He condemned the PEP report, which had been sponsored by the Foreign Office, as 'very uneven . . . and on the economic side extremely superficial' and rightly judged the research profile on economics as a whole as 'sketchy and indefinite'.[63] He was more

---

[60] Loveday to Avenol, 31 Oct. 1939, and Loveday's 'Memorandum on the League of Nations' Economic Intelligence Work', undated, LON R4592 10C/39238/3679.

[61] Memo by Loveday, 'Division of Work, Annex I', 5 Oct. 1939, and more detailed instructions from Loveday to Koopmans, 4 Oct. 1939, LON R4468, 10A/39148/39148.

[62] Avenol declared he was squarely behind Loveday's plans to Halifax on 8 Nov. 1939. Avenol to Halifax, AMAE, Papiers Argents: Avenol, vol. 30.

[63] Memo by Loveday, 'Report on Mission', LON R4605, 10C/34535/9854.

bemused by radical plans for a post-war European order, taking comfort from what he regarded as wise old birds, among whom he clearly saw himself as one of the 'more serious-minded persons', who believed such federalism 'must be allowed to run its course like measles and when the rash had gone there would probably be a reversion of opinion towards some form of the original League idea'.[64]

Loveday was similarly assiduous in his trawl for American support for the EFO's focus on 'the problems of relief, [international] reorganisation and reconstruction', and his lengthy exchanges with the State Department and the US Treasury were particularly noteworthy. In October 1939, he sent Rasminsky on an extended mission to Washington, New York, Ottawa, Toronto, Buenos Aires, and Bolivia to cement these contacts and to show that the EFO's work reflected the interests of all the Americas.[65] Here, too, there was significant engagement with non-governmental organizations, notably the Council of Foreign Relations. It had initiated a study by Viner and Hansen on post-war reconstruction, which expressed deep interest in Loveday's plans and their determination to stay in touch. Equally comforting to Loveday's embattled team was Rasminsky's conclusion that there was a new tone and boldness in the administration. Its leaders were now 'showing an encouraging awareness of American responsibility' in public, and the need for the USA to 'be ready to make its contribution to economic reconstruction when war is over'.[66]

The research effort in the United States seemed more advanced to the Geneva economists than that in Britain, in part because it chimed more closely with their own preoccupations. Loveday emphasized this when he presented the EFO's new research agenda to its financial supporters in the USA. There was the grave danger that governments who had fought the war would 'face the economic issues of peace exhausted and largely unprepared', and the challenge before them would be all the greater because the period that had preceded it was 'a decade of quasi-emergency'.[67] There would be no great wish to return to the pre-war economic world of 1939 as there had been in 1918. When the fighting was over, the world had to plan a path of recovery and reconstruction, not just from the war, but from the Great Depression too. But, despite the enthusiastic endorsement from a host of groups in the USA for the EFO's new emphasis on post-war reconstruction, it remained impossible for the administration to support the League more broadly. Whatever scope the Bruce Report had opened up for wider political involvement on the part of the Americans, the advent of an election year and more significantly the outbreak of

[64] Memo by Loveday, 'Report on Mission', LON R4605, 10C/34535/9854.

[65] Loveday to Grady, 9 Oct. 1939, LON, Loveday, P146/A-Loveday Letter Book, 2nd half 1939; Loveday to Riefler, 9 Oct. 1939, and Loveday to Riefler, 27 Nov. 1939, LON R4468, 10A/39148/39148.

[66] Loveday to Rasminsky, 2 Dec. 1939, and Rasminsky to Loveday, 13 Jan. 1940, LON R4605, 10C38822/9854.

[67] 'Memorandum on the League of Nations' Economic Intelligence Work', undated, LON R45592, 10C/39238/3679; Loveday to Tracy B. Kittredge, 3 Nov. 1939, LON R4592, 10C/39238/3679; Tittmann to Hull, 10 Nov. 1939, NARA RG59 500.C/994.

war in Europe had quashed the potential of the League reform, however cast, to deliver FDR to the League.[68] As Tyler put it in a widely discussed report,

if any question relating to US relations with the League were to come before Congress in the present atmosphere, it would in all likelihood be handled not on its merits, not even according to the wishes of the majority when sober. Mr Roosevelt's enemies would grab it as further proof that he is plotting to rush the country into war and make himself Dictator. The degree of collaboration now in progress might become impossible for years to come . . . Determined forces are out to kill Mr Roosevelt politically between now and the election, and a shot meant for him might hit the League.[69]

In the meantime, the British and French foreign ministries and treasuries became increasingly anxious over the implications of where the proposal for a Central Committee might take them now that war was under way. It heightened the risk that member countries would opt to leave the League of Nations, because the Bruce committee reforms held out the possibility of becoming members of the Central Committee. Members of the Bruce committee had not considered this eventuality at any length, largely because their preoccupation had been to bring in existing non-members, not imagine new defecting nations, and because continued Anglo-French support for the League had been taken for granted. (The dangers of this assumption became very clear after the Fall of France.) While it might once have been better to have 'an effective non-political League than an ineffective mixed League', circumstances now stood against this option. Unusually, in January 1940 there were also extensive direct discussions between the British and French foreign ministries—in other words, without the mediation of delegates in Geneva— regarding the real motivation behind the Secretary-General's continued promotion of the Central Committee plan. The French view that Avenol intended to use the Central Committee as a means to affect the pretence of League activity in the war did little to reassure officials in London or the Economic and Financial Section in Geneva.[70] Loveday began to square up to Avenol. With Stoppani's retirement in October 1939, the Economic and Financial Sections and the EIS were merged as one under Loveday's direction, and equally portentous was the gusto with which the new joint director reported to Avenol that Bruce, Britain, and the USA were now hostile to the idea of a Central Committee.[71]

At this stage McDougall interjected to pose a critical question. The attention given to reform and the EFO's research plans for the post-war order were all very

---

[68] For the most candid response, see Roosevelt's rejection of the American League of Nations Association proposal that he nominate a 'personal representative' to Geneva to support the League's efforts 'in the economic, humanitarian, intellectual and moral fields' in the wake of the Assembly's acceptance of the Bruce Report. See FDR to Clark M. Eichelberger, 29 Dec. 1939, and Hull to FDR, 29 Dec. 1939, NARA RG59, 500.C/999.

[69] Memo by Tyler, 'Visit to USA by R. Tyler, 9 June to 12 July 1939', p. 3, LON R4605, 10C/3367/9854, 20 July 1939; for the EFO's views, see minute by Loveday, 8 Dec. 1939, LON R4605, 10C/3367/9854.

[70] Conversation between Bourgois and Charron, 26 Jan. 1940, AMAE, SDN, Questions Économiques/Organisation Économique et Financier/Œuvre économique et financière de la SDN, 1939–40, no. 1156.

[71] Loveday to Avenol, 16 Feb. 1940, AMAE, Papiers Argents: Avenol, vol. 30.

well, but what was to be the agency's contribution in the here and now. In short, what was the League to do *in* the war? Of course, the 'irrepressible' McDougall had the answer: the EFO should form a rallying point for the Allied powers, led by Britain and its Commonwealth and imperial allies, and France.[72] It would become the basis on which the League could 'carry to neutral and American opinion a sense of allied confidence and will also underline the international soundness of allied peace aims'.[73] The Australian was all too conscious of the 'explosive' implications of this suggestion for the cohesion of the League because it was predicated on a divided world, but he was certainly not alone in thinking along these lines in the winter of 1939–40. His proposal was presaged in the American suggestion that Geneva 'may fulfil a useful purpose in maintaining contacts between the Democracies and States which are particularly exposed to totalitarian pressures but which may not desire to have their foreign policy managed for them by the Axis'.[74]

In March 1940, the impact of the war being waged beyond the frontiers of neutral Switzerland manifested itself in a variety of ways in the Palais des Nations. Although the secretariat went through the motions of taking the Bruce reforms further by convening a meeting in The Hague on 7 February 1940, with the former Dutch Prime Minister and long-serving League activist Hendrik Colijn as its chair, without British, French, or American support the reform initiative was dead. Instead, Colijn had meetings in Paris and London on what would become of the League, where he expressed his hope that the League would be used to facilitate solidarity between the neutral states of western Europe and with Britain and France. But these meetings created only greater uncertainty among Loveday's staff and state officials: it was not clear to them how Colijn's vision of allied and neutral solidarity related to the values and purpose of the League, especially as he also appeared to hope that the Italians might be included in this bloc.[75]

Uncertainty over Colijn's motives in Paris was further clouded by the fact that a close aid to Avenol accompanied Colijn, but when he was not there Colijn sang a rather different tune.[76] He was more forthright that the League should act as a support to the Allied powers, for example, in meetings with Joseph Paul-Boncour, a leading opponent of the Vichy government in 1940.[77] When Colijn arrived in London, he told Leith-Ross and Phillips that the League was dead, but that a reformed EFO could be used by Britain and France as a basis from which to rally support for liberal economic values and to forge closer links to neutral European

[72] Shackle's description of McDougall and his plans. See minute by Shackle, 'Re-organisation of Economic etc. Work of the League of Nations', 11 Apr. 1940, TNA: PRO BT11/1254.
[73] McDougall to Loveday, 10 Oct. 1939, LON, Loveday, P146/A-Loveday Letter Book, 2nd half 1939.
[74] Memo by Tyler, 20 July 1939, p. 4, LON R4605, 10C/3367/9854.
[75] In Paris Colijn met Paul-Boncour, Coulondre, and Champetier de Ribes. A planned meeting with Daladier was cancelled at the last minute. See Vitrolles (The Hague) to the Quai d'Orsay, 10 Feb. 1940, AMAE, SDN, Questions Économiques/Organisation Économique et Financier/Œuvre économique et financière de la SDN, 1939–40, no. 1156.
[76] Pelt to Avenol, 7 Mar. 1940, AMAE, Papiers Argents: Avenol, vol. 30.
[77] Paul-Boncour went on to lead the French delegation to the UN conference in San Francisco in 1944, and signed the UN charter on France's behalf in June 1945.

states, which were in great danger, because, 'whether they like it or not, they will be gradually drawn into the enormous economic bloc constituted by Germany and Russia'.[78] In the event, however, these countries did not have to wait to be sucked into the Third Reich by the power of its economy. The German army launched an attack on Denmark and Norway on 9 April and invaded the remainder of western Europe on 10 May. On 22 June, France was the last of these countries to surrender.

THE FALL OF AVENOL

The invasion tipped what remained of the League deeper into crisis. With each Axis victory, of course, the organization forfeited members and financial sponsorship. By January 1940, the secretariat had lost more than 50 per cent of its already low complement of staff members in a year.[79] But the sense of physical diminution was as nothing compared with the climate of suspicion that gripped the institution. Much of this was a result of the increasingly erratic, if not downright alarming, behaviour of the Secretary-General in the autumn of 1939. Correspondence between members of the secretariat made repeated reference to censorship and the need to take 'care' when communicating information about their plans and the League's future. There were also shocking reports that Avenol planned to hijack the planned Central Committee as part of a larger scheme to 'disband the Council and the Assembly in order to put himself at the top of a "Directory"'. The talk may have been true, but there was no serious risk this would happen.[80] As we have seen, key figures in Britain, France, and the United States were alive to this danger and stood in its way. However, by the spring of 1940, there was mounting evidence in support of rumours that had been circulating since 1939 that Avenol had become deeply hostile to British membership of the secretariat—the Greek Under-Secretary-General Thanassis Aghnides claimed Avenol had told him he wanted to rid it of British representatives altogether, so that he could 'create a new economic block consisting of Germany, Italy, France and Spain' from which England would be excluded and made to 'expiate for her crimes'.[81]

What was certainly clear was that Avenol was keen to exploit the crisis to shape the secretariat in his own image, and the expulsion of the USSR provided the opportunity to move against its lone communist member. The unfortunate Vladimir Sokoline, the only Russian member of the secretariat, was hastily pushed out, despite his desperate efforts to stay in Geneva as some sort of liaison between the League, the Red Cross, and the USSR. 'Natural' wastage also helped Avenol's cause.

---

[78] See Makins's record of conversation with Colijn, 22 Mar. 1940, and Leith-Ross to Makins, 1 Apr. 1940, TNA: PRO BT11/1254.

[79] Diary entry, 31 Jan. 1940, Sean Lester's Diary, UNOG <http://biblio-archive.unog.ch/Detail.aspx?ID=32586> (accessed 1 Aug. 2008).

[80] For the Parisian view, see note by Arnal, 30 Jan. 1940, AMAE, Y/Carton 81/dossier 1, 1937–40.

[81] Livingston to Halifax, 21 June 1940, TNA: PRO FO371/24440, C7931/6953/98. For details of the rows between Loveday and Avenol, see minute by Makins, 25 June 1940, TNA: PRO FO371/24440, C7391/6953/98.

Stoppani, for example, retired from the secretariat on 15 October 1939, six months beyond the statutory age limit of 60, because he was organizing the European Conference on Rural Life—the extension had to be fought for by Loveday, and paid from EFO's supplementary budget.[82]

These machinations were but a foretaste of what was to come after the fall of France. Since the start of the war the secretariat as a whole had been preparing for the possibility that the German government might violate Swiss neutrality. Avenol had insisted that the archives of the League be transferred to Vichy, and intended that, should Switzerland be invaded, Vichy would form the first 'halting place' of a reduced League headquarters.[83] The proposal caused uproar in Geneva, London, and Washington. Avenol had made the arrangements without consultation, although, when questioned by the British, he announced he was under pressure from Paris for 'maintaining an extravagantly large League'—a claim for which there is no evidence. In May 1940, some officials took the view, later supported by Dubin, that Avenol was incompetent rather than malevolent. The 'real trouble', as the British Foreign Office put it, was 'that M. Avenol is incapable of taking a decision, and if he does take a decision it is usually wrong'.[84] The Secretary-General claimed he was indecisive, because he did not want to take responsibility for breaking up the League; yet it was some of his decisions that came close to destroying it. In the middle of June, news reached London that Avenol was negotiating with officials in Vichy and was close to liquidating the organization. With France defeated the Battle of Britain began, and negotiations regarding American aid essential to Britain entered a delicate stage, the Foreign Office was forced to give urgent attention instead to the League. The reports grew only more alarming, with intelligence from Lester that Avenol was determined to forge a new Europe-only League of which Avenol would 'make himself leader'.[85]

There followed word that Avenol planned to sack all non-Europeans in the secretariat, had jettisoned the League's financial plan for the forthcoming year, and was attempting to establish contact with the German Consul General in Geneva, Wolfgang Krauel. It was also rumoured he had sent an emissary to Laval to secure Vichy's agreement to use the League's infrastructure for a 'New European League', assuring Laval that, if Hitler was not interested in it, Mussolini most certainly would be 'to counter German military might'.[86] The charitable version of these dark days for the League was that Avenol had had some kind of breakdown; the more likely explanation was that he had decided to throw in his panicky lot with the dictators, although, given the Nazi–Soviet Pact, it was hard to see any

---

[82] Stencek to Avenol, 10 Jan. 1939, and Avenol to Stoppani, 19 Sept. 1939, LON S888, Personnel Files, Stoppani.

[83] Walter to Makins, 14 May 1940, TNA: PRO FO371/24440, C6953/6953/98.

[84] Minute by Warr, 28 May 1940, TNA: PRO FO371/24440, C6953/6953/98.

[85] Livingston to Foreign Office, 27 June 1940, TNA: PRO FO371/24440, C7391/6953/98.

[86] Barros, *Betrayal from Within*, 236–7. Avenol's efforts to contact the German government were later confirmed by Goodrich; see Neville Butler to Makins, 7 Aug. 1940, TNA: PRO FO371/24441, C8375/6953/98. Avenol also attempted to use Stoppani to act as an intermediary with the Italian government, but the latter refused.

ideological consistency behind his ideas. The French government in Vichy, however, wanted nothing to do with his proposal. Rather, it wanted Avenol to resign
from his post as Secretary-General, because it was politically inconvenient to have a
Frenchman at the head of an international organization that was still identified,
despite Avenol's recent best efforts, with the values of liberal internationalism.[87]
Avenol's reaction to the news was to attempt a further purging of those officials
he deemed 'unreliable', and to cultivate a small cluster of League staff around him as
a *de facto* League, which he might control were he no longer in charge. In the
meantime, Lester, Aghnides, Renborg, Skylstad, and Loveday did all that they
could to oppose his plans. This involved extensive discussions with diplomats and
advisers in London, Washington, and New York. The fate of the League had
important implications for these world powers, and their position had profound
repercussions for the League.

It is ironic that Vichy was the first authority to request Avenol's resignation, but
it was not the last. Anxious not to counter Avenol's behaviour with an act contrary
to the values that the League was supposed to uphold, without acting against him
directly, the British Foreign Office cast around for a legal way for member states to
rid themselves of the maverick Secretary-General, maintaining extensive contacts
with Australia, Canada, New Zealand, the Union of South Africa, Eire, and the
Dutch and Norwegian governments in London.[88] The legal adviser to the Foreign
Office, William Malkin, however, discovered, 'strange as it may seem in a sup-
posedly democratic institution, the Secretary-General in fact exercises powers
which are almost dictatorial'.[89] When he proved so difficult to unseat, it was
proposed Avenol be deprived of his salary and his house, because he was 'greatly
attached to his comfort and well-being'.[90]

The affair had gone beyond trying to smoke him out. The most direct route to
sack him was through the Organizing Committee, but, given the war and the
increasing isolation of Geneva, this seemed unworkable. So leading officers of the
secretariat who opposed Avenol drew on their own resources to protect their
sections and the honour of the League, and did not wait for directions from
London. Loveday, Lester, and Frank Walters, the British head of the political
section of the League, agreed that the highest priority should be given to saving the
technical organizations. These were not only emblematic of the values of internationalism; their expertise and intelligence were useful to the Allied cause. Walters
argued that, should Switzerland be invaded, the League should be moved *en masse*
to London or Oxford. Lester and Loveday disagreed. Both believed it was essential
that some element of the League remained alive in Geneva to support the Allies and
to keep the ideals of international cooperation and organization alive for the post-
war era. At the same time, Loveday argued vehemently that the technical agencies

[87] Loveday to Makins, 23 July 1940, TNA: PRO FO371/24441, C7839/6953/98.
[88] Circular telegram to the Commonwealth, South Africa, and Eire, 8 Aug. 1940, TNA: PRO
FO371/24441, C8136/6953/98.
[89] Malkin to Makins, 17 July 1940, TNA: PRO FO371/24441, C7839/6953/98.
[90] Perl to Jebb, 11 July 1940, TNA: PRO FO371/24441, C7839/6953/98.

of the League were best relocated to where they would be most useful to the processes of intelligence-gathering and lesson-learning intrinsic in the task of reconstruction. It meant being as near to the source of future power as was possible, and this was the United States.[91]

Given the complexities of relations between the League and the USA, communications were inevitably circuitous. Loveday whispered something into the ear of Sweetser, who sailed to the USA to consult among others Riefler, who in turn approached the Director of the Institute for Advanced Study (IAS), Frank Aydelotte, a specialist in English literature, a graduate student of Brasenose College, Oxford, and a 'stalwart friend of the League of Nations'.[92] Sanctuary to some of the most famous refugees of National Socialism, including Albert Einstein, the IAS had a reputation for rescue, and Aydelotte quickly put together a tripartite response to Loveday's call for help, which included Carl Tambroek, Director of the Rockefeller Institute for Medical Research (who helped to finance the move), and Harold W. Dodds, President of Princeton University, who was later to make great play of 'Wilson's University' saving the League in its hour of need. Aydelotte also approached Cordell Hull, to ensure the State Department and the White House would privately support the invitation. They warmly endorsed the proposal.

The IAS was the ideal location for an extended League 'mission' to the USA. Together with the resources offered to the League by Princeton University, it was an educational and research venue of the first rank on the Atlantic seaboard. It had the essential infrastructural resources to support the section's work and, most importantly, was intellectually and physically close to the powerbrokers in Washington and New York. The EFO already enjoyed established relationships with all members of the IAS School of Economics and Politics, including its founding director, Flexner; Riefler, who remained on secondment to the US Treasury, and Mitrany, who spent most of the war working for the Institute for International Affairs at Chatham House as an adviser to the British Foreign Office.[93] The practical slant to the institute's work would not sit so easily with its commitment to advanced study, but, at a time when the USA was preparing to mobilize its resources against the threat of war, the Institute was gripped by efforts to marshal 'the scholarly resources of the nation'. This worked to the League's advantage. Edward Meade Earle, an expert in the history of American diplomacy at

---

[91] It is clear that the idea originated with Loveday. See Sweetser to Loveday, 4 June 1940, IAS, Box 38, GFILE, 'League of Nations (Transfer re. Economics Group)'; Walters to Makins, 14 May 1940, TNA: PRO FO371/24440, C6953/6953/98.

[92] Jacklin to Aydelotte, 19 Feb. 1941, IAS, Box 38, GFILE 'League of Nations Association Conference'; Institute for Advanced Study, *A Community of Scholars: The Institute for Advanced Study Faculty and Members 1930–1980* (Princeton, 1980), 3. Aydelotte was also a leading member of the US Association of the League of Nations in Philadelphia, where he had once lived, and New Jersey.

[93] He advised on both south-eastern Europe and on peace-making more generally, but was desperate to leave Britain and return to the IAS. Loveday was given his office. Brought to Chatham House by Arnold Toynbee, Mitrany and Toynbee regularly exchanged papers with the 'University Committee for the Study of Post-War International Problems' run by Edwin Gay and Aydelotte. See Toynbee to Mitrany enc., 29 Aug. 1942, LSE, Mitrany, 20.

the IAS, became the chairman of the American Committee of International Studies in 1939. The organization, funded by the Rockefeller Foundation, was also based at the Institute and assembled key American scholars from the fields of international relations, many of whom were notable League favourites, including Alvin Hansen, Jacob Viner, James Shotwell, and J. B. Condliffe, to explore and research America's role in the world in response to the wars now raging in south-east Asia and Europe.

The first formal exchange between the Americans and the League came in May 1940, when Aydelotte extended an invitation to Avenol that the technical sections of the League be relocated to the IAS. But the proposal, at a time when the EFO and especially Loveday were becoming a particular irritant to Avenol, was met with a stony rejection from the Secretary-General, who did not even see fit to consult member states for advice because the invitation had not come (nor could it have) from the American administration.[94]

When the British learned that Avenol had rejected the Institute, they were incensed. Matters came to a head on 21 June 1940 with a violent quarrel between Avenol and Loveday, the result of which was not just that Avenol opposed the move to Princeton, but wanted to sack Loveday and rid the EFO of its British component, and threatened to subordinate the entire organization and its programme for post-war reconstruction to the ILO. At this point it was mooted by the ILO's Director-General, John Winant, that the ILO might move to the USA, and take the EFO's place at the Institute, although, in the end, the ILO went on to spend the war in Canada: while the State Department was keen to find a home for the EFO, it was less enthusiastic about accommodating the ILO. There followed a series of tense meetings between first Lester and Avenol, and then the British consul in Geneva and Avenol, to 'encourage' the Secretary-General to accept the Princeton invitation. The most undiplomatic language was now the norm in meetings, which frequently disintegrated into shouting matches.[95]

The international backdrop only heightened the tensions in Geneva. Belgium surrendered to Nazi Germany on the day Sweetser's boat docked in New York, and he hastened to Princeton. Meetings at the State Department to discuss the move coincided with Britain's desperate and 'glorious retreat' from the beaches of Dunkirk, and the first letter of invitation was wired to Avenol the day after Italy had entered the war. The Americans were not about to give up. By the time their second invitation landed on Avenol's desk, France had been defeated.

On 10 July 1940, the IAS reiterated its invitation to the EFO and extended it also to the Health, Social, and Opium Sections of the League.[96] Avenol again rejected the offer, only then to propose, on 23 July, that Loveday, Lester, and Skystad, the Norwegian director of the Minorities and Intellectual Cooperation

[94] Lothian to Halifax, 19 July 1940, TNA: PRO FO371/24441, C7839/6953/98. Winant helped the ILO move to Montreal but resigned his post in 1941 to become the US Ambassador to the Court of St James; Avenol to Costa du Rels, 16 Aug. 1940, TNA: PRO FO371/24442, C8819/6953/98.
[95] Kelly to Foreign Office, 23 June 1940, TNA: PRO FO371/24442, C6953/6953/98.
[96] The State Department was an important source of support at this stage and also conferred with the British government over the invitation. See Lothian to Halifax, 19 July 1940, TNA: PRO FO371/24441, C7839/6953/98.

Section, move to Princeton but without their staff. All three refused. Loveday said he would go only if he could take with him key EFO members and if he received the necessary financial guarantees to support their research and publication pro-gramme. Within twenty-four hours Avenol relented. He wanted finally to be rid of this most troublesome Scotsman. Because the British government had articulated strongly its view that as many EFO staff as possible should be allowed to move to Princeton, Avenol finally agreed to transfer Loveday and twelve members of his core employees, along with their families, to Princeton 'on a standard League mission with funding running until the end of 1940', with the possibility of an extension until early in 1941.[97] There was a last minute spat over whether Avenol would release Nurkse, essential to Loveday's plans for an investigation into post-war monetary relations, but again the Secretary-General was forced to capitulate, and the matter was agreed.[98]

Or so it seemed. The deal did not come without two further acts of drama. The first was the bus carrying the EFO group, many of whom were travelling with their wives and young families, collided with a tram car in Grenoble, injuring three members of the party. They continued their journey three days later undeterred. The second, more farce than tragedy, came a few hours after the bus crash when, on 23 July 1940, Avenol declared he would resign as Secretary-General of the League, but it soon became apparent that announcing an intention to resign was not the same as leaving. Two days later there followed a long and disjointed communi-cation from Avenol distributed individually to member states, which Makins judged 'so garbled and dislocated that the whole business might be shown up as an example of propaganda persuasion'. (The British were sufficiently suspicious to sent the text for analysis by the Ministry of Information for evidence of being written under Nazi direction.)[99] In among the confused and self-aggrandizing account of Avenol's role in the reform movement and praise for the 'great eco-nomic, social and humanitarian work started and developed by the League', the note contained three points whose meaning became clear in the following days.

The first was the assertion that he had not resigned but that, with the Council and Assembly meetings adjourned, his constitutional powers as Secretary-General were in suspense. Secondly, he insisted this entitled him to convene a special meeting of the Supervisory Commission to decide the institution's future and only then would he announce the date on which his resignation would take effect. Thirdly, he claimed he remained in control of the League's financial resources and therefore, in effect, of the League.[100] There were other worrying developments. Despite his assurances of support for the League's technical divisions and its humanitarian work, Avenol had made no effort, practical or financial, to help the EFO move to the USA, and he now obstructed attempts of the Opium and Social Sections to accompany the EFO to Princeton. Nor were his relations with the

[97] Loveday to Makins, 23 July 1940, TNA: PRO FO371/24441, C7839/6953/98.
[98] Loveday to Avenol, 22 July 1940, LON, Princeton Office, C1624/No. 5, 40–4.
[99] Minute by Makins, 30 July 1940, TNA: PRO FO371/24441, C7982/6953/98.
[100] Memo by Avenol, 23 July 1940, TNA: PRO FO371/24441, C7982/6953/98.

Vichy government any clearer. Not only did he seemingly now intend to stay in Geneva, where once he had planned to move to Vichy, but the Vichy government, which had intended to resign French membership of the League, decided to remain a member for the time being. The British did not see the decision to stay as marking a stiffening of the French government's attitude towards their German masters, but rather 'that for purposes of their own, [they] want France to remain in the League'.[101] The analysis reflected a rising fear in the Foreign Office that the Germans intended to use the League in some way and that 'the League building might appeal to Hitler's imagination in the same way as did the railway carriage at Compiègne'—this theatrical scene of Nazi armistice with France on 22 June representing a dramatic role (and seat reversal) of the French armistice with Germany in 1918.[102] With most of the secretariat leaving for North America, there would be fewer impediments to whatever plans Avenol was hatching.

But it was the decisive intervention of Seymour Jacklin, the South African Treasurer of the League of Nations, that caused alarm bells in London to ring loud enough above the din of other emergencies for it to take action. Jacklin learned that Avenol intended to set up a subcommittee of the Supervisory Commission to take charge of the League finances that was to comprise Avenol, Jacklin as the treasurer, and a third person selected by Avenol. This, of course, meant that Jacklin would be outvoted by Avenol, and the latter left in a position to spend the League's money as he wished. Jacklin's grounds for suspicion grew when the Secretary-General asked him to transfer League gold back from the USA and place it in the custody of the BIS.[103] British opinion now turned resolutely against him.[104] There were four issues before the British government: how to regain control of the League's finances; how to get Avenol out; whom to appoint in the Secretary-General's place; and how to ensure the EFO made it safely to the USA.

Thanks, finally, to decisive intervention by the British, supported behind the scenes by the US State Department, the IAS, and the Rockefeller Foundation, an ad hoc committee was convened (rather than the Supervisory Commission meeting planned by Avenol) and the Secretary-General's resignation was put into effect. Working in cooperation with Jacklin, by late July 1940 the Foreign Office had control of the League's finances. The easy part was securing control of the league's liquid assets, some £3 million pounds, of which some £700, 000 were held in gold in London, and the remainder in New York. As the account was managed by the Lloyds & National Provincial Foreign Banks Ltd, which also had a branch from which these assets might be drawn in Geneva, so the British government, in liaison

[101] The decision was announced on 17 July. Livingston to Halifax, circulated to War Cabinet, 17 July 1940, TNA: PRO FO371/24441, C7839/6953/98. Paul Baudouin, appointed Vichy's Foreign Minister the day before, told Charron that the League afforded a 'bridge' to Britain, which Vichy wanted to keep.

[102] Minute by Warr, 18 July 1940, TNA: PRO FO371/24441, C7839/6953/98.

[103] Jacklin to the Treasury, 27 July 1940; for Avenol's request regarding the BIS, see telegram from Kelly (Berne) to Halifax, 13 Aug. 1940, TNA: PRO FO371/24441, C7982/6953/98.

[104] When he haggled over severance pay, Churchill acerbically asked 'how much will this Pétanist get?' See, Colville to Lawford, 27 July 1940, TNA: PRO FO371/24441, C7982/6953/98.

with the US Treasury, prepared to block these accounts in the event that Germany invaded Switzerland, or the Swiss government followed through on its threat to revoke the League's diplomatic immunity, and arrangements were made for states to make future contributions to the League to Lloyds in London or the South American Bank in New York.[105]

Ensuring that Avenol went through with his declared intention to resign on 31 August remained a path fraught with anxiety: it was feared the efforts to preserve the League might trigger a reaction from Nazi Germany and Vichy France; and there remained the risk that the League would disintegrate in the face of the twin problems of transferring the technical sections to Princeton while legally shoring up the executive functions of the League. But, regardless of the difficulties before them, Britain, its allies (including exiled governments), and the USA believed it 'essential to maintain the League as a basis of whatever co-operative international effort is built up after the war'.[106] After much deliberation between the Foreign Office, the Treasury, the War Office, and the Ministry for Labour (representing the perspective of the ILO and Social Section), and in consultation with the Dutch, Norwegian, American, and Latin American governments (through Adolfo Costa du Rels, the Bolivian President of the Council and plenipotentiary to Switzerland, and the Argentinian permanent delegate Carlos Pardo), it was possible to sustain a united front against Avenol.[107] With no allies left inside the League, with no coherent support from Axis forces outside it, and without money, he now had no alternative but to resign. Avenol stepped down on 31 August, and, forced to give up his beloved official residence, 'La Pelouse', he moved to Vichy. The Swiss authorities were not alone in breathing a sigh of relief.[108] The line of succession took care of who to appoint in his place: Sean Lester was the preferred candidate of Britain and the Empire and his role as Deputy Secretary-General meant he automatically stepped into the role.

While Lester gathered together the hundred or so remaining officials of the secretariat and began preparations for an urgent meeting of the intergovernmental Supervisory Committee in Portugal (which was easier for Allied members to reach than Geneva), the EFO began its hazardous journey to Princeton. The EFO's centrality to plans for the survival of the League was underlined on 1 October 1940 at a meeting of the Supervisory Commission held in Estoril, a small town just outside Lisbon, because the latter's hotels were so full of refugees there was no room

---

[105] Memo by Maxwell, 31 July 1940, TNA: PRO FO371/24441, C8365/6953/98.

[106] Kisch to Makins, 12 Aug. 1940, TNA: PRO FO371/24441, C8566/6953/98.

[107] Halifax to Kelly, 20 Aug. 1940, TNA: PRO FO371/24441, C8566/6953/98. Costa du Rels's extraordinary career as a bilingual writer in Spanish and French of drama, novels, and essays, which earned him considerable distinction in Bolivia, Argentina, and France, is also worthy of note as a further demonstration of the intellectual distinction of individual members of the League.

[108] His attempt to call a special meeting of the Supervisory Commission was scotched because members refused to attend and he required four or more to reach a quorum. Avenol continued to bombard the Allies with memos and to court Vichy. See minute by Makins, 19 Aug. 1940, TNA: PRO FO371/24441, C8566/6953/98.

for the League.[109] The meeting sanctioned the future for the League that had been set out first by Loveday and then by the Foreign Office in the preceding months. The committee endorsed the view that the EFO's presence in Princeton was essential to maintaining the value and reputation of the League in the war, and its successful transfer, the new financial arrangements, and the move of the ILO to McGill University in Montreal—with the expectation that it would soon join the EFO in the USA—were presented as causes for optimism.

But the difficulties of travel, the increasing disruption to its lines of communication, and the loss of yet more staff and resources brought home to Lester anew how isolated the Palais des Nations had become. Few personnel remained, and its grand committee rooms were given over to storing the possessions of secretariat members who had left. The future now lay elsewhere. Even the Swiss government made clear it would like to see the back of the League; yet, when Lester asked the British government to consider again whether the League in its entirety might be evacuated elsewhere, the rebuke was swift. The Swiss government, Lester was told by London, was 'none the worse for being a little embarrassed by the presence of the League organisation on Swiss soil'.[110] When it came to the more important question of a future home for the League, the only viable option was the USA. It remained essential that Lester did all he could to support the continuation of the League's technical work from afar, because FDR could not make a political commitment to internationalism.

By now the League was primarily a technocratic organization. Divorced from political engagement by events rather than design, in many ways the League had become the agency dedicated to economic and social cooperation proposed by the Bruce committee. But life after Geneva was to demonstrate anew the value of wide-ranging political contacts and support. Once in Princeton, Loveday believed he was living 'in what was really the hub of the universe today', and there was 'a constant flow of people from Canada, Latin America, the Dutch East Indies with whom one can and does get in touch'.[111] It was precisely because the EFO had such extensive experience of, and contacts with, European governments that it was of special interest to the US administration. This, and its unrivalled experience of international organization, combined with its relationships with the wider social scientific community, meant that it was able to make an important contribution to economic and financial planning from its new home.

---

[109] With many key members unable to travel and with Spanish visas desperately hard to come by, the meeting reached quorum only because Kisch, Pardo, and Costa du Rels insisted that the reluctant Finnish member Harri Holma attend (although he confined himself to procedural comment), 'for all the League had done for Finland the year before', while recognizing that Finland was 'scared of doing anything to offend the Axis powers who were pressuring it to leave the League altogether'. See Vereker to Halifax, 26 Aug. 1940, TNA: PRO FO371/24442, C9053/6453/98.

[110] Minute by Makins, 19 Oct. 1940, TNA: PRO FO371/24441, C11192/6953/98.

[111] Loveday to Lester, 2 July 1941, LON, Princeton Office, C1619/No. 2, 41.

8

Made in the USA, 1940–1943

On Sunday, 29 September 1940, eight employees of the League of Nations arrived with their families in New Jersey City. The group included citizens of Ireland, Sweden, the Netherlands, Belgium, Czechoslovakia, Switzerland, France, and New Zealand. Dishevelled after nights spent onboard SS *Exeter* sleeping on mattresses in the public lounge and shorn of their diplomatic status, they were subject to lengthy 'alien registration' proceedings. But their discomfort was temporary.[1] They were soon in the welcoming arms of the Princeton delegation—Aydelotte, Sweetser, and Loveday (who had arrived by clipper some three weeks earlier)—come to meet them. Every effort was made to ensure their comfort. The warmth of the reception prompted the normally reserved Loveday to reflect that, although Geneva still felt like his 'home town', its chilly atmosphere compared unfavourably with the 'neighbourly relations' of Princeton. Of course, this was partly due to his department being the guest of 'various learned bodies in Princeton and no hosts are so full of spontaneous kindness as the Americans'. More decisive, however, was the 'essential fact that when a mixed foreign group is small it is, and when it is large it is not, possible to ingest it'.[2]

So what did it mean to be consumed by the United States? For Loveday, who was by agreement the Acting Secretary-General of the League in the USA, and his colleagues, life was far more congenial and secure than in their last months in Geneva, a particular relief for those with young families.[3] They did not live in splendour, and finances were tight, as they were for the colleagues they had left behind. In 1941, the League's income fell by 50 per cent from that of 1940, which, in turn, was 66 per cent down on the already parsimonious year of 1939.[4] Loveday and his group were assisted by a supplementary grant of $50,000 over two years from the Rockefeller Foundation and the IAS, which charged them a notional

---

[1] They were Chapman, Deperon, Hilgerdt, Nurkse, Rosenborg, Baroness van Ittersun, Macguire, and Polak. Rasminsky and Lindberg joined them later.

[2] Loveday, *Reflections on International Administration*, 3.

[3] Memos, 'Arrangement between Loveday, Felkin and Renborg', 10 Feb. 1941, which designated Loveday Acting Secretary-General in the USA with regard to the Princeton Mission, the Opium Supervisory Body, and the Permanent Central Opium Board in Washington. See LON R5341, F17/40910/40910. Most of the Geneva exiles had young families with children aged between 5 and 11, although Loveday brought his two sons, aged 15 and 17, who returned to the UK to complete their military service when the time came.

[4] The figure set for the secretariat in 1940 for 1941 was 3,729,302 Swiss francs and the budget for the League as a whole was 10,659,7111 Swiss francs. 'Report of the Supervisory Commission for the Year 1940', 15 Oct. 1940, TNA: PRO FO371/24442, C 11192/6953/98.

dollar a day for their accommodation, although the group put considerable pressure on its physical resources.[5] The newly built and as yet unused dining hall was opened and put into service as a workspace, while on the floor below members of the School of Economics and Politics were forced to share offices, and the secretaries were consigned to desks in the corridors.[6] Within a few months, the Princeton Mission had more than doubled in size, and by the middle of 1942 it numbered more than thirty-five employees, supplemented by new talent, including a young Kenneth Boulding.[7] By then it had moved out of the central Fuld Hall building of the IAS and into the gently decaying buildings of the Hun Junior School nearby.

During its time in Princeton, the League group found resources of all kinds in short supply, but frequently managed a creative response. Not long after arriving, Loveday emptied the New York warehouse where artefacts and furniture from the League of Nation's Pavilion at the world's fair had been stored since it had closed in 1939. He helped himself to a typewriter, two desks, chairs, special sound-absorbing linoleum, and assorted League knick-knacks (including a brass tree that outlined the structure of the League of Nations). The re-creation of the 'Economic, Finance and Transit Organization Room' of the League Pavilion on the fourth floor of the Institute in Princeton was a poignant reminder of the hard times on which the League had fallen.[8] But League officials, including the Opium Section that also found a home there, had not come to Princeton to reconstruct a living League 'doll's house'. In their straitened circumstances, they drew strength from one another and what they believed was the distinct value of their expertise. The officials' intention was not to give their identity over to their American host, but to 'dovetail discreetly' into American efforts to forge a new basis on which economic, financial, and political relations might be built, and to place their concern with international governance at its heart.[9]

In February 1941, the Princeton group was confident it could direct the 'whale-like' US administration. Its members were boosted by the arrival of new colleagues from Geneva, including John Lindberg, a member of the ILO's League section for most of the 1930s, and reunion with old friends exiled from Nazi-occupied Europe.[10] Loveday was relieved and delighted that 'everyone here in Washington

[5] Final accounts of mission, LON F17/44116/40910; Makins to Kisch, 4 Nov. 1940, TNA: PRO FO371/24442, C11192/6953/98.

[6] See extensive correspondence in IAS, GFILE, Box 38 'League of Nations (Correspondence re Transfer of Economics Group)'.

[7] Boulding's supervisor in Chicago, Viner, recommended Boulding to Loveday, and Boulding recalled that his time with the Princeton Mission 'introduced me to what we might call the geography of statistics . . . [which] revealed that national frontiers were not very significant. See Kenneth Boulding, *Towards a New Economics* (Aldershot, 1992), 11. Boulding did not take direction easily even before he was fired for promoting pacifism in June 1942. See, e.g., Nurkse to Boulding, 'Notes on Price Policy', 21 June 1941, Mudd, Nurkse MC 173, Box 1, Folder 1.

[8] Loveday to Aydelotte, 29 Oct. 1940, and Gerig to Aydelotte, 30 Oct. 1940, IAS, GFILE, Box 38, 'League of Nations'.

[9] Loveday to Makins, c.25 Jan. 1941, TNA: PRO FO371 C 979/972/98.

[10] Loveday to Lester, 30 July 1943, LON, Princeton Office, C1619/No. 4, 43, 'Correspondence with Mr Lester'. Bonn, now in the USA, enjoyed renewed contact with old friends from Geneva, notably Condliffe, Pasvolsky, and Viner, whom he had first met through the League. He wrote a

and New York is as helpful as possible . . . and enthusiastic about our programme'. The League group regularly visited the State Department, the Federal Reserve, and the Treasury, and these departments sent officials to Princeton to review reports being compiled by the League, and to use the microfilmed records brought from Geneva.[11] The prospects of influencing the development of policy were judged immeasurably better from Princeton than from the 'rat trap' that Geneva had become.[12]

American internationalists, and particularly the US League of Nations Association, also concluded that the League presence in the USA, and State Department and White House support for it, would serve as a new launch pad for their cause. To this end, in April 1941, the IAS, Princeton University, and the Rockefeller Foundation assembled for the first time Americans who during the previous twenty years had participated in the 'technical' work of the League, the ILO, and the International Court as a formal group. The numbers involved were considerable. Three hundred invitations were issued—more could have been invited—and one hundred people came, including sixteen serving government officials from the departments of State, Treasury, Labor, Commerce, Tariff, Social Security, Federal Reserve, and Housing.[13] The central theme of the two-day meeting was that, whatever its shortcomings, the League had 'built up something new in the world: an effective international civil service' and that America's commitment to the 'preservation of these groups with their records and traditions would add greatly to the usefulness of whatever type of international organization the world may adopt once the war is over'.[14] It was followed by an open public meeting under the banner 'Building a New World Order', a commonplace war aim of fascist, communist, and liberal democratic powers that was so potent with regenerative validity that it had not yet become a cliché.

While these events and others gave League officials and their American supporters a 'real emotional stimulus and pickup' in the dark days of 1940 and 1941, neither Loveday nor his colleagues were seduced by the enthusiasm of American internationalists for a revived League as the basis of the new order.[15] Having witnessed the institution's failings for more than twenty years, and promoted the reform of the League for over a decade, the Princeton Mission's commitment was more to the cause and practices of internationalism embodied in the League, and less to the constitution of the organization itself. It was for this reason that Loveday and his co-workers were prepared to align with the widely held view among British

number of articles that supported the agenda of the Princeton Mission in the US press. See, e.g., 'Commonwealth out of Empire', *Saturday Evening Post* (1943), p.104, BAK, Bonn Papers, NL1982:17, and Mudd, Viner, MC 135, Box 4, Folder 22.

[11] Thanks to the beneficence of Rockefeller, the League was able to microfilm the EFO's entire archive before leaving Geneva, while the IAS bought the entire print run of League publications for its library. See memos in IAS, GFILE, Rockefeller Correspondence, 'League of Nations Fund, 1940–1941'.

[12] Loveday to Makins, *c*.25 Jan. 1941, TNA: PRO FO371 C 979/972/98.

[13] Sweetser to Lester, 23 Apr. 1941, IAS, GFILE, Box 38, 'League of Nations'.

[14] Welcome speech by Aydelotte, 29 Nov. 1941, IAS, GFILE, Box 38, 'League of Nations'.

[15] Loveday to Janet Smith, *c*.30 Apr. 1941 TNA: PRO FO/371/26661, C4144/3124/28.

policy-makers that the League had 'failed' and, with the emerging position of
FDR's administration, that it was better to found a new international organization
than compromise an American commitment to global leadership with uncomfortable associations to the past. Loveday's view was that the responsibility for this
'failure' lay with the major nation states (members and non-members), and the
primacy accorded to their rights in the configuration of the League—an issue that
he had long regarded as ripe for reform. Indeed, it was to preserve the secretariat's
work, and the lived experience of the League, that the Princeton Mission made an
early, hard-headed calculation not to challenge the generalized narrative of the
failure of the League of Nations.

Adhering primarily to the League's agenda on economic and financial relations
alone afforded the Princeton Mission a better chance it would be heard in framing
the lessons of history out of which the new institutions for world organization
would be built. The EFO's secretariat in America was anxious to make headway in
areas where it could have an impact: on issues relating to the revival of international
trade, on the adoption of a new monetary system, and on developing strategies to
combat economic depressions. But to make a contribution it had first to find a
voice amid the contradictory trends in US foreign policy. The key challenge was
that, while the US administration had absorbed the Princeton group into the
diffuse networks that were developing post-war policy, the implications of this
for formal League and US relations were unclear. The State Department now had
limitless access to the technical agencies of the League it had long valued, but the
EFO's arrival coincided with high-level political contacts between the White House
and the ILO that were to prove troublesome.

The ILO, like the Princeton Mission, enjoyed warmly cooperative relations with
members of the US administration and, notably, the community of social scientists
that informed the New Deal. But, unlike the EFO's orientation towards the
internationalist, free-marketeers of the administration, the ILO's ties were more
to New Dealers, including the ILO Director-General between 1939 and 1941,
John 'Gil' Winant, the former Chairman of Roosevelt's Social Security Board.[16]
Despite their more cooperative relations in the 1930s, which continued in some
measure during the war, the ILO and the EFO had different, distinctive priorities
for the post-war order. Which agency of the League would the USA draw upon as
the institutional template for its vision of the post-war world?

The answer depended as much upon the configuration of international relations
as the content of reconstruction policies. The Atlantic Charter and the Lend-

[16] Winant was also an alumnus of Princeton University and a Republican progressive in the 1920s,
who become increasingly estranged from his party and had what Churchill regarded as 'sound liberal
credentials'. See David Reynolds, 'Roosevelt, the British Left, and the Appointment of John G. Winant
as United States Ambassador to Britain in 1941', *International History Review*, 4/3 (1982), 393–413.
Even Reynolds, who recognizes the importance of Winant's ILO career to his ambassadorial role,
follows the common trend to neglect Winant's internationalism in preference to his importance to
Anglo-American relations. See also Dallek, *Frankin D. Roosevelt and American Foreign Policy*, 533, and
Lynne Olson, *Citizens of London: The Americans who Stood with Britain in its Darkest, Finest Hour*
(New York, 2010).

Lease Agreement, made law in March 1941, clearly showed US support for Britain and its Allies, and for a new world order with the values of liberal democracy and capitalism at its heart. But the launch of Operation 'Barbarossa' by Germany in June brought the USSR back into the mix, and, with the Japanese assault on Pearl Harbor, the reconfiguration of international relations demonstrated the power of contingency to reshape the intellectual agenda. The year 1941 was one in which the future of the world lay in the balance, with Germany, Italy, and Japan advancing a new and alternative world constellation. As far as the League was concerned, what they thought would not matter if the Axis won, and therefore the likely constellation of power after an Allied victory was set, although the place of the USSR in international relations remained to be determined.[17] Loveday's breathless account of events around Pearl Harbor concluded: 'the net balance seems to me favourable with very great immediate risks'.[18] Preparations for post-war relief, trade, monetary relations, and the international institutions needed to sustain them could therefore begin in earnest.

PLANNING WITHOUT PLANS

The Princeton Mission calculated that the disruption of the move meant nine lost months, but that the price had been worth it. Princeton afforded the opportunity to 'feel in command of one's work, able to keep in touch with realities, able to form a policy, and to seek and find co-operation in carrying it out'.[19] They were liberated from Avenol's machinations, and surrounded by an enthusiastic and large audience: 'a long list of people from Washington, New York, various universities, etc. . . . the people who matter, or the people who are going to matter later.'[20] Loveday knew such attention did not equal influence, but the mission was drawn into US post-war planning so rapidly that every member found himself playing 'several instruments, with each limb and another with his nose'.[21] Loveday continued to display the circumspection and acuity that had characterized his service in Geneva, and facilitated the forging of productive and sustained connections with the State Department, the US Treasury, the Federal Reserve board, and key advisers, such as Viner, Hansen, and Pasvolsky. His counsel that there should be 'no planning, no blue prints' guided the Princeton Mission, whose focus was 'the assessment of past experiences and failures, and the collection and comparison of data'.[22] Around the world this was the era of planning for war and for peace, yet the language of planning was to be eschewed by the League.

[17] For the remarkable story of how the NS Deutsche Kongress-Zentrale, under the leadership of Alfred Rosenberg, monitored and mimicked international organizations, culminating in the systematic plunder of archives in occupied territories, see Herren, *Internationale Organisationen seit 1865*, 74–9.
[18] Diary entry, 13 Dec. 1942, Nuffield, Loveday Diary, 1942.
[19] Loveday to Janet Smith, 10 Mar. 1941, TNA: PRO FO371/26661, C3124/3124/98.
[20] Loveday to Janet Smith, 10 Mar. 1941, TNA: PRO FO371/26661, C3124/3124/98.
[21] Loveday to Janet Smith, 10 Mar. 1941, TNA: PRO FO371/26661, C3124/3124/98.
[22] Loveday to Janet Smith, 10 Mar. 1941, TNA: PRO FO371/26661, C3124/3124/98.

The strategy was neither value nor ideology free. It remained the same as in Geneva: to establish conditions conducive to an open world economy, and to avoid repeating 'the tragedy of the past decade that began with the financial collapse in the autumn of 1929'.[23] The immediate challenge was to continue collating economic and financial intelligence, and to develop what were called 'practical' policy recommendations from it. The EFO's publication programme was hampered by wartime censorship, a problem with which economic agencies around the world grappled. In part, the impact of censorship on the Princeton Mission was limited because it owned a unique historical repository of global intelligence on the interwar economy out of which post-war planners could extrapolate, and because the British and US administrations supplied the mission with a wealth of top secret wartime data—notably on the control and supply of food and fertilizer in Europe—that kept it abreast of changes in the world economy.[24] In contrast to the pre-war years, where the priority of the League's commitment to open diplomacy made publishing paramount, now it decided 'to keep a completely open mind about publication'. The aim was to have several important papers on key topics ready for dissemination, but to keep them open to last-minute revision and 'only to release them when the time was right, when there was demand' from policy-makers.[25]

The mission's main preoccupation was to mine the past in building a shared vision with the Roosevelt administration. To claim there was 'no planning, no blueprints', when the League's work in Princeton was largely about anticipating the future, was a diplomatic strategy. Of course it developed schema and proposals, designed with sufficient flexibility to assure the secretariat of its continued relevance as national plans changed. But, because Loveday and his colleagues were the focus of suspicion in circles beyond the elite of Democrat internationalists and outward-looking Republicans, they did not want to look as though they were telling FDR what to do, and were mindful that 'planning' had potentially unwelcome associations with the New Deal, and with National Socialism and Communism. The approach left the Princeton group well positioned to deal with the evolution of US policy, as the progressive element of its agenda fell away, but led to an awkward schism with the British government and the ILO for whom post-war planning was the imperative goal.

The British government was taken aback by the enthusiasm of the League secretariat for its new American home, especially when in March 1941 the mission,

---

[23] Loveday to Janet Smith, 10 Mar. 1941, TNA: PRO FO371/26661, C3124/3124/98.

[24] At first it was proposed that the Princeton group would be responsible only for the collation of current non-European data; European data would remain the prerogative of the officers remaining in Switzerland. But this proved unworkable in the face of unquenchable US demand for League data on Europe. David Ekbladh takes the mission's frustration with wartime censorship too much at face value in 'Exiled Economics: The Transnational Contributions and Limits of the League of Nations' Economic and Financial Section', *New Global Studies*, 4/1 (2010), 1–6. Secret intelligence supplied to the mission was destroyed in 1946. See memo, 'Documents Burned—5th February 1946', LON, Loveday, P150/24–5. Among these documents were monthly reports from the Ministry of Information, and the Economic Intelligence Weekly of the British Foreign Office.

[25] Loveday to Lester, 6 Nov. 1941, LON S562/No. 6, 40–6.

supported by Hambro in New York and Sweetser in Washington, told it the time had come to bring the rest of the League to the USA.[26] Lester disagreed. Certainly, he was hugely frustrated in Geneva and missed his family in Ireland, but he remained persuaded of the argument, forcefully articulated by the Foreign Office, that the League must retain a nominal headquarters in Switzerland.[27] The British counselled that abandoning what was left of the League in Geneva would be a gift to enemy propaganda. Privately, the Foreign Office also worried that if the whole League moved to the USA it would soon be over-run by American states, North and South (the latter group now dominated the Organizing Committee). To their mind, the fact remained 'that the British Empire was now the bulwark of the League... Indeed, it was India which was paying the largest financial contribution to the organisation after Britain.'[28] But, more importantly, it was concerned to 'preserve and yet further develop the informal co-operation between the British Empire and the United States which has grown up in this war [and] is by far the greatest practical contribution that we can make to world peace in the future'. Churchill and his cabinet wanted to safeguard what is described as the primacy of its 'Anglo-American understanding' and did not want to put it at risk 'by any fancy project of European or world reconstruction, however attractive'.[29] The British government did not want the prerogatives of the League muddying the waters of Anglo-American relations. Therefore, not only did the Princeton Mission believe that its strategy of supporting and shaping US internationalism held the key to post-war reconstruction; it was clear that Britain was much less supportive of its work. It also had to stave off the ILO as a rival source of policy advice on global economic reconstruction, which was a recurrent theme between 1941 and 1943, reflecting, on the one hand, the coherence and timeliness of the ILO's emphasis on Labour rights and productivity for wartime governments, and, on the other, its strong ties to key American actors.[30]

The ILO's re-emergence as a force in international economic and social relations in the spring of 1941 signified a growing sensitivity to the social dimension of post-war economic planning, and the continued movement in the plate-tectonics of world power. Britain was increasingly alive to the, potentially painful, implications of the American continent's likely dominance of any global institutions (a conclusion reinforced by British experience of pan-American cooperation). The British Foreign Office and Ernest Bevin's Ministry of Labour believed it was worth

---

[26] Loveday to Smith on conversation with Hambro, Frederick Phillips, and Malik, 1 Apr. 1941, TNA: PRO FO/371/26661, C4144/3124/28.

[27] Record of conversation between Makins and Reber, 5 Aug. 1941, TNA: PRO FO371/26662, C9274/3124/98.

[28] Kisch to Makins, 14 June 1941, TNA: PRO FO371/26661, C6940/3124/98

[29] L.S.A. (Leo Amery), 'A Note on Post-War Reconstruction', 29 Oct. 1940, TNA: PRO CAB 21/1582. Amery's appointment as Secretary of State for India, though a post defined as cabinet rank minister outside the war cabinet, provided him with the opportunity to act against League internationalism (and freer trade) and for the imperial solidarity that had long characterized his views.

[30] The ILO's contribution culminated in the 'Declaration of Philadelphia', 10 May 1944, which remains essential to its self-conception <http://www.ilo.org/declaration/thedeclaration/textdeclaration/lang–en/index.htm> (accessed 10 Nov. 2010).

supporting the ILO against the EFO's ambition to be the voice of post-war economic planning because of 'its great measure of support among organized Labour in Britain and in the Dominions'. The activities of the EFO, by contrast, were connected to a wider 'group of interests based on the American continent and predominately committed to the primacy of the market'.[31]

But the ILO did not have much support within the US State Department, which generally considered its work as 'too ambitious', and its acting Director-General, Irishman Edward Phelan, 'unimpressive'.[32] There Loveday reinforced the League's claim to primacy by arguing that, whereas the ILO had so far done little to counter what he believed was the potentially unhealthy concentration of world planning 'along Anglo-American lines', the Princeton Mission afforded the all-important global dimension. Although the Anglo-American alliance was essential for the purposes of the war and had saved the League in its darkest hour, it was 'inadequate from the point of view of other countries because we need a more explicit "moral" and "altruistic" basis for a long-term policy'.[33] There were inherent dangers to the power of the Anglo-American axis, just as there had been in 1939 when the future of the free world 'crystallized' around the decisions taken by the Anglo-French bloc. Ultimately, Loveday argued, national ministries such as the State Department and the British Foreign Office were unable to take a genuinely global perspective, and it was vital to get international agency back into the picture as soon as possible, while at the same time moderating American internationalists' untargeted enthusiasm for the League.[34] Lester and Loveday understood the importance of circumspection, given that FDR's administration faced fiercely contested Congressional elections, and agreed it was not the time to articulate specific goals or to induce governments, notably Roosevelt's, to commit themselves to a particular architecture for international relations. (Unlike the artificial truce of National Government in Britain, it was business as usual for American politics in the war.) The ILO, however, had other ideas.

THE CHALLENGE OF THE ILO

In the summer of 1941, the governmental consensus in Britain, the USA, the exiled governments of Belgium, the Netherlands, Czechoslovakia, Greece, Norway, Poland, and Yugoslavia, with which Princeton was in contact, was that the League probably could not, or perhaps should not, be revived. The priority was to retain its considerable physical and intellectual assets, and personnel. Yet the gap left by the demise of the intergovernmental dimension of League operations created a void

---

[31]   Minute by Makins, 17 June 1941, TNA: PRO FO371/26661, C6940/3124/98.

[32]   Record of conversation between Makins and Reber, 5 Aug. 1941, TNA: PRO FO371/26662, C9274/3124/98.

[33]   Walters to Sweetser, 12 July 1941, LON, Princeton Office, C1617/No. 1, 40–1.

[34]   Loveday and Lester fought shy of many of Sweetser's initiatives, including his Institute for World Organization. See Lester to Sweetser, 1 Aug. 1941, and Lester to Sweetser, 22 Sept. 1941, LON, Princeton Office, C1619/No. 2, 41.

that the ILO sought to exploit.[35] The squabble between Princeton and Montreal that followed, as in many family fights, began as a row about money but was about more fundamental issues: seniority, authority, political favour, and ideology. Since its inception, the EFO had been distinguished by its strong intergovernmental dimension, institutionalized in its relationship to the Council and Assembly and mediated through the Second Committee, which had been eliminated by the war. It had become clear that the absence of an intergovernmental powerbase left the Princeton Mission vulnerable, especially as the ILO continued to be supported by local offices situated in member countries around the world, and received financial contributions from members who were not in the League, most notably the USA and Brazil.

At a meeting of the League Supervisory Commission in Montreal in July 1941, the contrast was stark. The ILO fielded fifty-seven staff members compared to one or two representatives from each of the other League agencies, and suggested that what was left of the League in Geneva move in with the ILO to save money.[36] Lester bridled at the suggestion: life was already 'damned hard for the secretariat', and now it faced 'disembowelling' by the ILO.[37] Two months later the ILO went a step further in casting itself as heir apparent to the League. Between 27 September and 4 October, it convened a special International Labour Conference in New York City, with a concluding session at the White House on 5 November 1941, where delegates were addressed by FDR. This first meeting of the ILO since the outbreak of the European war dramatically brought together on US soil 187 governments, employers, and workers' representatives, including deputations of exiled governments named above, and delegations from France and Luxembourg. The step change in the ILO's ambition and vision was clear. Phelan presented the ILO as *the* international agency to deal with the economic and social aspects of reconstruction, and the agenda of the British Labour movement as the model for other nations to adopt in the battle for higher wages and improved standards of living.[38] The organization was now overtly competing with the Princeton group's claim to articulate the lessons of history as seen from Geneva. The ILO referenced the Atlantic Charter of 14 August 1941 in its call for 'the fullest collaboration between all nations in the economic field, with the object of securing for all improved labour standards, economic advancement, and social security'—a global goal tempered by the New Deal rhetoric and intended to counter Hitler's vision of a European 'New Order'.[39] Other clauses in the Atlantic Charter, however, were a reminder of the persistent tensions in FDR's political vision, notably an emphasis on the

[35] Memo by Princeton Mission, 'Record of Inter-Allied Meeting to Discuss the Work of the League of Nation's Supervisory Commission', *c.*16 July 1941, TNA: PRO FO371/26662, C7906/3124/98.

[36] Memos by Makins, 'Report of the Meeting of the Supervisory Commission of the League of Nations, Montreal, 29th and 30th July 1941', 25 Aug. 1941, TNA: PRO FO371/26662, C9845/3124/98.

[37] Lester to Sweetser, 1 Aug. 1941, LON, Princeton Office, C1619/No. 2, 41.

[38] 'Asks World Unity on Welfare Plans', *New York Times*, 5 Oct. 1941, p. 46.

[39] Smith Simpson, 'The International Labor Conference', *American Political Science Review*, 36/1 (1942), 104; minute by Strang, 16 Nov. 1941, TNA: PRO FO371/26649, C12419/111/98.

primacy of the market and the value of free trade that were referenced in the agenda of the Princeton Mission.[40]

But national delegates at the meetings in Montreal and New York were less attuned to the tensions between the League and the ILO, and, when they spoke of the need for international agency, their priority was to convey their own domestic vision and concerns, and to encourage the USA and the Anglo-American alliance to act multilaterally. Delegates who addressed the question of organizational agency directly, notably Hambro, on this occasion acting as a representative of the Norwegian government in exile, acknowledged the valuable work of the Princeton Mission, while both the Belgian delegate Paul Spaak and the British employers' representative John Forbes complained that ILO ambition to act as the world's primary international organization was beyond its remit and its competence.[41] The simple fact remained, however, that the ILO was the only international body with which FDR's administration had congressional authority to work, and the link was useful to the administration for 'the transaction of international business in a regular and organised international machine'.[42]

By the end of 1941, respite for the Princeton Mission from the ILO challenge came from a number of directions, notably US entrance into the war, which, alongside developments on the Eastern Front, moved world power relations to a predominantly East–West axis. In 1942 and 1943, the economic and geo-political landscape continued to change in ways that would shape the next half century. From the perspective of post-war planning, the geo-political shift confirmed FDR's determination that the USA should dominate the post-war economic order, and cemented a conception of economic internationalism focused on the reopening and domination of international markets, and the promotion of consumption with the promise of higher living standards for all. This perspective was reinforced in 1942 by Congressional elections delivering a stronger coalition of Republicans and conservative Democrats that rejected the New Deal. US politics now struck a different note to the ILO's foregrounding of social rights, and the aim of rebalancing of the relationship between employees and employers.

If, at the beginning of 1942, the mindset of US reconstruction was moving closer to that of the Princeton group, the networks to which the mission was connected also contributed to the latter's revival. With the support of the State Department, and a variety of prominent ILO, American, Canadian, British, and exiled European economists, the mission mapped out a wide-ranging programme.[43] It confined

---

[40] The fourth point also contained the problematic caveat 'with due respect for their existing obligations'. See 'Text of the Atlantic Charter', 14 Aug. 1941 <http://avalon.law.yale.edu/wwii/atlantic.asp> (accessed 10 June 2009).

[41] Report by Loveday, 'Note on the World of the Conference of the International Labour Organization, New York, 27th October to 6th November', c.8 November 1941, LON, Princeton Office, C1745/No. 7 (1), 41.

[42] Minute by Ronald, TNA: PRO FO371/26649, C12419/111/98.

[43] The breadth and fluidity of this network make it difficult to chart consistently over time while simultaneously drawing out the skeins of policy. A snapshot of Loveday's correspondents in one week in December 1941 draws out the scale of this personal network: members of Nuffield College Social Reconstruction Survey, the Twentieth Century Fund, New York, and the National Institute of

itself to three major themes that shaped and reflected the priorities of US policy: world trade; international monetary policy; and emergency relief and the short-term challenges of post-war reconstruction, beneath which lay three principles. The first was that it was essential to study the lessons of the past and learn from them. Although it smacked of 'fighting the last war', it reflected the historical orientation of economic science at the time, and these economic 'generals' were as preoccupied with the experience of the Great Depression as with the lessons of the 'Great War' and its immediate aftermath. The second was that, while it was important to appreciate the impact of changes triggered by the war, 'fundamental economic forces' and cycles would surface at the war's end, which needed to be understood and countered. The group argued with considerable force and prescience that the problem of economic depressions, and their relationship to peace and security, would remain the most important challenge facing the modern world long after the impact of the war had faded.[44] The third guiding idea was that these examinations should be grounded in a firm empirical basis.[45]

In November 1941, the Princeton group produced the most comprehensive agenda for national and international reconstruction available anywhere at this stage of the war. It addressed ten issues (Loveday's original list had comprised twenty-four): commercial policy; access to raw materials; demographic questions; how to combat economic depression; post-war relief and reconstruction; currency problems; international capital movements; capital supply; national and international debts; and agriculture and nutrition.[46] Given the rapidly changing geo-political context, investigation of topics relating to the architecture of international relations was postponed. These included: 'the method of international progress, e.g. conferences, collective agreements, a regional or bilateral model; the economic and financial organization of the future; colonies; and the status of Europe as an economic unit'.[47] But the future organization of international affairs remained an important subtext for the Princeton Mission, particularly given its position as a point of triangulation in Anglo-American relations.

Friction between the ILO and Princeton gradually dissipated, although tensions between numerous and disparate elements involved in US administration and post-war planning rumbled on during the war and, unhelpfully, into the period of

---

Economic and Social Research in London. It also included American economists especially interested in monetary questions, notably Viner, Hansen, William Adams Brown, and Frank Southard of the US Treasury; also E. F. Penrose, formerly of the ILO and now serving as special assistant to the US Ambassador in London to Winant; Leo Pasvolsky, special assistant to the Secretary of State; A. Ramasawami Mudaliar, a former member of the League's Demographic Committee and member of the Governor General's Executive Council in India; and other economists working on questions relating to post-war reconstruction in India, Australia, Canada, and New Zealand; and the extraordinary envoy of the Finnish government, H. J. Procopé. He also met John Boyd Orr to discuss agriculture and nutrition.

[44] Memos by Loveday, 'Post-War Problems—Plan of Work', *c.*Nov. 1941, LON, Princeton Office, C1755/No. 1 40–4.

[45] Loveday to Lester, 6 Nov. 1941, LON S562/No. 6, 40–6.

[46] Loveday to Lester, 6 Nov. 1941, LON S562/No. 6, 40–6.

[47] Memo by Loveday, 'Post-War Problems', *c.*Sept. 1940, LON, Princeton Office, C1755/No. 1 40–4.

reconstruction itself.[48] In April 1942, the White House made it clear it wanted the ILO to focus solely on the 'social aspects' of post-war issues. It did not require the organization to confine itself to issues related to the protection and organization of labour, but it no longer wanted it to act as a formal negotiating body. Instead, the ILO should address 'informational and educational tasks', taking 'care to avoid' recommendations that might commit either the ILO or its members to specific policies.[49] The USA no longer needed the fig leaf of the ILO to cover its internationalism, and as its war economy developed, so the influence grew of businessmen and financiers who were less interested in labour codes than in opening up international markets. The conduits through which post-war reconstruction and a new economic order were to be negotiated were repositioned once more.

The squabble between the ILO and Princeton-based agencies of the League illustrated how the competing demands of the national and international political economy gave rise to divisions within states, such as the competition between New Dealers and the State Department, which favoured a more conventionally internationalist and orthodox economic foreign policy. The history of this rivalry, reaching back into the origins of Roosevelt's first electoral victory in 1932, is well known, but historians who map these cleavages within individual governments often fail to see how particular departments or groups within an administration sought out international connections and alliances to support their position. Seen from the vantage point of the ILO and the League, these transnational constellations were readily apparent, and during the war underwent significant and sometimes rapid change. The short-lived competition between the ILO and the Princeton Mission also revealed the political will, in some quarters of the American administration, to open up aspects of reconstruction policy to international agency: the ILO proposal for the Advisory Committee suggested that the Chinese, Indians, and South Americans all be given a prominent role. (This willingness to widen global involvement in debates about reconstruction was one of the saving graces of the proposal for Loveday.[50]) In this, Britain begrudgingly acted as a partner, notably renegotiating the re-entry of the USSR in the ILO.[51]

---

[48] At a meeting of the ILO emergency committee in London, Phelan implied that he carried with him the State Department and other leading members of the administration, notably the former Secretary of Agriculture and the current vice-president Henry Wallace. However, negotiations with British, Dutch, Canadian, and US officials revealed that Phelan and Goodrich were not so much in receipt of Presidential support as making a vigorous case for it, backed by a small group of New Dealers, notably Isadore Lublin, Adolph Berle, and Francis Perkins. See Phillips to Leith-Ross, 13 Jan. 1942, TNA: PRO FO371/30980, C2115/23/98; record of meeting between Phelan and Makins, 10 Apr. 1942, TNA: PRO FO371/30981, C4248/23/98; memo by Makins, 17 Apr. 1942, TNA: PRO FO371/30981, C4082/23/98.

[49] Telegram from State Department to Foreign Office, 3 Apr. 1942, TNA: PRO FO371/30980, C3617/23/98.

[50] Loveday to Lester, 30 Apr. 1942, LON S558/No. 4, 40.

[51] British support for the move was essential because of its long-established relationship with the ILO, and League members had to be brought on board to secure the governing body of the ILO's approval (notably Canada, the Netherlands, and India). It prompted considerable unease in some

THE LEAGUE IN PRINCETON

The British Treasury's support for the ILO in its bid for dominance over the League revealed how far its economic and strategic ethos had altered since its advocacy of international economic orthodoxy in the 1920s and then conservative-flavoured economic imperialism of the 1930s. Closer in public policy to US New Dealers in ways that would have been unimaginable in Chamberlain's Treasury, however, the USA and Britain remained far apart on trade policy.[52] Britain presented its move to general and imperial protection as necessary retaliation in response to, rather than the consequence of, a long-term shift in its domestic priorities. In the war, the diminution of Britain's economic power and its reliance on the sterling area made trade protection more important than ever to Britain's post-war prospects. But the British Ministry of Information's propaganda campaign narrated Anglo-American relations as a 'special relationship' that would deliver a 'partnership on equal terms' to lead the world and necessarily played down the difference between the two powers on trade policy.

On board HMS *Prince of Wales* moored in Placentia Bay, Churchill had been able to negotiate some wiggle room for imperial preference through a last-minute amendment of point four of the Atlantic Charter's commitment to 'further the enjoyment by all States . . . of access, on equal terms to the trade and to the raw materials of the world' on terms that granted 'due respect for their existing obligations'.[53] This, however, left the matter unresolved from a US and League perspective, and the tensions and challenges ahead in forging an economic and monetary order based on the Anglo-American partnership were spelt out in memoranda that were exchanged, albeit by way of organized 'leaks', between the State Department, and the British Treasury and Foreign Office in December 1941. Central to Anglo-American discussions was Pasvolsky's memorandum on 'Possibilities of Conflict in British and American Official Views in Post-War Economic Policy'. It became a famous exposition of the difference in bilateral relations between the two countries, which was powerfully shaped by the history of their encounters at the League of Nations and intelligence afforded by the Princeton Mission. Pasvolsky warned of the 'diametrically opposed' impulses in future Anglo-American trade policies: the British Empire and its global trading relationships would seek to retain economic controls for as long as possible; the Americans wanted to see 'free trade' established worldwide. The difference, he argued, had the potential to disrupt the most important relationship in international relations at a time when a vast number of countries including 'the rest of Europe and a large part of Asia would also face serious trading and account deficits'. The only way to save

British quarters. Makins to Leggett, 6 Apr. 1942, and Makins to Stephenson, 11 Apr. 1942, TNA: PRO FO371/30980, C3617/23/98.

[52] George Peden, *The Treasury and British Public Policy, 1906–1959* (Oxford, 2000), 292–7, 308–13.

[53] For Churchill's annotated copy see <http://history.state.gov/milestones/1937-1945/AtlanticConf> (accessed 24 July 2011).

the world from a new wave of economic nationalism would be to supply these countries with the 'necessary food, raw materials and capital equipment free or on credit'. The implication was that these resources would have to come from the United States, and the price to be paid was open markets. Here Pasvolsky adopted, almost verbatim, a formulation of the problem articulated in documents produced by the EFO. He saw the challenge for states as coming from the need, not so much to find the 'right policy' (although for Pasvolsky free trade was the 'right policy') as to develop the correct institutional context in which effective policies might be implemented on a cooperative basis. Paramount was the need for 'a clear and unequivocal declaration of the determination to do everything necessary for the creation of all conditions indispensable to the functioning of a multilateral system of international economic relationships'.[54]

The memorandum revealed that Pasvolsky did not have the sophisticated understanding of the economic challenges before the world evident in the work of Viner, Hansen, or John Maurice Clark, who were also writing influential policy papers at this time, but his sensitivity to the impact of transnational and inter-national networks and organizations on the prospects for liberal economic policy was striking. He dissected British protectionist opinion into three groups: those who believed that the dire state of Britain's balance of payments after the war meant that the government would have no choice but to continue foreign exchange and trade controls indefinitely (typified by Keynes); those who favoured the controlled economy on principle (advocates of economic planning on the Left of British politics); and those who wanted some measure of free trade, but were resistant to the unconditional application of MFN (advocates of imperial preference found in large number in the Conservative Party).[55]

Pasvolsky's concern was not merely to underline to the US and British govern-ments the danger posed to their relations, but the risks to global prosperity and security if protection continued to dominate British policy. On the one hand, he wanted to strengthen the hand of British Liberals such as Robbins, Meade, Robertson, and Harrod, all well known to him via the EFO, and, on the other, challenge groups in the USA, notably American farmers, whose views were closer to those of British protectionists than to those of the US administration. His experi-ence at Geneva had taught him of the 'predatory protectionist interests' well entrenched in Europe. These could work together to obstruct, and possibly even reverse, America's new commitment to free trade. Not that US policy needed to be 'completely free trade'. What it required was 'a large measure of flexibility in trade movements'.[56] It was the same formulation as that advanced by Stoppani at the 1933 World Economic Conference. Pasvolsky also wanted constituencies in the

[54] Memo by Pasvolsky, 12 Dec. 1941, TNA: PRO T247/94. For Loveday's and Pasvolsky's exchanges, see Loveday's 1940 diary entries of 4 Dec., 6 Dec., 24 Dec., and 1941 diary entries of 15 Apr., 1 June, 23 Aug., 22 Oct., Nuffield, Loveday Diary, 1941.
[55] Memo by Pasvolsky, 12 Dec. 1941, TNA: PRO T247/94; Douglas A. Irwin, *Against the Tide: An Intellectual History of Free Trade* (Princeton, 1996), 200–1.
[56] Memo by Pasvolsky, 12 Dec. 1941, TNA: PRO T247/94.

USA, the British Empire, and Europe, who supported the application of unconditional MFN to be as integrated and strong as possible, and that international organizations be established to safeguard these values and relationships. The creation of 'effective international machinery' to promote a liberal trade regime, therefore, had to 'find a means of influencing and coordinating certain important domestic policies'. Pasvolsky's emphasis on the value of effective international institutions had grown out of his close working relationship with the EFO in the 1930s and is notably similar to theories of the 'new political economy' of the twenty-first century.[57] Between 1940 and 1942 this conviction was reinforced by his front-row seat in the spats between the League, the ILO, and national representatives.[58]

The growing number of voices seeking to shape post-war economic policy triggered anxiety in London too. While the outbreak of war and the negotiations for Lend-Lease had increased the intensity and variety of bilateral intergovernmental contacts between the UK and the USA (from the Prime Minister and President downwards and across a wider range of departments than ever before), multiplicity sometimes threatened cacophony. Other Allied nations wanted a say, and, for post-war planning to be effective, the perspective of countries that were currently enemies also needed to be included. Here was a new use for the Princeton Mission: Britain and the USA used the involvement of the secretariat as a way to claim they were taking the views of other powers into account, and to retain control of the agenda at the same time.[59]

It prompted further reflection on the role of global institutions within the British government. Meade, now on secondment to the Economic Section of the War Cabinet, drafted an influential paper in which he proposed the creation of connected international bodies to coordinate economic policies after the war. He incorporated Keynes's blueprint for an International Clearing Union, an international investment board for developing countries, and a plan to supervise and stabilize the prices of primary goods (a buffer stock scheme that would reduce fluctuations in price), and proposed a raft of other schemes too. These included an international monetary arrangement that differentiated between creditor and debtor nations, a global programme for commodity controls, a charter that established best practice for international commercial relations, and, most importantly,

---

[57] Pasvolsky's account of the 'Failures and Mistakes of the 1920s', in his memo of 12 Dec. 1941, p. 8, TNA: PRO T247/94, was strikingly similar to that found in League of Nations, *The Transition from War to Peace Economy*. That this Anglo-American group knew one another well is often remarked upon in the literature; that they knew one another through the agency of the League was not. See Susan Howson, and Donald Moggridge, *The Wartime Diaries of Robbins and Meade, 1943–45* (London, 1990), 62.

[58] Memo by Pasvolsky, 12 Dec. 1941, TNA: PRO T247/94; memo by Keynes, 'My Notes on Mr Pasvolsky's Memo', 5 Jan. 1942, TNA: PRO T247/94.

[59] Leggett to Quintin Hill, 4 Apr. 1942, TNA: PRO FO371/30980, C3628/23/98. Lindsay Rogers told Loveday that the USA wanted the EFO to take the lead. See letter to Riefler, 9 Mar. 1942, TNA: PRO FO371/30980, 9 Mar. 1942. On Rogers, see Amy Fried, 'The Forgotten Lindsay Rogers and the Development of American Political Science', *American Political Science Review*, 100/4 (2006), 555–61.

an international commission that would coordinate the *internal* depression policies of nation states. This was an issue very close to the League secretariat's heart that had surfaced time and again in the work of the Depression Delegation and in the EFO's post-war planning documents. In the UK it now became a key theme in the Economic Section's work on post-war employment policy, on which Meade took the lead.[60]

The imprint of the League was found elsewhere, as the outline of a new architecture of international relations, and the organizations to support it, began to emerge. It was, as Loveday put it, 'a square with many roads leading to it... They are innumerable, and there must inevitably be much intermixture, bisection and overlapping.'[61] One road that he helped to pave at Pasvolsky's invitation was a joint Anglo-American economic declaration to accompany the Atlantic charter. In it, Loveday brought together the divergent Anglo-American goals for reconstruction by steering a careful path between Keynesian aspirations for a controlled return to multilateralism, and the US intention to reopen markets as soon as possible. The first shared aim, the declaration proclaimed, was the pursuit of national economic policies that would 'promote the fullest possible employment, increasing production, raising living standards and economic stability'. That weakened countries such as Britain would require the retention of state control over key levers in the economy, Keynesian or not, was left unsaid. The second goal pulled in a different direction, although it was not wholly disconnected from the first: the promotion of international collaboration and appropriate commercial policies to enable all countries to maximize their productive resources. Loveday's ability to articulate a common international vision was praised widely, as was his contribution to associated proposals. His input, for example, caused Hansen and Luther Gulick to revise their earlier, simpler plan for an International Development Corporation into a more sophisticated scheme that would combine 'London experience' with 'New York money' to revive international lending after the war.[62] Hansen and Gulick were impressed by Loveday's insistence that the corporation should provide advice and policy recommendations, and needed to have adequate and representative staffing by hiring experienced workers from member states around the world.[63] Arnold Toynbee told Halifax and Keynes the idea had great potential because 'the US in recent years had bungled its foreign lending and its citizens, after the war,

[60] Alec Cairncross and Nita G. M. Watts, *The Economic Section, 1936–1961: A Study in Economic Advising* (London, 1989), 99.

[61] Kisch to Loveday, 3 Nov. 1941, TNA: PRO FO371/26662, C12220/3124/98.

[62] Diary entry, 23 Dec. 1941, Nuffield, Loveday Diary, 1941, Luther Gulick, *Administrative Reflections from World War II* (Tuscaloosa, AL, 1948), 108–9. Skidelsky underlines the importance of Hansen's and Gulick's memos in firing up Keynes and British planning, though is unaware of the role played by the League. See Robert Skidelsky, *John Maynard Keynes*, iii. *Fighting for Britain, 1937–1946* (London, 2000), 218. The degree of multilateral exchange facilitated through the Princeton Mission must also nuance his presentation of proceeding 'in isolation from the other in 1942' (p. 233). Meade, by contrast, characterizes Anglo-American exchanges over the same period 'so large as to preclude any intimacy or at personal exchanges they petered out in inaction'. Howson and Moggridge, *The Wartime Diaries of Robbins and Meade*, 18.

[63] Loveday to Hansen, 25 Oct. 1941, LON, Princeton Office, C1629/No. 2, 41–2.

would have great sums available to be lent abroad but would be unwilling to lend under American direction'.[64] Of course, Loveday was too diplomatic to express it in these terms—he spoke more of the need for partnership and collaboration and the redistribution of wealth across nations—but Toynbee was right to recognize the scheme as having 'sprung from the old League of Nations'.[65] Although the British Treasury, rightly as it turned out, believed it would be insufficient to revive international lending on its own, the International Development Corporation was the first salvo in negotiations that led eventually to the Keynes–White plans, the World Bank, and the IMF. By then, reference to the League's pioneering contribution to institutionalized cooperation was knowingly cast aside to spare new organizations, intended to inject confidence and growth in the world economy, from association with failed interwar order.[66]

The Princeton Mission sought to ensure neither Britain nor the United States overlooked the close link between relief and reconstruction: Britain preferred to focus on the former, and the USA on the latter. The group's programme of work, and Loveday's barrage of correspondence to policy-makers in both nations, consistently highlighted the ties between them and that aid was as much about providing finance as it was about offering food. Its provocations, however, were not always taken up, although history was to prove their value. The Mission, for example, repeatedly asked how countries were expected to pay for their immediate needs—a question only finally resolved some five years later with the Marshall plan.[67] Where it had more effect was in inserting an international perspective more generally on post-war relief, and, once again, the Anglo-American team primarily engaged with the issue was led by a man who had been intimately involved with the EFO's work in the 1920s and 1930s, Frederick Leith-Ross.

In the spring of 1942, Leith-Ross became chairman of the new Inter-Allied Commission on Post-War Requirements. One of his earliest acts was to chair a meeting of familiar faces and some new ones at the first wartime session of the League's Economic and Financial Committee on US soil, held between 27 April and 1 May 1942. Among the established League hands were Loveday, Leith-Ross, McDougall, Riefler, and Fernand Van Langenhove (now Secretary-General of the Belgian Foreign Ministry in exile and recent architect of the plan for a Dutch–Belgian customs union, which became one of the founding pillars of the European Union). Among the 'new' were important representatives of other exiled European governments, including Georgios Mantzavinos, the current Deputy Governor (and future Governor) of the Bank of Greece in exile in London, and Jan

[64] Exposition on the Hansen–Gulick plan by Toynbee, c.6 Oct. 1941, TNA: PRO T247/70.
[65] Toynbee to Keynes, c.6 Oct. 1941, TNA: PRO T247/70.
[66] Loveday to Hansen, 25 Oct. 1941, and Loveday's annotations on 'Tentative Draft of Joint Economic Declaration by the Governments of the United States and Great Britain', Oct. 1941, LON, Princeton Office, C1629/No. 2, 41–2. Keynes's draft was extensively revised by Loveday; see Halifax to Keynes, 1 Nov. 1941, TNA: PRO T247/70.
[67] Explored at length in Loveday's correspondence with Hansen in 1941 and 1942. See LON, Princeton Office, C1629/No. 2, 41–2.

Nowak-Jeziorański, the 'Courier from Warsaw', an indefatigable emissary of the Polish government in exile who was later significant in shaping Poland's relations with the West, right up to its inclusion in NATO in 1999. The Economic and Financial Committee's role as a third, distinctive voice, neither British nor American, thereby made room for the wider world in the close, but never easy, 'special relationship'.

The reconvened committee encapsulated how the EFO continued to facilitate transnational networks in the war. Although small, its membership was diverse, able, and overwhelmingly European. Indeed, Lester believed the committee met a vital need to reassert a European perspective in Anglo-American wartime planning and vigorously argued that, despite the additional cost, the EFO's publications should continue to be published in French. (Lester lost the argument—an indication of the future Anglophonic direction of international diplomacy.[68]) It is true that these men probably would have met in some other Allied forum on reconstruction, but the meeting of the Economic and Financial Committee was a fertile affair. Loveday was taken aback by the enthusiasm of the delegates, who declared their home governments had a huge appetite for the mission's work, and included a wish list of additional topics for it to study.

Some proposals recycled familiar League themes; other discussions reflected entrenched fears among European members that the icy wind of free trade blowing from Washington would prove more than their economies, empires, and peoples could bear. McDougall suggested that the Princeton group look to launching a regional development scheme for the Danube Valley along the lines of the Tennessee Valley Authority, itself a reworking of older League and ILO public works for the region. Leith-Ross wanted the Princeton group to study how developed countries would be affected by industrialization of agricultural nations, while several participants argued that studies seeking to promote the liberalization of world trade should examine how this would affect individuals' standards of living. But critical reflections also emerged, of which two were key: the first was the tendency of reconstruction in the 1920s to deal with 'problems at their apex rather than at their base—international finance in terms of central banks instead of financing production; commercial policy in terms of tariffs instead of in terms of the economics of production'. Secondly, however well informed and refined the economic, financial, and social policies of the Allies, they would come to nothing unless related to the question of security. These were errors that 'should not be repeated'.[69]

But such views risked putting the cat among the Anglo-American pigeons, and threatened to set policy-makers in Washington and London against the mission. As a result, they were omitted from the published report, preferring to focus on themes that became familiar refrains in the EFO's many wartime publications: the

[68] Lester to Loveday, 4 May 1942 and 10 June 1942, LON, Princeton Office, C1631/No. 4 (1), 41–2.

[69] Note by Loveday, 'Economic and Financial Committees; Report to the Council on the Work of the Joint Session, London, 27 April–1 May, Princeton, 7–8 August 1942', Aug. 1942, and Lloyd to Vigier, 5 Nov. 1942, LON R4384, 10A/41803/1778.

challenges facing the world would be greater than at the end of the First World War; trade policy should be formulated on a bilateral and eventually multilateral and liberal basis—great play was made of Article VII of the Mutual Aid Agreement (the master document of Lend-Lease); and reconstruction schemes should be formulated and coordinated on an international scale. In short, there was need for 'a much larger degree of international collaboration than anything yet achieved' in history.[70] The challenge before the Allied Nations was to put flesh onto these bones. The committee indicated that the economic and financial work of the League had gone a long way to help. It provided a list of 'Work Undertaken by the League of Nations', and noted the rising demand for its reports around the world. It also underlined, drawing on the work of the Nutrition and Bruce reports of the 1930s, that one of the central challenges before policy-makers was the 'problem of economic advancement with social security'. In short, the League offered a 'system of collaboration' to help what Loveday called 'baby governments' to face the challenges of growing up.[71]

It is worth pausing on the mission's ringing endorsement of Article VII of the Mutual Aid agreement, or the 'consideration', as it was subsequently dubbed, because the mission defined what was due from the UK and its Allies in return for US aid. Churchill's escape clause in the Atlantic Charter that recognized 'existing obligations' was gone, to be replaced by a second, more precise and categorical definition of an Anglo-American commitment 'directed to the expansion, by appropriate international and domestic measures, of production, employment, and the exchange and consumption of goods'. Keynes was wrong to lambast 'the lunatic Mr Hull' and the US State Department alone for the priority of free trade that underpinned the Atlantic charter. The League of Nations, whose history reached deep into nineteenth-century European liberalism, promoted by the free-trading Dutch as much as by the British before 1931, was also responsible.[72]

THE TRANSITION FROM WAR TO PEACE ECONOMY

The extent of the challenges facing governments after the war was underlined in one of the most consulted and sought-after publications of the League: *The Transition from War to Peace Economy*. Widely circulated among Allied and exile governments in draft form throughout 1942, its publication in May 1943 came on the eve of renewed bilateral Anglo-American negotiations amid signs that British plans for a Clearing Union in London were losing out to the Stabilization Fund proposed by Washington.[73] The League report made passing reference to the new

---

[70] League of Nations, Economic and Financial Committees, *Report to the Council on the Work of the Joint Session* (Geneva, Aug. 1942), 5.
[71] League of Nations, Economic and Financial Committees, *Report to the Council on the Work of the Joint Session* (Geneva, Aug. 1942), 22; Loveday to Lester, 30 Apr. 1942, LON S558/No. 4, 40.
[72] Alfred E. Eckes Jr, *A Search for Solvency: Bretton Woods and the International Monetary System, 1941–1971* (Austin, 1975), 39.
[73] Skidelsky, *John Maynard Keynes*, iii. 301.

financial structures, but its primary intention was less to prescribe the details of policy than to frame and inform the context in which policy operated, and to stress the necessity for coherent and co-ordinated planning.

The Transition from War to Peace Economy presented a stark representation of a world

with no functioning international system to which to revert, moving rudderless into an unforeseeable future from a present in which the whole structure of production and trade, national and international, will be distorted, and in large areas of which many will have been killed or crippled, civilian populations uprooted from their homes, [industrial] plant destroyed, and the means of transport, the docks and railway terminals will have been battered and blasted.[74]

The picture recognized and responded to national reconstruction plans that were beginning to emerge, including one of the earliest and most significant, the British Beveridge Report, published to public acclamation in November 1942.[75] The League report, like that of Beveridge, opened with a set of guiding objectives that had radical potential. None was more ground-breaking than that the first objective for post-war economic policy should be to ensure that the fullest possible use was made of the 'resources of production, human and material, of the skill and enterprise of the individual . . . to attain and maintain *in all countries* a stable economy and rising standards of living'.[76]

In the 1930s many in the West continued to view their own societies as distinct from those of Africa or Asia. Through its work, however, the EFO's experts had come to place all societies of the world on a single continuum from the least to the most developed, with the presumption that it was in the interests of global prosperity and security if the world was seen as unified in following the same economic path heading towards a common goal of higher living standards. It was a proto theory of modernization, offering a view that is more widely identified with 'development economics', emerging in the USA after 1945.[77] The League's message had an aspirational quality, setting out a concept of world unity among the United Nations that had grown from 'the principle of equality of sacrifice and a pooling and sharing of the resources available for war and of the risks of war'.[78] In 1943, this characterization was some distance away from the rivalries that bedevilled relations within the Grand Alliance, where the perception was that the burden of sacrifice was anything but shared.

The Transition from War to Peace Economy was the first of two major publications of the Delegation on Economic Depressions, which had begun work in 1938, and

[74] League of Nations, *The Transition from War to Peace Economy*, 40.
[75] HMSO Social Insurance and Allied Services, *The Beveridge Report*, CMND 6404 (London, Nov. 1942). Harris, *William Beveridge*, 412–18.
[76] League of Nations, *The Transition from War to Peace Economy*, 11, emphasis added.
[77] See, e.g., Nils Gilman, *Mandarins of the Future: Modernization Theory in Cold War America* (Baltimore, MD, 2003), and David Engerman, *Modernization from the Other Shore: American Intellectuals and the Romance of Russian Development* (Cambridge, MA, 2003).
[78] League of Nations, *The Transition from War to Peace Economy*, 12.

was a project very close to the heart of the director, who, from the moment he arrived in Princeton, sought to reconvene the Depression Delegation. Three of the original committee members were now lost, their disparate fates illustrating the vagaries of war. Jacques Rueff's career as Deputy Governor of the Bank of France ended abruptly with the implementation of anti-Semitic legislation in Vichy France, while Ohlin was trapped inside Sweden, living a quieter life as professor of the Stockholm Business School, with his career as a Liberal parliamentarian held in abeyance. Most dramatic was the fate of the Finn Risto Ryti, who was appointed Prime Minister at the start of the Winter War in 1939. He sought to 'save Finland', first from the USSR, which resulted in the Moscow Peace Treaty in 1940, and then as President by moving closer to Germany, a quest that culminated in the ignominious deal signed with Ribbentrop in the summer of 1944. At the war's end, he was controversially tried as a war criminal and sentenced to ten years' imprisonment, much against the wishes of the majority of Finns. Although released after three years and later pardoned, it would take another forty-five years before his reputation was officially restored.

The wartime careers of delegation members Phillips, Riefler, McDougall, Haberler, and Morgenstern were far less dramatic. Each undertook important war work and remained in regular contact with Loveday and with the wider network of expertise the League had helped to generate. Phillips and Riefler were ensconced in national treasuries where much of the planning for the post-war monetary regime and supporting institutions were under way. McDougall moved to Washington in 1941 as part of the Australian economic mission. Haberler was still a member of the faculty in Harvard, while Oskar Morgenstern, his German-born successor as director of the Rockefeller-funded Österreichesches Institut für Konjunkturforschung in Vienna after Hayek's short-lived tenure, moved to Princeton in 1938. Although formally associated with the university, where Rockefeller continued to pay his salary costs, Morgenstern gravitated increasingly towards the IAS. The story of the friendship that developed there between Morgernstern and the Hungarian-born John von Neumann and its intellectual product, the first book on game theory, is famous.[79] What is much less well known is that his comfortable berth in Princeton, from which he was to declare in 1943 'a completely new era has started for me', also reunited him with economists from Vienna and Europe, thus connecting him to the Continent and a past from which he had yet to break.[80]

In 1941 and 1942, redrafting the Depression Delegation report, in abeyance since 1939, took priority over other projects.[81] With Rasminsky now running

---

[79] Oskar Morgenstern and John von Neumann, *Theory of Games and Economic Behaviour* (Princeton, 1944).

[80] Robert Leonard, 'The Collapse of Interwar Vienna: Oskar Morgenstern's Community, 1925–1950', *International Centre for Economic Research Working Paper Series*, 4 (2010), 48–9, draws out the diversity of views within the Austrian school, but is unaware of the degree to which the EFO's sojourn at the IAS reunited him with former colleagues from Austria or the wider network of business cycle research to which he had been integral. For further details on the work with Neumann, see Robert Leonard, *Von Neumann, Morgenstern, and the Creation of Game Theory: From Chess to Social Science, 1900–1960* (Cambridge, 2010).

[81] Loveday to Phillips, 17 July 1942, LON, Princeton Office, C1739/No. 1 (1), 40–5.

the Foreign Exchange Control Board of the Bank of Canada, it fell to Loveday to rewrite the earlier report, drawing on the opportunities the war presented for this work. The membership of the delegation was widened to ensure the breadth of perspective that had characterized its earlier incarnation was sustained.[82] A sign of the rehabilitation of the Netherlands in allied relations and the new importance of the Pacific countries was evident with the inclusion of G. H. C. Hart, the leading adviser in the Dutch Colonial Office, who had a particular interest in the relationship between agriculture and industry and the distribution of wealth in the Dutch empire. Loveday asked Gunnar Myrdal, who was living in Princeton with his wife, to replace Ohlin, but he declined. Zygmunt Karpinski, the exiled Governor of the Bank of Poland, and Gerald Towers, Governor of the Bank of Canada, however, were officially co-opted into the delegation, as was the American ILO economist Carter Goodrich.

Goodrich was engaged in developing the ILO's post-war programme, and his ILO colleagues E. F. Penrose and Arthur Winant provided additional ILO input.[83] Loveday also sought as much feedback as he could secure from economists among the League's current and former members, including exiled Germans in the USA, and most of the proposed amendments were minor. Anonymity was not just proffered to participants but was seen as desirable: the Princeton Mission preferred to work with advisers and economists who 'could be relied upon to do a job from an international point of view without becoming confused by any national political distractions'.[84] There was little disagreement over the political direction of the report among the eminent commentators who responded to the League's call, including Robbins, Robertson, Hansen, McDougall, Leith-Ross, US Director of Trade Agreements Harry Hawkins, Haberler, and Meade (the final two responding in the greatest depth).[85] Meetings were held to discuss the drafts in Princeton, Washington, London, and Ottawa in the winter of 1941 and spring of 1942, with a final gathering in Washington in August 1943 with supplementary members from China, Brazil, Venezuela, Colombia, Mexico, India, and Yugoslavia. Every corner of the world except Africa was represented. Loveday was especially pleased with the Latin American and Indian participation, and their reflections on the global dimension of the reconstruction challenge.[86] Sanctioned by the White House and the US State Department, the final event formally constituted as a session of

---

[82] Haberler argued that 'the special value' of the study was its 'stress on the international aspects and the consideration given to countries other than the USA and Britain'. Haberler to Loveday, 23 Mar. 1943, LON, Princeton Office, C1739/No. 1 (1), 40–5.

[83] See, e.g., E. F. Penrose, 'Economic Organization for Total War', pp. 3–41, and other essays in International Labour Office, *Studies in War Economics*, series B, no. 33 (Montreal, 1941); Carter Goodrich, 'The Developing Programme of the ILO', *Annals of the American Academy of Political and Social Science*, 224 (Nov. 1942), 183–9. ILO studies were more explicitly focused on the industrialized world than those of the EFO.

[84] Contributors were assured that their views would remain anonymous. Jessup to Loveday, 3 Apr. 1943, LC, Sweetser, Box 39.

[85] For correspondence and suggested amendments, see LON, Princeton Office, C1739/No. 1 (1), 40–5.

[86] Loveday to Lester, 10 Aug. 1942, LON, Princeton Office, C1619/No. 3, 42.

the Economic and Financial Committee was a landmark, being the first official meeting of the League on American soil. Sweetser was amazed that this remarkable precedent provoked so little controversy among the general public.[87]

That same month, the *New York Times* published a lengthy article under the banner 'League Urges New Economy', which heightened US demands that the as yet unpublished report be printed and widely circulated as soon as possible. The level of US official interest surpassed all Loveday's expectations. The Executive Office of the White House, the State Department, the Department of Commerce, the Department of Agriculture, the National Institute for Public Affairs, and the National Foreign Trade Council all made reference to it in their own works.[88] By November 1942, the 121-page report was approved and completed. Tellingly, though published in New York, it retained the League of Nations' Geneva imprimatur—a decision calculated to reinforce the League's claim as the guardian of internationalism, to generate interest 'as widely as possible and more particularly among leaders of public opinion', and to distinguish the lessons of history from plans for the present.[89] There were English and Spanish editions dispatched under a distribution list put together by the State Department. Although it was decided not to send a copy to every member of the Senate and House of Representatives, to avoid any 'unfortunate reactions', the catalogue of recipients was a *Who's Who* of the leading politicians and high-ranking officials of the American continent, North and South.[90] The report was also widely circulated among European governments in exile, though they were not the focus of the Princeton group's concern. The principal intentions were to educate American opinion leaders, to set the agenda for forthcoming Allied peace negotiations, and to shape policy, notably American, on reconstruction and international relations. Goodrich identified labour groups, employers' associations, and the press, while Henry Grady consulted public relations' experts to identify 'strategic newspaper people' across the USA.

The Transition from War to Peace Economy was composed for its audience to 'read as they run', and was testimony as to the extent the Princeton Mission had disengaged from the restrictions of the League constitution. It described it as a 'manifesto', a statement of policy not a document of economic analysis. The usual statistical and technical materials that had dominated the EFO's reports in the past were consigned to a series of supplementary publications. The key objective was to set out the likely challenges of national reconstruction while emphasizing the international context, to ensure 'the fruits of production are widely distributed'.[91] Although revised and honed from its 1939 form, its essential message remained

---

[87] Sweetser to Lester, 11 Aug. 1942, LON S564/No. 3, 40–6.
[88] For correspondence with the relevant US government departments and the press, see LON, Princeton Office, C1742/No. 8 (3), 42–5.
[89] Loveday to Lester, 10 Aug. 1942, LON, Princeton Office, C1619/No. 3, 42.
[90] Hill to Sweetser, 16 Nov. 1943, LON, Princeton Office, C1742/No. 8 (3), 42–5; 'Distribution List for Economic and Financial Committee's Report', Dec. 1942, LON, Princeton Office, C1742.
[91] Rasminsky felt this especially strongly. See Rasminsky to Loveday, 19 Sept. 1942, LON, Princeton Office, C1739/No. 1 (4), 42–3.

unchanged: the war may have heightened the expectations of states' economic policy and generated a dynamism of its own, which would, one way or another, come to an end, but the essential challenge remained that posed by the economic depression, the destructive consequences of which had extended over the first half of the twentieth century and outlasted those of war.

The publication was distinctive, because it advanced the international over nationally oriented reconstruction plans that were being developed at this stage in the war. In a familiar refrain, it argued there was every risk that the world would return to depression unless the challenges before national economies were supported by a viable international framework and was redolent with the language of a new social contract forged in the depression. There were echoes, too, of the rhetoric of world democracy that had accompanied the creation of the League: the depression was a worldwide event that meant industry had ceased to be the private concern of shareholders and trade unions and had become 'a social function carried out in the interest of all'.[92] The global humanitarian quality of this interpretation drew on the League's sensitivity to the social, psychological, and physiological effects of unemployment: 'the helpless feeling of insecurity, the anxiety regarding the future of dependents, the frustration of idleness, the sense of counting for nothing in the community.'[93]

Where the language of war and peace divided the world into 'winners' and 'losers', the report's narration of the seminal impact of the economic crisis highlighted the commonality of experience across nations and its devastating effects on all sectors of the economy regardless of specialism. Under the headline 'no return to the past', it offered a pithy assessment of the causes of the Great Depression. Recognizing the importance of the downswing in 1928–9 that the EFO's own pioneering research into business cycles had demonstrated, it argued that what had turned an 'ordinary' downturn into an unparalleled crisis was the long-term impact of the First World War. The list of its consequences were extensive: the overexpansion of agricultural production; the destruction of savings and currencies in the post-war inflation; the rapid growth of industry in neutral and non-European states and the difficulty of established economies adapting themselves to the new situation; the disturbances to balance of payments caused by large political debts (war debts and reparations); the growth of economic nationalism; the irregularities in the flow of capital between nations; and the failure of some countries, notably the United States, to adapt their tariff policy to reflect their new international status as a creditor. Aside from underplaying the deflationary role of the gold exchange standard after the Wall Street Crash, the account has stood the test of time. It anticipated aspects of the structural emphasis in Ingvar Svennilson's widely praised account of *Growth and Stagnation in the European Economy* published eleven years later, and many subsequent historical accounts. Equally importantly, it shaped the

[92] League of Nations, *The Transition from War to Peace Economy*, 16.
[93] League of Nations, *The Transition from War to Peace Economy*, 20.

architecture of economic and financial policy through its globalized interpretation of the crisis.[94]

International cooperation, it argued, held the key to recognizing and facing these challenges, a conclusion reaffirmed in late twentieth-century scholarship on the Great Depression and a lesson painfully learnt by statesmen and citizens during the first major economic crisis of the twenty-first century. This emphasis on inter-national cooperation between governments, industry, banks, farms, economists, employers, and employees was not new. It lay at the root of every narrative that had underpinned the technical work of the EFO since preparations for the World Economic Conference had begun in 1931. It argued that the construction of a new world economic system had to be central to planning for the transition from war to peace, otherwise a 1930s-style depression, or a post-war slump as occurred in the 1920s, was the very likely outcome.

The challenges facing individual nations were not ignored, but, the report argued incisively, national plans drafted in war had to factor in two as yet unknown elements: first, the degree to which socio-economic systems of individual states were likely to be significantly reshaped in response to the 'demands of the people'— a hugely important dynamic to sustaining public consent for the war effort; and, secondly, the ways in which peace might come about in different territories. Both these challenges meant it was all the more important that the international system was strong and flexible. It would frame the context in which states and societies faced tests that would be beyond their sole capacity to control, and the means by which states mediated their relations to one another. History would be an import-ant guide to the future, and the League had plenty of relevant history on which to draw. *The Transition from War to Peace Economy* ranged widely across the multifa-ceted impact of war on national economies: the shift in production patterns, labour relations, and the relationship between industry and agriculture were all afforded concise treatment. But the overriding concern was to analyse how these broader changes posed immediate questions of national economic policy, how they might be answered, and the likely international consequences of any chosen route. Fundamental to all these matters, and uppermost in the collective mind of the Depression Delegation: the threat posed by inflation.[95]

Drawing on its experience as an international actor in the inflationary crises of central and eastern Europe, the League argued that the gravest danger to economic stability would be the pent-up demands of consumers against the backdrop of the switch from military to peacetime production. At the same time, there would be a great temptation for states to print money to meet their citizens' expectations of

[94] The connection was not accidental. Many of the experts who advised Svennilson on his study had long-standing ties to the EFO. Ingvar Svennilson, *Growth and Stagnation in the European Economy* (Geneva, 1954); Erik Lundberg, 'Ingvar Svennilson: A Note on his Scientific Achievements and a Bibliography of his Contributions to Economics', *Scandinavian Journal of Economics*, 74/3 (1972), 313–28.

[95] However, the delegation did not downgrade the threat of inflation to the degree suggested by, among others, Endres and Fleming, *International Organizations*, 232. See also Pauly, 'The League of Nations and the Foreshadowing of the International Monetary Fund', 32.

employment and welfare. Governments were advised that growth should be nurtured by retaining control over some aspects of the economy by relinquishing it over others. Calling for the careful balancing of liberal and planned economics, the report offered a comprehensive treatment of the tools, financial and physical, available to governments to manage production and consumption. It stressed that governments' ability to deliver would rest on their national authority, but crucially, too, the degree to which the international context facilitated their access to capital, and states' sense of political legitimacy and national security. In short, liberalization would come from the actions of a strong state, not from the removal of governmental controls, contained within a coherent international order.

There was also a new objective that came to be seen as decidedly at odds with the liberal economics that had shaped the EFO's work for much of its history: full employment. It did not feature in earlier drafts but surfaced only as an explicit goal in 1942. Although the League's orthodoxy had made some notable shifts over the years—the move from unconditional support of the gold standard to a more open-minded approach towards currency movement, and the coupling of economic to social policy, for example—the resounding endorsement for full employment as a key goal of government here was striking, and facilitated by a variety of elements. In much the same way that the Beveridge Plan encapsulated views on social planning that were widely held, these same currents of thought were evident in the Depression Delegation.[96] Key contributions were made by Ohlin and Myrdal, significant figures in the pre-history of Keynesian thought, and after 1940 the Keynesian perspective grew as others in the delegation gradually shifted their position, perhaps none more strikingly than Loveday, who hosted a seminar at the IAS on the Beveridge Plan attended by Beveridge himself.[97] The move was easier, too, because members of the Depression Delegation who had vociferously orthodox views, notably Rueff and Ryti, were no longer part of it. Indeed, as a political economist, Beveridge had a broad approach that was very similar to many in the EFO and the ILO, which sought to promote individual and collective welfare, not by acts of policy, but by the discovery and enforcement of universally valid socio-economic laws.[98]

The Depression Delegation's commitment to full employment was a desired goal, but not the primary one; that remained the liberation of international capitalism. Nor did everyone in the delegation endorse it. The goal of full employment was subject to constant review, thanks to a sustained attack mounted by Haberler.[99] For the League group as a whole, full employment was not intended to challenge free market economics. Rather, governments had to exercise care not to 'launch too many schemes or to launch them at the wrong moment'. The repair of

[96] José Harris, 'Social Aspects in War-Time: Some Aspects of the Beveridge Report', in Jay Winter (ed.), *War and Economic Development: Essays in Memory of David Joslin* (Cambridge, 1975), 239–56.
[97] Correspondence relating to the Beveridge Seminar, IAS Faculty, 'Stewart, Walter, 1932–1945'. Toynbee was also a regular visitor to the IAS.
[98] John Hills, John Ditch, and Howard Glennerster, 'Introduction', in Hills, Ditch, and Glennerster (eds), *Beveridge and Social Security: An International Perspective* (Oxford, 1994), 10.
[99] See Chapter 9.

war damage would obviously be pressing, but, when possible, projects should be postponed until the free domestic economy has recovered: 'governments should endeavour to fill in gaps in demand rather than compete with the market.'[100] The key to success lay in knowing when to intervene, and when to step back— intelligence and advice from international organizations should help here—and in the availability of international capital and credit. These two elements provided the lubricant that would ease the world economy back from state-led wartime control to liberal capitalism. The report was shaped here by a critique of the impact of the international capital on the stability of the European economy during the interwar period, a perspective reinforced by the British government's fears for its own financial future articulated during the Second World War. While leaving the specific details of any international agreements to be resolved by the relevant governmental representatives, the expert network sustained by the League set out a few essential guidelines that, in very large measure, accompanied Bretton Woods. The echoes should not be surprising. The report appeared just as White, Keynes, and their advisers, many of whom had been in touch with the Depression Delegation since its inception, began drafting plans for an international clearing union. *The Transition from War to Peace Economy* was a barometer of the wider shift in the political economy that sustained the march to Bretton Woods, and a reflection of the EFO's twenty-five-year history, which had helped the world to see that such institutions were not only possible but necessary. The Princeton Mission made a powerful case for institutionalized cooperation, although the questions regarding its configuration had yet to be resolved.

Repeating a narrative that had surfaced in its rawest form in the preparatory materials for the World Economic Conference of 1933 on the need for international capital to release the vice of economic nationalism gripping the world economy, the League argued that international credit would be required for four purposes at the war's end. The first three areas of concern were to meet the immediate demand for food, raw materials, and essentials in stricken areas; to repair the physical damage caused by the war; and to supplement the reserves of banks of issue and, crucially, to support them during the inevitable balance of payments difficulties. Finally, it argued, credit was needed 'for the development and industrial re-organization of the industrial structure in countries whose boundaries have changed, whose industry no longer matches the pattern of global demand, and whose populations are too large for their current productive capacity and who find themselves too poor in capital to change the situation'.[101]

Loveday and his colleagues had long argued that international lending held the key to the revival of international trade on a multilateral basis. The report contained an account of the manifold pressures that had led to the rise and rise of tariffs and quotas in interwar protectionism. Significantly, it also marked the move away from the League's long-established narrative of American irresponsibility, in part because that message had been renewed by the US administration and its advisers, if not by

---

[100] League of Nations, *The Transition from War to Peace Economy*, 114–15.
[101] League of Nations, *The Transition from War to Peace Economy*, 70–91.

the wider American public, as the battle over the International Trade Organization and international aid was to show.[102] Instead, it called for a programme of trade liberalization, best facilitated on the basis of unconditional MFN by an international organization, which would provide economic intelligence, give advice, and mediate between states on tariff reductions and customs unions. It was the mission to which the EFO had aspired since the World Economic Conference of 1927, and which eventually was taken up by the General Agreement on Tariffs and Trade (GATT), the European Free Trade Association (EFTA), and the European Economic Community (EEC).

Although the report downplayed longer-term issues relating to credit and trade—the group returned to them in part two of their findings published in 1944—it firmly underlined that reconstruction must ultimately address the uneven distribution of wealth around the world. The commitment to global development was striking, all the more so because this preoccupation was largely absent from Keynesian economic thought of the period, and challenges the presumption that global development emerged as a primarily American concern in the war.[103] For the League, the conflict had exacerbated the uneven character of the world economy that had been its focus in the 1930s, and capital would be required to develop and reorganize 'the industrial structure where boundaries are modified, where existing structure has been rendered inappropriate to the post-war distribution of productive capacity'. While the League acknowledged that its work dealt 'more directly with the problems of industrial states than with the great areas of food and raw material production in Asia, America, Africa and elsewhere', this was justified because 'the great industrial markets of the world mainly determine the degree of economic stability enjoyed in the world as a whole and therefore by the produce of crude products'.[104] Moreover, it argued, the challenges before primary producers had to be kept in view, and principles governing international, preferably long-term, loans should be established to ensure they worked to the benefit of primary producing and industrial countries alike. These included low rates of interest, the possibility of suspension in times of particular hardship, and adequate labour standards for workers in the borrowing countries. The transition from war to peace, the League reminded the postwar planners, was a global challenge, and intergovernmental and non-governmental organizations needed to conceive a coordinated and integrated response to meet it.

FOOD ORGANIZED

The League's concern with primary production and its relationship to the supply of food resurfaced dramatically with the announcement of a US-sponsored UN Food

---

[102] Irwin, Mavroidis, and Sykes, *Genesis of GATT*, 8–15, rightly centres on the significance of Hull, but misses how the Geneva network promoted his ideas.

[103] See, e.g., Richard Peet, *Unholy Trinity: The IMF, World Bank and the WTO* (New York, 2003), 27–57.

[104] League of Nations, *The Transition from War to Peace Economy*, 37–8.

Conference to be held in Hot Springs, Virginia, from 18 May to 3 June 1943. *The Transition from War to Peace Economy*, and the fourteen supplementary studies that accompanied it, was published to coincide with the announcement. News of the food conference had first surfaced publicly three months earlier in a speech given by Sumner Welles in Toronto, where the assistant Secretary of State and a member of FDR's inner circle talked of 'a machinery for the purpose of assembling and studying all international aspects of problems under the general heading of freedom of want'.[105] There is no doubt that FDR's acute political antenna was behind a move intended to deflect the interest of US public opinion in the Bengal famine, which threatened to reinsert the troubling issue of Indian independence back into Anglo-American relations. But its tie to interwar internationalism was clear to the government in London, where Keynes confessed that, whenever he read anything about nutrition, his 'attention wanders'. News that FDR now believed 'food', not money or trade, would be a 'good starting point', Keynes feared, could have disastrous implications if talks devoted to 'agricultural questions' meant 'issues of wartime relief were ignored'.[106] There were worries, too, about an economic conference on a single issue, and a guest list that included the USSR and China. All told, it was an infinitely less attractive prospect than the desired 'comprehensive programme to deal with subjects, all of which are interrelated' negotiated first between the British and American governments.[107]

But, despite the fact that US ambitions for the UN Food Conference had come directly from the League, the Princeton Mission knew it would not be invited to attend. The secretariat had long 'camouflaged' the fact that US involvement in the organization had become 'as complete as that of any member of the League'.[108] Loveday knew FDR believed the subject of US public opinion and the League was a 'closed chapter', but, in contrast to Lester, he was relaxed about it.[109] There was no need for an overt presence at the Virginia conference, because the League's work had laid deep roots that nourished the conference: a nexus of expertise on nutrition and its relationship to agricultural production and rural life; and schemes for commodity regulation, tariff reduction, and increased food production. McDougall remained at the centre of the action, or, as the ILO put it, the 'father of the bridge'.[110] It was his 1942 report, prepared for the UN's programme for Freedom from Want of Food, and based extensively on his work for the League and the

[105] Radio Bulletin No. 49, Department of State, 26 Feb. 1943, LON S566.
[106] Keynes to Meade, cited in Skidelsky, *John Maynard Keynes*, iii. 300. 'Record of Third Treasury–Foreign Office Meeting on 2nd March 1943', TNA: PRO FO 371/35331, 393/147/70, where the Treasury argued food was 'a bone thrown to the United Nations dogs'; the FO took the view it was one 'of the general economic questions which would have to be solved by international means'.
[107] 'Text of Invitation from the United States Government', TNA: PRO FO371/35364, U1088/320/70.
[108] Loveday to Pasvolsky, 15 Mar. 1943, LON, Princeton Office, C1617, No. 8 42–3; 'Memorandum of Meeting between Churchill, Wallace, Stimson, Ickes, Connally, and Welles', 25 June 1943, LC, Pasvolsky, Box 7.
[109] 'Note on Section Meeting held on 6th March 1943', LON, Princeton Office, C1624/No. 3, 42–6; 'Record of Conversation between Loveday and Jebb', 23 Mar. 1943, TNA: PRO FO371/34519, C3872.
[110] Riches to R. M. Campbell, 18 May 1943, ILO, Winant and Phelan Files, Z 6/3/13.

Princeton Mission, that was read 'by chance', as the conventional history tells it, by Eleanor Roosevelt, who then invited McDougall to discuss his ideas over dinner with the President.[111] FDR's adoption of agriculture and nutrition as an essential topic on which the United Nations might score an early and easy success vindicated the League's promotion of the issue in the 1930s as an approach to global security and cooperation that would have popular appeal, on the one hand, and address the fundamentally important issues of the politics of hunger, on the other. Hot Springs laid the foundations from which the FAO eventually emerged at the Quebec conference two years later.

All this lay in the future. In 1943, the architecture of international relations was emerging, not set; however, the exclusion of the League from the UN Food Conference marked the end of the League as an internationally recognized agent. Although the Princeton group sought to steer clear of debates on the institutional configuration of the United Nations, Hot Springs prompted Loveday to argue for 'the more organic conception of the United Nations' than appeared to be developing in Washington—one that combined the 'tried technical services of the League' as well as its 'old political structure' that appeared to be the basis of US thinking for what would become the United Nations Organization (UNO).[112] The next twelve months were to reveal that the USA had absorbed the League's emphasis on the primacy of economics and finance, and the value of technocracy to international relations, but, in contrast to the League, had compartmentalized these priorities into discrete organizations.[113]

Given that the Grand Alliance had now firmly hitched its star to a new organization to replace the League, the latter's remaining European members argued that the League should concentrate more overtly on representing the interests of Europe and the rest of the world, and serve as a 'rallying agency for the smaller among the United Nations and the neutrals'.[114] Indeed, this was an obligation of which the Princeton Mission never lost sight, although, while reinforcing its contact to member states, it believed the League's objectives ultimately were best served by remaining as close as possible to the sources of power and agency in post-war planning, and they were American.[115] The impact of the US decision not to invite the League to Hot Springs should not be exaggerated. The League remained in the shadows of international relations. This was where it had

[111] O'Brien, 'F. L. McDougall and the Origins of the FAO', 171. Henry Wallace was so enamoured of McDougall he 'urged [Meade] very strongly that "somebody like McDougall" should be put on the air every night' to boost US support for post-war planning. See Howson and Moggridge, *The Wartime Diaries of Robbins and Meade*, 24.

[112] Memo for Eden, 'His Majesty's Government's Policy towards the League of Nations', 3 Apr. 1943, TNA: PRO FO371/34513 C3672.

[113] If the Americans did not want direct League involvement in the conferences to shape the post-war order, then the British would not fight the USA to secure it. Minute by Williams, 22 Apr. 1943, TNA: PRO FO371/34519 C3872.

[114] Rosenborg to Loveday, 23 Aug. 1943, LON, Princeton Office, C 1617/No. 8, 42–3.

[115] In June 1943 W. J. Hinton was seconded from the British Ministry of Information to act as a liaison between the Princeton group and the various governments of League members and Allied states in London. Hinton to Loveday, 5 June 1943, and Loveday to Hinton, 15 June 1943, LON, Princeton Office, C1618/No. 6, 43.

been forced to exist since 1936, and was where members of the secretariat had always lived. Its service to international relations, acting as a hub of intelligence and expertise, socializing and 'educating' those who came into contact with it, remained important. It was kept informed as to what went on at the Food Conference by a variety of sources, and the absence of public recognition was not an impediment to involvement in the development of US policy. In April 1943, the EFO was invited to meet members of Governor Herbert Lehman's staff to discuss 'tentative plans for a United Nations Relief and Rehabilitation Administration', which provided a new outlet for its expertise, and to represent the interests of the League's wider membership.[116]

RELIEF AND RECONSTRUCTION

Loveday met Lehman for the first time shortly after his appointment by Hull as Director of the Office of Foreign Relief and Rehabilitation Operations (OFRRO) in November 1942. Lehman was inexperienced in foreign policy: Hull had appointed him because his Congressional connections meant he stood a better chance than many of securing the necessary financial support from the House and Senate to pay for reconstruction.[117] Although it took time for OFRRO to refine its mission in the alphabet soup of Allied organizations for post-war planning, its focus on relief was clear from the outset. Intergovernmental negotiations between the 'Big Four' began formally in 1943, and the Princeton Mission was asked for practical help because, as the State Department put it, it offered both the United Nations Relief and Rehabilitation Administration (UNRRA) and associated UN organizations unparalleled expertise on the 'problems involved in making an international organization work successfully'.[118] In its plans for UNRRA, OFRRO leaned heavily on the League's experience of how to recruit staff and to manage relations between the international organization and the intergovernmental representatives who were sent to work with it. Both Leith-Ross's and Lehman's committees saw post-war relief mainly as a matter of procurement: matching raw material supplies to populations in greatest need. The challenges before them were viewed as logistical and international; nations were urged not to earmark essential items for their own populations or to build up reserves, but to be prepared to pool supplies and deliver them where shortages were most acute.[119] The questions before them centred on the practice of international coordination and cooperation

---

[116] Lionel Robbins was a particularly important source of intelligence. See also Sayre to Loveday, 30 Apr. 1943, LON, Princeton Office, C1770/No. 1, 43.

[117] George Woodbridge, *UNRRA: The History of the United Nations Relief and Rehabilitation Administration* (2 vols; New York, 1950), i. 21–6. The reasons for Lehman's appointment were not lost on Loveday. See Loveday, 'Note on Washington Mission, 30th January–5th February 1943', LON, Private Papers, P150/'Miscellaneous—Correspondence December 40–December 45'.

[118] Sayre to Loveday, 30 Apr. 1943, LON, Princeton Office, C1770/No. 1, 43; 'Memorandum by the Treasurer: Evolution of the Financial System of the League', 10 Jan. 1945, LON R5352, 17/43323/x.

[119] Woodbridge, *UNRRA*, i. 3–32.

regarding transportation, supply, and demography—the essence of the League of Nations' working life in Geneva. The Princeton Mission was able to help them with intelligence and experience of it all, while stressing that organization and preparation, as well as supply and execution, were paramount. Confirmation of the entangled history of UNRRA and the League manifested itself when the former established its headquarters at the Palais des Nations, with Arthur Salter as one of its Deputy Directors.

The invitation that summoned Loveday to Washington in April 1943 to advise the State Department on the UN recovery programme was redolent of League-style talk of the need to bring about immediate relief and coordinated reconstruction in the longer term. There followed a series of meetings and committee member-ships that came the Princeton group's way, and that reunited a considerable number of officials who had once been either in the employ, or associated with the League, during the 1920s and 1930s. But, while UNRRA's adoption of the League's long-trumpeted link between relief and reconstruction as its central tenet was viewed very positively by Loveday, he and his colleagues saw American determination to limit UNRRA's Council to the 'Big Four' as 'absolutely disastrous'.[120] Leith-Ross sup-ported great power domination by invoking the failure of the League, yet the EFO's long-standing connections to alternative clusters of expertise, especially in central and eastern Europe, left it in no doubt as to the region's deep frustration with their very limited input into UNRRA's work.[121] It was echoed by Rajchman, the former director of the LNHO, who was also in Washington during the war, and in 1942 and 1943 drafted plans for UNRRA's medical programme and a future international organization.[122] He, too, argued against great-power dominance, and complained that the region's needs—especially those of Poland—featured insufficiently in Anglo-American minds. His critique was connected to a wider view held by the European powers that UNRRA's planning, expressed largely through a drive to raise and safeguard living standards, needed to be more sensitive to local needs.[123] In the world of humanitarian agency there was no escape from power politics, and the world's smaller powers remained suspicious as to the political aims of the world's larger states. While the Americans and Russians made great public play of their fight against the economic exploitation of the Axis powers, the Princeton Mission sought to give a voice, with limited success, to smaller countries' growing fears that relief efforts and the wider architecture of international relations would be biased against them in favour of great-power interests.[124] Under UNRRA the rhetorical shift from reconstruction towards rehabilitation, with its connotations of moral improvement, increased their suspicions.[125] The British government was not alone

---

[120] Sayre to Loveday, 11 June 1943, LON, Princeton Office, C1770/No. 1, 43.

[121] Grace Fox, 'The Origins of UNRRA', *Political Science Quarterly*, 65/4 (1950), 561–84.

[122] On the Health Section's utility for UNRRA, see Iris Borowy, *Coming to Terms with World Health: The League of Nations Health Organization, 1921–1946* (Frankfurt am Main, 2009), 432–4.

[123] Its characterization as left-leaning is complicated by the Princeton Mission's endorsement of this view. See Feliks Gross, *Crossroads of Two Continents: A Democratic Federation of East–Central Europe* (New York, 1945).

[124] Loveday to Leith-Ross, 22 June 1943, LON, Princeton Office, C1629/No. 2 (2), 43.

[125] Foster to Loveday, 15 Feb. 1943, LON, Princeton Office, C1617/No. 3, 43–4. See also Peter Gatrell, 'Trajectories of Population Displacement in the Aftermaths of the Two World Wars', in Jessica

in seeking Loveday's advice on how to secure 'special' agreements with the American administration.

In late August 1943, Loveday, the League's Treasurer Jacklin, and his former Assistant Jean Bieler, led an interdepartmental meeting in Washington on how best to raise funds for international organizations. Although the discussion, in the words of Roy Veatch, Chief of the US Division of International Relations, broadly addressed 'the principal financial problems of any international organisation', UNRRA was uppermost in everyone's thoughts, because it was first among the planned agencies to take life as 'an operating organisation'. Following advice from the Princeton Mission, under the terms of its constitution, the Director-General and the secretariat were given more authority than first planned, and the mission also advised on how to finance and monitor UNRRA's operations.[126] The Americans initially intended to calculate members' net worth and contributions according to the same proportions allocated by the League, until Loveday advised otherwise, demonstrating how far members' economic capacities had altered during the course of the 1930s and the war. As a result, it was agreed that UNRRA should be funded under a scheme of 'present circumstances', which would then be revised once circumstances had 'normalized' or by the end of five years—whichever came first.[127] The Princeton Mission also told the Americans how these monies, once collected, should be managed and controlled.[128]

The advice was as much political as practical. The mission wanted to shape arrangements for post-war relief and the reconstruction of liberal capitalism in the interests of small and large countries. In preparation for further meetings with the US administration and future conferences, it accelerated its publication programme.[129] *Relief Deliveries and Relief Loans, 1919–1923* (drafted, in the first instance, by Polak) and *Commercial Policy in the Interwar Period*, published in 1942, notably offered an 'explosive' critique of failures of US policy during the interwar period.[130] These widely circulated reports had intellectual bite, and were reinforced by leading figures in the US foreign policy elite, including Pasvolsky, Viner, who at this stage played a key role in developing the rationale for the White plan, and Hansen, who was involved in revising the proposals for Bretton Woods.

Reinisch and Elizabeth White (eds), *The Disentanglement of Populations: Migration, Expulsion and Displacement in Post-War Europe, 1944–9* (London, 2011), 17.

[126] 'Some Notes on the Organisation and Function of UNRRA', prepared by OFFRO, Aug. 1943, in LON, Princeton Office, C1619/No. 1 (1), 43.

[127] Memo by Pearson, 'United Nations Interim Commission on Food and Agriculture', 3 Feb. 1944, LON, Princeton Office, C.1629/No. 1 (1), 43.

[128] Memo of meeting, 'Some Financial Problems of UNRRA etc.—Discussion in Governor Lehman's office Monday 30th August 1943', LON, Princeton Office, C1629/No. 1(1) 21, 45.

[129] Sayre to Loveday, 11 June 1943, LON, Princeton Office, C1770/No. 1, 43.

[130] Loveday claimed that Lehman, Acheson, and White 'attached a good deal of importance' to these reports. See Loveday to Leith-Ross, 20 Aug. 1942, and Leith-Ross to Loveday, 21 Aug. 1942, LON, Princeton Office, C1617/No. 2, 42. Ikenberry argues the war was an 'extra-ordinary vehicle for the concentration of expertise and planning' both among American economists and between US and British economists, but is unaware that this committee reflected US participation in the EFO's activities since 1927. See G. John Ikenberry, 'A World Economy Restored: Expert Consensus and the Anglo-American Postwar Settlement', *International Organization*, 46/1 (1992), 301.

Together, these men ran the Economic and Financial Group of the Council of Foreign Relations. Also among the preparatory papers for UNRRA was Viner's *Trade Relations between Free-Market and Controlled Economies*, published in July 1943 under the imprimatur of the League of Nations. Writing on his own, but relying heavily on the EFO's data recorded in the 1930s, Viner concluded that German protectionism was motivated primarily by political not economic considerations (encouraging because it suggested political change would reap immediate economic benefits), and he called for an international convention that would lead to the abolition of direct controls. An unremarkable conclusion on its own, Viner's work was important because it reinforced the case for an international agency to promote tariff reductions and multilateral trade under the convention of the MFN.[131] Viner repeated the League's critique of British policy, with sufficient vehemence to prompt members of the British War Trade Department to argue it was time to close down the Princeton Mission. The secretariat's former British employees, notably Meade, came to its defence, arguing that the League's position was not one of unadulterated free trade. It knew it was 'unrealistic to generalise about freer individual trading as a general teleological conception', and that the world could not 'burst into multilateral trade'. Nevertheless, the world needed national and international facilitation to bring national political economies to this ambitious goal.[132]

Viner's argument was supplemented by an additional report by Haberler, aided by Martin Hill of the Princeton group, entitled *Quantitative Trade Controls: Their Causes and Nature*. (James Meade and Lionel Robbins offered comments on the report.[133]) It, too, drew on the EFO's work of the late 1920s and 1930s, to explore how and why governments resorted to quantitative trade restrictions, notably quotas, when they had made firm political declarations to the contrary. Protectionism was sometimes the logical response to a grave economic climate, but it had serious political, and long-term economic, implications.[134] The report argued the emerging post-war world should be the beneficiary of its hard-won knowledge and experience, and that this time, unlike 1919, states could not and should not rush to liberate themselves from economic controls. A reformed monetary order would help—as had the gold standard—to shape the behaviour and expectations of markets, but the reliberalization of the world economy had to be facilitated more by state and international management than by market forces. The process was to be supported by a technocracy of experts and civil servants in new organizations dedicated to international coordination, cooperation, and oversight. Unlike after

[131] League of Nations, *Trade Relations between Free-Market and Controlled Economies* (Geneva, 1943).

[132] Noel Hall to Loveday, 3 July 1943, LON, Princeton Office, C1617/No.3, 43–4; Howson and Moggridge, *The Wartime Diaries of Robbins and Meade*, 62–79. On Meade's importance to post-war trade policy, see John Toye and Richard Toye, *The UN and Global Political Economy: Trade, Finance and Development* (Indiana, 2004), 23–4.

[133] Hill to Meade, 29 Sept. 1943, C19630/No. 2 (3), 43–5.

[134] Economic, Financial, and Transit Department, *Quantitative Trade Controls: Their Causes and Nature* (Geneva, 1943), preface.

the First World War, this time governments should 'agree in advance to some orderly process of decontrol and some financially and economically sane system of reviving the economic life of countries impoverished by the war'.[135] International management and coordination needed to be coupled with the development of a coherent national strategy, with the goals of full employment and the prevention of economic depression at their centre. If there was something incongruous about the degree to which the League and its associated economists had come to advocate managerial solutions to promote free market economics, it went unnoticed. Their message both informed and reflected the dominant features of the international order that was constructed in 1944, and then reconstructed as economic recovery faltered in 1947, and as ideological tensions between capitalists and communists broke out into cold war.

In the late summer of 1943, the Princeton-based League officials had also offered OFFRO and UNRRA advice on personnel recruitment, and how best to organize and manage their relations with member states. The effort was supplemented by the third, major EFO report, *Europe's Overseas Needs 1919–1920 and How They Were Met*. This was not so much a guide on what to do as a history of what had gone wrong at the end of the First World War, which detailed the disastrous consequences of international inaction, and, coupled with the *Transition from War to Peace Economy* and supplementary reports, it largely fulfilled the State Department's plea that the League provide an 'annotated agenda' for UNRRA's work.[136] By then, the Princeton group's involvement in UNRRA had become all consuming. Loveday had mixed feelings about this. It was clear that this new organization, alongside others on the drafting board, would duplicate the work of the League and render it redundant, but it was not this that troubled him. He was happy to make a contribution in the handover to what he hoped would be more effective and empowered organizations, serving full-time also on the panel of economists offering advice on a proposed Food and Agriculture Commission.[137] His concern was the multiplicity of international organizational heirs to the League that sought the Princeton group's advice, for it was difficult to see how these institutions' functions would relate to one another. He was anxious there should be one 'overall political and/or economic world organization of which these various functional bodies should be a part'.[138] He saw his role, and that of every League official acting in a consultative capacity, to stress it was essential that each new organization be created with an eye to its place in the system as a whole. In 1943, this seemed a long way off.

Equally prescient was Loveday's frustration with the American preference for a bureaucratic rather than a political approach to the challenges of international cooperation. Although he had long advocated a depoliticized, technocratic

[135] Economic, Financial, and Transit Department. *Quantitative Trade Controls*, 42.
[136] Report by Loveday, 'Report on Washington Mission—30th January–5th February 1943', p. 2, undated, LON, Private Papers, P150/'Miscellaneous Correspondence, December 40–December 45'.
[137] Loveday to Lester, 13 Sept. 1943, LON, Princeton Office, C1619/No. 4, 43.
[138] Loveday to Lester, 20 Oct. 1943, LON, Princeton Office, C1619/No. 4, 43.

approach to international cooperation, technocracy alone, he argued, would not advance the cause of a liberalized world economy after the war. He complained that American officials showed 'a naïve bureaucratic innocence which is almost unbelievable'. They needed to wake up to the reality that international life was 'not identical with the Department of Agriculture and that a naked bureaucracy left almost uncontrolled by governments is not likely to be popular'.[139] But American inexperience was also Loveday's route to influence. He persuaded the committee developing McDougall's draft constitution for the FAO to spend a week in Princeton and joined them at committee meetings in Washington in December 1943.[140]

That winter, the US administration, responding to criticism, decided to rationalize the brief and the number of organizations dedicated to post-war planning.[141] In the meantime Dean Acheson took over UNRRA, while the US Foreign Economic Administration (FEA) continued to study the likely needs for post-war relief. All these agencies drew on the EFO's empirical studies. On 20 September 1943, the US government, with the Princeton group's help, completed the third draft of the agreement covering UNRRA's programme of work. It was then forwarded to the Allies three days later, and discussed and approved at a conference in Atlantic City, which opened on 9 November 1943. As with the UN Food Conference, the US administration restricted the invitation list to representatives of member governments, with the Princeton Mission invited to join UNRRA's Council as observers 'and not members'.[142] Formally they represented the past, but their ideas and experience had fed into conference preparations, and there were many old Geneva hands among the conference and national Council members, including James Brigden from Australia (close to both McDougall and Bruce), Alain DuParc representing Belgium, Aake Ording from Norway, Leith-Ross from the UK, and Francis Sayre and Thomas Parran from the USA.

In Atlantic City it was agreed that UNRRA's focus should remain 'relief and related operations' that necessitated the creation of a purely temporary organization. (British hopes that the organization might have greater resources at its disposal and a longer-term remit, along the lines of the supreme Allied Economic Council, were dashed.) However constrained the League's role might have appeared in formal terms, its officials discovered they were 'entitled to [join] any committee ... and could, in fact, intervene with discretion'.[143] Indeed, Loveday told Lester, 'the

[139] Loveday to Lester, 20 Oct. 1943, LON, Princeton Office, C1619/No. 4, 43.

[140] Loveday's diaries reveal the regularity of their contact. See Loveday Diaries, 1941, 1942, and 1943, Nuffield, Loveday.

[141] OFFRA was merged with the Office of Lend-Lease Administration and the Office of Economic Warfare (which had once been called the Board of Economic Warfare). The resultant body was the Foreign Economic Administration, and Lehman was made FDR's special assistant tasked with coordinating the development of the United Nations Organization. Loveday remained close to Lehman, for whom, he declared, he had nothing but 'the highest respect'. See Loveday to Lester, 20 Oct. 1943, LON, Princeton Office, C1619/No. 4, 43.

[142] Shaw to Sweetser, 8 Nov. 1943, LC, Sweetser, Box 39; Acheson to the Economic Section of the League of Nations, 13 Nov. 1943, C1770/No. 1, 43; Woodbridge, *UNRRA*, i. 24–6.

[143] Loveday to Lester, 9 Dec. 1943, LON, Princeton Office, C1619/No. 4, 43.

conference was working so completely along the lines which I had hoped—lines which are set out in the Transition Report—that I said nothing publicly and really had very little to do even behind the scenes.'[144] But his satisfaction in this achievement turned into dust, as UNRRA's relief mission faltered on the ground in 1945, as donor nations reasserted their sovereignty, and as world war became cold war. Loveday was never content for the League to settle into the role of stage hand to American players in the drama of reconstruction. He used the conference in Atlantic City as the opportunity to convene a meeting of the Economic and Financial Committee of the League to provide an additional platform to articulate European perspectives on UNRRA.[145] It was an indication of the continued political and intellectual value of the League, even as the institution was being inexorably consigned to the past. So, too, was the intergovernmental (rather than purely expert) composition of the committee, which, as well as assembling old friends, included new representation, notably Henry Grady, who attended for the first time as a US governmental (not expert) delegate.[146]

Given that planning for the FAO, UNRRA, the financial and trade institutions, and the United Nations organization was now advanced, what was the purpose of reuniting member states with the League secretariat? Most obviously, of course, it validated the Princeton Mission and gave it the opportunity to gauge international opinion, which demonstrated 'quite useful' commonality on a number of key issues.[147] Everyone was agreed on the target of 'reviving' and 'reintegrating' the world economy and 'raising living standards', but were divided as to the best tools for the job. The Chinese and Indian delegates stressed the need for developing countries to retain tariffs to protect their drive to industrialize; and the Norwegians argued that similar protection would be needed for fledgling European industries. The demand for protection by European nations—the resurrection of a spectre that reached back into the nineteenth century—allied British and Americans delegates in their opposition to it, and all participants argued that, whatever the differences between them, decisions on trade policy needed to be taken swiftly 'to prevent vested interests' from seizing control. Viner's treatment of *Trade Relations between Free-Market and Controlled Economies* for the League was used as the basis of their discussions, but aspects of its treatment were hotly contested, notably Viner's emphasis on 'two blocs' in global trade—the free and the controlled. The Czech delegate Josef Hanc was not alone in fearing that this representation encouraged discrimination between the planned economies of the Soviet Union and the West, which would only lead to a further deterioration of relations between the two sides.[148]

---

[144] Loveday to Lester, 9 Dec. 1943, LON, Princeton Office, C1619/No. 4, 43.
[145] Domaniewski (Poland), Loridan standing in for Langenhoven (Belgium), Crena de Iongh (Netherlands), Alphand, Constatin Fotich (Yugoslavian Ambassador in London), Sardar Malik (India), Josef Hanc (CSR), Kan Lee (China, Commercial Counsellor at the Chinese Embassy), and Arne Skaug (Norway). Their numbers were supplemented by eight EFO secretariat members.
[146] Grady to Hill, 30 Nov. 1943, LON, Princeton Office, C1629–C1630/No. 2 (3), 43–5.
[147] Loveday to Lester, 9 Dec. 1943, LON, Princeton Office, C1619/No. 4, 43.
[148] Loveday to Lester, 9 Dec. 1943, LON, Princeton Office, C1619/No. 4, 43.

Monetary relations were similarly contested. A few delegates were horrified that the gold standard was to be abandoned, but most were enthused by the prospective new financial arrangements sketched out for them by Nurkse. The last major issue discussed, but like monetary policy kept from public view, was the suggestion that the League should devote more time to examining the possibilities of intensifying economic relationships among European countries. The suggestion, of course, was Monnet's. But it was agreed not to disclose that it had come from the Free French delegate, and to present it as a League initiative, to give it the air of 'impartiality', on the understanding that the League's experience and expertise left it extraordinarily well placed to comment on European union.

Many Europeans also complained of the Anglo-American desire to consign the League to history because the organization was still useful to them. Their stance was illustrated by the degree of US public interest in the meeting: the US Office of War Information reported news of the meeting and European views on reconstruction in twenty-eight separate broadcasts made in fourteen different languages, giving the Europeans access to channels of communication and opinion exiled governments generally lacked.[149] League-sponsored meetings in the USA provided the opportunity to learn of, and potentially coordinate, reconstruction policies with other European governments, and an additional chance to influence Anglo-American delegates who attended. For the League officials, on the other hand, contact with the Europeans gave them the occasion to gauge the views of the rest of the world on Anglo-American plans, and to take advice on how what was left of the League should relate to the emerging organizations of a new international order. The general view was that what was likely to emerge was a 'League under another name', and this would be an 'acceptable' outcome. Ironically, this was not Loveday's view. He wanted the successor organizations of the League to be new and distinct. It gave credence to the Princeton Mission's claim to be a disinterested 'intelligence centre and adviser', and for the new UN organizations, through comparison with the failed League, to be branded a success.[150] Experience had also taught him that great powers should be less prominent, and the understanding of security more wide-ranging, than in the League. The next two years would sorely test this aspiration.

---

[149] Loveday to Leith-Ross, 3 Jan. 1944, LON, Princeton Office, C.1630/No. 2 (3), 43–5.

[150] 'Summary of the Meetings of the Economic and Financial Committees—Joint Session—Princeton', 6–7 Dec. 1943, LON, Princeton Office, C.1630/No. 2 (3), 43–5.

9

The Architecture of the New World Order, 1944–1945

'If you take positions, you are exposed to dangers.' So counselled Goldenweiser at the annual meeting of the American Statistical Association, but, 'if you do not take positions, the dangers are much less, but your usefulness is almost reduced to vanishing point . . . It is better to take a position openly than to continue to appear completely impartial.'[1] In this address of 9 December 1943, Goldenweiser recognized the importance of the relationship between 'Research and Policy', and the challenges faced by social scientists feverishly preparing policy materials for a new world order. His acknowledgement of the central role being played by what he called the 'partially, impartial expert' was an unusual public commentary on the politics of science. Rarely, if at all, did social scientists reflect on why one idea was selected over others to shape government policy, or that social scientists' proposals were shaped by political partiality as well as 'impartial' science.

Yet debates about governance were at the heart of scientific work in the field of international economics, where there was a pronounced move to institution building. If the League of Nations had failed, its chronicle generated the impulse to build not just one new organization to facilitate international coordination and cooperation, but many. It generated the International Monetary Fund (IMF), the International Bank for Reconstruction and Development (IBRD or the 'World Bank'), and, of course, the United Nations (UN) in 1944.[2] The IMF was endowed with a $8.8 billion fund, which members could draw upon when their balance of payments fell into deficit, so as to prevent currency and banking crises of the kind that had gripped Europe in 1931. The IBRD, despite its title, was focused less on funding post-war reconstruction than on facilitating private funding to that end, and on generating investment in the world's less developed economies in much the

---

[1] Lecture by Goldenweiser, 'Policy and Research, 9 December 1943', LC, Goldenweiser, Box 1. Goldenweiser was another of the US government's economic elite to have been born in Eastern Europe, in his case Kiev. He graduated from the First Kiev Gymnasium in 1902, moving to the USA the same year and taking a Bachelor's degree at Columbia and an MA and Ph.D. at Cornell. He became a member of the IAS in 1946 and died in Princeton in April 1953.

[2] Holger Nehring and Helge Pharo, 'Introduction: A Peaceful Europe? Negotiating Peace in the Twentieth Century', *Contemporary European History*, 17/3 (2008), 283. Anne-Marie Slaughter, *A New World Order* (Princeton, 2004), juxtaposed the shortcomings of international institutions, notably the UN, 'perched above nation-states enforced by global rules' (p. 7), with new networks of governance, yet the early history of these institutions was deeply interwoven in states' scientific, political, and financial networks.

same way that the EFO had for Austria, Hungary, Bulgaria, and Greece after 1919, and its initial loans totalled some $500 million. The planned triumvirate of institutions was to have been rounded off by an International Trade Organization (ITO), a high-profile initiative that was fleshed out in its fullest form in September 1945, though left unratified because of the same sort of political pressures—from farming groups in the USA, the imperative of imperial preference, and developing countries' unease—that stymied the work of the League.

The history of the new economic and financial order established at the small New Hampshire town of Bretton Woods in July 1944 is ordinarily recounted through the competitive and cooperative relationship of the brilliant and charismatic John Maynard Keynes and the canny, determined, and enigmatic Harry Dexter White. It was framed in the wider dynamic of the 'special relationship', and their rival schemes developed with the support of their respective Treasuries; the British more creative, the US more organized. But the formal title of the Bretton Woods meeting, the Economic and Financial Conference of the United Nations, was a stark reminder of its deeper origins. On both sides of the Atlantic, the starting point for preparatory papers of plans for the International Monetary Fund was the records relating to the World Economic and Financial Conference of the League of Nations hosted in London in 1933, while materials relating to tariff holidays negotiated at the World Economic Conference in Geneva in 1927 were among documents compiled for the planned ITO discussions.[3]

More important than this historic paper trail was a shared understanding of the recent history of the world economy, facilitated through the agency of the League. Goldenweiser, a key member of the US delegation at Bretton Woods, had represented the USA at the World Economic Conference in 1933, and vowed at the time to learn from his country's uncoordinated performance, which had allowed other nations to blame America for a failure to cooperate.[4] Eleven years later, participants and witnesses of the London farrago, including Berle, Lubin, White, Feis, Viner, Hansen, Loveday, Robertson, and Keynes, were among the first to congratulate 'Goldy' in ways that reflected how all of them were mindful of the lessons of their interwar experiences.[5] Keynes and Robertson were now in the driving seat of British Treasury policy, while White, a junior member of the Tripartite Stabilization Agreement negotiation team, Hansen, and Goldenweiser were acting for the USA. Other US negotiators from outside the Treasury were also familiar figures in the committee rooms of the League and at the seminars hosted at the IAS: Pasvolsky, Frederick Livesey, Dean Acheson, and Arthur Sweetser, who

---

[3] In Nov.1941, for example, Kisch asked Loveday for a copy of the 'proposals of the Preparatory Commission of Experts of 1933', which 'has definite bearing on the steps necessary to get rid of economic nationalism'. Kisch to Loveday, 3 Nov. 1941, TNA: PRO FO371/26662, C12220. 3124/98.

[4] Correspondence between Morgenthau and Goldenweiser, Aug. 1944, NARA RG56, Entry 360, Box 17.

[5] Correspondence relating to 'Policy and Research', LC, Goldenweiser, Box 1.

was now in charge of the information programme of the United Nations.[6] Between 1943 and 1944, these men set about determining the scale, structure, function, financing, and location of the international organizations to enshrine and safeguard the practice of economic and financial cooperation in ways that were very different from the First World War. But the immediacy of the shifting international context and the scale of the challenges frequently threatened to overwhelm officials, who often complained they were short of skilled and experienced personnel. As in the field of reconstruction and food agency, the technical resources of the League, though publicly unacknowledged, were an important support and helped to fill the gaps.[7]

This was the end game for the League of Nations in Switzerland, and its mission in Princeton. In the period of transition between 1943 and 1944, as one world order subsumed the next, the League of Nations served as both support and critic, as it was consulted by a variety of parties on the proposals for the Bretton Woods institutions. Indeed, it is striking how, if we take our gaze away from the dominant Anglo-American axis, the remaining participants at the Bretton Woods negotiations come into view, states that had continued to support the League, and the EFO in particular, in its darkest hours: India, Canada, Australia, the governments of Latin American countries, and the exiled governments from Nazi-occupied western Europe. Their negotiators had cut their teeth and developed important contacts with one another and with the Americans at League meetings.

Aside from facilitating international sociability, the League provided essential scaffolding in intellectual and practical terms. The Princeton Mission told the Americans how to recruit, manage, and sustain the bureaucracy of the new institutions, and directed their likely agenda. It also supplied the historical narrative and definition of an interconnected world economy against which the novelty of the new institutions was set in vivid contrast.[8] Indeed, its experience and emphasis on institutions to promote financial stability and global development, presented in embryonic form in the Bruce Report of 1939, were enshrined in both the IMF and the World Bank, and in the, often forgotten, Economic and Social Council (ECOSOC). It was intended to act as a lynchpin in relations between the Bretton Woods institutions and the humanitarian agenda of a new organization to replace the League—without a name in the summer of 1944, it was announced as the United Nations Organization at Dumbarton Oaks in meetings that ran from 21 September to 7 October 1944. The publicity for the UN may have proclaimed its difference from the League, but its organization, institutional

---

[6] In the early 1950s, as the battle to define the United States' relations with the world turned in on the American nation, the history of this internationalism contributed to charges of un-Americanism in the early 1950s for Lubin, Pasvolsky, and White.

[7] The Federal Reserve Board began its studies on post-war international monetary organizations, for example, by studying the work of the Financial Committee. See memo by Klopstock, 'The League of Nations Financial Committee', 17 May 1943, FRBNY 4608/Postwar Monetary Organization.

[8] Pasvolsky to Hull, 9 Aug. 1943, NARA RG59.3.1, Entry 0558, Box 4, file 4; memo by Eleanor Dulles, 'Financial Relief', 29 May 1943, NARA RG59.3.1, Entry 0558, Box 4, file 6. The failure of the League usually forms the opening reference point in early histories of Bretton Woods too. See, e.g., Eckes, *A Search for Solvency,* 19–31.

infrastructure, and workforce all drew heavily on its predecessor in Geneva. For Loveday and Lester, as for the remaining League employees, the handing of 'their' world order to new institutions and agents was to prove a bitter-sweet experience.

HISTORY MEETS MONETARY POLICY

Of all the varied ways in which the League shaped the emerging architecture of international relations in the Second World War, its contribution to the history of monetary relations has been the prime focus of interest. Here, the role of Ragnar Nurkse was pivotal. Born in 1907 to an Estonian father and Swedish mother, he studied Economics in Edinburgh (1928–31) and Vienna (1932–4), where he participated in salon gatherings hosted by Ludwig von Mises, alongside Hayek, Haberler, and Fritz Machlup. Nurkse was gifted, erudite, and cosmopolitan. He was also a talented pianist, and, aside from being fluent in his father's tongue of Estonian and his mother's Swedish, had an excellent command of German, Russian, English, French, and Italian. In 1934, at the same time as the Nazi influence drove Ludwig von Mises from Vienna to the Graduate Institute in Geneva, Nurkse took up a research post with the EFO, the only Estonian member of the secretariat of the League of Nations. In an organization where expertise could count for much more than official rank, he rose to prominence thanks to his lucid command of international finance. Loveday came to rely on him and helped to keep the 27-year-old Nurkse from being drafted in 1935, and five years later listed Nurkse foremost among the economists he wanted to take to Princeton. Then at the centre of a bitter tug of war between Avenol and the Scotsman, much to Nurkse's joy, Loveday prevailed.[9]

As a member of the Princeton Mission, at first Nurkse was not required to publish his views, producing instead discussion papers to supplement preparations for the publication of the work of the Depression Delegation. But, by 1942, the need to offer a League perspective on monetary policy became pressing for two reasons: first, because the Depression Delegation's field of inquiry had broadened so far as to include almost every aspect of interwar economic relations, and it had been decided to break the work into two publications with a number of specialized supplementary reports. The monetary gap in this otherwise comprehensive series of publications was serious and limiting. Secondly, the Princeton Mission's role as consultant to UNRRA and to assorted governmental and non-governmental agencies of the Allies placed a considerable and unpredictable demand on its resources. Anglo-American intergovernmental negotiations on monetary policy, of which the League was kept fully apprised by Phillips for the British in Washington, and by

---

[9] Kalev Kukk, '(Re)Discovering Ragnar Nurkse', *Kroon and Economy*, 1 (2004) 1–7. During the war, Nurkse became increasingly important to the morale of the personnel. Loveday respected the brilliant Nurkse's loyalty to the League and mission, which was 'quite admirable but not really in his own interest'. See Loveday to Lester, 12 Feb. 1942, LON, Personnel File, S844, 'Nurkse, Ragnar'.

Stewart and others in the US Treasury on the US side, highlighted the strength of the emerging Anglo-American consensus on monetary policy. If the Princeton group was to provide the necessary international corrective and capitalize on its twenty-four-year expertise in international monetary affairs to shape this agenda, the time to intervene was now.

When it came to monetary policy, the League's outpost in Princeton was not short on ambition. Loveday and his colleagues believed they finally had the opportunity to create 'a real international bank with powers to grant credits to central banks, rediscount bills and influence national policy'. To this end, Nurkse, directed by Loveday, began work on 'an historical account of the interwar experience of monetary problems . . . with the object of determining some principles of future monetary agreements'.[10] Nurkse's authority in the field was critical, and he acted as the gatekeeper: no memorandum or document collection on monetary policy was disseminated without his say-so.[11] At the same time, it was the collaborative process established by the mission at the IAS that helped bring Nurkse's ideas to fruition. Much of the raw material for the book came from his previously circulated League memoranda, and these, alongside draft chapters, were discussed at the Economic Discussion Club at Princeton, which regularly mingled Princeton-based economists with anyone interesting en route to Washington or New York.[12] The overworked Nurkse also hired William Adams Brown, an economist at Brown University, to help. The author of *The International History of the Gold Standard Reinterpreted, 1919–1934*, published by the US National Bureau of Economic Research in 1940, Adams Brown assisted Nurkse in analysing the performance of the exchange equalization accounts, although his contribution was short-lived because he went to work on a full-time basis for the State Department early in 1943. His arrival in Washington reinforced the group's link to the State Department, and Adams Brown remained in close touch with Nurkse.[13]

Out of these labours came Nurkse's seminal study *International Currency Experience, 1919–1939*, published in 1944, renowned in economic science for its preoccupation with the lessons of history, notably the turbulent periods of inflation

---

[10] Loveday to Riefler, 9 Mar. 1942, LON, Princeton Office, C1629/No. 2, 41–2. By Mar. 1942, the Princeton group had finished and circulated memos that gave information about UNRRA's plans and Anglo-American monetary negotiations, notably 'Europe's Post-War Capital Needs', 'Exchange Stabilisation Funds', the 'Operation of the Gold Exchange Standard System of the 1920s', and the 'Sterling Exchange Standard of the 1930s', but it lacked an authoritative account of the world's monetary order. Work on this began in earnest in the spring of 1942. Nurkse coordinated the drafting of these memos, which then provided the source material for his study. Chapter One of *International Currency Experience*, for example, is redrafted from the previously circulated 'League of Nations: The Total Volume of International Currency. Changes in Demand and Supply', 6 Oct. 1943, Mudd, Nurkse, MC 173, Box 1, File 6.

[11] See, e.g., his comments on assorted memos in Mudd, Nurkse, MC 173, Box 1, File 5.

[12] The networks' dynamics are difficult to reconstruct because they met in person at the IAS, but the surrounding arrangements surface in Nurkse's and Viner's correspondence. See, e.g., Nurkse to Loveday, 12 June 1942, Mudd, Nurkse, Box 1, File 1; Rosenborg to Viner, 27 May 1944, Mudd, Viner, MC 135, Box 17, File 7.

[13] For their correspondence, see LON, Princeton Office, C1755/No. 1–2, 42.

and deflation in the interwar period.[14] Nurkse's interest in history was as much the product of the EFO's mission in the USA as a scientific disposition that stressed the importance of the past. The study met Loveday's requirement that the EFO's wartime work on trade and economic relations should involve 'the assessment of past experiences and failure'.[15] As Nurkse was the chief monetary adviser to the delegation, his report was conceived as complementary to its work, and it was to his colleagues in the EFO past and present that he turned when he circulated the first draft of the *International Currency Experience*, early in 1943. Among the most prominent were Rasminsky, Haberler, who was advising the Board of Governors of the Federal Reserve, and Polak, who was then at the Dutch economic mission and, like Haberler, based in Washington. The revisions they and other commentators suggested were minor. It says much for the quality of Nurkse's work that the proposed changes were more about enhancing the presentation than the content of the argument, which was certainly more readable than many of the later academic commentaries published upon it.[16] Among the minor quibbles of Nurkse's colleagues was the request for 'pointed conclusions' rather than 'leisurely argument . . . for the sake of clarity', and Loveday's complaint that the draft's 'use of the word "liquidity" as a substance is really quite intolerable', for there were 'limits to the extent to which economics are justified in abusing the English language by the employment of terms which they excuse on the grounds of being technical'.[17] The lucidity, range, and power of Nurkse's exposition were evident to all who read it, as the varied and many tributaries of thought and debate on monetary policy in the League from 1920 to 1944 were now distilled into this single stream.

The mission's preoccupation with communication was a potent reminder of the text's original intention: to complement and support, as well as to test, the detailed and sensitive monetary negotiations under way between the US and British Treasuries. Historical analysis has seen the *International Currency Experience* as a path-breaking critique, taken up subsequently by others, of the way the resultant pegged exchange rate system and the IMF operated.[18] But, before we turn to the substance of Nurkse's treatise, it is important to underscore that the work was anchored firmly in efforts to facilitate negotiations at Bretton Woods, not to oppose them. Nurkse intended his study, which was also widely circulated in draft form beyond the Princeton network, to support the work of the Bretton Woods planners. Indeed, he and his colleagues distributed copies of the *International*

---

[14] Nurkse, *International Currency Experience*. It was also issued as *Conditions of International Monetary Equilibrium* and published by the Princeton International Finance Section, Princeton University, in 1945.

[15] Loveday to Janet Smith, 10 Mar. 1941, TNA: PRO FO371/26661, C3124/3124/98.

[16] For full details of the commentaries, see LON, Princeton Office, C1738/No. 1–4, 42–4.

[17] Loveday to Nurkse, 13 Apr. 1944, LON, Princeton Office, C1738/No. 1–4, 42–4.

[18] For Nurkse miscategorized as a critic, see Endres and Fleming, *International Organizations*, 196–7. For a more careful assessment, see Michael Bordo and Harold James, 'Haberler versus Nurkse: The Case for Floating Exchange Rates as an Alternative to Bretton Woods', Oct. 2001, NBER Working Papers 8545 <http://www.nber.org/papers/w8545> (accessed 7 Sept. 2009), which traces why Haberler, having presented the case for floating exchange rates, was not an advocate until 1953.

Currency Experience and other League documents at the Bretton Woods conference to delegates who did not already have copies and, when the Bretton Woods Agreements were complete, helped to explain the importance of the New Hampshire deal to the wider public.[19] The subsequent stress on the difference between the Princeton group and the Anglo-American camps downplays that there was a transnational consensus at a time when beggar-thy-neighbour economics of the 1930s meant that no one was yet ready openly to advocate floating exchange rates.[20] The confluence of academic, civil service, and political support owed much to the EFO's efforts at education and facilitation on monetary policy during the last quarter of a decade, and the flurry of detailed, technical correspondence that crossed the Atlantic between the economists battling to determine the precise operation of the new institutions relied on strong ties the EFO had helped to create.[21] The *International Currency Experience* was a reflection of this process, and, at the same time, brilliantly articulated the historical context in which plans drawn up by Keynes and White had been developed.

The study cemented Nurkse's international reputation, although he was already an economist of considerable renown, in a career sadly foreshortened by his premature death aged 51 in 1959.[22] It also illustrates that he was a fine historian, systematically exploring episodes of financial disturbance and currency upheaval in the interwar period, and drawing heavily on the League's archive of comparative, if not always comprehensive, economic and financial data. Nurkse's grasp of the character of the nineteenth-century gold standard was nuanced and sophisticated, and placed great stress on the system's multilateral character.[23] He saw the gold standard as a convention that emerged almost 'spontaneously through the recognition by various countries [not the actions of the hegemon] of certain common objectives, chief among them being currency stability'.[24]

The power of Nurkse's history came from his vivid retelling of the story of monetary disorder in both the 1920s and the 1930s, which established an overwhelming case for international monetary coordination and cooperation, and the way he linked it to development of economic nationalism, political radicalization,

[19] See extensive correspondence in LON, Princeton Office, C1738/No. 2–2, 42.

[20] For the Anglo-American dimension see Ikenberry, 'A Word Economy Restored'.

[21] See, e.g., Viner to Keynes, 9 June 1943, and Keynes to Viner, 12 July 1943, Mudd, Viner, MC 135, Box 16, File 21.

[22] Viner had cause to regret disparaging remarks made in 1935 to Haberler, who had encouraged him to read 'the Mr Murske [*sic*.]', in Viner to Haberler, *c.* Mar. 1935, Mudd, Viner, MC 135, Box 12, File 20. Viner wrote a fulsome review of Nurkse's posthumous collection of essays, Ragnar Nurkse, *Equilibrium and Growth in the World Economy: Economic Essays by Ragnar Nurkse* (Cambridge, 1961). His reputation is undergoing something of a renaissance. See Rainer Kattel, Jan A. Kregel, and Erik S. Reinert (eds), *Ragnar Nurkse (1907–2007): Classical Development Economics and its Relevance for Today* (London, 2009); Kukk, '(Re)Discovering Ragnar Nurkse', 1–7; Harold James, *International Monetary Cooperation since Bretton Woods* (Oxford, 1996).

[23] The analysis stands up well, for example, to Eichengreen, *Golden Fetters*, while the gold standard's multilateral qualities have been underlined by Marc Flandreau, *The Glitter of Gold: France, Bimetallism, and the Emergence of the International Gold Standard, 1848–1873* (Oxford, 2004).

[24] Press Release, Columbia University Department of Public Information, 30 June 1944, LON, Princeton Office, C1738, No. 2, 2, 42.

and war. It was a tragedy told in five parts, with the Keynes–White team arriving as heralds of a new order in the final act of the drama. The wide circulation of Nurkse's study, in draft form in 1943 and in cloth- and paper-bound copies after its publication in 1944, was followed by extensive second and third print runs in 1946 and 1947, and was evidence of the broad appeal and the merit of his approach.[25] His monetary history of these two crucial decades was the first of its kind and had an important, if not incalculable, impact, because it was well constructed and contained in its period. As the propaganda strategies of the US Office of War Information and the British Ministry of Information recognized, history was an exceptionally powerful tool, because it engaged audiences emotionally and intellectually, and because the past played a central role in framing society's expectations of the future. Nurkse's historical approach also helped him avoid abstract or technical language, and enabled him to set out how the ideas and structures that shaped financial life had changed in ways that, if the lessons of history were heeded, would deliver a bright, prosperous future.[26]

If *International Currency Experience* was good history, it was also a first-rate work of economics. It posed fundamental questions and sought to distil essential rules by asking, on the basis of what Nurkse called 'practical experience', 'what were the conditions required for a system of stable exchanges in the future?' Stable exchanges, of course, did not mean fixed or even pegged. Drawing on work of the League's 1931 Gold Delegation report, Nurkse explored the implications of using gold as the sole and primary means of international settlement. Important questions followed from this. What methods were there for regulating its supply in relation to demand? What were the prerequisites for the successful functioning of an exchange reserve system such as the gold exchange standard or the sterling area? (Again, each topic had been the subject of systematic study by the League.) How were 'correct' exchange rates to be determined between different countries, and when might it be appropriate to adjust them? And, crucially, what were 'the basic factors governing the need, the desire, and the ability of various types of countries to hold reserves for this purpose?' He also posed questions about the impact of currency speculation on stability and how exchange control might be avoided.[27]

These questions were used to guide the reader through the historical detail, and to frame rules that would make for a stable monetary order on the basis of sustained multilateral coordination. Those who have sought to emphasize the difference between Nurkse, on the one hand, and Keynes and White, on the other, underline that Nurkse, rather like the BIS, had set his face against a 'rigidly planned, global treaty for the solution of specific crisis difficulties and for governing international

---

[25] The book was marketed at the general and student audience as well as at people in high places. See Schatz to Watterson, 29 Aug. 1944, and Rosenborg to Schatz, 1 May 1944, LON, Princeton Office, C1738/No. 2–2, 42.

[26] On history in propaganda, see Susan A. Brewer, *To Win the Peace: British Propaganda in the United States during World War II* (Ithaca, NY, 1997), 89–103.

[27] Nurkse, *International Monetary Experience*, 210–32.

relations in general'.[28] But his focus on norms not institutions lay, at least in part, on the League's self-denying ordinance against offering a detailed commentary on the role of international institutions, because it did not want to contaminate the new agencies with the failed history of the League. In writing its historical prelude, Nurkse made an important contribution to the framing of Bretton Woods and he did the same for notions about regional monetary coordination, notably in Europe, that developed subsequently.

Nurkse was strongly in favour of 'placing international cooperation on an organized and permanent basis', and he, alongside his Princeton colleagues, spent almost their entire careers advancing the cause of international economic cooperation from within the League of Nations.[29] Institutions were important to them, but they believed that, for an international organization to be effective in the longer run, the monetary policies of each government had to be informed by, and be sensitive to, the national and global context; states needed to coordinate their actions in good times and in bad, but monetary regimes through which that coordination found expression were prone to change. The real disruption to international relations came when individual states, often without warning, abandoned the agreed rules. He stressed multilateral coordination, emphasizing that the ground rules needed to be sufficiently accommodating so that they would not need to be modified constantly, but revisited regularly, and, when necessary, renegotiated on an open and multilateral basis. The rules were to be founded on 'publicly recognized criteria', with the implication that states would have to exercise restraint in macroeconomic policy for the sake of currency stability, and it was incumbent upon governments to keep the public informed and involved.

Three elements lay at the base of the Nurkse's monetary framework. First, states shared common policy objectives. Top of the list was the combined goals of high levels of employment and economic stability, which, according to Nurkse, surfaced explicitly in state policy around the world in the Great Depression.[30] Secondly, the world's principal economies needed to exercise discipline over levels of inflation in their own countries, with any future international institutions charged with controlling inflation (and deflation) worldwide. Thirdly, there needed to be an internationally shared view of what might comprise advisable levels of inflation, and Nurkse's framework allowed scope for some variation in national norms from the international standard. All three elements were intended to send a strong anti-inflationary message to policy-makers. At the same time, Nurkse remained alive to the risks of deflation. Indeed, he was one of the few students of the gold standard to acknowledge that, while the system helped to generate the deflationary crisis of the Great Depression, it had been intended as an anti-deflationary device. He pointed

---

[28] Endres and Fleming, *International Organizations*, 197.

[29] Nurkse to Coolidge, 1 Apr. 1944, LON, Princeton Office, C1738/No. 1,1.

[30] This may have been true for the USA, but historians of West European states tend to identify the relationship between a regime's legitimacy and employment emerging in, or immediately after, the First World War. See Conway and Romijn (eds), *The War for Legitimacy*, 45–6. It was, however, the slump that prompted European states to recognize the need for more active economic policies to match claims in their manifestos and electorates' expectations.

out there were no viable alternatives to the gold standard available at the time, and without it there would have been a general shortage of international currency to facilitate commerce and trade and risk the possibility of a deflationary crisis in 1924 and not 1931.[31]

At the same time, the League had moved on from its preoccupation with blocked accounts and the disruptive effects of short-term capital flows that had distinguished Haberler's and Nurkse's publications for the League in the mid-1930s. By now both men had come to the conclusion, increasingly widely shared, that short-term capital movements would be less disruptive if contained within a broadly agreed, rule-based approach to international monetary relations, and made an important 'distinction between normal conditions and crises (including periods of reconstruction after war)', although Nurkse later came to believe that the distinction between 'crisis' and normal conditions was somewhat overdrawn.[32] The timeframe of Nurkse's analysis was a wide one, ranging from the late eighteenth century until the outbreak of the Second World War, a much wider canvas than was usual for the League, and by drawing together the most dramatic and divergent episodes of monetary history in the modern world, *International Currency Experience* underlined the multiplicity of forces acting on currency stability and international monetary relations in the medium to long term. With so many currencies and reserve assets of variable quality, the turbulent history of the gold exchange system demonstrated the inherent temporality and susceptibility of international monetary orders. Indeed, if increased capital mobility (and therefore potential vulnerability) was indispensable to the world's plans for higher levels of international trade, then production and employment were goals better served by an open international economy; there was also an increased need for coordination, cooperation, and scientific vigilance.

Nurkse and Loveday may have doubted the ability of the pegged exchange rate system, with currencies fixed within agreed bands in relation to a gold-backed dollar, endorsed at Bretton Woods, to safeguard monetary stability and economic growth indefinitely. They were sceptical, too, of certain member currencies' ability to meet the American-defined criteria, but they viewed the need for regime and institutional change at some stage in the future positively. The history of the League demonstrated the need for institutional reform, and multilateral dialogue to stay in touch with the ever-changing world around it. As history's witness, the Princeton Mission recognized the immense achievement of Bretton Woods when compared to economic conferences of the past, underlining that economic and financial cooperation was progressive not finite. Nurkse, Loveday, and other members of the mission joined the 730 delegates from 45 nation states at Bretton Woods, and they were eloquent and convincing spokesmen on the value of

---

[31] Nurkse, *International Currency Experience*, 42.

[32] 'While I still feel that the disequilibriating capital movements of the inter-war period were due partly to political fears, speculation regarding exchange rates and other "abnormal" factors described in *International Currency Experience*, it seems likely that they were based in part also on the perfectly "normal" play of private profit incentives' (Ragnar Nurkse, *Problems of Capital Formation in Underdeveloped Countries* (Oxford, 1953), 27).

international organizations to facilitate currency stabilization and international development in particular. Much of their publicity effort was directed inside the United States, for it was here that Congressional and public opinion, as the League knew only too well, had the power to derail the entire project. At the start of 1944, the Secretaries of State, Commerce, Treasury, and the Chairman of the Board of Governors of the Federal Reserve System 'all agreed more had to be done to develop . . . Congressional and public opinion on the inter-relation of international security and international economic institutions'.[33]

The general US approach was to write articles and give lectures to as wide a public as possible. In this task, the Princeton group worked closely with American-based economists who had been associated with the EFO in a variety of capacities over the years, including Bell Condliffe and Viner. They coordinated their publication drive with the US Treasury and Office of Economic Affairs in the State Department. The latter, while 'not expected to underwrite these papers 100 per cent', wanted them to 'reflect fairly accurately the lines of policy' the administration were aiming at. And they did.[34] Although not vetted by the United States government, the *International Currency Experience* was conceived as part of this educative programme. Loveday appeared on British radio giving his impressions of Bretton Woods, and he and Nurkse gave newspaper interviews setting out the meeting's achievements and importance.[35] In the months to follow they also gave individual tutorials and detailed answers to queries on the new world monetary order that came from a variety of directions, including members of the US public and exiled government members of the League. To those diehards who wanted a return to the gold standard past, Nurkse argued that there was 'nothing in either the Keynes or the White plans to prevent a country from maintaining its currency legally convertible to gold, if it has any gold'. And, of course, this point was key; only the USA had sufficient gold to take such a step as the dollar remained fully convertible to gold in the new system.[36] Nurkse's gifts as a communicator and educator were appreciated in other directions too. Arthur Young, of the Chinese Supply Commission, for example, drew on the *International Currency Experience* to understand the challenges before Chinese monetary reconstruction.[37]

The study was framed in explicitly global terms. Although it had a strong focus on European monetary history, a result of where monetary 'power' and the sources of its disruption were located, it also discussed the monetary relations of the Americas, the Dominions, India, China, Japan, and Iran in the world monetary system, with the United States afforded a central role. The euro-centricity of much of the discussion was a tantalizing glimpse of the future, because the rule-based approach to monetary coordination and international cooperation set out by Nurkse became

---

[33] Memo by Collado to Hull, 21 Mar.1944, NARA RG59.3.1, Entry 0558, Box 5, File, 4.
[34] Condliffe to Viner, 27 July 1943, Mudd, Viner, MC 135, Box 7, File 5.
[35] Newspaper clippings, July–Aug. 1944, LON, Princeton Office, Box C1777, No.3, 44.
[36] Nurkse to Coolidge, 1 Aug. 1944, LON, Princeton Office, C1738/1/1/43/44. He greatly enjoyed the conference. See his 'Notes on Bretton Woods Conference', 23 July 1944, LON, Princeton Office, C1777/3/4/4.
[37] Young to Nurkse, 11 Sept. 1944, LON, Princeton Office, C1738/No. 1, 1.

a consistent feature of European monetary cooperation and integration in the post-war period, which culminated in the European Exchange Rate Mechanism and the introduction of the Euro in January 1999.

Although the Princeton group's direct input into post-war monetary schema was less direct than its involvement with UNRRA, it was appraised of plans for the new monetary order as they were developed by contacts in the British and US treasuries in the spring and summer of 1943, as debate raged between financiers and economists in the Allied and exiled powers. In March 1943, Frederick Phillips solicited the mission's views of the White and Keynes plans as they stood. The League officials commented on the likely bases for calculating members' contributions to the fund, preferring to take 'gold as the factor determining the amount of contribution' rather than to use the volume of participating countries' trade, because this way the USA would contribute a great deal more. Next, they analysed the merits of the intentions behind the competing proposals. They preferred White's plan for the fund to 'buy, exchange, accept deposits, issue its own bonds, etc.' in preference to Keynes's scheme, which was 'simply a clearing union'.[38] There was nothing simple about it, of course, but their dismissal belied a deeper concern that Keynes's scheme for a multilateral International Clearing Union denominated through a new international unit of account, the Bancor, was based on credit that would ultimately have to be supplied by the USA. It was likely to be too ambitious and expensive for Congress to swallow, and provided states with too much freedom to defend their interests, which Loveday believed could ultimately threaten the stability of the system as a whole. By contrast, the appeal of White's scheme was that it left 'a special reserve at the disposition of the Fund'. Loveday's team also endorsed the US notion that members' gold and foreign exchange reserves should form part of the basis on which contributions were calculated. However, in contrast to Britain's worries that the White fund would not have sufficient reserves to meet its immediate needs, the Princeton Mission worried that White's proposals would not deliver enough reserves for the fund to be effective in the longer term. Loveday argued he had 'always thought that one might have a system under which each country should always keep X per cent of its gold reserve with the Fund on deposit'. Then the fund reserves would be sufficient 'to meet the difficulty of any country's quota becoming depleted'.[39] A percentage, rather than a fixed-sum approach, he argued, would also increase the American contribution to the fund, to the benefit of the world's poorer economies.

For the same reason, Loveday opposed White's proposal that fluctuations in national balance of payments be used as one of the bases for determining contributions, because the world's poorer countries would lose out. The Princeton Mission shared Keynes's desire that the only state rich enough to make a difference, the

---

[38] Loveday to Phillips, 16 Mar. 1943, and Loveday's memo 'Certain Points of Difference Considered', *c.* Mar. 1943, LON, Loveday, P150/Miscellaneous Correspondence, Dec. 40–Dec. 45.

[39] Loveday's memo 'Certain Points of Difference Considered', *c.* Mar. 1943, LON, Loveday, P150/Miscellaneous Correspondence, Dec. 40–Dec. 45. The mission also surveyed the opinion of key figures from the USA, the UK, and Europe in Washington regarding the emergent plans. See LON, Loveday, P150/Miscellaneous Correspondence, Dec. 40–Dec. 45.

USA, should contribute more, although it disliked Keynes's determination to privilege British self-interest in future plans over what they believed to be the best interests of the world as a whole.[40] The mission was also less enthused by White's intention that the fund would fix exchange rates, and manage the process by which they would be changed. In an echo of Nurkse's stress on the contingent and episodic character of monetary relations in the *International Currency Experience*, Loveday feared the approach would make the fund too rigid to withstand what were likely to be very challenging circumstances in the first year of operation, especially in the first post-war years, 'when the danger of error is greatest'.[41] The Princeton Mission rightly identified that both schema did not deal with the biggest challenge before them: how would countries finance the transition from wartime to peacetime economies, and reconstruct their infrastructure and industry, as well as their trade links?[42] League economists now working for national governments endorsed the League's democratic sensibility in their critique of the scheme; Rasminsky was not alone in bridling at 'the idea of the Bank of England and either the Federal Reserve or the US Treasury dominating the situation'.[43] When he complained of small countries' resentment of Anglo-American dominance embedded in the Keynes and White plans, he could claim he was not just expressing Canadian self-interest because of his work in Geneva.[44] Indeed, Viner shared Rasminsky's rising unease about the growing concentration of power in the hands of the most powerful states and disapproved, 'on non-economic grounds', of individual countries holding the power of veto, 'unless it was granted to all countries regardless of their quotas'.[45] Nurkse and Rasminsky also urged the architects of Bretton Woods to remain sensitive to the complexity of power relationships in the international political economy. National economies were not as homogenous as national polities, and a failure to recognize this might (and as it turned out did) undermine support for the liberalization of international trade: 'For American wheat-growers, Canada is the largest country in the world. Danish exchange matters for New Zealand. New Zealand exchange for Australia, the Argentine, Canada etc.'[46] Nurkse, looking on from the observer gallery at the Bretton Woods conference with a League-seasoned eye, observed it was all 'too

---

[40] Richard N. Gardner, *Sterling–Dollar Diplomacy: The Origins and Prospects of International Order* (2nd edn; New York, 1969), 71–95; Skidelsky, *John Maynard Keynes*, iii. 218–56.

[41] Loveday to Phillips, 16 Mar. 943, LON, Loveday, P150/Miscellaneous Correspondence, Dec. 40–Dec. 45.

[42] Loveday to Phillips, 16 Mar. 1943, LON, Loveday, P150/Miscellaneous Correspondence, Dec. 40–Dec. 45; James, *International Monetary Cooperation*, 38–67.

[43] Record of conversation between Pasvolsky and Rasminsky, 24 June 1943, NARA RG59.3.1, Entry 0558, Records of Leo Pasvolsky, Box 4, File 7. Rasminksy and Viner agreed that White had been 'too hard' on the Keynes plan, although they accpeted it was 'not generally good banking [practice] to have the debtors control the bank and this the Keynes plan would provide'.

[44] Rasminsky went on to become chief reporting delegate of the primary commission overseeing negotiations for the creation of the IMF under the chairmanship of Harry Dexter White.

[45] Viner to Keynes, 12 July 1943, Mudd, Viner, MC 135, Box 16, File 21.

[46] Viner to Keynes, 12 July 1943, Mudd, Viner, MC 135, Box 16, File 21.

much of a US show', which alienated other countries.[47] In these circumstances, it was all the more important that non-US negotiators were able to test the American position, and here Nurkse and other League representatives at the New Hampshire conference believed the performance of negotiators, notably those representing Britain, were frequently deficient.[48] Nation states were also too self-interested. To their mind, the putative IMF needed more money and more power to enable it to act as 'definitely a Central Bank of central banks'. As it stood, the institution was designed 'to make reports and bring pressure to bear and even compel countries to take certain action without, however, having day-to-day business influence on credit policy'.[49]

But Rasminsky's and the League's critique of the White and Keynes plans, and the institutions that resulted from them, did not amount to a sustained attack on institutionalized cooperation. Rather it sounded the cautionary note that these institutions would face greater and more varied challenges than their architects could anticipate. They reasoned that the IMF and the IBRD needed to be strengthened, while at the same time acquiring greater flexibility and adaptability. Although the American administration intended the fund to have more power than the British desired, the mission argued that White's plans, in some ways, did not go far enough. It gave the board 'too much power without consultation and the member states too little latitude, while at the same time failing to indicate the measures required for national adaptation when balance in national finances is lacking'.[50]

The *International Currency Experience* expressed the League's commitment to global development and established Nurkse's credentials in the field. He argued that more money would need to be found than currently planned for the IBRD and the IMF, because the experience of the 1920s and 1930s had demonstrated that poor nations would use up monetary reserves on more immediate needs, especially when 'impoverished or devastated by war'. Post-war financial arrangements needed to fund currency stability, reconstruction, and global development, and credit facilities granted 'for the general purpose of currency stability', without attention being paid to the broader issues of economic development of post-war relief, were

[47] Nurkse handwritten 'Notes on Bretton Woods', undated, Mudd, Nurkse, MC 173, Box 2, File, 3.
[48] Nurkse complained that Brand was 'too old, cold & slow', that Robertson made a 'mess at least twice' at key moments in the negotiations, and that the British delegation was noticeably diminished when Keynes was not present. See Nurkse, 'Notes on Bretton Woods', undated, Mudd, Nurkse, MC 173, Box 2, File, 3. For details of the observer status accorded the League and the ILO, see Kelchner to Loveday, 18 June 1944, NARA RG59, 800.515/6-2844.
[49] Loveday proposed that the fund should have the power to 'discount the domestic paper of central banks at rates of interest that varied from day to day' to influence the credit policy of all the countries whose central banks were 'in the Bank'. This grew out of his own plan for a global central bank developed when he first arrived in Princeton in 1940. See Loveday to Phillips, 16 Mar. 1943, and his memo 'Certain Points of Difference Considered', c. Mar. 1943, LON, Loveday, P150/Miscellaneous Correspondence, Dec. 40–Dec. 45
[50] Record of conversation between Pasvolsky and Rasminsky, 24 June 1943, NARA RG59.3.1, Entry 0558, Box 4, file, 7.

simply 'wasteful'.[51] Although sensitive to the humanitarian case for development and reconstruction aid, Nurkse and his League colleagues did not couch the case for international loans in these terms. From their perspective, the best way to think about the problem of currency stabilization and international loans was to consider what was best, first and foremost, for 'the maximum long-run benefit to the borrowing countries and to the world as a whole'.[52] This emphasis on the *Problems of Capital Formation in Underdeveloped Countries* was taken up in a series of lectures given by Nurkse in Buenos Aires in 1951 and expounded in a publication of the same name that marked an important part of his contribution to post-war development economics—a voice that was as often critical as it was supportive of the work of the UN.[53]

THE GHOST OF REPARATIONS PAST

The spectre of reparations, which rose again to haunt international negotiations among the Allies after 1941, touched on elemental issues about the moral basis of Allied claims for a new post-war order, and the distribution of power and wealth within it. We shall see that here, too, as in so many other apparently discrete debates about post-war planning, the League played a hitherto undetected role. Although not involved in the inter-allied discussions of reparations in the run-up to the Yalta, Cairo, Tehran, and Potsdam Peace Conferences between December 1943 and February 1945, the Princeton Mission nevertheless kept a wary eye on developments because recent history had demonstrated the implications of reparations for the viability of the countries on which they were imposed, and for the international system that facilitated their payment. For the EFO, moreover, the chequered experience of inter-war reparations was woven into the fabric of its own history, despite the fact the League and the EFO did not have authority to intervene in international reparations. (The BIS, of course, was created to help to facilitate their repayment, but became as much a rival as an ally.) The potency of political debts to poison international relations among supporters of League-style internationalism was demonstrated at the World Economic Conference in 1933, and in the Anglo-French war debt defaults that destroyed the possibility of further intergovernmental loans in the run up to the Second World War. The one useful outcome was the hire-purchase agreement that needed no repayment: the Lend-Lease programme of American aid to its Allies. This is not to say that Lend-Lease did not come without its own conditions, as in the Atlantic Charter, but these were terms, notably the commitment to open trade, that League internationalism supported.

The history of war debts did not evaporate with the advent of Lend-Lease. Surveys of the American public revealed the deep, continued suspicion harboured

---

[51] Nurkse, *International Currency Experience*, 219.
[52] Nurkse, *International Currency Experience*, 219.
[53] Nurkse, *Problems of Capital Formation*, and Ragnar Nurkse, *Patterns of Trade and Development* (Uppsala, 1959).

by the Americans towards the British Allies on economic issues, fuelled in particular by their failure to pay back wartime bonds, and this was part of the reason why the public education programme around Bretton Woods and other United Nations' organizations needed careful handling.[54] The USA wanted constant reassurance that the new institutions of international economic and financial cooperation were not a fancy way of 'hornswoggling' the American people out of their hard-earned wealth for nefarious ends, including the protection of European empires.

Although the mission sought to avoid expressing any public views on reparations, it was well aware of its potential to tear asunder the hard-fought sense of hemispheric solidarity, and to cast a pall over any successor organization in much the same way as Maynard Keynes's salvo *The Economic Consequences of the Peace* hung a dark cloud over the League. Its prominence meant the League at war did try to shape discussions on reparations covertly when opportunities presented themselves. The topic resurfaced in international discourse from 1941 and more immediately after the decision to impose reparations against Germany and its allies was taken at the inter-allied conference in Moscow in late 1943. Among the Allies, the USSR was the most determined to secure reparations from Germany and its allies 'to compensate for all the damage they had done during the war'.[55] It insisted that compensation should be paid first to those countries that had suffered the greatest damage in proportion to their national wealth, prime of which was the USSR. The Netherlands and Britain, who also staked an early interest in the subject at the Moscow conference, claimed to speak for all interested parties by arguing that reparations should be made simultaneously to all claimant countries in agreed proportions to the total amount levied.

The British government knew reparations could divide the Allies, especially as it carried the extra burden of being 'charged with emotional content and suffer[ing] from their association with past failure'.[56] However, it was reluctant to take a lead on the issue and sought instead to follow US policy in the hope that this would secure a favourable American treatment on other issues that were more important to Britain. On both sides of the Atlantic, Keynes remained influential. Members of the American State and Treasury Departments interviewed him on the topic, sometimes alone, on several occasions. Yet the man, who had pronounced so famously in 1919, was now very reluctant to be drawn on the lessons of history, simply declaring any settlement ought to 'appear just now and ten years hence', that an 'elastic formula' should be used to determine German capacity to pay, and that payments be made over as short a period as practicable. In contrast to 1919, he was

[54] Patricia Clavin, 'Shaping the Lessons of History: Britain and the Rhetoric of American Trade Policy, 1930–1960', in A. Marrison (ed.), *Free Trade and its Reception: Freedom and Trade* (London, 1998), i. 287–307.

[55] Memo by Eugene Varga, 'Payment of Reparations by Hitler, Germany and her Accomplices', *Information Bulletin, Embassy of the USSR*, NARA, RG59.3.8, Economic Committee, 1940–6, Box 49.

[56] See State Department memo, 'British Thought on Reparations and Economic Security', Sept. 1943, NARA RG59.3.8, Box 50.

less interested in how much Germany should pay than with whom would receive payments and how: 'Would anyone', Keynes asked his American counterparts, 'want German industry [to be] run by Soviet Commissars?'[57]

Keynes's perspective strongly shaped that of the British government, which was pragmatic and present-minded—features it liked to believe were characteristic of its foreign policy as a whole. The American administration instead sought to approach the issue in what it regarded as a 'long-term' and 'less self-interested' fashion, in part because it recognized in 1944 that the admissible claims 'it would be able to present for reparation will in probability be small in comparison with the claims of the devastated nations'.[58] The administration's perspective echoed that of the League group in Princeton, for whom the primary focus of reparation policy ought to be the bearing it would have on the new architecture of international relations.[59] Yet, while the objective was agreed, the road to achieving it was far from clear, as the League discerned a wide divergence of thinking on reparations among US policy-makers alone. And, once again, the American preoccupation with the lessons of history provided the mission with a means to help the USA establish what it believed would be a more coherent policy.

At the most fundamental level, much of the statistical information that under-pinned the US administration's historical accounts as to the effects of reparations on the wider world came from the League.[60] League intelligence filtered into the variety of other departmental and research group memoranda on the subject too. Indeed, despite the divergent views within the administration as to how best to approach the problem, all sides were agreed that the increased availability of economic intelligence and the development of economic science since the 'Great War' had greatly increased the chance of measuring Germany's capacity to pay. Before the Paris Peacemakers were castigated, it was worth remembering, they argued, 'that there were no national incomes series available, that there were no measures of production, that trade statistics were fragmentary, and that there was little understanding of the relation between budgetary practices, currency conditions, and the value of money on the exchanges'.[61] The League had made important contributions to the dissemination and interpretation of comparative data. More specifically, it helped governments decipher some of the technical and potentially wide-ranging aspects of reparations payments on the stability of the world economy, notably sponsoring Ohlin's work on transfer mechanisms in the

[57] See State Department memo, 'British Thought on Reparations and Economic Security', Sept. 1943, NARA RG59.3.8, Box 50.

[58] Memorandum by the Reparation Committee, 'Draft Memorandum by Reparation Committee on Part One, II, B, 3, of Agenda (Reparation I)', 18 Feb. 1944, NARA RG59.3.8, Box 49.

[59] Memorandum by the Reparation Committee, 'Draft Memorandum on Part One, II, B, 3, of Agenda (Reparation I)', 18 Feb. 1944, NARA RG59.3.8, Box 49.

[60] See the statistical bases of histories consulted by the Interdivisional Committee on Reparation, Restitution and Property Rights, including Philip Mason Burnett, *Reparation at the Paris Peace Conference from the Standpoint of the American Delegation* (2 vols; New York, 1940).

[61] Memorandum by the Reparation Committee, 'The Reparation Problem: Experience after World War 1', 28 Feb. 1944, NARA RG59.3.8, Box 49.

Dawes plan, which was now understood to have significantly accelerated and deepened the financial pressures on Germany after 1928.[62]

Although in 1944 the United States anticipated its decisions would be informed by higher-quality information than in 1919, it remained uncertain as to the place of reparations within the context of its global 'economic and political programs'.[63] Its ambivalence was rooted in deep divisions between its government departments, and within the American public on the issue, which was exposed by Henry Morgenthau Junior's dramatic intervention in September 1944 with a plan 'for the complete shutdown of the Ruhr'.[64] Although the intervention shocked British and some West European exiles, Morgenthau's plan marked the opening gambit, not the closing bid, in an intricate process of negotiations between different government departments and the American public. It was evidence of the democratic context in which FDR's foreign policy was framed and the tensions inherent in the President's position on this, as on so many other, questions.[65] FDR, like most Americans, agreed that Germany should and could afford to pay reparations—the productive strength of the German war economy crudely demonstrated the point; the difficult question was how to measure its capacity to pay in an evolving geo-political context. Here, again, League intelligence and expertise were important grist to the US mill. Harry Dexter White drew up the earlier, less draconian version of the Morgenthau plan, which said nothing about mining or other industries or areas. His position was closer to that of the State Department and the Office of Strategic Services, both of which were sensitive to Germany's role as a key importer and exporter at the heart of the European economy. And, once again, many of the Americans who wrote memoranda on the reparations issue and participated in international conferences at Yalta and Quebec had been schooled in the issue through Geneva.[66]

Privately, the Princeton Mission argued that Germany had the capacity to pay reparations. The challenge was to determine the means and volume of payment to ensure justice was done, while bearing in mind the wider, central role Germany played in the European economy. Twenty years of studying and attempting to negotiate with both Weimar and National-Socialist Germany had taught the Princeton group the importance of strong and coherent international will in the face of German obstruction. It argued that there had been too much stress in

[62] Ritschl, *Deutschlands Krise*, 104–41.
[63] Memorandum by the Reparation Committee, 'The Reparation Problem: Experience after World War 1', 28 Feb. 1944, NARA RG59.3.8, Box 49. American planners, like the League, did not see a strong causal relationship between inflation and reparations.
[64] John Morton Blum (ed.), *From the Morgenthau Diaries*, iii. *Years of War, 1941–1945* (Boston, 1967), 354–77.
[65] Wilfried Mausbach, *Zwischen Morgenthau und Marshall: Das wirtschaftspolitische Deutschlandskonzept der USA, 1944–47* (Düsseldorf, 1996); Michaela Hönicke, 'Morgenthau's Programme for Germany', in Robert Garson and Stuart Kidd (eds), *The Roosevelt Years: New Perspectives on American History, 1933–45* (Edinburgh, 1999), 168.
[66] Memorandum by the Reparation Committee, 'The Reparation Problem: Experience after World War 1', 28 Feb. 1944, NARA RG59.3.8, Box 49, pp. 8–9; John Lamberton Harper, *American Visions of Europe: Franklin D. Roosevelt, George F. Kennan, and Dean G. Acheson* (Cambridge, 1994), 105.

the interwar period on German rights over those of the international community. The Allies needed to be more robust when facing German determination to protect its sovereignty than they had been in 1919, and they were. With the Allied victory in Europe on 7 May 1945, the German state effectively ceased to exist, the debate about reparations became a cause and symptom of escalating tensions between members of the Grand Alliance, and, by 1948, the Anglo-American drive for national defence, defined in global terms, was the paramount concern in their treatment of the German zones of occupation. This put paid to American, and with it Western, aspirations to collect monetary assets, and assets in kind, from their zones of occupation, although the USA still recovered some $98.6 million from German holdings in the USA and $12.6 million from neutral countries to whom Nazi Germany had economic and financial ties: Sweden, Portugal, Spain, Afghanistan, Tangiers, and Ireland.[67] In the East, reparations were paid, but the price included a divided world.

Yet between 1943 and the summer of 1945, the issue of reparations remained unresolved, and threatened to disrupt what, for the Western powers, were more substantive issues regarding UNRRA, new financial institutions, and currency and trade reform. Although Keynes had little inclination for a fight over reparations this time, his name was used in one of the most potent external critiques of the reparations settlement of the First World War intended to shape the outcome of the Second: *The Carthaginian Peace or the Economic Consequences of Mr Keynes*. The book was written by the French economist Étienne Mantoux in 1942 and 1943. It appeared to international acclaim in 1946, and became the first of many distinguished critiques of Keynes's position on reparations.[68] Mantoux's study was a systematic challenge to the economic calculations that underpinned Keynes's assessment that Germany could not afford to pay reparations, and a call on the Allies to recognize the importance of reparations, too, for peace terms concordant with concepts of international justice. Mantoux's central concern was 'nothing else than what the coming Peace is to be'.[69] The book was a tour de force, made all the more remarkable by the biography of its author, a 31-year-old captain who died in the service of the Free French forces in Bavaria on 29 April 1945, eight days before the war ended, while his book was in the final stages of production.

Mantoux's study has long been interpreted as the work of a lone scholar—an individual's expression of French frustration with German resurgence in the 1930s and the determination to secure justice for France and for Europe after the Second World War. In 1945, his publisher, Oxford University Press, highlighted how his perspective and experience as an economist—he had taught briefly at the London School of Economics—had shaped his ideas, and the important influence of his father, Paul Mantoux, who had served the French government at the Paris Peace Conference and taught at the Graduate Institute in Geneva. But the press and the

---

[67] See Martin Lorenz Mayer, *Safehaven: The Allied Pursuit of Nazi Assets Abroad* (Missouri, 2007).

[68] Étienne Mantoux, *The Carthaginian Peace or the Economic Consequences of Mr Keynes* (London, 1946).

[69] Mantoux, *The Carthaginian Peace*, p. xv.

book's reviewers praised Mantoux's independence, writing 'while America was still neutral', and singled out his uncanny ability to proffer 'well-marshalled and informative economic data', despite the near statistical blackout of the war.[70]

Yet, although the text was Mantoux's own, the context in which it was written, and the materials on which it was based, were heavily reliant on the League of Nations. Mantoux's statistical compilations and the stress on the 'patient effort needed to build up a future world opinion' strongly invoked the Geneva spirit.[71] Indeed, from 1941 to 1943 he was a visiting member of the IAS, reunited with members of the Geneva secretariat he knew so well from the time when his father had served as head of the Political Section. Mantoux made ready use of the economic and financial materials amassed in Princeton to inform his study, and debated his ideas with members of the mission, many of whom shared his views. IAS seminars and faculty members, notably Riefler, his sponsor at the IAS, also gave him access to the US administration, all the way up to the top of the US Treasury. Intriguingly, both he and White expressed very similar ideas to Mantoux at US Treasury meetings.[72] (Mantoux's analysis of the productive capacity of the Ruhr finds a striking parallel in White's proposals.[73]) In much the same way as US economic foreign policy was framed and articulated by years of engagement with the League, so, too, it seemed, was this accredited French take on the question of reparations.

There are other echoes of the Princeton Mission in Mantoux's work: 'we must first take care of economics and politics will then take care of themselves'; 'it might not be a bad idea to begin discovering *what* was done at Versailles before deciding not to do the same'.[74] Yet his writing was not bound to the technocratic world that confined League officials. Mantoux could write passionately of how it 'was not the League that failed, but the nations', and, when it came to building peace and a new world organization, the world's statesmen would do well to remember 'the numbers and character of peoples must enter as much as the figures for wheat, coal or petroleum output'.[75] The fundamental question, therefore, was how to reconcile plans for the open world of the future with 'the ever increasing nationalisation of economic life'?[76] This was the conundrum that had preoccupied the League's post-war planners since 1940, and loomed large in Allied peace-making in 1944 and 1945.

[70] See, e.g., R. C. K. Ensor, 'Introduction', in Mantoux, *Carthaginian Peace*, p. vi; review of *The Carthaginian Peace* by Melchior Palyi, *Review of Politics*,.9/3 (1947), 390–3.
[71] Mantoux, *The Carthaginan Peace*, p. x.
[72] Record of meeting between White and Riefler, 3 Mar. 1943, NARA II, RG56, Entry.360.O, Box 20. Mantoux was also on friendly terms with Viner. See Mantoux to Viner, 26 Nov. 1941, Mudd, Viner, MC138, Box 18, File 8.
[73] e.g. Mantoux, *Carthaginan Peace*, 72–5.
[74] Mantoux, *Carthaginan Peace*, 183.
[75] Mantoux, *Carthaginan Peace*, 188.
[76] Mantoux, *Carthaginan Peace*, 182, 189.

DUMBARTON OAKS

With plans for the IMF and the World Bank agreed at Bretton Woods in July 1944, action had to follow, and the next building block in the institutional edifice, in Pasvolsky's words, to a 'peace built stone by stone' came with the Dumbarton Oaks Conference that opened on 21 August 1944 in Washington. The meetings, conducted in camera between small, specialized delegations from the USA, Great Britain, the USSR, and China, were intended to address security issues, notably the composition and powers of the new international organization to replace the League of Nations.[77] On 9 October the conference closed with the announcement of arrangements for the UNO, which were to be ratified by a subsequent conference in San Francisco in 1945. But, despite the fanfare, in many ways Dumbarton Oaks marked the end of more expansive interpretations of security for the world centred on collective security, and an independent, UN-run military force.[78] The institution that emerged was remarkably similar to its 1920 predecessor. The Assembly of the League was reborn as a General Assembly, and reasserted a public claim to Wilsonian-style international democracy. The eleven-nation membership of the Security Council, too, echoed the League, although its focus was more clearly on 'hard security' and its structure reflected what was understood as the special responsibility of the major powers to make the world safe. Its five permanent members, the USA, Britain, Russia, China, and France preserved great power domination in the new world order, in ways that were troublingly similar to the interwar period.[79]

The narrative developed to introduce the new United Nations to the American public: 'another, better sustained effort to achieve the objectives of international peace and co-operation', did not flatter the League.[80] Nor could it afford to, given the stalemate that had emerged at Dumbarton Oaks, and the increasing tension in Anglo-American relations with the USSR (though British relations with the USA were often far from harmonious) played out across the backdrop of the Warsaw Uprising. The novelty and relative merits of the Dumbarton Oaks proposals were consistently presented in relation to the 'failed' League: the latter had not preserved peace because its covenant was simplistic; its organization lacked great power support and it was without military muscle. The League's denigration helped to foreground the innovations that trumpeted the fact that, when the tools of arbitration and embargo failed, the new organization would have the means, through the powers invested in the Security Council and armed forces supplied

---

[77] Pasvolsky's comment recorded by Collado, 21 Mar. 1944, NARA RG59.3.1, Entry 0558, Box 5, File 4.

[78] Robert C. Hilderbrand, *Dumbarton Oaks: The Origins of the United Nations and the Search for Postwar Security* (Chapel Hill, NC, 1990), 122–208, 244–7.

[79] Harper, *American Visions of Europe*, 120; Warren Kimball, *The Juggler: Franklin Roosevelt as Wartime Statesman* (Princeton, 1994), 84–105.

[80] Memo by Sweetser, 'Dumbarton Oaks and League Covenant', LC, Sweetser, Box 40.

by the organization's membership, to act against what it deemed a serious threat to world peace.

Sweetser was asked to explain this new overt hostility to the League to members of the American League of Nations Association, who declared themselves to be 'shocked' by the strength of these denunciations of the League's record in comparison with the proposed UN.[81] The need to make the new organization 'seem different' and better from the League was 'inevitable', despite the fact that the new organization, too, had its shortcomings, and League supporters everywhere, he replied, 'needed to bring everyone together in a common programme'.[82] For Sweetser and the Princeton Mission, the need to distort, even forsake, the history of the League had become a painful necessity, although there was a growing sense of unease among Princeton officials, because Dumbarton Oaks had not delivered all they had hoped, and because the UNO placed such great emphasis on great power collaboration. The League officials acknowledged that great power support was important; indeed, it had spent twenty-five years making the case for it on behalf of the League. But also of importance were the League's claim to global democracy and its embodiment of the recognition, acknowledged in the opening words of Cordell Hull, in a promotional film on Dumbarton Oaks, that 'the whole world today is more and more a single inter-dependent area. This inter-dependence means that we must either develop close co-operation in common economic, social, and political matters or develop frictions that will inevitably lead to war.'[83] Here Hull echoed a wider understanding of peace and security evident in the late nineteenth century that had been recovered by the League in the 1930s and enshrined in the Bruce Report.[84] But, to the Princeton Mission's frustration, the outcome of Dumbarton Oaks left the humanitarian dimension of the UNO grossly underplayed and underdeveloped. History had taught the League that economic, financial, social, and security concerns had to be woven together as much as possible. For the value of an international organization to be made 'real to the general public', complained Loveday, 'one must connect it more directly with the day-to-day activities and interests, in the narrow sense of the word, of the great mass of people. One must render it less purely political and more economic, cultural and social.'[85]

[81] Berdahl to Gerig, 30 Nov. 1944, and Sweetser to Pasvolsky, 22 Dec. 1944, LC, Sweetser, Box 40.
[82] Sweetser to Berdhal, 12 Dec. 1944, LC, Sweetser, Box 40; Hilderbrand, *Dumbarton Oaks*, 245–6.
[83] Memo by Sweetser, 'Opening Statement by the Secretary of State for the Dumbarton Oaks Film', 9 Jan. 1945, LC, Sweetser, Box 40.
[84] Memo by Sweetser, 'The Gist of Dumbarton Oaks', 22 Dec. 1944, LC, Sweetser, Box 40.
[85] Loveday to Sweetser, 19 Jan. 1944, LC, Sweetser, Box 39. Loveday was especially scathing of the activities of the Executive Committee of the League of Nations Union (LNU). He condemned the LNU, despite calling for the 'full import of the League' to be 'realised by the general public' in an LNU Pact published in London in 1943, for failing to recognize or demonstrate any interest in the non-political activities of the League. The pact was signed by the Lords Cecil, Layton, and Perith, and by K. D. Courtnay and Gilbert Murray. Only Layton and Murray, in Loveday's estimation, recognized the value of the non-political agenda to the organization's appeal to the public.

Indeed, the economic and social dimension of international security had been included in the American delegation's proposal to Dumbarton Oaks for an Economic and Social Council (ECOSOC). It was a carbon copy of the agency proposed by the Bruce Committee in 1939 and was presented by Geneva hands Pasvolsky and Harley Notter, a close associate of Henry Wallace and Head of the State Department's Division of International Security and Organization. ECOSOC was to be a discrete, primary organ of the UNO intended to sit alongside the General Assembly, the Security Council, an international Court of Justice, and a permanent secretariat. But it was dropped from the Dumbarton Oaks agenda on day two of the conference, because the delegation from the USSR did not want to include the objective to foster economic and social cooperation among the purposes of the new body.[86] Edward Stettinus, leading the US delegation, did not put up much of a fight. As we have seen, the welfare, 'new deal' aspects of US post-war planning had begun to dissipate as early as 1942, and welfare issues were a source of friction among American peace-planners, some of whom, such as FDR's Chief of Staff, Admiral William D. Leahy, were opposed on ideological grounds, and among others who feared conflating welfare with peace would disrupt plans for reconstruction and aid (the provenance of UNRRA) and post-war security. For the USA, the primary aim now was to demonstrate leadership and unity within the ranks of its delegation, and its post-war planners felt 'the whole world was watching' to see whether the USA 'means business in its whole programme of international organization for security and economic expansion'.[87] Given the composition of Dumbarton Oaks, it was not possible for League officials or the rest of the world to resist. Bretton Woods had established a framework for the governance of economic and financial relations to bring prosperity, negotiations for the security provisions of the UNO had concluded, and the ILO was still in business. It was, therefore, easy for the Dumbarton Oaks negotiators to ignore the fact that security and the economy needed to be brought together in some formal way or to accept that a means to coordinate and integrate the new institutions of global governance had to be agreed.

The downgrading of ECOSOC at Dumbarton Oaks was deeply disquieting for the Princeton Mission, which believed the conference had botched the chance to safeguard economic prosperity and ignored the needs and rights of smaller powers.[88] While historians of the conference are critical of the meeting's failure to address questions of human rights, the dominance of the great powers, the impact of the veto on the efficacy of the Security Council, and the failure to set up an independent military force, the mission's critique recovers the contemporary

---

[86] The creation of each organ was left to the discretion of a different committee respectively, so the proposal for an Economic and Social Council lived on, but remained undeveloped at the Washington meetings. See Hossein Fakher, 'The Relationships among the Principal Organs of the United Nations', unpublished Ph.D. thesis, Institut Universitaire de Hautes Études Internationales, 1950, 15.

[87] Memo by Collado (discussed with Pasvolsky, Hiss, and Acheson) to Hull, 21 Mar. 1944, NARA RG59.3.1, Entry 0558, Box 5, File 4.

[88] League officials were in close contact with the delegates. See, e.g., Record of Conversation in New York and Washington between Loveday, Hambro, Capel-Dunn, Gore-Booth, and Gerig, 'The League and the New World Organization', 21–24 Aug. 1944, LON, Loveday, P150/24–5.

expectation that the UNO would also be charged with a responsibility of helping to combat economic crises. In response, the Princeton Mission redoubled its efforts to make a final, major effort to shape the new global agenda in the name of the League. It cut back, where possible, on its consulting activities to UNRRA and government agencies, and concentrated on revising and, by early 1945, publishing and disseminating *Economic Stability in the Post-War World: The Conditions of Prosperity after the Transition from War to Peace*, the second part of the report of the Delegation on Economic Depressions. In the same way that the focus of planning by the Allied governments had moved on from the immediate needs of reconstruction to long-term planning, so, too, *Economic Stability and the Post-War World* marked League efforts to articulate what should be the priorities of the new world order in the long term. It was to be the EFO's swansong.

Extant since 1938, the Depression Delegation continued to afford the Princeton group an important intellectual and political network preoccupied with what its members believed to be the greatest threat to peace, which was not great power confrontation, but economic depression. For the delegation, the prospect of continued military conflict at the end of the Second World War remained a real possibility, for, if state's policies were 'based on fear and not on confidence and mutual aid, they are bound to be essentially negative, restrictive, self-destructive'.[89] History showed 'depressions which occur in the first decade or more after major wars to be of exceptional violence and duration'.[90] The delegation had been trying to complete the final report to underline the point for over a year.[91] But, unlike the *International Currency Experience*, which made it to press in time for Bretton Woods, the second volume of the Depression Delegation's findings was the work of a dislocated group, which had to convene to write and agree on the final text of the report. Loveday had taken advantage of the Montreal UNRRA Council and the Dumbarton Oaks meetings to reconvene its authors, many of whom were acting as advisers or observers to national delegations. It took until December 1944 before they were able to make real progress, and the pressures they faced redoubled as Europe was liberated and members of the mission were recalled home to help out with the challenge of reconstruction. By then, the tide of history had moved more firmly against it, as the Princeton group became victims of their own failures and successes: failure because the future architecture of international relations was almost fully formed, and it now formally excluded the League, so that there were fewer spaces into which its influence and perspectives could seep; success because many of the ideas and individuals who were part of it had been part of its history.[92]

---

[89] League of Nations, *Economic Stability in the Post-War World: The Conditions of Prosperity after the Transition from War to Peace* (Geneva, 1945), 20.

[90] League of Nations, *Economic Stability in the Post-War World*, 16.

[91] McDougall, in particular, grew increasingly exasperated, and repeatedly urged the Princeton Office to publish part two of the Depression Delegation report 'before any further United Nations Conferences on economic questions are summoned'. See McDougall to Loveday, 31 May 1944, LON, Princeton Office, C1740/No. 1, 43–4.

[92] Among the notable absentees were Ohlin, Redvers Opie (who temporarily replaced Frederick Phillips after his death in 1943), G. F. Towers, Governor of the Bank of Canada, and the Pole Zygmunt Karpinski, on secondment to the Bank of England.

Loveday, of course, was tenacious and skilled in 'make-do and mend' inter-nationalism. Between October 1944 and February 1945, he managed to convene five meetings of a makeshift delegation. R. H. Brand, based at the British Supply Council in Washington, replaced Phillips, W. Domaniewski, Commercial Counsellor at the Polish embassy, represented the central and eastern European perspective; Crena de Iongh substituted the now deceased Hart, and Rasminsky stood in for Towers. The latter was barely a substitution at all, given Rasminsky's long-standing involvement in the section. Although it did not come naturally to him, Loveday now ignored the formal League conventions that governed such appointments; with the League wound up, there was nothing to lose.[93] The delegation additionally comprised: Morgenstern, McDougall, Winfield Riefler (back from London), and Carter Goodrich, representing the International Development Works Committee of the ILO, aided by Christie Taite and E. J. Riches on questions relating to trade unions and wages. So as to ensure *Economic Stability in the Post-War World* represented the breadth and depth of the League's economic credentials, he also circulated drafts of the final report to Ohlin, Myrdal, Pasvolsky, John Williams, Henry Grady, and Robert Marjolin, economic adviser to the French Commissariat of Supply and Reconstruction based in Washington, a former assistant to Charles Rist and a key economic adviser to de Gaulle.

THE QUEST FOR ECONOMIC STABILITY

The general character and objectives of economic policy advanced by Loveday and his colleagues, among whom there was remarkably little disagreement, were global in engagement, egalitarian in aspiration, and underpinned by the promise of economic growth through consumption. The world should aspire to the fullest possible use of the resources of production in all countries, a stable economy, and rising standards of living. No man or woman who wanted work should be unemployed for any time longer than it takes to train for a new form of employment; goods and services had to be provided to meet the physiological needs of all classes of people; society should distribute the financial cost of unemployment as fairly as possible; and individual liberty should be respected when it comes to employment choices; and educational opportunities be brought on a par with one another. Equality between states was also important: all should share in the markets of the world through the liberalization of trade barriers; and the benefits of modern methods of production should be available to all peoples of the world through trade, and 'courageous' international measures of reconstruction and development.[94]

---

[93] Loveday did not bother to approach governments formally, but rather negotiated directly with the individuals concerned. He also exceeded his authority in giving committee documents to non-committee members. See Loveday to Marjolin, 31 Aug. 1944, LON, Princeton Office, C1740/No. 11, 43–4.

[94] League of Nations, *Economic Stability in the Post-War World*, 21–2; League, *The Transition from War to Peace Economy*, 14.

These priorities were both a reiteration and an extension of previous reports. In the earlier phase of its work, the Depression Delegation placed greater emphasis on the need for international institutions to facilitate coordination and cooperation and to help identify and address the cyclical downturn as and when it occurred. Bretton Woods had seen the creation of specialist monetary institutions, which was a source of both gratification and concern for the Princeton Mission: the IMF was a landmark institution, but one that asserted the primacy of the world's major powers—hardly surprising given that that was where the capital on which the institution depended lay. The World Bank was a modest but significant advance, because it recognized and promoted the interests of poorer nations. But the value of both institutions to the wider prospects of economic security was now at risk, given that the proposal for an Economic and Social Council had stalled at Dumbarton Oaks, and plans for an international trade organization were less advanced than Loveday and his colleagues would have liked. There was now a grave risk that, as the Allies wrestled to secure the world in conventional ways with weapons and treaties, the relationship between economy, society, and peace would not receive the attention than the League secretariat believed it demanded.

Everyone who participated in the writing of *Economic Stability and the Post-War World* knew it was the League's last word on the subject, and were convinced it was important. The Princeton Mission's involvement with UNRRA, and its contacts with Allied and exiled governments, left it in no doubt as to the rising domestic pressure for governments to deliver on promises of renewal at the war's end. With the dissolution of the League nigh, time was running out to combat the nationalism embedded in so much of the rhetoric of reconstruction and its uncomfortable echoes of Great Depression recovery programmes. Given the concentration on the imminent prospect of peace, the group agreed to cut back the historical account of the interwar years from over a hundred pages in the first draft to a sharp pointed account of no more than twenty. History was being jettisoned and so, too, were Princeton Mission inhibitions. The time had come to be 'as explicit as possible regarding the nature of the policies open to individual governments' and the importance of coordination and oversight on an international plane.[95] Essential to its case were the findings and conclusions of both its scientific work and its practical experience.

The report's overview of the cyclical and structural sources from where depression might emanate was drawn from around a hundred years of global economic history, including a quarter of a century of learning on the job by the League. Twenty-first-century economists would add little that was new to it. But, as much as the officials sought to make a case for their own authority and recommendations, the report conveyed their awe at the creative and destructive powers of the world economy. It demonstrated how far the League had come from its endorsement of laissez-faire in the 1920s. Viewed from the world of the twenty-first century facing new economic and geo-political challenges, the perspective of advisers who spent

---

[95] League of Nations, *Economic Stability in the Post-War World*, 315.

their whole lives grappling with questions of international security and prosperity speaks to us as much today as it did to the new international society of 1945.

Most striking was the note of caution and, in places, humility about facing the future: despite the advances and achievements of economics in the Second World War, the world must remain ever vigilant to the threat of depressive forces and shocks, and flexible in its policy response. Economic crises 'have many causes. They vary in nature, and may require the adoption of different policies on different occasions. There is no single simple remedy or specific.'[96] The one constant was that they are 'international phenomena', the response to which required international coordination. Equally arresting in this condensed rendition of the League's labours of the 1930s was the lucid and sustained focus on global capitalism. It was not a story of individual states operating in an amorphous world economy; rather the text advanced the concept of a world economy with discussion in chapters organized around the themes of: the strategic role of investment; primary production; and the means by which booms and depressions were communicated through different economies around the world. The perspective climaxed in the second section of the text, with thirteen chapters dedicated to setting out current academic research on how best to combat the varieties of depression that the League believed governments were obliged to combat, with the global consequences of any policy action kept firmly in view.

The central theme was a long-established one in the EFO's analysis: the importance 'of the great industrial countries' to the position of the smaller ones, which, without access to international reserves and resources of all kinds, 'were forced to seek shelter' in restrictive national economics that helped to shatter 'the weakened fabric of world economic relationships'.[97] The report was sensitive to the inequalities of wealth within, as well as between, countries: the more equal the distribution of income between groups in society, the greater the stabilizing effect on the national economy. This tension could be eased by close government focus on 'the lower-income groups...by increasing their productivity or their purchasing power'.[98] An alternative approach, it recognized, would be to direct taxation policy to redistribute national wealth, but this could act as a disincentive on business and check economic progress. For all their focus on the international economy, modern methods of tax avoidance and offshore tax havens did not feature in the imagination of a group engaged in its own battle for diplomatic status to avoid the imposition of US taxes on 'meagre' League salaries paid from Switzerland. In so doing, it drew on the EFO's research into the penalties of double taxation.[99] By contrast, its advice that 'selective policies of credit control are preferable to a general contraction of credit' in the face of a significant speculative boom in a stock exchange or real-estate

---

[96] League of Nations, *Economic Stability in the Post-War World*, 291.
[97] League of Nations, *Economic Stability in the Post-War World*, 19.
[98] League of Nations, *Economic Stability in the Post-War World*, 294
[99] For a pioneering study of the League's work on fiscal evasion and double-taxation, see Christophe Farquet, 'Lutte contre l'évasion fiscal: L'Éche de la SDN durant l'entre-deux guerres', *L'Économie politique*, 44 (2009), 93–112, and 'Expertise et négociations fiscales à la Société des Nations, 1923–1939', *Relations internationals*, 142/2 (2010), 5–21.

market had a very modern ring; the anxiety that excessive saving on the part of consumers might trigger a depression (rather than prolong one) rather less so.

Consumption, not production, was centre-stage: how its growth might be facilitated, sustained, and managed to fight depression. Consumer economies, the League argued, were more equal, prosperous, and stable, and this emphasis on the relationship between consumption and stability signified the shift in the League's economic thought over the previous fifteen years. Every economy should be understood as a consumer economy, and, in a global context, this invested particular responsibilities in the world's major industrial countries to the less developed economies. Their emphasis on the plurality of world power was striking. So, too, was the conspicuous absence of any consideration of the imperial dimension that helped to sustain British and French pretensions to global power in the minds of both the small remaining band of League officials and the American administration. Although colonialism was not addressed directly, the text's emphasis on 'responsibility', 'development', 'equality', and the importance of 'national sovereignty in shaping economic policy', as well as the limits that confronted it when battling for growth or against depression, indicated where its attitude lay. The major challenge, as the Princeton group saw it, 'for democratic statesmen and administrators' was to maximize 'material wealth without jeopardizing human liberties'.[100] It could be read as a criticism of colonialism, although the stress on economic development could still be accommodated within the conception of humanitarian imperialism, and posed a more overt challenge to the policies and values of the USSR.

Taken together, *Economic Stability and the Post-War World* and its supplementary reports were intended as a manual for governments on how to manage the political economy, a guide to the potential sources of trouble in the national and international economy, and how best to tackle issues relating to: labour mobility, the responsibilities of the trade union and business communities, employment and inflation, unemployment in special areas and industries, unemployment due to chronic depression, measures to be adopted by raw-material and food-producing countries, and how to relate these national measures to the well-being of the international economy as a whole. There was no space here for empires, Soviet, Fascist, or otherwise.[101]

An implicit critique against colonial trade protection came through, too, in the report's reflection of the League historical battles with trade restrictions that spanned three decades. Tariffs and quotas had destroyed the world economy of the 1930s. At the same time, protectionism for smaller countries and small-scale producers was presented as a matter of necessity, not choice. The danger for the future was that the world's major economies would continue to set one standard for themselves, and another for the rest of the world. It was a prescient warning. After the Second World War, the plans for the ITO were scuppered by American agricultural

---

[100] League of Nations, *Economic Stability in the Post-War World*, 23.
[101] League of Nations, *Economic Stability in the Post-War World*, 315.

interests, while developing countries found themselves squeezed by international agencies who demanded freer trade as a condition of development aid.[102]

But, for all the agreement among the report's authors, there were two areas of controversy. The first arose from Haberler's continued opposition to the sections relating to government expenditure and employment policy, which represented the broadly Keynesian aspirations of key committee members. This was a long-standing headache for Loveday. The second was the delegation's, notably the secretariat's, increasingly critical take on the new architecture of international economic and financial relations in the wake of Dumbarton Oaks.

THE BATTLE OVER EMPLOYMENT

In the winter of 1944 Haberler tried to recover ground given in the past to delegation members who had been enthused by Keynes's or Beveridge's ideas.[103] Loveday and Rasminsky had drafted most of the 1939 and 1943 Depression Delegation reports, and employment policy had been contentious then too. Once again, Loveday proffered a detailed explanation of the means by which 'government expenditure may create employment in the same way as private expenditure'. He retained earlier material, but noted that, when it came to depression policy, 'public spending alone would not do the trick', and that public finance should 'help to maintain demand by the monies paid out in bad times, and to curtail it in good times'. The private sector remained as important to the prospects of recovery as public expenditure, if not more so, along with the international context—nationally oriented strategies needed international coordination.[104] This formulation was not enough for Haberler, who never missed a meeting of the delegation in Princeton, though he was not formally a member, nor returned a draft of the Depression Delegation report to Loveday without extensive suggested revisions. After much batting back and forth, the unrelenting Haberler joked, the long-suffering Miss Joseph, the senior secretary to the Princeton Office, must be 'writing the chapters on the role of national spending to combat depression'. It was probably she, he teased, who was responsible for addressing questions relating to the problem of maintaining aggregate demand 'in a 100 per cent Keynesian spirit', while Haberler complained that his qualifications and alterations had not 'been worked into the text in a coherent, logical manner'.[105] He wanted the document to make a clearer distinction between problems associated with general depressions

---

[102] The intolerance for local views or protectionism shaped the behaviour of major international institutions after the Second World War. See, e.g., Daniel Maul, 'Help Them Move the ILO Way: The International Labour Organization and the Modernization Discourse in the Era of Decolonization and the Cold War', *Diplomatic History*, 33/3 (2009), 387–404.

[103] There had been a very lively and heated debate between Haberler and Hansen as to the merits of the Beveridge plan at the seminar hosted by the IAS in 1943. See Loveday to Opie, 31 Aug. 1944, LON, Princeton Office, C1740, No. 1, 43–4.

[104] Loveday to Haberler, 14 Dec. 1944, LON, Princeton Office, C1740/No.1, 43–4.

[105] Haberler to Loveday, 4 Sept. 1944, LON, Princeton Office, C1740/No.1, 43–4.

that 'can be solved in terms of broad aggregates, such as total spending, saving, investment and consumption', and 'the more difficult problems which do not lend themselves to such easy solutions', notably when partial depressions affected particular elements of the national or international economy that produced structural unemployment.[106]

To reinforce his point, Haberler forwarded Pigou's attack on the 'windy hopes of a post-war Beveridge millennium' to Loveday, with a brisk note that the report should include a reflection of the view that the 'current discussion of post-war full employment takes far too naïve a view of the efficacy of establishing a gross money demand sufficient to take the output of industry while keeping aggregate demand stable'.[107] Haberler believed that, in the immediate post-war period, a particular problem would be the rapid contraction of some industries and the considerable growth of others, resulting in wildly different employment patterns. The answer to the conundrum, he argued, was greater labour mobility. The report needed to ask, 'on what does mobility depend, and how can it be developed?'[108] How did state support for the unemployed shape labour mobility and flexibility?

His intention was to do more than sharpen the text. He wanted to use it as a means publicly to challenge the Beveridge Report, which he regarded as an 'extremely well written and a very able performance', but one that went 'too far into recommending doubtful reforms... some way beyond the anti-cyclical policy'.[109] Of course, Haberler's sights were trained not solely on Beveridge but on his rival Keynes. He believed Beveridge's work would 'inevitably draw comparisons with the League report', which made it 'all the more important that the latter should be of really first class quality'.[110] Again and again he argued that the fiscal policy chapter should receive 'some more working-over' by him.[111] The offers were politely but steadfastly declined.[112]

Loveday, although acknowledging what he believed was the potentially 'pernicious' national focus of Beveridge's proposals, was not about to dance to Haberler's tune.[113] He cut back the report's sustained consideration of employment policy to emphasize instead Beveridge's call for equality of opportunity and treatment. Loveday valued the democratic quality and significance of these ideas for international relations, and this was his primary concern: 'to add some important suggestions' to the Bretton Woods and Dumbarton Oaks proposals to ensure that they were 'adequate machinery for the general co-ordination and synchronization of policies for dealing with economic depressions'.[114] The death of the gold

---

[106] Haberler to Loveday, 4 Sept. 1944, LON, Princeton Office, C1740/No.1, 43–4.

[107] Haberler to Loveday, 15 Dec. 1944, enclosing a note on Pigou's article in *The Statist*, London, 13 Nov. 1943, 758, LON, Princeton Office, C1740/No.1, 43–4.

[108] Haberler to Loveday, 15 Dec.1944, LON, Princeton Office, C1740/No. 1, 43–4.

[109] Haberler to Loveday, 11 Dec.1944, LON, Princeton Office, C1740/No. 1, 43–4.

[110] Haberler to Loveday, 23 Oct. 1944, LON, Princeton Office, C1740/No. 1, 43–4.

[111] Haberler to Loveday, 11 Dec. 1944, LON, Princeton Office, C1740/No. 1, 43–4.

[112] Loveday to Haberler, 8 Dec. 1944, LON, Princeton Office, C1740/No. 1, 43–4.

[113] Loveday to Haberler, 14 Dec. 1944, LON, Princeton Office, C1740/No. 1, 43–4.

[114] Quoted by Brand in letter to Riefler, 15 Nov. 1944, LON, Princeton Office, C1740/No. 1, 43–4.

standard and the growing responsibility of the state to offer economic security to its citizens articulated by Beveridge only heightened the need for international coordination, and the dangers to world peace should it fail. Theory and history demonstrated that the cyclical fluctuations in an 'economically integrated world are not a national but an international phenomenon, and require not only national but international action'. Global coordination and cooperation held the key both to meeting consumers' needs as a first priority, and as a frame in which to think about how the world's 'mechanical, scientific and human' resources might be mobilized to meet those needs. Anything less would result in 'wide differences in the standards of living of different peoples . . . a menace to social order and international understanding, the growing sense of world unity'.[115]

A WATCHTOWER FOR THE WORLD

Economic Stability in the Post-War World, like the *International Currency Experience*, both endorsed and challenged the emergent architecture of international relations. The report explained the value of the new specialist monetary agencies, the World Bank and the IMF, although Loveday privately continued to doubt how far the world's large governments would tolerate and submit to their 'extraordinary executive powers'.[116] Publicly, his critique focused more on the IMF and World Bank's authority to supervise the character and overall trends in international lending and whether they had sufficient financial resources at their disposal in the face of the challenges ahead. The scars from the 1931 meltdown of international finance and its bitter economic and political legacies ran deep within him.

To this end, Loveday proposed there should be a third international institution to have oversight 'of all long term loans where ever they were made'. Although the proposal was rejected by other delegates who regarded it as 'going a bit far' and 'impractical', the text remained peppered with strong statements as to the importance of contra-cyclical lending for the stability of the world economy and the need for financial probity.[117] It sonorously declared: 'the wide-spread collapse of financial institutions which so frequently occurs in depressions does not arise solely because of deflation. It reflects also in most cases the presence of over-extended positions that could have been avoided in the preceding period of prosperity.'[118] When it came to the operation of private financial institutions, the Depression Delegation wanted the new economic and financial institutions to adopt a particular state of mind—an ever-present vigilance to the threat of depression—which it believed was more important than a precise set of policy recommendations.

The external members of the Depression Delegation may have scotched the secretariat's proposal for an international agency to monitor and supervise

---

[115] League of Nations, *Economic Stability in the Post-War World*, 17.
[116] Loveday to Brand, 5 Oct. 1944, LON, Princeton Office, C1740/No. 1, 43–4.
[117] Brand to Loveday, 2 Oct. 1944, LON, Princeton Office, C1740/No.1, 43–4.
[118] League of Nations, *Economic Stability in the Post-War World*, 277.

international credit movements, but the latter's call for an international buffer stock agency did make it into the final report. Following the lead of the ubiquitous McDougall, it argued that the agency should be invested with the power to purchase key commodities when prices were in a long downward trend, and sell them when prices were rising. Its operations would thereby act as a stabilizing influence on international prices, and 'consuming as well as producing countries should participate'. After an initial investment, it was imagined the organization would be self-funding, with the authority to raise additional funds whenever market conditions proved the most favourable, and producers and consumers would have a say in its funding and operation. It was developed very much with the 'small farm' and key primary industries (notably mining) of the world's less industrialized economies in mind.[119] It reflected the wide framing of *Economic Stability in the Post-War World*, which was written with careful 'application' and attention to the world's non-industrial countries. The report emphasized how global stability and taking special care of this group would enhance the prospects for peace and prosperity. It demonstrated how the income of countries dependent largely on the export of a few primary products was subject to particularly wide fluctuations when demand turned downwards, a trend that was accompanied and reinforced by a sharp decline in international investment. The proposed World Bank, the League hoped, would help by pursuing 'a contra-cyclical investment policy' and that this additional machinery would maintain demand in both primary producing and industrial countries. The proposal was not made lightly. Its architects 'were fully conscious of the practical and political difficulties... errors of judgement will be inevitable'.[120] At the same time, the administrative machinery and technical storage facilities built up to accommodate and handle stocks of basic commodities during the war offered a tremendous opportunity—one missed after the 'Great War'.

The potential efficacy of a buffer stock agency was contrasted to the impact of schemes to control production, an area in which the League had significant practical experience. These generally emerged as a means 'to limit the effects of long-term or structural change in the economy' rather than cyclical downturn, but overproduction was almost always the inevitable result.[121] The new agency was intended to work within a world of open markets and was to respond, and when necessary moderate or shape, market trends rather than dictate them, to prevent the severe fluctuations in prices and demand that 'devastate and destroy'.[122] Never adopted worldwide, although also considered by UNRRA and promoted by Boyd Orr and McDougall during the former's period as director of the FAO, these ideas were to become a cornerstone of the EEC's Common

[119] League of Nations, *Economic Stability in the Post-War World*, 265–71. It also explored why it was difficult and inappropriate for farmers to set up their own buffer stock schemes.
[120] Haberler commended Loveday for it. See Haberler to Loveday, 11 Dec. 1944, LON, Princeton Office, C1740/No. 1, 43–4.
[121] League of Nations, *Economic Stability in the Post-War World*, 271.
[122] League of Nations, *Economic Stability in the Post-War World*, 270–5.

Agricultural Policy, whose wine lakes and butter mountains became the stuff of farmers' dreams and finance ministers' nightmares.[123]

The second, new international agency proposed in the report was what it called a Central Committee that would be positioned between the UN and ECOSOC, and the more specialist IMF, the IBRD, and the proposed ITO. ECOSOC should not be allowed to wither on the vine—the implication of Dumbarton Oaks—and its precise functions needed to be developed as a matter of urgency. To this end, Loveday and his colleagues had recourse to the Bruce Report's call for a Central Committee and invested it with the particular responsibility to guard the world against economic depressions by rebranding it as a 'central advisory body' and appointing to it experts and government ministers selected by UNO and ECOSOC. Above all, they should be 'persons whose views carry weight not only about technical monetary questions, but also about broad issues of commercial policy, of labour policy, of agricultural policy, of public finance'.[124] Their primary concern would be to keep issues relating to the balance of the world economy firmly in view. Its body should meet at regular and frequent intervals to study and assess the policies pursued by different governments affecting economic activity and economic fluctuations, both locally and universally. As always, the League also stressed the importance of public, as well as official, communication and the need for coordination. The committee was charged, when promoting its findings, to suggest clear policy alternatives; to arrange joint discussions with international bodies and government representatives; and to take the lead in identifying when it was appropriate for the UN and others to take action 'against the common enemy which depressions constitute'.[125]

On one level, as Loveday acknowledged, the proposal for the committee was 'not really either very new or radical'.[126] He was effectively arguing for some sort of reformed Economic and Financial Organization (with civil servants, experts, and government ministers now enjoying an equal voice) with an enlarged, permanent Depression Delegation to live on after the dissolution of the League. Nor was Loveday clear whether the agency should be located within ECOSOC, whether it would be separate from council but within the United Nations, or whether it should be distinct from the UNO altogether. But it would be wrong to dismiss the central advisory body as merely a poorly conceived attempt to secure 'jobs for the boys' in Princeton. By 1945, Loveday and his colleagues in Princeton all had new positions. Indeed, most of them had turned down offers, in many cases repeatedly, from universities, government departments, and international agencies before settling on their final choice. Rather, the delegation promoted the idea of the Central Committee because it believed the new architecture of international capitalism was being fashioned with a gaping hole in the middle. Indeed, it was to be

[123] Amy Staples, *The Birth of Development: How the World Bank, Food and Agriculture Organization, and the World Health Organization Changed the World, 1945–65* (Kent, OH, 2006), 88–96.
[124] League of Nations, *Economic Stability in the Post-War World*, 288.
[125] League of Nations, *Economic Stability in the Post-War World*, 287.
[126] Loveday to Brand, 5 Oct. 1944, LON, Princeton Office, C1740/No .1, 43–4.

filled in a piecemeal fashion in coming decades: the IMF offered reports on the world economy's health; associations such as the Mont Pèlerin Society brought together economists to forge the shared scientific and political agenda of classical liberalism (and included many League regulars among its attendees); the Group of 7 major industrial powers was created to meet the need for prompt intergovernmental action after a confluence of economic and security shocks in the 1970s. Its composition, excepting the formal inclusion of the USA, effectively recreated the Council of the League and the EFO.[127] Latterly, the annual World Economic Forum at Davos restored a touch of Geneva magic by affording the opportunity for experts, journalists, academics, and politicians with what was now called 'name recognition' to meet to discuss the issues of the day and enjoy good skiing in Switzerland.

However, the central question raised by the proposal for a central committee was never answered: whose responsibility was it to stand sentry for the world economy against crisis and depression? What was distinctive about Loveday's proposal was that this 'body be tightly focused . . . on the fluctuations of economic activity' and thereby provide an early warning system of impending economic crisis to save capitalism from itself. Equally important, he argued, would be the organization's ability to respond quickly when it perceived the need for 'urgent action' by calling for immediate intergovernmental and institutional cooperation along recommended lines outside the usual cycle and pattern of cooperation (another lesson drawn from the League's experience). What Loveday and Brand, the delegate who expressed the greatest enthusiasm for the idea, failed to explore in depth was how the central advisory body would retain a fresh and detached outlook on the world. What would prevent the Central Committee from reflecting, rather than monitoring and questioning, prevailing economic orthodoxy?

Part of this neglect can be put down to the Depression Delegation's (over) confidence in the impartiality of economic science. The group failed to think sufficiently about the politics of economic science—still comparatively little understood—and how the public and political demands for absolutes would shape the interpretation of its work. But it was also because for most of the period after 1930, as capitalism was in crisis and a tide of economic nationalism swept the world, the efforts of the League secretariat in Geneva and of the Princeton Mission to reconnect and restore the world economy had put them outside the political mainstream. So, too, had their continuing faith in internationalism and international organization at a time when much of the world had renounced such beliefs. Personal circumstances and temperament were also important. By 1945, the ethnically mixed group of League troubadours in Princeton had become a group of professional outsiders—employees of an organization out of time and place, and citizens of countries in which they had not resided for decades (indeed some were stateless because their country had rescinded their citizenship, been occupied, or dissolved), and residents in a country that registered them as aliens.

[127] The G7 comprised Britain, Japan, Canada, France, Germany, Italy, and the USA.

Variously labelled as 'statisticians', 'economists', and 'international civil servants', they had professional training and position that placed great importance on intellectual detachment, but there was no denying the pessimism that had come to infect their outlook on the world.[128]

The slide into depression was most pronounced in Loveday, though it was soon to affect Nurkse too. He had been a doughty fighter for his organization and his beliefs when he arrived in Princeton in 1940 and for much of the war, but the deterioration of Loveday's mood and health in the wake of Dumbarton Oaks was marked. That the end of the League was approaching did not help, although it hardly came as a surprise to him. Overwork was a greater factor. So, too, was his growing conviction that, while much energy had gone into planning Europe's post-war reconstruction needs, much remained unresolved. The same was true on a global level where, if the world was fortunate enough to evade an immediate post-war economic crisis (and the stuttering recovery of 1946 and 1947 was evidence it did not), then serious deficiencies in the proposals for economic and military security remained.

Loveday's pessimism was inductive of a useful clear-headedness, and the final observations of *Economic Stability in the Post-War World* ended on a sobering note penned by the man from Fife

'Nothing could be more dangerous, nor more untrue, than to assume that the maintenance of the fullest measure of employment can be left to each government acting in isolated independence. All will be affected by the success or failure of others. All must co-operate in their attempts to attain the end on which we believe we all agree. Even granted such co-operation, success will not be achieved lightly or rapidly. There will be many experiments, many disappointments and failures . . . but failing co-operation there can be no success.[129]

The Princeton group may have set out as 'clearly as possible the policies which might have stabilizing results', but Loveday declared himself 'far from being optimistic about the extent or the rapidity with which these results might be achieved'. He was attacked within the League and outside it for this sentiment, but successfully resisted efforts to replace it 'by any sort of superficial optimism'.[130]

Loveday believed the voice of the gloomy outsider had its place in the global political economy. He was right. But, of course, the more significant outsider in the emerging global capitalist order planned for the world economy was the USSR. Soviet-style command economies, like the imperial skeins that shaped the European distribution of wealth and power, were barely mentioned in *Economic Stability in the Post-War World*, or in any other policy-oriented documents by the Princeton group for that matter. (Statistical compilations were a different issue.) The League order was explicitly liberal and capitalist. Indeed, the expulsion of the USSR had helped to put paid to League aspirations that it might be reformed and revived after the war, and the Princeton group's subsequent approach to its soured

---

[128] It is very different from the optimism that characterized the views by development pioneers. See Staples, *Birth of Development*, 22–3.
[129] League of Nations, *Economic Stability in the Post-War World*, 290.
[130] Loveday to Brand, 5 Oct. 1944, LON, Princeton Office, C1740/No. 1, 43–4.

relations with the USSR was along the lines of 'least said, soonest mended'. In 1945, how command and capitalist economies would relate in the new, liberal capitalist world remained an open question. *Economic Stability in the Post-War World* suggested tolerance. There was a repeated stress on the need of economies for freedom—'an appraisal of the advantages and costs of greater, or greater apparent, economic stability as contrasted with the freedom of action to which many peoples are accustomed'. But the delegation also suggested the question be posed at a different level, one that emphasized standards of living or, put another way, the freedom to consume. Here, East could meet West.[131] The resources for consumption were best secured by access to foreign trade and foreign investment—an openness that was inimical to the USSR—for resources are 'not scattered evenly around the globe'. Yet Russia was a special case, 'a continent of her own which is endowed with almost every variety of agricultural resources and materials'.[132] It was presented as a separate world outside the capitalist global economy, a sleight of hand that the EFO had used often in the 1930s. And this separately imagined world was about to be made real. With peace fast approaching, the time had come to turn the blueprints of international relations into institutions made of stone, capital, and souls. The communist vision of the world had begun to collide with the capitalist one, as Soviet troops met fellow members of the United Nations on German soil, and diplomats convened in San Francisco for the inaugural conference of the United Nations Organization.

---

[131] For the centrality of consumption to the USSR, see Kotkin, 'Modern Times'.
[132] League of Nations, *Economic Stability in the Post-War World*, 266.

Conclusion

The end of the League came, as it had begun, with the world in conference. It was a death of two parts. The first was the conference in San Francisco that inaugurated the United Nations in April 1945, and marked an infamous, public affront to the League. Although the Geneva Headquarters and the Princeton Mission were invited to represent the League, there was a mix-up over the seating arrangements. As the national delegations took centre-stage at the War Memorial Opera House, a striking beaux arts building reminiscent of the League and distinguished as the first opera house in the USA raised by public subscription from thousands of citizens, Lester, Loveday, and Manley Hudson of the International Court were initially without seats and then found themselves consigned to the gods. Squabbles with the Russians over whether the League had the right to select its own delegation, and the spectacle of 'the dress circle crowded by San Franciscans from the age of ten upwards', added insult to injury.[1] While Lester demurred politely that no offence had been taken, Loveday and his colleagues groused more openly at the slight to the League, and the State Department flapped in response. It was the outcome of administrative incompetence, not a policy choice, they claimed.[2] While not doubting the State Department's capacity for incompetence, the officials saw the episode as unequivocal proof of the League's diminished status in the pecking order of international affairs, and evidence of the renewed primacy of the national. With its intellectual contribution to post-war planning drawing to a close during 1944, and its insight and advice into the practical questions of how to set up and run an international organization used up, Lester and Loveday were guests at their own funeral. Indeed, they had helped to arrange it.

A more fitting memorial came twelve months later with the convocation of the final meeting of the Assembly in Geneva, and the first since 1939. Here, Lester and Loveday were centre-stage as the League was formally consigned to history. During eleven heady days in the Palais des Nations, the past, present, and future collided. Delegates reminisced about the noble sentiments and the dreams that had founded the League, commending its officials for keeping 'the sacred flame of hope of a

---

[1] Douglas Gageby, *The Last Secretary General: Sean Lester and the League of Nations* (Dublin, 1999), 240–6. The USSR disputed the League's right to nominate delegates from nation states that were neutral. This covered Lester, Phelan, and the Spaniard Julio López-Oliván, representing the International Court. Soviet objections centred on López-Oliván, and Alger Hiss mediated on the League's behalf. He negotiated a temporary solution, which replaced López-Oliván with the American Manley Hudson.

[2] Lester to Loveday, 11 Apr. 1945, Lester to Winant, 14 Apr. 1945, and Lester to Jebb, 14 Apr. 1945, LON S563/San Francisco Conference. US League enthusiasts were especially incensed; see, e.g., '"Snub" is Charged of 3 League Aides', *New York Times*, 23 June 1945.

better and richer future alive in the storm' as the internationalism of peace was replaced by the internationalism of war, and expressed their fears for a future under the shadow of the emergent superpowers.[3] Only the contrarian Churchill could assert it was precisely because there were 'grievous and deep-seated divisions in the UNO' that it had a better chance of success than the 'homogenous League'.[4]

Loveday's claim the the UNO was 'a *new* League' (his emphasis) captured that it was neither very new nor very different from its predecessor.[5] Despite the concerted attempt to present a world made new in 1945, there were important continuities between the new architecture of international relations and the old. One of them was that the UNO from the start faced a ceaseless quest for international legitimacy and the need to demonstrate 'success' in terms of its founding charter. (Before being moved to its permanent location, the organization was temporarily housed, ironically, in Lake Success, New York City.) But there were important discontinuities, in particular the effective uncoupling of many of the League's 'technical' services into discrete new institutions—notably in the field of economics and finance—from a direct association with the United Nations Organization that were to make the quest for that success all the more elusive. There was to be such a great proliferation of these separate agencies, especially in the field of development, that they became known as the 'second UN', but, while they were associated with the 'first' UN organization in the mind of specialists in the field of international relations, they were rarely so in the minds of politicians or the general public.

CONTINUITIES

The UNO was a 'warmed-up' League, most obviously in the configuration and practices of the General Assembly where the primacy of national sovereignty reinforced notions that the nation state, in preference to imperial or federal alternatives, became the expression of statehood to which peoples aspired.[6] Architects of the new home of the international organization in Manhattan quickly altered the planned seating arrangements for its membership, which rapidly grew in excess of the 51 states that had signed the founding charter in 1945. By 1955, it had 76 members, rising to 147 thanks to successive waves of decolonization and the admission of China by 1975, and 193 by 2012.

---

[3] Hambro's opening speech to the 21st Assembly meeting, *Manchester Guardian*, 8 Apr. 1946, p. 5.
[4] Speech made by Churchill at the presentation of the Cecil bust at the Royal Institute of International Affairs. 'Mr Churchill on Why the League Failed', *Manchester Guardian*, 30 May 1946, p. 6.
[5] Record of Conversation between Loveday, Hambro, Capel-Dunn, Gore-Booth, and Gerig, 'The League and the New World Organization', 21–24 Aug. 1944, LON, Loveday, P150/24–5.
[6] Mazower, *No Enchanted Palace*, 28–65; Susan Pedersen, 'Getting out of Iraq—in 1932: The League of Nations and the Road to Normative Statehood', *American Historical* Review, 115/4 (2010), 975–1000. Although Kennedy places greater stress on differences between the UN and the League through his greater preoccupation with 'hard security', he is alive to continuities too. Paul Kennedy, *The Parliament of Man: The Past, Present, and Future of the United Nations* (London, 2006), 41–7.

The Security Council, though smaller in membership than the Council of the League, was a more potent expression of great power dominance. There was now much more talk of 'rights', but recognition and enforcement proved as thorny as they had after 1919.[7] The Security Council and what was to become the infamous element, the veto, were novel attributes of the new organization, although the divided cold war world that was to stymie operations of the council was a familiar impediment. As the history of the EFO illustrated, the League represented a familiar vision of a world divided into separate spheres, with one world largely presented as supporting the values and practices of liberal capitalism, and the other as opposed to them.

There were echoes of the past, too, in the universal claims made for the UNO in its founding Charter, and by its principal national sponsors in 1945, the USA and Britain. Where Presidents Roosevelt and Truman used a language of 'freedom' to invoke the mission of the new organization, Churchill and Attlee preached a doctrine of 'responsibility' to secure US financial and military aid to rebuild Europe, and to ensure the USA would take over what they believed had been the British mantle as guardian of global stability. That task included the preservation of empires, where the responsibility remained the development of the colonial world. Here, the British Empire sought to 'save herself', as Jawaharlal Nehru had predicted in 1927, by inciting 'the imperialism and capitalism of America to fight by her side'.[8] But so did the multiversal qualities of the League, with Nehru at the same time invoking the more radical aspirations articulated in the UN's claim to represent one world and oppose colonialism and racism. A concern for individual rights now took priority over the preoccupation with collective rights, notably those of minority groups that distinguished the interwar period.[9] However, the more expansive rights talk of the war years—evident, for example, in the 1944 Philadelphia Declaration, which argued that the quality of the new international organizations, 'in particular those of an economic and financial character', should be judged by their ability to promote social justice—was abandoned in preference to a more constrained approach to social rights in an international order that privileged the rights of the market.[10]

---

[7] For Mazower, in a reading of the UN's founding that focuses on a strand of British imperial internationalist thinking on rights, the charter of the UN 1945 marked a move away from more substantive commitments. Sluga's reading of San Francisco, by contrast, recovers Ralph Bunche's concerns for aspiring Black nations, and Virginia Gildersleeve's rewriting of Smuts's and the author of its famous summons: 'We the People'. See Glenda Sluga's review of Mazower, *English Historical Review*, 125/516 (2010), 1280–2.

[8] Nehru cited in H. W. Brands, *India and the United States: The Cold Peace* (Boston, 1990), 8; Brewer, *To Win the Peace*, 244.

[9] Mazower, *No Enchanted Palace*, 149–53. For an overview of how human rights gained international traction only after the 1940s as a means of staking political claims and counter claims, see Stefan-Ludwig Hoffman (ed.), *Human Rights in the Twentieth Century* (Cambridge, 2011).

[10] Report by the ILO, 'International Labour Conference: Declaration Concerning the Aims and Purposes of the International Labour Organization Adopted by the Conference at its 26th Session, Philadelphia, 10 May 1944', *Official Bulletin*, 26/1 (June 1944), 3. The declaration was welcomed, though not unequivocally, by FDR. His speech in response to the declaration is reported in the same issue <http://www.ilo.org/public/english/century/download/roosevelt.pdf> (accessed 9 Dec. 2010.)

It would be wrong to assume that, among others, policy-makers in Britain and the United States were united in abandoning the international campaign for social rights. Ernest Bevin, the incoming British foreign secretary, remained a staunch supporter of the ILO, for example, and believed preserving the Empire was to the detriment of the British worker, who had never got very much out of it. He was bitterly disappointed to see Philadelphia cast aside.[11] Nevertheless, in short order the vocabulary of peace—social and international—deployed in the war was replaced by the language of security directed at markets and the state.

The economic and financial regime that emerged after 1945, widely heralded as a clear break with the past, also held deep continuities with the interwar and war years. The novel elements were eye-catching. In the Second World War, economic and financial issues were first when it came to imagining and building the peace, unlike in the First World War, when they had come last. There was a marked shift in emphasis in international relations from the 'regulation of inter-state relations to the deliberate promotion by collective measures of economic and social progress'.[12] Discrete institutions—the IMF, IBRD, and to some extent the FAO and UNRRA, were intended to 'liberate' the world from economic protection, and to safeguard it from the destabilizing effects of financial crises. The self-same ambition was embedded in the planned trade organization. The power arrangement in these institutions replicated the primacy of western power relations and liberal capitalism. Although we still lack a systematic appreciation of FDR's take on the international political economy in the war years—he anointed Treasury and State Department plans for Bretton Woods with the words 'I think this is all right'—there was no doubting members of his executive sustained a deep interest in international relations on economic, financial, and social questions from late 1932 that culminated in these institutions' foundation.[13] Even if the policies of FDR's administrations pulled in different directions, the President consistently explored the relationship between international relations and economic prosperity. This much can be said of a President whom historians have been able to interpret only by inference, in what, throughout his three terms in office, remained a deeply contested presidency.

If the Bretton Woods institutions were new, they were born of a twenty-five-year struggle to found, legitimate, and develop an economic and financial dimension to intergovernmental relations, which both supported and challenged the power of the state. Out of this effort came the Economic and Financial Organization of the

The declaration marked the concerted attempt of the ILO to reassert itself into post-war international institutional arrangements, but to limited effect. See also Eddy Lee, 'The Declaration of Philadelphia: Retrospect and Prospect', *International Labour Review*, 133/4 (1994), 467–84.

[11] Anne Deighton, 'Ernest Bevin and the Promotion of Human Rights in Europe, 1945–1950', in Ann-Christina L. Knudsen (ed.), *Locating Europe: Ideas and Individuals in Contemporary History* (Aarhus, forthcoming). For a contemporary take on the lost opportunity of the Philadelphia Declaration, see Alain Supiot, *L'Esport de Philadephie: La Justice sociale face au marche total* (Paris, 2010).

[12] Loveday, *Reflections*, 20.

[13] FDR to Hull, 3 Apr. 1944, NARA RG59, 800.515/4-344/CS/LE; Harper, *American Visions of Europe*, 259–74.

League. The title of organization took over a decade to secure, and it was later denied by an eminent former member of the Economic and Financial Section, Per Jacobsson. He left the EFO in 1930, for the newly founded BIS, which enjoyed financial resources the EFO could not match, before moving to the pre-eminent financial organization, the IMF, of which he became director.[14] It is hardly surprising that in retrospect he challenged the EFO's entitlement to the term 'organization', for it was its 'shortcomings' that allowed the IMF to shine.

Central to the EFO's claim for legitimacy, and the basis on which coordination and cooperation within the world economy would take place, were the collation and dissemination of economic and financial intelligence. Embedded within League-invented classifications were implied rules about sound capitalist practices, and these functions were transferred wholesale to the UNO, the IMF, and the World Bank.[15] The EFO's mission to offer policy prescriptions came later, hesitant at first in the 1920s, but increasingly assertive and defined by key initiatives such as its work on food security, and advice on how states should combat economic depression. It was based on the notion of 'practical' economics that were sensitive to context, and sought to bridge protectionism and free trade, state intervention, and market freedom. By the 1930s, its view was distinguished in initiatives that included, for example, its work on food security, and the global fight against financial crisis and economic depression. The scientific underpinnings of this work were drawn from the increasingly distinct, but not yet separate, scientific fields of international relations, economics, sociology, and biology.

The secretariat's effort to secure recognition as a discrete 'organization' within the League was an indication of its faith in the value of institutionalized cooperation. There was strong continuity from interwar to post-war in some of the satellite institutions that were bequeathed from the League in what became known as the 'UN family', including ECOSOC, the LNHO, now the rebranded World Health Organization, and the ILO, although the latter felt more marginal to international relations in the two decades that came after the Second World War than it had after the first.[16] There was continuity to pre-First World War

[14] Pauly, *Who Elected the Bankers?* 60; Erin E. Jacobsson, *A Life for Sound Money. Per Jacobsson: His Biography* (Oxford, 1979), 35–95.

[15] Economic Intelligence Service, the League of Nations, *Statistical Yearbook of the League of Nations Monthly Bulletin of Statistics*, alongside its *Money and Banking*, the *Review of World Trade*, and the *World Economic Survey*, for example, fell largely in the purview of the IMF. The work of the EIS was taken up and developed in publication and digital information series, such as the IMF's *World Economic and Financial Surveys*, the monthly *International Financial Statistics*, and the *Global Financial Stability Report*. For a full list, see *IMF Periodicals* http://www.imf.org/external/pubs/pubs/per.htm (accessed 1 Oct. 2010). Loveday believed UN and IMF publications to be inferior to those of the League, at least for the first decade, and his heirs at the UN acknowledged as much. See Loveday, *Reflections*, 1, and William Leonard (Director UN Statistical Office) to Loveday, 27 Oct. 1950, LON, Loveday, P 151/26–7.

[16] The staff from the League agencies formed what the UN described as a 'sizeable nucleus' of its new organizations. See Morrissey to Tomlinson, 'Memo on Budget Estimate for Work of the Economic and Social Council', 17 Nov. 1945, UNO, S-0 991-0001. On the ILO, see Eddy Lee, Lee Swepston, and Jasmien Van Daele, *The ILO and the Quest for Social Justice, 1919–2009* (Geneva, 2009), 182–4.

institutions, too, when the IIA in Rome was subsumed into the new FAO. The IIA bequeathed the FAO its statistical know-how on the global agricultural market, a bank of information on plant disease and its prevention, and a range of connections to farmers' associations and academic institutions that represented their interests.[17] But the EFO's work in the field of agriculture, led by McDougall and supported by Loveday and the EFO, was the key link. The FAO was firmly under the umbrella of the UN, bringing to a conclusion the EFO's efforts to control the IIA since its capture by Italian fascists in the 1930s. It was there that the League team of McDougall and Boyd Orr were reunited, the latter becoming the first Director-General of the FAO, represented the cutting edge of nutritional science, and McDougall grounding the FAO in the League's and the IIA's long-standing links to producers. In the 1940s, these two men discovered the immense challenges of turning the FAO from an organization dedicated to nutritional research and education, the original framing of the FAO proposal at Hot Springs, into an organization with the power to build a world of plenty from which social stability, and international peace, would come. Empowered by science, and a new institution founded with US presidential support, in 1945 these men had the confidence to imagine a world free of hunger and famine. But Boyd Orr left the FAO within three years, disillusioned by the failure of Britain and the USA to endorse his plan for a world food board to regulate the global market, and by the US government's decision to distribute Marshall Aid without involving the FAO.[18] McDougall remained in Rome until his sudden death in 1958, much of the time working alongside Walter Boudreau of the LNHO section, who joined him there, and Dag Hammarskjöld, the UN Secretary-General whom he had first met through the latter's work on business cycles. The allies now treated the FAO and the UN with pointed disregard as the internationalist vision of the war stalled in the global polity of the cold war.

The EFO's imprint on the new organizations of the international political economy may not have been overt, but it was not inconsequential. It was certainly viewed with a great deal more benevolence by the US administration to which it had sought to move closer in the 1930s than by its old rival the BIS. Much to the 'extreme anxiety' of US Treasury officials, the liberation of Europe freed the officials of the BIS trapped in Basle, who promptly travelled to the USA to involve themselves in post-war planning; the USA complained that 'it smells of the Norman–Schacht period', under which it most certainly wanted to draw a

[17] Tosi and Trentmann underestimate the importance of the League connection. The IIA had put its toe in the water when it came to articulating farmers' needs for credit, insurance, and new trade arrangements, but the EFO's work was much more significant. Luciano Tosi, *Alle origini della FAO. Le relazioni tra L'Istituto Internazionale di Agricoltura e la Società della Nazioni* (Rome, 1991), 210–22; Frank Trentmann, 'Coping with Shortage: The Problem of Food Security and Global Visions of Co-Ordination, *c.*1890s–1950', in Frank Trentmann and Just Fellming (eds), *Food and Conflict in Europe in the Age of the Two World Wars* (New York, 2006), 13–48.

[18] Vernon, *Hunger*, 155–6; Tim Boon, 'Agreement and Disagreement in the Making of "A World of Plenty"', in David F. Smith (ed.), *Nutrition in Britain: Science, Scientists, and Politics in the Twentieth Century* (London, 1997).

line.[19] Institutional inheritances, then, had limitations and dangers, as well as benefits.

But the pre-eminent link between the worlds of international organizations before and after 1945 was the continuing emphasis on the value of technocracy. As Salter had put it, the League demonstrated the unparalleled value of bringing together '*expert* advice' and '*representative* advice' (his emphasis).[20] While the functions of the post-war organizations were built out of the experience of the League, and the positive, if limited, contribution that the EFO could claim, the secretariat's critique of its history underlined, on the one hand, the constraints state behaviour could impose on international organizations, and, on the other, the value of a dedicated international secretariat supported by the worldwide web of science. The scientifically current, apolitical, and internationally regarded expert was associated with the, generally highly regarded, 'technical agencies' of the League, and became an especially pronounced feature of the international and regional organizations that emerged in the second half of the twentieth century. The primacy of expert advice in the new specialist agencies represented the continued power of the idea that the world could be directed by using figures, numbers, and statistical categories. In 1945, many hoped the battle for peace could be won by developing agreed rules for international accounting. These were not the dreams of science fiction. The impact of national income accounting in Britain, for example, demonstrated the potency of technical tools to deliver economic and social good, and the League's work on clearing, mediated by Stoppani as a member of the Italian delegation, was to inform the creation of the European Payments Union in 1950.[21] National statesmen, too, continued to harbour hopes that difficult intergovernmental relations could be circumvented by reaching out to the scientific communities in hostile states, a prescient analysis that stressed the importance of transnational society to the peaceful end of the cold war.[22]

In contrast to expert advice, in 1945 the place of 'representative advice'—the views of lobby groups, activist communities, and national governments—was less clear. Many social scientists believed politics were best left out of the equation. Myrdal was not alone in arguing that technocratic cooperation needed to be conducted in camera. International commissions were more likely to be effective, he argued, by stressing 'the technical, non-political nature and by avoiding all publicity'. Privacy was all, and only when expert decisions had been reached should the outcome be fed to states. For him, the United Nations Economic Commission for Europe was a model, because 'the greatest secrecy was kept up: the committees

---

[19] David Waley, cited in Toniolo, *Central Bank Cooperation*, 272.

[20] Arthur Salter, *The Framework of an Ordered Society* (Cambridge, 1933), 46–7.

[21] See Ralf Magagnoli, 'Anregungen zu einer Neubewertung der Europapolitik Alcide De Gaspersis', *Journal of European Integration History*, 4/1 (1998), 27–54. In 1945, Stoppani tried to re-enter international service but was prohibited by the fact that Italy, a former enemy power, was not yet a member of the new organizations. Stoppani to Lester, 23 Nov. 1946, LON, Personnel Files, S888, 'Stoppani, Pietro'.

[22] Thomas Risse-Kappen, 'Ideas Do Not Float Freely: Transnational Coalitions, Domestic Structures, and the End of the Cold War', *International Organization*, 48/2 (1994), 185–214.

met in private, had no formal rules of procedure, no records were kept except an account of agreements reached between all or a number of states, and no votes were ever taken'. The state officials acted together with the secretariat as 'restricted "clubs", keeping as much independence as possible from their home governments, and avoiding public interest and debate'.[23]

But the preference for a lack of transparency that came to characterize the IMF, the World Bank, and the EEC—organizations all dedicated to the primacy of technocracy and economic and financial cooperation—held dangers for their futures as well as, more obviously, for the interests of the peoples they claimed to serve. Avoiding public interest, debate, and democratic norms robbed regional and international organizations of their claim to legitimacy, and eroded support for their activities on the state level, as the attacks on the democratic deficit of the IMF, the World Bank, and the EEC/EU, although differently composed in each case, all came to illustrate. Although these institutions sought to represent and inculcate notions of good governance, their distance from 'the people' contradicted this claim. Similarly, the focus on performance indicators, and the scientific hubris in much development policy of the 1950s and 1960s, illustrated the dangers of failing to talk to, or engage with, the locals. Social democracy had an international, as well as a national, value. Indeed, the Princeton Mission's experience of life on the margins in the Second World War brought the point home. It was from there, far more than in Geneva, that League officials were confronted with difficult questions about the marginalization of small states in the global political economy, and stressed the importance of reaching out to as wide a base as possible in society, not just the opinion-forming elite.

In the interwar period, the League had helped to orientate action and create a social reality for the secretariat and the networks of expertise and government delegations it sustained. During and after the Second World War, many of the individuals who were members of these groups directed their ideas, their friendships, and rivalries, their own (or inherited) memories of the interwar period, and their connections into new organizations and networks. As we have seen already from the origins of the FAO and the WHO, many League staff—the secretariat of the League or those who worked for the organization in an advisory capacity—found ready employment in the new international organizations.[24] Both Jacobsson and Polak ended up

[23] G. Myrdal, 'Increasing Interdependence between States about the Failure of International Cooperation', from *The Essential Gunnar Myrdal*, cited in Johan Schot and Vincent Lagendijk, 'Technocratic Internationalism in the Interwar Years: Building Europe on Motorways and Electrical Networks', *Journal of Modern European History*, 6/2 (2008), 197.

[24] Memo of meeting between League and UN officials, 'Notes on Questions of Procedure Discussed between Messers Lester, Pelt and Hill', 7 Apr. 1946, UNO, S-0369, Martin W. Hill, Box 37, File 13, Acc. 92/3. The administrative structure of the League formed the basis of the UN, and acted as its lodestar in the early years. See memos relating to the work of the Preparatory Commission of the United Nations, UNO, S-0991-000-01 to S-0991-0001-08. Attacks on the abilities and professionalism of the UN secretariat by member states, notably the Belgian delegate Roland Lebeau, compared the new organization very unfavourably with the efficacy of the League secretariat. See memo by UN secretariat, 'Notes on the 194th meeting of the Fifth Committee on the Morning of 11 October 1949', UNO, S-0991-0002-05.

at the IMF. Polak was there at its birth, and maintained an office at the fund until his death at the age of 95 in 2010, while Rasminsky was Canada's executive director at the IMF and executive director of the IBRD from 1952 to 1962.[25] A continuity of ideas and practices regarding economic and financial oversight passed from the EFO to the IMF. These men also influenced the new organizations to be pragmatic in ways that did not always satisfy their critics, and sought to interpose their institutions between capital markets and states along lines first developed by the League. From the beginning, these institutions were inured to unpopularity because the League had been.

Others with experience of international coordination and cooperation, such as Monnet, sought to propagate new organizations; the promotion of regionalism through the League stretched further than this former Deputy Secretary-General, and gave a strongly technocratic direction to efforts to rebalance Franco-German relations, and with it the prospects for Europe. Technical expertise garnered at the League was deployed by Stoppani and Frère in the European Payments Union, and participation in international negotiation facilitated by the League was invaluable to government figures such as Van Zeeland and Paul-Henri Spaak. Political and ministerial relationships, for better and for worse, benefited from the experience of the League, as generations of government delegates acquired the habits of international engagement, with much of their familiarity centred on European economic security.[26]

The ideas and practices fostered in Geneva lived on in contexts that were nourished and developed by the new international organizations, but that also existed beyond their walls. Universities and think-tanks, producers' groups and trade unions, remained connected to the EFO, and regarded it as a model long after the organization had ceased to function formally in Geneva. On his way to the Bretton Woods Conference as part of the Indian delegation, Dr B. K. Madan, the first director of the statistics and research department of the Reserve Bank of India and its future Deputy Governor, took a detour to visit the Princeton Mission 'to acquaint himself with the general lines and organisation' of its research activities, 'the published results of which are regularly received and studied by us'.[27] More diverse and difficult to categorize, yet all the richer for it, were the careers of the young statisticians and economists recruited into the EFO who advised governments, taught the next generation, and expanded the frontiers of modern economics. The illustrious and diverse list includes Meade, Koopmans, Nurkse, Haberler, Tinbergen, Viner, Morgenstern, and Boulding.[28] Other economists,

[25] His work was very highly valued by Loveday. See Loveday, 'Reports on Mr Polak', 1941 and 1942, LON, Personnel Files, S857, 'Polak, J.J.'. On his contribution to IMF practices and ideas, see Jacob A. Frenkel and Morris Goldstein, *International Financial Policy: Essays in Honour of Jacques J. Polak* (Washington, 1991), 3–37.

[26] Stoppani was reconciled with Italy after 1945 and by the same token helped to rehabilitate Italy. His biography carries echoes of research that suggest the enduring significance of interwar encounters with the League among Japanese progressives. See Burkman, *Japan and the League*, 213–21.

[27] Deshmukh to Loveday, 31 May 1944, LON, Princeton Office, Box C1777/No. 3, 44.

[28] Pauly traces precisely EFO staff who later rose to prominence in the IMF. See Pauly, 'The League of Nations and the Foreshadowing of the International Monetary Fund', 16.

who would not be included on any list of those associated with the League, such as Ludwig von Mises, nevertheless had their lives touched by it. Thanks to the Anschluss in March 1938, travel for Austrian passport-holders became difficult, and it was only because of the League's intercession to enable Haberler to attend a meeting of the Depression Delegation that he was able in the same week to act as a witness at Mises' wedding in Geneva just after the latter had been afforded refuge by the Graduate Institute of International Studies.[29] As we have seen of Loveday's efforts to help economists whose ethnicity or politics put them at risk from Europe's dictators, the EFO was engaged in the business of academic rescue more broadly.

The EFO made a rich and varied contribution to the history of economic ideas that defies generalization, especially when traced through the professional histories of individuals that, in some cases, span six decades or more. At the fulcrum of this history lies these economists' preoccupation with the relationship between the market, the state, and international security. The problems they studied, and a stress on pragmatic, policy-oriented, and empirically informed responses that characterized their early work in Geneva, became pronounced features of their work later in their careers, and the institutions to which they were connected. So, too, did dependence of economic science on EIS data, which continues to provide the backbone of studies of the global economy in the Great Depression. More is known about these economists' individual contributions to the history of economic ideas. Reconnecting their work for the League and, in particular, the institutional context and imperative of the studies they authored, or the committees and conferences they informed, draws out how League prerogatives shaped their published work, as demonstrated in Nurkse's *International Currency Experience.* Indeed, his participation in uniting apparently opposing views of the global economy in his work for the Depression Delegation left him well placed to bring together the work of Keynes and Schumpeter to explain how poor countries were kept poor by a lack of real capital in their economies. He was one of a number of former League economists who moved into the field of development economics in the 1950s.[30] Most retained a strong interest in what had become a central preoccupation for the EFO after 1930: what its expert nexus believed to be the close relationship between economic stability, the distribution of economic wealth, and the origins of war. The depth of this conviction, and the longevity of the network that sustained it, were underlined by the fact that Jan Tinbergen was a founding trustee of the organization of 'Economists against the Arms Race' set up in 1989.[31]

[29] Haberler to Loveday, 30 May 1938, LON, Personnel Files, S786, 'Haberler, G.'; Jörg Guido Hülsmann, *Mises: The Last Knight of Liberalism* (Auburn, AL, 2007), 731.

[30] Hans H. Bass, 'Ragnar Nurkse's Development Theory: Influences and Perceptions', in Kattel, Kregel, and Reinert (eds), *Ragnar Nurkse*, 10; Marc Blaug, 'No History of Ideas, Please, We're Economists', *Journal of Economic Perspectives* 15/1 (2000), 145–64.

[31] Jan Tinbergen was a founding trustee of 'Economists for Allied Arms Reduction', renamed 'Economists for Peace and Security' in 2005. James Meade's and Kenneth Boulding's careers, too, were marked by a lifelong interest in the relationship between war and prosperity. See, e.g., James Meade's involvement with the campaign group 'War on Want', and Susan Howson (ed.), *The Collected Papers*

The participation of these individuals in new policy networks that emerged after the Second World War demonstrated, as in the interwar period, the difficulty of corralling expert positions under a single banner, and the benefits to economic science of bringing together colleagues whose views diverged as well as converged. One such network was the Mont Pèlerin Society founded in 1947.[32] A significant number of its founder members were associated with the dissolved League—now with a new reason to come back to Switzerland—including Haberler, Rueff, and Rappard, the erstwhile Director of the League's Mandate's Commission. The society has been credited with forming the basis of an international network that fuelled an international revival in the economics of the Austrian school and the advent of monetarism, particularly in Britain and the United States in the late 1970s. (It should not be taken as read that a small state was a concomitant of their world view.[33]) Loveday took some persuasion to join the Mont Pèlerin Society, whose work was overtly political in its intention to strengthen the principles and practice of a free society and to study the workings, virtues, and defects of market-oriented economic systems.[34] Others who had been important members of the League nexus rejected the invitation outright. Viner was among them, declaring his preference 'in principle to keep out of any collective activity' that might be described as 'political', in a decision Hayek declared as 'crushing'.[35] This very public mix of politics and economic science, in the heady atmosphere of the early cold war, was a very clear break made by some members of the secretariat and advisers with the past. There were others that underlined some of the fundamental cleavages between the post-war order and that which had preceded it.

DISCONTINUITIES

The UNO was more focused on hard security, was more hierarchical, and was an even greater expression of the power of the nation state than the League had been. As Loveday put it to Sweetser, the UN spent too much time worrying about the security interests of states, and not enough time trying to 'connect to the day-to-day activities and interests of the great mass of people'. The organization needed to be made 'less political and more economic, cultural and social'.[36] Although the powers invested in the Security Council meant the constitution of the new UN was less favourable as a whole to individual national sovereignty, small powers appeared decidedly

of James Meade (3 vols; London, 1988, 1989). See also Kenneth Boulding, *The Economics of Peace* (New York, 1945).

[32] Philip Mirowski and Dieter Plehwe (eds), *The Road from Mont Pèlerin: The Making of Neo-Liberal Thought Collective* (Cambridge, MA, 2009).

[33] Ben Jackson, 'At the Origins of Neo-Liberalism: The Free Economy and the Strong State, 1930–1947', *Historical Journal*, 53/1 (2010), 233–51.

[34] Charles Rist took the same view. An overview of the society's membership and the agenda of its meetings has been compiled by Marc Haegeman, *The General Meeting Files of the Mont Pèlerin Society, 1947–1988* <http://www.liberaalarchief.be/MPS2005.pdf> (accessed 26 Jan.2009).

[35] Hayek to Viner, 3 June 1947 and 13 July 1947, Mudd, Viner, MC 138, Box 13, File 6.

[36] Loveday to Sweetser, 91 Jan. 1944, LC, Sweetser 39, File 'UN Beginnings'.

disadvantaged against the large ones, despite the Charter's rhetorical commitment to show 'respect for the principle of equal rights and self-determination of peoples'. It looked more a 'concert of Europe in modern dress'.[37] For Loveday and his colleagues in the League secretariat, this was a sorry turn of events. For others, however, the harnessing of the world's major powers in the Security Council, the organization's enhanced abilities of military enforcement, were markers of the UN's success when compared to the record of the League. Such a favourable assessment was boosted further by the post-decolonization application by new nation states for UNO membership.

So, too, was the greater emphasis on technocracy and specialization from the outset in the assortment of new or rebranded institutions that formed part of the UN family in 1945: the IMF, IBRD, ILO, WHO, and the International Court of Justice (formerly the Permanent Court). Specialization undoubtedly brought some advantages and far greater resources, but it reinforced challenges that the League had experienced when it came to coordinating the activities of different agencies, including questions of how to ensure equality of access; to secure 'expert' and 'representative' advice; and to make their activities both accountable and accessible to the public. These challenges expanded as the number and range of intergovernmental agencies multiplied, alongside their connections to a proliferating number of NGOs, whose numbers swelled dramatically in the 1970s, as the wider processes of globalization regained momentum lost in the Great Depression, and decolonization caused the number of states to multiply.[38] In 1944 and 1945, Loveday and his colleagues promoted ECOSOC as the agency to take the lead connecting the UN's economic and social agenda with the IMF, the IBRD, what became GATT, the WHO, and the ILO. The Princeton Mission believed it was well placed to appreciate the importance and potential of ECOSOC, and the problems the UNO and the technical organizations would face if its coordinating function remained unrealized. Those that have puzzled over the grand claim that ECOSOC 'replicated the work' of the Security Council in chapter IX ('International Economic and Social Co-Operation') and chapter X ('The Economic and Social Council') in the UN's Covenant, demonstrate the limitations of attempting to understand its role solely through the lens of the UNO and the cold war.[39] In many ways, ECOSOC was the distillation of the EFO and notions of 'positive security' developed in the League. More directly, the idea for ECOSOC came from reforms proposed in the Bruce Committee in 1939, and its staff, structures, and early programme of work were inherited directly from the EFO's secretariat and the Princeton Mission. Indeed, so trapped was it by its history that ECOSOC remained based in Geneva when the Palais des Nations was ceded to the UNO.[40] But the cold war, and the communist states' determination that the UN should not

[37] *Observer*, 6 Jan. 1964, p. 4.

[38] Akira Iriye, *Global Community. The Role of International Organizations in the Making of the Contemporary World* (Berkeley and Los Angeles, 2002), 96–156.

[39] Kennedy, *Parliament of Man*, 43.

[40] The Preparatory Commission of the United Nations recruited from lists of staff prepared by the Princeton Office. See memo, 'Members of the Secretariat of the League of Nations Engaged in

be used to promote the interests of global capitalism, proved of greater hindrance to its early work, and the debate about its underdeveloped role in the global order continued into the twenty-first century. Nor did the financial interests of the USA emerge untarnished by charges of egoism by members of the Princeton Mission; it viewed the insistence that the IMF and World Bank be located in Washington, away from the UNO in New York, and ECOSOC in Geneva, as 'disastrous'.[41]

More immediately apparent after 1944 was the break between technical agency and open diplomacy. The League's claim to be open and accountable was a requirement with which the EFO had long wrestled. The search for legitimacy in the face of bankers' opposition in the 1920s, and frustration at the failure of state internationalism in the 1930s, prompted the EFO's secretariat and nexus of experts to favour efficacy over democratic legitimacy, but the Princeton Mission's experience during the Second World War prompted it to think again about the balance between state engagement and expertise. By the 1950s, states' determination to control their experts meant international organizations comprised, in Loveday's judgement, 'only persons who receive prior instructions from their governments and bargain rather than discuss. The best solution is rarely sought, only the easiest compromise.'[42] His charge has resonated through history, rephrased into a complaint less about 'compromise' than about the ability of wealthy countries—either the USA as hegemon, or the West—to shape these institutions and their priorities. In the determination to ensure that the world was made secure by the provision of bread, questions about who would get the butter, and whether butter was to their taste, were pushed aside. Weaker states or non-state actors with alternative viewpoints began to complain it was impossible to gain access to the exclusive normative realm.[43]

The departure of the UN family of organizations from the grand claims to open diplomacy that heralded the founding of the League was matched by a shift in popular attitudes to the two organizations. Whereas the League was greeted by an outpouring of popular support in its response to claims to global democracy, the UN was met with a whimper.[44] National associations dedicated to supporting the UN still exist, but they are far less popular than the British League of Nations Union or the US League of Nations Association, for example.[45] The fashion of marching on the world organization in search of rights fell out of vogue. The people who thronged the early images of the League of Nations became the ghosts of history. Indeed, it remained easier to access the UN in Geneva (the UNO took

Economic and Social Work provided by the Princeton Mission, and Used its Programme of Work as the Starting Point', undated, UNO, S-0991-000-08.

[41] Philip Noel-Baker to Loveday, 10 Apr. 1946, LON, Loveday, P151/26–7.

[42] Loveday, *Reflections*, p. xv.

[43] Ngaire Woods, *The Globalizers. The IMF, the World Bank and their Borrowers* (Ithaca, NY, 2006), 1–23.

[44] 'UNO', *Observer*, 6 Jan. 1946, p. 4

[45] In 1946, membership of the United Nations Association was reported to stand at around 50,000 in Britain compared to 500,000 at the peak period of the League of Nations Union. See 'UN Association', *Manchester Guardian*, 31 May 1946, p. 3.

over the Palais des Nations as its European Headquarters once it had been vacated by UNRRA) than in New York, thanks to the comparatively open quality of its architecture. Old League hands claimed the 'physical conditions of work' in the new Turtle Bay buildings opened in 1952 had a detrimental effect 'on the social atmosphere' in the new skyscraper 'on the top of which are perched the higher directorate, who, it is currently believed "speak only to God"'.[46]

If the architecture and image of the UN marked a break with the League, so, too, did the tone of its public diplomacy. The 'plain speaking' of the Security Council found favour in some quarters, but others complained that in the new organization the 'power of the Word is simply forgotten'.[47] When it came to mobilizing public opinion, for all its shortcomings, the League was judged to be 'subtler and more delicate', qualities deemed essential if the organization was 'flexible enough to inform and mobilize public opinion without enervating or exciting it'.[48] The League had a variety of voices and tones available to it—pedals of crescendo that ranged from the Council in secret, the Council in private, the Council in public, the Assembly, to the Secretariat's contacts to lobbyists and supporters' associations. The UN, on the other hand, had two: fortissimo through the Security Council; and deliberately muted through the Assembly, with the voices of smaller states under a permanent dampener thanks to the onset of the cold war.

For Loveday and Nurkse—notably, both men turned down the opportunity to work for the new international organizations—the faltering new architecture of international relations was confirmation of some of the shortcomings they had identified in the war. While the UN failed to prevent tensions rising between East and West—with the world's smaller nations, most immediately in central and eastern Europe, the obvious losers—the IMF and the World Bank had insufficient capital to revitalize the world economy at peace; UNRRA faltered, and plans for the ITO were abandoned. Loveday, there at the beginning of the battle for the League, had little fight left in him. Life as educator, researcher, and adviser back in Britain now offered greater rewards than that of the international civil servant, and he followed Butler's footsteps to become Warden of Nuffield College in Oxford.[49] He undertook some consultancy work for the UNO and ECOSOC, but his heart was not in it.[50] After 1945 there was a striking loss of energy and drive from a man who had steered the EFO through its darkest days. For much of the 1930s and the war, the pressures of work and the uncertainty over whether he could retain his staff—he kept a surprising number of them for much of the war—were immense. 'Every single member of staff could get a higher salary if he left', and he faced regular requests from governments and the new agencies as they emerged in the war.

---

[46] Loveday, *Reflections*, 6.

[47] Salvador de Madariaga, 'United Nations and League', *Manchester Guardian*, 2 Mar. 1946, p. 4.

[48] Salvador de Madariaga, 'United Nations and League', *Manchester Guardian*, 2 Mar. 1946, p. 4.

[49] Loveday, like Butler, was attracted to Nuffield College because both men shared Beveridge's hopes that Nuffield would establish 'a neutral and empirical social science tradition where the LSE had failed'. See Harris, *William Beveridge*, 363.

[50] He complained ECOSOC's Economic and Employment Commission was 'completely useless'. Loveday to Harrod, 29 Jan. 1948, LON, Loveday P150/26–7.

Yet, as long as his staff had a choice, they opted to remain with the mission in Princeton, where, Loveday regularly reported to Lester, morale was 'quite excellent'.[51] How can this be explained? In part, Loveday was obviously keen to boost the morale of the isolated Lester with this claim, but his conviction was genuine: confidence remained high until the end of 1944, because Loveday's staff believed they made a contribution, if not always on the technical content of policy, then to the overall direction and evolution of a new commitment to internationalism and international organization. Their personal sense of value was sustained because of the respect accorded to them as social scientists, as analysts of the shortcomings of governmental policy, and as witnesses of the failures of international relations in the past. Important, too, was their ability and capacity to exercise independent judgement, which included pointed criticisms of great power dominance and of interdepartmental chaos within the US administration, and their fears this chaos would be mirrored in an institutional chaos in a new world architecture.

Nurkse, like Loveday, was afforded shelter for a second time when the Princeton Mission was dissolved in 1945. Both men were made members of the IAS until they could take up their new posts, which for Nurkse was especially important, as the turn of events in Eastern Europe meant a return to his native Estonia was out of the question.[52] Nurkse, whom Loveday regarded as 'one of the ablest members the department has ever had', like Loveday, opted for an academic career, turning down the invitation to work for the IMF in preference for an appointment as Professor of Economics at Columbia University.[53] But, although his career in Columbia was distinguished, he found the transition to life in New York difficult: the city was 'polluted', full of 'noise, dust', and 'the university a redbrick, slumming, slump place' from which one had to commute to live in a 'suburban vacuum'. It became clear that Loveday's secretariat, despite its pressures, had provided a sheltered and supportive context for Nurkse's work that he now lacked, and that the mountains of Geneva and the woodland of the IAS were equally important to sustaining his sense of well-being. 'Change was desirable.'[54] Within days of writing these words in a notebook kept at his bedside, and two weeks before he was due to take up Viner's post at Princeton University, he died suddenly, aged just 52.

There were other possibilities in the League's record in economics and finance that remained unrealized in the post-war world. The first was the stress the EFO's secretariat, in particular, had placed on the need for constant global review and

---

[51] e.g. Loveday to Lester, 30 July 1943, LON, Princeton Office, C7619/No. 3, 43.

[52] See Loveday to Lester, 4 Jan. 1946, LON, Section Files, Personnel Files, S844, 'Nurkse, Ragnar'. Between 1945 and 1947, aside from Loveday and Nurkse, EFO section members at the IAS included John H. Chapman (New Zealand), Paul Deperon (Belgium), Folke Hilgerdt, J. Ansgar Rosenborg and John Lindberg (Sweden), Martin Hill and Constantine F. MacGuire (Ireland), Miroslav A. Kriz (Czechoslovakia), Phyllis W. van Ittersum (Netherlands), and Percy Gill Waterson (Britain). Other staff members had transferred to Long Island to work with the UN. See Institute for Advanced Study, *Bulletin, No. 12, 1945–1946* (Princeton, Oct. 1946), pp. ix–xiii, 3–4.

[53] Loveday to Stencek, 16 May 1945, LON, Personnel Files, S844, 'Nurkse, Ragnar'.

[54] Undated diary entry found in 1959 notebook found by his 'desk and table (bedroom)', Mudd, Nurkse, MC 173, Box 4.

institutional reform so that the organizations created to facilitate coordination and cooperation in the global economy would stay in touch with the ever-changing world around them. Economics, too, needed to remain in touch with the flourishing discipline of international relations.[55] Questions relating to reform should be framed not around the implication that the organization was 'failing', but rather around the idea that it was a necessary response to the evolving character of the political economy. The second was its view that economic crisis and depression remained a constant, and potentially the gravest, threat to global stability. As the Depression Delegation had argued, the creative nature of economic change meant it was difficult to predict how and when it would strike. Informed vigilance was the most the world could manage, and this was best achieved by the creation of a global, independent 'central advisory body', independent of the IMF, to watch for and take action 'against the common enemy which depressions constitute'.[56] Moreover, the Princeton Mission was mindful of the fact that the architects of Bretton Woods had forfeited the opportunity to coordinate economic and financial policy on an intergovernmental level when it abandoned the integrated architecture of the League for the specialist structure of the UN organizations. The creation of the G7 in 1973 in response to the global financial crisis, which marked the end of the Bretton Woods settlement, signalled also the marginalization, if not the end, of the institutions to which it had given birth, and a renewed recognition of the need for structures of intergovernmental as well as expert cooperation.

Equally lost from view with the end of the League was the organization's recognition in the mid-1930s of the central challenge before the modern world: how to recognize, respect, and protect the world's diversity, while attempting to improve the quality of life, or its living standards—an important distinction in its work. In April 1946, Goldenweiser, in his capacity as President of the American Economic Association, publicly expressed the association's appreciation of the League's work in the field of economics, which 'will forever stand as a mighty contribution to the advancement of well-being throughout the world'.[57] It was an open recognition of the organization's efforts to insert a third voice into the debate of whether state or market was best. The League's reaction to the alternative between state and market liberalism that divided the world in the interwar period was to put the problem in the hands of experts. They did not see

[55] The integration of social sciences, notably economics and international relations, had distinguished the League's work and Anglo-American wartime planning. As the specialization of the social sciences became increasingly pronounced, individuals associated with the League fought back. The drive to reintegrate the social sciences, for example, was a pronounced feature of Boulding's career. See Philippe Fontaine, 'Stabilizing American Society: Kenneth Boulding and the Integration of the Social Sciences, 1943–1980', *Science in Context*, 23/2 (2010), 221–65.

[56] League of Nations, *Economic Stability in the Post-War World*, 287, and memo by Economic, Financial and Transit Department, 'Note on International Economic and Social Organization', 6 Mar. 1944, LON, Loveday P150/24–5. The council bore a striking resemblance to calls in 2008, led by Josef Ackermann of the Deutsche Bank, for a 'global council of wisemen' to develop concerted action by 'governments, central banks and market participants' to combat the effects of the credit crunch, and to anticipate financial crises in the future. See 'Deutsche Bank Head Calls for Government Help', *Der Speigel*, 18 Mar. 2008.

[57] LON, Loveday P150/24–5, Goldenweiser to Hambro, 25 Apr. 1946.

the choice between market and state as a binary opposition. Rather, the answer was to engage both options, as each challenge needed to be understood in its particular context, and in relation to the needs of the world's economy and of its citizens (as articulated by experts). In Loveday's words, to be 'dogmatic is to be stupid'. For him and the network he helped to build, the insertion of international agency between state and market, though 'still in an experimental state, was essential for global prosperity and peace'.[58] The new internationalism that emerged in 1945, as a hot war ended and a global cold war began, opted for the path to development that was more statist and productivist than envisaged in the interwar period. The EFO's history demonstrates the 'revolution of expectations' in relation to international development that began in the interwar years, not in the Second World War. What altered dramatically after the Second World War was the scale of operations, which were powerfully linked to ideas of conformity, social control, and pacification, as the numbers of specialist staff and agencies involved grew to unprecedented levels. In a speech to commemorate the first ten years of the UN given by the EFO's former employee and first historian, Martin Hill contrasted the EFO's 30 staff in 1930 to the 400 working in the UN's department of Economic and Social Affairs, and the more than 1,000 in the employ of the World Bank, the IMF, and the FAO.[59]

CHRONICLE OF A DEATH FORETOLD

The League was formally consigned to history with the convocation of the 21st Assembly of the League of Nations on 8 April 1946 at the Palais des Nations.[60] The advertised purpose of the meeting was twofold: formally to abrogate the obligations of the League's Covenant to allow functions attributed to the League to be transferred to the new UN family of organizations; and, secondly, to decide what should happen to the League's assets—its archives, library, buildings, and the monies it had on account.

Although other agencies of the League had met during the war, this was the first session of the Assembly since 14 December 1939, when it had decided to expel the USSR—an issue that was awkwardly evoked when the USSR declared it wanted to rejoin the organization so that it could collect its share of the League's financial assets that were to be returned to its existing members. It was turned down, albeit with a fulsome acknowledgement of 'the fundamental contribution of the USSR to the overthrow of the Fascist enemies of civilization and . . . the collaboration of the USSR in building on the foundations so successfully laid the new edifice of international solidarity'.[61]

---

[58] Loveday, *Reflections*, p. xviii.

[59] 'Martin Hill Address to the Nassau Club', 3 Mar. 1955, UNO, S-0369, Martin W. Hill, Box 369, File 36, Sub-File 8, Acx 92/3.

[60] For a full list of participants of the Twentieth and Twenty-First Ordinary Session of the Assembly, 8–18 Apr.1946, see <http://www.indiana.edu/~league/2021thordinaryassemb.htm> (accessed 9 Apr. 2011).

[61] See 'Russia not to receive Share of League's Assets', *Manchester Guardian*, p. 8.

The unseemly circling of family members around the deathbed of this dying relative exposed chronicles of the League that were embarrassing to those present. Austria, barred from membership of the UNO, also tried to get back in by claiming that it withdrew in 1938 only as a result of German pressure. (In this case, the legality of its claim to attend was more complex, as the Assembly had never acted upon Austria's decision.[62]) Among the thirty-six members deemed eligible for a share of the assets, several, including Mexico and Yugoslavia, had to make up arrears in their membership fees before they could be considered eligible. Financial questions took more than two years to resolve, and it was decided in a common plan thrashed out between the League and the UNO, agreed on 6 March 1946, that, rather than the monies being refunded, the balance, some $10,809,273, would be transferred directly across from the former organization to the latter as member contributions. It meant that League members that were deemed ineligible for UNO membership, which in 1946 included the neutral Portugal, Finland, Ireland, and Switzerland, received a refund.[63]

Questions of diplomatic protocol, though complex, were decided with greater expedition. By 18 April 1946 everything was agreed, thanks to the steely determination of those gathered to commemorate the end of the League with dignity. Among their number was the Assembly President Hambro, Adolfo Costa du Rels, the Bolivian President of the Council, and the indefatigable British internationalist Philip Noel-Baker, serving under Bevin in the Foreign Office, and back in Geneva at the side of the now 81-year-old Lord Robert Cecil, who was the meeting's elder statesman. Although behind the scenes the secretariat of the League and the Princeton Mission were working closely with the Preparatory Commission of the UNO, after 1944 the tendency of the United States to wish the League into oblivion was unmistakable. The 21st Assembly marked the delegates' desire that their experience of the League's 'disappointments and disruptions may be turned to use in cementing the structure of a new world security'.[64]

But politics were also part of the mix. Bevin's insistence that the conference take place in Geneva, and not in London or New York, offered a platform to smaller nations that had been bit-part players in the wartime summits, notably the European powers that were embroiled in battles for relief with UNRRA only metres away from the assembly hall in Geneva, to recover their international voice. If there was disappointment in the unfulfilled promise of the League, greater disenchantment was already being expressed in the UNO. As the French delegate Paul-Boncour put it, 'those of us who were at San Francisco and London certainly did not find there the atmosphere of enthusiasm and faith we found when the League was being built up in Geneva'.[65] Both in spite, and because, of its history, even in 1946 the hollowed-out League commanded a zeal and loyalty from its early

[62] See 'Austria's Claim not Recognized', *Manchester Guardian*, 13 Apr. 1946, p. 5.
[63] Lester to Trygve Lie, 4 Aug. 1947, LON, 17F, R5352, 97/44133/43187.
[64] Taken from Hambro's speech on the final day of discussion, '1919–1946: End of the League. Experience that Can Help UNO', *Manchester Guardian*, 20 Apr., p. 6.
[65] 'Lack of Enthusiasm for the UNO', *Manchester Guardian*, 11 Apr. 1946, p. 5.

supporters that the UN did not. The Europeans also felt their loss of prominence in the new organization acutely, which acted as a further spur to talk of European union.[66] The end of the League signalled the end of European predominance in the arrangement of world affairs. The promise of the 'world's first parliament' faded rapidly from memory, as did its record in promoting coordination and cooperation in economic and financial affairs.[67] (Keynes, the man who did so much to fire public interest in the question at the League's birth, died two days after the League.) As the great doors to the assembly hall closed to delegates for the last time on 18 April, Cecil's final words were more a warning from history than a valediction: 'The League is dead; long live the United Nations.'[68]

[66] See, e.g., memo by the secretariat, 'Notes on the 209th Meeting of the Fifth Committee on the Afternoon of 27 October 1949', UNO, S-0472-0080.

[67] Within three years the UN was sufficiently concerned that the people of Europe needed to be 'made aware of the UNO' to seek to move more of its operations to Europe. See memo by the secretariat, 'Notes on the 209th Meeting of the Fifth Committee on the Afternoon of 27 October 1949', 28 Oct. 1949, UNO, S-0472-0080, RAG-1.

[68] Walters, *History of the League of Nations*, 815.

Archival Sources and Bibliography

ARCHIVAL SOURCES

International Organizations
Archives of the League of Nations, Library of the United Nations, Geneva, Switzerland (LON)
Registry (R) series
1 Political
10A General
10B Economic Intelligence
10C Finance
10D Economic
10E Finance
10E Gold
17 F Legal (Finance)
50 General
Comité Économique Procès-Verbaux (P.V.), 1926–1939
Comité Financier Procès-Verbaux (P.V.), 1920–1939
Documents du Comité Économique (E.) 1926–1939
Documents du Comité Financier (F.) 1926–1939

Section Files (S) series
Hill, Martin
Loveday, Alexander
Office of the Secretary-General
Personnel Files
Princeton Office
Salter, Arthur

Archives of the International Labour Office, Geneva, Switzerland (ILO)
Series EP: Economic Committee
Series L: League of Nations Files
Series P: Social Economic Section
Series XE: Butler Files
Series Z: Winant and Phelan Files

United Nations Archives and Records Centre, New York, NY (UN)
Central Registry
Chef de Cabinet
Papers of Martin Hill
UNCIO Records, 1941–6

Archives of the Bank of International Settlements, Basle, Switzerland (BIS)
2/92 Papers relating to the World Economic Conference
6/14 Relations with the League of Nations; Relations with the United Kingdom

7.18 McGarrrah/Fraser Correspondence, 24–92
7/18 Per Jacobsson Papers

Central Banks
Bank of England, London (BoE)
Norman diaries (ADM20)
Secretary's Files (G15)
Secretary's Letterbooks (G23)

Records of the Federal Reserve Board, New York, NY (*FRBNY*)
BOG Monetary Policy, 1936–1938
C798/League of Nations
Council of Foreign Relations—Economic and Financial Group 1942
Harrison, George Papers
Post-War International Monetary Organization, 1943
Sproul, Allan Papers

State Archives
The National Archives, Kew, London, UK (TNA)
Board of Trade (BT)
Cabinet Office (CAB)
Colonial Office (CO)
Foreign Office Series (FO)
Kent Catalogue of Files and Microfilms of the German Foreign Ministry Archives, 1924–45 (GFM)
MacDonald, James Ramsey (PRO 30/69)
Prime Minister Office files (PREM)
Treasury Series (T), including the papers of the following officials:
  Hawtrey, Sir Ralph (T208)
  Hopkins, Sir Richard (T175)
  Leith-Ross, Sir Frederick (T188)
  Niemeyer, Sir Otto (T176)
  Phillips, Sir Frederick (T177)
War Office (WO)

Archives du Ministère des Affaires Etrangères, Paris (AMAE)
Y. Série Internationale 1918–1940
Y. Série Internationale SDN
Y. Guerre 1939–1945
Z. Europe
Papier Agents: Avenol, Josef

Centre des Archives Économiques et Financières, Paris (CAEF)
Fonds Tresor
B12.617 until B2.678
B31.716–F 30 7892 until B33.675–F 30 3101
B32.320–F30 1415 until B32.299–F 30 1393
B32.418–F 30 1514 until B32.422–F 30 1518

Bundesarchiv, Abteilung Potsdam (BA)
Reichsfinanzministerium (R2)
Reichswirtschaftsministerium (R7)
Reichskanzlei (R43)

National Archives of Ireland, Dublin
Department of Foreign Affairs

National Archives and Records Administration, College Park, Maryland, VA (NARA)
Department of Labour (RG174)
Department of State: Decimal Files (RG59)
Department of State: Inter- and Intradepartmental Committees (RG353)
Department of the Treasury (RG56)
Office of the Secretary (RG40)
Records of Secretaries of State and Principal Officers (RG59.3.1)

National Archives of Australia, Canberra (NAA)
Bruce, Stanley Melbourne
McDougall, Frank Lidgett

Personal Papers
Nuffield College, Oxford (Nuffield)
Loveday, Sir Alexander, Papers and Diaries

Western Manuscripts Division, Bodleian Library, University of Oxford (Bodl.)
Simon, Sir John

University Library, University of Cambridge (ULC)
Baldwin, Stanley

LSE Archives, London School of Economics, London (LSE)
Meade, James
Mitrany, David

University Library, Birmingham University, Birmingham (Birmingham)
Chamberlain, Neville

Bundesarchiv, Abteilung Koblenz (BAK)
Bonn, Moritz Julius

Manuscript Division, Library of Congress, Washington DC (LC)
Davis, Norman
Feis, Herbert
Frankfurter, Felix
Goldenweiser, Emanuel
Hull, Cordell
Nielsen, Frederick K.

Pasvolsky, Leo
Sweetser, Arthur

Seeley G. Mudd Manuscript Library, Princeton University, Princeton, NJ (Mudd)
Derso and Kelen Collection
Krock, Arthur
Nurkse, Ragnar
Viner, Jakob
White, Harry Dexter

Franklin D. Roosevelt, Roosevelt Presidential Library, Hyde Park, NY (FDR)
President's Personal File (PPF)
President's Official File (POF)
President's Secretary's File (PSF)

Butler Library, Oral History Collection, Columbia University, New York, NY (Butler)
Dodds, Harold
Lubin, Isador
Perkins, Frances
Shotwell, James T.
Viner, Jakob
Warburg, James

Shelby White and Leon Levy Archives Center, Institute for Advanced Study, Princeton, NJ (IAS)
Records of the Office of the Director: Frank Aydelotte Files (Aydelotte)
Records of the Office of the Director: General Files (GFILE)
Records of the Office of the Director: Files by School series (FAC)
Records of the Schools of Economics and Politics/Humanistic Studies

BIBLIOGRAPHY

Adams Brown, William, *England and the New Gold Standard, 1919–1926* (London, 1929).
Aglan, A., Feiertag, O., and Kevonian, D. (eds) 'Albert Thomas, société mondiale et internationalisme, réseaux et institutions des années 1890 aux années 1930, actes des journées d'études des 19 et 20 janvier 2007', *Cahiers d'IRICE*, 2 (2008), 127–55.
Ahamed, Liaquat, *Lords of Finance, 1929: The Great Depression—and the Bankers who Broke the World* (London, 2010).
Aldcroft, Derek, *From Versailles to Wall Street, 1919–1929* (London, 1977).
Allain, Jean, 'Slavery and the League of Nations: Ethiopia as a Civilised Nation', *Journal of the History of International Law*, 8 (2006), 213–244.
Amrith, Sunil, *Decolonizing International Health: India and Southeast Asia, 1930–1945* (London, 2006).
Amrith, Sunil, "Food and Welfare in India, c.1900–1950', *Comparative Studies in Society and History*, 50/4 (2008), 1010–35.
Anderson, Warwick, *The Cultivation of Whiteness: Science, Health and Racial Destiny in Australia* (Melbourne, 2002).
Angell, Norman, *The Peace Treaty and the Economic Chaos of Europe* (London, 1919).

Angell, Norman, *The Economic Functions of the League* (London, 1920).

Archer, Clive, *International Organizations* (3rd edn; London, 2003.).

Armstrong, David, Lloyd, Lorna, and Redmond, James, *From Versailles to Maastricht: International Organization in the Twentieth Century* (Basingstoke, 1996).

Asso, Pier Francesco, and Fiorito, Luca, 'A Scholar in Action in Interwar America: John H. Williams' Contributions to Trade Theory and International Monetary Reform', *Quaderni*, 430 (2004), 1–38.

Aufricht, Hans, *Guide to League of Nations Publications. A Bibliographic Survey of the Work of the League, 1920–1947* (New York, 1966).

Ausch, Karl, *Als die Banken fielen: Zur Soziologie der politischen Korruption* (Vienna, 1968).

Auswärtiges Amt, *Akten zur deutschen auswärtigen Politik 1918–1945* (Baden-Baden, 1950–).

Backhouse, Roger E., and Bateman, Bradley W., *Capitalist Revolutionary: John Maynard Keynes* (Cambridge, MA, 2011).

Backhouse, Roger E., and Bateman, Bradley W., *The Cambridge Companion to Keynes* (Cambridge, 2006).

Badger, A. J., *The New Deal: The Depression Years, 1933–1940* (London, 1990).

Balderston, Theo (ed.), *The World Economy and National Economies in the Interwar Slump* (New York, 2003).

Barber, William J., *From New Era to New Deal: Herbert Hoover, the Economists, and American Economic Policy, 1921–1933* (Cambridge, 1985).

Barnett, Michael N., and Finnemore, Martha, 'The Politics, Power, and Pathologies of International Organizations', *International Organization*, 53/4 (Autumn 1999), 699–732.

Barros, James, *Betrayal from Within: Joseph Avenol, Secretary-General of the League of Nations, 1933–1940* (New Haven, 1969).

Barros, James, *Office without Power: Secretary-General Sir Eric Drummond* (New York, 1979).

Bashford, Alison, 'Nation, Empire, Globe: The Spaces of Population Debate in the Interwar Years', *Comparative Studies in Society and History*, 49/1 (2007), 170–201.

Bass, Hans H., 'Ragnar Nurkse's Development Theory: Influences and Perceptions', in Rainer Kattel, Jan A. Kregel, and Erik S. Reinert (eds), *Ragnar Nurkse (1907–2007): Classical Development Economics and its Relevance for Today* (London, 2009).

Bayersdorf, Frank, '"Credit or Chaos"? The Austrian Stabilisation Programme of 1923 and the League of Nations', in Daniel Lacqua (ed.), *Internationalism Reconfigured: Transnational Ideas and Movements between the World Wars* (London, 2011).

Beale, Marjorie, *The Modernist Enterprise: French Elites and the Threat of Modernity, 1900–1940* (Stanford, CA, 1999).

Becker, Josef, and Hildebrand, Klaus (eds.), *Internationale Beziehungen in der Weltwirtschaftskrise, 1929–1933* (Munich, 1980).

Berend, Ivan T., *Decades of Crisis: Central and Eastern Europe before World War II* (Berkeley and Los Angeles, 1998; 2003 edn).

Berger, Peter, *Im Schatten der Diktatur. Die Finanzdiplomatie des Verters des Völkerbundes in Österreich, Meinoud Marius Rost van Tonnigen, 1931–1936* (Vienna, 2000).

Berghahn, Volker R., and Kitchen, Martin (eds), *Germany in the Age of Total War* (London, 1981).

Beveridge, William, *Full Employment in a Free Society* (London, 1944).

Billig, Michael, *Banal Nationalism* (London, 1995).

Birn, Donald S., *The League of Nations Union, 1918–1945* (Oxford, 1981).

Bjerkholt, Olav, 'Ragnar Frisch's Business Cycle Approach: The Genesis of the Propagation and Impulse Model', *European Journal of the History of Economic Thought*, 14/3 (2007), 449–86.

Blaug, Marc, 'No History of Ideas, Please, We're Economists', *Journal of Economic Perspectives*, 15/ 1 (2001), 145–64.

Blum, John Morton (ed.), *From the Morgenthau Diaries* (3 vols; Boston, 1959–67).

Boianovsky, Mauro, and Trautwein, Hans-Michael, 'Haberler, the League of Nations, and the Quest for Consensus in Business Cycle Theory in the 1930s', *History of Political Economy*, 38/1 (2006), 45–89.

Boon, Tim, 'Agreement and Disagreement in the Making of "A World of Plenty" in David F. Smith (ed.), *Nutrition in Britain: Science, Scientists, and Politics in the Twentieth Century* (London, 1997).

Borchardt, Knut, 'Could and Should Germany Have Followed Great Britain in Leaving the Gold Standard?', *Journal of European Economic History*, 13/3 (Winter 1984), 471–94.

Bordo, Michael D., *The Gold Standard and Related Regimes. Collected Essays* (Cambridge, 1999).

Bordo, M., Godin, Claudia, and White, Eugene M. (eds), *The Defining Moment: The Great Depression and the American Economy in the Twentieth Century* (Chicago, 1998).

Borowy, Iris, *Coming to Terms with World Health: The League of Nations Health Organization, 1921–1946* (Frankfurt am Main, 2009).

Bosmans, J. L. J., *De Nederlander Mr A. R. Zimmerman als Commissaris-Generaal van de Volkenbond in Oostenrijk 1922–1926* (Nijmegen, 1973).

Boulding, Kenneth, *The Economics of Peace* (New York, 1945).

Boulding, Kenneth, *Towards a New Economics* (Aldershot, 1992).

Boyce, Robert W. D., *British Capitalism at the Crossroads, 1919–1932: A Study in Politics, Economics and International Relations* (Cambridge, 1987).

Boyce, Robert W. D., *The Great Interwar Crisis and the Collapse of Globalization* (London, 2009).

Brands, H. W., *India and the United States: The Cold Peace* (Boston, 1990).

Brewer, Susan A., *To Win the Peace: British Propaganda in the United States during World War II* (Ithaca, NY, 1997).

Burk, Kathleen, *Britain, America and the Sinews of War, 1914–1918* (London, 1985).

Burke, Bernard V., *Ambassador Frederic Sackett and the Collapse of the Weimar Republic, 1930–1933: The United States and Hitler's Rise to Power* (Cambridge, 1995).

Burkman, Thomas W., *Japan and the League of Nations: Empire and World Order, 1914–1938* (Honolulu, 2008).

Burnett, Philip Mason, *Reparation at the Paris Peace Conference from the Standpoint of the American Delegation* (2 vols; New York, 1940).

Cain, P. J., and Hopkins, A. G., *British Imperialism: Crisis and Deconstruction, 1914–1990* (London, 1993).

Cairncross, Alec, and Watts, Nita G. M., *The Economic Section, 1936–1961: A Study in Economic Advising* (London, 1989).

Carlson, Benny, 'Who was the Most Famous Economist in the World—Cassel or Keynes?', *The Economist as Yardstick, Journal of the History of Economic Thought*, 31/4 (2009), 519–30.

Carlson, Valdemar, 'The Education of an Economist before the Great Depression: Harvard's Economics Department in the 1920s', *American Journal of Economics and Sociology*, 27/1 (Jan. 1968), 101–11.

Carr, E. H., *Twenty-Years Crisis* (London, 1939).

Cassel, Gustav, *The World's Monetary Problems* (London, 1921).

Cassel, Gustav, *Post-War Monetary Stabilization* (New York, 1928).

Cassel, Gustav, *The Crisis in the World's Monetary System: Being the Rhodes Memorial Lectures Delivered in the Trinity Term 1932* (Oxford, 1932).

Cassiers, Isabelle, *Croissance, crise et régulation en économie ouverte: La Belgique entre les deux guerres* (Brussels, 1989).

Cassimatis, Louis P., *American Influence in Greece, 1917–1929* (London, 1988).

Cayet, Thomas, Rosental, Paul-André, and Thébaud-Sorger, Marie, 'How International Organizations Compete: Occupational Safety and Health at the ILO, a Diplomacy of Expertise', *Journal of Modern European History*, 7/2 (2009), 174–96.

Ceadel, Martin, *Living the Great Illusion: Sir Norman Angell, 1872–1967* (Oxford, 2009).

Chandler, Lester V., *Benjamin Strong, Central Banker* (Washington, 1958).

Charvet, J. F., *L'Influence Brittanique dans la S.D.N (des origines de la S.D.N jusqu'à nos jours)* (Paris, 1938).

Chatterji, Joya, 'Right or Charity? The Debate over Relief and Rehabilitation in West Bengal, 1947–50', in Kaul Suvir (ed.), *The Partitions of Memory* (Dehli, 2002), 74–110.

Christ, Carl F., 'The Cowels Commission's Contributions to Econometrics at Chicago, 1939–1955', *Journal of Economic Literature*, 32/1 (1994), 30–59.

Cini, M., and Bourne, A. (eds), *Palgrave Advances in European Union Studies* (Basingstoke, 2006).

Clarke, Peter, 'The Treasury's Analytical Model of the British Economy between the Wars', in Mary O. Furner and Barry Supple (eds), *The State and Economic Knowledge: The American and British Experiences* (Cambridge, 1990), 171–203.

Clarke, Stephen V. O., 'The Reconstruction of the International Monetary System: The Attempts of 1922 and 1933', *Princeton Studies in International Finance*, 33 (1973).

Clarke, Stephen V. O., *Exchange-Rate Stabilization in the Mid-1930s: Negotiating the Tripartite Agreement* (Princeton, 1977).

Clavin, Patricia, 'The World Economic Conference, 1933: The Failure of British Internationalism', *Journal of Modern European Economic History*, 20/3 (1991), 489–527.

Clavin, Patricia, ' "The Fetishes of So-Called International Bankers": Central Bank Cooperation for the World Economic Conference, 1932–3', *Contemporary European History*, 1/3 (1992), 281–311.

Clavin, Patricia, *The Failure of Economic Diplomacy, Britain, France, Germany and the United States, 1931–1936* (London, 1996).

Clavin, Patricia, 'Shaping the Lessons of History: Britain and the Rhetoric of American Trade Policy, 1930–1960', in A. Marrison (ed.), *Free Trade and its Reception: Freedom and Trade* (London, 1998), i. 287–307.

Clavin, Patricia, *The Great Depression in Europe, 1919–1939* (London, 2000).

Clavin, Patricia, 'Europe and the League of Nations', in Robert Gerwarth (ed.), *Twisted Paths: Europe 1914–1945* (Oxford, 2006), 325–54.

Clavin, Patricia, 'Interwar Internationalism: Conceptualising Transnational Thought and Action, 1919–1939', in Daniel Lacqua (ed.), *Internationalism Reconfigured: Transnational Ideas and Movements between the World Wars* (London, 2011).

Clavin, Patricia, and Patel, Kiran Klaus, 'The Role of International Organizations in Europeanization: The Case of the League of Nations and the European Economic Community', in Martin Conway and Kiran Klaus Patel (eds), *Europeanization in the Twentieth Century: Historical Approaches* (London, 2010), 110–31.

Clavin, Patricia, and Wessels, Jens-Wilhelm, 'Another Golden Idol? The League of Nations' Gold Delegation and the Great Depression, 1929–1932', *International History* Review, 26/4 (Dec. 2004), 709–944.

Clavin, Patricia, and Wessels, Jens-Wilhelm, 'Understanding the Work of the Economic and Financial Organization of the League of Nations', *Contemporary European History Review*, 14/4 (2005), 475–6.

Coffin, Judith G., 'A "Standard" of Living? European Perspectives on Class and Consumption in the Early Twentieth Century', *International Labor and Working-Class History*, 55 (1999), 6–26.

Cohrs, Patrick O., *The Unfinished Peace after World War I: America, Britain and the Stabilisation of Europe, 1919–1932* (Cambridge, 2006).

Colijn, H. J., 'The World Economic Conference of 1927', *Annals of the American Academy of Political and Social Science*, Special Issue, 'Europe in 1927: An Economic Survey', 134 (Nov. 1927), 140–4.

Collingham, Lizzie, *The Taste of War: World War Two and the Battle for Food* (London, 2011).

Connelly, Matthew, *Fatal Misconception: The Struggle to Control World Population* (Cambridge, MA, 2008).

Constantine, Stephen, *The Making of British Colonial Development Policy, 1914–1949* (London, 1984).

Conway, Martin, and Romijn, Pieter (eds), *The War for Legitimacy in Politics and Culture, 1936–1946* (Oxford, 2008).

Conze, Eckert, Frei, Norbert, Hayes, Peter, and Zimmermann, Moshe, *Das Amt und die Vergangenheit: Deutsche Diplomaten in Dritten Reich und in der Bundersrepublik* (Munich, 2010).

Costa Bona, Enrica, *L'Italia e la Società Delle Nazionia* (Padova, 2004).

Costigliola, Frank C., 'Anglo-French Rivalry in the 1920s', *Journal of Economic History*, 37/4 (December 1977), 911–34.

Cottrell, Philip L., 'Norman, Strakosch and the Development of Central Banking: From Conception to Practice, 1919–1924', in Philip L. Cottrell (ed.), *Rebuilding the Financial System in Central and Eastern Europe, 1918–1994* (Aldershot, 1997), 30–75.

Cottrell, Philip L. (ed.), *Rebuilding the Financial System in Central and Eastern Europe, 1918–1994* (Aldershot, 1997).

Cowan, Jane, 'Justice and the League of Nations Minority Rights Regime' in Kamari Maxine Clarke and Mark Goodale, (eds.), *Mirrors of Justice: Law and Power in the Post-Cold War Era* (Cambridge, 2010).

Crombois, Jean, *Camille Gutt and Postwar International Finance* (London, 2011).

Crozier, Andrew, *Appeasement and Germany's Last Bid for the Colonies* (London, 1988).

Cumpston, Ina Mary, *Lord Bruce of Melbourne* (London, 1989).

Dallek, Robert, *Franklin D. Roosevelt and American Foreign Policy, 1932–1945* (New York, 1979).

Darwin, John, *The Empire Project: The Rise and Fall of the British World-System, 1830–1970* (Cambridge, 2009).

Davies, Thomas R., *The Possibilities of Transnational Activism: The Campaign for Disarmament between the Two World Wars* (Leiden, 2007).

Davis, Joseph S., 'World Currency and Banking: The First Brussels Financial Conference', *Review of Economics and Statistics*, 2/12 (Dec. 1920), 304–25.

Davis, Joseph Stancliffe, *Wheat and the AAA* (Stanford, CA, 1935).

De Marchi, Neil, 'League of Nations Economists and the Ideal of Peaceful Change in the Decade of the Thirties', in Craufurd D. Goodwin (ed.), *Economics and National Security: A History of their Interaction. Annual Supplement to Volume 23, History of Political Economy* (London, 1991), 143–78.

Decorzant, Yann, *La Société des Nations et la naissance d'une conception de la régulation économique internationale* (Brussels, 2011).

Decorzant, Yann, 'Internationalism and the Economic and Financial Organization of the League of Nations', in Daniel Lacqua (ed.), *Internationalism Reconfigured: Transnational Ideas and Movements between the World Wars* (London, 2011), 115–33.

Dell, Robert Edward, *The Geneva Racket, 1920–1939* (London, 1941).

Donnelly, J. B., 'Prentiss Gilbert's Mission to the League of Nations Council, October 1931', *Diplomatic History*, 2/4 (1978), 373–88.

Drummond, Ian A., *The Floating Pound and the Sterling Area, 1931–39* (Cambridge, 1981).

Drummond, Ian A., *London, Washington and the Management of Franc 1936–1939* (Princeton, 1979).

Dubin, Martin D., 'Towards the Bruce Report: The Economic and Social Programs of the League of Nations in the Avenol Era', in United Nations Library, *The League of Nations in Retrospect* (Geneva, 1983), 42–72.

Dunbabin, J. P. D., *The League of Nations Place in the International* System (Oxford, 1993).

Duroselle, J. B., 'The Sprirt of Locarno: Illusions of Pactomania', *Foreign Affairs*, 50/4 (1972), 752–64.

Eckes, Alfred E., Jr., *A Search for Solvency: Bretton Woods and the International Monetary System, 1941–1971* (Austin, 1975).

Economic and Financial Organization, *Remarks on the Present Phase of International Economic Relations* (Geneva, 1935).

Economic, Financial, and Transit Department, *Quantitative Trade Controls: Their Causes and Nature* (Geneva, 1943).

Edgerton, David, *Britain's War Machine: Weapons, Resources and Experts in the Second World War* (London, 2011).

Egerton, George W., *Great Britain and the Creation of the League of Nations: Strategy, Politics and International Organization, 1914–1919* (London, 1979).

Eichengreen, Barry, 'The Bank of France and the Sterilization of Gold, 1926–1932', in Barry Eichengreen, *Elusive Stability: Essays in the History of International Finance, 1919–1939* (Cambridge, 1990), 83–112.

Eichengreen, Barry, *Elusive Stability: Essays in the History of International Finance, 1919–1939* (Cambridge, 1990).

Eichengreen, Barry, *Golden Fetters: The Gold Standard and the Great Depression, 1919–1939* (Oxford, 1992).

Eichengreen, Barry, 'The Origins and Nature of the Great Slump', *Economic History Review*, 47/2 (1992), 13–39.

Eichengreen, Barry, *Globalizing Capital: A History of the International Monetary System* (Princeton, 1996).

Eichengreen, Barry, and Temin, Peter, '"Afterword": Counterfactual Histories of the Great Depression', in Theo Balderston (ed.), *The World Economy and National Economies* New York, 2003), 183–207.

Ekbladh, David, 'Exiled Economics: The Transnational Contributions and Limits of the League of Nations' Economic and Financial Section', *New Global Studies*, 4/1 (2010) 1–6.

Emmett, Ross B., *Frank Knight and the Chicago School in American Economics* (London, 2009).

Emmett, Ross B., *The Elgar Companion to the Chicago School of Economics* (Cheltenham, 2010).

Endres, Anthony M., and Fleming, Grant A., *International Organizations and the Analysis of Economic Policy, 1919–1950* (Cambridge, 2002).

Engerman, David, *Modernization from the Other Shore: American Intellectuals and the Romance of Russian Development* (Cambridge, MA, 2003).

Ensor, R.C.K., 'Introduction', in Étienne Mantoux, *The Carthaginian Peace or the Economic Consequences of Mr Keynes* (London and New York, 1946), v–vii.

Fakher, Hossein, 'The Relationships among the Principal Organs of the United Nations', unpublished Ph.D. thesis, Institut Universitaire de Hautes Études Internationales, 1950.

Fakhri, Michael, 'The 1937 Sugar Agreement: Neo-Colonial Cuba and Economic Aspects of the League of Nations', *Leiden Journal of International Law*, 24/4 (2011), 899–922.

Farnham, Barbara, *Roosevelt and the Munich Crisis: A Study in Political Decision-Making* (Princeton, 1997).

Farquet, Christophe, 'Lutte contre l'évasion fiscale: L'Échec de la SDN durant l'entre-deux-guerres', *L'Économie politique*, 44 (2009), 93–112.

Farquet, Christophe, 'Expertise et négociations fiscales à la Société des Nations, 1923–1939', *Relations internationals*, 142/2 (2010), 5–21.

Fearon, Peter, 'Hoover, Roosevelt and American Economic Policy during the 1930s', in W. R. Garside (ed.), *Capitalism in Crisis: International Responses to the Great Depression* (London, 1993), 114–47.

Feiertag, Olivier, 'Albert Thomas, les débuts du BIT et la crise économique mondiale de 1920–1923', in A. Aglan, O. Feiertag, and D. Kevonian (eds), 'Albert Thomas, société mondiale et internationalisme, réseaux et institutions des années 1890 aux années 1930, actes des journées d'études des 19 et 20 janvier 2007', *Cahiers d'IRICE*, 2 (2008), 127–55.

Feis, Herbert, *Nineteen Thirty Three: Characters in Crisis* (New York, 1966).

Ferguson, Niall, 'Constraints and Room for Manoeuvre in the German Inflation of the Early 1920s', *Economic History Review*, 49/4 (1996), 635–66.

Fink, Carole, *The Genoa Conference: European Diplomacy, 1921–22* (Chapel Hill, NC, 1984).

Fink, Carole, Frohn, Axel, and Heideking, Jürgen (eds), *Genoa, Rapallo and European Reconstruction in 1922* (Cambridge, 1991).

Finnemore, Martha, *National Interests in International Society* (Ithaca, NY, 1996).

Flandreau, Marc, *The Glitter of Gold: France, Bimetallism, and the Emergence of the International Gold Standard, 1848–1873* (Oxford, 2004).

Flandreau, Marc, Holtfrerich, Carl-Ludwig, and James, Harold (eds), *International Financial History in the Twentieth Century: System and Anarchy* (Washington, 2003).

Fontaine, Philippe, 'Stabilizing American Society: Kenneth Boulding and the Integration of the Social Sciences, 1943–1980', *Science in Context*, 23/2 (2010), 221–65.

Forbes, Neil, *Doing Business with the Nazis: Britain's Economic and Financial Relations with Germany, 1931–1939* (London, 2000).

Fosdick, Raymond, *Letters on the League of Nations* (Princeton, 1966).

Fox, Grace, 'The Origins of UNRRA', *Political Science Quarterly*, 65/4 (1950), 561–84.

Fraser, Drummond D., *Credit or Chaos: The Ter Meulen Credit Scheme of the League of Nations* (London, 1921).

Frenkel, Jacob A, and Goldstein, Morris, *International Financial Policy: Essays in Honour of Jacques J. Polak* (Washington, 1991).

Fried, Amy, 'The Forgotten Lindsay Rogers and the Development of American Political Science', *American Political Science Review*, 100/4 (2006), 555–61.

Furner, Mary O., and Supple, Barry (eds), *The State and Economic Knowledge: The American and British Experiences* (Cambridge, 1990).

Gageby, Douglas, *The Last Secretary General: Sean Lester and the League of Nations* (Dublin, 1999).

Gardner, Richard N., *Sterling–Dollar Diplomacy: The Origins and Prospects of International Order* (2nd edn; New York, 1969).

Garside, W. R. (ed.), *Capitalism in Crisis: International Responses to the Great Depression* (London, 1993).

Garson, Robert, and Kidd, Stuart (eds), *The Roosevelt Years: New Perspectives on American History, 1933–45* (Edinburgh, 1999).

Gatrell, Peter, 'Trajectories of Population Displacement in the Aftermaths of the Two World Wars', in Jessica Reinisch and Elizabeth White (eds), *The Disentanglement of Populations: Migration, Expulsion and Displacement in Post-War Europe, 1944–9* (London, 2011), 3–26.

Gelfand, Lawrence G. (ed.), *Herbert Hoover: The Great War and its Aftermath, 1914–1923* (Iowa, 1979).

Ghébali, Victor-Yves, *La Réforme Bruce, 1939–1940: 50 ans de la Société des Nations* (Geneva, 1970).

Ghébali, Victor-Yves, 'The League of Nations and Functionalism', in A. J. R. Groom and Paul Taylor (eds), *Functionalism: Theory and Practice in International Relations* (London, 1975), 141–61.

Ghébali, Victor-Yves, and Ghébali, Catherine, *A Repertoire of League of Nations Serial Documents*: Répertoire des series de documents de la Société des Nation, 1919–1947 (New York, 1973).

Gilman, Nils, *Mandarins of the Future: Modernization Theory in Cold War America* (Baltimore, MD, 2003).

Goodrich, Carter, 'The Developing Programme of the ILO', *Annals of the American Academy of Political and Social Science*, 224 (Nov. 1942), 183–9.

Goodrich, Carter, 'Possibilities and Limits of International Control Migration', *Millbank Memorial Fund Quarterly*, 25/2 (1947), 153–60.

Goodwin, Craufurd D. (ed.), *Economics and National Security: A History of their Interaction. Annual Supplement to Volume 23, History of Political Economy* (London, 1991).

Gravenitz, Fritz Georg von, "Internationalismus in der Zwischenkriegszeit Deutschland und Frankreich in der globalen Agrarkrise', unpublished Ph.D thesis, European University Institute, 2011.

Grayson, Richard S., *Liberals, International Relations and Appeasement: The Liberal Party, 1919–1939* (London, 2001).

Grazia, Victoria de, *Irresistible Empire: America's Advance through 20th Century Europe* (Cambridge, MA, 2005).

Grenzebach, William S., *Germany's Informal Empire in East-Central Europe: German Economic Policy towards Yugoslavia and Rumania, 1933–39* (Stuttgart, 1988).

Griffiths, Richard T., 'Free Traders in a Protectionist World: The Foreign Policy of the Netherlands, 1930–1950', in S. Groenveld and M. Wintle (eds), *Britain and the Netherlands: State and Trade, Government and Economics in Britain and the Netherlands since the Middle Ages* (Zutphen, 1992), 152–68.

Groenveld, S., and Wintle, M. (eds), *Britain and the Netherlands: State and Trade, Government and Economics in Britain and the Netherlands since the Middle Ages* (Zutphen, 1992).

Groom, A. J. R., and Taylor, Paul (eds), *Functionalism: Theory and Practice in International Relations* (London, 1975).

Gross, Feliks, *Crossroads of Two Continents: A Democratic Federation of East–Central Europe* (New York, 1945).

Gulick, Luther, *Administrative Reflections from World War II* (Tuscaloosa, AL, 1948).

Haberler, Gottfried, *The Theory of International Trade with its Applications to Commercial Policy* (London, 1936).

Haberler, Gottfried, *Prosperity and Depression: A Theoretical Analysis of Cyclical Movements* (1937; rev. edn; Geneva, 1938).

Haegeman, Marc, *The General Meeting Files of the Mont Pèlerin Society, 1947–1988* <http://www.liberaalarchief.be/MPS2005.pdf> (accessed 26 Jan. 2009).

Hall, Noel F., ' "Trade Diversion"—An Australian Interlude', *Economica*, 5/17 (1938), 1–11.

Hankey, Maurice, *Diplomacy by Conference: Studies in Public Affairs, 1920–1946* (London, 1946).

Hantos, Elemér, *Die Weltwirtschafts-Konferenz: Probleme und Ergebnisse* (Leipzig, 1930).

Hantos, Elemér, *L'Économie mondiale et la Société des Nations* (Paris, 1930).

Harper, John Lamberton, *American Visions of Europe: Franklin D. Roosevelt, George F. Kennan, and Dean G. Acheson* (Cambridge, 1994).

Harris, José, 'Social Aspects in War-Time: Some Aspects of the Beveridge Report', in Jay Winter (ed.), *War and Economic Development: Essays in Memory of David Joslin* (Cambridge, 1975), 239–56.

Harris, José, *William Beveridge: A Biography* (Oxford, 1977).

Hawtrey, Ralph G., *Monetary Reconstruction* (London, 1923).

Healy, M., *Vienna and the Fall of the Habsburg Empire: Total War and Everyday Life in World War I* (Cambridge, 2004).

Helmreich, Jonathan E., *United States Relations with Belgium and the Congo, 1940–1960* (Newark, NJ, 1998).

Henig, Ruth, *The League of Nations* (London, 2010).

Herren, Madeleine, *Hintertüren zur Macht. Internationalismus und modernisierungsorientierte Aussenpolitik in Belgien, der Schweiz und den USA, 1865–1914* (Munich, 2000).

Herren, Madeleine, *Internationale Organisationen seit 1865: Eine Globalgeschichte der internationalen Ordnung* (Darmstadt, 2009).

Hilderbrand, Robert C., *Dumbarton Oaks: The Origins of the United Nations and the Search for Postwar Security* (Chapel Hill, NC, 1990).

Hill, Martin, *The Economic and Financial Organization of the League of Nations: A Survey of Twenty-Five Years' Experience* (Washington, 1946).

Hills, John, Ditch, John, and Glennerster, Howard (eds), *Beveridge and Social Security: An International Perspective* (Oxford, 1994).

Hilton, John, 'International Wage Comparisons', *Economic Journal*, 43/171 (Sept. 1933), 479–83.

HMSO Social Insurance and Allied Services, *The Beveridge Report*, CMND 6404 (London, Nov. 1942).

Hochschild, Adam, *King Leopold's Ghost: A Story of Greed, Terror, and Heroism in Colonial Africa* (New York, 1998).

Hoffman, Stefan-Ludwig (ed.), *Human Rights in the Twentieth Century* (Cambridge, 2011).

Hogan, Michael J., *Informal Entente: The Private Structure of Cooperation in Anglo-American Economic Diplomacy, 1918–1925* (Columbia, 1977).

Holtfrerich, Carl-Ludwig, 'Economic Policy Options and the End of the Weimar Republic' in Ian Kershaw (ed.), *Weimar: Why did German Democracy Fail?* (London, 1990), 58–91.

Hönicke, Michaela, 'Morgenthau's Programme for Germany', in Robert Garson and Stuart Kidd (eds), *The Roosevelt Years: New Perspectives on American History, 1933–45* (Edinburgh, 1999), 155–72.

Hoover, Herbert, *Three Years World of the American Relief Administration in Austria* (Vienna, 1922).

Hoover, Herbert, *The Memoirs of Herbert Hoover, 1929–1941* (New York, 1953).

Horn, Martin, *Britain, France and the Financing of the First World War* (Montreal, 2002).

Howson, Susan, 'Sterling's Managed Float: The Operation of the Exchange Equalisation Account, 1929–1939', *Princeton Studies in International Finance*, 46 (1980).

Howson, Susan (ed.), *The Collected Papers of James Meade* (3 vols; London, 1988, 1989).

Howson, Susan, and Moggridge, Donald, *The Wartime Diaries of Robbins and Meade, 1943–45* (London, 1990).

Hubback, David, *No Ordinary Press Baron: A Life of Walter Layton* (London, 1985).

Hülsmann, Jörg Guido, *Mises: The Last Knight of Liberalism* (Auburn, AL, 2007).

Ikenberry, G. John, 'A World Economy Restored: Expert Consensus and the Anglo-American Postwar Settlement', *International Organization*, 46/1 (1992), 289–321.

Imlay, Talbot C., *Facing the Second World War: Strategy, Politics and Economics in Britain and France, 1938–1940* (Oxford, 2003).

Innes, A. M., 'The Ter Meulen Scheme', *Economic Journal*, 31/124 (Dec. 1921), 544–7.

Institute for Advanced Study, *A Community of Scholars: The Institute for Advanced Study Faculty and Members 1930–1980* (Princeton, 1980).

International Labour Office, *Studies in War Economics*, series B, no. 33 (Montreal, 1941).

Iriye, Akira, *Global Community: The Role of International Organizations in the Making of the Contemporary World* (Berkeley and Los Angeles, 2002).

Irwin, Douglas A., *Against the Tide: An Intellectual History of Free Trade* (Princeton, 1996).

Irwin, Douglas A., Mavroidis, Petros C., and Sykes, Alan O., *The Genesis of GATT* (Cambridge, 2008).

Jackson, Ben, 'At the Origins of Neo-Liberalism: The Free Economy and the Strong State, 1930–1947', *Historical Journal*, 53/1 (2010), 233–51.

Jackson, Julian, *The Popular Front in France: Defending Democracy, 1934–38* (Cambridge, 1988).

Jackson, Peter, *France and the Nazi Menace: Intelligence and Policy-Making, 1933–1939* (Oxford, 2000).

Jacobsson, Erin E., *A Life for Sound Money: Per Jacobsson: His Biography* (Oxford, 1979).

Jaitner, Klaus, 'Aspekte britischer Deutschlandpolitik' in Josef Becker and Klaus Hildebrand (eds), *Internationale Beziehungen in der Weltwirtschaftskrise,1929–1933* (Munich, 1980), 21–38.

James, Harold, *International Monetary Cooperation since Bretton Woods* (Oxford, 1996).

James, Harold, *The German Slump: Politics and Economics, 1924–1936* (Oxford, 1986; new edn, 2007).

James, Harold, *The End of Globalization: Lessons from the Great Depression* (Cambridge, MA, 2009).

James, Harold, 'International Order after the Financial Crisis', *International Affairs*, 87/3 (2011), 525–37.

Jebb, H. M. G., *The Memoirs of Lord Gladwyn* (London, 1972).

Johnson, Helen, 'Frederick Leith Ross. The Career of an Economic Diplomat', unpublished D.Phil. thesis, University of Oxford, 2008.

Kaiser, David, *Economic Diplomacy and the Origins of the Second World War, 1930–1939* (Princeton, 1980).

Kamminga, Harmke, and Cunningham, Andrew (eds), *The Science and the Culture of Nutrition, 1840–1940* (Amsterdam, 1995).

Kaplan, Edward S., *American Trade Policy, 1923–1995* (Westport, CT, 1996).

Kattel, Rainer, Kregel, Jan A., and Reinert, Erik S. (eds), *Ragnar Nurkse (1907–2007): Classical Development Economics and its Relevance for Today* (London, 2009).

Keeton, E. D., *Briand's Locarno Policy: French Economics, Politics and Diplomacy, 1925–1929* (New York, 1987).

Kelen, Emery, *Peace in their Time: Men who Led us in and out of War, 1914–1945* (New York, 1963).

Kennedy, David M., *Freedom from Fear: The American People in Depression and War, 1929–1945* (Oxford, 1999).

Kennedy, Michael, 'The Irish Free State and the League of Nations, 1922–1932: The Wider Implications', *Irish Studies in International Affairs*, 3/4 (1992), 9–23.

Kennedy, Michael, *Ireland and the League of Nation, 1919–1939* (Blackrock, 1996).

Kennedy, Paul, *The Parliament of Man: The Past, Present, and Future of the United Nations* (London, 2006).

Kent, Bruce, *The Spoils of War: The Politics, Economics, and Diplomacy of Reparations, 1981–1932* (Oxford, 1989).

Keynes, John Maynard, *The Economic Consequences of the Peace* (London, 1919).

Keynes, John Maynard, *A Treatise on Money*, ii. *The Applied Theory of Money* (London, 1930).

Keynes, John Maynard, 'The Policy of Government Storage of Foodstuffs and Raw Materials', *Economic Journal*, 48 (Sept. 1938), 449–60.

Keynes, John Maynard, 'The League of Nations: Professor Tinbergen's Method', *Economic Journal*, 49/195 (1939), 558–69.

Keynes, John Maynard, *The Collected Writings of John Maynard Keynes*, xix. *Activities 1922–1929: The Return to Gold and Industrial Policy, Part II*, ed. Donald E. Moggridge (Cambridge, 1981).

Kimball, Warren, *The Juggler: Franklin Roosevelt as Wartime Statesman* (Princeton, 1994).

Kindleberger, Charles P., *International Short-Term Capital Movements* (New York, 1937).

Kindleberger, Charles P., *The World in Depression, 1929–1939* (Berkeley and Los Angeles, 1973; 2nd edn, 1986).

Kindleberger, Charles P., 'Commercial Policy between the Wars', in P. Matthias and S. Pollard (eds), *The Cambridge Economic History of Europe*, viii. *The Industrial Economies: The Development of Economic and Social Policies* (Cambridge, 1989).

Klemperer, K., *Ignaz Seipel: Christian Statesman in a Time of Crisis* (Princeton, 1971).

Knutsen, Torbjörn L., *A History of International Relations Theory: An Introduction* (Manchester, 1992).

Kotkin, Stephen, 'Modern Times: The Soviet Union and the Interwar Conjuncture', *Kritika: Explorations in Russian and Eurasian History*, 2/1 (2001), 111–64.

Kroener, B. E., Müller, R. D., and Umbreit, H., *Germany and the Second World War: Organization and Mobilization of the German Sphere of Power: Wartime Administration, Economy and Manpower Resources, 1942–44/5* (Oxford, 2003).

Krüger, Peter, 'A Rainy Day, 6 April 1922: The Rapallo Treaty and the Cloudy Perspective for German Foreign Policy', in Carole Fink, Axel Frohn, and Jürgen Heideking (eds), *Genoa, Rapallo and European Reconstruction in 1922* (Cambridge, 1991), 49–64.

Kukk, Kalev, '(Re)Discovering Ragnar Nurkse', *Kroon and Economy*, 1 (2004), 1–7.

Lacqua, Daniel (ed.), *Internationalism Reconfigured: Transnational Ideas and Movements between the World Wars* (London, 2011).

Lagendijk, Vincent, *Electrifying Europe: The Power of Europe in the Construction of Electricity Networks* (Amsterdam, 2008).

Layton, Walter, and Rist, Charles, *The Economic Situation of Austria* (Geneva, 1925).

League of Nations, *Permanent Staff List of the Secretariat* (Geneva, 1920).

League of Nations, *Official Journal* (Geneva, 1920–40).

League of Nations, *Supplement to Report No. XIII. (3.): Summary of Recommendations Included in the Memorandum on the World's Monetary Problems by Gustav Cassel* (London, 1921).

League of Nations, *Brussels Financial Conference, 1920: The Recommendations and their Application* (2 vols; Brussels, 1922).

League of Nations, *Staff List of the Secretariat* (annual edns; Geneva, 1922–38).

League of Nations, *The Settlement of Greek Refugees* (Geneva, 1924).

League of Nations, *The Settlement of Bulgarian Refugees* (Geneva, 1926).

League of Nations, *Report and Proceedings of the World Economic Conference* (2 vols; Geneva, 1927).

League of Nations, *Report of the Economic Work of the League of Nations* (Geneva, 1927).

League of Nations, *World Economic Conference, Geneva 1927: Final Report* (Geneva, 1927).

League of Nations, *League of Nations A Pictorial Survey* (Geneva, 1929).

League of Nations, *Legislation on Gold* (Geneva, 1930).

League of Nations, *Interim Report of the Gold Delegation of the Financial Committee* (Geneva, 1930).

League of Nations, *Principles and Methods of Financial Reconstruction Work Undertaken under the Auspices of the League of Nations* (Geneva, 1930).

League of Nations, *Selected Documents Submitted to the Gold Delegation of the Financial Committee* (Geneva, 1930).

League of Nations, *Interim Report of the Gold Delegation of the Financial Committee* (Geneva, 1931).

League of Nations, *Second Interim Report of the Gold Delegation of the Financial Committee* (Geneva, 1931).

League of Nations, *World Economic Survey* (annual editions, 1931–9).

League of Nations, *Final Report of the Gold Delegation of the Financial Committee* (Geneva, 1932).

League of Nations, *Review of World Production, 1925–1931* (Geneva, 1932).

League of Nations, *Enquiry into International Clearing* (Geneva, 1935).

League of Nations, *Remarks on the Present Phase of International Economic Relations* (Geneva, 1935–9).

League of Nations, *Economic Committee, Equality of Treatment in the Present State of International Commercial Relations: The Most-Favoured-Nation Clause* (Geneva, 1936).

League of Nations, *Final Report of the Mixed Committee of the League of Nations on the Relation of Nutrition to Health, Agriculture and Economic Policy* (Geneva, 1937).

League of Nations, *European Conference on Rural Life: Report of the Preparatory Committee on the Work of its First Session* (Geneva, 1938).

League of Nations, *Report on Exchange Control* (Geneva, 1938).

League of Nations, *The Development of International Co-operation in Economic and Social Affairs: Report of the Special Committee* (Geneva, 1939).

League of Nations, *Europe's Trade: A Study of the Trade of European Countries with Each Other and with the Rest of the World* (Geneva, 1941).

League of Nations, *Economic Fluctuations in the United States and the United Kingdom, 1918–1922* (Geneva, 1942).

League of Nations, *Commercial Policy in the Interwar Period: International Proposals and National Policies* (Geneva, 1942).

League of Nations, Economic and Financial Committees, *Report to the Council on the Work of the Joint Session* (Geneva, Aug. 1942).

League of Nations, *Europe's Overseas Needs 1919–1920 and How They Were Met* (Geneva, 1943).

League of Nations, *Relief Deliveries and Relief Loans, 1919–1923* (Geneva, 1943).

League of Nations, *Trade Relations between Free-Market and Controlled Economies* (Geneva, 1943).

League of Nations, *The Transition from War to Peace Economy: Report of the Delegation of Economic Depressions, Part I* (Geneva, 1943).

League of Nations, *The Committees of the League of Nations: Classified List and Essential Facts* (Geneva, 1945).

League of Nations, *Economic Stability in the Post-War World: The Conditions of Prosperity after the Transition from War to Peace* (Geneva, 1945).

Lee, Eddy, 'The Declaration of Philadelphia: Retrospect and Prospect', *International Labour Review*, 133/4 (1994), 467–84.

Lee, Eddy, Swepston, Lee, and Van Daele, Jasmien, *The ILO and the Quest for Social Justice, 1919–2009* (Geneva, 2009).

Leith-Ross, Frederick, *Money Talks: Fifty Years of International Finance: The Autobiography of Sir Frederick Leith-Ross* (London, 1968).

Leonard, Robert, 'The Collapse of Interwar Vienna: Oskar Morgenstern's Community, 1925–1950', *International Centre for Economic Research Working Paper Series*, 4 (2010), 1–63.

Leonard, Robert, *Von Neumann, Morgenstern, and the Creation of Game Theory: From Chess to Social Science, 1900–1960* (Cambridge, 2010).

Likaka, Osumaka, *Naming Colonialism: History and Collective Memory in the Congo, 1870–1960* (Madison, WI, 2005).

Lloyd, Lorna, *Peace through Law: Britain and the International Court in the 1920s* (Woodbridge, 1997).

Lochner, Paul Louis *Herbert Hoover und Deutschland* (Boppard am Rhein, 1961).

Lojkó, Miklós, *Meddling in Middle Europe: Britain and the 'Lands Between', 1919–1925* (Budapest, 2006).

Long, David, *Towards a New Liberal Internationalism: The International Theory of J. A. Hobson* (Cambridge, 1996).

Loucheur, Louis, *Carnet secrets, 1980–1932*, ed. and annotated Jacques de Launay (Brussels, 1962).

Loveday, Alexander, *The History and Economics of Indian Famines* (Oxford, 1914).

Loveday, Alexander, *Reflections on International Administration* (Oxford, 1958).

Lundberg, Erik, 'Ingvar Svennilson: A Note on his Scientific Achievements and a Bibliography of his Contributions to Economics', *Scandinavian Journal of Economics*, 74/3 (1972), 313–28.

McCarthy, Helen, 'Leading from the Centre: Foreign Policy and Political Agreement in the 1930s', *Contemporary British* History, 23/4 (2009), 527–42.

McCarthy, Helen, *The British People and the League of Nations: Democracy, Citizenship and Internationalism, c.1918–1945* (Manchester, 2011).

MacDonald, Callum A., *The United States, Britain and Appeasement* (London, 1981).

McKercher, B. J. C., *Transition of Power: Britain's Loss of Global Pre-eminence to the United States, 1930–1945* (Cambridge, 1999).

MacMillan, Margaret, *Paris 1919: Six Months that Changed the World* (New York, 2001).

Magagnoli, Ralf, 'Anregungen zu einer Neubewertung der Europapolitik Alcide De Gaspersis', *Journal of European Integration History*, 4/1 (1998), 27–54.

Magnasson, Lars, *Gustav Cassel, Popularizer and Enigmatic Walrasian* (London, 1991).

Magnus, Jan R., and Morgan, Mary S., 'The ET Interview: Professor J. Tinbergen', *Econometric Theory*, 3/1 (1987), 117–42.

Maier, Charles, *In Search of Stability: Explorations in Historical Political Economy* (Cambridge, 1987).

Malinvaud, Edmond, 'The Scientific Papers of Tjalling C. Koopmans: A Review Article', *Journal of Economic Literature*, 10/3 (1972), 798–802.

Manela, Erez, *The Wilsonian Moment: Self-Determination and the International Origins of Anticolonial Nationalism* (Oxford, 2007).

Mantoux, Étienne, *The Carthaginian Peace or the Economic Consequences of Mr Keynes* (London, 1946).

March, J. G., and Olsen, J. P., 'The Institutional Dynamics of International Political Orders', *International Organization*, 52 (1998), 943–69.

Marcus, Nathan, 'Credibility, Confidence and Capital: Austrian Reconstruction and the Collapse of Global Finance, 1921–1931', unpublished Ph.D. thesis, New York University, 2010.

Marks, Sally, *The Illusion of Peace: International Relations in Europe, 1918–1933* (Basingstoke, 2003).

Markwell, Donald, *John Maynard Keynes and International Relations. Economic Paths to War and Peace* (Oxford, 2006).

Marshall, Dominique, 'The Formation of Childhood as an Object of International Relations: The Child Welfare Committee and the Declaration of Children's Rights of the League of Nations', *International Journal of Children's Rights*, 7/2 (1999), 103–47.

Martin, Charles, and Montpetit, Édouard, *La Conférence de Gênes en vue de la reconstruction économique de financière de l'Europe* (Ottawa, 1922).

Matthias, P., and Pollard, S. (eds), *The Cambridge Economic History of Europe*, viii. *The Industrial Economies: The Development of Economic and Social Policies* (Cambridge, 1989).

Maul, Daniel, 'Help Them Move the ILO Way: The International Labour Organization and the Modernization Discourse in the Era of Decolonization and the Cold War', *Diplomatic History*, 33/3 (2009), 387–404.

Mausbach, Wilfried, *Zwischen Morgenthau und Marshall: Das wirtschaftspolitische Deutschlandskonzept der USA, 1944–47* (Düsseldorf, 1996).

Mayer, Martin Lorenz, *Safehaven: The Allied Pursuit of Nazi Assets Abroad* (Missouri, 2007).

Mazower, Mark, *No Enchanted Palace: The End of Empire and the Ideological Origins of the United Nations* (Princeton, 2009).

Mazumdar, Pauline H., '"In the Silence of the Laboratory": The League of Nations Standardizes Syphilis Tests', *Social History of Medicine*, 16/3 (2003), 437–59.

Meade, James, *An Introduction to Economic Analysis and Policy* (Oxford, 1936).

Metzger, Barbara, 'Towards an International Human Rights Regime during the Inter-War Years: The League of Nations' Combat of Traffic in Women and Children', in

K. Grant et al. (eds), *Beyond Sovereignty: Britain, Empire and Transnationalism, 1880–1950* (Basingstoke, 2007), 54–79.

Meyer, Margaret G., 'The League Loans', *Political Science Quarterly*, 60/4 (1945), 492–526.

Ministère des Affaires Étrangères, *Documents diplomatiques français* (Paris, 1929–86).

Mirowski, Philip, and Plehwe, Dieter (eds), *The Road from Mont Pèlerin. The Making of Neo-Liberal Thought Collective* (Cambridge, MA, 2009).

Mitrany, David, *The Progress of International Government* (London, 1933).

Mitrany, David, *The Functional Theory of Politics* (London, 1975).

Moggridge, Donald, 'Keynes and his Correspondence', in Roger E. Backhouse and Bradley W. Bateman (eds), *The Cambridge Companion to Keynes* (Cambridge, 2006), 136–59.

Moorhouse, Frank, *Grand Days* (London, 1993).

Moorhouse, Frank, *Dark Palace* (London, 2000).

Morgan, Mary S., *The History of Econometric Ideas* (Cambridge, 1991).

Morgenstern, Oskar, and Neumann, John von, *Theory of Games and Economic Behaviour* (Princeton, 1944).

Mouré, Kenneth, *Managing the Franc Poincaré: Economic Understanding and Political Constraint in French Monetary Policy, 1928–1936* (Cambridge, 1991).

Mouré, Kenneth, *The Gold Standard Illusion: France, the Bank of France, and the International Gold Standard, 1914–1939* (Oxford, 2002).

Mouton, M.-R., *La Société des Nations et les Intérêts de la France, 1920–1924* (Bern, 1995).

Myers, Denys P., 'The Liquidation of the League of Nations Functions', *American Journal of International Law*, 42/2 (1948), 220–354.

Navari, Cornelia, 'Origins of the Briand Plan', *Diplomacy and Statecraft*, 3/1 (1992), 74–104.

Navari, Cornelia, *Internationalism and the State in the Twentieth Century* (London, 2000).

Nehring, Holger, and Pharo, Helge, 'Introduction: A Peaceful Europe? Negotiating Peace in the Twentieth Century', *Contemporary European History*, 17/3 (2008), 277–99.

Neilson, Keith, *Britain, Soviet Russia and the Collapse of the Versailles Order, 1919–1939* (Cambridge, 2006).

Newton, Scott, *Profits of Peace: The Political Economy of Anglo-German Appeasement* (Oxford, 1996).

Nicols, Beverly, *Cry Havoc!* (London, 1933).

Nixon, J. W, 'Work of [the] International Labour Office', *Statistical and Social Inquiry Society of Ireland*, 91 (1937–8), 69–86.

Northedge, F. S., *The League of Nations: Its Life and Times, 1920–1946* (Leicester, 1986).

Nurkse, Ragnar, *International Currency Experience: Lessons of the Inter-War Period* (Geneva, 1944).

Nurkse, Ragnar, 'International Monetary Policy and the Search for Economic Stability', *American Economic Review*, 37/2 (May 1947), 569–80.

Nurkse, Ragnar, *Problems of Capital Formation in Underdeveloped Countries* (Oxford, 1953).

Nurkse, Ragnar, *Patterns of Trade and Development* (Uppsala, 1959).

Nurkse, Ragnar, *Equilibrium and Growth in the World Economy: Economic Essays by Ragnar Nurkse* (Cambridge, 1961).

O'Brien, John B., 'F. L. McDougall and the Origins of the FAO', *Australian Journal of Politics and History*, 46/2 (2000), 164–74.

Offner, Arnold A., 'Appeasement Revisited: The United States, Great Britain and Germany 1933–1940', *Journal of American History*, 64/2 (1977), 373–93.

Ohlin, Bertil, *The Course and Phases of the World Economic Depression* (Geneva, 1931).

Olson, Lynne, *Citizens of London: The Americans who Stood with Britain in its Darkest, Finest Hour* (New York, 2010).

Overy, Richard J., *Hermann Göring: The Iron Man* (London, 1984).

Parker, R. A. C., *Chamberlain and Appeasement* (London, 1993).

Parrish, Michael, *Anxious Decades: America in Prosperity and Depression, 1920–1941* (New York, 1992).

Pashtuhov, Vladimir D., *Experience in International Administration: Memorandum on the Composition, Procedure and Functions of Committees of the League of Nations* (Washington, 1943).

Pasvolsky, Leo, *Economic Nationalism and the Danubian States* (New York, 1928).

Pasvolsky, Leo, *Bulgaria's Economic Position with Special Reference to the Reparation Problem and the Work of the League of Nations* (Washington, 1930).

Pasvolsky, Leo, *War Debts and Economic Prosperity* (Washington, 1932).

Pasvolsky, Leo, *Gold: A World Problem* (Philadelphia, 1933).

Pauly, Louis W., 'The League of Nations and the Foreshadowing of the International Monetary Fund', *Princeton Essays in International Finance*, 201 (Dec. 1996), 1–52.

Pauly, Louis W., *Who Elected the Bankers? Surveillance and Control in the World Economy* (Ithaca, NY, 1997).

Peden, George, *The Treasury and British Public Policy, 1906–1959* (Oxford, 2000).

Pedersen, Susan, 'Back to the League of Nations', *American Historical Review*, 112/4 (2007), 1091–1117.

Pedersen, Susan 'Getting out of Iraq—in 1932: The League of Nations and the Road to Normative Statehood', *American Historical Review* 115/4 (2010), 975–1000.

Peet, Richard, *Unholy Trinity: The IMF, World Bank and the WTO* (New York, 2003).

Pegg, Carl Hamilton, *Evolution of the European Idea, 1914–1932* (Chapel Hill, NC, 1983).

Pentzopoulos, Dimitri, *The Balkan Exchange of Minorities and its Impact on Greece* (Paris, 1962).

Peter, Matthias, *John Maynard Keynes und die britische Deutschlandpolitik. Machtanspruch und ökonomische Realität im Zeitalter der Weltkriege, 1919–1946* (Munich, 1997).

Poidevin, Raymond, 'La Tentative de rapprochement économique entre la France et l'Allemagne, 1938–1939', in Jacques Bariéty et al (eds), *La France et L'Allemagne entre des deux guerres mondiales* (Nancy, 1987), 59–69.

Polyani, Karl, *The Great Transformation: The Political and Economic Origins of our Time* (Boston, 1944).

Ranshofen-Wertheimer, Egon, *Victory is not Enough: The Strategy for a Lasting Peace* (New York, 1942).

Ranshofen-Wertheimer, Egon, *The International Secretariat: A Great Experiment in International Administration* (Washington, 1945).

Rappard, William E., *The Common Menace of Economic and Military Armaments: The Eighth Richard Cobden Lecture* (London, 1936).

Reinalda, Bob (ed.), *The Ashgate Companion to Non-State Actors* (London, 2011).

Reinalda, Bob, and Verbeek, Bertjan (eds), *Decision Making within International Organizations* (London, 2004).

Reinisch, Jessica, and White, Elizabeth (eds), *The Disentanglement of Populations: Migration, Expulsion and Displacement in Post-War Europe, 1944–9* (London, 2011).

Renoliet, J.-J., *L'UNESCO oubliée: La Société des Nations et la cooperation intellectuelle, 1919–1946* (Paris, 1999).

Reynolds, David, 'Roosevelt, the British Left, and the Appointment of John G. Winant as United States Ambassador to Britain in 1941', *International History Review*, 4/3 (1982), 393–413.

Rhodes, Benjamin D., 'Reassessing "Uncle Shylock": The United States and the French War Debt, 1917–1929', *Journal of American History*, 55/4 (1969), 787–803.

Ribi, Amalia, 'Humanitarian Imperialism. The Politics of Anti-Slavery Activism in the Inter-War Years', unpublished D.Phil. thesis, University of Oxford, 2006.

Ribi Forclaz, Amalia, 'A New Target for International Social Reform: The International Labour Organization and Working and Living Conditions in Agriculture in the Interwar Years', *Contemporary European History*, 20/3 (2011), 307–29.

Richard-Picchi, Anne-Isabelle, 'Colonialism and the European Movement in France and the Netherlands, 1925–1936', unpublished Ph.D. thesis, Cambridge University, 2010.

Rickett, Denis 'Salter, (James) Arthur, Baron Salter (1881–1975)', *Oxford Dictionary of National Biography*, online edn, October 2009.

Rietzler, Katharina, 'American Foundations and the "Scientific Study" of International Relations in Europe, 1910–1940', unpublished Ph.D. thesis, University College, London, 2009.

Rietzler, Katharina, 'American Philanthropy and Cultural Diplomacy in the Interwar Years', *Historical Research*, 84/223 (Feb. 2011), 148–64.

Risse-Kappen, Thomas, 'Ideas Do Not Float Freely: Transnational Coalitions, Domestic Structures, and the End of the Cold War', *International Organization*, 48/2 (1994), 185–214.

Ritschl, Albrecht, *Deutschlands Krise und Konjunktur 1924–1934: Binnenkonjunktur, Auslandsverschuldung und Reparationsproblem zwischen Dawes-Plan und Transfersperre* (Berlin, 2002).

Rodgers, James Harvey, *America Weighs her Gold* (New Haven, 1931).

Rodgers, James Harvey, and Hayes, Carlton J. H., *The Process of Inflation in France, 1914–1927* (New York, 1929)

Rolfe, J. Simon, *Franklin Roosevelt's Foreign Policy and the Welles Mission* (London, 2007).

Rooth, Tim, *British Protectionism and the International Economy: Overseas Commercial Policy in the 1930s* (Cambridge, 1993).

Roskill, Stephen, *Hankey Man of Secrets*, ii. *1919–1931* (London, 1972).

Rötheli, Tobias F., 'Business Forecasting and the Development of Business Cycle Theory', *History of Political Economy*, 39/3 (2007), 481–510.

Rovine, Arthur W., *The First Fifty Years: The Secretary-General in World Politics 1920–1970* (Leiden, 1970).

Royal Irish Academy, *Documents on Irish Foreign Policy* (Dublin, 2000).

Rutherford, Malcolm, 'Chicago Economics and Institutionalism', in Ross B. Emmett (ed.), *The Elgar Companion to the Chicago School of Economics* (Cheltenham, 2010), 25–39.

Ryder, Oscar, 'Foreign Trade Policy of the United States', *Political Quarterly*, 8/4 (1937), 565–76.

Salter, Arthur, *The Framework of an Ordered Society* (Cambridge, 1933).

Salter, Arthur, *Memoirs of a Public Servant* (London, 1961).

Salter, Arthur, *Slave of the Lamp: A Public Servant's Notebook* (London, 1967).

Samuelson, Paul, 'Interactions between the Multiplier Analysis and the Principle of Acceleration', *Review of Economists and Statistics*, 21/2 (1939), 75–8.

Samuelson, Paul A., 'Gustav Cassel's Scientific Innovations: Claims and Realities', *History of Political Economy*, 25/3 (1993), 515–27.

Sayers, R. S., *The Bank of England, 1891–1944* (3 vols; Cambridge, 1976).

Scarf, Herbert E., *Tjalling Charles Koopmans, 1910–1985* (Washington, 1995).

Schot, Johan, and Lagendijk, Vincent, 'Technocratic Internationalism in the Interwar Years: Building Europe on Motorways and Electrical Networks', *Journal of Modern European History*, 6/2 (2008), 196–217.

Schröder, Hans-Jürgen, *Confrontation and Cooperation: Germany and the United States in the Era of World War I, 1900–1924* (Oxford, 1993).

Schuker, Stephen A., 'Origins of American Stabilization Policy in Europe: The Financial Dimension, 1918–1924', in Hans-Jürgen Schröder (ed.), *Confrontation and Cooperation: Germany and the United States in the Era of World War I* (Providence, RI, 1993), 377–401.

Schuker, Stephen A., 'The Gold Exchange Standard: A Reinterpretation', in Marc Flandreau, Carl-Ludwig Holtfrerich, and Harold James (eds), *International Financial History in the Twentieth Century: System and Anarchy* (Washington, 2003), 77–94.

Schulz, Matthias, *Deutschland, der Völkerbund und die Frage der europäischen Wirtschafsordnung, 1925–1933* (Hamburg, 1997).

Shields, Sarah D., *Fezzes in the River: Identity Politics and European Diplomacy in the Middle East on the Eve of World War II* (Oxford, 2011).

Self, Robert, *Chamberlain: A Biography* (Vermont, 2005).

Simmons, Beth, *Who Adjusts? Domestic Sources of Foreign Economic Policy during the 1930s* (Princeton, 1994).

Simpson, Smith, 'The International Labor Conference', *American Political Science Review*, 36/1 (1942), 102–4.

Siven, Claes-Henric, 'Heertje Heemeijer and Samuelson on the Origins of Samuelson's Multiplier-Accelerator Model', *History of Political Economy*, 35/2 (2003), 323–7.

Skidelsky, Robert, *John Maynard Keynes*, i. *Hopes Betrayed, 1883–1920* (London, 1984).

Skidelsky, Robert, *John Maynard Keynes*, ii. *The Economist as Saviour, 1920–1937* (London, 1992).

Skidelsky, Robert, *John Maynard Keynes*, iii. *Fighting for Britain, 1937–1946* (London, 2000).

Slaughter, Anne-Marie, *A New World Order* (Princeton, 2004).

Sluga, Glenda, 'The Hancock Lecture, 2009: Was the Twentieth Century the Great Age of Internationalism?', *Australian Academy of Humanities Proceedings 2009* (Canberra, 2010).

Smith, David F. (ed.), *Nutrition in Britain: Science, Scientists, and Politics in the Twentieth Century* (London, 1997).

Smouts, Marie-Cloud, *Les Organizations internationales* (Paris, 1995).

Smuts, Jan C., *The League of Nations: A Practical Suggestion* (London, 1919).

Social Science Research Council and the International Labour Office, *International Wage Comparisons: A Report of Two International Conferences and a Critical Review of Available Statistical Data* (New York, 1932).

Staples, Amy, *The Birth of Development: How the World Bank, Food and Agriculture Organization, and the World Health Organization Changed the World, 1945–65* (Kent, OH), 88–96.

Steiner, Zara, *The Lights that Failed: European International History, 1919–1933* (Oxford, 2007).

Steiner, Zara, *Triumph of the Dark: European International History, 1933–1940* (Oxford, 2011).

Stirling, A., *Lord Bruce: The London Years* (London, 1974).

Strandmann, Harmut Pogge von, 'Rapallo—Strategy in Preventative Diplomacy: New Sources and Interpretations', in Volker R. Berghahn and Martin Kitchen (eds), *Germany in the Age of Total War* (London, 1981), 123–43.

Sumner, Scott, 'Roosevelt, Warren, and the Gold-Buying Program of 1933', *Research in Economic History*, 20 (2001), 135–72.

Supiot, Alain, *L'Esport de Philadephie: La Justice sociale face au marche total* (Paris, 2010).

Svennilson, Ingvar, *Growth and Stagnation in the European Economy* (Geneva, 1954).

Szejnmann, Christian (ed.), *Rethinking History, Dictatorship and War* (London, 2009).

Tavlas, George S., 'Chicago, Harvard and the Doctrinal Foundations of Monetary Economics', *Journal of Political Economy*, 105/1 (1997), 153–77.

Thomas, Martin, *Britain, France and Appeasement: Anglo-French Relations in the Popular Front Era* (Oxford and New York, 1996).

Thorne, Christopher, *The Limits of Foreign Policy: The West, The League and the Far Eastern Crisis of 1931–1933* (London, 1972).

Tiltman, H. Hessell, *Peasant Europe* (London, 1936).

Tinbergen, Jan, *Statistical Testing of Business-Cycle Theories* (Geneva, 1939).

Tinbergen, Jan, *Business Cycles in the United States of America 1919–1932* (Geneva, 1939).

Tinbergen, Jan, 'On a Method of Statistical Business-Cycle Research: A Reply', *Economic Journal*, 50/197 (1940), 141–54.

Tomás Rangil, Maria Teresa, 'The Role of Self-Interest and Rationality in the Explanation of International and Civil Wars, 1942–2005', unpub. Ph.D. Thesis, Université de Paris Ouest Nanterre-La Défense (2010).

Toniolo, Gianni, *Central Bank Cooperation at the Bank for International Settlements, 1930–1973* (Cambridge, 2005).

Tooze, Adam, *The Wages of Destruction: The Making and Breaking of the Nazi Economy* (London, 2006).

Tosi, Luciano, *Alle origini della FAO: Le relazioni tra L'Istituto Internazionale id Agricoltura e la Societàdella Nazioni* (Rome, 1991).

Tournes, Ludovic, 'La Philanthrope americaine et l'Europe: Contribution à une histoire transnationale de L'Americanisation', Université Paris-I Panthéon-Sorbonne, unpublished habilitation, 2 vols, 2008.

Toye, John, and Toye, Richard, *The UN and Global Political Economy: Trade, Finance and Development* (Indiana, 2004).

Tracy, Michael, *Government and Agriculture in Western Europe* (3rd edn; London, 1989).

Trentmann, Frank, 'Coping with Shortage: The Problem of Food Security and Global Visions of Co-ordination, *c.*1890s–1950', in Frank Trentmann and Just Fellming (eds), *Food and Conflict in Europe in the Age of the Two World Wars* (New York, 2006), 13-48.

Trentmann, Frank, *Free Trade Nation: Commerce, Consumption, and Civil Society in Modern Britain* (Oxford, 2008).

Trentmann, Frank, and Fellming, Just (eds), *Food and Conflict in Europe in the Age of the Two World Wars* (New York, 2006).

Tucker, Rufus S., 'Gold and the General Price Level', *Review of Economic Statistics*, 16/1 (Jan. 1934), 8–16.

Turnell, Sean, 'F. L. McDougall: Éminence grise of Australian Economic Diplomacy', *Australian Economic History Review*, 40/1 (2000), 51–70.

Turner, Arthur, 'Anglo-French Financial Relations in the 1920s', *European History Quarterly*, 26 (1996), 31–55.

United Nations Commission on Human Security 2003, *Human Security Now* (New York, 2003).

United Nations Library, *The League of Nations in Retrospect: Proceedings of the Symposium* (Berlin and New York, 1983).

United States Department of State, *Papers Relating to the Foreign Relations of the United States* (Washington, 1947–).

Veatch, Richard, *Canada and the League of Nations* (Toronto, 1975).

Végh, Carlos, A., 'Stopping High Inflation: An Analytical Overview', *Staff Papers—International Monetary Fund*, 39/.3 (1992), 626–95.

Verma, Dina Nath, *India and the League of Nations* (Patma, 1968).

Vernon, James, *Hunger: A Modern History* (Cambridge, MA, 2007).

Wallis, John Joseph, 'Lessons from the Political Economy of the New Deal', *Oxford Review of Economic Policy*, 26/4 (2010), 442–62.

Walters, Frank P., *A History of the League of Nations* (Oxford, 1952; 2nd edn, 1965).

Wasserstein, Bernard, *Barbarism and Civilization: A History of Europe in our Time* (Oxford, 2007).

Watt, D. C., *Personalities and Policies: Studies in the Formulation of British Foreign Policy in the Twentieth Century* (Notre Dame, IN, 1965).

Webster, Andrew, 'The Transnational Dream: Politicians, Diplomats and Soldiers in the League of Nations' Pursuit of International Disarmament', *Contemporary European History* 14/4 (2005), 493–518.

Webster, Andrew, 'Absolutely Irresponsible Amateurs: The Temporary Mixed Commission on Armaments, 1921–1924', *Australian Journal of Politics and History*, 54/3 (2008), 373–88.

Wehrli, Yannick, 'Sean Lester, Ireland and Latin America in the League of Nations, 1929–1946', *Irish Migration Studies in Latin America*, 7/1 (2009), 39–44.

Weinbaum, A., Thomas, L., Ramamurthy, P., Poiger, U., Dong, M., and Barlow, T. (eds), *The Modern Girl around the World: Consumption, Modernity and Globalization* (Durham, NC, 2008).

Weindling, Paul, 'The Role of International Organizations in Setting Nutritional Standards in the 1920s and 1930s', in Harmke Kamminga and Andrew Cunningham (eds), *The Science and the Culture of Nutrition, 1840–1940* (Amsterdam, 1995), 319–32.

Weindling, Paul, 'The League of Nations Health Organization and the Rise of Latin American Participation', *História, Ciências, Saúde—Manguinhos*, 13/3 (2006), 1–14.

Weissman, Benjamin, *Herbert Hoover and Famine Relief to Soviet Russia, 1921–1923* (Stanford, CA, 1974).

Wendt, Bernd Jürgen, *Economic Appeasement: Handel und Finanz in der britischen Deutschland-Politik* (Düsseldorf, 1971).

Wessels, Jens-Wilhelm, *Economic Policy and Microeconomic Performance in Inter-War Europe. The Case of Austria, 1918–1938* (Stuttgart, 2007).

Whitney, N. R., *The American Economic Review*, 12/3 (1922), 515–17.

Wicker, Elmus, 'Terminating Hyperinflation in the Dismembered Habsburg Monarchy', *American Economic Review*, 76/3 (1986), 350–64.

Wicker, Elmus, *The Banking Panics of the Great Depression* (New York, 1996).

Wilt, Alan F., *Food for War: Agriculture and Rearmament in Britain before the Second World War* (Oxford, 2001).

Winter, Jay (ed.), *War and Economic Development: Essays in Memory of David Joslin* (Cambridge, 1975).

Winter, Jay, *Dreams of Peace and Freedom: Utopian Moments in the 20th Century* (New Haven, 2006).

Wintzer, Joachim, *Deutschland und der Völkerbund, 1918–1926* (Paderborn, 2006)

Woodbridge, George, *UNRRA: The History of the United Nations Relief and Rehabilitation Administration* (3 vols; New York, 1950).

Woods, Ngaire, *The Globalizers: The IMF, the World Bank and their Borrowers* (Ithaca, NY, 2006).

World Peace Foundation, *Report on the Brussels Financial Conference* (Boston, 1920).

Yearwood, Peter J., *Guarantee of Peace: The League of Nations in British Policy, 1914–1925* (Oxford, 2009).

Zagoroff, S. D., Vegh, J., and Bilimovich, A. D., *The Agricultural Economy of the Danubian Countries, 1935–45* (Stanford, CA, 1955).

Zanasi, M., 'Exporting Development: the League of Nations and Republican China', *Comparative Studies in Society & History*, 49/1 (2007), 143–69.

Zimmerman, Alfred R., *Principiële Staatkunde* (2nd edn; Rotterdam, 1932).

Zweig, Stefan, *The Post Office Girl* (London, 2009).

Index

Brussels Conference (1920) 17–23, 19 n.17, 22 n.31, 24, 26, 42
business cycle inquiry/world economic conference proposal 71–8
Covenant, *see* Covenant of the League of Nations
economic appeasement 185–93
economic depressions 198–230
Economic and Financial Committee, *see* Economic and Financial Committee
end game/legacy of 305–14, 320–1, 325–6, 341–56, 345 n.16, 356n., 357–9
Genoa Conference (1922) 23–5
and the gold standard 51–7, 57–65, 66–71
introduction 1–10, 6 n.10, 10 n.21
new approaches to global security 159–84, 181 n.70
politics and trade 39–46, 41 n.93
rural life 193–8
Secretariat, *see* Secretariat of the League of Nations
stabilization/development 25–33
and the United States 47–51
in the US 1940–43 267–304, 276–7 n.43
working patterns 33–9, 35 n.77
World Conference 1933 78–84, 84–5, 88–99, 99–105, 106–15, 116–23
and World War 2, 251–66, 251 n.55
years of transition 1933-36, 124–59
League of Nations Association (US) 269
League of Nations Disarmament Conference 85
League of Nations Health Organization (LNHO) 165–6, 169–71, 191, 250, 345
League of Nations Library 37
League of Nations Union 26
League Supervisory Commission 194, 275
Leahy, William D. 327
Lehman, Herbert Henry 297
Leith-Ross, Sir Frederick 90, 100, 106, 109, 127, 131, 139–40, 146–7, 153, 155, 183–4, 237, 244, 257, 283–4, 297–8, 302
Lend-Lease Agreement 271, 281, 285, 319
Lester, Sean 242, 244, 259–60, 262–3, 265–6, 273–4, 284, 302, 308, 341, 355
liberalism:
classical 40
economic 142, 159, 218, 232, 237
and Great Depression 46
revival of British 105
Lindberg, John 268
Lippmann, Walter 120
Lloyd George, David 21, 24, 35
Lobo, Helio 243
Locarno Treaty 39, 41, 41 n.92, 149
London School of Economics (LSE) 254
Loucheur, Louis 41–2
Loveday, Alexander 5, 19, 27, 34–5, 54, 58–9, 58 n.39, 63–4, 63 n.64, 66–9, 72, 74–6, 86, 88–9, 92, 96, 99–100, 105, 108–12,

115–24, 128–38, 140–5, 147, 149–50, 157, 159, 161, 168–71, 175–6, 178, 184, 184 n.81, 187–94, 201–3, 205–8, 210, 212, 215, 218, 218 n.60, 219–23, 228–9, 231–4, 237–9, 243–63, 261 n.91, 265, 267–72, 267 n.3, 274, 277, 282–4, 288–9, 293, 295, 297–9, 299 n.130, 301–3, 308–9, 309 n.10, 314–18, 318 n.49, 329, 329 n.93, 333–42, 346, 350–1, 354–6

MacDonald, Ramsay 40, 81, 88, 98, 106, 108, 110–11, 113, 116, 173
McDougall, Frank Lidgett 149–50, 165, 166–71, 175–9, 190–3, 195, 212, 228, 234–6, 238, 256–7, 283–4, 287, 295–6, 302, 328 n.91, 336, 346
McGarrah, Gates W. 70
Machlup, Fritz 308
Madan, Dr B. K. 349
Makins, Roger 200, 263
Malkin, William 260
Mant, Reginald 56, 58, 70
Mantoux, Étienne 323–4
Mantzavinos, Georgios 283
Marschak, Jacob 210
Marshall Aid 283, 346
Massigli, René 129, 151
Matsudaira, Tsunco 113
Meade, James 202, 210, 212, 226, 254, 280–2, 300
'Measurement of the Volume of Saving, The'(secretariat study) 217
Mellon-Bérenger Accords 79
'Memorandum on the World's Monetary Problems' (Cassel) 19–20
Mexico 358
Milhaud Plan 147
Mills, Ogden 92
Mises, Ludwig von 308, 350
Mitrany, David 164, 261, 261 n.93
Mixed Committee on the Problem of Nutrition (1935) 161, 161 n.6, 164, 166, 169–72, 212
Miyoji Ito 144
Mlynarski, Feliks 56
Moley, Raymond 104, 120–1, 121 n.109, 133
monetarism 351
Monetary Commission 90
monetary demand 230 n.101
Monnet, Jean 14, 17, 35, 304, 349
Mont Pèlerin Society 338, 351
Montevideo Conference (1933) 121
Montreal UNRRA Council 328
Moreau, Émile 52, 54, 62
Moret, Clément 86, 110, 118
Morgan, John Pierpoint 16
Morgenstern, Oskar 37, 212, 287
Morgenthau, Hans 116, 237
Morgenthau, Henry Junior 322

and agriculture 196–7
and the Clearing Committee 139
financial stability in 31
foreign debt obligations of 183
and gold 120
and hunger problems 179, 181
international financial aid imperative 18
stabilization needs of 33
and trade 143, 153, 239
political debts, *see* war debts
Political and Economic Planning group
(PEP) 254
Politis, Nicholas 33
Popular Front 172–3
population 195
Portugal:
consequences of loss of British import
market 44
ineligibility for UNO membership 358
'positive security' notion 168
Pospisil, Vilem 56
Posse, Hans Ernst 91
Post-War Requirements Commission 283
Potter, Pitman 163
Preparatory Committee (London Conference
1933) 91–2, 94, 96, 99–102, 104
second 105–6, 109
Princeton Mission (1940–1945):
and the achievement of Bretton Woods,
314–17
and the 'Big Four' negotiations (1943) 297–8
case for institutionalized cooperation in the
War 293
claim to be disinterested intelligence centre/
adviser 304
close link between relief and
reconstruction 283
configuration of the United Nations 296
confused purpose of 303
disengaged from restrictions of League
constitution 289
and downgrading of ECOSOC 327
and Dumbarton Oaks 326
endgame 307, 337–40, 341, 349,
352–6, 358
establishment of 265–6, 270, 272, 272 n.24
final effort to shape new global agenda,
328, 330
and Food Conference at Hot
Springs 1943 295–6
and German reparations 322–3
and the ILO challenge 274–9
monetary policy 309
and post-war reparations 319
preoccupation with communication 310
regional development scheme proposal 284
threats to close down 300, 348
and UNRRA/OFFRA 299, 301, 302,
308, 316
working with advisers/economists 288
Princeton University 261

Princeton University Press 204
Progress of International Government, The
(Mitrany) 164
Prosperity and Depression (Haberler) 203–4
protectionism:
disagreement on schemes 104–5
logical response to grave economic
climate 300
resurrection of a spectre 303
and the *Second Interim Report* 63
for small countries 332–3, 333 n.102
strangling the global economy 79
in the UK 157
way out of 236
Provisional Economic and Financial
Committee 26
purchasing power parity (PPP) 20

Quantitative Trade Controls (Haberler) 300
Quesnay, Pierre 35

Radice, Edward Albert 252–3, 252 n.57
Rajchman, Ludwik 75
Ramsay, Sir Malcolm 123, 123 n.114
Rapallo Treaty 23
Rappard, William Emmanuel 162–3, 175,
177, 351
Rasminsky, Louis 212, 214–16, 216 n.56, 219,
223, 228, 255, 287–8, 310, 317–18,
317n., 329, 333, 349, 349 n.25
Reciprocal Tariff Agreement Act
(RTAA) 111, 114, 121, 126, 128, 134–5,
141, 146, 154, 157
Refugee Settlement Commission 32, 32 n.65,
33 n.69
'Relation of Nutrition to Health, Agriculture and
Economic Policy' 171
Relief Deliveries and Relief Loans 1919–1923
(Polak) 299
'Remarks on the Present Phase of International
Economic Relations'
(economics report) 144
Renborg, Bertil 247, 260
reparations 13, 18, 29, 68, 78–9, 319–25
Reparations Commission 17, 26, 30–1, 34
Report of the Gold Delegation 203
Reynaud, Paul 109
'Rhodes Memorial Lectures' (Cassell) 69,
69 n.90
Riefler, Winfield 212, 224, 261, 283, 287, 324
Rist, Charles 55, 91, 95
Ritter, Karl 91
Robbins, Lionel 222, 280, 300
Robertson, Dennis 219, 223–4, 228, 280, 306
Rochat, Charles 145
Rockefeller Foundation 36–7, 39, 74, 74 n.95,
202–3, 262, 264, 267–9, 287
Rogers, James Harvey 142–3, 142 n.60,
151, 154
Romania:
and French ties 192